The Purse and the Sword

The Purse and the Sword

The Trials of Israel's Legal Revolution

DANIEL FRIEDMANN

TRANSLATED BY HAIM WATZMAN

OXFORD
UNIVERSITY PRESS

Library of Congress Cataloging-in-Publication Data

Names: Friedmann, Daniel, 1936- author. | Watzman, Haim, translator.
Title: The purse and the sword : the trials of Israel's legal revolution /
 Daniel Friedmann ; translated by Haim Watzman.
Other titles: Haarnak yeha-ḥerev. Hebrew.
Description: New York : Oxford University Press, 2016. | Includes bibliographical
 references and index.
Identifiers: LCCN 2016013103 | ISBN 9780190278502 (hardback)
Subjects: LCSH: Political questions and judicial power—Israel. | Judicial independence—Israel. |
 Courts of last resort—Israel. | Law—Israel— History. |
 BISAC: LAW / Legal History. | LAW / Comparative.
Classification: LCC KMK2244 .F7513 2016 | DDC 349.5694—dc23 LC record available at
http://lccn.loc.gov/2016013103

9 8 7 6 5 4 3 2 1

Printed by Edwards Brothers Malloy, United States of America

Note to Readers
This publication is designed to provide accurate and authoritative information in regard to the subject matter covered. It is based upon sources believed to be accurate and reliable and is intended to be current as of the time it was written. It is sold with the understanding that the publisher is not engaged in rendering legal, accounting, or other professional services. If legal advice or other expert assistance is required, the services of a competent professional person should be sought. Also, to confirm that the information has not been affected or changed by recent developments, traditional legal research techniques should be used, including checking primary sources where appropriate.

(Based on the Declaration of Principles jointly adopted by a Committee of the American Bar Association and a Committee of Publishers and Associations.)

> **You may order this or any other Oxford University Press publication
> by visiting the Oxford University Press website at www.oup.com.**

CONTENTS

TIMELINE CHART

The Timeline Chart refers to the major cases and other legal developments described in the book and to the parallel political events in Israel.

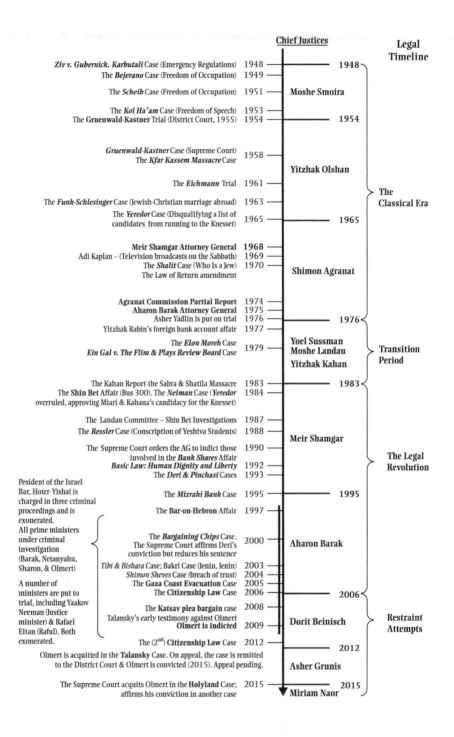

Chief Justices   **Legal Timeline**

Ziv v. Gubernick. Karbutali Case (Emergency Regulations) — 1948

The *Bejerano* Case (Freedom of Occupation) — 1949

1948

The *Scheib* Case (Freedom of Occupation) — 1951

Moshe Smoira

The *Kol Ha'am* Case (Freedom of Speech) — 1953

The **Gruenwald-Kastner** Trial (District Court, 1955) — 1954

1954

Gruenwald-Kastner Case (Supreme Court)
The *Kfar Kassem Massacre* Case — 1958

Yitzhak Olshan

The *Eichmann* Trial — 1961

The *Funk-Schlesinger* Case (Jewish-Christian marriage abroad) — 1963

The *Yeredor* Case (Disqualifying a list of candidates from running to the Knesset) — 1965

1965

The Classical Era

Meir Shamgar Attorney General — **1968**

Adi Kaplan – (Television broadcasts on the Sabbath) — 1969

The *Shalit* Case (Who Is a Jew) — 1970
The Law of Return amendment

Shimon Agranat

Agranat Commission Partial Report — 1974

Aharon Barak Attorney General — 1975

Asher Yadlin is put on trial — 1976

Yitzhak Rabin's foreign bank account affair — 1977

1976

The *Elon Moreh* Case
Ein Gal v. The Flim & Plays Review Board Case — 1979

**Yoel Sussman
Moshe Landau
Yitzhak Kahan**

Transition Period

The Kahan Report–the Sabra & Shatila Massacre — 1983

The **Shin Bet** Affair (Bus 300). The *Neiman* Case (*Yeredor* overruled, approving Miari & Kahana's candidacy for the Knesset) — 1984

1983

The Landau Committee – Shin Bet Investigations — 1987

The *Ressler* Case (Conscription of Yeshiva Students) — 1988

Meir Shamgar

The Supreme Court orders the AG to indict those involved in the **Bank Shares** Affair — 1990

Basic Law: Human Dignity and Liberty — 1992

The *Deri & Pinchasi* Cases — 1993

The Legal Revolution

Pesident of the Israel Bar, Hoter-Yishai is charged in three criminal proceedings and is exonerated.

The *Mizrahi Bank* Case — 1995

1995

The **Bar-on-Hebron** Affair — 1997

All prime ministers under criminal investigation (Barak, Netanyahu, Sharon, & Olmert)

The **Bargaining Chips** Case.
The Supreme Court affirms Deri's conviction but reduces his sentence — 2000

Aharon Barak

Tibi & Bishara Case; Bakri Case (Jenin, Jenin) — 2003

Shimon Sheves Case (breach of trust) — 2004

A number of ministers are put to trial, including Yaakov Neeman (Justice minister) & Rafael Eitan (Raful). Both exonerated.

The **Gaza Coast Evacuation** Case — 2005

The **Citizenship Law** Case — 2006

2006

The **Katsav plea bargain** case — 2008

Talansky's early testimony against Olmert
Olmert is indicted — 2009

Dorit Beinisch

Restraint Attempts

The (2nd) **Citizenship Law** Case — 2012

2012

Olmert is acquitted in the **Talansky** Case. On appeal, the case is remitted to the District Court & Olmert is convicted (2015). Appeal pending.

Asher Grunis

The Supreme Court acquits Olmert in the **Holyland** Case; affirms his conviction in another case — 2015

2015

Miriam Naor

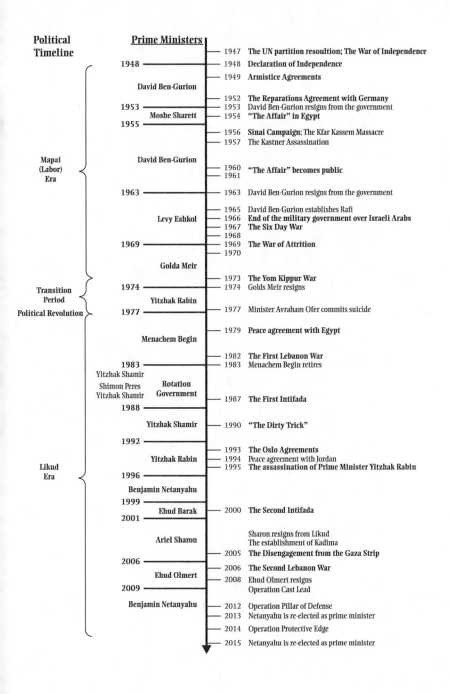

**Political
Timeline**

Prime Ministers

1947 — The UN partition resoultion; The War of Independence

1948 — 1948 Declaration of Independence

1949 — Armistice Agreements

David Ben-Gurion

1952 The Reparations Agreement with Germany
1953 — 1953 David Ben-Gurion resigns from the government
Moshe Sharett — 1954 "The Affair" in Egypt
1955

1956 Sinai Campaign; The Kfar Kassem Massacre
1957 The Kastner Assassination

Mapai
(Labor)
Era

David Ben-Gurion

1960 "The Affair" becomes public
1961

1963 — 1963 David Ben-Gurion resigns from the government

1965 David Ben-Gurion establishes Rafi
Levy Eshkol — 1966 End of the military government over Israeli Arabs
1967 The Six Day War
1968
1969 — 1969 The War of Attrition
1970

Golda Meir

1973 The Yom Kippur War
1974 — 1974 Golds Meir resigns

Transition
Period

Yitzhak Rabin

Political Revolution — 1977 — 1977 Minister Avraham Ofer commits suicide

1979 Peace agreement with Egypt

Menachem Begin

1982 The First Lebanon War
1983 — 1983 Menachem Begin retires

Yitzhak Shamir

Shimon Peres   Rotation
Yitzhak Shamir   Government

1987 The First Intifada

1988

Yitzhak Shamir — 1990 "The Dirty Trick"

1992

1993 The Oslo Agreements
Yitzhak Rabin — 1994 Peace agreement with Jordan
1995 The assassination of Prime Minister Yitzhak Rabin
1996

Likud
Era

Benjamin Netanyahu

1999

Ehud Barak — 2000 The Second Intifada
2001

Sharon resigns from Likud
Ariel Sharon   The establishment of Kadima
2005 The Disengagement from the Gaza Strip
2006

2006 The Second Lebanon War
Ehud Olmert — 2008 Ehud Olmert resigns
2009   Operation Cast Lead

Benjamin Netanyahu — 2012 Operation Pillar of Defense
2013 Netanyahu is re-elected as prime minister

2014 Operation Protective Edge

2015 Netanyahu is re-elected as prime minister

Introduction

When the state of Israel declared its independence on May 14, 1948, it had 650,000 Jewish inhabitants, a majority of them of European origin. The public was largely united around the Zionist idea and the belief that the individual needed to serve the nation. A socialist ideology took center stage in the Yishuv, the Jewish community in Palestine, during the three decades of British Mandate rule that preceded independence, and continued to dominate for nearly three decades after independence. In its early period, Israel had a strong government based on a single large governing party. At its helm was one of the greatest Jewish leaders of the modern age, David Ben-Gurion. Economic disparities were relatively modest, and the kibbutz, the commune in which individuals eschewed private property and fashioned a society based on social cohesion and equality, was seen by most Israelis as an ideal. Religion took second place to a secular outlook. The law played a modest, if not marginal, role.

Sixty-eight years have passed since then. Israel is now, in 2016, an entirely different country. Nearly nothing is left of the distinctive nature it had when it was young. The population has grown twelvefold, to more than 8 million. The cohesion emblematic of that earlier time has been replaced by division and multiculturalism. The principle that the individual should stand at the service of the nation has been replaced by individualism and the proposition that the state should serve the individual. Socialism has been abandoned; today Israel is a patently capitalist country, with economic disparities not unlike those of the United States. Some remnants of social democracy remain, however—there is practically universal health insurance, and organized labor remains strong in many sectors of the economy. Israeli society and the public milieu have been colored by religion, and the law emerged from the corner it was relegated to in the past and moved into center stage. The legal system—the courts, prosecutors, government attorneys, and police—has grown immensely powerful, to the point where it threatens to take over the other branches of government.

No longer is there a strong central leadership like that the state enjoyed until the Yom Kippur War of 1973. Since then, most governments have been weak and have faced frequent political crises. The weakness of the central government has empowered two minority groups far beyond their numbers. The Israeli settlers in the territories Israel captured in the Six Day War of 1967 and the Haredim (ultra-Orthodox) have been able to dictate the country's political and social agenda. At the same time, the ineffectuality of the executive and legislative branches created a vacuum that enabled the legal system to seize new powers for itself, transforming it into a central force in the running of the state. A side effect has been repeated clashes between the newly empowered legal institutions and the two new and powerful interest groups, the settlers and the Haredim.

This book is a history of Israel's legal system and its interactions with the country's politics. At its center is Israel's legal revolution, in which appointed officials, specifically judges, state attorneys, and bureaucrats, acquired powers that had previously been invested in elected officials—the prime minister, his cabinet, and the Knesset, Israel's parliament.

The legal revolution began three decades ago, in the 1980s, although its first glimmerings were apparent a few years earlier, during Yitzhak Rabin's first government, in the period just following the Yom Kippur War of 1973. The fall of that government was an outcome of the growing power of the legal system.

Prior to the revolution, that system had developed impressively, but also diffidently and humbly. I will concisely summarize that initial period in order to provide the background to the seismic events that followed.

This book is a considerably revised version of one published in Hebrew in 2013. I am grateful to my research assistant Etia Rottman-Frand for her help in preparing this book for publication and checking the references. I am also particularly grateful to Haim Watzman for translating the manuscript and for his helpful comments and suggestions.

PART ONE

The Classical Court

A State Is Born

On May 14, 1948, just a few hours before the end of the British Mandate over Palestine, David Ben-Gurion declared the establishment of a Jewish state in the Land of Israel. Its Declaration of Independence was promulgated by the People's Council, the parliament of the Yishuv, the Jewish community in Palestine. At the same moment, the People's Council renamed itself the Provisional State Council, and under that name served as the new state's legislature until elections were held. The Council chose thirteen of its members to serve as the People's Administration, the provisional government of the upcoming state.

A few days later the council enacted the Law and Administration Ordinance (in keeping with the Mandate's practice, the term "ordinance" meant "law"). Section 11 of the law stated that the laws as they had been on the eve of the establishment of the state would remain in force "insofar as there is nothing therein repugnant to this Ordinance or to the other laws which may be enacted by or on behalf of the Provisional Council of State, and subject to such modifications as may result from the establishment of the State and its authorities," but without subordination to Britain.[1]

In this, the council established the principle of legal continuity with British rule. Israeli law owes a large debt to the British Mandate, which established its three-tiered court system (Magistrates, District, and Supreme Courts) and endowed it with a legal culture of high quality. However, the White Paper laws, the Mandate acts that had restricted Jewish immigration and the purchase of land by Jews, were declared null and void. This step was greatly reinforced in 1950 by the enactment of a most important statute—the Law of Return. It opens with the words "Every Jew has the right to immigrate to Israel." In this it reflects the state of Israel's fundamental tenet that it is the home of the entire Jewish people. The law leaves open the question of who counts as a Jew, and that question, as one might expect, came before the court, as I will relate further on.

The religious parties and numerous other citizens of the new state had expected that Jewish law, the legal system originating in biblical law and subsequently developed in the Mishnah, the Talmud, and by generations of rabbinic authorities, would become the central pillar of its legal system, but that did not happen. The shapers of Israeli's legal infrastructure understood that Jewish law, at least as it stood at the time, was not consistent with the fundamental democratic principles on which the state had been founded. In particular, it did not invest legislative authority in an elected parliament. Furthermore, Jewish law, inasmuch as it discriminates between women and men, conflicts with the egalitarian values that were fundamental to the Zionist movement. Finally, Jewish law simply did not address a long list of important issues that face modern states: insurance, intellectual property rights, corporations, and financial instruments, to name just a few. Nevertheless, the rabbis were able to retain their control over marriages and divorces, with problematic consequences.

Israel's War of Independence had started even before the state was declared. Arab guerrilla forces began to attack the Yishuv as soon as the U.N. General Assembly passed, on November 29, 1947, a resolution partitioning Palestine into Jewish and Arab states. The Yishuv leadership supported the resolution, but the Arabs rejected it and preferred to fight a bloody war. Following the passage of the resolution, the British began a gradual evacuation of the country.

Just as that evacuation was coming to an end, and as the legal end of the Mandate approached, David Ben-Gurion, the Yishuv's leader, decided that the Yishuv had to declare the establishment of the Jewish state. He was able to convince a bare majority of the provisional government to support this decision. Following the declaration, made on May 14, 1948, the armies of the surrounding Arab states invaded the new country, in flagrant violation of the United Nations' decision and international law.

Despite being outnumbered and possessing inferior weaponry, Israel won the war, although it suffered heavy losses. In the process, it gained control of some of the territory that the partition resolution had designated for the Palestinian Arab state. The rest of the Palestinian territory ended up under Jordanian (the West Bank) or Egyptian (the Gaza Strip) control. During the course of the war, most of the Arabs living in the areas controlled by Israel either fled or were expelled, creating a refugee problem that persists to this day. But a substantial number of Arabs remained, and their numbers have greatly increased since then. In contrast, when Arab armies took control of areas where Jews lived, such as Jerusalem's Old City, no Jews were ever allowed to stay there, and these areas became, to use the German term, *Judenrein*.

The new state held its first general election on January 25, 1949. Israel's citizens chose a Constituent Assembly of 120 members, which was to draft a constitution. But rather than do that, the assembly resolved to change its name to the Knesset and constitute itself as Israel's parliament. About a year later, the Knesset passed what has come to be called the Harari Resolution, named after its sponsor, Knesset member Yizhar Harari. This internal Knesset decision was not a formal law but simply charged the Knesset's Constitution, Law, and Justice Committee with drafting a series of basic laws that would eventually be combined together to form a constitution. Precisely how that constitution would eventually be ratified—by national referendum, special majority of the Knesset, or in some other way, was left open. It was as if the Constitutional Convention of 1787, called by the thirteen American states, had declared itself, without any ratification process, to be the U.S. Congress, empowering itself to enact federal laws while retaining a role in the drafting of a constitution as it went along. Given that constitution-writing and lawmaking are two distinct activities and that a constitution is by definition a document with higher status than regular legislation, the Harari Resolution raised a snarl of legal questions to which satisfactory answers have never been found.

Mapai, the socialist-Zionist party led by Ben-Gurion, which had been the Yishuv's dominant political force, won the first election.* The elections were conducted according to the proportional system that had been used in the Yishuv and in the Zionist Congresses, with each party assigned seats in the Knesset according to the percentage of votes it received. Under this system, Mapai received forty-six seats. While not an absolute majority, this was a large plurality that ensured that it would be the dominant force in any ruling coalition. In seeking coalition partners to gain a governing majority, Ben-Gurion from the start ruled out any cooperation with the parties of the far ends of the political spectrum—Menachem Begin's hyper-nationalist Herut** Party on the right and the Jewish-Arab Communist Party (Maki) on the left.*** He also made a momentous decision that has affected Israeli politics to this day. Despite their ostensible shared socialist ideology, Ben-Gurion preferred to leave another party out of his government—the socialist-Zionist Mapam Party,**** which at the time was of Marxist inclinations and declared allegiance to the Soviet Union. Instead, Ben-Gurion preferred a partnership with a block of religious parties, both Zionist and Haredi non-Zionist, that had run as a single slate in the elections.

To cement the coalition with the religious parties, Ben-Gurion made a number of concessions that constituted a significant departure from secular Zionist ideology. The most important of these was the Rabbinical Courts Jurisdiction (Marriage and Divorce) Law of 1953, which invested all jurisdiction over marriage and divorce in the Jewish community to state-sponsored rabbinic courts, with Muslim, Druze, and Christian marriage and divorce controlled by the state-sponsored religious courts of their respective communities.[2] While this simply continued the status quo that had been established by Ottoman law and carried on by the British Mandate, many Israelis had expected the new state, as a democracy, to eliminate the discrimination against women that prevails under Jewish religious marriage and divorce law. In fact,

---

* Mapai was a Hebrew acronym for the Workers of the Land of Israel Party. Mapai remained Israel's largest and ruling party from 1948 until it was voted out of power in 1977. Ben-Gurion led it until 1963, with the exception of a single brief interval. In the mid-1960s Mapai merged with two other parties to become the Labor Party. In recent years the party has run in elections under various names—most recently, in 2015, as the Zionist Camp.

** Herut was a right-wing nationalist party with roots in the Revisionist Zionist movement of Ze'ev (Vladimir) Jabotinsky. It was formed by veterans and supporters of IZL, the Hebrew acronym for the National Military Organization, the Revisionist underground militia that Begin had commanded during the British mandate period. The British viewed IZL as a terror organization.

*** Maki later joined with smaller radical factions to form Hadash, the Front for Peace and Equality. In the 2015 elections it ran on a joint slate with three Arab parties, the United Arab List.

**** Mapam won nineteen seats in the election of 1949, making it the second-largest party after Mapai. In 1954 it split, and the breakaway faction, Ahdut HaAvodah–Poalei Tzion ran separately. In 1965 the latter faction allied with Mapai, eventually forming the Labor Party. Mapam continued as a separate party but, for a time in the 1970s and early 1980s, it ran on a joint slate with Labor, called the Alignment. In 1992 it joined with two other small parties of the left to form Meretz, a small party that remains active today.

the very opposite happened—the new law actually somewhat augmented the rabbinic courts' powers.

The decision to forswear government control of such a central aspect of life and to hand it over to rabbis—who owed their primary allegiance not to the laws of the state but to religious edicts—was diametrically opposed to the vision of Theodor Herzl, the founder of the Zionist movement. In his seminal work *The Jewish State*, Herzl declared: "We shall therefore prevent any theocratic tendencies from coming to the fore on the part of our priesthood. We shall keep our priests within the confines of their temples in the same way as we shall keep our professional army within the confines of their barracks."[3]

Some of Ben-Gurion's close advisers, notably Haim Cohn and Dov Yosef, warned him that the law would have serious consequences, but the prime minister believed the promise made by his first minister of religions, Rabbi Yehuda Leib Maimon, that the rabbinic courts would display flexibility and would adapt religious law to the needs of the state and the requirements of the modern age. In practice, the rabbinic courts have repeatedly and painfully shown that the opposite is the case—they have, more often than not, construed Jewish law in the most severe and exacting possible way.

The Rabbinical Courts Jurisdiction (Marriage and Divorce) Law stands opposed to the secular character of the Zionist movement, and to the principle of equality for women that has been a Zionist principle from its very inception. Zionism was a progressive movement not just in the Jewish context but on the world stage. From the start it granted women the right to vote for and be elected to its institutions, at a time when, in many Western countries, women were denied these rights. To acknowledge this, and to a certain measure to compensate for the injury to women's rights done by the religious jurisdiction, the Knesset also passed the Women's Equal Rights Law of 1951.* That law states: "Women and men shall be equal for purposes of every legal act" (Section 1a). But the law limited this equality in Section 5: "This law shall not infringe any legal prohibition or permission in connection with marriage and divorce."[4] In other words, Israeli women were equal, but not when it came to marriage and divorce. The religious monopoly in the area of marriage and divorce stood opposed to the worldviews of many of Israel's inhabitants and to the principles of its nonreligious political parties, including Mapai. It had social consequences that manifested themselves in legislation and judicial rulings. The liberal public did not consider itself bound by religious law. As such, couples often preferred to cohabit and raise families without marriage, a practice that began in the Yishuv period and expanded after the state was founded. This sort of partnership was officially recognized in Israeli law immediately after independence, in the Disabled Persons Law (Provident Payments and Rehabilitation), enacted in 1949, which awarded pensions to Israelis wounded in the War of Independence, as well as to their families. The law defined "wife" to include "a woman who lives together with the disabled person and

---

* The Women's Equal Rights preceded the Rabbinical Courts Law, but, as noted, at the time it was passed the rabbinical courts already enjoyed an almost complete monopoly over Jewish marriage and divorce in Israel by virtue of Mandate legislation, which remained in force until it was replaced by the Rabbinical Courts Law in 1953.

who is publicly known as his wife." A few years later a similar rule was established, granting such a "common-law" spouse* the same rights as a legal wife in a range of legislation, including those addressing compensation or pensions, such as the Social Security Law and others addressing property and inheritance rights. The existence of such laws and standards in a country that grants a monopoly to religious law in personal matters is a paradox unique to Israel.[5]

The courts followed the Knesset in recognizing cohabitation outside of marriage and granting such couples rights not specified by legislation. They ruled that there was no fault associated with a couple's decision to enter into such an arrangement, and that an agreement to do so is not contrary to public policy. This position is, of course, opposed to that of religious law, which takes a negative view of conjugal relations outside of marriage. Likewise, the courts applied to such couples the rules that they developed regarding co-ownership of property acquired by legally married husband and wife, including real estate purchased while they were married but registered only in the name of one of them.[6]

Ben-Gurion also diverged, for the same reasons, from his principle of state neutrality when he agreed to exempt religious women from the military service that was mandatory on other Israeli women (leaving open the option that they could perform volunteer service). He also consented to the establishment of a system of state-run religious schools, and recognized an independent but state-funded Haredi system.

Immediately following independence, a huge wave of immigrants entered the country. Within three years the country's Jewish population had doubled. The new state suffered from insecurity on its borders and severe economic depression, exacerbated by the arrival of so many newcomers. To address its economic problems, the government instituted strict regulation of the economy, requiring licensing and oversight of most economic activity, including foreign currency. Many economic controls remained in force for many years thereafter.

In time, the Israeli economy recovered and grew stronger, thanks in large measure to an influx of foreign capital. Jewish and Zionist organizations brought in donations and investments, and West Germany made reparations payments to Israel after the two countries reached an agreement in 1952, one fiercely opposed by Begin and Herut.

In the meantime, the Arab countries used all means at their disposal—diplomatic, economic, and military—to harm Israel. Terrorists based in the West Bank and Gaza Strip staged terror attacks within Israel, and Israel responded with reprisals. The tensions on Israel's southern border exploded when Egypt's ruler, Gamal Abdul Nasser, signed a large weapons deal with Czechoslovakia, just a short time after he nationalized the British-administered Suez Canal. Under a secret British-French-Israeli compact, the Israel Defense Forces (IDF) launched the Sinai Campaign (Operation Kadesh) on October 29, 1956. A week later Israel had seized control of the entire Sinai Peninsula. But the United States and Soviet Union were aghast and together forced Israel to withdraw its forces to the ceasefire line of 1949.

---

* The literal translation of the Hebrew term describing this relationship is "publicly known [spouse]." It is not considered a legal marriage. Thus, for example, a person who is legally married and then cohabits with another spouse (without divorcing his first partner) does not commit the offense of bigamy.

On the first day of the operation, Israeli security forces were involved in a horrifying incident. At that time, Israel's Arab citizens lived under military law and those who lived close to the Jordanian border had been regularly subject to a nighttime curfew lasting from 9 p.m. until 6 a.m. On the eve of the operation it was decided to move the start of the curfew up to 5 p.m. Inhabitants of one village, Kfar Kassem, returned from their day's work not long after that hour, not having heard of the change. Border Guard troops opened fire on them, massacring forty-seven Arab civilians, about half of them women and children. Eleven soldiers and commanders were brought before a military court on murder charges.[7] In their defense, they claimed that they had acted under military orders. The court rejected this defense on the grounds that a soldier, despite his duty to obey orders, is morally and legally bound to refuse to comply with an illegal command over which "a black flag waves." Eight of them received long prison terms, but were pardoned not long thereafter.[8]

Ben-Gurion served as prime minister until 1963, except during a brief retirement from 1953–1955 in which he was replaced by Moshe Sharett. During that time his leadership went practically unchallenged. But the Ben-Gurion era ended when he resigned in 1963, angry over the handling of what came to be called simply "the affair" (a botched operation by an Israeli spy ring in Egypt that had occurred some nine years earlier, during Sharett's term as prime minister). The result was a break between him and his colleagues in the Mapai leadership. Ben-Gurion went so far as to form a new party, Rafi, and was expelled from Mapai, the party he had helped found and had led for decades.

Elections were held in 1965 and were won by Mapai, allied with Ahdut HaAvodah and now led by Levi Eshkol. Rafi, led by Ben-Gurion and including younger leaders such as Moshe Dayan and Shimon Peres, received only ten seats in the Knesset. Eshkol pursued a new set of domestic policies. Two of his most notable moves were abolishing the military regime under which most of Israel's Arab citizens had lived and ending the political boycott of Begin and Herut.

In the meantime, Herut had gained legitimacy by joining forces with the middle-class, pro-free-enterprise Liberal Party (previously known as the General Zionists), which had in the past at times been a coalition partner of Mapai. The Liberals had generally pursued a dovish line in foreign policy. By the mid-1960s, however, the party's leaders believed that they needed to offer the country an alternative to Mapai rule and that the only way to challenge the ruling party's hegemony was to partner with Herut in an electoral alliance they named Gahal. They seem to have felt that whatever differences the two parties had on foreign policy and security issues were not all that significant, given that by this time Israel had achieved relative calm on its borders and a major war was not in sight. Furthermore, Herut's dream of a Greater Israel seemed such a remote possibility that it could be disregarded. But just two years later the Six Day War erupted, and foreign and defense policy returned to the foreground—in particular, the issue of the future of the territories that Israel captured from Jordan, Egypt, and Syria in that war. Herut saw much of them as part of a Greater Israel. Ironically, the moderate liberals found themselves bound to support Begin's hard-line position on negotiations with the Arab states and on the new territories.

The first rumblings of the Six Day War began in 1967, when Nasser ordered the U.N. peacekeeping forces that had been stationed there and in the Gaza Strip to evacuate. Nasser also closed the Red Sea's Straits of Tiran to Israeli vessels and deployed the Egyptian army in the Sinai Peninsula. In parallel, Egypt signed a military cooperation agreement with Syria, Jordan, and Iraq. The Israeli public was alarmed and called for a broad national unity government to face the crisis. Eshkol gave in, bringing Rafi and Gahal into the government. Moshe Dayan assumed the defense portfolio, which Eshkol, like Ben-Gurion before him, had up until then reserved for himself. Begin became a government minister for the first time, gaining further legitimacy. It was a critical step in his road toward the prime ministership.

When war broke out on June 5, Israel quickly decimated the armies of Egypt, Jordan, and Syria and took control of the Sinai Peninsula, the Gaza Strip, the West Bank including East Jerusalem, and the Golan Heights. This placed a million Palestinians under Israeli rule. The huge victory bolstered Israel's self-confidence, but did not lead to peace.

Prime Minister Eshkol died about a year and a half after the war and was replaced by Labor's new leader, Golda Meir. Nasser also died and was succeeded by Anwar Sadat. Sadat was less charismatic than Nasser but much more capable, proving himself to be one of the greatest statesmen in the modern history of the Middle East, second in rank only to Kemal Ataturk and David Ben-Gurion.

Sadat evinced a willingness to reach an accommodation with Israel, but negotiations between the two countries failed. On October 6, 1973, in mid-day on Yom Kippur, Israel was attacked in the south by Egypt and in the north by Syria. The attack surprised Israel's army and civilian leadership and the IDF suffered heavy losses in its early stages. But in a series of bloody battles Israeli forces retook the territory captured by Syria in the Golan Heights and turned the tide on the Egyptian front as well. Egypt nevertheless managed to hold its own and maintain some of its territorial gains in Sinai. By the end of the war, 2,656 Israeli soldiers had been killed and more than 7,000 wounded, huge numbers for such a small country. Israel's economy suffered a serious blow and did not recover for more than a decade.

The elections originally scheduled for October 1973 were postponed to the end of December. Prior to the election the government appointed a national commission of inquiry chaired by Chief Justice Shimon Agranat to determine why Israel had been surprised by the attack and why its military deployment had not been able to hold back the invading forces.

The Alignment—the Labor Party running on a joint slate with the much smaller and no longer pro-Soviet Mapam—won the election as if nothing had happened. It lost a few seats to a broadened right-wing block, Likud, which added some small factions to the Herut-Liberal alliance. But Labor remained by far the largest party and the only one that could form a government. Meir formed a coalition along the lines of the previous one. In early April 1974, the Agranat Commission placed full blame for the initial setbacks of the war on the army's high command, including the chief of staff, the head of military intelligence, and the general of the Southern Command. It exonerated the political leadership—setting off a public uproar. Meir, already disheartened by the shambles the war had left in its wake and battered by the protests against the political leadership, in particular against Defense Minister Dayan, resigned later that month, just a few weeks after forming her government.

Labor chose Yitzhak Rabin to replace Meir. But the man he defeated in the party's internal leadership contest, Shimon Peres, did not give up. A new and previously unknown phenomenon made its first—but hardly its last—appearance in Israeli politics. Instead of accepting defeat, either by retiring from politics or loyally serving the victor, the losing candidate, in this case Peres, continued to vie for the top spot with all means at his disposal.

The first battleground was the cabinet. Peres and his supporters made it clear that if Peres was not given the defense portfolio, his Rafi faction would bolt and Rabin would not have the votes he needed to form a government. Rabin gave in. Peres then proceeded to lend his support to Israeli settlers in the West Bank heartland, where most of the area's Palestinians lived. This contradicted Rabin's policy, which favored settlement in the Golan Heights and in the Rafiah salient in northern Sinai while strongly opposing settlements in that part of the West Bank densely populated by Palestinians. The government was put to the test by Gush Emunim, a movement, largely composed of young messianic religious Zionists, that campaigned for a Greater Israel incorporating much of the new territories, notably the West Bank. Members of the organization set up a squatter settlement alongside the Palestinian Arab village of Sebastia in Samaria, not far from Nablus, a large city in the northern West Bank. The government ordered their evacuation, but they returned. After several rounds of this, the government agreed to a compromise that Peres reached with the settlers, under which the squatters agreed to move to a nearby army base, establishing a civilian Jewish settlement.[9] This set the pattern for the establishment of many more Jewish settlements in the midst of the Palestinian cities and villages of Judea and Samaria, as the settlers called the West Bank, terminology that was eventually adopted by the Israeli government and public.

Rabin's government fell three years later as the result of a dispute with one of its coalition partners, the National Religious Party, over a violation of the Sabbath. New elections were set for May 17, 1977. Soon before them, the press reported that Rabin and his wife maintained an account in a bank in the suburbs of Washington, D.C., in violation of Israeli law at the time. Rabin resigned as Labor's leader and was replaced by Peres. Likud won forty-three seats, becoming the largest party. The Labor-led Alignment plunged from fifty-one seats in the previous Knesset to just thirty-two.

It was an astonishing juncture in Israeli politics, much more momentous than an opposition party winning an election, as often happens in democracies. Mapai and its successor Labor Party had led the Yishuv uninterrupted for three decades during the British Mandate and the state of Israel for another three. Now the Israeli public had sent it packing.

Furthermore, Likud, with Begin's Herut at its center, was not a standard opposition party. Labor's leaders viewed Herut as a faction fundamentally foreign to the Zionist movement, irresponsible and dangerous, a group of extremists who had played no role in building the country. Many in the old Labor elite felt as if the country had been stolen from them. They were replaced by new elites, members not only of Begin's Revisionist cadre but also Mizrahim—Jews from the Islamic world who had immigrated during the mass influx of the 1950s—and Orthodox Zionists of the National Religious Party and the Haredim.

Begin's mentor, Ze'ev Jabotinsky, had been an advocate of a thoroughly secular Zionism, but Begin comfortably allied with the religious parties. The Haredim soon came to hold the balance of power on Israel's political map, and have since 1977 been members of nearly every governing coalition. They were generously rewarded in coalition agreements. One of the great catastrophes that the Begin government brought on Israel was the sweeping exemption from military service that he granted to all full-time students in religious seminaries, *yeshivot*. Ben-Gurion had granted such an exemption to a small number of *yeshiva* students, agreeing that this was necessary to rehabilitate the *yeshiva* world that had been destroyed in the Holocaust. But now all limits were removed. The exemption from military service, coupled with increased financial support to the *yeshivot* and their students, has created a strong incentive to pursue religious studies for years on end. The number of *yeshiva* students skyrocketed while the numbers of Haredim who worked for their living greatly declined, thus creating an economic problem with which the Israeli government is trying to grapple to this day.

To Judge But Not to Rule

When the state was established, the Magistrates and District Courts that had operated under British rule continued to do so in the new country, staffed by the Jewish
judges that had served on these courts under the Mandate administration. But the
Mandate's Supreme Court had for all intents and purposes ceased to exist. Its British
and Arab justices were gone, leaving the single Jewish justice, Gad Frumkin.

The vacuum was filled just a few months later, while the War of Independence
still raged. A new Supreme Court came into being on September 14, 1948. During
the few interim months, the Tel Aviv District Court had been granted the power to
review actions of the executive branch by means of prerogative writs—orders which
form the basis of judicial review of the executive's exercise of its powers.* This authority was then transferred to the new Supreme Court when it was established. In
this the new Supreme Court retained the character of its Mandate predecessor—
in addition to being the highest appellate court for civil and criminal cases, it also
served as the court of original jurisdiction in matters regarding the legality of the
actions of the state or other bodies and persons performing public functions. In this
latter guise, it is officially known as the High Court of Justice, for which the Hebrew
acronym is *Bagatz*. The court's hybrid nature was, however, now further complicated by the fact that there was no body to which to appeal its decisions. Under
the Mandate, rulings issued by the Supreme Court could be appealed to the Privy
Council in London. Now that Israel was independent of Britain, this possibility no
longer existed. Consequently, a fundamental right, that of appeal of court decisions,
no longer existed in cases that the Supreme Court heard as the High Court of Justice.
(True, in certain exceptional cases there is a possibility of a further hearing by a
larger panel of a case decided by a panel of three justices, but that is very limited in
scope.) An attempt to redress this anomaly was made in February 1950, when the
justice ministry proposed legislation to transfer High Court of Justice powers to the
District Courts. The justices of the Supreme Court fiercely opposed the initiative.
Among their reasons, so it seems, was their desire to maintain the prestige that its
government oversight functions had brought the court during its brief history thus
far. Justice Minister Pinhas Rosen, respectful of the justices, withdrew the bill.[10]

---

* Habeas corpus, the best known of these, can be invoked not only against the government but
also against private individuals who hold another person in illegal captivity.

It was Rosen who selected the justices who were appointed to new court's bench, and while his choices were technically recommendations, they were all approved by the cabinet and, in the case of Supreme Court justices, also by the People's Council and subsequently by the Knesset that replaced it. His candidate for chief justice, Moshe Smoira, had been his law office partner. Both of them had immigrated to Palestine from Germany. Imagine the pandemonium that would break out today if a justice minister were to promote the candidacy of a former law partner to the Supreme Court, all the more so its chief justice.

Appointed along with Smoira were another two private attorneys, Menahem Dunkelblum and Yitzhak Olshan; Rabbi Simha Assaf, a Hebrew University professor and expert in Jewish law who did not have a law degree or familiarity with secular law; and Judge Shneur Zalman Cheshin of the Tel Aviv District Court, the only one of the five with judicial experience.

The choice of justices aimed at gaining the court broad public support. To that end, its membership was meant to reflect, more or less, the political composition of the Provisional People's Council. Smoira and Olshan were close to Mapai; Dunkelblum, president of the Bar Association, was associated with the General Zionists; Rabbi Assaf was meant to represent the religious population. Cheshin was not associated with any political grouping. For reasons that remain obscure, Rosen firmly opposed appointing Frumkin, the only Jew who had served on the Mandate Supreme Court, to the new court—even David Ben-Gurion's support was to no avail. As a result, the bench was an entirely new one. None of its members had ever served as a high court justice, and only one, Cheshin, had been a judge of any sort at all.

The original bench did not have much luck. Only one of the five, Olshan, remained on the court until he reached the mandatory retirement age of seventy. All the others died before they reached that age or resigned their seats because of illness. Olshan served until 1965, when he was replaced as chief justice by the senior member of the bench, Shimon Agranat, who led the court for eleven years. The Agranat court was the Supreme Court's golden age, the period in which it reached the high point of its public and moral authority. Its rulings were attuned to the need for stability and continuity, while advancing the law in a sound and gradual way and protecting private citizens from arbitrary actions of the state.

One of the most important and precedent-setting rulings Agranat and his court issued established the irresistible impulse defense against criminal liability, reflecting a liberal approach that exonerates a defendant unable to control his actions.[11] The court's pioneering ruling in the Kol Ha'am case, which I will discuss below, is to this day considered a foundation of free speech in Israel. Agranat may well have been the greatest judge Israel has produced, but his reputation suffered after he presided over the commission of inquiry into the Yom Kippur War debacle, which absolved the country's political leadership of all responsibility.

When Agranat retired in September 1976 he was replaced by Yoel Sussman. Sussman, however, soon fell ill and was unable to perform his duties; he finally resigned in February 1980, about a year before his seventieth birthday. He was a brilliant justice, with few if any equals in his analytic abilities and original approach to the law. His opinions are eminently clear, brief, precise, and persuasive. He opposed the practice of including obiter dicta in judicial opinions, those tangential digressions in which judges discuss issues and make pronouncements that are not required for deciding the legal issue at hand. In one case he even called the practice a contravention of judicial authority. Later, during the period of the revolutionary court, the practice would become common.

The inclusion of Rabbi Simha Assaf on the original court set the precedent of a "religious chair" on the high court. Ostensibly the justification was that the court needed an expert in traditional Jewish religious law, but it was understood that the court would always include a justice who lived an Orthodox Jewish lifestyle and had a traditional outlook.

Ben-Gurion also wanted a Sephardi judge. The Sephardi community consists of a number of groups. One is Jews whose ancestors came from Spain or Portugal. The other group of Sephardi population, the Mizrahim (Oriental or Eastern), were those whose families had come to Israel from the Islamic world. The two groups shared customs and liturgy, but the first group included families who had lived for generations in Palestine and who during the Ottoman era belonged to the Yishuv's elite. While originally the dominant group in the Yishuv, under the British Mandate they lost their dominant influence as Ashkenazi Jews immigrated from Europe. Nevertheless, they remained well established socially and economically. The members of the other Sephardi group, the Mizrahim, were much less well off and felt sidelined and discriminated against. Despite Ben-Gurion's insistence, it was only in 1967 that a Sephardi District Court Judge, Eliahu Manny, was promoted to the Supreme Court.[12] From that time onward, at least one of the justices was traditionally Sephardi, and he was always chosen from that community's elite. In other words, he did not represent the "other Israel," the Mizrahi immigrants who had arrived after the founding of the state and most of whom, no matter what their educational and economic background in their countries of origin, had suffered poverty and discrimination in the Jewish state. It took until 2001 for that community to see one of its members appointed to the high court, one of the last bastions of the Ashkenazi elite in Israel.

At first, appointments to the courts on all levels were made in accordance with the Mandate practice—that is, the executive branch appointed judges. Appointments to the Supreme Court, however, required ratification by parliament (originally the Provisional State Council and subsequently the Knesset). The method was changed in 1953 with the enactment of the Judges Law. This vested the power to make judicial appointments in a Judicial Selection Committee of nine members. It was chaired by the minister of justice and its members, the law stipulated, included another cabinet minister, two members of the Knesset, two attorneys chosen by the Israel Bar Association, the chief justice of the Supreme Court, and two associate justices from that court. In passing the law, the country's elected officials agreed to transfer powers they had held to a body that, while it included political representatives, operated independently of the political system. The presumption behind this change was that the justice system should be shielded from political influence and its independence bolstered.

Notably, the composition of the committee guaranteed that a majority of its members would be "professionals" in the legal field—three justices and two attorneys, in addition to the justice minister himself, who almost always held a law degree. The professional majority made sense in the Supreme Court's classic period, in which it operated on a purely professional basis. It is not clear that this is the best composition today, now that, in the wake of the revolutionary period, the high court rules on questions of politics and values and even voids laws passed by the Knesset.

During Israel's early years its politicians regarded the law as of secondary, if not marginal importance. Until the Six Day War, Mapai kept all the major cabinet port-folios for itself—defense, foreign affairs, finance, and education. The justice min-istry was not considered critical, and as such Mapai had no problem giving it to Pinhas Rosen of the small Progressive Party, who held that post almost continuously until 1961.

At that time, Israeli political leaders looked askance at judges and jurists. The Mapai leadership emerged from a workers' movement that esteemed agriculture and physical labor over "unproductive" occupations such as commerce and deal-making. The law, a profession Jews had served in eminently in the Diaspora, fell into the second category.

When the Nazis came to power, a wave of immigrants from Germany arrived in Palestine. Many of them were white-collar professionals in the field of law, medicine, banking, insurance, and business. Among them were Yoel Sussman, Moshe Landau, Alfred Witkon, Ze'ev Zeltner, and other important legal figures.

Politicians were also dismissive of the Supreme Court. This attitude was evident, for example, in 1952, when Justice Minister Dov Yosef declared that the courts were issu-ing overly mild sentences to citizens convicted of attacking policemen. He submitted a bill setting a minimum sentence for this crime. Members of the opposition faulted the proposal for limiting judges' discretion. Yosef responded with a fierce polemic against judges and their lenient approach. Were judges, he asked, "winged saints who have descended from heaven . . . who know what is right and what is wrong?"

Chief Justice Moshe Smoira and his colleagues sent an angry letter to Knesset Speaker Joseph Shprinzak, advising him that Yosef's offensive outburst against the judiciary was unsettling relations between the branches of government and dele-gitimizing the courts. Shprinzak returned the letter to Smoira. This act of deliberate discourtesy, he said, was meant to underline the Knesset's sovereignty, but it dealt the court yet another blow.

The government's attitude was evident in the building which housed the high court. Unimposing and dilapidated, it was located far from the hill on which the Knesset and the prime minister's office were built. But, as the years went by, the Supreme Court's achievements and the respect in which it was held by the citizenry and the academy magnified the glaring contradiction between its standing and the dismal building in which it was housed. Despairing of public funding for the con-struction of a new building worthy of the court, Chief Justice Meir Shamgar finally sought philanthropic support. The Rothschild Foundation provided the funds and in 1992, almost forty-five years after the court was founded, the Supreme Court moved into an impressive home adjacent to the Knesset.

Despite their chilly attitude toward the Supreme Court and lower courts, the government and the Knesset displayed good judgment when it came to critical issues such as judicial independence, authority, and appointments. For its part, the Supreme Court respected the Knesset's sovereignty and did not hand down rulings that were likely to incur the ire of the other branches of government. The legislature and executive almost always respected and acted in accordance with the high court's decisions. But, during the country's early years, there were some painful exceptions.

One of the most prominent of these was the case of two Arab villages in the Galilee, Ikrit and Biram, which had been taken by the Israel Defense Forces (IDF) during the War of Independence. In October 1948 the inhabitants were ordered to evacuate their homes. They were told that the order was a temporary one and that they would be allowed to return. But the promise was not kept. The villagers petitioned the Supreme Court, which ruled that there was no legal basis for preventing these Israeli citizens from moving back into their villages. The court ordered the army to return all their land and property to them.[13] The government ignored the ruling. The case came before the government and the court several more times over the years that followed.[14] But to this day the villagers have not been allowed to return and successive governments have not abided by the court's decisions.

The supremacy of parliament legislation is one of the pillars of British law, and as such it was inconceivable, given the legal tradition that took form in Palestine during the Mandate, that a court might void a law. During its classic period, Israel's Supreme Court continued to see the supremacy of the Knesset as a fundamental principle. For example, in one case petitioners claimed that the state was availing itself of the power to expropriate private property granted to it under the Defense (Emergency) Regulations that had been enacted by the Mandate government and that had remained in force after the establishment of the state. The petitioners claimed that the Defense Regulations stood in contradiction of Israel's Declaration of Independence. The court denied the petition, thus affirming the expropriation. The grounds were that the Defense Regulations had the standing of a statute, whereas the Declaration of Independence was not a constitutional document that empowered the courts to void parliamentary legislation that was inconsistent with that document.[15]

Nevertheless, there were cases in which the court was able to soften the negative impact of laws through interpretation or in other indirect ways. In September 1948 Ahmad al-Karbutali asked the Supreme Court to issue a writ of habeas corpus for a friend, Ahmad Abu-Laban, who had been arrested by Israeli forces in his home in Jaffa in July 1948. He was not informed why he had been detained or even whether he was being held by the civil or military authorities. In August he was brought before a magistrate who extended his detention by ten days, after which he was released. In September he was again detained and was not permitted to see his lawyer, nor was he told the reason for his arrest. Upon receiving the petition, the court issued an order nisi requiring the state to respond to the question of why Abu-Laban had been arrested. The state replied that the arrest had been carried out under Regulation 111 of the Defense (Emergency) Regulations, which granted military commanders expansive powers to arrest any person the commander deemed necessary without stating his reasons for doing so.

While Regulation 111 was certainly draconian, the court maintained that it had no power to void it. However, the language of the regulation provided an opening— it required the establishment of an advisory committee to which the detainee could apply to ask for his release. No such committee had yet been set up at the time Abu-Laban was arrested. Justice Olshan (who heard the case along with Justices Smoira and Cheshin) ruled that "if, against the enormous power granted to the military commander, the detainee has been granted such a minuscule right," it was only proper that this right be "guarded unblinkingly." Given that the advisory committee had not been formed, the arrest order was invalid; the fact that such a committee had been set up after the arrest did not validate the arrest itself. The court ordered Abu-Laban released.[16]

The ruling was a considerable achievement—don't forget that the case was heard at the height of the War of Independence, in which there were moments in which the new country's very survival hung in the balance. On the other hand, clearly the military authorities were free to simply arrest Abu-Laban once again, now that the advisory committee had been set up.

The court did make one exception to its principle that legislation passed by the Knesset was absolutely binding, but it was not much of one. The case was *Bergman v. Minister of Finance and State Comptroller*, handed down in July 1969.[17] Bergman was an attorney who petitioned against the law governing elections to the Knesset and local authorities. One of his arguments was that the campaign finance method established by the law denied funding to new parties and was thus inconsistent with Section 4 of Basic Law: The Knesset, a section that was "entrenched," meaning that it could only be amended by a majority of all members of the Knesset—that is, at least sixty-one Knesset members had to vote for the change.

In his opinion, Justice Landau acknowledged:

> This petition raises potentially weighty preliminary questions of a constitutional nature, relating to the status of the Basic Laws, and to the justiciability before this court of the issue of the Knesset's actual compliance with a self-imposed limitation in the form of an "entrenched" statutory provision, such as section 4 of the above-mentioned Basic Law.[18]

But the attorney general, Meir Shamgar, relieved the court of the need to decide this point. He announced that the state would not take a position on the question of whether the issue of the law's force was justiciable since, on the facts of the case as he saw it, the petition was without foundation.

The court found that the law did indeed violate the principle of equality. Given the attorney general's position and the urgency of the matter, the court decided not to discuss the issue of justiciability and ruled on the merits of the case that the minister of finance should make public campaign funds available also to slates not represented in the current Knesset. But, at the end of their judgment, the justices also pointed the way out of the complication. The Knesset, the judges said, could act in one of two ways. It could re-enact the provisions of the law as they were, despite their manifest inequality, but passing them with the special majority required by the Basic Law. Alternatively, it could amend the law so as to remove the inequality. In other words, the ruling did not contradict the justices' fundamental doctrine that the Knesset was sovereign and that its legislation could not be challenged by the other branches of government. Justice Landau stated it unambiguously: "It need hardly be said that in making this suggestion we in no way presume to encroach upon the sovereignty of the Knesset as the legislative authority."[19]

At that time, no one conceived that there could be anything wrong with a law circumventing a Supreme Court ruling. The court then recognized that the Knesset was fully empowered to do so, and even offered advice regarding how to accomplish that.

Furthermore, the court recognized at that time that there were issues that were not justiciable. When Ben-Gurion established diplomatic relations with the Federal

Republic of Germany, the German government appointed Rolf Paulus as its first ambassador to Israel. Paulus had served as an officer in the Wehrmacht during World
War II. The Supreme Court was petitioned to prevent his entry into the country,
but the court dismissed the suit. Justice Sussman needed only a few lines to lay out
the Court's reasoning: "The government has decided as it sees fit ... The Knesset
endorsed the government's decision ... The considerations are not legal ones but
rather of foreign policy and the candidate's fitness for the position, and this court is
not authorized or able to decide those questions."[20]

This self-restraint was also evident in the principle that the Supreme Court refrained from intervening in the government's economic and security policy decisions. Another important requirement further limited the court's reach: It would
hear petitions only by those who had standing. In other words, only persons whose
individual interests are at stake can seek redress in court.

Along with other limitations it took upon itself, the recognition that it had to defer
to Knesset legislation rather than seek to void it still left the Supreme Court with a
broad field of action and enabled it to play a critical role in defending human rights.
In *Kol Ha'am v. Minister of the Interior*, for example, the court examined an order
issued by Interior Minister Israel Rokach suspending publication of the daily newspaper *Kol Ha'am* for ten days and that of its sister Arabic-language daily, *al-Itihad*,
for fifteen days.[21] Both newspapers, associated with Israel's Communist Party, had
printed articles attacking the possibility that Israel might provide troops to assist
the United States in a war against the Soviet Union and its allies (the government
denied that it had made any promise to do so). Rokach issued his order by invoking the Press Ordinance, a law dating back to the Mandate that granted him the
power to suspend the publication of a newspaper that had published anything that,
in his opinion, was likely to endanger public safety. In a leading opinion authored by
Justice Agranat, the court declared that there were limits to the freedom of speech,
which could be constrained when the speech in question would almost certainly
endanger public safety. The court ruled, however, that such near certainty did not
pertain with regard to the pieces published in the two newspapers. It ruled that the
interior minister had exceeded his authority and voided the suspension of publication. The decision remains to this day a cornerstone of free speech law in Israel.

Another important test case came when Ben-Gurion refused to allow Israel
Scheib (later Israel Eldad) to be employed as a teacher. Scheib had been a leader of
Lehi (also known as the Stern Gang), an extremist underground militia during the
Mandate period and the War of Independence. Ben-Gurion justified his decision on
the grounds that Scheib had advocated the use of arms against IDF troops. But the
government did not present the court with any document showing that Scheib had
in fact incited anybody to do so. Justice Cheshin wrote: "If the opinions of a citizen
are rejected, that does not mean that he loses the right to live or that his life may be
taken, he may not be kept from earning his livelihood, nor is he to be harassed by
administrative action."[22] The court issued this ruling, which enabled Scheib to be
employed, in 1951, when Ben-Gurion and Mapai were at the height of their power.

Other rulings protected individuals from bureaucratic abuse. One of these, *Peretz
v. Kfar Shmaryahu Local Authority*, grew out of a local government's refusal to rent
a public hall to residents of the town who wished to hold Reform Jewish services
there.[23] The Supreme Court ruled that a public authority could not act prejudicially

against a particular group, even though the hall was its property. Since the town government rented the hall out to a variety of organizations, the justices found that its refusal to do the same in the case of this Reform community constituted indefensible discrimination.

The Supreme Court also intervened in a long series of cases involving religion-state conflicts. In Chapter 1, I have already noted its recognition of the rights of unmarried spouses. Another such ruling, the leading Funk-Schlesinger case, required the Interior Ministry to register as married couples who wed outside Israel. The ministry had to do so, the court ruled, even when one member of the couple was not Jewish and the marriage was thus not recognized by the rabbinic courts.[24] Such overseas marriages produced a tangle of legal questions given that the civil courts generally recognized them while religious courts refused to do so. The situation was even more complicated when such a couple wished to divorce. By law, divorce fell under the sole purview of the religious courts, but how could that apply when those courts did not recognize the marriage to begin with? The Knesset took up this question, passing the Jurisdiction in Dissolution of Marriage Act (Special Cases), 1969, creating a limited space for civil divorces, even though Israel still does not allow civil marriages.[25]

Another important ruling voided a municipal bylaw prohibiting gas stations from opening on the Sabbath.[26]

Of special interest is a case involving television broadcasting in Israel, which began after the Six Day War. In 1969 the Israel Broadcasting Authority (IBA) decided to broadcast television programming daily, including on Friday nights and Saturdays. The question was whether this was in line with the promise Ben-Gurion gave the Haredi Party Agudat Yisrael on the eve of Israeli independence on matters of state and religion—what came to be known as the "status quo agreement." Prime Minister Golda Meir suspended the Sabbath programming prior to the first scheduled Friday night broadcast. Attorney Yehuda Ressler petitioned the Supreme Court in the name of one of his clients, Adi Kaplan, and the justice on duty, Zvi Berinson, who received the petition at home, issued a temporary injunction requiring the IBA to proceed with the broadcast. Israel's nonreligious population, which felt it was subject to religious coercion, was ecstatic. The enthusiastic response to the ruling deterred the government from contesting the interim order, which ended up creating an established fact.

The court also made two seminal rulings in the context of the "who is a Jew" controversy. The first, in 1962, involved Oswald Rufeisen, who had been born a Jew in Poland and had taken refuge in a monastery there during the Holocaust. While there he converted to Catholicism and after the war joined the monastic community under the name Brother Daniel. Despite his Catholic faith, he decided to immigrate to Israel.

Brother Daniel argued that he was a member of the Jewish nation, but his request to receive an immigration card as a Jew returning to his homeland under the Law of the Return and to be listed as of Jewish nationality on his identity card, was refused. He petitioned the Supreme Court. The majority on the bench that heard his suit voted to deny it, with Justice Haim Cohn dissenting.[27] The majority found that the term "Jewish" as used in Israeli legislation should be interpreted in its secular sense, that is in accordance with accepted societal use of the word and not necessarily in its *halakhic* sense. Under those terms, the justices in the majority found, a Jew who had converted to another religion had severed himself not only from the Jewish religion but also from the Jewish people.

The issue resurfaced in 1970 in *Shalit v. Minister of the Interior*. Benjamin Shalit, an IDF officer, married a non-Jewish woman. They had children, and when Shalit registered them with the Interior Ministry, he asked that they be listed as Jews. The registration included two lines, religion and nationality. In Israel, the term "nationality" is not equivalent to "citizenship," as it is in many Western countries, but rather designates the national group to which the citizen belongs, such as Jewish or Arab. Shalit did not contest that his children could not be listed as of Jewish religion, given that their mother was not Jewish, but he demanded that they be registered as being of Jewish nationality. The Interior Ministry maintained that the two went hand in hand; a person who was not of Jewish religious could not be of Jewish nationality.

The registration had no practical legal significance, but it was at the center of a profound ideological controversy. The Supreme Court preferred not to get involved in that polemic. Justice Landau worded himself cautiously: "We have taken an unusual step in this unusual case, and have suggested to the government that it demolish the basis of the controversy . . . by removing the actual cause of the debate, that is by removing the 'nationality' line from the registration." The government rejected the proposal because it, too, preferred not to get involved in such a divisive issue. With the issue left to the court to decide, an expanded bench of nine justices, in a five-to-four decision, allowed Shalit's petition and ordered the ministry to list the Shalit children as being of Jewish nationality.[28]

The decision set off a public and political storm. The National Religious Party, a member of the coalition, demanded that only Jews in the Orthodox sense count as Jews for the purposes of the Population Registry Law and, even more important, the Law of Return. Finally a compromise was achieved, and the two laws were revised. On the one hand, the *halakhic* standard that a Jew was "a person who was born of a Jewish mother or has become converted to Judaism and who is not a member of another religion" was inserted.[29] But the question of what constituted conversion—that is, whether it had to be an Orthodox conversion—was left open. That issue remains in debate to this day.

The Shalits petitioned the court again, demanding that their son Tomer, born in 1971, be registered as a member of Jewish, or alternatively Hebrew, nationality. The court denied the petition, holding that the terms "Hebrew" and "Jew" were synonymous.[30]

Nonreligious Jews received compensation for the inclusion of the *halakhic* definition of who is a Jew in the law in the form of another provision stating:

The rights of Jew under this Law and the rights of an *oleh* [Jewish immigrant] under the Nationality Law . . . , as well as the rights of an oleh under any other enactment, are also vested in a child and a grandchild of a Jew, the spouse of a child of a Jew and the spouse of a grandchild of a Jew, except for a person who has been a Jew and has voluntarily changed his religion.[31]

In other words, intermarried couples had the right to immigrate to Israel and to take up Israeli citizenship, as were their children and grandchildren, even if the latter were not recognized as Jewish by the *halakhah*. It was this provision that made possible, two decades later, the mass immigration of close to a million immigrants from the Soviet Union, many of whom were not Jewish by Orthodox standards but who nevertheless view themselves as Jews and Israelis.

Another ruling of constitutional importance was rendered in 1965 in *Yeredor et al. v. Chairman of the Central Elections Committee for the Sixth Knesset*.[32] That year the Elections Committee, the body responsible for organizing the national elections of that year and approving the slates that would compete, disqualified the Socialist List. The grounds were that the slate was illegal because its initiators rejected Israel's existence and territorial integrity. The committee based its finding on the fact that most of its candidates belonged to a group called al-Ard. The year before that group had been the subject of *Jiryis v. Haifa District Commissioner*, in which Justices Berinson, Witkon, and Landau had found that "[n]o government can be expected, in the name of preserving the freedom of association, to grant its seal of approval to the establishment of a fifth column within the borders of its country."[33]

Against the dissent of Justice Haim Cohn, Justices Agranat and Sussman affirmed the Election Committee's decision. Sussman explained: "Just as a person is not required to consent to another killing him, so a state is not required to being destroyed and expunged from the map." The justices cited the historical example of the Weimar regime in Germany, a democracy that had not protected itself from a movement that exploited democratic means to destroy democracy. The court, which had proved itself a defender of human rights, comprehended that it also needed to defend Israeli society. The democratic right to run a slate in elections and be elected to the Knesset had to give way when it constituted a clear and present danger to democracy and the state itself.

This approach was reversed later, during the court's revolutionary era, when it abandoned this balanced opinion in favor of a radical interpretation of human rights. The need to defend the collective was pushed into the margins and *Yeredor* was reversed.

The Six Day War, which brought with it Israeli rule over the West Bank and Gaza Strip and their inhabitants, as well as Israeli settlement in those territories, created a new and complicated legal situation.

A clear distinction needs to be made, of course, between those territories that were annexed to Israel—East Jerusalem and the Golan Heights—and other territories. In the case of the first two, Israeli law was declared by the Knesset to apply to them, without explicit use of the word "annexation." Yet, in terms of Israeli law, East Jerusalem and the Golan Heights are part of the state of Israel, and its laws apply to them in full, despite the fact that other countries do not recognize these annexations and despite the difficult question of whether they are valid under international law.

Israeli law was not, however, applied to most of the territories captured in 1967. In the West Bank and Gaza Strip the guiding principle has been that the sovereign is the military commander, and that he has the authority to promulgate laws. However, it has also been clear that these commanders act in accordance with instructions received from the defense minister, meaning the political leadership.

Israel has argued that the West Bank is not occupied territory because it did not have a legal sovereign prior to being taken by Israel. The territory was conquered by Jordan in 1948, but most of the world's countries never recognized that country's right to the territory. Israeli governments eventually preferred to use the term "administered territories" (rather than "occupied territories"). But after Likud came to power and the Israeli settlers in the territories gained more influence, an additional change took place, one that was more than just semantic—the Israeli government began to refer to the West Bank as "Judea and Samaria."

The military governor, as the sovereign, is meant to continue to apply the same Jordanian law system that was in force the day before the war, on June 4, 1967, subject to additional legislation on his part. As the years of Israeli rule grew longer, however, more and more legislative changes were required.

The establishment of Israeli settlements in these territories produced an especially complex legal situation. The settlers were Israeli citizens, living outside the state of Israel but in territory it controlled. What law should apply to them? The question arises in a huge variety of issues. But as the settlers—and, as it turned out, the state—saw it, it was inconceivable that these Israelis would have to live under Jordanian law, ruled by a military government, and subject to the military justice system. The solution, a very problematic one, was to apply Israeli law to the Israelis living in the territories, while their Arab neighbors from across the road continued to be subject to Jordanian law and the laws legislated by the military governor. The result is that when an Israeli and a Palestinian are involved in an incident, the Israeli's case is generally heard in an Israeli court according to Israeli law and procedure, while the Palestinian's case is heard in a military court. The situation is intolerable. In contrast, when an Israeli and a Palestinian in the territories sign a business agreement, a single law has to apply to the contract. In a case in which the question arose regarding labor relations between an Israeli employer and his Palestinian workers, the Supreme Court ruled in 2007 that Israeli law was to be applied to both sides.[34]

Questions of principle also arose. For example, can Israel's Supreme Court, as part of its power to oversee government authorities, hear cases involving the actions of the military government in the West Bank and Gaza Strip? And if so, can an inhabitant of those territories petition the Supreme Court against the military commander, arguing that the latter is violating the Hague Conventions regarding the laws of war, or the Geneva Conventions regarding the protection of civilians?

The public debate over these issues was a subdued one, and these kinds of issues were barely addressed in judicial rulings over the years. In practice, a single person decided such issues. That was Meir Shamgar, who was appointed attorney general in 1968. He accepted the premise that the Supreme Court was empowered to hear cases involving Israeli actions in the territories. When petitions were submitted he, the government's attorney, did not argue that the issues lay outside the court's authority. That was an exceptional position to take, because in countries with legal systems similar to Israel's, such as the United States and Britain, the courts refrain from overseeing territories conquered in war by those countries. With regard to the status of the territories and the application of international law and international treaties regarding occupied territories, Shamgar adopted a theoretical approach according to which the territories were not occupied. But he also declared that Israel would take upon itself to act in accordance with the humanitarian directives of those treaties. The Supreme Court has indeed applied them in its rulings.

The result was a chimera representing Israel's ambiguous attitude toward the territories. Judea and Samaria are not, according to Israel, occupied territories, except that humanitarian rules of international law apply to them as if they were occupied territories. But neither are they parts of the state of Israel.

This legal snarl grew exponentially more complicated in 1977. The Begin government allowed a group of settlers to move onto the site of Elon Moreh near Nablus. To provide the new settlement with land, the government expropriated lands, including private Palestinian land. Supreme Court petitions against this move exposed an ideological dispute within the Israeli establishment and some of the legal problems raised by Israel's control of the territories.

The Supreme Court had been petitioned about land confiscations in the past, but it had always denied the petitions on the grounds that the expropriation was for military purposes. In the Elon Moreh case the state, and the IDF chief of staff, also claimed that the expropriated private land was needed for military purposes, but other military experts disputed that.[35]

The dispute heated up when Defense Minister Ezer Weizman, one of the respondents to the petitions, acknowledged that "[t]he security needs can be achieved without establishing a settlement in the place under discussion." Yigal Yadin, the leader of the centrist Democratic Movement for Change,* who had years before served as the IDF's second chief of staff, opposed the establishment of the settlement and asked that the government reconsider its decision. In addition, Gush Emunim, the settler movement, declared that Jews should settle all parts of the historical Land of Israel. Prime Minister Begin, for his part, stressed that "the Jewish people has a right to settle in Judea and Samaria, and these things are not necessarily connected ... to national and state security concerns." The conclusion was that the dominant consideration in expropriating the land was ideological and not military. The court, which had issued a temporary injunction halting the expropriation, turned it into a rule absolute.

Begin did not try to deal with this ruling or change it via legislation. He understood very well that it was not an obstacle to his plans. The legal trick was to establish settlements on state-owned land, a category that applied to large swathes of West Bank territory. This was land that had belonged to the Jordanian state in accordance with Ottoman law and came under Israeli state control after the Six Day War. The Supreme Court did not prevent settlements on this category of land, just as it did not prevent settlements built on private land for security reasons.

The issue first arose in 1967, after the Six Day War and well before the legal revolution. In those days a person could petition to the high court only if he had standing. In the case of state land, nobody had a personal interest that would grant him the standing required to bring a suit. Moreover, in 1981, still in the pre-revolutionary era, a case concerning a dispute about whether a certain piece of land was private or state-owned, and whether the procedures established to decide such issues was legal, came before a bench consisting of Justices Aharon Barak and Dov Levin and

---

* The Democratic Movement for Change (DMC) was a centrist party that sought to reform Israeli politics and administration. It won fifteen seats in the 1977 elections, an unprecedented performance for a new party, but that was not enough to grant it the balance of power. Begin formed a government without it, but kept cabinet portfolios open in the hope that it would give him its support—as it indeed did not long thereafter.

chaired by Shamgar. In his ruling, Shamgar stated that Article 55 of the Fourth Hague Convention of 1907 requires the military governor to "safeguard the capital" of public properties "and administer them in accordance with the rules of usufruct [the right to use property and enjoy its profits]." The land could therefore not be sold but may be leased or rented.[36] It is, however, very doubtful whether the settlers consider themselves mere leaseholders who can be evicted when the lease expires.

Issues relating to the settlements arose again in 1991, when the legal revolution was well on its way. A panel chaired by Chief Justice Shamgar, joined by Justices Eliezer Goldberg and Theodor Or, held that the settlements reflect governmental policy in which the court will not intervene. The petitioners claimed that such settlements violated both international law and Israel's own constitutional principles. The court pointed out that the petitioner was challenging a general policy of the Israeli government, not some specific act, and as such the court would not address it. The opinion the court issued includes phrases reminiscent of the old court, before the legal revolution, such as "[the court] must refrain from discussing issues of foreign policy, which are invested in other branches of government." In other words, the matter is not justiciable.[37]

This is clearly not in line with Justice Barak's position on justiciability. But on this specific issue the court never changed course, not even after the appointment of Barak as chief justice in 1995. Presumably this was a matter crucial to the government. An attempt by the court to stop the settlements might well have led it to a collision with the government on a scale that could have jeopardized the legal revolution.

The bottom line is that settlements have not been blocked for legal reasons (except when built on Palestinian private land and when there were no security reasons to justify it), although they have sometimes been stopped for political ones.

Thus, paradoxically, the Elon Moreh ruling failed to put the brakes on Israeli settlements in the territories, after which they actually proceeded at an ever-increasing pace.

3

The Attorney General and His Powers

Did the new state need an attorney general? The answer was not obvious to its founders. The Mandate administration had such an officer, who served as the regime's minister of justice and its chief lawyer and legal adviser. After the establishment of Israel, the country's first minister of justice, Pinhas Rosen, was invested with many of the powers that, under the Mandate, had been wielded by the chief justice of the Supreme Court and the attorney general. Prime Minister David Ben-Gurion maintained that the minister himself, aided by his staff, could advise the government on legal issues. He advocated concentrating full legal authority in the office of justice minister, subject however to the appointment of an independent state attorney, to head the state prosecution. Rosen thought otherwise. He sought and achieved the appointment of an attorney general, subordinate to the justice minister but responsible for providing the government with legal counsel. Notably, the Hebrew term for "attorney general" translates literally as "legal adviser," and thus stresses this office's duties as counselor to the government. However, in addition to his position as adviser he was also made head of the prosecution.

The first person to fill the post was Yaakov-Shimshon Shapira, a member of Mapai, a well-regarded private attorney, and a man of great authority. He did all he could to enhance the powers and influence of the post. He also demanded that the attorney general participate in cabinet meetings, but Ben-Gurion refused. Apparently it was this refusal that prompted Shapira to resign in 1950.

The post was offered to State Attorney Haim Cohn, who was not identified politically but had close relations with Ben-Gurion. He served in the post for a decade, until his appointment to the Supreme Court, to the seat vacated by Justice Shneur Cheshin. In the area of criminal law, Cohn took an entirely independent stance, reflected in his decisions on who and when to indict. He had no hesitations about filing charges even when the government was less than enthusiastic. One case in point was the libel suit he filed in the name of the state, over the opposition of Justice Minister Pinhas Rosen and Minister of Commerce and Industry Dov Yosef,* against Malchiel Gruenwald. Gruenwald had denounced Israel Kastner, then the spokesman of the Ministry of Commerce and Industry. Kastner had sought to save Hungary's Jewish community by negotiating with Adolf Eichmann, the German Nazi who played a

---

* Dov Yosef, a very well-known lawyer, had previously served briefly as minister of justice.

major role in the implementation of the Final Solution in countries conquered by Germany during World War II. Gruenwald had accused Kastner of collaborating with the Nazis in order to save his relatives and friends. Furthermore, Gruenwald alleged, Kastner had received economic benefits, which made him for all intents and purposes an accessory to the plundering of Jewish property by the Nazis. He also charged Kastner with intervening in the case of a Nazi officer, Kurt Becher, to enable him to escape punishment after the war.

The lawsuit proved to be a mistake and turned into a debacle. The Kastner trial, as it came to be called, raised questions about the conduct of Jewish leaders during the Holocaust and unnecessarily tangled the government up in a highly emotional controversy. It proved that the attorney general's professional judgment is not necessarily better than that of his political superiors. Moshe Sharett, who replaced Ben-Gurion as prime minister for a two-year period, appreciated Cohn's abilities and integrity, but wrote in his diary (not in connection with the Kastner affair) that Cohn "is devoid of all public astuteness."[38] The District Court's findings against Kastner were devastating, even as it acquitted him of economic gain and abetting the plunder of Jewish property. (The court found Gruenwald guilty of libeling Kastner on this charge and imposed a nominal fine of one Israeli pound). Kastner, the court declared, had "sold his soul to the Devil." The affair shook Sharett's government. In the end the major part of the District Court's severe findings against Kastner were overturned in a majority decision on appeal (although not the finding that he had testified in Germany after the war in favor of Nazi war criminal Kurt Becher).[39] Gruenwald, who was found guilty of libel in charging Kastner with collaborating with the Nazis in addition to charging him of gaining from the plundered Jewish property, received a suspended sentence of one year in prison.[40] But Kastner was already dead then, felled by an assassin's bullet.

Cohn's decisions about who not to indict were even more interesting, reflecting as they did his liberal outlook. For example, he did not file charges against an abortionist who had performed the procedure on a woman with her consent and without negligence, even though the procedure was illegal. He also refused to bring homosexuals to trial when the relations were between consenting adults (the Knesset later decriminalized such relations). Cohn also instigated a fundamental change in the legal code in 1954—the elimination of the death penalty for the crime of murder. The death penalty remained in force, however, for other crimes, such as those contained in the Nazi and Nazi Collaborators (Punishment) Law, the law Adolph Eichmann was later convicted under by an Israeli court. He was the only person against which the death penalty has been carried out in the history of the Israeli state.

Cohn's successor was Gideon Hausner, an active member of Rosen's Progressive Party. As in the case of Shapira before him, his was the appointment of a political figure to the post of attorney general. During Dov Yosef's tenure as justice minister, he and Hausner vied over legal powers. The dispute between them reached the cabinet, which in June 1962 decided to form a committee of jurists to study the issue and make recommendations. The chairman of the committee was Justice Shimon Agranat and his colleague Justice Zvi Berinson, along with a well-known attorney, Avraham Levin. The committee endorsed Hausner's position that the attorney general had the final say in all decisions regarding indictments. Nevertheless, the committee stated that the attorney general was required to take government penal policy into account in making his decisions. Furthermore, in cases with security, political, or public implications, he was to consult with the minister of justice, or in some cases with the full cabinet. But, following such consultation, the final decision lay in his hands.

On the other hand, the committee fully accepted the justice minister's position about the attorney general's role as legal counsel to the government. "The proper order of government requires that, in general, the government respect the attorney general's *legal* opinions" (emphasis in the original). Nevertheless, "the government is permitted ... to decide for itself how to act in a specific instance, in accordance with its discretion."

The committee favorably cited one of the examples the justice minister had brought before it—a case in which the attorney general recommends bringing a particular case to trial, on the grounds that he thinks the state has a good chance of success. The government, the committee said, was nevertheless permitted to decide to reach a compromise rather than go to court. (Obviously, the committee was not referring to criminal cases, in which plea bargains also involve a form of compromise. In such cases, however, the decision is exclusively that of the attorney general and the government may not intervene.) On the other hand, the freedom not to act in accordance with the attorney general's position is available only to the government. All other authorities in the executive branch must accept the attorney general's opinions on legal issues as binding.

The climax of Hausner's tenure was his appearance as chief prosecutor in the Eichmann trial, which earned him a place in history. This very public role strengthened his position against the justice minister. Nevertheless, after the trial Hausner realized that his differences with the minister were too great for him to remain in his post. It is hard to believe, but back in those days, when the attorney general did not see eye-to-eye with the justice minister, it was the attorney general who resigned. Later the positions reversed, and on occasion an attorney general caused a justice minister, and sometimes even a prime minister, to resign. In those cases the attorney general continued to hold his post as if nothing had happened, and, if anything, his position was strengthened.

In 1968, after the Six Day War, Justice Minister (and former attorney general) Yaakov-Shimshon Shapira proposed to appoint Meir Shamgar to the post of attorney general. Shamgar served as the Israel Defense Forces' chief military advocate general during the war. In his youth, Shamgar had been a member of the IZL (the Revisionist underground militia that Begin had commanded during the British mandate period). His appointment to the post of attorney general was a step in Prime Minister Levi Eshkol's policy of ending Ben-Gurion's ban on the appointment of former IZL operatives and members of the Herut Party to senior public positions.

Shamgar had a commanding personality and used that to augment the powers of his new job. He made major changes in the attorney general's manner of operation. One of these was that he began issuing directives. In theory, these were meant to provide guidance and assistance on legal issues to government offices, but over the years they were gradually imbued with legislative force. He also subordinated the legal counsels serving in the individual ministries to him, creating a situation in which the ministries gradually came to see themselves as subject to his centralizing authority. Seven years later, Shamgar was appointed to the Supreme Court. His successor as attorney general was Aharon Barak, a professor of law who just a year before had taken up the post of dean of the Hebrew University of Jerusalem's law school.

4

The Legal System Topples Rabin

The idea that a cabinet minister might be investigated for criminal offenses and even indicted would have seemed fantastic during the state's early years. True, there were some exceptional cases. Minister of Defense Moshe Dayan, an avid collector of artifacts and amateur archaeologist, was alleged to have pilfered items that, by law, should have been turned over to the Israel Antiquities Authority. Dayan made no secret of his collecting, but his status as an unchallenged national hero left the authorities powerless to do anything about it.[41]

That changed after the Yom Kippur War, when the public utterly lost confidence in the country's leadership. The ruling party, Mapai, was increasingly accused of corruption and favoritism. Paradoxically, this happened after Mapai had made important changes in the way it operated. It no longer filled government positions only with party members, as the appointment of IZL (the Revisionist underground militia that Begin had commanded during the British Mandate period) veteran Meir Shamgar to the post of attorney general demonstrated. Similarly, Shamgar's successor, Aharon Barak, had not been politically active and was not identified with Mapai.

The weakening of the central government meant that the law-enforcement system now enjoyed public support for investigations of political figures. At the end of 1974, soon after Yitzhak Rabin formed his first government and while Shamgar was still attorney general, the police began investigating Michael Tsur, CEO of the Israel Corporation, a holding company chartered in 1968 to funnel foreign investment into Israel. Minister of Industry and Commerce Pinhas Sapir had appointed Tsur the ministry's director general at the age of thirty-five, and Tsur later held other important economic posts. Tsur was convicted on several counts of corruption and sentenced to fifteen years in prison. His appeal of the severity of his sentence was denied, but after serving about six and half years in prison he received a presidential pardon and was released.

Even worse for Mapai was the Yadlin scandal. Asher Yadlin had served in two top posts in the Histadrut labor union, which then controlled a large sector of the economy and functioned almost as a second government in the social and economic realm. He had been CEO of Hevrat HaOvdim, the holding company that oversaw the Histadrut's economic enterprises; and of Kupat Holim Clalit, the Histadrut's medical services provider. In early September 1976, the government decided to appoint him governor of the Bank of Israel. A police complaint had been filed against him by Yigal Laviv, a journalist at a sensationalist weekly, *Ha'olam Hazeh*. Laviv claimed that Yadlin had taken bribes as part of a deal in which Kupat Holim had purchased a vacation village at Sharm el-Sheikh in the southern Sinai Peninsula. The police investigated the charges at length but found nothing to incriminate Yadlin. But a second set of suspicions followed, involving Yadlin's dealings with a friend named Hava Ehrlichman, with whom he claimed to have had intimate relations.

Yadlin later related that on a Friday afternoon two weeks after the government decided to nominate him as governor, he received a phone call from Attorney General Aharon Barak, inviting him to a meeting at his office. There Barak told Yadlin of the two investigations and suggested that he speak to the chief of the Police Investigations Department, Jacob Kedmi (who would later serve on the Supreme Court). Yadlin, an experienced political operative, evinced considerable naivety. He was not acquainted with the legal world. A criminal investigation against a person of his stature was exceptional at that time, and he had just met with the attorney general, the person whose job it ostensibly was to help the government get Yadlin confirmed quickly as the Bank of Israel's governor. He was apparently not aware that the attorney general wears two hats, that of counsel and that of prosecutor, and that in his case the two were in conflict. Which attorney general had suggested that he meet with Kedmi—the government's chief counsel or the one in charge of the state prosecution?

In a memoir he wrote about the affair, Yadlin recalled how he felt. "Sitting across from me was a trustworthy man, who spoke to me gently—trust me, the matter will be over in the blink of an eye." Yadlin did not even think of consulting a lawyer, so sure was he that Barak was offering him a way of putting the whole matter to rest quickly.[42]

As they spoke, Kedmi and his deputy arrived. At this point Yadlin realized that he was being interrogated, yet he did not reach the obvious conclusion. He was still hoping to be the Bank of Israel's next governor. When Kedmi phoned him the next day and asked for some clarifications, Yadlin could not resist the temptation to offer a further defense of himself. The conversation ended up going on for hours. At the end Kedmi told him that he hoped that the matter would soon come to an end, but that he had to speak to Barak. Kedmi called again on Saturday afternoon to tell Yadlin that they would be pleased if he would consent to a lie detector test. It would take only ten minutes, just three questions, and then he would be able to notify the attorney general that everything was fine.[43]

Yadlin's trust in the police investigator was beginning to unravel, but he still had perfect confidence in the attorney general. He asked to speak to Barak. Barak told him on the phone, so Yadlin later related, that he was under no obligation to agree to the procedure. But, Barak said, he thought that the polygraph could bring the whole matter to an end that same evening. Still seeking an easy way out of the thicket he had gotten caught in and hoping to avoid a lengthy police investigation, he again refrained from consulting an attorney. He reported for the examination, but the promised ten minutes soon turned into hours. He later claimed that Kedmi had told him that the examination took a long time because the device was giving unclear data about his answers.

On October 17, 1976, Yadlin's appointment again came up before Rabin's cabinet. Barak presented the ministers with a document relating to several real estate deals that Kupat Holim had been involved in, with Ehrlichman as the agent. The suspicion was that Yadlin had received bribes totaling 48,000 Israeli pounds (IL). The investigation had to be continued, Barak said, noting that Yadlin denied all the charges against him. At this point, after the Sharm el-Sheikh case had collapsed, the prosecution's case did not look at all impressive. Nevertheless, the only cabinet member to defend Yadlin was Housing Minister Avraham Ofer. While the cabinet did not cancel the appointment, it endorsed Barak's recommendation that the investigation proceed. The police now had a free hand.

Yadlin was arrested the next day. At a later stage, when charges were filed, the prosecutor asked the court to extend his detention until the end of the trial. The prosecution request was heard and approved by District Court Judge Dov Levin. Yadlin appealed the decision to the Supreme Court, which affirmed Levin's ruling.

Yadlin's incarceration prior to his conviction was the harshest and most serious element in the whole affair. It stood in opposition to the theory that the courts always seek to protect human rights, while the legislature always threatens them. In this case the Supreme Court grossly violated Yadlin's rights, while the Knesset subsequently passed legislation respecting the rights of suspects and defendants in criminal trial. Jailing a man who has not yet been convicted of a crime, a person who is supposed to be presumed innocent, is a clear violation of his rights. Courts have the power to order a suspect incarcerated until the end of proceedings, but up until 1988 the law did not specify in what cases this was justified. At the time, the decision was at the sole discretion of the courts, who looked to British law for the grounds on which they could do so: the fear that the defendant would abscond, or that he was dangerous to the public, or that he would seek to influence witnesses or otherwise disrupt the trial.

In the Yadlin case the courts enormously broadened the rules of detention. In dismissing Yadlin's appeal to the Supreme Court, Chief Justice Yoel Sussman ruled that "[i]t is necessary to take into account the public repercussions of releasing a prisoner of this rank . . . This consideration in and of itself requires, when the evidence in possession of the state proves a method of bribe-taking that continued over a long period . . . that such a defendant not walk free until his case has been heard."[44] This decision, by one of Israel's greatest judges, is regrettable. The idea that freeing a public figure on bail until the end of his trial will have negative public repercussions and this requires keeping him incarcerated—even though he might be found innocent—is unacceptable and outrageous.

Such arrests clearly make it much easier for the prosecution to obtain conviction, even when the defendant is innocent, if only through a plea bargain. Men and women with no criminal record who find themselves mixed up in a criminal case for the first time in their lives find it difficult to endure incarceration, coming as it does on top of the public humiliation they have suffered, the tension involved in the trial, and the expense of defending themselves. They also find it difficult to conduct their defense, since that requires, especially in complex business cases, putting material together, examining documents, and conducting inquiries. Obviously, it is extremely difficult to do all this from a jail cell. The result is that such detainees are often willing to reach plea bargains, even if they truly believe they are innocent.

The courts' harsh incarceration policy was sharply criticized, and the Knesset took action in 1988. It passed a liberal amendment to the Criminal Procedure Law to remedy the courts' unjustified severity, so detrimental to human rights. But the change was only a partial solution. The courts continue on occasion to keep suspects in jail without regard to their rights, including during police investigations.

The prosecution seemed at first to have little chance of obtaining a conviction in the Yadlin case, but with the defendant in jail the picture changed. Along with the pressure that his detention exerted on him, it signaled to others that Yadlin was a lost cause. It did not take long for the prosecution to find two witnesses who were willing to help incriminate Yadlin in return for immunity from prosecution. Yadlin later claimed that, had jail not broken him and had his friend and supporter Avraham Ofer not committed suicide, he would have been able to prove that the sums he received from the two witnesses were not bribes given to him personally but were rather designated for a fund that would be made available to him for party political purposes. Other senior members of the party had similar funds, he said.[45]

Yadlin's lawyer, Shlomo Tusia-Cohen, who had come into the case very late, thought that, under the circumstances, there was now a fairly high chance he would be convicted.

Ofer, the housing minister in Rabin's cabinet, had come under investigation at about the same time as Yadlin. Ofer was suspected of corrupt practices in Shikun Ovdim, a public housing company. His investigation also grew out of a series of exposés written by Yigal Laviv, on the basis of which the journalist also submitted a complaint to the police. The charges Laviv made were then echoed in banner headlines in other newspapers as well. The police investigated each of Laviv's allegations and found that most of them were baseless. Prime Minister Rabin, who was very fond of Ofer, was furious about how the lengthy investigation was disrupting the government's work. He demanded that the inquiry be expedited, but without success. In the end, Attorney General Barak agreed to report on the case to Rabin.

The two men met on Saturday, January 1, 1977. Also in attendance were Finance Minister Yehoshua Rabinowitz, Justice Minister Haim Zadok, and Police Minister Shlomo Hillel. The meeting was supposed to be a secret one, but word of it leaked and journalists and photographers staked out Rabin's private home. The next day's headlines vilified Ofer. Rabin was displeased. "I can promise," he said, "that no notification of the time and place of the meeting came out of my office."[46] He again demanded that Barak at the very least provide him with confirmation, in writing, that the police had found no evidence to prove the great majority of the allegations against Ofer and that the investigation still underway only had to do with four or six other charges. Rabin later claimed that Barak's response was: "Fine, tomorrow morning you'll receive a status report from me, regarding the counts for which no basis had been found and those on which the investigation will continue." But when the cabinet convened the next morning for its weekly meeting, Rabin related, "the reverse happened—Barak notified me that the police opposed providing Rabin with a letter, as we had agreed in my home on Saturday."[47] Rabin was thus unable to make a statement regarding where the investigation stood. Presumably the police were interested in maintaining ambiguity so as to put pressure on Ofer. Such pressure sometimes leads suspects to confess. (According to another version of the story, Barak backtracked on his promise to report to Rabin on Ofer's case because in the interval new evidence against Ofer had reached the police.[48]) But if the intention was to exert pressure on Ofer, it worked better than intended. Ofer, who had expected some relief, could take no more. On January 3, 1977, his body was found in his car.

He had shot himself. The note he left said: "For the last weeks and months they are spreading rumors about me, spilling my blood, leveling unfounded accusations against me, abusing me. I have no doubt that the truth will come to light, that I have not embezzled and I have not stolen, that they are all false accusations, but I don't have the strength to bear it any longer."

The affair led to a rupture between Rabin and Barak. In his memoir, Rabin wrote: "My confidence in him was shaken by the Avraham Ofer affair. It seemed to me that, seeking for himself the image of a brave and impartial man, he had actually given in to public opinion."[49] When Yadlin heard of Ofer's suicide, he broke out in tears and suffered bad chest pains, requiring his hospitalization in a hospital intensive care unit.

In the end Yadlin chose to agree to a plea bargain. He confessed to several counts of taking bribes and other lesser offenses, in the hope that that would put an end to the affair. But in the end it did him no good. Whatever chance he might have had of acquittal was lost, and the sentence he received was a harsh one—five years in prison and a fine of IL250,000. The Supreme Court dismissed his appeal.[50]

Subsequent proceedings against Yadlin involved Mordechai Ellison, who was arrested on suspicions that had no connection to Yadlin. Under interrogation, he told the police that he had given Yadlin's sister $30,000. In exchange for his testimony about this, he was made a state's witness and granted immunity from prosecution in the case against him.

Yadlin and his sister were indicted on the basis of Ellison's testimony. Yadlin pleaded innocent and his lawyer, Tusia-Cohen, tried to persuade Attorney General Barak to withdraw the indictment. Yadlin had already been punished severely, Tusia-Cohen argued, and there was no reason to conduct a new trial. But he did not succeed. Yadlin was again offered a bargain—he could plead guilty on lesser charges, and in light of his already heavy sentence, the prosecution would make do with a fine of IL5,000. Yadlin refused.

One possible explanation for Barak's insistence on charging Yadlin in the new case is that Ellison had been made a state's witness and it was necessary to justify the grant of immunity. In my view, however, it is best not to indict a person for lesser crimes committed prior to those included in an earlier indictment. But that is in fact done in Israel from time to time.

Yadlin's second trial did not arouse much interest because it was conducted after Mapai lost power and the public no longer had any interest in the defendant. But this time the prosecution suffered an embarrassing defeat. District Court Judge Menachem Ilan dismissed the charges against Yadlin's sister at the end of the prosecution's presentation, ruling that there was no case for her to answer. Yadlin himself was acquitted, with Judge Ilan declaring that "Ellison's entire account . . . is artificial and forced, fabricated in order to save his own skin."

Then it was Rabin's turn. In March 1977, shortly before the national elections slated for June of that year, Dan Margalit of *Ha'aretz* revealed that Leah and Yitzhak Rabin had a bank account in the United States. The dollars deposited there dated to Rabin's service as Israel's ambassador in Washington. But the law at the time forbade them to continue to hold such an account once they had returned to Israel.

While this was an offense, the law empowered the minister of finance to allow the offender in such cases to pay a fine as a way of avoiding prosecution. Rabin met with

Barak and understood from him, so it seems, that he could resolve the issue in this way. "Barak spoke gently and soothingly, as if the matter were a minor one. Leah was very much surprised and her fears were allayed."[51] Barak later explained that he spoke then on the assumption that the sum residing in the account was a relatively modest one. When he learned that it was about $20,000, he said, he saw no way of avoiding a trial. And there were indeed precedents for going to trial because of sums of this size.[52]

The authority to decide whether to forego prosecution and to allow the payment of a fine lay in the hands of the finance minister. A ministry committee that addressed the matter recommended a fine. Finance Minister Rabinowitz very much wanted to accept the recommendation. But Barak officially notified him that he should not do so.

There are two versions regarding what Barak told Rabinowitz. According to one account, which appears in Rabin's memoir, he told the finance minister that if he were to decide to impose a fine and a citizen were to petition the Supreme Court, Barak would not defend Rabinowitz's decision before the court.[53] The problem is that at that time the rule was that a petitioner had to have standing to petition the court—that is, he had to demonstrate that he had a personal interest in the matter. As such, there could have been no real chance that such a petition would be filed, and if one was, it would almost certainly be dismissed by the court. This is exactly what happened when a private individual petitioned the court demanding the opposite— that a fine be imposed on the Rabins. Justices Alfred Witkon, Haim Cohn, and David Bechor denied the petition on just these grounds, that the petitioner had no standing.[54] Did Rabin know that? His book indicates that he did not.

A slightly different account appears in Nomi Levitsky's biography of Barak,[55] as well as in a book-length interview with Barak by Ariel Bendor and Ze'ev Segal.[56] In this version, Rabinowitz told Barak that no one had standing to petition the Supreme Court in the matter, to which Barak replied that in such a case he, Barak, would file a suit. In such a case, Barak warned Rabinowitz, the finance minister would have to retain a private attorney to represent him, at his own expense.*

Both versions highlight the conflict of interest inherent in the attorney general's two roles—that of prosecutor and that of legal counsel to government officials liable to or seeking to avoid prosecution. Paradoxically, here the attorney general prosecuted the prime minister while at the same time "advising" (but actually demanding

---

* At the time, while I served as dean of the Tel Aviv University law school, I met with Minister of Justice Zadok. He related to me the first version of the story, according to which Barak declared that he would not defend Rabinowitz before the Supreme Court. I told him that, as far as I could see, there was no person with standing in the matter and suggested that Rabin be granted a pardon. Zadok asked whether a pardon could be issued prior to conviction. I explained that I saw no difficulty in doing so, citing the pardon that President Gerald Ford had granted to his predecessor, Richard Nixon. That pardon was issued before Nixon was tried in connection with the Watergate scandal and was aimed at heading off such a trial. (Of course, there was no similarity between the crimes of which Nixon was accused and Rabin's offense.) Zadok responded that, even if a pardon were possible, he did not think it was right. As, in Israel, a pardon without the recommendation of the justice minister is highly unlikely, that was the end of the idea.

that) the finance minister not take an action that would obviate the criminal proce-dure that the attorney general wishes to pursue. It is highly probable that had the Rabins and Rabinowitz received independent legal advice, they might have been able to settle the matter without trial.

Barak's conversation with Rabin, just after the revelation about the American bank account, is reminiscent of Barak's conversation with Yadlin. Who did Rabin think he was talking to, the head of the state prosecution, with an interest in prosecuting the case, or the government's legal counsel, seeking to extricate Rabin from the mess he found himself in? Rabin had learned something from the Ofer affair and wrote in his memoir that he did not have much faith in Barak. Yet in his own case he did not seek out independent legal advice, believing that it would not be proper for a prime minister to do so.

Rabin might well have been able to save himself had his wife taken full respon-sibility for the account, as it would have not changed anything for her and would have rendered his culpability technical. But Rabin refused to make any distinction between himself and his wife, and insisted that he was equally responsible for the failure to close the account. In fairy tales, such chivalric behavior pays off. In Israel, not necessarily.

When Rabin realized that the possibility of a fine had been blocked and that Barak was determined to indict him, he announced his resignation and declared that he would not be a candidate in the upcoming elections. In fact, the government had become a transitional one, and Israeli law did not allow resignation in that case, so in April Rabin went on leave and leadership of the government was handed over to Shimon Peres. Here, too, Rabin's dignity was on display. He did not seek an ar-rangement under which he would not be charged if he resigned. Nevertheless, Barak realized that under the circumstances there was no point in an indictment, and al-lowed Rabin to pay the fine and thus avoid a criminal charge. But Barak was not prepared to do the same for Leah Rabin. He brought her to trial, where she pleaded guilty. District Court Judge Dov Levin imposed a heavy fine of IL250,000 or a year in prison. In her memoir, she pointed out that the fine was equivalent to the cost of a very nice apartment in those days.[57]

Was it right to deny Rabin the option of a fine? Rabin had been a prominent Palmach (Hebrew acronym for strike companies, the elite force of the Yishuv's para-military defense organization, during the British Mandate) commander during the War of Independence and Israel Defense Forces chief of staff in the Six Day War—the man responsible for the victory that saved Israel from destruction. Should that not have been taken to account? Furthermore, the foreign currency in the Rabin ac-count had not been purchased on the black market. The account had been opened lawfully and had simply not been closed when the Rabins returned to Israel. In ad-dition, putting a prime minister on trial shakes the government and can have fateful consequences for the country. Should that consideration be set aside in the case of a minor offense?

At around that time the Supreme Court issued a ruling in which it declared that foreign currency violations were not ones of moral turpitude. As Justice Cohn put it, "an offense that carries a fine by discretion of an administrative authority is by its very nature an offense that bears no turpitude, whether or not the fine was im-posed."[58] Should a prime minister have been brought to resign over such an offense?

It should be noted, however, that the public accepted and appreciated the handling of the Rabin affair. That may have been one more aspect of the Labor Party's decline following the Yom Kippur War and of changing public attitudes toward the country's leaders. Barak enjoyed public support and popularity. The prime minister's resounding resignation did much to enhance Barak's prestige and was an important milestone in establishing his elevated position in the public eye.

Another scandal involving a leading figure in Labor came in the wake of the Rabin affair. Abba Eban, who had served as foreign minister in the Eshkol and Meir cabinets, was discovered to have more than $300,000 in a foreign bank account—more than ten times what the Rabins had had. Eban, who was not in the cabinet at the time, learned from the Rabins' experience. He hired top-flight private attorneys. His claim, supported by his secretary, was that he had been given special permission by the Ministry of Finance to keep this sum overseas—but that he had lost the document proving this. No copy of such a permit could be found in the Finance Ministry, nor any reference to its existence. But this time Barak overruled the Jerusalem district attorney and closed the case without bringing Eban to trial.

Under such circumstances, the payment of a fine in lieu of prosecution seems eminently reasonable. Presumably, had Eban been given the alternative of paying a fine or going to trial, he would have chosen the former. Barak, however, did not see that as an option, because it would have looked problematic for him to agree to a fine for a foreign bank balance so much higher than that of the Rabins, who had not been given that option. The choice was thus between indictment or nothing. Barak chose nothing.

"Law? Justice? I learned an instructive lesson in the meaning of those concepts," Leah Rabin wrote. "First, [Eban] was not a political target at the time. Second, he apparently had a very skillful defense attorney (he needed it!)."[59] Her sense that she had been treated unjustly stayed with her throughout her life. She refused to shake Barak's hand even at her husband's funeral, following his assassination.

Another similar case arose fifteen years later, when Rabin was serving as prime minister for the second time. In November 1992 the government decided to appoint Itamar Rabinovich, a professor of Middle Eastern history at Tel Aviv University, to be Israel's ambassador to the United States. An opposition member of the Knesset, Gonen Segev, demanded that the appointment be withdrawn on the grounds that Rabinovich had maintained a bank account in the United States without a permit, apparently from the period while he was on sabbatical there. Rabinovich had already paid a fine for this income tax and foreign currency violation. The cabinet confirmed the appointment in January 1993. Segev petitioned the Supreme Court.

The petition was heard before a panel headed by Barak. No issue of standing came up (as it almost certainly would have had the court received a petition in Rabin's case in 1977), since in the course of the legal revolution, then well underway, the requirement of standing had been almost completely abolished. It looked as if the government might have to cancel the appointment. But, as Levitsky relates in her biography, "Rabin was unconcerned." According to Shimon Sheves, director general of the Prime Minister's Office at the time, Rabin's reaction said a lot about what he thought about the legal system. "I know them," Rabin said. "They'll defend Rabinovich because he is one of them."[60] He was right. This time the state attorney defended the appointment, even though the sum in Rabinovich's account was similar to what had been in the Rabins'. The petition was denied, and the new ambassador flew to Washington.

The court did not offer its grounds for the decision, simply stating that it would do so at a later date. But time passed, month after month, and nothing happened. Everyone was curious to see what the court would say, but the reasons were not forthcoming.

Rabin was assassinated in November 1995. Immediately thereafter, while the country was in turmoil, several important legal developments occurred. First, when the traditional seven-day mourning period came to an end, while the government was still operating in a caretaker capacity, Dorit Beinisch was appointed to the Supreme Court. A month and a half after the assassination, on December 19, the court finally issued its opinion in the Rabinovich case. It is a brief document, certainly in comparison to other similar judgments, just four pages long. It does not explain why it was necessary to wait so long for such a brief opinion. Chief Justice Barak, who chaired the panel, simply stated that "only when the offense is not serious in nature and circumstances is there room to impose a fine."[61] Does that mean that in the Rabins' case the nature and circumstances of the violation were serious enough to obviate that option?

In fact, there were no grounds for the court to invalidate Rabinovich's appointment. There is no justification for the Supreme Court to intervene on ostensibly moral grounds and to claim that a government appointment is not reasonable, just as the attorney general had no business intervening in the decision of the responsible authorities to impose a fine on Rabin in lieu of prosecution. Yet there are three difficulties with the decision in Rabinovich's case. First, it left an impression of discrimination between Rabin and Rabinovich, underlining the problematic nature of the severe line taken in Rabin's case. Second, the lengthy, unreasonable delay in issuing the opinion, without any adequate explanation, raises the question of whether the cause was the court's concern about an inevitable comparison between the two cases. Third, is it legitimate for the court to put off issuing a judgment or opinion to a date convenient to the court for public or political reasons? In other words, should the court exercise the kind of discretion in this regard that might be appropriate in the case of political bodies? Does that not amount to a politicization of the process of justice, resulting from judicial activism and the fact that the court itself had become a player in the political arena?

5

Menachem Begin

Temporary Justice Minister

In 1977, after Yitzhak Rabin was ousted from the prime ministership, Israel experienced the first change of government in its history. The Labor Alignment went into the election led by Shimon Peres, who was much less popular than Rabin. The Labor Party, the Alignment's principal component, had (under the name Mapai) ruled the Yishuv during most of the Mandate period and the state of Israel for the nearly three decades since it had been founded. Now it lost the election. Likud, which had no experience in running a country, won. Its leader, Menachem Begin, became prime minister.

Begin was a great admirer of Aharon Barak and probably felt that he owed Barak a great deal. After all, in bringing down Rabin Barak had helped Begin win the election. Begin asked Barak to stay on as attorney general, and Barak agreed. At first Begin formed a narrow government based on a bare majority in the Knesset. But, hoping to lure a new and successful center party, the Democratic Movement for Change, into his coalition, Begin kept several portfolios in reserve, among them the justice ministry. In the meantime, he himself served as minister of justice. During his short tenure in the post he managed to do quite a bit. One notable initiative was in the area of extradition. Israel had an extradition treaty with Switzerland and, under its terms, Switzerland demanded that Israel deliver into its hands an Israeli citizen named Reuven Pesachowitz, for whom a Swiss investigating magistrate had issued a warrant. Pesachowitz stood accused of fraudulently obtaining credit of close to 10 million Swiss francs from a local bank. The extradition process had begun in Israel a few years previously, when the attorney general asked the Tel Aviv District Court to declare Pesachowitz extraditable. The court did so, and the Supreme Court unanimously rejected his appeal.[62]

The final determination regarding extraditions is, however, vested in the minister of justice. Begin, as temporary justice minister, ruled that Pesachowitz would not be handed over to the Swiss. It was a scandalous decision. While the final power of decision was indeed vested in the justice minister, the minister needed to have serious reasons to refuse to extradite after the accused had exhausted his recourse to the courts and they had declared him extraditable. But Begin had an emotional opposition to turning over Jews to gentiles. Jewish tradition took a severe attitude toward talebearers and informers. And Begin had sharp memories of the Season, in which members of the Haganah (the Yishuv's paramilitary defense organization, the forerunner of the Israel Defense Forces [IDF]) and Palmach (an elite force of the Haganah) turned over IZL (the Revisionist underground militia that Begin had commanded during the British Mandate period) operatives to the British.

All the effort that the attorney general and his staff had put in to extradition had thus been in vain. Begin's decision struck a blow against the attorney general and against the rule of law, a value Begin often waxed eloquent about. He could make the technical claim that he had simply exercised the power vested in him, but in fact he had misused his power. This time Barak made no response and did not threaten to petition the Supreme Court himself. In practice, he accepted Begin's action. There was also no petition to the Supreme Court. Apparently no one is Israel had the necessary standing to do so.*

A few years later, with the advent of the legal revolution, the picture had changed completely. In February 1983 an Arab was murdered in France, and the local authorities suspected a French Jewish citizen, William Nakash, of being involved in the crime, along with several others. Nakash fled to Israel, where he took an assumed name and claimed Israeli citizenship on the basis of the Law of Return. When his true identity was revealed, the French demanded his extradition. The Jerusalem District Court ruled that he was extraditable, but Minister of Justice Avraham Sharir decided not to return Nakash to France. Sharir claimed that there was reason to fear for Nakash's life if he were arrested in France. Shulamit Aloni, member of the Knesset, joined by some other members and public figures, petitioned the Supreme Court to force Sharir to extradite Nakash. A bench of five justices headed by Chief Justice Shamgar heard the case.

By this time a new spirit pervaded the court. In a decision rendered in 1987, some ten years after Begin's decision regarding Pesachowitz, the majority on the panel reversed the court's traditional position on standing and ordered the Nakash extradition to be sent back to the justice minister, who was enjoined to examine whether the danger to Nakash, were he extradited, was indeed any greater than that in other such cases.[63] A commission Sharir appointed to examine the question found that there were no adequate grounds for Nakash's claims and recommended his extradition. Nakash then himself petitioned the high court, but his suit was denied and he was sent back to France.[64]

But the Pesachowitz affair took place at a time when the Supreme Court was still reluctant to second-guess the decisions of political leaders. Begin felt that the decision he had made in Pesachowitz's specific case was insufficient. He sought a fundamental change in the extradition law. In short order he prepared and had the Knesset pass an amendment to the Foreign Offenses Law, which came to be known as the Begin Law. It provided that no Israeli citizen would be extradited for any offense committed after he became an Israeli citizen, and that citizens could be tried in Israel for a range of specific offenses, specified in the law, committed in other countries. The legislation was extremely problematic, as became painfully evident in September 1997, when a brutal murder was committed in the state of Maryland. One of the suspects

---

* The Swiss authorities, as well as the Swiss bank involved, might conceivably have had the required standing, but they did not apply.

in the crime was a seventeen-year-old Jewish youth named Samuel Sheinbein. He managed to obtain an Israeli passport and fled to Israel. American-born, Sheinbein was a U.S. citizen who had lived there all his life, but he held Israeli citizenship as well thanks to a grandmother who had lived for a time in Israel and taken citizenship there. By Israel law, Israeli citizenship devolved on her children and grandchildren even though she no longer lived in the country. The American government opened extradition proceedings. The case reached the Israeli Supreme Court, where it was heard by a bench of five justices. A majority of three justices ruled that the Begin law made it impossible to extradite Sheinbein. Chief Justice Aharon Barak remained in the minority, along with Justice Jacob Kedmi.[65]

The Sheinbein case was "a diplomatic, moral, and legal nightmare," as David Weiner, a senior attorney in the Public Defender's Office, wrote.[66] American officials and members of Congress attacked Israel, causing the country untold damage. There was no choice but to amend the Begin law, which the Knesset did in 1999, so that persons of Sheinbein's status could be extradited.* But, obviously, the change did not apply to Sheinbein, who, in accordance with the Begin law, was tried in Israel. He reached a plea bargain with the prosecution, according to which he was sentenced to twenty-four years in prison. That was a much lighter sentence than he would have received in the United States. He was jailed in Israel but did not serve out his term. On leave from jail he obtained a pistol and was able to smuggle it into his prison cell. In February 2014 he opened fire on his jailers and was killed in the gunfight that followed.

During his term as justice minister, Begin also recommended the pardon of the former director of the Israel-British Bank, Yehoshua Ben-Zion, who had been convicted of embezzling a huge sum of money from the bank, which eventually collapsed. Ben-Zion claimed that he suffered from a medical condition that required his release from prison and provided documents supporting his claim. Israel's president, Ephraim Katzir, accepted Begin's recommendation and pardoned Ben-Zion, who was released after serving only three years of his twelve-year sentence. The pardon was questionable in the extreme, given that the court that sentenced Ben-Zion had taken into account his medical condition when meting out his punishment.[67] Furthermore, just a year previously the Supreme Court had denied a petition by Ben-Zion to release him for the same reason.[68]

The pardon was hugely controversial. In formal terms, Begin could claim that he had acted in accordance with the law. The power to pardon lies with the president, and Begin, as justice minister could make whatever recommendations he saw fit. But in practice the pardon dealt a heavy blow to the legal system.

In this case, too, the attorney general kept his peace. His biographer claims that Barak "was deeply shocked" and even considered resigning. In the end he decided not to do so at the urging of Chief Justice Sussman.[69] Presumably, had Barak resigned he would not have been appointed to the Supreme Court a year later.

.

---

* In addition, an Israeli citizen who is a resident of Israel can be extradited subject to the condition that, if sentenced to prison abroad, he will be allowed to serve his prison term in Israel.

Ben-Zion, who won a pardon on the basis of his tenuous medical situation, lived on for many years thereafter, all the while proclaiming his innocence. He died in 2004, twenty-five years after his pardon, outliving Begin by a dozen years.

Begin served as justice minister for several months, until the Democratic Movement for Change (DMC) finally agreed to join the government. The justice portfolio was given to Shmuel Tamir, a DMC leader who had previously been a bitter political rival of Begin's within the Herut Party. Begin had no choice but to accept the appointment, given his desire for the DMC to bolster his coalition, but he did all he could to clip Tamir's wings. The real victim was the post of justice minister itself. One way Begin limited Tamir's influence was by having the attorney general participate regularly in cabinet meetings. This enhanced Barak's standing and hurt Tamir's. He also refused to involve Tamir in negotiations with Egypt, making Barak the leading legal member of the negotiating team instead. Barak also participated in the Camp David negotiations after his appointment to the Supreme Court.

Begin's term as prime minister was full of surprises and crises. One of the biggest surprises occurred on Saturday night, November 19, 1977, when Egypt's president, Anwar Sadat, arrived in Israel. In a historic speech to the Knesset, he declared himself willing to enter into peace negotiations. These eventually produced a peace treaty between Israel and Egypt, signed in March 1979 on the White House lawn.

The agreement granted Egypt all its territorial demands—the return of the entire Sinai Peninsula. That required Israel to evacuate all the settlements it had built there. The agreement also recognized "the legitimate rights of the Palestinian people." Israel's principal achievements were the fact of signing a peace treaty with the largest and strongest Arab country; reaffirmation of its right to free navigation of international waterways, including the Suez Canal; the demilitarization of Sinai; and the end of Egypt's participation in the Arab boycott.

The severe economic crisis that Israel faced following the Yom Kippur War worsened under Begin. A few months after the election, in October 1977, the government declared an "economic revolution" that included an end to foreign currency controls. The new policy sent inflation spiraling. In 1978 it reached 116 percent and was still rising. Likud found itself in a problematic position going into the 1981 elections, but three weeks before the poll Begin ordered the bombing of a nuclear reactor under construction in Iraq. The successful strike helped Begin win the election and form his second government.

Begin, who had been vilified on the right for making concessions to Egypt and, in particular, for agreeing to evacuate the Sinai settlements, pursued a more hawkish line in his second term. In December 1981 he quickly pushed through the Golan Heights Law, which applied Israeli law to the territory taken from Syria in 1967, thus effectively annexing it. Half a year later, in June 1982, with Palestinian guerillas ensconced in southern Lebanon, Begin sent the IDF into Lebanon, starting the First Lebanon War. Begin and his defense minister, Ariel Sharon, believed that by allying with the Christian Phalange forces commanded by Bachir Gemayel they could drive Palestinian terror groups out of Lebanon and end once and for all their use of southern Lebanon as a base for attacks on Israel. Israeli forces quickly pushed northward and reached Beirut, Lebanon's capital, but suffered heavy losses.

In August Gemayel was elected Lebanon's president. Yet before he could take office he was felled in an explosion. Angry Phalange forces were given a green light by

Israel to enter the Sabra and Shatila Palestinian refugee camps in Beirut. On the night of September 16, seeking to avenge their murdered leader, the Christian forces slaughtered hundreds of Palestinian men, women, and children.

A week later hundreds of thousands of Israelis turned out in central Tel Aviv to protest not only the massacre but also the war itself. Begin gave in to the protestors' demands for an independent commission of inquiry to examine the massacre and the events that led up to it. Chief Justice Yitzhak Kahan, by law charged with appointing such a commission, decided to head it himself. As its other members he chose Justice Aharon Barak and IDF Major General (ret.) Yona Efrat.

Begin now encountered Barak in a different guise, and this time it did not end with Begin extolling the rule of law and the judges of Jerusalem. In its report, issued in February 1983, the Kahan Commission found that no one among the Israeli political or military leadership intended or wished the massacre to happen, and yet the decision to allow the Phalange forces into the refugee camps without any oversight was made without proper consideration of the risks involved. The commission held a number of Israeli leaders and IDF commanders personally responsible for what had happened, declaring that "it should have been foreseen that the danger of a massacre existed if the Phalangists were to enter the camps without measures being taken to prevent them from committing acts such as these." While Begin had testified that "no one conceived that atrocities would be committed," the commission asserted that "we are unable to accept the position of the prime minister that no one imagined that what happened was liable to happen."[70]

Kahan and his two colleagues also implicated Sharon and recommended that he leave the post of defense minister. That did not, however, prevent him from later being elected prime minister.* Thirty years later Dov Weissglas, who had served as Sharon's legal counsel before the Kahan commission and later as director of his office during his service as prime minister, issued a sharp critique of the commission. He claimed that no one in the intelligence community had anticipated the massacre and that information that arrived later indicated that the atrocity was instigated by the Syrians, who were seeking to stymie the possibility of an agreement between Israel and Lebanon.[71]

Begin was deeply wounded by the conclusions. Yehiel Kadishai, a close associate, related that Begin had been deeply disappointed with Barak and that "from that day to his last he never again pronounced the name of Aharon Barak."[72]

On August 28, 1983, Begin announced that he could no longer lead the government. Two months later he resigned and left politics. A few weeks later, in November 1983, Meir Shamgar was named chief justice. The war in Lebanon was not yet over and inflation was soaring to new heights. The government, battered by these events and without its charismatic leader, was weak and riven by dissension. It was about to face a newly assertive and confident Supreme Court.

---

* A commission of inquiry is, of course, free to establish facts and reach conclusions, both positive and negative, regarding cabinet ministers, but in my opinion it is not proper for such a commission to rule whether a given person is fit to hold a political position and serve in the cabinet. The government certainly is not obligated to act on such a recommendation. Nevertheless, given the difficult political position of the government following the war, it was unable to oppose the recommendation or refrain from acting on it.

PART TWO

The Legal Revolution

6

The Legal Revolution Takes Off

I. THE TRANSITIONAL PERIOD

In the classic period, the Supreme Court was small, composed of justices who were generally appointed at a relatively young age. As such, most of them served fairly long terms, guaranteeing stability and cohesion on the bench. That does not mean, of course, that the court was an idyllic place where consensus always reigned. But most of the justices during that period had studied law overseas, more often than not in England or Germany, and while working as private attorneys, judges, and scholars during the Mandate had absorbed the English tradition of self-restraint.

The change began in 1975, at the tail end of the classic period, when Meir Shamgar, then the attorney general, was appointed to the court at the age of fifty. Shamgar was much younger than all the other justices on the court at the time, many of whom had been appointed some twenty years earlier. Soon after he took up the gavel, Menachem Begin was elected prime minister. Begin's six years as Israel's leader, from 1977 to 1983, were a transitional period for the court. There were clear signs that it was moving in a new direction. One notable instance came in 1980, when Justice Aharon Barak, two years after his appointment, asserted that the court had the authority to void acts of government on the grounds that they were not reasonable.[73] As a result of Shamgar's young age at his appointment, and the retirement of his older colleagues in the few years that followed, by late 1983, just after Begin resigned the prime ministership, Shamgar was the most senior justice on the court. Under the customary seniority system, he thus became chief justice. (The seniority system, determined by the number of years served on the Supreme Court, has no legislative basis, but the justices of the Supreme Court have been able to convince the Judicial Selection Committee to select each time the most senior justice as chief justice. The committee is not bound by this tradition and can in principle deviate from it, but has never done so.)

Nevertheless, during the transitional period, between 1975 and 1983, the court continued to issue rulings that evinced the same aspiration for stability that had characterized the classic court. Yet the composition of the court underwent rapid change. Within seven years, between 1976 and 1983, four men served as chief justice— Shimon Agranat, Yoel Sussman, Moshe Landau, and Yitzhak Kahan. Compare this with the previous twenty-eight years, during which only three chief justices served— Moshe Smoira, Yitzhak Olshan, and Agranat.

Shamgar's appointment marked the passing of the baton to a younger generation. Up to that point all the chief justices (with Olshan being the single exception) had immigrated only after completing their legal studies. Shamgar, in contrast, arrived at the age of fourteen and sometime later joined the IZL, the underground militia headed by Menachem Begin. He studied history and philosophy for one year at the Hebrew University in Jerusalem. In 1944 he was deported by the British to detention camps in Eritrea, Sudan, and Kenya, where he spent nearly four years. During his incarceration, he studied law by correspondence with the University of London and obtained an Ll.B. degree. The two chief justices who followed him, Barak and Dorit Beinisch, studied law in Israel.

There was another difference as well. All the previous chief justices had worked as private attorneys, and some of them had been District Court judges. Starting with Shamgar, Israel's chief justices have come from another direction entirely. With the exception of Asher Grunis, who was appointed chief justice in 2012 and served for less than three years, none had worked as a private attorney or served on the District Court bench.* Their principal legal experience was in the public service, as attorney generals or state prosecutors.

The retirement of the older generation of justices led to a wave of new appointments under Shamgar. One noteworthy phenomenon, which continued afterward as well, was a rapid turnover of associate justices. They were appointed at advanced ages and retired after serving relatively short terms. Nevertheless, some of the appointments were quite significant. Miriam Ben-Porat, the first woman named to Israel's Supreme Court, served for eleven impressive years. Menachem Elon, a professor of Hebrew law, held the court's "religious seat" for almost sixteen years.

Barak was appointed not long after Elon, in 1978. He was only forty-two years old at the time. His young age not only ensured that he would eventually become chief justice but also that he would serve on the court for twenty-eight years (of which eleven were as chief justice), the longest term served by any justice in the new era. The fact that Chief Justices Shamgar and Barak served on and led the court for very long periods, at a time when most other justices served relatively short terms, made them hugely influential.

The appointment of Shamgar as chief justice in November 1983 came at about the time that Menachem Begin resigned as prime minister. The national elections of 1984 were close, and the new court issued a ruling that notably affected the nature of the Knesset—the Knesset elected that year and those that followed.

II. SHAMGAR AS CHIEF JUSTICE

The legal revolution, the dramatic upheaval in which the legal establishment would come to overshadow the other branches of government, can be dated to Meir Shamgar's accession to the post of chief justice of the Supreme Court in November

---

* Grunis retired in 2015, and Justice Miriam Naor was appointed chief justice. Naor never practiced as a private attorney. She served in the State Attorney's Office, after which she became a judge in the Magistrates Court, was promoted to the District Court, and was subsequently appointed to the Supreme Court.

1983. His appointment also marked the final step in a changing of the guard on the Supreme Court. At that point, not a single member of the founding generation remained on the bench, a personnel shift that was a central factor in the empowerment of the judicial branch at the expense of the government and the Knesset. The first generation of Supreme Court justices, educated in Europe or in the Anglo-American world, did all they could to avoid intervening in political issues, recognizing the sovereignty of the Knesset and the need for self-restraint. But as these judges retired they were replaced by judges of native Israeli background and education who, making good use of the prestige that the court had gained under their predecessors, sought to involve the court in matters that had heretofore been outside its purview. And this was precisely the time when a weakened political establishment was helpless to oppose the judicial activism that was eating away at its powers.

A new chief justice at first presides over judges appointed to the court during the tenure of his predecessors. But, under Israel's method of appointing judges, a chief justice who serves an extended term can, especially if many of the judges on the bench when he comes into office are of an advanced age, to a great extent mold the court in his image. In Shamgar's case, there were twelve other judges on the court when he became its chief, two of those holding temporary appointments. By the time he retired, only five of the original justices remained. The other eight had been appointed under his watch and with his direct involvement, since the chief justice serves as one of three Supreme Court justices who are among the nine members of the committee that chooses new judges.

When, after eight years on the court, Shamgar became chief justice, there were three justices who had come to the court straight from the public prosecution. Gabriel Bach had been state attorney, while Shamgar himself and Aharon Barak had been attorneys general. During Shamgar's tenure as head of the court this number grew. Two key appointments were Jacob Kedmi, who had served as chief military prosecutor and then headed the Investigations Branch of the Israel Police before being appointed a District Court judge, and Itzhak Zamir, who had served as attorney general. Another such appointment that Barak promoted, that of State Attorney Dorit Beinisch, was aborted at the last minute when Shamgar withdrew his support. To this day he has not offered any explanation for that change of heart. He may well have been wary of the positions Beinisch had taken on security matters, for example when she refused, in 1993, to represent the government when the Supreme Court heard a petition opposing the cabinet's decision to deport to Lebanon 415 Palestinian members of Hamas who had been arrested by Israel (the case will be discussed below). He may also have been swayed by Prime Minister Yitzhak Rabin's opposition to Beinisch's appointment, and perhaps he had other reasons.[74] Whatever the case regarding Beinisch, the security issue seems to have been a factor in another appointment, that of Mishael Cheshin in January 1992.

Cheshin, the son of Justice Shneur Zalman Cheshin, one of the five original members of Israel's Supreme Court, completed his law degree at the Hebrew University summa cum laude. His early career was spent mostly in the Ministry of Justice; during Shamgar's service as attorney general, Cheshin was his deputy. But when Shamgar was appointed to the Supreme Court, Cheshin was skipped over for the attorney general's position, and Aharon Barak was appointed attorney general instead. The two men worked together closely until Barak himself was appointed to the Supreme Court, at which time Cheshin was skipped over one more time in favor of Itzhak Zamir, a close friend of Barak's. Cheshin left the ministry and went into private practice.*

His legal talent had never been disputed, although his short temper and sharp tongue might have blocked his path to the top, but in 1992 Shamgar decided to seek Cheshin's appointment to the Supreme Court. Shamgar did not state his considerations, but most likely the chief justice, who then stood just three years before mandatory retirement, wanted the court to have counterweight to Barak. Under the traditional seniority system, Barak was slated to succeed Shamgar as chief justice. Despite his activist judicial philosophy and his long collaboration with Barak, Shamgar was much less extreme in his approach than his imminent successor and rejected Barak's contention that "all is justiciable."

Another important subject on which Shamgar and Barak differed was security. Shamgar recognized the limitations the court faced in addressing issues of war, counterterrorism, and the existential issues faced by the state. Barak's position was that, when it came to the court's authority, there was no distinction to be made between war and peace and all other issues. In his view, the court can examine the reasonableness of an action carried out by the country's security forces on par with a case regarding a decision made by a building contractor. The difference between the two came to the fore in the cases, to be discussed below, of the pardon granted to the Shin Bet operatives involved in the Bus 300 incident and the expulsion of Hamas members to Lebanon. Shamgar seems to have viewed Cheshin as a candidate who could restrain Barak's agenda of inserting the court into security and matters relating to the survival of the state.

Cheshin proved to be a justice to be reckoned with. But he did not have the power to overcome Barak's rulings in the security realm. Barak benefited from his superior status and wielded huge clout with the majority of the justices. Cheshin found himself repeatedly in the minority, including the case of the repatriation of Hezbollah prisoners to Lebanon. A rare exception was the slim, one-vote majority Cheshin led against Barak in a ruling that affirmed the Knesset's power to prevent Palestinians from gaining a right to reside in Israel by virtue of marriage to Israeli citizens.

Cheshin's temper was on display when he was asked about this ruling by Yuval Yoaz, a reporter for *Ha'aretz*. The interview was published in May 2006, shortly after Cheshin's retirement from the court. Speaking of Barak, who at the time was still chief justice, he said: "Justice Barak can live with thirty to fifty people getting blown up so long as there are human rights. I am not. He thinks one way, I think another. I'm very glad I was in the majority." (Cheshin issued a public apology to Barak immediately after the article appeared.)

III. THE LEGAL REVOLUTION'S MAIN FEATURES

The legal revolution that began under Shamgar and reached its climax during Barak's tenure as chief justice was characterized by the rapid annulment of a long series of legal rules and principles that had previously constituted the foundation of the Israeli

---

* I thought Cheshin was the appropriate candidate and said so publicly in an article I published in *Ma'ariv*.

system. They were replaced, one after the other, with new rules that expanded the powers of the Supreme Court and transformed it into a major actor in the governance of the state. The new approach was diametrically opposed to the legal tradition that had prevailed under the British Mandate and during the first thirty-five years of Israeli independence, a tradition firmly based on the principle of the separation of powers and cautious judicial development.

Part of the new system was a radicalization of certain civil rights, in particular freedom of speech and the freedom to be elected to office, in total disregard for the price to be paid. It also did away with the convention that certain issues lay beyond the purview of the courts, replacing it with an approach that viewed any, or almost any, subject as justiciable in principle. Another rule that was cast aside was the one requiring a petitioner to the Supreme Court to have legal standing in the case at hand. Furthermore, the Supreme Court asserted its power to revoke decisions of the cabinet and even the Knesset for being unreasonable, adopted a new standard of legal interpretation centered on a law's purpose or intention, as that seems to the judge, rather than on the actual wording of the law. This enables judges at times to determine that a law means something completely different from what it says. It led to legislation by interpretation, turning the court into a super-legislator.

Nevertheless, the Shamgar court of 1983–1995 and the Barak court of 1995–2006 are clearly distinguishable. Under Shamgar, the court still recognized in principle that there were nonjusticiable issues, at least to a limited extent. In particular, the justices of the Shamgar court exercised self-restraint in the area of national security, and this ensured public confidence in the court. Shamgar led a court that still included figures like Miriam Ben-Porat and Menachem Elon, who opposed what they viewed as Barak's overreach, often leaving him in the minority on matters of principle.[75] All this changed when Barak became chief justice. The judges who were prepared to contend with him reached retirement age. Barak's approach that even political and national security issues were subject to judicial review became dominant. The relative restraint that characterized the Shamgar court evaporated, and along with it so did the public's absolute trust in the court.

The Supreme Court's new and central role in running the country rested on three legs: the abrogation of the requirement of legal standing, the doctrine that all government actions and decisions were subject to judicial review ("everything is justiciable"), and the rule that any decision of a public authority can be quashed on the ground of unreasonableness. These principles created a situation in which, for all intents and purposes, every decision made by a governmental authority could be appealed to the Supreme Court. Examples of cases brought before the court included agreements reached by the government with terrorist organizations in which convicted terrorists were traded for Israeli captives or the bodies of soldiers. Prior to the Barak court no one would have dreamed of suggesting that such a matter was subject to judicial review. Yet, as the legal revolution became ensconced in the court's practice, it became inevitable that a subject of such public import be brought before the court. While it is true that the court did not in fact intervene in these matters (even though some of the agreements were patently unreasonable), the very fact that it heard the cases and granted opponents of the agreements an additional platform for making their arguments shows just how far the court's reach had extended.

The legal revolution also involved a drastic change in the working practices of the Supreme Court, and thus of other courts as well. When the Supreme Court took up issues of great importance, it seemed only proper to the court and the public that these cases be heard by large benches. Bringing such a case before a large panel of justices underlined its importance and provided a more persuasive result. Unlike the U.S. Supreme Court, in which all nine justices sit on every case, the Israeli Supreme Court assigns smaller panels of judges—usually three. In the court's first decades, larger panels were rare. In the wake of the revolution, panels of seven, nine, and even eleven justices became routine. At the same time, the old practice of writing concise and methodical opinions was replaced by a new fashion of long, taxing opinions hundreds of pages long, full of *obiter dicta* (tangential remarks), to which the court sought to give the force of legislation. One prime example is the ruling handed down in 1995 that first established the court's power to annul a law passed by the Knesset on the ground that it conflicts with Basic Law: Human Dignity and Liberty. The opinion, all of which was obiter—namely, not required for the decision actually reached—is nearly 340 pages long. Former Justice Haim Cohn remarked that this is the longest obiter ever written in Israel.

As a result of these developments the court found itself flooded with petitions that in the past would have been rejected on the grounds of a lack of standing or justiciability, but which were now accepted with open arms. The court's work was thus thrown into disarray. One consequence is that four or five years, and sometimes longer, goes by between the court's hearing of a case and its handing down of its decision. The central role initially assigned to the Supreme Court, that of hearing civil and criminal appeals, has been shunted aside. The entire legal system is paying a heavy price for the Supreme Court's decision to assume, at its own initiative, a role entirely different from that assigned to it by the Knesset. It has presumed to become a constitutional court in a country that lacks a constitution.

The malfunctioning of the Supreme Court cascaded into the lower courts, where judges also began to write unnecessarily long opinions. They also adopted the new standard of legal interpretation, which was taken to grant the courts discretion in every area and in all matters.

Another less familiar aspect of the legal revolution is that it greatly expanded criminal liability at the expense of fundamental principles of human rights. That is the subject of chapters 24 and 25.

7

Undermining the Political System

I. THE NATIONAL UNITY GOVERNMENTS (1984–1992)

Israeli elections are conducted on a national-proportional basis, with a large number of political parties, movements, and factions running slates each time. Any party that gets over a fairly low threshold wins seats in the Knesset in proportion to the percentage of the votes it receives.* To form a government, a candidate for prime minister needs to cobble together a coalition of parties supported by a majority of the Knesset's members (MKs), meaning, in the case of Israel's 120-member parliament, usually at least 61 (though a minority government is also conceivable). This arrangement functioned reasonably well during the period in which the Labor Party (previously known as Mapai) was in the ascendant and no other party received enough seats to be able to be the lynchpin of a government. But Labor hegemony began to unravel following the Yom Kippur War of 1973.

In the elections of 1977 Labor's fortunes declined drastically and Likud won. Likud's leader, Menachem Begin, formed a government with the support of religious and Haredi parties, later adding the Democratic Movement for Change, a new but short-lived center party that made an impressive showing at Labor's expense. In the following elections, in 1981, Labor (running in the framework of the Alignment) recovered and received almost as many votes as Likud, but Begin again formed a government. However, two years later Begin suddenly resigned and withdrew from public life. The years that followed were marked by intense rivalry between the two major parties, Likud and Labor, which remained more or less equally matched. The small parties thus held the balance of power and upped their demands, which provided the incentive for the two large parties to form a series of national unity governments. The jockeying for power between Labor and Likud at times led both parties and their leaders to disregard the most minimal rules of political decency. In some cases they "acquired" parliamentarians who were willing to cross the aisle in exchange for benefits and perks. This reached its height in the 1990 episode that came to be known as the Dirty Trick, that is discussed later in this chapter.

---

* The threshold was 1 percent until 1992. It was then raised gradually, most recently in 2014, when it was set at 3.25 percent.

As the large parties grew weaker and dependent on their coalition partners, Israel's judicial system gained power dramatically. The Supreme Court was able to assert its power and pursue a much more activist role, further attenuating the power of the Knesset and the cabinet.

After Begin's resignation in November 1983, Likud, following a grueling intraparty struggle, chose a new leader, Yitzhak Shamir, who became prime minister. But turmoil within his party continued. Elections to the Knesset were set for July 1984. The country at that time was on the brink of despair. The Lebanon War of 1982 and its aftermath, during which Israeli forces remained deep inside Lebanese territory and suffered many casualties, had deeply divided the country. The massacre at the Sabra and Shatila refugee camps in Beirut in September 1982, committed by Lebanese Phalangist forces after Israel's occupation of the southern part of the Lebanese capital, had severely damaged Israel's international standing. At the same time, Israel was in the throes of a severe economic crisis. Inflation had reached astronomical levels (191 percent in 1983, 445 percent in 1984), and Israel's citizens felt that the country was on the brink of disaster. Despite the crisis, the results of the 1984 elections were ambiguous. Labor received more votes and Knesset seats than Likud, but when the small parties lined up behind each of the large ones there was a tie. As a result, Likud and Labor formed a national unity government and agreed to rotate the premiership between them. Labor leader Shimon Peres took the top post first. According to the agreement, he would serve as prime minister and Shamir as foreign minister for two years, after which they would switch.

Despite this tenuous political balance, the unity government was able, under Peres's leadership, to successfully address the two central crises it had inherited from Begin's tenure—the Lebanon quagmire and hyperinflation. The government pulled back Israeli forces from most of the territory they had occupied during the war, leaving them only in a security zone in southern Lebanon, and put in place an economic program that halted and reduced the inflation rate. Another ray of light was the crisis in the Soviet Union, which led to the easing of restrictions on Jewish emigration and a growing influx of new *olim*—as Jewish immigrants to Israel are called—from that country that changed the face of Israeli society.

As the rotation agreement dictated, Peres and Shamir changed places in November 1986. In his new capacity as foreign minister, Peres reached understandings with King Hussein of Jordan regarding the future of the Israeli-occupied West Bank, but Shamir aborted the agreement and refused to bring it before the cabinet for consideration. In December 1987 a Palestinian uprising in the West Bank and Gaza Strip, the Intifada, began, first with Palestinians throwing stones at Israelis and their vehicles, and then escalating into more severe violence.

National elections were held again in November 1988, with Shamir entering the campaign as the incumbent prime minister. The results perpetuated the virtual dead heat between the two major parties, with Likud winning forty seats and Labor thirty-nine. Once again the smaller parties held the fate of the larger ones in their hands. But given that the Haredi parties and the National Religious Party preferred Likud, Shamir was assured the support of sixty-five members of the Knesset. While this meant that he could form a right-wing government, Shamir preferred once again a national unity government with Labor. However, given the majority he enjoyed even without Labor's support, he was not compelled this time to agree to rotation in the premiership.

This government proved volatile and lasted barely a year and a half. In March 1990 Labor left the coalition and the government fell in a no-confidence vote. President Chaim Herzog appointed Peres to form a new government; to gain a Knesset majority, however, Peres needed the support of all the Haredi factions. But Rabbi Elazar Menachem Shach, the spiritual leader of one of the Haredi factions, declared his inalterable opposition to a Peres government. His position influenced the spiritual leader of another Haredi party, Rabbi Ovadiah Yosef of the Sephardi-Mizrahi* Shas movement, to withhold his support from Peres as well.

Peres was, however, determined to form a government. At this point he could count on only sixty MKs, comprising his natural left-wing allies and one small Haredi party. He thus needed one more vote and found it in a disgruntled former Likud minister, Avraham Sharir, who agreed to cross the aisle in exchange for the promise of a guaranteed Knesset seat and other privileges. This gambit came to be called the Dirty Trick, and by common consensus it was one of the low points of Israel's political history. The move was aborted on the Knesset floor when Peres presented his new government. Two of his putative Haredi supporters absented themselves, and it transpired that they had no intention of supporting the new government. Peres had to inform the president that he had failed.

Herzog then asked Shamir to form a government. Shamir's methods were hardly more impressive. He issued a humiliating public plea for Sharir to "come home" and then gained the support of a wayward Labor Knesset member who transferred his support in exchange for appointment as a deputy minister. This gave Shamir a bare majority, producing a weak and contentious government. Shamir was unable to enforce discipline in his party and among his coalition parties, creating a situation in which the government was unable to steer the legislative process.

In the wake of the Dirty Trick, public confidence in Israel's government plunged. The political system was debilitated and the government increasingly unable to function. All this happened at a time of fierce ideological dissension over religion and state, security policy, and Israeli settlement in the territories taken in the Six Day War. The Supreme Court moved into this vacuum, taking advantage of the opportunity to enlarge its powers at a time when the government and the Knesset were in no position to hold it back. Only in one particular instance, the Bus 300 affair, which will be addressed below, did the two large parties display a rare common front, enabling the government to overrule Attorney General Itzhak Zamir's demand for a police investigation of the Shin Bet, Israel's internal security service, and to oust him from his post.

II. THE GOVERNMENT LOSES CONTROL OVER LEGISLATION

The weakening of the central government had another consequence. As coalition discipline loosened, members of the chamber were increasingly able to pass laws over the objections of the government. Active MKs passed sweeping reforms in the areas of civil and labor rights in 1988–1992. The Knesset's Constitution, Law, and

---

* The Mizrahi (Oriental or Eastern) is a sub-group of the Sephardi community. See chapter 2 above.

Justice Committee, under its Likud chairman, Uriel Lynn, sent the Knesset a series of laws of huge import. At the initiative of Labor Knesset Member Ora Namir, the Knesset passed the Employment (Equal Opportunities) Law of 1988, which forbade discrimination between workers and job applicants "on account of their sex, sexual tendencies, personal status or because of their age, race, religion, nationality, country of origin, views, party or duration of reserve service." This advanced liberal law had profound consequences for Israeli life and culture.

One major consequence of this expansion of labor rights came in 1989 and received much public attention. As part of its collective bargaining agreement with its workers, El Al airlines granted once a year a free airline ticket to the spouse or partner of each of its tenured employees. The language of the agreement made it clear that the term referred to a partner of the opposite sex. Jonathan Danilowitz, a flight steward, requested a ticket for his male partner, and when El Al refused he took his case to court. The Regional Labor Court ruled that the restriction of the benefit to partners of the opposite sex stood in violation of the Employment (Equal Opportunities) Law, which forbade discrimination on the basis of sexual orientation. Thus, a steward whose life partner was a man should receive the benefit as well. This ruling was upheld on appeal to the National Labor Court.[76]

El Al petitioned to the Supreme Court, which had previously ruled that the Labor Courts were subject to its review. A three-judge panel upheld the Labor Court ruling, with Justice Aharon Barak and Justice Dalia Dorner issuing a detailed opinion. Justice Jacob Kedmi remained in the minority.[77] The majority opinion devoted considerable attention to the right to equality, with Barak suggesting that the plaintiff would have been deserving of legal remedy even in the absence of the 1988 law.

The Supreme Court ruling was welcomed by Danilowitz and Israel's homosexual community, but was sharply condemned by the Haredim. Given that the Knesset had forbidden discrimination in the labor market on the basis of sexual orientation, the Labor Courts' rulings were hardly surprising. The Supreme Court could simply have issued a brief decision stating that, in light of the provisions of the law, it saw no cause for intervening in the Labor Courts' purview. Instead, the justices chose to take up the legal question at stake in its broadest sense. The result was that the court, rather than the Knesset, received the credit for this liberal turn that improved the standing of single-sex couples. At the same time, it opened itself up to severe and gratuitous criticism from the religious community, who should have directed their ire at the legislature rather than the court.

In addition to regular legislation in the area of human rights, the Knesset also took significant steps in the area of basic laws. Lynn, chairman of the Constitution, Law, and Justice Committee, had belonged to the Liberal Party, one of the components that had allied to form Likud, often disregarded the government's instructions. For example, a group of Knesset members, among them law professors Amnon Rubinstein and David Libai, sought the passage of a basic law on human rights, and the Likud minister of justice, Dan Meridor, also lent his support. Such an initiative had been unsuccessful in the past. But now the political situation created a unique opportunity. Two bills were introduced: Basic Law: Human Dignity and Liberty, and Basic Law: Freedom of Occupation. In negotiations with the religious parties, the bills' sponsors and supporters agreed to significant compromises, and both laws were enacted in 1992.

The compromises reflected the fact that a range of issues that one might have expected such basic laws to include are not addressed. For example, the Basic Law: Human Dignity and Liberty does not mention the right to equality, most likely because of the religious parties' concern that if it did so it might affect Jewish religious marriages and divorces, which grant different rights and prerogatives to men and women. However, the law's first section refers to the principles contained in Israel's Declaration of Independence, which was formulated in a liberal way and includes the right to equality.

For the same reason, that is, to ensure the support of the religious parties for the Basic Law: Human Dignity and Liberty, the law makes no mention of the right to marry. Furthermore, Section 10 states: "This Basic Law shall not affect the validity of any law . . . in force prior to the commencement of the Basic Law." This provision was inserted to ensure that the law not mandate any change in Israel's marriage and divorce law, even though the fact that the monopoly that Israeli law grants to religious courts in these areas means that there is in fact no right to marriage. For example, people of no religion cannot be married in Israel, nor can a Jew marry a non-Jew.

Another provision reflecting a major compromise states that the basic law's purpose is "to establish in a Basic Law the values of the State of Israel as a Jewish and democratic state." The combination "Jewish and democratic" has since been the source of reams of commentary and disputation.

The Basic Law: Freedom of Occupation is "entrenched" by virtue of its Section 7, according to which "[t]his basic law shall not be varied except by a basic law passed by a majority of the members of the Knesset." However, the broader and much more important Basic Law: Human Dignity and Liberty enjoys no special status. Nothing prevents its revision or annulment, or requires a special Knesset majority to do so. Nor does Basic Law: Human Dignity and Liberty include provisions authorizing the courts to review legislation passed by the Knesset. That power derives entirely from judicial rulings. The interpretation that the activist court has given to this basic law is that the Supreme Court has the power to nullify laws the Knesset has passed subsequent to its enactment (if these laws are not basic laws themselves) when this later legislation is inconsistent with the Basic Law: Human Dignity and Liberty.* In this it reversed the rule that had previously been the standard, that a later law always takes precedence over a previous one, even a basic law, unless the basic law requires a special majority for its amendment or revocation.

The actual passage of the two basic laws proceeded almost without protest and attracted little attention. Less than half the Knesset's members were present for the vote, the press barely noted the event, and it seemed as if no one noticed that something important had taken place. But it did not take long for the Basic Law: Human Dignity and Liberty to generate profound divisions and controversies. That same year, Deputy Chief Justice Barak published an article entitled "The Constitutional Revolution: Protected Basic Rights,"[78] and continued to promote the idea contained

---

* This interpretation is less problematic with regard to the Basic Law: Freedom of Occupation in view of Section 7 quoted above, and Section 8 of the law, enacted in 1998, which clearly indicates that subject to certain qualifications, legislation which conflicts with this basic law is invalid.

in its title, both in writing and orally. In reaction, Justice Mishael Cheshin questioned whether Israel had, in promulgating these basic laws, in fact adopted a constitution.[79] Likewise, former Chief Justice Moshe Landau stated in a panel discussion in 2000 that Israel's constitution was "the only one in the world to be created by judicial fiat." Numerous legislators claimed after the fact that they had no idea that they were passing a constitution, and that they had had no intention of changing the balance of power between the Supreme Court and the Knesset or their respective powers. MK Michael Eitan of Likud, for example, declared in a Knesset debate in 1995 that he and his colleagues had never dreamed at the time of the vote on Basic Law: Human Dignity and Liberty, which became the major source of judicial review of Knesset legislation, that they were perpetrating a constitutional transformation. It was, he maintained, "the first revolution carried out without public knowledge."[80]

During the debate that preceded passage of the laws, Lynn had stated specifically: "We are not shifting the balance to the Supreme Court . . . this is not the establishment of a constitutional court . . . that is receiving special power to nullify laws."[81] Nevertheless, Meir Shamgar, chief justice at the time the two basic laws were enacted, viewed the Knesset debate differently. In his concurring opinion in *Mizrahi Bank v. Migdal*, he pointed to what seemed to him as a lack of clarity and concluded that Basic Law: Human Dignity and Liberty granted the Supreme Court the authority to nullify legislation, thus establishing a rule of great import.

Indeed, other members of the Knesset claimed that it was clear that the intention of the basic laws was to serve as the basis for a judicial review process, and that most members of the Knesset at the time had actually intended this consequence. One of them, Amnon Rubinstein, maintains this position even while acknowledging that an explicit provision requiring a special majority for amending or revoking Basic Law: Human Dignity and Liberty was defeated in votes on the floor.[82]

In other words, the very fact of whether Basic Law: Human Dignity and Liberty was meant to have constitutional status was debated, and on top of that it was claimed that at least some members of the Knesset were misled regarding its nature. The most trenchant statement of this view came from Aryeh Deri of Shas, who spoke of a "deliberate deception of the religious and Haredi public."[83]

The Supreme Court went on to interpret the Basic Law: Human Dignity and Liberty broadly, in a way that is difficult to ground in the language of the law. Even Rubinstein, one of the law's sponsors and central supporters, evinced astonishment when a substantial minority of the court cited it as grounds for voiding a law that prevented Palestinians from the territories who had married residents of Israel from entering the country. Such use of the basic law, Rubinstein warned, could be self-defeating.

During the same period in which these two basic laws were passed, the Knesset passed laws relating to the structure of government and political parties. One of the changes was to institute direct elections for prime minister, although it was revoked in 2003. Other changes made then still remain in force.

One of these was a provision specifying that a no-confidence motion could not topple a government unless at least sixty-one members of the Knesset voted for it (instead of simply a majority of those voting). Furthermore, the motion had to specify which member of the Knesset would form the next government. This measure, aimed at strengthening the prime minister and preventing fortuitous pluralities from toppling a government, was termed "constructive no-confidence."* In addition, in response to the Dirty Trick of 1990, the Knesset amended the Basic Law: The Knesset (1958) to make it more difficult for members of that body to switch from one party to another. While these changes improved the situation somewhat, the system remained fundamentally the same. In other words, the central government remained weak, which enabled the Supreme Court to accrue more power.

Three months after the passage of Basic Law: Human Dignity and Liberty and Basic Law: Freedom of Occupation, in June 1992, elections were held for the Thirteenth Knesset. Likud lost, leading to a brief period of Labor rule under Prime Minister Yitzhak Rabin. Rabin's government reached the Oslo Agreements with the Palestinians, but the central government remained weak, as it is to this day. Exacerbated by deep-seated ideological differences among Israel's citizens regarding the future of the territories and religion-state relations, this weakness has prevented the political branches of the government from curbing the court's growing activism.

---

* The constructive no-confidence rule was first enacted in 2003 as a provision to Basic Law: The Government, and was later reinforced in the 2014 enactment of the Governance Law.

8

Jewish Racists Meet Palestinian Nationalists in the Knesset

I. THE COURT RESHAPES THE KNESSET

One of the first things the Supreme Court did after Meir Shamgar took the chief justice's chair in November 1983 was to intervene in the next round of national elections. In doing so it affected the nature of Israel's parliament, its membership, and Jewish-Arab relations in Israel.

In June 1984 the Supreme Court took up the case *Neiman v. Chairman of the Elections Committee*,[84] which was an appeal of a decision made by the Elections Committee, the body charged with organizing Israel's national elections. The committee had disqualified two slates from running in the elections. One was Kach, led by Rabbi Meir Kahane, and the other the Progressive List for Peace. The first was disqualified on the grounds that the party's principles were racist and antidemocratic; Kach, the Elections Committee ruled, supported terrorism and sought to stir up hatred between different parts of the Israeli population. The Progressive List for Peace was a joint Jewish-Arab list that supported the Palestinian national demand for Palestinian Arab self-determination. A majority of the committee's members decided that "this slate indeed includes subversive elements and tendencies, and central figures on the list identify with enemies of the state." The Progressive List for Peace, they ruled, "advocates principles that threaten the integrity and existence of the state of Israel as well as the preservation of its uniqueness as a Jewish state." The evidence used by the committee to reach its decision included an affidavit by General Avigdor Ben-Gal concerning Mohammed Miari, who headed the slate. Miari had previously been active in al-Ard, an Israeli Arab movement, whose application to be registered as an association was denied in 1964 on the grounds that there is no room to grant a "seal of approval to the establishment of a fifth column" in the country.[85] It was not Miari's first attempt to run for the Knesset—he had numbered among the candidates of the Arab Social List, which the Supreme Court had disqualified from participating in the elections held in 1965, in the *Yeredor* decision. Ben-Gal maintained that Miari had appeared at a gathering of Israeli Arab mayors that had discussed how to respond to the attacks committed by the Jewish Underground against the mayors of Arab cities in Judea and Samaria, where he had taken an "inflammatory and inciting" approach. Miari, Ben-Gal said, had called on the mayors to stage a general strike.

The Central Elections Committee based its decision in 1984 on the *Yeredor* precedent, but now, twenty years after the Supreme Court took up that previous case, its approach had changed entirely. A panel of five justices (Meir Shamgar, Miriam Ben-Porat, Menachem Elon, Aharon Barak, and Moshe Bejski) stressed that the right to vote for and be elected to the Knesset were fundamental rights. Led by Shamgar, with the other four justices concurring, it reversed the committee's decision and allowed both slates to participate in the elections.

The new standard they set is not all that clear, given that all five justices wrote separate opinions. Shamgar maintained that any restriction on the right to be elected needed to be based on an explicit statutory provision, and that disqualification was "an extreme and last measure in the face of 'near certainty' " of imminent danger, a standard not met, in his opinion, in this case. Miriam Ben-Porat endorsed the minority opinion written by Justice Haim Cohn in the *Yeredor* case, according to which the Central Elections Committee had no authority, in the absence of an explicit statutory grant of such power, to disqualify any slate, neither on the basis of a fundamental principle of the legal system nor on any other basis. Elon accepted the majority opinion in the *Yeredor* case, but maintained that the authority to disqualify a slate applied only to one that denied Israel's territorial integrity or right to exist, and that this had not been proven, or did not exist, in the case of the two lists in question.

The differing opinions may have left the reasoning hazy, but the result was clear—the Supreme Court overturned the decision of the Central Elections Committee and also overturned the *Yeredor* rule. Both slates, it declared, were permitted to run in the elections. When the poll was held, Kach won a single seat in the Knesset and its controversial leader, Meir Kahane, became a member of Israel's parliament. The Progressive List for Peace won two seats, one of which went to Miari and the other to General (ret.) Mattityahu Peled, a Jewish peace activist.

The difference between the *Yeredor* and *Neiman* rulings is obvious, not only in regard to the result but also in terms of the efficacy of the process and its scope. *Yeredor* was heard by a panel of three justices, with hearings held in the first half of October 1965. The decision, twenty-two pages long including both majority and minority opinions, was handed down two weeks following the final hearing. The *Neiman* case, in contrast, was heard by five justices. The operative ruling was issued one day after arguments were heard, affirming that both slates could participate in the elections. But the opinions, totaling nearly one hundred pages, were not issued until nearly a year later. This inflated length reflected the court's new approach each time it encountered a complex issue—to respond with a large quantity of verbiage. Sometimes this takes the form of disputations by the justices among themselves or their colleagues, while at other times it reflects a feeling that the longer the decision and the more justifications it offers the more persuasive it will be.

A comparison of the two decisions also reveals some fundamental differences. *Yeredor* exemplifies the balanced activist approach of the old court. The judges recognized that a slate of candidates could be disqualified despite the lack of an explicit statutory provision authorizing this, but they imposed limits on their own power. They neither rejected the force of the relevant statute nor did they claim the right to do so. Rather, in *Yeredor*, they in essence completed the legislation in an area that the legislature had not addressed. Furthermore, the judicial activism on display in this decision was aimed at defending the Zionist state from what the court saw as a real danger. That is an entirely different goal than that pursued by the activism of the new court.

In fact, in a certain respect the *Neiman* decision was the reverse of activism. The court made a show of modesty, claiming its reluctance to assume the power to disqualify slates for the Knesset, in the absence of a statutory provision authorizing it to do so. But the truth is that the decision actually takes activism to an extreme, reversing a precedent set previously by the Supreme Court that had been binding for decades. In *Neiman*, the Supreme Court established a new rule that instituted a change in the nature of the Knesset. This was only one of many cases that set aside precedents of the classic Supreme Court, thereby entirely altering the nature of law and politics in Israel.

The new Supreme Court did more than display a much higher level of activism than its predecessor had. It entirely changed the direction of the court. Previously the court had been mildly activist, seeking to protect Zionism and the Jewish state. Now it became sweepingly activist, giving maximum weight to the rights of individuals or some groups, while almost completely disregarding the heavy damage and risks its decisions imposed on other groups or on the public as a whole. When a racist party such as Kach entered the Knesset, Kahane's right to be elected was prioritized. At the same time, the court disregarded the public interest that a racist movement of this sort not gain strength or exploit the status, perquisites, and means that membership in the Knesset provides. When representatives of the Progressive List for Peace were seated in the Knesset, it created a situation that has, since then, enabled extensions of the Palestinian national movement to sit in the Israel legislature.

II. THE KNESSET GRAPPLES WITH THE NEW RULING

The legislative branch had no practical way of responding to *Neiman* prior to the elections of 1984. But after the elections the new Knesset amended Section 7a of the Basic Law: The Knesset to mandate that slates and candidates would be forbidden to participate in elections if their stated goals or actions negate the existence of Israel as the state of the Jewish people, if they reject the democratic nature of the state, or if they engage in racist incitement. In accordance with this amendment, Kach was disqualified by the Central Elections Committee from running in the next elections, to the Twelfth Knesset in 1988. The Supreme Court affirmed this decision in a second *Neiman* case (and then reaffirmed it prior to the elections for the Thirteenth Knesset in 1992), on the grounds that the party's publications and agenda constituted racist incitement and a rejection of Israel's democratic character.[86]

However, by a vote of three (Shamgar, Bejski, and Shlomo Levin) to two (Elon and Dov Levin) the court rejected an attempt to prevent the Progressive List for Peace from running in the 1988 elections.[87] In that decision, Shamgar added a condition, one not mentioned in the law, that needed to be met for disqualifying a slate that rejected the existence of the state of Israel as a Jewish state. He ruled that a fundamental right should be restricted "only in the face of certain and immediate danger" and that a precondition for invoking the new Section 7a was "the existence of a clear and present danger." The obvious question is why Kach was seen as presenting a "clear and present danger," even though it was clear that the slate of such a racist party should be disqualified regardless of the answer.

After the Supreme Court's refusal to disqualify the Progressive List for Peace, the Knesset passed, in May 2002, another amendment to Section 7a stating: "A list of candidates will not participate in elections to the Knesset and no person will be a candidate for election to the Knesset if the goals or actions of the list or the actions of the person . . . explicitly or implicitly do one of the following: 1. Negate the existence of the state of Israel as a Jewish and democratic state; 2. Racist incitement; 3. Support the armed struggle of an enemy state or terrorist organization against the state of Israel." However, the Knesset also added a reservation: "The decision of the Central Elections Committee that a candidate is prevented from participating in elections requires the confirmation of the Supreme Court."

This last amendment was passed while Aharon Barak was chief justice. It was tested in a case involving Balad (sometimes called the National Democratic Alliance), an Israeli Arab party founded and led by Azmi Bishara. It filed a slate for the Knesset elections of 2003 (after Bishara had represented it in the previous Knesset as part of an electoral alliance with Hadash, a faction dominated by Israel's Communist Party). The Central Elections Committee disqualified it, and the case came before the Supreme Court, where it was heard before a panel of eleven justices. The majority, which allowed the appeal of the Central Elections Committee's decision and ordered that Balad should be allowed to run in the elections, consisted of seven justices (Aharon Barak, Eliahu Matza, Dalia Dorner, Dorit Beinisch, Izhak Englard, Eliezer Rivlin, and Ayala Procaccia), while four opposed the decision (Shlomo Levin, Tova Strasberg-Cohen, Jacob Turkel, and Edmond Levy).[88]

It is difficult to square the majority opinion with the amended Section 7a of the Basic Law: The Knesset, given the material on Bishara that was presented to the court. "It should be said immediately," Chief Justice Barak wrote in his opinion, "that we accept that the actions attributed to Knesset member (MK) Bishara in the matter of rejecting the existence of the state of Israel as a Jewish state and in the matter of supporting the armed struggle against it stand at the center of his goals and actions, and they constitute for him a dominant objective. Furthermore, these actions are not a theoretical idea, but rather a political potential that MK Bishara has taken from theory into practice in ongoing activity, and with great force." But Barak added a reservation to this incisive account. The question at hand, he wrote, is "whether the evidence on which the positive answer to the two questions we have raised are 'persuasive, clear, and unambiguous' . . . Only this high level of evidence can resolve the democratic paradox and revoke one of the central rights of democracy—the right to vote and be elected."

It is hard to see how this is consistent with Barak's earlier statement. The meaning of this last paragraph would seem to be that the court sets such a high standard of evidence that, in practice, it becomes impossible to disqualify any candidate, even in the most severe circumstances. A wealth of evidence supporting Bishara's disqualification was presented to the court, but the justices of the majority simply rejected what should have been inarguable.

Deputy Chief Justice Levin, in his dissent, put the issue succinctly:

> The disqualification of MK Bishara and Balad would seem . . . to be obligatory also because of their support for the armed struggle of an enemy state or terrorist organization against Israel . . . in my view the evidence in this regard is

unequivocal. We might also mention . . . MK Bishara's speech in June 2001 in the city of Qardaha in Syria, at an event attended by Arab leaders and personages, among them the secretary general of Hezbollah and the vice-president of Iran, at which MK Bishara called for promoting the armed struggle ("the resistance") against Israel. Is not this public appearance in an enemy country in and of itself, without considering the other public speeches made by MK Bishara, sufficient to qualify as support for an enemy country or terrorist organization? It looks to me like Lord Haw-Haw [an Irish-British Fascist who broadcast Nazi propaganda to Britain during World War II] asking, on the basis of the law parallel to the Basic Law: The Knesset, to vote for [Levin seems to have meant "to be elected to"] the British Parliament.

What happened in practice was that the court's majority used its interpretation of the law to frustrate the intent of the legislature, thus allowing an extreme Arab nationalist movement to be elected to the Knesset. Some argue that this is, in fact, a desirable result,[89] on the grounds that the participation of such elements in Israel's elections increases the Arab public's sense of belonging to and identification with the Israeli state. But if that is the case, why should it not apply also to the racist Kach party? Why should it not also be true that its supporters would, by participating in the election, come to identify with and feel a sense of social unity with the rest of the groups in the country?

In fact, there is no proof that the decision encouraged the Arab public to identify with the state. One could easily argue the opposite. The fact is that Israel's Arab citizens rarely resorted to violence as a means of protest as long as the *Yeredor* rule stood. Such violence became more and more common when Palestinian Arab nationalists gained representation in the Knesset. This is hardly firm proof of a causal connection between the two, but it is highly questionable whether a wholesale grant of representation to Palestinian nationalists has bolstered a sense of belonging to the Israeli polity among the country's Arab citizens.

The report of a national Commission of Inquiry into the Clashes between the Security Forces and Israeli Citizens in October 2000, headed by Justice Theodor Or (the Or Commission) describes the growth of extremism and the escalation of violence in Israel's Arab community. The commission, whose other members were District Court Judge Hashim Khatib and Professor Shimon Shamir, an academic expert on Arab affairs and a former Israeli ambassador to Egypt and Jordan, was established following a series of violent demonstrations by Israeli Arabs that took place at the time of the outbreak of the Second (al-Aqsa) Intifada. That Palestinian uprising in the West Bank and Gaza Strip began after Ariel Sharon, then leader of the opposition Likud party, made a visit to the Temple Mount along with several other Knesset members of his party. Arabs at the site rioted; dozens of policemen and about ten Palestinians were injured in the clash. Rioting then spread through the territories and Israel as well. Israeli Arabs blocked roads, cutting off transportation arteries. They also threw stones at passing vehicles, in one case killing a Jewish driver. The riots in Israel were suppressed by the police, but thirteen Arab citizens were killed in the process.

The Or Commission also examined the role played by two Arab members of the Knesset, Azmi Bishara and Abdulmalik Dehamshe, specifying articles and statements made by them in the period leading up to the riots. According to the commission, "Bishara and his movement also consistently praised Hezbollah during and after its war with the state of Israel . . . In doing so, they conveyed a message that Hezbollah should be seen as an example to be emulated in conflict with Israel." While presumably the riots would have broken out even without such pronouncements by Bishara, it added, "it seems that [they] added fuel to the fire. They contributed substantially to inflaming the atmosphere and encouraged the inclination to commit violent acts." In Dehamshe's case, the commission found that his statements addressed issues regarding which the Arab public felt injured and threatened—homes, land, and mosques— but "his statements encourage a turn to violence and are made in the virulent style of 'breaking hands and feet' and martyrdom. In this he contributed to firing up the public in advance of and during the violent events of October 2000."

Hence, the presence of a person like Bishara in the Knesset, where he received a platform that amplified his voice, did not serve as a positive influence on Israel's Arab community. Moreover, it had a negative effect on the Jewish majority, which tends to view the Israeli Arab public through the lens of its most extreme leaders. The result is ever more suspicion, alienation, and hostility between Jews and Arabs inside Israel.

The Supreme Court's decision regarding Bishara's candidacy effectively eviscerated the provision of the Basic Law: The Knesset that denied the right to be elected to the Knesset to a person or party whose effective goal is to subvert Israel's existence as a Jewish and democratic state, or one who supports armed resistance against Israel. It adopted an approach that rendered the actual implementation of the law impossible in practice. The judgment was based on a radical approach to human rights that puts the rights of the individual or the group to which he belongs in the center, while attaching almost no importance to the need to defend the public at large and the state.

Bishara continued to contribute to the shaping of Israeli law. Following the Second Lebanon War, at the end of 2006, he was indicted under the Prevention of Terror Ordinance, following a Knesset decision to strip him of procedural parliamentary immunity. The charges related to two speeches he had made. In the first, in the Israeli Arab city of Um al-Fahm, he declared: "Hezbollah has won, and for the first time since 1967 we have tasted victory. Hezbollah has the right to be proud of its achievement and humiliation of Israel . . . Lebanon, the weakest of Arab countries, has offered a tiny model, that if examined deeply can offer the conclusions needed for success and victory: a clear goal, a potent will to win, and the preparation of the means required to achieve this goal . . . Hezbollah . . . saw to it that its guerrilla war was well-publicized in the media, and all its achievements significantly affected the morale of the people of Israel, who slowly lost patience in the face of the losses it incurred."

The second speech was one Bishara gave in Syria, at a ceremony also attended by Ahmed Jibril, leader of the Popular Front for the Liberation of Palestine–General Command, and Hassan Nasrallah, the leader of Hezbollah. In this speech Bishara laid out a strategy that cannot be interpreted as anything other than vigorous support for the "resistance," that is, armed struggle, against Israel. Bishara petitioned his protector, the Supreme Court. The court did not let him down. In a majority decision (Barak and Rivlin, with Justice Esther Hayut dissenting), it ruled that Bishara's speeches were covered by his substantive parliamentary immunity, and that the criminal procedure against him in the magistrates court should be annulled.[90]

The end of the story—so far—came when Bishara was investigated for serious violations of state security. He fled Israel and has not returned to this day. If the suspicions against him are confirmed, it will show that he took one more step consistent with the views he openly expressed in speeches that were brought before the Supreme Court, and which the justices of the majority chose to disregard.

The issues Bishara raised remain on the public agenda and most recently came to the fore in the elections of 2015. The Central Elections Committee decided to disqualify the candidacy of another Balad parliamentarian, Haneen Zouabi (in these elections, Balad ran as part of the United Arab List*), as well as that of Baruch Marzel, a Kach leader who was running on the Yachad-Otzma Yehudit list and who claimed to have shed his racist beliefs. The Supreme Court overturned both bans.[91]

Thus, every attempt by the Knesset since 1984 to prevent the election of representatives of the Palestinian nationalist movement has been frustrated by the Supreme Court through its interpretation of the law. There is no parallel in the world for the fact that Palestinian nationalists sit in Israel's parliament. Of course, there are examples of representatives of a group or people seeking secession or autonomy sitting in a national parliament, as do representatives of the Scottish national movement in the British parliament. But the Scots are not in armed conflict with the English, nor do they seek sovereignty over London and the entire British Isles. The situation between the Palestinian national movement and Israel is completely different. Palestinian terror against Israel has not ceased, and Hamas, which won a majority of the vote in the Palestinian territories, seeks to destroy Israel and replace it. The upshot is that support for "resistance" is voiced by Arab representatives in Israel's Knesset. Some of these parliamentarians have even participated in memorial events for terrorists who have killed Israelis, as well as in other events in which terrorists have also participated. True, the court has preserved a measure of balance by approving the candidacy of a man who in the past was a leading figure of a racist movement, but it is not clear that this benefits Israeli democracy.

Another development relates to Jewish-Arab cooperation in political parties. In the past there was such cooperation. Arab candidates ran on satellite slates linked to Mapai, forerunner of the Labor Party, and since the 1980s have been included in that party's own slate. These satellite slates were included in the coalition, and their members sometimes served as deputy cabinet ministers. Over time the significance of this phenomenon has been greatly reduced. The percentage of Arabs participating in the national elections is relatively small, and most of them vote for the Arab parties. Arab and other minority members are sometimes included in lists of other parties, and Raleb Majadele of the Labor Party served as a cabinet minister under Prime Minister Ehud Olmert. But these are the exceptions to the rule.

The number of Knesset members representing Arab slates (Hadash, Balad, Raam, and Taal) has grown in recent Knessets to about ten and in the 2015 elections rose to thirteen. But it has been impossible to bring them into a governing coalition because of the manifestly pro-Palestinian line that they take. However, the left has used them

---

* Raising the minimum percentage to 3.25 percent in 2014 prompted all the Arab parties to run a combined slate in the March 2015 elections. They won thirteen seats, two more than they had won collectively in the previous election, when they ran on three different lists.

on occasion to form a "blocking majority," that is a Knesset majority opposing the appointment of a Likud prime minister. In one case, in 1992 under Rabin, Labor used such a blocking majority to put together a government along with religious and center parties without including the Arab parties in the coalition. The presence of Palestinian nationalist parties in the Knesset has soured Jewish-Arab relations in Israel and caused a reaction that has probably also strengthened the Israeli right wing parties. One can easily understand the feelings of large parts of the Jewish public when they heard in 2010 that MK Zouabi was participating in a flotilla from Turkey intent on breaking through the Israeli siege of Gaza, especially when the participants in the flotilla violently attacked Israeli commandos who sought to halt the ships. Israelis were no less upset when Bishara made his statements extolling Hezbollah's "victory" in the Second Lebanon War.

9

The Supreme Court and Military Service for Yeshiva Students

Justiciability and Public Suits

Soon after the establishment of the state, Prime Minister David Ben-Gurion approved a deferment of military service for a limited number of *yeshiva* students. In practice, this amounted to an exemption, as these young men continued to study full time until they were married and had children and were thus no longer eligible for the draft. The stated justification for the deferment was the need to enable the world of Jewish religious study to recover following the devastation wreaked by the Holocaust. At that time, the Haredi community was a tiny proportion of Israel's population. They had a handful of representatives in the Knesset but were never part of the governing coalition under Ben-Gurion.*

That changed in the elections of 1977, which ejected Labor from power. Likud emerged as the largest party, and its leader, Menachem Begin, was tapped to form a government. But to gain a Knesset majority he needed the support of the Haredi public's representatives in the Knesset, the four-member Agudat Yisrael faction. Begin, while not religious in his personal practice, had a much deeper respect for and admiration of those who did than had the left-leaning leaders of the Labor Party. As such, he had no problem with asking them to join his coalition, and they were happy to accept. One of the major concessions he made to Agudat Yisrael was agreeing to remove the limitation on the number of yeshiva students who could claim exemption. Excusing yeshiva students from the military draft is tantamount to exempting them from an onerous tax, given that young Israeli men serve in the military for three years. The deferment-exemption in turn led to a huge increase in the number of yeshiva students excused from army service. It also led to a growth in the Haredi population as a whole, because the system provided an incentive for young religious men who had not previously identified as Haredim (among them from the Sephardi

---

* In Israel's first elections, in January 1949, a group of religious parties, among them the Haredi Agudat Yisrael Party, ran together as the United Religious Front. The united party joined the coalition, and one of its Haredi members, Rabbi Meir Levin, became a minister in Ben-Gurion's cabinet.

community) to enroll in Haredi *yeshivot*. The growth in the Haredi population in turn meant that the strength of the Haredi parties in the Knesset increased over the years.

In 1970, prior to the legal revolution, a reserve officer filed a petition against the deferment. At the time the number of deferments qua exemptions granted to yeshiva students was still fairly modest—the total number had reached about 5,000. The court rejected the suit on the grounds that the petitioner had no standing in the case. Justice Alfred Witkon put it concisely:

> It is clear that there can be no judicial proceeding unless there is a dispute (*lis*). A particular person must come and assert his or her right or grievance. In this respect judicial proceedings differ from proceedings before the legislature or the executive. Without a complainant, there is no place for adjudication, and if a complainant who is nothing but the spokesman for the general public were sufficient, judicial proceedings would be likely to obscure the borderlines [between the judicial and the legislative and executive branches] and be interpreted as a breach of the principle of the separation of powers.[92]

Sixteen years went by, during which the number of exemptions granted to yeshiva students grew by leaps and bounds. The question again came before the Supreme Court in 1986 in a petition submitted by Yehuda Ressler, a major in the Israel Defense Forces.[93] The Supreme Court ruling in the case is a classic display of the new penchant for long opinions. It goes on for seventy-five pages, so it is hardly surprising that it was issued a full two years after the petition was submitted. In comparison, Justice Witkon needed only ten pages and issued his decision just a few weeks after the earlier petition had been filed.

The detailed opinion, written by Justice Aharon Barak, rejected the central claim made by the respondent, the Ministry of Defense, that Ressler had no standing to sue. "I see nothing in the nature of the judicial role which necessitates holding that only the person whose right is violated is entitled to plead his case," he declared.

A full twenty-five pages of the opinion were devoted to the question of justiciability. Barak distinguished between normative and institutional justiciability, finding that, with regard to the normative aspect, all issues are justiciable. His reasoning was that all behaviors are either permitted or forbidden by the law, and that every human action can be measured according to this standard. This rather simplistic test is disputable, given that, as Justice Menachem Elon wrote in a different case, there are many human behaviors that the law does not address and regarding which it does not seek to take a position. We do not say, he noted, that "the law 'permits' eating, speaking on the telephone, hiking, running, or dancing simply because it does not 'forbid' these actions." The law simply does not address such actions. It disregards them, just as it disregards many other matters of morality that fall outside its purview. Elon also severely criticized the attempt by his colleague, Barak, to use unreasonableness as a rationale for judicial review of decisions such as establishing relations with a foreign country, or the organization, structure, deployment, equipping, and missions of the army. In Elon's view, all these subjects lie outside the court's jurisdiction.[94]

The significance of the institutional justiciability to which Barak referred is that even if a subject is justiciable, it may be that the authority to do so has been invested in another body, such as the legislature or government, rather than the court. But he rejects the court's lack of institutional justiciability, arguing that it "is most problematic; that its legal foundations are shaky, that it is based to a great extent on irrational grounds." Hence, even though Barak excluded some cases from judicial review, the ambit of the exclusion he offered is so narrow that, in practice, no actual instance fits it. In short, everything is justiciable.

In Barak's view, even the matter of establishing diplomatic relations with another country can come before the court. In making this determination, he rejected the rule established by Justice Yoel Sussman according to which the considerations surrounding such a decision are not matters of law but rather of foreign policy, and are thus not justiciable. According to Barak, since all government authorities are required to act reasonably, and given that unreasonableness, a term he broadened greatly, exists as grounds for judicial intervention, it is possible to apply judicial review to the question of with what countries the state of Israel will or will not establish diplomatic relations.

This entire long discussion is essentially obiter, given that with regard to the matter at hand Barak determined that it had not been proven that, given the authority invested in him by law, the defense minister's decision to exempt yeshiva students from military service was unreasonable. The petition was therefore denied, while obiter became a defining trait of the judicial revolution, and in the process was turned into binding rules.

In this same case regarding military service for yeshiva students, Chief Justice Shamgar agreed with Barak regarding the expansion of the right of standing and to the determination that a "public petitioner" could apply to the Supreme Court in a variety of instances. He rejected, however, Barak's claim that everything is justiciable, which Shamgar saw as inconsistent with the separation of powers. In Shamgar's view, when the dominant character of a subject is political, the court should refrain from addressing it. For example, the court should not intervene in matters of peace and war, the reasonableness of the method of combat chosen by the army, and many other subjects. Justice Ben-Porat inclined in this regard toward Shamgar.*

Barak remained in the minority on the matter of justiciability, but he had a huge advantage—he was more than a decade younger than Shamgar, Ben-Porat, and Elon, and could look forward to serving for more than ten years as chief justice—by which time none of them would sit on the bench any longer. During this period he was able to act as he saw fit and to instill his views in the other justices. The fact that he had in the past been in the minority was no obstacle as far as he was concerned.

Opening the doors to all comers entirely changed the court's character and function. Justices even encouraged petitions by refraining from imposing costs on public petitioners who lost their cases, as is common practice in Israel and Britain. Justice Cheshin famously complained: "It would be only a slight exaggeration to say that

---

* Shamgar reiterated his position in an interview he granted, following his retirement, to Arye Carmon and Amira Lam, in *Yedioth Ahronoth*, April 17, 2009, and more recently in MEIR SHAMGAR, AUTOBIOGRAPHY 194–98 (2015) (Isr.). His approach was also reflected in the decision, discussed previously in chapter 2, regarding the nonjusticiability of the government's policy of settlement in territories conquered in the Six Day War.

today a person picks up the morning or evening newspaper and his eye flits through the news items until it finds a certain item, and having found it he calls his friends and says: Let us arise and go now to Zion, to the Supreme Court. And he acts on his words. It's as if Supreme Court petitions are written on the way [to Jerusalem]."⁹⁵ Cheshin was widely quoted, but nothing changed. The court continued to encourage such petitions, and even in the case cited above, the court, while rejecting the petition, did not impose costs on the petitioners. The consequence is not only the multiplication of suits but also the appearance of "serial petitioners" on matters relating to politics, the Jewish-Arab conflict, the status of women, the protection of a specific sector of society, and corruption. It does not cost much to file a Supreme Court petition, and there is little risk of incurring costs. On the other hand, the petitioner gains clear benefits—often in the form of publicity. Even if the suit is rejected, the petitioner generally succeeds in drawing media attention to the subject he seeks to promote.

If we carry this logic to its ultimate and absurd end, why should it even be necessary for the court to wait for a petitioner to take up a public issue? If the justices themselves read about an issue in the newspaper and decide that they want to rule on it, why should they not, like the state comptroller, simply take it up, subpoena the relevant state officials to receive their responses, and issue orders as they see fit?

The subject of military service for yeshiva students continued to occupy the Supreme Court. Ten years following Ressler's initial petition, in 1998, the court, this time a bench of eleven justices headed by Barak, issued another lengthy judgment. The justices ruled that the minister of defense was not empowered to defer or exempt yeshiva students from mandatory service. The decision was based on a new principle established by the court under which a general arrangement that is tantamount to a fundamental policy requires primary legislation. In other words, the defense minister could not use his discretion to defer the military service of citizens so as to create a general rule exempting entire groups from military service. In the absence of explicit Knesset legislation exempting or deferring yeshiva students from military service, the minister would no longer be able to do so. The court also ruled that its decision overruling the defense minister's policies would come into effect only a year later.⁹⁶ The court subsequently granted three extensions of this period, and the Knesset granted itself a further extension. In 2002 the Knesset passed a law providing for the deferment of military service for full-time yeshiva students. It was known as the Tal Law, after retired Justice Tzvi Tal, who headed a public commission that drew up recommendations for legislation on the issue. The law permitted the deferment of service for yeshiva students but also contained provisions to provide incentives for students to enlist at an older age and then to enter the workforce. The legislation contained a sunset provision limiting its force to five years. As soon as it was passed, a petition was submitted to the Supreme Court arguing that it should be invalidated—after all, this was the height of the legal revolution, in which the court had declared its power to overrule Knesset legislation. Four years later the majority of a nine-judge panel headed by Chief Justice Barak handed down a 160-page decision stating that, at this point, there were no grounds for negating the law.⁹⁷

The Knesset later extended the law's term for another five years. A petition demanded that the court invalidate the extension. Once again the case was heard by a panel of nine justices. Barak had retired in the meantime, so the panel was headed by the new chief justice, Dorit Beinisch. Once again the court delayed, this time for five years, before issuing a 130-page decision. Once again the court refrained from invalidating the law, but ruled that it could not be extended again.[98] This was in 2012, just when the term of the five-year extension came to an end. In the meantime Chief Justice Beinisch retired as well, but the saga continued. According to the court's decision, once the law expired, the defense ministry was required to draft yeshiva students, but this was not done. The status quo ante continued. A small number of Haredim enlisted, but most Haredi yeshiva students do not. In March 2014 the Knesset passed a new law, which its supporters called the Equal Burden Law, yet it was anything but. This law, slated to go into force by 2017, establishes a special and prejudicial rule that favors Haredim. Furthermore, it does not correct other discriminatory aspects of the enlistment law, such as that which grants religious women a right to a complete exemption from military service, instead of which they may, but are not required, to perform alternative national service. As could have been expected, a petition to void the Equal Burden Law has been submitted to the Supreme Court. While this petition is still pending, the Knesset amended the law making further concessions to the Haredim. A petition against the amendment was not long in coming. The two petitions join the pile of cases awaiting decision.

The bottom line is that complex political and social forces are at play in the controversy over whether Haredi yeshiva students should be drafted. While many Israelis find the fact that Haredim do not serve intolerable, other political forces support the exemption. Another factor is that the Haredi population is Israeli's poorest population, in part because its young men spend so many years in religious study rather than gaining practical skills and working to support their large families. Many would like to improve their standard of living, and Israeli society as a whole has an interest in bringing them into the workforce. The Supreme Court inserted itself into this struggle with a series of long and learned judgments and, as such, can be seen as having taken part in the public debate on the issue. But clearly the court, despite its tremendous exertions, cannot solve the problem, and can play only a small role in the series of unsatisfactory arrangements that have and will continue to govern this issue for the foreseeable future.

10

The Secret Services Affair

I. TERRORISTS HIJACK BUS 300

On April 12, 1984, four terrorists seized a crowded bus on its way from Tel Aviv to Ashkelon. The assailants ordered the driver to continue past Ashkelon into the Gaza Strip, intending to use the dozens of passengers as hostages to compel Israel to release terrorists held in its jails. They may have planned to issue other demands as well. Israel Defense Forces (IDF) and police forces pursued the bus and intercepted it in the central Gaza Strip. High-ranking IDF commanders and government officials arrived at the scene, among them Minister of Defense Moshe Arens; Avraham Shalom, chief of the Shin Bet, Israel's secret internal security service; and Yitzhak Mordechai, commander of the Infantry and Paratroop Corps, who oversaw the rescue operation.

Early the next morning a special task force stormed the bus. Two of the terrorists were killed in the battle, as was one of the passengers. The two remaining terrorists were photographed by news photographers at the scene as they were taken for questioning. Following the interrogation the two assailants were driven away. It subsequently emerged that they were liquidated by agents of the Shin Bet, in accordance with an order given by Shalom.

But that was not the story the Shin Bet told. The organization tried to conceal the fact that the two terrorists had been captured alive and executed without trial. But the cover-up ran into a problem. A photographer, Alex Levac of the daily newspaper *Hadashot*, had snapped a shot of one of the terrorists just after he had been removed from the bus by two members of the security forces. The photograph shows him apparently unhurt and able to walk. The military censor banned the publication of this information, but without success. The story appeared in the foreign press, and the news spread from there throughout Israel as well. Three days after the incident, *Hadashot*, a new and upstart newspaper founded not long before by the publishers of the liberal daily *Ha'aretz*, quoted a story from a foreign newspaper about the fate of the terrorists. A few days later it printed Levac's photograph on its front page. The fact that Israeli forces had killed prisoners who no longer presented a danger, in violation of international conventions and its own declared standards, set off a blaze of controversy in Israel, as did the attempt to prevent the public from learning about it.

In response to the public uproar, Arens appointed a commission of inquiry under the provisions of the Military Justice Law, headed by Res. General Meir Zorea. At the insistence of the Shin Bet, one of its officials, Yossi Ginossar, was included on the panel. Chief Military Defense Counsel Ilan Shiff served as legal counsel to the commission.

But the Shin Bet did not stop trying to cover up the affair. Shalom, in cooperation with his Trojan Horse, Ginossar, sought to conceal the truth. In his testimony before the commission, Mordechai confirmed that he had interrogated the terrorists to extract vital information—how many terrorists had been on the bus and whether they had left a booby-trapped bomb on the vehicle. He related that he threatened and pistol-whipped one of the terrorists. The blow, he insisted, had not been life-threatening and did not cause any real harm. After obtaining the information that there were no more terrorists on the bus and that the charge they had left on the bus was not booby-trapped, Mordechai handed the two men over to the Shin Bet. Mordechai testified that the terrorists were not at that time suffering from any serious injury.

The Shin Bet agents continued to interrogate and beat the two prisoners. They then took the terrorists to an isolated location and used rocks to smash their skulls. But the Shin Bet claimed that the two were taken to a hospital, where they were declared dead.[99]

The Zorea Commission's full report and the testimonies it heard remain classified to this day. What we know for certain is that the Shin Bet's witnesses coordinated their testimonies with Shalom and Ginossar and perjured themselves, while implicating Mordechai in the terrorists' deaths. One of the commission's members advised Mordechai to retain legal counsel, and when rumors of what was going on in the commission's deliberations began to spread and word of it was provided by soldiers who testified, the IDF itself retained the services of Amnon Goldenberg, who assumed representation of Mordechai.

The Zorea Commission submitted its report a month after it was constituted. It found that the terrorists' death had been caused by fractures to their skulls. It was unable to determine who had killed them, but the report stated that there was reason to suspect that members of the security forces had committed a crime. The full report was not made public, but Itzhak Zamir, who held the post of attorney general at the time of the affair, later wrote that the commission found that the two terrorists "were beaten to death by enraged soldiers during their interrogation. Only one suspect was identified by the commission—the chief paratroop officer."

Mordechai and his advisers knew that the facts were entirely different, and the IDF leadership also had doubts about the commission's version of events.

Attorney General Zamir called for a police investigation. The Shin Bet, which had never been investigated by the police, opposed the idea and was backed by Prime Minister Shimon Peres. As a compromise, an "investigative team" headed by State Attorney Yona Blatman was appointed. The team also included another lawyer, a police officer, a Shin Bet official, and Chief Military Prosecutor Menachem Finkelstein. Blatman and the police officer were granted the legal powers of police investigators.

Given the commission's finding "of fact" that there was only one suspect, the State Attorney's Office focused on Mordechai. Shin Bet officials were given instructions by their superiors before testifying to the investigative team and repeated the version of events they had provided to the Zorea Commission. Mordechai, Goldenberg, and another lawyer, Dror Hoter-Yishai, who had served with Mordechai in the paratroops and now advised him, realized that nothing could challenge the unshakeable and almost automatic confidence the State Attorney's Office displayed regarding the Shin Bet testimonies.

Their idea was to take a different track. There was no dispute regarding the three stages at which the terrorists had been beaten—first on the bus during the raid, when the commandos had struck them on the backs of their necks; then when they were interrogated by Mordechai; and finally, when they were further interrogated by the Shin Bet at the scene. (At this point, no one but the Shin Bet knew about the deadly blows the terrorists were dealt at the fourth stage, after they were taken away by Shin Bet agents and their skulls were crushed.) A "battle of the pathologists" ensued.[100] In his testimony before the Blatman team, Dr. Moshe Feinsod of Rambam medical center in Haifa supported the theory that the terrorists' deaths could have been caused by the blows they received during the raid on the bus. In contrast, the State Attorney's Office enlisted the help of Dr. Avraham Sahar, of Hadassah hospital in Jerusalem, whose report implied that Mordechai was responsible for the terrorists' deaths.

This disagreement brought another one in its wake. The director of the National Center of Forensic Medicine, Dr. Bezalel Bloch, was prepared to support the hypothesis that the cause of death might have been the beatings on the bus. Mordechai's counsel, Goldenberg, contacted Bloch, but the Ministry of Health's chief counsel instructed the latter that he was not permitted to intervene in the case. At the same time, the ministry's director general notified Goldenberg that "following consultation with the attorney general, I am compelled not to consent to your request to permit Dr. Bloch to offer testimony, as you wish."

At the beginning of January 1985, Attorney General Zamir wrote a letter to the director general laying out his reasoning. He noted that the sanction against Dr. Bloch testifying "was based on a standing order . . . according to which physicians employed by the state may not offer medical opinions that may serve as legal testimony against the state . . . This order expresses a general principle that applies beyond the Ministry of Health. Thus it is unreasonable that a jurist employed by the state would be permitted to offer a legal opinion that can serve a suit against the state." Zamir concluded by stating that he did not understand "why it is necessary to insist on receiving an opinion from Dr. Bloch . . . [when] it is possible to obtain an opinion from other physicians who are not employed by the state."

Zamir's position is discomfiting. Why was Dr. Bloch's opinion "against the state"? After all, this was not a claim for damages against the state. It was a preliminary fact-finding inquiry that would make recommendations. Only on the basis of the ungrounded assumption that the inquiry was aimed specifically against Mordechai could a finding clearing Mordechai of suspicion, or even casting doubt about his culpability, be considered "against the state." But even if that were the case, the state could not claim that its goal was to prove Mordechai's guilt regardless of the facts. Dr. Bloch was, by virtue of his position as the chief of the state's forensic and pathology institute, the government's top expert on the subject. If Mordechai's attorneys believed that Dr. Bloch's testimony could clarify the case, even if this meant testifying in Mordechai's favor, then the Blatman team was duty-bound to hear what he had to say.

In the end, after the intervention of the state comptroller, Mordechai's counsel were permitted to invite Dr. Bloch to testify.

In the meantime, Blatman's team was riven with disagreement. Finkelstein requested access to the testimonies heard by the Zorea Commission. He believed that there was good reason to suspect that most of the violence against the terrorists had been committed by Shin Bet agents. Factually and legally, he maintained, Mordechai could not be held responsible for the terrorists' deaths.

The team submitted its conclusions in July 1985, a little more than a year after it was constituted. It adopted the position of Finkelstein and Mordechai's attorneys regarding the lack of a causal connection between the acts attributed to Mordechai and the death of the two assailants. As such, he could not be brought to trial for manslaughter. A month later Zamir's opinion, which was meant to remain classified, was reported by the media. Zamir pointed out that the terrorists had been beaten by many people, among them five Shin Bet agents and three policemen. All these should be brought up before disciplinary tribunals, he ruled. Zamir addressed Mordechai's case separately and severely. While he wrote that the Blatman team had found that Mordechai could not be held responsible for the death of the terrorists, there was nevertheless evidence suggesting that he was guilty of causing severe injury and of unbefitting behavior.

Zamir's recommendation was submitted to Chief Military Advocate General Ben-Zion Farhi. Accepting the recommendations meant bringing Mordechai to trial before a military court, since the charges against him were too serious for disciplinary procedure before a superior officer. "I revolted," Farhi later said in an interview published in April 2012 on the website of the advocate general. "It was an error to go public with this recommendation" and to send the case to the military prosecutor. He summoned his staff, and "the impression was that the material was very much deficient and that the Shin Bet testimonies were shallow and deficient." Insisting that he was empowered to exercise his own judgment, he decided, against Zamir, on a less serious procedure—to bring Mordechai before a disciplinary panel on lesser charges.

Fortunately, in those days the attorney general had not yet become the most powerful figure in Israel's public administration. Other officials were able to exercise more reasonable discretion. Had the same question come up a few years later, someone would no doubt have petitioned the Supreme Court in the name of the public interest in order to invalidate Farhi's decision. The court would have most probably have decided, in the name of reasonableness, to compel Farhi to act unreasonably—that is, to defer to the attorney general's recommendation to court-martial Mordechai. Indeed, Justice Dorit Beinisch, who served as state attorney before her appointment to the court, later ruled that "like all governmental bodies, the chief military advocate general is also subordinate to the professional instruction of the attorney general and to his legal opinions."[101]

This determination is inconsistent with one of the basic rules of Israeli law, according to which any authority that has been granted discretion to make decisions, the chief military advocate general in this case, is free to exercise that discretion independently and is not subject to the instructions of superior authority. As will be explained below, at a later stage the Supreme Court eventually decided that the principle of the rule of law requires the government and every public official to snap to obedience at the attorney general's every command even when it is unfounded or based on wrong interpretation of the law. Luckily for Yitzhak Mordechai, back then this odd perception of the rule of law had not yet been adopted, and as such the advocate general was free to wield his personal discretion and reject the attorney general's recommendation. In the event, Farhi's judgment was ultimately shown to be much more reasonable than that of the attorney general.

On August 16, 1985, Yitzhak Mordechai reported to Brigadier General Haim Nadal for a disciplinary hearing. Two days later Nadal announced that he had decided to acquit Mordechai, on the grounds that Mordechai had exercised reasonable force. The five Shin Bet suspects, for whom Zamir had recommended only a disciplinary proceeding, were subsequently acquitted as well. The attorney general decided that the policemen involved in the incident should not even face a disciplinary hearing.

This was only the end of Act I, in the course of which Mordechai was not only falsely accused but also found himself vilified by the media as a brutal murderer of prisoners. Zamir did not let it go at that—he wanted Mordechai suspended from his military command. As Yoel Marcus of *Ha'aretz* would later write, "Itzhak Zamir, unwittingly maneuvered by several Shin Bet officials, stood in the forefront of the campaign against Mordechai. First he wrote to Mordechai's attorney demanding that Mordechai suspend himself from the IDF. He then approached the chief of staff twice, and when he was rebuffed he turned to the minister of defense." According to Marcus, Zamir took advantage of a "public ceremony to level a serious accusation that the IDF scorned the law."

But, to repeat, at this time the Israeli version of "the rule of law" had not yet taken root, and the Supreme Court was still not in the picture. As a result, Chief of Staff Moshe Levy was able to use his own discretion, which turned out to be better than Zamir's, and keep Mordechai on active duty.

Then criminal charges relating to a different matter were brought against Dr. Bloch, who had testified in Mordechai's favor. The criminal investigation seems to have been conducted during the period in which the Bus 300 affair was at its height. At the time, Mordechai was still considered the central suspect in the latter case. The charges against Bloch had to do with a private opinion that he had provided in a civil suit involving a death in a traffic accident. Bloch received a modest fee of $70 in exchange for his opinion. But it led to a very serious charge of bribery—according to the prosecution, it was payment for doctoring his professional opinion.

The mountain turned into a molehill by July 1986, when the case ended with a plea bargain. The bribery charge was withdrawn. Bloch pled guilty to a charge of breach of trust and was sentenced to a fine of 1,000 Israeli shekels (in those days, about $667). Bloch was represented by Dror Hoter-Yishai, who argued that the payment had not been a bribe but simply a professional fee for a private consultation. The individuals who had served as directors of the institute all claimed that they were permitted to issue private opinions of this sort, but that, according to the provisions of this permit, a certain sum was to be deducted from their salaries when they did so. In this case, no deduction had been made. Whatever the case, the result of the plea bargain proves that the matter should at most have been dealt with by a disciplinary rather than a criminal proceeding. There is no way of proving that the bribery charge against Dr. Bloch was connected in any way to his testimony "against the state," but presumably it left him with the feeling that it is preferable to be on the right side of the fence.

II. THE ATTORNEY GENERAL IS FORCED TO RESIGN

The show seemed to be over; in fact, Act II was just beginning. Mordechai's disciplinary proceeding had come to an end, and all the suspects were acquitted. But in October 1985 internal dissension in the Shin Bet broke out of the bounds of the organization itself. The service's deputy chief, Reuven Hazak, demanded that the chief, Avraham Shalom, resign on the grounds that he had fabricated evidence in the Bus 300 case and that the Shin Bet had deliberately misled the Zorea Commission. He told Shalom that he was prepared to resign as well—up to this point he had been seen as Shalom's certain successor. Hazak was backed by two of the organization's division chiefs, Rafi Malka and Peleg Radai. Shalom rejected the demand, leading to a severe crisis in the organization that eventually required the attention of the prime minister's office.

On the night of the Bus 300 hijacking Yitzhak Shamir had been prime minister. By this point Shimon Peres had assumed the premier's post, following that year's July elections and the subsequent rotation agreement reached by Labor and Likud. Hazak met with him and told him who had killed the terrorists. Peres, who had already been briefed by Shalom, evinced no interest in intervening. He even asked Hazak the obvious question—where had he been all this time, in particular during the height of the investigation that followed the incident. Hazak, after all, had known who killed the terrorists almost from the start, and had participated in meetings at which the cooking of the evidence was planned. (Radai had not been involved, and Malka had learned of it only after Mordechai's acquittal.)

Hazak was disappointed, but Peres's point of view can be understood, if not justified. The subject dropped out of public view, no one took any interest in it. Reopening, especially given that Shamir categorically opposed doing so, would have caused a severe political crisis and could well have toppled the government. Alongside the severe damage that the Shin Bet would suffer, Peres was aware that Hazak had not demanded that the alleged culprits be brought to trial, nor that they apologize or even compensate Yitzhak Mordechai, even symbolically, for the damage to his career and reputation. Hazak only wanted Shalom, and perhaps a few other people, ousted from the Shin Bet. And Shalom was scheduled to retire not long thereafter in any case.

Following Hazak's meeting with Peres all seemed calm on the surface, but the turbulence within the Shin Bet did not die down. A few months later, in February 1986, Hazak provided Dorit Beinisch, then deputy state attorney, with the details of the affair. A meeting with Attorney General Itzhak Zamir followed. Up to that point Zamir had not clashed in any serious way with the political leadership, but this time he took a firm stand. Clearly, this was a scandal of the most serious sort.

At first, Zamir was prepared to take into consideration the politicians' position and to accept an arrangement under which Shalom and several other Shin Bet agents would resign. But Peres and Shamir unwisely refused. Zamir then ordered the police commissioner to investigate. But the political leadership—not just Peres and Shamir but also Defense Minister Yitzhak Rabin and other members of the cabinet—was unanimous in believing that an investigation would inflict heavy damage to state security and destroy the Shin Bet. This rare unity doomed not only the criminal investigation but also Zamir's tenure.

Information slowly began to leak to the media about a serious rift between the attorney general and the government. Most of the press supported the attorney general, whom they portrayed as a heroic figure and defender of the rule of law, withstanding heavy pressure from the government. The Knesset debated the matter when the opposition tabled no-confidence motions against the government. Peres denied pressuring Zamir, while the attorney general gave an interview to *Ha'aretz* in which he criticized the use of military censorship to keep the affair secret and demanded that the Shin Bet chief suspend himself until the investigation was completed.

Then something new happened. A few weeks before the outbreak of the Shin Bet affair, and without any connection to it, Zamir had informed the cabinet that he was prepared to resign. Justice Minister Moshe Nissim did not immediately commence a search for a candidate to replace him. In the meantime, political infighting in the government unrelated to the Shin Bet affair led to Nissim being switched to the finance portfolio. Yitzhak Moda'i replaced him as justice minister. Now, at the height of the crisis, Moda'i, in coordination with Peres and Shamir, resolved that it was time to act, and began a search for a new attorney general. During a cabinet meeting on June 1, 1986, Moda'i asked Zamir to step outside with him for a moment. The justice minister told him that a few minutes later the cabinet would approve the appointment of Zamir's replacement, Yosef Harish, a judge on the Tel Aviv District Court. What made the process easier, and made it possible to present it as an acceptance of Zamir's resignation rather than a dismissal, was Zamir's previous notification that he wished to end his tenure.

Presumably, if a scenario like this one played out today, any number of citizens and organizations would petition the Supreme Court to halt it. But then no one doubted that the government had the power to decide who would be its attorney general, and to replace that person if it saw fit. Even if an attorney general is dismissed and a new one appointed in a questionable procedure, there were, in those days, no grounds for denying that the government is perfectly within its rights to do so.

Harish received a chilly welcome. "They put out a contract on me," was his way of putting it. The media vociferously attacked the appointment, and the staff of the State Attorney's Office was hostile and derisive. All Harish had done was to consent to replace Zamir, but that was enough to make him complicit in the ouster of the champion of the rule of law. In retrospect, he was clearly the victim of a great injustice. Because the State Attorney's Office refused to cooperate with him, Harish often had to address difficult issues alone or nearly on his own. Despite this, he displayed better judgment than Zamir and his supporters in the State Attorney's Office on a series of complex legal questions.

Regarding the Shin Bet, Harish told of a meeting he had with Zamir upon assuming his new position. He asked the outgoing attorney general if he would indeed have laid the affair to rest had Shalom moved his retirement up by a few months. Zamir, according to Harish, answered in the affirmative. "And in that case there is no affair and no nothing?" the new attorney general queried. "If that's the case . . . I am astounded. You speak so highly of the rule of law, you fought here . . . against the executive branch . . . In what law . . . does it say that a person who takes two people off a bus alive, healthy and uninjured . . . smashes their heads in . . . and then does his best to pin the blame on others . . . and who fabricates evidence for a year and a half . . . [gets off] and his only punishment . . . is that he is nicely asked to step aside . . . and there is no affair and no nothing. Is that the rule of law or the rule of compromise?" Harish says that Zamir did not answer.[102]

III. THE PRESIDENT GRANTS PARDONS

Zamir's order that the police pursue a criminal investigation remained in force. The government in fact demanded that Harish withdraw his predecessor's order, but Harish maintained that he had no authority to do so. He proposed that the government establish a national commission of inquiry (presumably in such a case the police investigation would be suspended). But, given that a statutory commission of inquiry would have the power to subpoena Shin Bet personnel, the government would not hear of it. The cabinet and the attorney general reached an impasse, at which point the former finance minister, Yoram Aridor, proposed that pardons be granted to all the Shin Bet officials involved.

Prime Minister Peres convened a consultation. The participants included two private attorneys, Ram Caspi and Yaakov Neeman, as well as Harish. The new attorney general did not rule out the idea of a pardon, even though the police investigation was still in progress and no charges had been filed. A short time later the cabinet asked Israel's president, Chaim Herzog, to issue the pardons. Herzog agreed, on condition that Shalom resign. A huge public uproar ensued. The media attacked Harish virulently, even though the pardon had not been his initiative, claiming that he should have prevented the pardons. Zamir, the dismissed attorney general, was depicted as a hero.

Neither did Prime Minister Peres emerge unscathed. He had not been involved in the Bus 300 affair, which took place while he led the opposition. The pardon proposal came up after he had served for nearly two years as premier of a national unity government, close to the date when, according to the rotation agreement, he would resign and be replaced by Shamir. He could have exploited the affair for political gain by refusing to consider a pardon, which may well have caused the government to fall and brought on new elections. But Peres preferred his integrity—a trait his opponents often derided him for lacking—by going through with the rotation. Presumably he also believed that the criminal investigation, and any subsequent indictments, trials, and convictions, could destroy the Shin Bet. He was not prepared to do that.

The pardons presented a legal question. Could the president pardon in advance a person who had not yet been convicted? The answer seems clear: If he could grant a pardon to a person who had been convicted, he obviously could do so, *a fortiori*, in the case of a person who had not yet been found guilty. But a year earlier, in June 1985, Herzog had asked Itzhak Zamir to render an opinion on this very issue. The case at hand was that of the Jewish Underground, a band of extremists who had carried out terrorist attacks against Palestinians over the course of several years. Sympathizers with the members of the Underground called on Herzog to pardon them for their crimes and thus avert their trial and punishment. Zamir responded with a document arguing that the president was empowered to pardon only a convicted criminal. Herzog refrained from issuing pardons, presumably not only because of Zamir's opinion but also because it was unjustified. Zamir, however, turned his opinion into a directive stating the president has no power to pardon before a conviction.

It is doubtful whether any general rule on this subject was necessary, but that question is dwarfed by the fundamental error in Zamir's reasoning. The subject had already been discussed in two Supreme Court opinions. In one, Justice Shimon Agranat wrote: "The president has the power to pardon offenders both before and after their conviction."[103] The second opinion was written by Zvi Berinson: "It seems to me that it is in the power [of the president] to pardon any offender, including before he is brought to trial."[104] Justice Haim Cohn took a similar position, asserting that the presidential pardon should be interpreted broadly. Zamir argued that these statements by Agranat and Berinson were obiter, that is, that they had addressed the issue in passing and were thus not binding. Yet there is something arrogant in a government official, even if a senior one and the attorney general, who assumes the authority to restrict the powers of the president in contradiction of language included in Supreme Court decisions, even if these were but obiter. If the attorney general indeed thought it necessary to issue a directive, he should at most have stated that there was doubt about the president's powers and that it was conceivable, though far from certain, that the court might rule contrary to the views of these past illustrious justices and determine that the president could not pardon an offender who had not yet been convicted.

This mistaken directive demonstrates that Israel's attorney general, nominally counsel to the cabinet, has assumed the authority to legislate, that is to establish laws that are incumbent on the government to obey. He also has judicial powers, in that he can issue what is tantamount to a judicial ruling against the government, even in matters that are open to dispute. No less interesting, however, is the ideological symbiosis that characterized the work of Attorney General Zamir and Justice Aharon Barak, as each of them promoted a doctrine of radical judicial activism from their respective perches.

As one might expect, the Shin Bet pardons were challenged before the Supreme Court, on the basis of petitions submitted by citizens, members of the Knesset, lawyers, and no less than twelve university faculty members. Lack of standing was no longer an obstacle, of course. The petitions were heard before a three-judge panel led by Chief Justice Meir Shamgar, accompanied by Miriam Ben-Porat and Aharon Barak. By a majority vote, the court recognized the validity of the pardons. Shamgar surveyed previous opinions on the subject and pointed out that, in legal systems similar to Israel's, pardons could also be granted prior to conviction. He then addressed Zamir's directive, offered a thorough critique of its reasoning, and rejected it completely.[105]

In a minority opinion, Barak maintained that President Herzog had exceeded his powers and that the pardons were void. "This issue," he wrote, "stands at the center of our constitutional life ... the arms of the law stand high but the law is higher than all of us." Barak claimed that "we are interpreting a constitution" even though Israel has no document by that name. At that point, the Basic Law: Human Dignity and Liberty had not yet been passed. In his long and detailed opinion, he rejected the opinions of Justices Berinson and Agranat, and of course rejected that of Chief Justice Shamgar as well.

After reading Barak's dissent, Shamgar added a few sentences to his opinion regarding Barak's use of the term "rule of law." Shamgar noted that the power to pardon prior to conviction was established "in countries whose regimes are among the most proper, and denying that there is effective rule of law in every country with such a broad scope of the power of pardon would be a radical conclusion lacking any real basis."

It fell on Deputy Chief Justice Miriam Ben-Porat to break the tie. She realized that Barak believed it of utmost importance that his position be accepted. He made every effort to persuade her,[106] but to no avail. She concurred in Shamgar's opinion and made it clear that, given the positions taken by Agranat, Berinson, and others, there was no doubt that in Israel the president could also pardon an offender who had not yet been convicted.

The specific question was the president's powers, but the case at hand could not be understood outside its security context. In the judgment of the political leadership, the case was severely detrimental to the nation's security. A more general question was whether the attorney general or the courts would decide a security issue of the highest importance, or whether it was not better for the decision to be made by the president in consultation with the political leadership. Barak's position was that the decision should be made solely by the legal profession. The chief and deputy chief justices maintained that the final decision can also be made by the country's elected leaders.

Barak is notorious for seeking to clip the wings of the other branches of government and expand the authority of the courts. Here, as in other cases, the fight was not over the rule of law. What was at stake was who would rule. Everyone agreed that the attorney general had the discretion not to file charges against a person even though he had committed an offense. Such a decision (which is subject to review by the Supreme Court) is for all intents and purposes similar to a pardon. What Barak and Zamir sought was for the prosecution and judiciary to have a monopoly over the use of discretion to absolve a suspect at the preconviction stage. They opposed the use of presidential power to grant a pardon at this stage, which they regarded as an encroachment into the area they considered to be solely under their control.

Furthermore, the Bus 300 case is a good example of Barak's attitude toward precedent. He in fact sought, and in many cases succeeded, to rewrite entire areas of Israeli law. Armed with the slogan "the rule of law," he tried to remove all restraints on the powers of the Supreme Court and to whittle away at the powers of the other branches of government.

In short, the truth of the case was the opposite of that presented by the media, and probably that ensconced in Israel's historical memory of the affair. The rule of law was in fact threatened by Zamir, who issued a mistaken directive and tried to deny the president authority he legally held. It was Harish who defended the rule of law. He represented the president and the government in the Supreme Court and won, thus proving that the attorney general (and the State Attorney's Office, which was under his authority) should not mix their personal views with professional matters. The attorney general should not interfere with the operation of the government simply because the government's actions are not consistent with his worldview. The press, of course, was free to criticize the pardon, but the pardon was legal and the attorney general had to defend it, which Harish did successfully.

The media also treated President Herzog unfairly. In his memoir *Living History*, Israel's sixth president was highly critical of Zamir's conduct. According to Herzog, 90 to 95 percent of the writing about him in the press was negative, at a time when 92 percent of the public supported him.

But the affair was not over yet. The police completed the criminal investigation and handed its findings over to the State Attorney's Office. The latter formed a committee to study the material, led by Deputy Attorney General Yehudit Karp. One of the dramatic questions was the role played by Shamir, who had been prime minister when the bus was hijacked. The Shin Bet chief claimed that the terrorists were killed and the judicial process sabotaged on Shamir's orders. The Karp Committee found that there was no possibility of determining whether Shamir was responsible. This removed the political leadership from the scandal. The other suspects clearly could not be brought to trial because they had been pardoned, but they were required to leave the Shin Bet.

11

Torture

Less than a year after the Bus 300 affair, described in the previous chapter, another Shin Bet (Israel's internal security service) scandal hit the front pages. Izat Nafso was an Israel Defense Forces officer from Israel's Circassian community, a small non-Arab group that is Muslim by religion and the members of which are, unlike most other Israeli Muslims, conscripted into the Israeli army. Nafso served in an army unit stationed in southern Lebanon. With the end of his military service in sight, he married a woman from his village. But a few weeks after his wedding, on January 4, 1980, while on his final leave but still officially in the service, he was arrested and taken for interrogation. The suspicions against him were based on information received from a Shin Bet informant who, it would later transpire, was a double agent feeding his operators trumped-up charges. Nafso was interrogated by a team of Shin Bet agents led by Yossi Ginossar, the same Ginossar who would later serve as his organization's Trojan Horse on the Zorea Commission's investigation of the Bus 300 affair. Nafso claimed that his interrogators broke him by using severe physical and psychological torture, leading him to confess to serious offences. He was tried before a special military court authorized to hear cases of treason. The panel of judges was headed by Ben-Zion Farhi, who, as we have seen, subsequently served as chief military advocate general. One of the other judges was Mordechai Kremnitzer, a member of the law faculty at the Hebrew University, an expert on criminal law and a prominent human rights activist.

Nafso told the court about the torture and claimed that his confession had been extracted under pressure. The Shin Bet agents lied, denying that torture had been used and claiming that Nafso had confessed of his own volition without any improper use of force. The court accepted the agents' testimony and admitted Nafso's confession as evidence. He was convicted of treason and abetting the enemy in wartime and sentenced to eighteen years in prison. An appeal submitted to the Military Court of Appeals by a former chief military advocate general, Tzvi Hadar, was dismissed. The decision on the appeal was handed down just a few weeks after the news broke that Shin Bet agents had flagrantly perjured themselves before the Zorea Commission and the Blatman investigation. But the appeals bench failed to connect the dots, basing its decision on the traditional approach that a court of appeal does not intervene in determinations of fact based on the credibility of witnesses made by the lower court.

Just a few days before the decision on the appeal was rendered, the Military Justice Law was amended so as to make it possible for a decision by this top military court to be appealed to the Supreme Court. Nafso, availing himself of this provision, was granted leave to do so.

A crucial development in the case took place within the Shin Bet. Avraham Shalom resigned and was replaced, temporarily, by former Shin Bet Chief Yosef Harmelin. Apparently, the obstruction of justice that came to light in the Bus 300 affair raised doubts within the agency with regard to Nafso's conviction. The Shin Bet decided to reopen the case and a re-examination of the evidence by the Shin Bet and the chief military advocate general revealed that most of Nafso's claims about pressure and torture were true.[107] The military prosecution concluded that Nafso had been wrongfully convicted and proposed a deal to the former officer and his attorneys: The conviction would be set aside, in exchange for which Nafso would plead guilty to a charge of "exceeding his authority to the point of endangering state security." This count was based on the fact that Nafso had, during his time in southern Lebanon, met with a man with ties to terrorists groups and had not reported the fact.

The plea bargain was reached while Nafso's appeal to the Supreme Court was still pending. The deal was submitted to a panel chaired by Chief Justice Meir Shamgar. It was an odd procedure—a plea bargain in a higher court that contradicted the findings of two lower courts, and involving the appellant's conviction of a much lesser crime than those of which he was originally accused. Furthermore, the connection between the original charges and the count contained in the new conviction seemed to be tenuous in the extreme. Cognizant of this, Shamgar declared that the Supreme Court needed to consider "whether the appellant is not doing himself evil, because he has no more strength and cannot bear imprisonment any longer."

Nafso reiterated that he indeed confessed to the lesser charge of his own volition and not because of the prison term he was serving. The court accepted the plea bargain and sentenced him to two years in prison. By this time, in 1987, Nafso had served seven and a half years,[108] so he was released forthwith. Five days later, *Yedioth Ahronoth* published an interview with him in which, while he did not say so explicitly, he implied that he was innocent of the lesser charge as well.[109]

The plea bargain reached with Nafso is hardly satisfactory. When a person has been accused of serious crimes, such as murder or treason, there is a high likelihood that, even if he is innocent, he will agree to a plea bargain involving conviction on a far lesser charge. Facing a long, expensive trial that can wreak severe damage on him, his reputation, and his family no matter what the final verdict, such a person is likely to be advised by his lawyers that he would be better off confessing to the lesser crime and even enduring a relatively short prison term rather than trying to prove his innocence. If it turns out that the defendant did not commit the serious crime of which he was accused, it is unseemly to charge him with some smaller and marginal offense, simply to save the prosecution's face.

The actions committed by the Shin Bet agents in Nafso's case would have justified a police inquiry. But, given that it was clearly not an isolated case of obstruction of justice by the Shin Bet, Attorney General Harish pushed for the case to be examined by an independent panel. This time the political leadership was not opposed—no political figures were implicated and as such none were threatened. Neither did the Shin Bet object, weakened as it was at this time by the embarrassing revelations that had emerged from the Bus 300 and Nafso scandals. Thus, a week after the Supreme Court decision, the cabinet voted to establish a national commission of inquiry to examine "the investigation methods and procedures of the [Shin Bet] on HTA [Hostile Terrorist Activity], and the giving of testimony in court in connection with these investigations."[110] The decision stated explicitly that the commission was being set up in the wake of the Nafso verdict. As provided by law, the members of the commission were appointed by the chief justice of the Supreme Court. Shamgar chose former Chief Justice Moshe Landau to chair the commission. Its other members were Supreme Court Justice Yaacov Maltz and Major General (ret.) Yitzhak Hofi, a former director of the Mossad, Israel's overseas espionage and special operations agency.

The commission's report was sharply critical of the Shin Bet's conduct in the Nafso case. "This case serves as an alarm and a warning," it stated, "not only because of the miscarriage of justice to [Nafso] himself, but no less because of the corruption inherent in perjury, which was exposed to the light of day and which must now be wholly eradicated."[111] Even more severe, the members of the commission wrote, was the discovery that the agency's conduct with Nafso was part of a practice that had become standard in the organization. The three members found that Shin Bet interrogators had, for the past sixteen years, used physical and psychological pressure of various kinds to gain confessions from suspects and to falsely deny in court that they had done anything of the sort. In the vast majority of cases the court had accepted the false testimony of the Shin Bet agents that appeared before it. Only in rare cases had courts rejected confessions obtained in this manner.

The justification offered by Shin Bet officials was that the goal justified the means. In cases like these they were certain the defendant was guilty, and their perjury was meant to ensure the conviction of people that they were certain were dangerous terrorists or involved in hostile activity against Israel. Some of the Shin Bet witnesses heard by the commission claimed that there had been an implicit compact with the prosecution, "a kind of tacit, winking agreement" regarding their falsehoods.[112] The prosecutors, both military and civilian, denied this categorically, and the commission accepted their testimony rather than that of the Shin Bet officials. Some Shin Bet agents even claimed that "the judges were also 'part of the game,'" a contention that the commission rejected as entirely unfounded.[113]

The Landau Commission declared that Israel was obligated to hold to moral values and to ban illegal interrogation methods. Nevertheless, its members recommended that no legal proceedings be instigated against Shin Bet interrogators who had in the past acted in accordance with the standard procedures in the organization, even if this involved criminal activity and perjury. The justification for this was that such proceedings would badly damage the organization. The approach was much like that of the cabinet and the president in the Bus 300 affair.

Nafso was not satisfied with the report. He petitioned the Supreme Court to order that his interrogators be brought to justice, arguing against the Landau Commission's recommendation not to charge them. His petition was heard by a panel presided over by Aharon Barak. In a surprisingly brief opinion, only four pages long, Barak rejected Nafso's petition on the grounds that he had presented the court with a very narrow question: whether the attorney general had acted in accordance with the Landau Commission's recommendations.[114]

This time Barak said nothing about the rule of law. In his decision, he concurred with the president, the government, and the attorney general, as well as a national commission of inquiry headed by a former Supreme Court chief justice, that it was best to avoid a criminal trial when security interests of the first order were involved. In this instance, Barak chose not to stand against all these others and turn the case before him into an impressive precedent. He understood that it was better to end the matter quietly.

The legal system's principal function is to ascertain the truth and expose lies. The most obvious lesson to be learned from the Bus 300 and Izat Nafso affairs is how badly the system failed at this task. In theory, a judge in the first instance, who hears witnesses and forms his opinion of them, is best equipped to determine how reliable they are, to decide which ones to believe and which not. This is the basis of the rule that appeals courts do not re-examine the lower court's findings of fact. But in the real world this theory clearly does not work—being a trained jurist does not necessarily enable a prosecutor or judge to discern whether a witness is lying. State Attorney Yona Blatman chose to believe Shin Bet agents who were in fact lying rather than army officers who were telling the truth. Attorney General Itzhak Zamir accepted Blatman's wrong opinion. Both these men stood at the pinnacle of the public legal system.

The same thing happened in the Nafso trial. The prosecution believed false witnesses, and the court preferred their testimony to that of Nafso himself, who was the one witness who told the truth. In neither case was it the legal system that uncovered the truth in the end. Furthermore, these were not isolated instances. Many judges, in many cases, over many years, have demonstrated a notable inability to discern who was speaking the truth and who lying. But the Landau Commission was appointed to examine what had happened in the Shin Bet, not within the legal and judicial machinery. No one dared suggest that there was a problem in the latter. No one even dared suggest such a thing out loud.

Another problematic phenomenon is a general tendency by prosecutors to disregard or even oppose evidence that contradicts their preconceptions about a case, as happened when the prosecutors in the Bus 300 affair dismissed testimonies inconsistent with their theory that Yitzhak Mordechai was guilty of killing the terrorists. An inner conviction that a certain party is guilty can violate the rights of an innocent person, as was the case when Zamir sought Mordechai's suspension from his army post.

Yet the state prosecution and attorney general emerged from both these embarrassing scandals not only unscathed and without having been subject to constructive criticism, but as heroes. Much was said about the danger presented by the Shin Bet and the need for oversight, but no one spoke of the danger presented by the public prosecution, even when it acts in good faith, and its own need for outside supervision.

The situation has only gotten worse since then. The Supreme Court has turned the attorney general into the country's supreme commander, despite the fact that in the Bus 300 case the position of the Chief Military Prosecutor Menachem Finkelstein and Chief Military Advocate General Ben-Zion Farhi were more balanced and reasonable. Increasingly, officials in the justice system have used leaks to the media to sully the reputations of suspects. Partly because of this, the percentage of cases ending in conviction has increased dramatically—and with it the danger that an innocent person will be convicted.

The Shin Bet's interrogation methods and procedures were the principal focus of the Landau Commission, which addressed both the Bus 300 and Nafso cases. Its members heard evidence about the use of torture in the questioning of suspected terrorists, and about how this was denied by Shin Bet agents in court, who would claim that the suspects provided their confessions of their own free will.

The commission categorically condemned the practice of perjury and sought to apply the rule of law to Shin Bet interrogations. Nevertheless, its members were well aware that the nature of the suspects the Shin Bet needed to get information from presented more difficult a problem than the criminal investigations that are the police force's principal work. The investigation of a conventional criminal offense, even if a murder, looks principally to the past. The question is whether the suspect or some other person committed the crime. In the case of terrorists, interrogators focus on the future. They must uncover and prevent hostile acts that are being planned or are likely to be committed in the future. (True, the future can be a consideration in some criminal cases, for example in the case of a serial offender or organized crime ring, but the scale of the likely damage is usually smaller.) Under these circumstances, interrogators face considerable pressure to discover not only what happened in the past but also to prevent the next terror attack.

The Landau Commission sought to find a way that would enable interrogators to do their job while still keeping their practices within bounds that would not exceed the accepted practices of similar organizations in democratic countries. Its recommendations were based on a distinction between torture and pressure. As such, it permitted the Shin Bet to use psychological pressure and deception, and in certain cases, when there is no other choice, in cases defined as "ticking bombs," also "a moderate measure of physical pressure." The commission added, however, that there should be guidelines "setting clear boundaries in this matter, in order to prevent the use of inordinate physical pressure arbitrarily administered by the interrogator."[115]

Immediately following the publication of the report the media launched an all-out attack on the report and on Landau himself. The central charge was that the report sanctioned torture. The expression "moderate physical pressure" became a term of abuse and was presented as if it were a cover for real torture. Criticism of the report also appeared in the legal literature.[116] Michal Shaked writes in her biography of Moshe Landau that the attacks on the report were "brutal, incorrect, and unjustified." The members of the commission were seeking to prevent torture, and the distinction they made between torture and pressure that does not reach the point of torture is well-grounded. Furthermore, incarceration for the purposes of interrogation for a limited period of time, prior to trial, is accepted practice in Israel.* Many detainees would claim that detention itself is a form of torture, but clearly it is not the type of torture forbidden in international treaties.

The second foundation of the Landau Commission report was the law, specifically the "necessity" defense that now appears in Section 34:11 of the Penal Code. This provision absolves a person of responsibility for "an act immediately necessary to save his own life, freedom, body, or property, or that of another person, from concrete danger of serious harm." Given that a terrorist endangers the life of innocent people, the commission reasoned that defense against a terrorist attack counts as a

---

* Under Israeli law, a police officer may detain a suspect for twenty-four hours, and in some cases forty-eight hours. Further detention requires a judge's approval.

necessity. The commission thus proposed, in the classified section of the report, to establish guidelines for Shin Bet interrogators defining what means were permitted and what forbidden. These guidelines would take into account the circumstances, including the risk presented by the suspect and his associates.

In December 1987, two months after the Landau Commission issued its report, the First Intifada broke out. The Shin Bet played a central role in Israel's response to the uprising, and in doing so its agents on more than one occasion violated the rules laid down in the report. Seven years later, in 1994, after the signing of the Oslo Accords and the end of the First Intifada, the Public Committee against Torture in Israel, a nongovernmental organization, petitioned the Supreme Court to forbid the Shin Bet to use torture in its interrogations. Five more years went by before the court issued its judgment in the case, in September 1999. Delays of this sort in cases that raise important questions is characteristic of the Supreme Court's conduct since the legal revolution.

In its judgment, the court forbade several specific methods of interrogation, among them "shaking" (violently agitating the suspect so that his head and neck jiggle rapidly back and forth), and issued a general order against the use of torture. At the same time, the court categorically rejected the Landau Commission's position that the necessity defense can serve as the basis for interrogation guidelines. Furthermore, it stated that neither the cabinet nor the Shin Bet's directors had the authority to lay down rules regarding the use of physical methods of interrogation. On the other hand, the court recognized that "a reasonable investigation is likely to cause discomfort. It may result in insufficient sleep. The conditions under which it is conducted risk being unpleasant." Likewise, "Within the confines of the law, it is permitted to resort to various sophisticated techniques."[117]

And what about an immediate danger, a "ticking bomb"? In such a case, Barak was prepared to recognize the necessity defense in a case in which exceptional methods, beyond those generally permissible, were used against a subject. In other words, while the necessity defense could not be used as a basis for guidelines given in advance, it could, after the fact, be invoked by an interrogator in a criminal proceeding lodged against him. This distinction, between advance instructions and ex post facto exemption, is not particularly attractive. It is even more difficult to comprehend in light of the sanction the judgment gives to the attorney general "to provide guidelines regarding the circumstances under which interrogators will not be brought to trial." The question that arises is why is it permissible for the attorney general to offer advance guidelines based on the necessity defense, regarding situations in which he will refrain from filing charges, yet impermissible to provide interrogators with guidelines based on the same defense. The not very persuasive solution to the paradox is that Barak distinguished between, on the one hand, guidelines to the interrogators regarding use of pressure or torture and, on the other hand, guidelines to the prosecution for avoiding indictment in cases in which pressure or torture has been used. The difference is too fine to be convincing.[118]

The attorney general of course refrained from laying down rules or providing advance guidance regarding instances in which interrogators would not be brought to trial. He had no reason to open himself up to attacks of the type that the members of the Landau Commission were subjected to. The upshot of the court decision was that, in the eye of the public, guided by shallow and one-sided reportage and opinion pieces in the press, Landau had permitted torture and Barak forbidden it. The report was also blamed for allowing the Shin Bet to use interrogation methods that Landau and his colleagues had never sanctioned. Barak's ruling was the death knell for the Landau Report. Landau himself was deeply hurt and offended. The Supreme Court's categorical rejection of the report's legal foundation was tantamount to a stinging condemnation of a former chief justice, one of our greatest judges, and the report his commission had produced. From Landau's point of view, the judgment should at least have stressed that the commission's intention had been to prevent torture, not to allow it. Presumably Landau would also have ruled out the specific interrogation methods that Barak forbade. In practice, the Shin Bet did not operate in accordance with the report and continued to use methods that had no grounding in that document. As Michal Shaked put it, "Landau felt betrayed." Barak's judgment holds forth at length on the human dignity of the suspects. According to his biographer, Landau wrote to Barak asking "What have you done to my human dignity?"[119]

Landau was highly critical of Barak's judicial activism, of the use he made of the concept of unreasonableness, and of the authority that the Supreme Court assumed to invalidate laws passed by the Knesset. Up until this point, Landau had confined his criticism to legal journals and professional forums. But a year after the ruling in the torture case, the former chief justice offered a lengthy interview to *Haʾaretz* in which he voiced a sharp and outspoken critique of Barak and the court he headed.

In 2002 the Knesset passed the ISA (Shin Bet) Statute, which granted Shin Bet agents the powers of interrogation, search, and even to access communications data. Section 18 states that "an employee of the service or a person acting on behalf of the service will not bear criminal or civil responsibility for an act or omission performed in good faith and reasonably in the framework of his position and in order to carry out his duties." The language "in good faith and reasonably" places limits on this grant of immunity. It hardly seems likely that Izat Nafso's interrogators could have invoked this section in their defense. The real protection that Shin Bet interrogators enjoy is that the public prosecution grants them immunity, tantamount to a pardon, just as it does to police investigators and the staff of the State Attorney's Office. This immunity is not anchored in any law. It derives from the prosecution's exercise of discretion. This is what happened in the Nafso case, where the interrogators were not put on trial, a decision by the prosecution that the Supreme Court saw no reason to invalidate. The controversy surrounding the Bus 300 case, which Barak, Zamir, and the media presented as a fight to enforce the rule of law, was in fact a battle for state power. Aharon Barak and Itzhak Zamir, who disputed the president's power to grant a pre-trial pardon, had no objection to achieving a similar result by abstaining from prosecution. They simply sought to have the power to do so vested solely in the hands of the legal apparatus.

12

The Second Rabin Government and the Oslo Agreements

In the wake of the news that he and his wife had maintained an illegal foreign bank account, Prime Minister Yitzhak Rabin resigned his leadership of the Labor Party in 1977. He was replaced by his arch-rival, Shimon Peres, who led the party through a string of electoral defeats. His best showing was a virtual tie in the elections held in 1984. The results led to a national unity government in which Peres served as prime minister for two years, under a rotation agreement. In the early 1990s Rabin began to seek to lead Labor once again, and in February 1992 he trounced Peres in an internal leadership contest.

Four months later, in the elections to the Thirteenth Knesset, Labor won a stunning victory, gaining forty-four seats in the Knesset. Labor's natural partner was the super-dovish Meretz Party, which won twelve seats. Together, Hadash, a Jewish-Arab front dominated by the Communist Party, and the Arab Democratic Party won five seats. While, because of their advocacy of the Palestinian cause, these two parties were not candidates to join the ruling coalition, neither they nor Meretz were under any circumstances going to support a right-wing government led by Likud. Rabin thus emerged from the election with a "blocking majority" of sixty-one members of the Knesset, making it impossible for Likud to form a government. Under these circumstances, he was able to reach across the political divide to invite the participation of parties that preferred Likud but had an interest in not remaining in the opposition. One of these was a new Haredi-Sephardi Party, Shas, which agreed to join the coalition and grant Rabin a narrow majority. The Rabin government increased funding for education and expanded development projects in the Arab community. In 1994 his government also revamped the Israeli health system with a National Health Insurance Law.

The Intifada, the Palestinian uprising that began in December 1987, was at that time fading out as a popular uprising. It metamorphosed into a wave of organized terror attacks. One of these was the kidnapping of a Border Guard policeman, Nissim Toledano, by agents of Hamas, an Islamist Palestinian faction. Hamas sought to force Israel to release its founder, Sheikh Ahmed Yassin, who was held in an Israeli prison. Toledano's body was found a few days after the abduction. He had been tied up and stabbed to death soon after being captured.

The murder shocked the Israeli public. In response, the government decided on the immediate deportation of a large number of Hamas activists from the West

Bank and Gaza Strip. In practice, the order was issued by the military commander in accordance with the Defense (Emergency) Regulations enacted during the British Mandate over Palestine and which remained in force in Israel. Terrorists had been deported in the past, but this had generally involved individuals who were banished for long periods. Before the order was carried out, they were usually given the right of hearing before a committee established under the terms of these regulations. This time the plan was to expel a large number of terrorists for a shorter period. Immediately after Toledano's body was found, deportation orders were issued expelling 415 Hamas activists for a specific term not exceeding twenty-four months. The deportees were not given a right of hearing before implementation began on December 16, 1992, when the men were loaded on buses that took them to the Lebanese border. But the attempt to keep the operation secret failed. Human rights organizations and Jewish and Arab members of the Knesset rushed to file Supreme Court petitions, some of which asked the court to issue interim orders to delay the expulsion until the court reached its decision on whether the order was legal.

The justice on duty that evening was Aharon Barak, who issued the requested stay order. The prisoners, who were still within Israel's borders, waited on the buses. The question was what would happen now, with international pressure on Israel already building up. At this point Chief Justice Meir Shamgar intervened. He convened a panel of seven justices that revoked Barak's stay and issued an order nisi. But the delay had given the Lebanese authorities an opportunity to prepare themselves. They refused to accept the deportees. The Hamas men were left in limbo, in tents on Lebanese territory just north of the security zone occupied by Israel.

As if that were not enough, there was a further complication. The deportation was carried out after Rabin consulted with Attorney General Yosef Harish. Harish was prepared to sanction the move, but it transpired that State Attorney Dorit Beinisch was inalterably opposed. With Beinisch and most of her staff unwilling to defend the government's position and to cooperate with Harish on this matter, Harish had no choice but to appear before the Supreme Court himself. Nili Arad, who headed the High Court of Justice Department in the justice ministry, consented to appear along with Harish and, exceptionally, Israel Defense Forces (IDF) Chief of Staff Ehud Barak joined them. The seven-justice panel handed down its verdict a little more than a month later, on January 28, 1993. The court ruled for the government and revoked the order nisi. This incident is a good demonstration of the problem with the currently accepted practice by which the state attorney or the attorney general can refuse to defend the government in court if they believe the government's policy to be legally problematic. In the present case, Harish's decision to defend the government was made in the face of stiff opposition by the state attorney and his office, who actually refused to cooperate with him. Another attorney general might have decided to adopt an approach in line with the dominant view in his office and allow the case against the government to remain undefended. But the fact that a case seems a hard one, or that the government's position is not in accord with the values of the government's lawyers, cannot be allowed to leave the state without counsel. This case, in which the dominant view in the Attorney General's Office was against representing the government, and yet the attorney general, acting almost alone, won a court victory, proves the point. Indeed, a few months later Prime Minister Rabin was less fortunate, when Harish declined to represent him in the Deri case that is discussed below.

In its decision on the deportation case, the court discussed at length a judgment rendered in 1980 in the case of *Kawasama v. Minister of Defense*,[120] regarding the deportation to Jordan of three Arab leaders—the mayors of the West Bank cities of Hebron and Halhul and the imam of the al-Ibrahimi Mosque in the Tomb of the Patriarchs in the former city. This earlier deportation had been carried out following the murder of six Jews who were on their way back from praying at the tomb. In that case also, the candidates for deportation were not given an opportunity to argue their case before the committee established under the defense regulation, on the grounds that the security situation was tense and explosive and immediate action was required. Justice Landau wrote for the majority then, stating that while, in principle, the deportees should be given a right of hearing prior to their deportation, the failure to grant it did not invalidate the deportation itself. Nevertheless, he recommended that two of the three deportees be allowed to plead their case. Justice Haim Cohn dissented. In his view the deportations were utterly null and void.[121] Following the majority decision, the two deportees who were the subjects of Landau's recommendation arrived at the Allenby Bridge, which connects Jordan with the West Bank, where they were immediately arrested. A hearing, in which the deportees were represented by their lawyers, was held before the committee near the bridge. The committee approved the deportation and a subsequent petition to the Supreme Court was dismissed.

Basing itself on the *Kawasama* precedent, the Supreme Court panel in the new deportation case ruled that the deportation of the Hamas operatives to Lebanon remained in force, but that the state should allow the deportees to plead their cases after the fact. To lend the judgment maximum force, the decision was unanimous, and no single judge was credited with writing the opinion. But in her book on Chief Justice Barak, *Your Honor*,[122] Nomi Levitsky tells of a fierce battle behind the scenes. She says that Barak, Theodor Or, and Eliahu Mazza drafted a minority opinion, in line with Barak's interim order, that was harshly critical of the deportation process. The four judges in the majority prepared their own opinion. In the end, however, Shamgar brokered a compromise that made a unanimous decision possible. The judgment sidestepped the issue of whether the explosive situation, that existed at the time the order was issued, justified deportation without prior right of hearing, and whether its denial constituted a violation of the law. Instead, it addressed only the deportation after the fact, that is, after the cancellation of Barak's temporary stay order, and held that, according to the *Kawasama* precedent, the failure to grant the deportees a hearing did not invalidate the deportation orders. Nevertheless, the state was required to grant the deportees a right of hearing after the deportation, similar to that which had been accorded to two of the *Kawasama* deportees.[123]

Operationally, the action was a total failure. It was not long—just a year to a year and a half—before the deportees returned. Their standing in Hamas and on the Palestinian street had been enhanced, and many of them quickly took on leadership roles, among them Mahmoud al-Zahar, Ismail Haniyeh, and Abel Aziz Rantisi. Haniyeh became the Hamas prime minister in the Gaza Strip, al-Zahar is a top figure in the organization, while Rantisi, a senior Hamas commander, was targeted in 2004. The deportees were also able to use their time in Lebanon to establish connections with the Iranian Revolutionary Guards and Hezbollah, both of which provided support and military know-how.

Rabin's second term as prime minister also produced the Oslo Accords, which in turn led to the signing of a peace treaty between Israel and Jordan. The first Oslo Accord was concluded in August 1993, about eight months following the deportation of the Hamas operatives to Lebanon. The agreement marked a sea change in Israeli policy. After long years of nearly wall-to-wall consensus in Israel that rejected negotiations with the Palestine Liberation Organization (PLO) and refused to accept the creation of a Palestinian state, Rabin's government commenced negotiations with the PLO and signed an agreement that set Israel on the road to accepting the creation of such a state.

This watershed was the product of a number of factors that influenced each side. In 1987, Shimon Peres, then foreign minister in the national unity government headed by Yitzhak Shamir, reached the so-called London Agreement with King Hussein of Jordan. That compact, the details of which were never officially made public but which was much discussed in the press and in the political arena, was reported to have called for an international peace conference. Peres and Hussein allegedly intended for it to lead to an agreement that would reestablish Jordanian rule over the West Bank. Shamir, however, rejected the agreement. Soon thereafter the Intifada broke out, and Hussein announced that he and his country no longer saw themselves as representatives of the Palestinians in the West Bank and recognized the PLO as the sole representative of the Palestinian people. This ended any hope of Israel reaching an agreement with Jordan over the territory it had captured from that country in 1967.

In fact, the PLO was not in good shape at the time. During the Lebanon War of 1982, the Palestinian organization and its militias were ejected from that country, losing its last base in proximity to Israel. Its leaders sought a way to return to center stage. The Oslo agreement provided a solution to the predicaments of both Israel and the PLO.

But the agreement caused dissension within Rabin's government, with its narrow Knesset majority. The parties of the right opposed the agreement, organizing rallies and campaigning vociferously against it and against Rabin personally. In the meantime, Shas leader Aryeh Deri faced corruption charges.

Shas had been founded in 1982, some thirty-five years after the establishment of the state of Israel. It quickly gained popularity among the Sephardi population, notably those whose families had come to Israel from the Islamic world (the Mizrahim). They were both religious and traditional, and felt that they had been sidelined and discriminated against. The established Haredi parties, dominated by Ashkenazim, had always explicitly rejected Zionism, while enjoying financial support that governments granted to Haredi schools, *yeshivot*, and other institutions in exchange for Haredi votes in the Knesset. While Ashkenazi Haredi politicians refused until very recently to accept ministerial portfolios, they were appointed as deputy ministers.*

---

* In August 2015 the Supreme Court ended this practice by holding that a deputy minister may not wield the powers of a minister. As a result, the Haredi leadership allowed the deputy minister of health, Yakov Litzman, to accept the position of minister.

In its commitment to placing strict religious observance at the center of public life, to seeking state support for religious schools and seminaries, and its veneration of rabbinic leaders to whom all major political decisions were referred, Shas modeled itself after the Ashkenazi Haredi parties. But in other respects it was different. While its Knesset representatives and leaders were all Haredim, many of its voters were not strictly observant and certainly not Haredi in their lifestyles. It adopted the nationalistic ethos of Zionism and was happy to participate fully in governing coalitions and the cabinet. As a result, the party has been a partner in nearly all Israeli governments of the last two decades.

Yet, despite its independent opinions on Zionism and the state of Israel, and despite the fact that many of its activists served in the army, Shas fell into line with the Ashkenazi Haredi parties on the issue of exempting *yeshiva* students from army service. Shas also founded dozens of independent schools throughout the country that, like Ashkenazi Haredi schools, segregate boys and girls and stress Torah study. The general studies offered by these schools are, when they are offered at all, usually of low quality. Shas also excludes women from its list of candidates to Knesset elections.

Shas's electoral power and its use to further a religious agenda caused a backlash among Israel's nonreligious citizens, some of whom lashed out in the media and in the Knesset against the Sephardi party. In turn, Shas's activists and supports sensed that they were being persecuted. These feelings were amplified when a series of central figures in the party, including members of the Knesset, were charged with and convicted of misusing their offices to line their own and their party's pockets. This reached its climax when the cases of two of them reached the Supreme Court: Raphael Pinchasi, who served as minister of communications from 1990 to 1992 and then as a deputy minister in Rabin's government, and party leader and Interior Minister Aryeh Deri.

At the age of twenty-seven, Deri's career took off in 1986 when he was appointed director general of the interior ministry by Shas's first political leader, Interior Minister Yitzhak Peretz. But two years later Deri replaced Peretz as party leader and cabinet minister under Prime Minister Shamir. He had not yet celebrated his thirtieth birthday.

Deri continued to hold the interior portfolio in the Rabin government. His voters idolized him, and he won trust and admiration among many nonreligious Israelis and politicians. His moderate stance on the Israel-Arab conflict included a willingness to trade territory for peace, in keeping with a ruling by the party's spiritual leader, Rabbi Ovadia Yosef. This position helped pave the way for partnership with Rabin.

The problem was that, two years earlier, the police had begun investigating allegations that Deri had taken bribes and committed other financial wrongdoings (this group of allegations would form the "personal case"). He was also accused of taking advantage of his post to funnel public funds to organizations affiliated with Shas (the "public case"). The investigation dragged on for a lengthy period while Deri continued to serve as a cabinet minister. But, in June 1993, the State Attorney's Office submitted a list of charges in the personal case to the Knesset, with a request that it revoke the immunity from prosecution to which Deri was entitled as a legislator. The most serious of these was accepting a bribe of more than $150,000. In short order a good-government nongovernmental organization (NGO), the Movement for

Quality Government in Israel, petitioned the Supreme Court, demanding his dismissal from his ministerial post.

A decade earlier, during Itzhak Zamir's term as attorney general, another cabinet minister, Aharon Abuhatssira, had been put on trial for financial offenses. At the time, Abuhatssira represented the religious-Zionist National Religious Party. He was charged with stealing funds from a charity he ran as well as breach of trust by a public official. Abuhatssira continued to serve in the cabinet during his trial. No one demanded that he resign. He left the government only after his conviction.[124] It was understood at that time that a minister did not have to resign if he was under criminal investigation or trial—he could continue to serve as long as he had not been convicted (of course, he was free to quit if he wished). Even Attorney General Zamir, who submitted the charges against Abuhatssira, did not maintain that he ought to resign and did not demand that he do so. But the Rabin government and Deri now found themselves facing a new Supreme Court that did not consider itself bound by the rules and conventions of the past. The press, NGOs, and a part of the public now realized that the Supreme Court was quite happy to take up issues that would previously have been considered political and thus outside its ken. Furthermore, the court now allowed nearly anyone to petition it on nearly any matter of supposedly public interest, without any requirement of standing.

In August 1993 the Knesset's legal counsel presented the charges against Deri to the Knesset and asked that his parliamentary immunity be withdrawn. And while this issue was still before the Knesset, the Supreme Court agreed to hear a petition demanding his dismissal from the cabinet.

Another petition, demanding the dismissal of Pinchasi, then a deputy minister, was submitted at the same time. Pinchasi's case was more complicated legally because his immunity remained in force, as I will recount below.

Harish often showed himself willing to support the government's position against the prevailing view in his office and against vociferous claims that doing so undermines the rule of law. He had done so on the issue of pardons for the Shin Bet operatives in the Bus 300 affair and again in the case of the deportation of Hamas operatives to Lebanon. But in the Deri and Pinchasi cases, which arose not long before the end of his tenure, Harish adopted the approach advocated by Zamir and supported by Barak, under which the attorney general may dictate the government's position on legal matters and may decline to defend the government in court. In the cases at hand Harish decided that the two Shas leaders should leave office. Consequently he refused to argue against their dismissal and refused to allow the prime minister to be represented by another lawyer.

Rabin desperately needed Shas to remain in the coalition. But with Harish refusing to represent his point of view, and forbidden to appoint another attorney to do so, he had no one to plead his position. The best Rabin could do was to write a letter, which Harish was gracious enough to allow to be read in court. In other words, the state attorney represented the attorney general rather than the prime minister and sided with the petitioners in demanding Deri's and Pinchasi's dismissal.

At that time, the law did not contain any provision regarding the tenure of an indicted minister or deputy minister. Did the silence of the legislature constitute a "negative arrangement," that is, did it in practice establish a rule against dismissing a member of the cabinet (or at least not requiring it) in such cases? For example, if the Knesset had enacted a law that a person aged at least seventeen who has passed an appropriate examination is entitled to a driver's license, it may be deduced that a person under that age is not entitled to a license, even though the law did not state this explicitly. The scope of what the law affirms can be used to deduce what it negates. And if it was not a negative arrangement, was the prime minister required to exercise his power to fire a minister? In other words, if the prime minister did not do so, was that unreasonable to the point of requiring the Supreme Court's intervention?

The two suits were argued before the same panel of five justices headed by Chief Justice Shamgar and including Barak, Eliahu Mazza, Dov Levin, and Eliezer Goldberg. Shamgar wrote the unanimous opinion in the Deri case,[125] while Barak authored the judgment in the Pinchasi case.[126] Both judgments were rendered on September 7, 1993, and were identical in their results. While the Basic Law: The Government did not at the time address criminal investigations or convictions of cabinet ministers or deputy ministers, the court ruled that the legislature's silence in this case did not constitute a negative arrangement. Such a state of affairs prevailed, the justices ruled, when the legislature had considered an issue and decided that there was no need to legislate in the matter because the relevant rule could be deduced from the law's other provisions. But that was not the case when the legislature had not discussed the issue at all.

More problematic was the answer the court gave to the second question—that the prime minister's decision to dismiss or not dismiss a minister was subject to the rule of reasonableness. Shamgar ruled that Rabin's failure to fire Deri was unreasonable in the extreme. But it is important to remember that this was a political matter. The revolutionary Supreme Court had refrained from ruling that a racist movement like Kach should be prohibited from running for the Knesset so long as the law did not mandate this. Yet now it saw fit to establish a new rule regarding when cabinet ministers and deputy ministers were fit to serve in their positions.

This ended the political careers of Deri and Pinchasi (although Deri would later resume his). While Shamgar wrote that he was not, in his judgment, "invoking moral norms, which the law provides no basis for," but the justices undoubtedly enforced what seemed to them a fitting ethical standard. These standards were not part of Israeli law, but became part of it after the court for all intents and purposes enacted them. The fact is that Aharon Abuhatssira continued to serve as a cabinet minister even after being indicted, resigning only after his conviction. At the time, no one thought this was against the law. In the Deri and Pinchasi decisions, the court expanded the scope of a rule it had established regarding appointments to public positions in the case of Yossi Ginossar, discussed below, to the political realm, without making any distinction between the two.

Shamgar held that the two men had to be relieved of their positions in order to maintain public trust in the government. But this statement lacks any empirical basis. On the contrary, there are indications that when Shas left the government following the dismissal of its two leaders, public trust in the government was diminished, as usually happens when the government loses support in the Knesset. Indeed, the period that followed proved that the concept of "public trust" was no more than a legal fiction.

The problematic nature of these rules was further complicated by the fact that Pinchasi's parliamentary immunity had not been revoked, because the Supreme

Court itself had overruled a Knesset decision to do so. Pinchasi thus could not be prosecuted at this stage. Yet the Supreme Court ignored his immunity and addressed the charges as if an indictment had been made, and Pinchasi was thus bound to resign.

The court's two rulings had wide-ranging consequences. For all intents and purposes, the court second-guessed a political decision by a prime minister, a matter lying within the purview of the person holding that office. It placed his decision on the same level as that of a civil service official granting a business license. But the two are in fact entirely different. The court's slide into determining the composition of the government constituted a grave violation of the separation of powers and led it straight into the political arena. The question was not whether the result was good or popular. It was whether the court was allowed under any circumstances to establish criteria regarding the composition of the cabinet.

The dismissals of Deri and Pinchasi resulted from the revolutionary court's desire to encroach into the political realm, impose its own wishes and the norms it saw fit, and to promulgate the laws it thought the country should have. But the fact that the targets of its gross intervention in politics and practice of judicial legislation were leaders of the Sephardi community had political and social consequences of the first order.

The problem with the concept of unreasonableness as a basis for judicial decisions is that it is never clear where its boundaries lie. The problem is particularly acute in the political area. Is it reasonable for a cabinet minister under criminal investigation to remain in his post? Is offering a cabinet or subcabinet post to a politician as part of political deal reasonable? Is it reasonable to award a politician a deputy minister post, simply to gain his party's support for a coalition government, when it is clear that the deputy minister is superfluous and perhaps even deleterious to the efficient prosecution of that government office's business?

Following the election of 2009, Benjamin Netanyahu put together the largest cabinet in Israel's history, with thirty ministers and nine deputy ministers. Is it reasonable to appoint such a large cabinet, consisting of more than half the coalition members of the Knesset, when it is clear from logic and experience that state's affairs can be conducted just as well, if not better, by a cabinet less than half that size? Is it moral? All we know is that up to now the Supreme Court has not intervened in such a matter.

It should also be noted that in 2001, after the Supreme Court's decisions in the cases of Deri and Pinchasi, the Knesset enacted a revised version of the Basic Law: The Government, which included a provision stating that if a cabinet minister is convicted of an offense and the court declares that the offense carries moral turpitude, the minister's tenure will end at the moment of conviction. It would seem reasonable to believe that in enacting this provision, the Knesset intended to override the rule the court had established in the Deri and Pinchasi cases and to prefer a presumption of innocence in similar cases. Nevertheless, the Supreme Court stated, in an obiter in another case, that the change in the law did not affect the rule that the prime minister should dismiss any minister who was indicted on criminal charges, at least when the charges were serious.

The Supreme Court's rulings in the Deri and Pinchasi cases were handed down just at the time the Oslo agreements were signed. On September 9, 1993, the day after the court declared that the prime minister must dismiss Deri, Israel's prime minister and the chairman of the PLO, exchanged letters of mutual recognition. Four days later, at a ceremony at the White House, Yitzhak Rabin and PLO chief Yasser Arafat shook hands in the presence of U.S. President Bill Clinton.

Legal procedures went on complicating the diplomatic processes. Shas left the coalition, leaving the government without a majority, at a most sensitive time for Israel's foreign relations. According to Yosef Harish, who was attorney general at the time, Rabin pressured him to refrain from pursing charges against Deri, but Harish, despite his past differences with the State Attorney's Office, this time made common cause with State Attorney Dorit Beinisch and insisted on seeking an indictment and on Deri leaving the government.

Two weeks following the court's decision regarding Deri, the declaration of principles between the PLO and Israel came before the Knesset. The debate was fiery. Two days later, on September 23, the Knesset voted on the declaration, which had been given the status of a vote of confidence in the government. Rabin squeaked by—the motion passed with the support of sixty Knesset members (MKs). Another fifty voted against and eight abstained. Rabin found himself in a problematic situation. Without Shas, he led a minority government with the support of only fifty-six MKs (Labor's forty-four and Meretz's twelve). To survive no-confidence motions and pass legislation, he depended on the support of two Arab parties, which opened him up to accusations that, in matters relating to agreements with the Palestinians, he was beholden to Palestinian interests rather than the best interests of the Jewish state. Furthermore, some members of his own party were discomfited by the Oslo Accord, weakening his government further.

In continuation of the Oslo Accord, Israel and the PLO signed another agreement in Cairo in 1994, under the stewardship of Egyptian President Hosni Mubarak. This was called the "Gaza and Jericho first" agreement, in which Israel agreed to hand over Jericho and the Gaza Strip to a PLO-run Palestinian Authority (PA). In September 1995 Israel and the PLO signed the Oslo II Accord. This divided the territory of the West Bank and Gaza Strip into three categories. Area A was placed under the rule of the Palestinian Authority; in Area B the PA would administer civilian affairs while security would remain in Israeli hands; in Area C Israel would control both security and civilian affairs, with the exception of a small number of matters that would be administered by the Palestinian Authority. In an extremely tense vote, the Knesset approved the agreement by a narrow sixty-one to fifty-nine majority. The deciding votes came from Hadash and the Arab Democratic Party, as well as from three MKs, Gonen Segev, Alex Goldfarb, and Esther Salmonovitch, who split away from the hawkish Tzomet Party. Their newly formed faction joined the coalition, with Segev receiving a cabinet seat and Goldfarb a deputy minister post. At the same time, two Labor MKs, Avigdor Kahalani and Emmanuel Zissman, voted against the agreement that their party leader had placed before the Knesset. A few months later they split from Labor and formed a new faction, the Third Way.

Shas voted against the agreement. This was one more stage in a political metamorphosis that began when the Supreme Court compelled Deri's dismissal and Shas left the coalition. The already fierce opposition to the first Oslo agreement was now reinforced by the claim that Oslo II had passed thanks only to Arab votes. While this charge may be illegitimate from a democratic point of view, it bore great emotional weight with a large part of the Jewish public.

On February 25, 1994, the holiday of Purim, just half a year after the first Oslo Accord was signed, a resident of the Jewish settlement of Kiryat Arba took the law into his hands. Dr. Baruch Goldstein, a physician, donned an IDF uniform, took a rifle, and strode into the Tomb of the Patriarchs in next-door Hebron, sacred to both Muslims and Jews. He entered a prayer hall used by Muslims, who were offering the prayers of the Friday preceding the Ramadan fast. He opened fire, killing twenty-nine worshippers and wounding more than a hundred, and kept firing until some of the Muslims managed to overpower and kill him.

Riots broke out in Palestinian cities and towns, and the measures taken by the security forces to curb them resulted in the deaths of nine Arabs, while many more were wounded. Hamas began to send suicide bombers into Israel proper. Left-wing Israel groups demanded the evacuation of the Jewish settlement in Hebron. Some government ministers thought the government should consider that, but Rabin vetoed the idea. He may well have believed that a minority government would be unable to execute such a dramatic change in policy. He limited himself to the establishment of a National Commission of Inquiry chaired by Chief Justice Meir Shamgar and to the implementation of its recommendations regarding arrangements for members of the two religions for visits to and prayers at the Tomb of the Patriarchs. Kach, the movement to which Goldstein belonged, was declared a terror organization.

Rabin's standing with the public weakened as a result of all these events. Hamas's suicide bombings shocked the public and began to turn it against his policy of accommodation with the Palestinians, and his loss of Shas's support as a result of the Supreme Court's ruling created a united religious-Haredi front in the Knesset that opposed the Oslo Accords. Right-wing demonstrators rallied nearly daily in front of the prime minister's home. This climaxed in October 1995 with a huge protest in Zion Square in the center of the capital's downtown at which demonstrators bore placards and shouted slogans branding Rabin as a murderer and a traitor. Some signs depicted him in an SS uniform. The leaders of the Likud opposition stood on the balcony overlooking the square that served as the speakers' platform. Some of them, disturbed by the extremism of the sentiments expressed in the slogans and signs, left the site. Others claimed that they were not aware of defamations the crowd was voicing and of the picture of Rabin portrayed as a Nazi.

About a month later, on November 4, 1995, Rabin was assassinated by Yigal Amir, a law student at Bar-Ilan University. Amir shot Rabin at the end of a peace rally at Tel Aviv's Malkhei Yisrael Square, which now bears Rabin's name. This act of political violence shook the Israeli public. Despite the huge controversy roused by the Oslo Accords, Rabin, who had led Israel's army to victory in the Six Day War of 1967 as the IDF chief of staff, was a beloved figure, both because of his long service to his country as a soldier and in government, and because of his gruff, modest, and honest demeanor. Not only the left was shocked by the assassination. So was Israel's right, where some figures expressed feelings of regret and responsibility for not speaking out against the wild attacks on Rabin, but still denied responsibility for his murder.

Shimon Peres took over as acting prime minister and shortly thereafter formed a new government under his leadership along the same lines as the Rabin government.

But nothing went right thereafter. On January 5, 1996, a senior Hamas leader, Yehiya Ayash, was successfully targeted when a cellular phone exploded in his hand. During the two months that followed, Palestinian suicide bombers committed several horrifying attacks in Israel, including exploding two crowded buses in Jerusalem, in the first killing twenty-six and in the second nineteen. Another suicide bombing at Dizengoff Center (a shopping mall) in Tel Aviv killed thirteen.

Elections were set for May 29. For the first time, Israeli voters cast separate ballots for prime minister and for a Knesset slate. Opposing Peres was the Likud's new young leader, Benjamin Netanyahu. Peres's half year as the country's leader did not put him in a good position. The public, buffeted and bloodied by terrorism that reached into its central cities, turned against the Oslo process that Peres personified. The forty-seven-year-old Netanyahu won and Likud returned to power.

13

The Deri Trial

The trial of former Interior Minister Aryeh Deri is the most important and dramatic criminal proceeding to be conducted in the era of the legal revolution. It alienated a large part of the public, which lost trust in the judicial system, and reinforced their sense that the leaders of the Mizrahi community (Jews who came to Israel from the Islamic world) suffered from discrimination. On top of this, both the government and the opposition sensed that Deri was a key figure and that his fall undermined the policies that the government sought to pursue.

Aryeh Deri was—and remains—a charismatic politician. He was born in Morocco, but received his education—a strictly religious one—in Ashkenazi *yeshivot*. In this he was typical of the Mizrahi elite. He has a special talent for finding a way into the hearts of the nonreligious public. As interior minister he devoted considerable attention to the problems of the Arab sector and as a result enjoyed much more support from that community than Jewish politicians normally get.

Ostensibly, the legal system emerged from its confrontation with Deri with the upper hand. It forced him out of the government even before he was convicted. But the victory came at a high price. One manifestation of that price was political—the dramatic strengthening of Israel's right wing. When Deri fell, he was replaced as Shas's leader by Eli Yishai, who had manifestly right-wing sympathies. (This would not be the first time that the work of the legal system, which is often characterized as tilting toward the left, has actually bolstered the right. Recall that the same thing happened when Yitzhak Rabin was forced to resign as prime minister in 1977. The end result was that the right, led by Menachem Begin, won power for the first time in Israeli history.) Deri's fall not only failed to increase public trust in government; it dealt a blow to public confidence in the Supreme Court and in the entire judicial system. Criminal proceedings against politicians of Mizrahi origin, especially but not only those associated with Shas, provided grist for those, usually the close associates and co-ethnics of the accused, who proclaimed that Israeli society was biased against Mizrahi, Haredi, and religious Jews. In Deri's case however, it was not only his supporters who condemned his trial and responded through the ballot box. A large swath of Israelis who were quite distant from Shas and its agenda felt the same.

The police investigation of Deri began in 1990 following news reports, and continued from that point on at a frantic pace for a long period. The press reports presented Deri's culpability as obvious and incontrovertible, while police investigators and prosecutors seemed to feel a personal duty to obtain a conviction, a duty that grows all the more acute as the clamor in the media grows louder and as the figure in question is more senior. The police investigation was not focused on specific allegations but rather searched for any scrap of evidence that could lead to Deri's conviction.* No other subsequent investigation of a public figure was so aimed at dredging up every possible allegation against and evidence of the wrongdoing of a public figure—that is, until the case of Ehud Olmert, which will be discussed in Chapter 28. In Olmert's case as well the police and prosecution, egged on by the press, scrutinized a man from head to toe in an effort to turn up evidence to convict him of something, anything.

The original charges against Deri and three others were submitted to the Jerusalem District Court in December 1993. A few days before this, when the charges were submitted to the Knesset so that this body could lift Deri's parliamentary immunity, the Supreme Court rendered the decision that required Rabin to end Deri's tenure as minister of the interior. The atmosphere surrounding the subsequent trial was hostile. "Without entering in to the question of the charges themselves," his attorney, Dan Avi-Yitzhak, said,

> I have no doubt that despite his long trial he did not have his day in court. The mass of articles in the media created preconceptions about Deri that were very difficult to shake free, and from the first moment, even before the presentation of the evidence, I had the feeling that the judges had determined his verdict in advance and that it was a "done deal. . . ."
>
> From the start, the judges were suspicious of all Deri's witnesses, and even when the prosecution's witnesses testified in his favor, they did not believe any of them. This was also evident in the unbounded and unreasonable trust they expressed in the judgment regarding the state's witness, [Yaakov] Shmuelevitch, despite the unequivocal evidence presented to the District Court that showed that there was no reason to do so.[127]

The major charges against Deri had to do with a charitable foundation that was called, for short, Lev Banim. This organization ran a *yeshiva* and *kolel* (a seminary for married students) for men who had become religious. At the end of 1983 Deri was invited to become involved in the organization and to give classes at the institutions it ran. His talents were evident and led to his appointment, soon thereafter, as the foundation's administrative director. Shas was founded in 1984. In September 1986 Deri was appointed director general of the interior ministry, and in 1988 minister of the interior. The police investigation commenced about a year and a half later. The District Court panel, made up of Judges Ya'akov Tzemach, Musia Arad, and Miriam Naor (who is now chief justice of the Supreme Court), found that Deri had received bribes totaling $155,000 from Lev Banim. These were paid to him by another employee of the organization, Yom-Tov Rubin (who was one of the other defendants in the trial). According to the judgment, Deri also received bribes in the

---

* While from the start I viewed the rise of Shas with concern and disagree with much of its program, that is irrelevant to my critique of the Deri investigation. See my article *Yesh Gvul* [*There Is a Limit*], HA'ARETZ, June 30, 1993.

form of payment for overseas trips for himself and members of his family and for hotel stays in Israel. The bribes were given, the court determined, in expectation that Deri would use his public position to obtain state support for the organization.[128]

After their marriage, Deri and his wife lived for a time in a prefab home, but Isser and Esther Verderber helped them buy an apartment in the Jerusalem neighborhood of Ramot, costing $42,000. The Verderbers were childless Holocaust survivors. They lived in New York and had adopted Yaffa Deri before her marriage. After the wedding they financially supported her and her husband. All this happened before Shas was founded.

Some time later the Deris sold their apartment in Ramot and bought a larger one. In February 1989, when Deri was already interior minister, he signed an agreement to purchase a new apartment on HaKablan Street in Jerusalem, a home that the court described as a "luxury apartment." The judges wrote that it was "a spacious apartment, comprising two stories" and offered lurid descriptions of its furnishings. The apartment cost $260,000, but the court found that the total cost of its purchase, renovation, and improvement reached at least $445,000 in 1989–1990 dollars.

The court also stated that Deri purchased this apartment at least five years after his public life began and that given his salary the purchase of the residence represented "an exceptional and surprising growth of capital." It also determined that Rubin, working for Lev Banim, transferred $120,000 to Deri to help finance the purchase of the apartment.

Deri claimed that he had deposited some of this money with Rubin or lent it to him, and that the rest came from a gift that the Verderbers gave him and his wife. Deri's defense was corroborated by the financial disclosure statement that he submitted to the state comptroller when he was appointed interior minister, as every member of the cabinet is required to do. This document, which predates the police investigation and was drawn up at a time when Deri did not imagine that there was any problem at all with his finances, states that Yom-Tov Rubin owed him about $50,000.

No one disputed that the Verderbers indeed supported Deri, but the court determined that they did not have resources of a magnitude that could explain the sums of money they gave to him. But the Verderbers never gave the police their version of the story. Isser Verderber died in 1990, before the police investigation began, and a year later—when the investigation was already underway—Esther was injured in an automobile accident in New York. She died in June 1991, before the police could depose her. Both of them were buried in Jerusalem. Deri's lawyers indeed asked Esther to sign an affidavit confirming his version of the story. Esther, however, refused to sign it. The prosecution claimed that she refused to sign it because it was not truthful. But she may well have had other reasons. For example, she may have been concerned that the tax authorities would begin to look into the source of the money. Whatever the case, her version of the story was not heard.

Esther Verderber's accident led to ugly rumors, suggesting that Deri had a hand in her death. While the rumors were baseless, they received much play in the media, where writers claimed that his motive was to prevent her from revealing that the financial support that they provided him was actually more modest than what Deri claimed. The Israel police asked their counterparts in New York to investigate whether the accident might have been deliberate. The Americans concluded that the claim was baseless and that she had died in a routine traffic accident. Yet the rumor, now disproved, continued to reverberate in the media and to give the public the impression that Deri was not only corrupt but also capable of much worse.

On top of this, the section of the judgment that mentioned the fact that Esther's testimony had not been heard noted that "Esther was blocked" from testifying, a wording that can be read as awkward for Deri. It went on to say that "Esther took the truth with her into the true [next] world. Defendant number 1 [Deri] has no desire for that truth [to come to light]."

When Deri appealed the verdict, his attorneys asked to submit as evidence a written statement by New York's deputy police chief confirming that Deri was not under investigation with regard to Esther Verderber's death. The Supreme Court rejected the request on the grounds that "the prosecution does not ascribe to Deri ... any part in the circumstances surrounding the death of Esther Verderber, and it is not at all clear to us for what reason and why the defense attorneys are seeking to bring this irrelevant subject up." Yet it is clear why Deri's lawyers sought to offer proof that Deri was not suspected of a role in her death. True, the prosecution had not explicitly accused him of such involvement, but the charge was in the air, part of the atmosphere surrounding Deri's trial.

The testimony of the state's witness, Yaakov Shmuelevitch, was an important building block of the prosecution's case. Shmuelevitch was a nonreligious private investigator who in 1984 became religious, along with his wife. He enrolled at the Lev Banim *yeshiva*. Some time later he was appointed its administrative director. Afterward, the people behind Lev Banim founded another nonprofit organization, the Center for Prisoner Rehabilitation (CPR), and Shmuelevitch was appointed to head it. With Deri's help, the new organization received government funding. The court found that the plan was that at least some of these funds were to be funneled to Lev Banim via the creation of fictitious debts by CPR to Lev Banim.

Some time later relations between Shmuelevitch and Deri soured. Shmuelevitch decided to use his experience as a private investigator to record their conversations. The court would later conclude that his aim had been to create evidence that, while he was CPR's director in name, he was not really responsible for what took place there. At a later date he shed his religious observances and left the *yeshiva*.

After being given the status of state's witness, Shmuelevitch told investigators that Deri had demanded that Lev Banim's staff deposit money in Deri's account, and that in private conversations "they would say in a kind of chant 'Aryeh needs grocery money,'" meaning money for his day-to-day expenses. The defense of course sought to undermine his testimony. Shmuelevitch had legal problems in Switzerland, and in the direct examination at Deri's trial, he testified that he was suspected in connection with a deal that "wasn't real." He added, however, that "those suspicious have been dropped, according to what the prosecutor told me ... What remains against me is a suspicion of a type of business negligence," as well as a matter of "work without a license."

In cross-examination, Avi-Yitzhak, Deri's attorney, asked how it was, given the benign nature of the charges Shmuelevitch claimed to be accused of, that he had been incarcerated for more than seven months in strict isolation. Avi-Yitzhak also asked whether it was true that "the act you committed in Switzerland was in fact international fraud to the tune of tens of millions of dollars, after you offered to sell at a bargain price non-existent letters of credit. The goal was that the person would hand over his money and the letters would not reach him." Shmuelevitch's reply was: "What the gentleman said is a total lie."

Shmuelevitch gained the court's full trust. The judges wrote that "despite a rigorous cross-examination … Shmuelevitch remained self-possessed and spoke judiciously. His testimony under cross-examination made him more believable. Only a witness telling the truth could have withstood such questioning as Shmuelevitch did—an unbudgeable rock."

Deri's trial took no less than 400 sessions, at the end of which Deri was convicted of one count of taking a bribe, one count of obtaining something by fraud, as well as three counts of breach of trust, but was acquitted of several other charges. He was sentenced to four years in prison and a fine of NIS* 250,000 (about $65,000). The three other defendants were convicted of paying bribes and several other counts, and received lesser sentences. The reading of the verdicts in the District Court was dramatic; large parts of the judgment were read out loud and broadcast on the radio. Deri's supporters were infuriated by what they saw as an injustice and insult to their revered leader.

Deri appealed to the Supreme Court. The case was heard by Shlomo Levin, Eliahu Mazza, and Jacob Kedmi, who rendered their decision in 2000. Details about the charges against Shmuelevitch in Switzerland had not yet come to light. Even so, the justices agreed that the District Court may have placed too much trust in the state's witness:

> The court ascribed too little weight to the fact that, before the agreement that he would turn state's witness was signed with him, Shmuelevitch also told the police and their agents false accusations against Deri and others (alleging that they were involved in smuggling funds overseas). It should be noted that during his examination in court, Shmuelevitch denied ever saying this, and in this at least gave an untruthful testimony.

Nevertheless, the Supreme Court affirmed the District Court's judgment, in keeping with the rule that an appeals court does not intervene in the first court's evaluation of the evidence that it received from witnesses it heard and of whom it had the opportunity to form an impression. The Supreme Court did, however, make significant modifications of the District Court's findings. The scope of the bribery conviction was narrowed, in part in consideration of the declaration of assets that Deri had submitted to the state controller. The Supreme Court panel determined that the sum total of the bribes Deri accepted was $60,000. Along with this, it found, other unspecified sums were deposited in Deri's bank account and trips overseas were paid for. Deri was acquitted on appeal of one of the counts of breach of trust, and the

---

* When the state of Israel was founded in 1948 it adopted the pound as the basic unit of currency. In 1980 the currency received a Hebrew name: Shekel (IS means Israeli Shekel). In the early 80s Israel suffered hyperinflation and in 1985, in the framework of an economic stabilization plan, a new Israeli shekel (NIS) was introduced, replacing the former IS at the rate of 1000 IS to 1 NIS.

findings on the other two counts were reduced in scope. The appeals of the other defendants were also allowed in part.[129]

As a consequence of these findings, Deri's prison sentence was reduced to three years. Deri petitioned for a further hearing before a larger Supreme Court panel, but that request was denied by Chief Justice Aharon Barak in September 2000.[130] The criminal proceedings against Deri thus ended here, and the former interior minister was ordered to report for incarceration on September 3, 2000. Thousands of his supporters gathered at the gates to the prison to see him off. They shouted that he was innocent and founded a *yeshiva*, Sha'agat Aryeh, that operated in tents just outside the prison for many months thereafter.

Deri has continued to maintain his innocence. He claims that he was persecuted and that he suffered an injustice. A short time after the verdict in the District Court a videotape began making the rounds. It was handed out by Deri's supporters at rallies, in synagogues, and on street corners. On it, Deri spoke of the discrimination he felt he and his supporters had suffered. The video's Hebrew title translates as *J'accuse!* In it, Deri showed his followers his apartment, the one the court had termed luxurious, where he and his wife raised their eight children under conditions that were certainly reasonable but by no means affluent.

In May 1999, some two months following the District Court verdict, elections were held for prime minister and the Knesset. Shas won more votes than ever before, giving it a full seventeen seats in the Knesset. Mizrahi voters flocked to the party in protest against what they felt was the court's bias against their kind. Benjamin Netanyahu was defeated by Ehud Barak, a former army chief of staff who led the Labor Party. Despite the calls of some of his supporters to ban Shas from government—calls that demonstrated how great the abyss between Haredi and non-religious Israelis had become, and how great profoundly Ashkenazim misunderstood Mizrahi grievances—Barak included the party in his coalition.

Soon after the Supreme Court's verdict in his appeal, Deri and his lawyers obtained information about the proceedings underway in Switzerland against the central prosecution witness. It transpired that, after his testimony in Israel, Shmuelevitch had been sentenced in Switzerland to eighteen months in prison. The time he had spent in custody (265 days) was deducted from the sentence, and the rest was suspended. He was banished from that country for eight years. The Swiss court had found him guilty of involvement (as an accessory rather than a principal) in an attempt to defraud thirteen investors of very large sums of money and of the actual defraudment of one investor.

Deri petitioned the chief justice that same year, asking him to order a retrial. He also asked Attorney General Elyakim Rubinstein to initiate a criminal investigation against Shmuelevitch for perjury. The attorney general rejected the request, and Deri petitioned the Supreme Court to overrule him. The petition was heard before Justices Dalia Dorner, Ayala Procaccia, and Edmond Levy. Levy, writing for the tribunal, said:

In July 1994, Shmuelevitch was arrested in Switzerland on suspicion of involvement in the commission of fraud on a large scale . . . For many months Shmuelevitch denied the facts attributed to him, but in his interrogation on January 19, 1995 . . . this changed . . . Shmuelevitch [declared] that, after additional thought, he had decided to make his contribution to reaching the truth. Immediately following this the prosecutor informed him that he was suspected of repeated commercial fraud, and then listed one by one, the incriminating facts attributed to him, and Shmuelevitch confirmed that they were correct, subject to a few reservations . . . Later in the interrogation, Shmuelevitch claimed that he had not acted with an intention to defraud, but I find it difficult to reconcile this declaration with the facts he acknowledged.

Levy enumerated the responses Shmuelevitch had given as testimony in response to his questioning at the Deri trial, where he claimed that "those suspicious have been dropped" and that "what remains against me is a suspicion of a type of business negligence." According to Levy, "Shmuelevitch's responses were, at best, incorrect and misleading." He added further on that "there can be no doubt that with regard to the investigation in Switzerland, Shmuelevitch did not do his duty to testify truthfully."

Despite this, the panel dismissed Deri's petition and did not order the attorney general to open a perjury investigation against Shmuelevitch. The justices ruled that the lie he had told did not touch on the actual accusation against Deri but was relevant only to the witness's credibility, and thus did not justify intervening in the attorney general's decision.[131]

Reinforced by Justice Levy's remarks on Shmuelevitch's responses in court, Deri pushed forward with his petition for a retrial. Chief Justice Barak affirmed that "Shmuelevitch 'did not tell the truth about the proceedings against him in Switzerland' . . . [and in so doing] contributed to misleading the District Court and 'did not do his duty to testify truthfully.'" The claim made by the attorney general's representative that the state's witness "did not lie in his testimony in court . . . but rather testified about the state of the accusations as he understood it" was rejected. Nevertheless, Barak turned down the request for a retrial on the grounds that even without Shmuelevitch's testimony there was sufficient proof to convict Deri and the other defendants.[132] Among other things, Barak noted that the basis of the Supreme Court's finding that Deri had taken bribes totaling $60,000 had been a rejection of Deri's and Rubin's claim regarding the source of the money. Once that version of events had been rejected, Barak reasoned, the unavoidable conclusion was that the money was a bribe. In other words, Deri's conviction was not built on the foundation of Shmuelevitch's testimony. This is a problematic and unpersuasive conclusion. Shmuelevitch was without a doubt the central prosecution witness, who had testified that an "atmosphere of bribery" had pervaded Lev Banim. His testimony, accepted without reservation by the District Court, could not but contribute to an atmosphere of distrust of Deri and cast doubt on his testimony. Moreover, the mere fact that the court did not accept Deri's account of how he had added $60,000 to his net worth is insufficient to prove that his money was received as bribe.

The end result is an uncomfortable one. It may be safely assumed that Deri was harmed by the false testimony of the state's witness, while Shmuelevitch suffered no consequences for evading the truth and enjoyed unjustified immunity for having provided testimony that helped the prosecution to obtain the conviction of the leader of a political party and a government minister. Once again, the affair demonstrates the limitations a court faces in distinguishing between truth and falsehood.

The District Court termed Shmuelevitch an "unbudgeable rock" and gave him its full trust, which turned out to be unjustified.

Another question is the prosecution's behavior. In the hearing regarding Deri's petition for a retrial, a representative of the attorney general argued that Shmuelevitch's testimony did not constitute a failure to tell the truth. That claim seems improper given the information that had come to light in the interim regarding the Swiss proceedings against Shmuelevitch. What did the prosecution in fact know about the proceedings in Switzerland at the time of Deri's trial? Clearly, if the prosecutors knew that their witness's testimony in this regard was not in accord with the facts, it was their duty to bring this to the attention of the court and the defense attorneys. But even assuming that the prosecutors did not know this, the question remains whether they did not have a responsibility to find out. Deri may have found it very difficult to ascertain the status of legal proceedings in a foreign country, but the prosecution is unlikely to have had that problem. The fact is that the prosecutors in each country cooperated fully—that is what made it possible to bring Shmuelevitch to Israel in the first place to testify in the trial. It was the prosecution's job to determine all the facts, even if they favored a defendant against whom it was at pitched battle.

Yigal Arnon, the attorney who represented Deri in his appeal against his criminal conviction, did not hesitate to say publicly[133] and bluntly that he thought Deri had suffered an injustice. He was not the only one. Amnon Dankner, a journalist at *Ma'ariv* and a well-known author and television personality, published an extensive article on the case in September 2000, following the ruling in Deri's appeal. The headline was "The Black Holes in His Conviction." Dankner argued that the Supreme Court ruling in the main undermined the very foundations of the District Court's conviction of Deri. The Supreme Court found that Shmuelevitch had made a false accusation against Deri in his police interrogation and had been caught lying. Once that determination had been made, the Supreme Court should have called into question the lower court's confidence in the state witness's testimony. That conclusion required not only reducing the sum of the bribe Deri supposedly accepted but his total acquittal. Dankner also argued that basis for the determination that Deri had accepted bribes was the increase in his wealth—yet there was no way of ruling out the possibility that this money had been provided by the Verderbers. The court had doubted whether the Verderbers had such sources, but it then turned out that in their will they had left their heirs, among them Aryeh and Yaffa Deri, a total of $300,000.

Deri was released from prison in July 2002 after his term in prison was reduced by a third for good behavior. Only then did a panel of the Jerusalem Magistrates Court, comprising Judges Shulamit Dotan, Haim Lakhovitzky, and Aharon Farkash, begin hearing the so-called "public" case against Deri. In this trial Deri stood accused of breach of trust, on the grounds that during his tenure as director general of the interior ministry and as minister of the interior, he had, on seven occasions, decided to transfer funds to institutions associated with his party. He was not accused in any of these cases of having derived personal benefit, only of providing support for these institutions because of their ties to his party rather than on the basis of equality and proper procedure.

Clearly, such transfers of public money cannot be tolerated, even if, as Deri claimed, other parties had done the same. Still, the question again arises of whether this second trial was not further evidence of the approach taken by the prosecution—that of persecuting this defendant with a list of charges, and then bringing him to trial once again, after the end of his first trial, for acts committed prior to his previous trial. Such a procedure violates fundamental rules of fairness, infringes on human dignity, and gives the impression of untrammeled persecution of the defendant.* In the end the court cleared Deri of four of the counts he had been charged with, but convicted him of one count of breach of trust and sentenced him to a three-month suspended sentence and an additional fine of NIS 10,000 (about $2,600).[134]

In November 2008 Israel held municipal elections, including in the capital city of Jerusalem. Deri wanted to run for mayor. Six years and three months had passed since he completed serving the prison term he had been sentenced to in his first trial. At the time he committed those offenses, and at the time he had been sentenced to prison, the law had provided that a person sentenced to more than three months in prison could not be included on a slate of candidates for a period of six years following completion of the prison term. In 2000 the Local Authorities Law (Elections) was amended, extending this period to seven years. In other words, Deri qualified as a candidate under the former term of the law, but not as amended.

Judge Moshe Sobel of the Jerusalem Administrative Court ruled, in *Deri v. the Jerusalem Municipal Election Administration*,[135] that the extension of the disqualification period was not a punishment, and as such the rule against retroactive punishment did not apply to it. Deri was thus not entitled to run in these elections. But those who hoped, or feared, that this would mark the end of Deri's political career were proven wrong. In the elections to the Nineteenth Knesset, held in January 2013, Deri was placed in the second slot on Shas's list of candidates and was elected to the Knesset. In May of that year, Rabbi Ovadia Yosef, the spiritual leader of Shas and of the religious Sephardi and Mizrahi community, appointed him as the head of the party. Deri led Shas in the election campaign leading up to the elections of March 2015, in which the party won seven seats. His party joined the coalition headed by Prime Minister Netanyahu, and Deri became minister of the economy. He left this post in November 2015 and remained minister of the development of the Negev and the Galilee.

---

* I wrote an article discussing this issue: *Highly Improper Technique: The Second Indictment against Deri Should Have Been Dismissed*, YEDIOTH AHRONOTH, Oct. 2, 2003.

14

The Bar-On–Hebron Affair

Following his election as prime minister in 1996, Benjamin Netanyahu appointed Yaakov Neeman, a leading private attorney, to the post of justice minister. The two men sought to replace the sitting attorney general, Michael Ben-Yair, who had been appointed by Yitzhak Rabin's government. Neeman was forced to resign from his post, in circumstances that will be described below, and was replaced by Tzachi Hanegbi. Attorney General Ben-Yair continued in his post following Neeman's resignation, but the efforts to replace him continued. In short order a scandal broke out and caused a public outcry. Dubbed the Bar-On–Hebron affair, it led to investigations against Netanyahu, Hanegbi, and others.[136] On the face of it, the affair fizzled out. None of those involved was put on trial, and all the investigations were closed. Yet it brought about a dramatic change in the structure of Israel's government and the power relations between its different branches. The executive branch—the cabinet—was weakened drastically, with its authority to appoint its own legal adviser, the attorney general, seriously impeded. In contrast, the power of the Supreme Court surged as it gained much more than a foothold in determining who would fill this essential post.

At the beginning of December 1996, Attorney General Ben-Yair announced that he intended to leave his post in a month's time. He may well have done so because he was aware that the prime minister intended to replace him, or he may have had other reasons. Netanyahu sought a replacement, interviewing several candidates, among them Dov Weissglas and Ronnie Bar-On. On January 1, 1997, when Ben-Yair's resignation took force, Netanyahu's personal attorney, David Shimron, proposed the candidacy of Dan Avi-Yitzhak, who at that time was defending Shas's leader, Aryeh Deri, in the criminal trial then underway.

Three days later Avi-Yitzhak met with the prime minister. He knew from Deri that Deri supported the candidacy of Bar-On, a private attorney and an active member of the Likud Party. Avi-Yitzhak spoke of what took place at this meeting only under a court order, and after Deri waived lawyer-client privilege. By his testimony, he had told Deri before the meeting that he would oppose Bar-On's appointment. Avi-Yitzhak said that he advised Netanyahu that the appointment would be a bad idea, both because the legal profession did not view Bar-On as fit for the post and because the appointment was liable to hurt all those involved, including the prime minister himself. Furthermore, he did not think that, as attorney general, Bar-On could be of any assistance to Deri in the criminal case being conducted against him. Avi-Yitzhak also told the prime minister, or at least hinted strongly, that Deri intended to topple the government if Netanyahu and the cabinet did not do as he wished in the matter of the attorney general appointment. Deri, it will be recalled, had been compelled to leave his cabinet post following the Supreme Court decision in his case, but he was still a Knesset member and the leader of Shas, which was part of Netanyahu's coalition.

The prime minister's version of the conversation was somewhat different. He claimed that he met with Avi-Yitzhak to offer him the post of attorney general. While Avi-Yitzhak had led him to understand that Deri was interested in Bar-On's appointment and that a rumor was going around about a connection between the two, but he did not remember the specifics and did not consider it important. Avi-Yitzhak's candidacy indeed was raised at this juncture, and he did not reject it. It would later transpire that Netanyahu had also broached the candidacy of another attorney, Yitzhak Molcho, who assisted the prime minister on state matters. Molcho, however, was not interested.

Deri was not pleased with the idea of appointing Avi-Yitzhak. He wanted his lawyer to continue representing him in the lengthy and complex criminal proceeding against him. He was also concerned that appointing his personal lawyer to this public post would look bad to the public and pushed for Bar-On. Hanegbi also preferred Bar-On—he had done his internship in Bar-On's office and the two were friends. But it was not Hanegbi who first suggested the appointment; he claimed to have heard about it from Netanyahu. The proposal to name Avi-Yitzhak soon fell by the wayside.*

On Friday, January 10, 1997, Hanegbi asked the cabinet to approve Bar-On's appointment to the post of attorney general. That same morning, about an hour prior to the cabinet meeting, Hanegbi had a routine meeting with Chief Justice Aharon Barak. The justice minister briefed Barak on the appointment, telling him that four candidates had been shortlisted for the job. Three had been ruled out for various reasons, leaving Bar-On. Hanegbi asked Barak what he thought of the candidate. Barak categorically rejected the idea, saying that Bar-On was not fit for the post. But at the cabinet meeting, when Hanegbi told his colleagues that he had briefed the chief justice about the upcoming appointment, he did not inform them of Barak's response. The cabinet approved Bar-On and a public uproar ensued. The designated attorney general was an active member of Likud and his appointment was strongly criticized in the media.** The next evening, Saturday night, Labor Knesset member Ophir Pines petitioned the Supreme Court to disqualify Bar-On. A hearing was held the next day. The three justices assigned to the case—Theodor Or, Mishael Cheshin, and

---

* Avi-Yitzhak told me that he was not interested in the position, but that out of courtesy to the prime minister he did not reject his proposal on the spot and said that he would consider it. Later, at the end of 2003, the then justice minister, Yosef (Tommy) Lapid, sought Avi-Yitzhak's consent to submit his name to the committee that, following the Bar-On–Hebron affair, was charged with finding a candidate for this post. Avi-Yitzhak declined.

** Ronnie Bar-On subsequently served as minister of finance in Ehud Olmert's government. Together with the prime minister, he successfully led the economy through the 2008 global financial crisis, which Israel passed unscathed.

Itzhak Zamir, suggested that Bar-On not assume the post until the court had ruled on the petition. The state attorney accepted the proposal, fearing that otherwise the court would issue a temporary injunction.[137] The hearing was then adjourned, to be resumed later, but events overtook the court. That same day, just two days after his appointment, Bar-On resigned.

That hardly brought the controversy to an end. Ten days after Bar-On's resignation, a reporter for Israel television's Channel One, Ayala Hasson, reported that Bar-On's candidacy had been proposed to Deri by an Israeli businessman, David Appel. Deri met with Bar-On and, Hasson reported, Bar-On had promised Deri that, if appointed, he would ensure that the prosecution would reach a plea bargain with Deri. Under the deal, there would be no conviction with turpitude, meaning that it would not be an obstacle to his political career. (Bar-On would subsequently deny categorically that he had made any such promise.) Hasson further informed the Israeli public that Deri had notified the prime minister and the director general of the prime minister's office, Avigdor Liberman, that "if Bar-On is not appointed, Shas will leave the government." Hasson noted that "these were the days prior to the Hebron Agreement [in which Netanyahu agreed to hand most of the city over to the Palestinian Authority]. Shas announced its opposition to the agreement and Liberman ran to do Deri's bidding and promised that Bar-On would be appointed . . . Shas withdrew its opposition to the Hebron agreement. That was the deal: an attorney general in exchange for the [Hebron] Agreement."[138]

When Hasson's investigation was aired, the government had yet to appoint an attorney general to replace Bar-On. State Attorney Edna Arbel thus served as acting attorney general. On the basis of the information revealed in the television report, she ordered a criminal investigation. The police subsequently recommended that charges of fraud and breach of trust be brought against Prime Minister Netanyahu (subject to a further investigation), Justice Minister Hanegbi, and Liberman. The police also recommended that, on top of the other counts against him, Deri be charged with extortion. The police investigation was completed with exceptional speed, in the space of less than three months, and the case, along with the recommendations, were submitted to Arbel on April 15. In the meantime, Elyakim Rubinstein, a judge on Jerusalem's District Court, had been appointed attorney general by the cabinet. Barak backed that appointment, ensuring that it would go through smoothly.

The case continued to proceed at an astounding pace for the Israeli state attorney's office. Three days after the police submitted their material, State Attorney Arbel presented it to the new attorney general with a detailed assessment of her own (although she wrote: "we pondered a great deal before reaching our conclusions"). Neither did the fact that "among us" (apparently the team of lawyers who dealt with the affair) were some who thought that "the evidence justifies charging the prime minister and justice minister" slow down the process. The major conclusions contained in Arbel's opinion, which she completed in three days, were that there was not sufficient evidence against the prime minister, justice minister, and Bar-On. Arbel did, however, conclude that there was evidence justifying charges against Deri (subject to a hearing). The result was the odd situation that Deri could be accused of threatening the prime minister to get him to appoint Bar-On, but that the prime minister would not be charged with agreeing to do so, even though he was responsible for actually carrying out the appointment. As Arbel put it: "We are aware of the difficulty . . . but this outcome is necessitated by analysis of the evidence." It is true that the law and rules of evidence sometimes allow such strange things to happen, but common sense dictates against it.

Developments continued at a rapid pace. Two days after receiving Arbel's opinion, Rubinstein decided to accept all her recommendations. However, following Deri's conviction in the principal trial, Rubinstein closed this case.

Another highly significant event occurred in the interim between Bar-On's resignation and Attorney General Rubinstein's decision—a committee chaired by former Chief Justice Meir Shamgar was appointed by Justice Minister Hanegbi "to examine the manner of appointing the attorney general and issues related to his tenure." This appointment was made at the height of the police investigation against the prime minister and Hanegbi himself.

What were the country's leaders thinking when they decided to appoint this committee, which would almost surely end up weakening the government by recommending that it hand over powers and reduce its authority with regard to the attorney general's duties and appointment? Presumably they thought that if they acted "properly," that is, as the legal establishment expected them to, the investigations underway against them would be resolved in their favor. Of course, there is not a shred of evidence that the leaders' "propriety" in any way affected the cases against the prime minister and justice minister. But the fact is that the cases were closed remarkably quickly, despite the fact that some lawyers in the State Attorney's Office were doubtful and skeptical, especially about Netanyahu's actions.

The Supreme Court's involvement in criminal proceedings brought on, as might be expected, petitions asking the court to overrule Rubinstein's decision to close the investigations in the Bar-On–Hebron affair.[139] These petitions were submitted by a number of Knesset members from the left, among them Yonah Yahav, Yossi Beilin, and Yossi Sarid. The petitions presented problems beyond the ones already cited, that of the status of public suits and the problematic nature of court involvement in the preparation of an indictment of a public figure. In this case, one cannot avoid the discomfiting feeling that the petitioners sought to change the political map by way of criminal charges against a political opponent. The suits were heard by a panel of five justices, headed by Shlomo Levin. Justices Eliezer Goldberg and Theodor Or, speaking for the majority, pointed out questionable elements in the opinions of the state attorney and attorney general regarding the prime minister's behavior in the affair. Justice Or even noted that "it may well be that the evidence could have led to another result." In the end, however, he ruled that there were no grounds for even an order nisi—not in the matter of the prime minister and certainly not with regard to the justice minister. Dalia Dorner, writing for the minority, maintained that it would be appropriate to issue an order nisi in the matter of the closing of the case against the prime minister, but not in Hanegbi's case.

From the point of view of the chief justice, the affair ended in the best possible way. Hanegbi, a very amenable justice minister from the court's perspective, one highly praised by Barak, remained in his post. Barak's choice for attorney general received the post and would later be appointed to the Supreme Court. No less important, the committee to examine the role and appointment of the attorney general was headed by Meir Shamgar, who had formerly served in that post and would thus bolster the authority of the attorney general at the expense of the cabinet and the government as a whole. As a former chief justice, Shamgar would also see to it that the Supreme Court would play a central role in choosing the person to fill the job.

During his first tenure as prime minister, Netanyahu was compelled to accept the Oslo agreements, even though he had opposed them when they were reached. Furthermore, following a summit meeting in Washington with Yasser Arafat and President Bill Clinton, Israel withdrew from most of Hebron, while retaining control of the Tomb of the Patriarchs and a small additional area. A second summit, the Wye Plantation conference convened by Clinton in October 1998, ended with an agreement on the transfer of additional territories in the West Bank to Palestinian control.

This latter agreement was not implemented in the main, but the opposition it aroused among right-wing members of the Knesset destabilized the government. In a national election held half a year later, in May 1999, Netanyahu was defeated by Ehud Barak, leader of the Labor Party.[140]

15

Ehud Barak's Commission of Inquiry

Prime Minister Ehud Barak withdrew Israeli forces, in May 2000, from the security zone that Israel had occupied in southern Lebanon since 1982. He also sought a peace treaty with the Palestinians. The negotiations he conducted with Yasser Arafat, the PLO chief and chairman of the Palestinian Authority, culminated at a summit meeting held at Camp David under the auspices of President Bill Clinton in July 2000. But the parley ended in failure. Soon thereafter, in September, a second Palestinian Intifada broke out. The violence was not restricted to the territories, however. Riots also swept through Israeli Arab villages, where protestors blocked main roads, cutting off transportation between different parts of the country. Demonstrators threw rocks at passing cars and, in one case, killed a Jewish driver. The riots were quelled by the police, but in the process thirteen Arabs, citizens of Israel, were killed.

Many Israelis, particularly the country's Arab citizens, were shocked and incensed by the deadly results of the suppression of the riots. They blamed Barak and his government. A month later, seeking to regain the support of the Arab population, the Barak government formed a statutory national commission of inquiry, chaired by Supreme Court Justice Theodor Or, to investigate the causes and response to the violence.

Dissension in the government, in particular involving the Haredi parties, along with the severe violence of the Second Intifada, destabilized Barak's coalition. He resigned in December 2000 after serving as prime minister for only a year and a half. Following his resignation, but while still serving as caretaker prime minister pending an election, Barak pathetically participated in another round of negotiations with the Palestinian leadership, held at Taba in the Sinai Peninsula, in the hopes of reaching a peace agreement. But a prime minister who has resigned after losing his Knesset majority has no moral or political mandate to embark on a major political or diplomatic initiative.[141] The new negotiations quickly reached an impasse and produced nothing, while the Second Intifada continued in full force.

Barak declared a special election for prime minister only. According to the Basic Law: The Government as it then stood, the prime minister had the authority, with the president's consent, to call elections to the Knesset as well. But he refrained from doing so, apparently out of concern that his party would be soundly defeated.

In the elections for prime minister, held in February 2001, Barak faced the new leader of the Likud, Ariel Sharon. Sharon defeated him soundly—Barak received only 37.4 percent of the vote. Only a little more than 62 percent of Israel's citizens voted, a record low turnout that was due in part to the fact that many of Israel's Arab citizens boycotted the election. If Barak thought that establishing the Or Commission would gain him and his party support from Israel's Arabs, he had clearly been mistaken. Sharon was thus prime minister when the Or Commission submitted its report to the government in August 2003.

Barak did not come out well in the commission's report. "Barak," it stated, "was not aware of or sufficiently attentive to the processes occurring in Israel's Arab society, which created during his tenure a real fear of the outbreak of widespread rioting." Furthermore, he "did not give enough thought to the need for appropriate preparation by the police force prior to the riots" and "took insufficient action to prevent the use of deadly force by the police or to limit it."[142] The commission refrained from any recommendation regarding Barak's eligibility for any post in the future, since he was an elected official. It did, however, make such a recommendation regarding Shlomo Ben-Ami, who was minister of internal security at the time of the riots, stating that he should not be allowed to serve in this post in the future.

In disqualifying Ben-Ami from holding a particular portfolio, namely a political position, the Or Commission repeated the mistake made by the Kahan Commission in its report on the massacre in the Sabra and Shatila refugee camps in Beirut during the First Lebanon War. That commission, it will be recalled, had ruled that Ariel Sharon was disqualified from serving as defense minister.

The Or Commission also made rulings regarding figures in the police force, and recommended that the Police Investigations Department investigate several incidents with the purpose of preparing criminal charges against some of the policemen involved in the deaths. The commission also examined the actions of several leaders of the Arab public (as noted above), but refrained from making personal recommendation in their regard. Beyond this, it made general recommendations regarding the state's, and in particular the police force's, treatment of the Arab population.

16

Protecting Human Rights

From the time Israel was founded, the Supreme Court has played a central role in protecting human rights. I have already discussed several such decisions.[143] Human rights issues were also central to cases dealing with issues religion and the state, which raised questions regarding women's rights and the severe consequences of imposing religious law on the public at large. It is often said that the role of the courts is to protect minorities against the majority. In Israel the opposite is often the case. The coalition system enables parties representing minorities to impose their will on the majority. Time and again the Supreme Court has needed to protect the majority against the power wielded by minorities, as in the matter of television broadcasts on Friday nights, the beginning of the Jewish Sabbath.

I. RELIGION AND THE STATE

On the whole, on matters of religion and the state the Shamgar court continued the line taken by the classic court. As we have seen, during the country's early years the Supreme Court played a central role in this area. For example, Israel national television was allowed to broadcast on Friday nights thanks to an interim order from Justice Zvi Berinson. Another case addressed the appointment of Leah Shakdiel, an observant Jewish studies teacher, to the Religious Council of Yeruham. The ministerial committee in charge of these appointments refused to allow her to serve on the council, on the grounds that, traditionally, only men served on these bodies, and that local and the Chief Rabbinate objected to the appointments of women to such a position. The Supreme Court overruled the veto on Shakdiel's appointment on the grounds that it violated the Equal Rights for Women Law.[144] Of special note in this case was the opinion written by Justice Menachem Elon, who held the seat traditionally reserved for an observant justice trained in Jewish religious law.

Elon surveyed the *halakhic* rulings touching on the matter, including Maimonides' interpretation of Deuteronomy 17:15, "Put a king over you." Maimonides cites this verse in ruling that "[a] woman may not be raised to kingship, as it says 'a king over you' and not 'a queen'; so it is for all leadership positions in Israel—only a man is appointed." However Maimonides' interpretation is problematic because in Hebrew, including legal discourse, the male gender is used generically, to refer to both men and women. Other *halakhic* authorities were, of course, aware of this problem, but nevertheless most of them ruled as Maimonides did. The majority of authorities maintained not only that women could not hold public posts but also that they could not be granted the vote.

Elon did not see his role as that of making a *halakhic* ruling. He did, however, point to other views, and concluded that Jewish law did not explicitly forbid a woman to serve on a religious council. The court's judgment that Shakdiel should be granted a seat on the Yeruham religious council was "in accordance with the opinions of great and good [authorities], well-grounded in the world of halakhah." He asserted that the court was free to choose between the range of opinions presented by traditional Jewish law and could choose to follow an opinion that did not reflect that of the majority of *halakhic* authorities recognized by the Orthodox community.

Another important religious question that came before the court on a number of occasions was the "who is a Jew" issue—that is, who qualifies as a Jew under Israeli law, and whether the state is required to accept the Jewish religious definition. In the court's early years the question was raised in the Benjamin Shalit[145] and Oswald Rufeisen ("Brother Daniel")[146] cases. Later it came up in particular in connection with cases dealing with the issue of conversion to Judaism. Throughout Jewish history rabbinic courts have been the gatekeepers in this regard. Since Judaism has no central authority, a conversion authorized by one set of rabbis will not necessarily be recognized by others. Such disputes arose from time to time within the framework of Orthodox Judaism. But Israel's official religious courts, controlled by the Orthodox and Haredi communities, have always refused categorically to accept conversions performed by Jewish movements it considered heretical, most notably the Conservative and Reform movements to which most affiliated American Jews belong. As far as Israel's rabbinic courts are concerned, a person who undergoes Conservative or Reform conversion has, when it comes to marrying or divorcing in Israel, the status of a non-Jew. But is such a convert a Jew within the meaning of the Law of the Return, which permits every Jew around the world to immigrate to Israel? And should the state population registry register such converts as Jews?

Initially, this issue arose with regard to people who had undergone Conservative or Reform conversions overseas. In these cases the Supreme Court ruled that, for the purposes of registration and the Law of the Return, the state must recognize conversions carried out in recognized Jewish communities in accordance with their accepted procedures.

A new stage was reached in 2005, in a suit brought by fourteen people who had immigrated to Israel from several countries and who commenced conversion procedures in Israel. They later chose to go overseas to undergo Reform or Conservative conversion, after which they returned to Israel and asked to be recognized as Jews under the terms of the Law of the Return. The Ministry of the Interior refused to do so on the grounds that the acceptance of a conversion performed overseas required that the person in question had joined a Jewish community there, a condition that the petitioners did not meet. Their conversions, popularly referred to as "hop-over conversions," presented the Supreme Court with a major difficulty. Secular Zionism had never instituted its own procedure for acceptance into the Jewish people. Neither had the Israeli state done so—it remained dependent on religious bodies on this fundamental question relating to the right to enter Israel and receive citizenship.

The case was heard by a panel of eleven justices and was decided by a majority of seven. The majority ruled that the "hop-over conversions" undergone by these specific petitioners was not a barrier to their enjoying the benefits of the Law of the Return.[147] However, the justices also authorized the Interior Ministry to draft regulations to prevent the abuse of this method of conversion—that is, to ensure that "hopover conversions" so recognized were performed in good faith by the converts and the communities that converted them.

The legislative compromise achieved in the Shalit case did not put an end to the controversy over who is a Jew, and neither did subsequent legal battles. The Population Registry Law requires the listing of each inhabitant's religion and nationality. And while nationality and citizenship are equivalent terms in many Western countries, that is not the case in Israel. The registry, and each inhabitant's identity card, notes whether he is Jew, Arab, Druze, or a member of another minority group. This has inevitably led to legal argument over how to classify people and who belongs to which group. Often this involves a cultural-ideological debate over matters of religion and the state.

Another case involved an Israeli who asked the deletion of his listing in the population registry and on his identification card, as being of Jewish nationality. He preferred not to be registered as the member of any nationality but simply as an Israeli citizen. The Supreme Court agreed. Justice Berinson made a distinction between belonging to a religion or national group and not belonging to or leaving such a group. He maintained that "when a person declares that he belongs to a given religion or nationality, there is no certainty that that religion or group will, according to its laws and rulings, take him in and recognize him as such. But unbelief or denial of religion, and a person's desire to see himself as a citizen of the world free of the bounds of nationality, is his own business and requires no outside consent or certification."[148]

The court ruled that a person could be registered as an Israeli resident or citizen and leave the line regarding his religion or nationality blank.[149] Yoram Kaniuk, a novelist, took advantage of this to change his registration, crossing out his previous designation as being of the Jewish religion and leaving the space blank.[150] That, however, relates to the registration of religion. When it comes to nationality, a person who accords with the law's definition of a Jew—one born to a Jewish mother or a convert—has a difficult time removing that designation.[151] The system has been even less amenable when people have asked that their nationality be listed as "Hebrew" or "Israeli."

The terms "Jew," "Hebrew," and "Israeli" were long synonyms. True, in biblical times, following the fracturing of the united realm into the kingdoms of Judah in the south and Israel in the north, the term "Israeli" generally referred to the latter state, the home of ten of the twelve tribes. Nevertheless, Israel was the second name of the patriarch Jacob, and thus the tribe of Judah, by the biblical account descended from Jacob's son of that name, were also "children of Israel."

The term "Hebrew," in Jewish tradition, was attached to the patriarch Abraham, who migrated from the land of his birth, Ur of the Chaldees, beyond the Euphrates. On one account, Abraham was given this name because he came from beyond the river—the root of the Hebrew word *Ivri*, Hebrew, bears the connotation of "beyond." The terms "Jew" and "Jewish" are Anglicizations of *Yehudi*, literally referring to a member of the tribe of Judah. The Jews of today are referred to as such because they are understood to be primarily the descendants of that tribe, since the ten northern tribes were sent into exile and disappeared following the Assyrian conquest of the Kingdom of Israel.

The term "Hebrew" appears elsewhere in the Bible as well. Pharaoh's chief cup-bearer refers to Joseph as a "Hebrew youth" (Genesis 41:12), and Exodus 21:2 legislates regarding Hebrew slaves. Today, we speak of the Jewish people, but their language is Hebrew. But II Kings 18:26 relates that King Hezekiah's counselors asked Rabshakeh, envoy of King Sennacherib of Assyria, "Please, speak to your servants in Aramaic, for we understand it; do not speak to us in Judean. . . ."[152]

The Hebrew University is located in Jerusalem, capital of the state of Israel, and the land in which it was founded is called the Land of Israel. Israel is defined as the Jewish state, homeland of the Jewish people. The country's Declaration of Independence opens with the words "The Land of Israel was the birthplace of the Jewish people," and the new state's relation to the Jewish people is reiterated several times more in the document. But the Declaration of Independence also refers to "the people of Israel," while the signers of the document are referred to as "representatives of the Hebrew Yishuv [the Jewish community in Palestine] and the Zionist movement," who are proclaiming "the establishment of a Jewish state in the Land of Israel." Toward its end, the document refers to "the independent Hebrew nation in its land." On the surface, it looks as if the term "Hebrew" is being used as a synonym for "Jewish." But it may well be that the new country's leaders were seeking to establish the term "Hebrew" as the proper term for referring to the Jews living in Israel. They may have wanted to have to avoid presenting themselves as representing the entire Jewish people. Nevertheless, they clearly viewed the people of the Yishuv as belonging to the Jewish people and not as part of some separate nation. The Law of Return uses the term "Jew," granting every person fitting that designation the right to immigrate to Israel. The Basic Law: Human Dignity and Liberty refers to Israel as a "Jewish and democratic state."

Israel's courts have consistently ruled that the terms "Hebrew" and "Jewish" are synonyms, but some people in the modern age have preferred the term "Hebrew." Under the British Mandate, the term was identified with the Young Hebrews movement, who were also called the Canaanites. This group sought to establish a Hebrew identity separate from the Jewish people and to seek its roots in the Israelite nation that lived in the land prior to the Exile. Hebrews were, they proclaimed, a new nation that had arisen in the Land of Israel, one that viewed itself as distinct and fundamentally different from the Jewish people of the Diaspora.[153]

Following the establishment of Israel, the Young Hebrews lost much of their support, and after the establishment of the state the use of the term "Hebrew" declined. It was increasingly replaced by "Israeli." The reason was obvious—the new country was called Israel, and thus its inhabitants held Israeli citizenship. This was true of all its inhabitants, no matter what their nationality or religion—Jews, Druze, Muslim Arabs, Christian Arabs, Circassians, Arameans, and others. Did that mean that there was now an Israeli nation, comprising all those who held Israeli citizenship?

The question arose in the case of George Rafael Temerin, who immigrated to Israel from Yugoslavia in 1949. He was registered as being of Jewish nationality and as of no religion. In 1970, Temerin asked the Population Registry to change his national affiliation to "Israeli," but his request was rejected.[154] His case reached the Supreme Court. In his ruling, Chief Justice Shimon Agranat discussed a number of categories and concepts, among them the ethnic identity of a group that sees itself as sharing a common culture. Such an ethnic group, Agranat argued, did not constitute a nation. That latter term referred to an ethnic group that wielded power or political influence so as to realize its national values.

Agranat cited books and other sources from the fields of sociology and political science, a clear sign that the question did not fall into the realm of the law. In any case, he and his fellow justices rejected Temerin's claim that a new Israeli nationality had come into being in the state of Israel, an Israeli nation distinct from the Jewish people. In a concurring opinion, Justice Yitzhak Kahan offered a more pointed statement, abjuring sociological questions of ethnic identity and the definition of the term "nation." He focused on the legal issue: the Population Registry Law, as amended following the Shalit case, mandated that anyone according with the definition of the Law of Return—that is, a person who had been born to a Jewish mother or who had converted to Judaism, and who did not profess another religion—was to be registered as being of Jewish nationality. According to the law, Kahan ruled, such a person could not demand to be registered as a member of another nation.

Forty years later the question came up before the Supreme Court once again. The petitioners were several individuals, some of them well known to the Israeli public. Among them were Uzzi Ornan, a professor of linguistics, and former members of the Knesset Shulamit Aloni and Uri Avnery. Ornan had in the past been registered, on his own declaration, as a member of the Hebrew nation. Now he sought to switch his nationality to "Israeli." Ornan had also established an organization called "I am Israeli," the members of which signed a petition declaring that they belonged to the Israeli nation rather than the Jewish nation.

What was new in this case was that the petitioners were registered as belonging to different nations. Most of them were Jews, but were joined by inhabitants of Israel of other groups, religions, and nationalities as well—an Arab, a Druze, a Buddhist, and a Burmese. They all claimed that a new nationality had come into being in the state of Israel, one that included all the country's inhabitants—the Israeli nation.

Their claim was based on the incongruence of the terms "Jewish" and "Israeli." These terms had once been synonymous. Yet, while the term "Jewish-Arab" seemed dissonant, "Israeli Arab" had become an accepted designation for the country's Arab citizens. It was a natural outcome of the fact that they were Israeli (not Jewish) citizens. However, this claim did not answer the question of whether common citizenship was a tie sufficiently strong to create a nation.

This takes us back to questions that properly belong to the fields of sociology and political science: What is the definition of "nation" and what kinds of group within a country can constitute a national minority? When the case came before the District Court, Judge Noam Sohlberg (now a member of the Supreme Court) maintained that the case was not justiciable, as the court had no means of determining whether or not an Israeli nation had come into being. He was right—the subject is by nature a political one. What should an Israeli court do if, for example, an Arab citizen of Israel petitions to have his nation listed as Palestinian? Do the courts want to grapple with such a question?

But the Supreme Court rejected Sohlberg's position. Justices Asher Grunis, Hanan Melcer, and Uzi Vogelman ruled (citing the Temerin case as a precedent) that the case was indeed justiciable. Clearly the legislature can mandate the court to take up a subject that is not ordinarily justiciable and thus make it such, but in doing so it may impose a burden that the court is unable to bear. The court's ruling will become legally binding, but its determination of the existence or nonexistence of a given nation will not necessarily persuade the public or the members of a given group who maintain that they constitute (or do not constitute) a nation.

Justice Melcer noted in his opinion that the Israeli legal system, as embodied in the Declaration of Independence and Knesset legislation, defines the state as Jewish and democratic. This constitutional definition of the state precludes the legal possibility of recognizing an "Israeli nation" distinct from the Jewish nation. In this he rejected the claim of those petitioners who were registered as members of the Jewish nation to belong to an Israeli nation. A distinction thus has to be made between citizenship and nationality. The state is Jewish, citizenship in the state is Israeli, and those citizens belong to different nationalities or, conceivably, no national group at all. As regards the petitioners of other nationalities, Melcer wrote, he doubted whether it was the court's role to decide whether, for example, a claim that might be made by a Belgian citizen living in Israel that his Israeli identity card should show his nationality not as Belgian but rather as Flemish. The best solution, he suggested, would be to eliminate the "nationality" line in the Population Registry, as in fact had been done on new identity cards.[155]

This takes us back to where we began—the problem of how a person joins the Jewish people and gains citizenship in its nation-state. The entry ticket for non-Jews is conversion, a process that is controlled by religious groups—the different streams of Judaism in and outside of Israel.

As it stands today, the state exercises no power or supervision over religious courts or rabbis (in Israel or abroad) that conduct conversions. This situation, in which entry into the Jewish people, and thus the right to Israeli citizenship, is in the sole purview of religious bodies—some of which do not recognize the state and over which the state has no control—is unacceptable. Tens of thousands of refugees from Third World countries are knocking on the doors of the state, and Israel invests huge sums of money and effort to build border fences and to pursue other means of halting this influx. At the same time, the government metes out heavy sanctions against illegal migrants and foreign workers whose work permits have lapsed, seeking to expel them from the country. What prevents all these people from entering the Jewish people through the main door by undergoing conversion supervised by one or another religious court? This is not just a theoretical possibility—it is already happening. The Supreme Court has been petitioned by foreign workers and residents who have undergone conversion by private religious courts operating in Israel outside the official rabbinate. As of this writing the court has made no ruling on these cases, and the Knesset has avoided dealing with it. At this time only a small number of foreigners are using this channel to attempt to gain Israeli citizenship, but the picture could well change if it turns out that this gate opens wide.

Another vexing problem in the area of state and religion relates to the monopoly that the rabbinical courts enjoy over the marriage and divorce of Jews in Israel (just as the religious courts of other faiths control marriage and divorce in their communities). There is no civil marriage in Israel; all such ceremonies are performed by and under the sole authority of clergy. Problems relating to couples that circumvented the system either by living together without marriage or by marriage abroad have oc-cupied the Knesset and the courts over the course of Israel's history.[156] In a number of rulings, Chief Justice Aharon Barak went a few steps further. He sought to grant civil marriages conducted outside Israel a status approaching official marriage within Israel. In one case he ruled that an Israeli couple who underwent a "Paraguayan marriage" were bound by Israel's laws requiring alimony and maintenance payments. (Paraguay permits couples living outside Paraguay to grant power of attorney to a representative in Paraguay who performs a civil marriage in their name, after which the couple receives a marriage certificate authorized by the Paraguayan govern-ment.)[157] In another judgment, Barak ruled that a same-sex couple who married outside Israel, in a jurisdiction that recognizes such marriages, should be registered as a married couple by the Population Registry and granted all the rights accorded to married couples under Israeli civil law.[158]

II. FREEDOM OF EXPRESSION

The right to free speech was recognized by the classic Supreme Court in *Kol Ha'am v. Ministry of the Interior* and a host of other cases. But at that time the court knew to set limits to this freedom. In the *Ein Gal* case, the Film and Play Review Board, a state oversight body, refused to allow the screening in Israel of a film entitled *The Struggle over the Land, or Palestine in Israel* on the grounds that it contained "provocation by minorities against the state and its citizens, and as such is liable to bring about . . . acts of violence." The Supreme Court rejected a petition challenging the disqualifi-cation of the film, noting that the film "adopts the claim that Arab terror organiza-tions and the country's other enemies are disseminating . . . around the world." The court stated that the misrepresentation of historical facts was not in and of itself sufficient to justify banning the film. In this case, however, the court maintained, "it comes on top of the fundamentally incendiary nature of the film." Furthermore, "the false propaganda that this film is meant to serve . . . constitutes a tool in the hands of those who seem to legitimize the murderous acts of terror organizations within the state."[159]

During Barak's tenure as chief justice this area underwent considerable change. Freedom of expression began to be referred to as a "constitutional" right, even though it is not mentioned in any of Israel's basic laws. The basis for this claim was the court's expansion of the concept of human dignity, which is explicitly protected by the Basic Law: Human Dignity and Liberty, to include all rights that the court sees fit to protect. Theoretically, certain restrictions remain on freedom of expression. So, for example, the court declared that "protected freedom of expression does not include the freedom to express abominations."[160] Likewise, freedom of expression may be constrained because it is detrimental to public peace or even public sensitivi-ties. But a close reading of the relevant judgments shows that these restrictions are in practice virtually meaningless. Attempts to rein in free speech on these grounds are nearly always doomed to failure.

The rule regarding harm to public peace applies only when the harm is "serious, grave and severe," and when it threatens to "shake the foundations" of society. An injury to sensitivities can justify restricting freedom of expression only if it threatens to "shake that society to its very foundations." Such an injury can justify restricting freedom of expression only "if it exceeds the standard of social tolerance," and "if it is capable of shaking the foundations of mutual tolerance...."[161]

The case involving the film *Jenin, Jenin*, a putative documentary about the Israel Defense Forces' (IDF) action in the West Bank city of Jenin during the Defensive Shield operation illustrates this new approach. The operation, in which Israeli forces re-entered West Bank cities and refugee camps that it had pulled out of in the framework of the Oslo Accords, was a response to a horrifying wave of terror that swept through Israel during the Second Intifada. The terror climaxed with the suicide bombing of the Park Hotel in Netanya on the eve of the Pesach holiday in 2002. By all reasonable accounts, the IDF did all it could to avoid injury to civilians and suffered many losses as a result. The worst of these losses came when a contingent of reserve soldiers was decimated by Palestinian guerrillas during a patrol of the Jenin refugee camp—which the IDF deliberately refrained from bombing from the air or shelling because of its dense civilian population, even though such a barrage would have in all probability saved the lives of the soldiers. A short time after the hostilities ended, Mohammad Bakri, an Israeli Arab actor, arrived in the refugee camp with a film crew and collected testimonies from its residents about their experiences during the combat in the camp. Many of the interviewees charged that Israel had fired on innocent civilians and had forced Palestinian children to perform combat-related missions. The District Court described one of the most shocking scenes: "The film shows a tank driving toward a group of people lying on the ground. It also shows a Palestinian whose hands are tied behind his back being led toward the row of supine people. The tank is seen driving toward the people, and then a voice is heard shouting that the tank is running them over. Immediately thereafter a volley of gunfire is heard, and the picture changes such that the tank stands there and people are evacuating a body on a stretcher."

In fact, this atrocity never took place. It also turned out that many other crimes that the film accused IDF soldiers of committing had not happened. Yet *Jenin, Jenin* was marketed as a documentary. This makes the case different from the ruling handed down by the classic Supreme Court in the Israel Film Studio Inc. case of 1962,[162] in which the court sanctioned the broadcast of a newsreel report about the evacuation of the residents of the Sumeil neighborhood in Tel Aviv. The footage included in the item was not pleasant to watch and perhaps did not provide a full view of the event, but they showed things that actually happened.

The Review Board refused to allow *Jenin, Jenin* to be screened. Bakri and several associates went to court. The Supreme Court allowed the petition and ordered that the film be screened.[163] The opinion gives the impression that the justices did not view the footage and that their decision was based on the material placed before them. They recognized that the film contained lies, but Justice Dalia Dorner wrote:

> The mere fact that an expression is false does not constitute a cause for the re-moval of protection. This is in contrast to the manner it is expressed, such as being racist. The use of such a manner of expression . . . violates a statutory pro-hibition and constitutes a cause for the restriction of that expression . . . Indeed, it has been established that "regarding the freedom of expression, we do not con-cern ourselves with the truth of the expression" . . . the restriction of false expres-sion would allow the authorities the power to distinguish between the true and the false....[164]

The rule established by the classic court in the Ein Gal case was thrown out, just as the new court rejected many of the rules established prior to the legal revolution.

The court agreed that upsetting sensibilities could be a reason for banning a film, but the interpretation it gave that term was so restricted that it was basically devoid of content. "[T]here is no doubt," Justice Dorner wrote in the main opinion,

> that the film injures the feelings of many members of the public, including the feelings of the soldiers who participated in the battle and their families, especially the parents, spouses and siblings of the fallen, including respondents 3–32. However, it should not be said that this injury, with all of its pain and anguish, is not within the bounds of that which is tolerated in our democratic society.[165]

In a concurring opinion, Justice Ayala Procaccia agreed, adding:

> Falsehoods should not be confronted by suppression. Rather, freedom of expression should serve as a means to present the truth and to challenge such falsehoods in the free and open market of ideas. In the free flow of information, opinions, ideas and values, the truth will ultimately prevail over lies.[166]

But is it really true that "the truth will ultimately prevail"? This language, like other clichés such as "justice wins out in the end," express an optimism that real life often fails to confirm. The Jewish people endured false blood libels for centuries, and many people today still believe that the *Protocols of the Elders of Zion* is a true account.[167] Under such circumstances, the court's avid defense of the right to lie is not very convincing.

Yes, there are cases in which the argument is about views or interpretation, or over matters about which truth is not clear and the facts are open to dispute. In such cases we would not want an administrative authority to decide the question and ban a controversial film. But when the lie is serious, blatant, and brazen, like the scene of a tank ostensibly running over bound Palestinians, and when the sensitivities of the public are seriously hurt, it is another matter entirely.

That is the idea behind laws forbidding racist provocation and Holocaust denial. These prohibit the dissemination of lies that cause serious harm to the sensitivities of a large public. In such situations the legislature is not prepared to put its faith in the ultimate victory of truth. It would be better, then, not to be blinded by abstract ideas stated in high language.

But the court decided to allow the film to be screened. After it was, a number of reservists who had fought in Jenin filed a libel suit against Bakri. In the district court, Judge Michal Nadav ruled that the film indeed constituted libel. Bakri, she claimed, could not claim legal protections, such as that he had told the truth. But the plaintiffs encountered another legal obstacle. While they had taken part in battles in Jenin, there was nothing in the film that identified them personally or that defamed them as individuals. It was the public and the army in general that had been libeled, and Section 4 of the Prohibition of Libel Law states explicitly that libel of the public is not grounds for a civil suit. As a result, the suit against Bakri was dismissed, a decision that was confirmed by the Supreme Court.[168]

But the sweeping view of freedom of expression as reflected in the opinions of Dorner and Procaccia that permitted the screening of *Jenin, Jenin* was moderated after Barak and Dorit Beinisch retired. The court now takes a more balanced view, recognizing that other values can sometimes take precedence over freedom of expression.[169]

III. EQUALITY

Alice Miller, a soldier, petitioned the Supreme Court in 1995, asking it to order the IDF to allow her to undergo the selection process to be an air force pilot. The IDF had refused on the grounds that, according to the regulations of Israel's high command, women are not to be placed in combat positions. One justification for this rule was that Israeli women serve a shorter period of regular army service and reserve duty than men do. Miller declared that she was prepared to serve the same amount of time as men, but this did not satisfy the IDF authorities. They also claimed that a woman would be disqualified from service when she was pregnant and after giving birth.

The suit was heard before a bench of five justices. The majority, composed of Justices Eliahu Mazza, Tova Strasberg-Cohen, and Dalia Dorner, rejected the army's position and ordered that Miller be summoned for the selection process.[170] In the end, she did not pass, but she opened the door for other young women, several of whom have served as combat pilots and navigators in recent years. The decision strengthened the position of women in the army and proved beneficial to the army itself. It is in line with the liberal approach already adopted by the Supreme Court in its earlier period and reflected in the case of Leah Shakdiel discussed above.

The case of *Ka'adan v. Israel Lands Administration*[171] proved to be more controversial. The petitioners were an Arab couple who lived in an Arab village. They wished to purchase a home or a lot in an Israeli community, Katzir, which had been built by the Jewish Agency on land provided by the state, not far from the Ka'adans' village. One of the Jewish Agency's functions is the settlement of Jews in the Land of Israel. It assigned the task of establishing the settlement to a cooperative society, and the society only accepted Jews to live there. (It should be noted that, not far away, an urban settlement, Harish, was also established, in principle at least, open equally to Jews and Arabs.)

The Jewish Agency defended the situation in part with the claim that the establishment of Katzir was pursuant to one of its missions, the settling of Jews in parts of the state of Israel in which the Arab population is dominant. It referred to its statement of purpose, which includes the language: "the settlement of Jews throughout the land, and in particular in rural areas and areas in which the Jewish presence is sparse . . . and by doing so increasing Israel's security." These claims were rejected, as was the state's claim that it was prepared to allot land for the establishment of an Arab community settlement. Chief Justice Barak stressed the principle of equality, and in the matter of a separate allotment of land to Arabs he adduced the U.S. Supreme Court's *Brown v. Board of Education* decision. In that case, which put an end to segregated schools for black Americans, the justices ruled that "separate educational facilities are inherently unequal."[172]

Barak was aware of situations in which Israeli court decisions had recognized separate treatment of a given population. Such was the case, for example, when the Israel

Lands Administration (ILA) decided to lease land only to Bedouin in the framework of its policy of moving them into permanent homes. A Jewish police officer from Beersheba who sought to lease a lot in a settlement set aside for Bedouin was turned down by the ILA, a decision that was confirmed by the Supreme Court.[173] Despite these precedents, in *Ka'adan* the majority decided to reject the policy of allocating land in Katzir only to Jews.

The *Ka'adan* decision has been much criticized. Ruth Gavison of the Hebrew University law school, for example, published an article in *Ha'aretz* under the headline "Jews Have a Right to Settlements of Their Own." Her position is clear: "While the Jews are a majority in Israel, they are a small minority in a hostile region. Within the state there is a large minority affiliated with the Arab nation, which is the large majority in the region. The desire to bolster control of an area in Israel is a legitimate interest, as long as it is not detrimental to the vested rights of the Arabs."

A similar critique was voiced by a former chief justice, Moshe Landau. In an interview with Ari Shavit, he asserted that the court's ruling "disregards the fact that we are a country engaged in self-defense that cannot commit suicide . . . there is the possibility that territories could be wrenched away from the state, of irredentism." Another critic was Shimon Shetreet, also a member of the law faculty at Hebrew University and a former Labor Party cabinet minister. He cited another Supreme Court decision in which the justices rejected "the suit of a Jordanian citizen to be permitted to lease an apartment in the Jewish Quarter in Jerusalem's Old City . . . from the Jewish Quarter Development Company . . . The court ruled that this did not constitute unacceptable discrimination but rather a legitimate distinction, against the background of the goal of the arrangement—the reconstruction of the Jewish Quarter and its designation for Jews, as well as for security reasons involving the lack of loyalty of Jordanian citizens to the state of Israel, and political considerations, that is the destruction of the Jewish Quarter by the Jordanian army."[174]

In fact, Israel has many residential areas populated by closed communities, among them Haredim and Arabs. The country also maintains separate educational institutions for nonreligious, religious, and Haredi Jews, and for Arabs.

In 2011 the Knesset responded to the *Ka'adan* decision by passing legislation authorizing communities consisting of no more than 400 households to establish admissions committees empowered to turn away applicants, including on grounds of incompatibility with the community's social life. The law was challenged before the Supreme Court on the grounds that its purpose was to exclude Arabs and members of other minorities. Three years later, under the leadership of Chief Justice Asher Grunis, the court ruled against the petitioners with a five to four majority.[175]

17

Trespassing on the Executive

As already noted, the new rules instituted by the revolutionary court were tripartite in nature: The demand that a petitioner have standing in a case was revoked; any, or nearly any, subject was now considered justiciable; and "unreasonableness" became a grounds for court intervention. This combination had the effect of making every decision by the executive branch provisional in nature, as it was subject to review by the court. I have already presented in chapter 9 one example of this triad of rules, from the first stage of the controversy over the enlistment of Haredim in the Israel Defense Forces (IDF). At that time the Supreme Court took upon itself to review whether a decision made by the defense minister, who had used his legal powers to exempt *yeshiva* students from the draft, was reasonable. Once again, it is important to distinguish between the Shamgar court, which continued to display a measure of self-restraint when it came to court intervention, especially on security matters, and the Barak court, which shed all such restraints. I will first highlight court intervention in decisions made by the attorney general with regard to indictments and appointments in the public sector, which began with the Shamgar court. Then I will examine the court's insertion of itself into policy-making, under the leadership of Chief Justice Aharon Barak.

I. THE ATTORNEY GENERAL AND INDICTMENTS

The attorney general is vested with the discretion to bring charges or to refrain from doing so. He may decide not to seek an indictment for any of several reasons— because he thinks no crime has been committed, because the evidence is insufficient for conviction, or due to lack of public interest in pursuing the case. In its classic era, the Supreme Court asserted its authority to review the attorney general's decisions in this regard, but restricted itself to the narrow grounds of whether the attorney general had acted in good faith. Back then, the mere claim that the attorney general had erred would not suffice to justify judicial intervention.[176] As one might expect under such a standard, only rarely were petitions filed asking the court to review a decision not to bring a suspect to trial, and in almost all cases such petitions were denied.

A few years after Barak left the attorney generalship and ascended to the Supreme Court, he declared that judicial review of the attorney general's actions should be grounded "on the same normative basis as its review of every other administrative authority."[177] The remark was incidental to the case at hand, but under the new court such obiter dicta often gained the force of new rules that replaced old ones. A major decision in this matter was handed down in December 1989. The petition in question had not been filed against the attorney general but rather against the chief military advocate general, but the issue at hand was similar.[178] The case was one of the many that grew out of the First Intifada. IDF soldiers had picked up some twenty young Arabs from the villages of Beita and Huwwarah, in accordance with lists of suspects given to the army by the Shin Bet. The suspects were bound and then beaten severely on their arms and legs. The blows were dealt with clubs, some of which broke in the process.

The soldiers involved apparently understood their action to be in accord with the government's iron fist policy against Palestinian rioters. The advocate general decided to bring up, on disciplinary charges, Colonel Yehuda Meir, the battalion commander who had issued the orders regarding the treatment of Palestinian detainees. The grounds were that the incident had occurred at the very beginning of the Intifada, just a few days after it was decided to use force against Palestinian insurgents. At the time, so the advocate general's reasoning went, the exact parameters of the force to be used remained unclear, as no specific orders had been given. Furthermore, he felt there was no justification for a criminal procedure because the IDF chief of staff had already resolved to terminate Meir's service in the IDF.

In December 1989, a bench headed by Justice Moshe Bejski held that the Supreme Court had the power to review decisions of the state prosecuting authorities, including the attorney general, when they are extremely unreasonable. Another justice, Jacob Kedmi, spoke of substantial unreasonableness. The court rejected the reasoning that the chief military advocate general gave for his decision and ruled that, in a case like this one, a disciplinary procedure was insufficient. The military advocate general's decision was quashed on the ground of unreasonableness, and the court ordered that Colonel Meir should be brought to trial.[179] Meir was tried before a military court, convicted, and stripped of his rank.

That same year the Supreme Court was petitioned in another case, this time against Attorney General Yosef Harish. Harish had decided not to indict the bankers and accountants involved in manipulating the prices of Israeli bank stocks. The manipulation took place during a period of runaway hyperinflation in the early 1980s. Back in the 1970s, Israel's major banks instituted a practice of buying back their own shares in order to keep their prices rising and thus encourage investors to buy their stocks. As a result of the manipulation, bank share prices rose independently of the banks' profitability or the value of their assets. The authorities, including the Ministry of Finance and the Bank of Israel, were aware of the practice but failed to stop it, even though they realized that the pyramid would eventually collapse. In the summer of 1983, when a wave of stock sales ensued, the banks found themselves without the resources to buy back their shares. The crisis peaked at the beginning of October, when the public panicked, lost confidence in the market, and began massively unloading its bank stocks, causing a run on the stock exchange. At this point the government intervened. It closed the stock market for two weeks while it put together an emergency package in which it guaranteed the value of the banks' stocks and eventually bought them at the cost of billions of taxpayer dollars. At the beginning of 1985 a national commission of inquiry was appointed to investigate the crash. It was headed by Justice Bejski, and I was one of its members. The

Bejski Commission recommended that a number of top bank officials be compelled to resign from their position, and the government accepted the recommendations. The question of their criminal liability was handed over to Harish, who decided not to press charges in the case.

When Bejski ruled in 1989 that the court should intervene in the chief military advocate general's decision not to file charges against Colonel Yehuda Meir, he knew very well that he was setting a precedent that would help the court intervene in the attorney general's decision in the bank case. In Bejski's view, the decision not to bring criminal charges against the bank officials was unacceptable. Having headed the commission of inquiry, he could not, of course, sit on the bench that considered the attorney general's decision in that case, but he was able to influence that case indirectly through the precedent he set in Colonel Meir's case.

The petition on the bank stock case was heard before a bench headed by Chief Justice Meir Shamgar, along with Justices Barak and Shlomo Levin. The attorney general informed the court that he had resolved not to file charges against the bankers for a number of reasons. Among them was that their case had already been examined by the Bejski Commission, whose report had resulted in "very severe sanctions of being dismissed from their jobs and cut off from the banking profession." Second, state authorities had been aware of the stock manipulation (if not all of its aspects), but had done nothing effective to stop it. Third, the Bejski Commission had in fact achieved the goals of punishing the guilty, deterrence, and instilling new norms. Beyond these considerations, seven years had passed since the crisis, and there was no reason "to impose on the public . . . the cost . . . trouble, and pain of rolling back the affair."

None of Harish's arguments convinced the court. The court ruled that the attorney general's decision constituted a substantial deviation from the balance required in such a case and that it was "entirely unreasonable." The decision not to put the bankers on trial because of a "lack of public interest" was voided. The court ordered the attorney general to render a decision on the matter based on whether the evidence was sufficient to bring the bankers to trial.[180]

Subsequent developments demonstrated that justice and reason lay on Harish's side. It took an additional seven years for the criminal procedure to wend its way through the courts, and the results were not impressive (with the exception of the length of the judgments handed down). Indictments against the bankers and accountants involved in the affair were submitted to the District Court in 1990. The case was heard by Judge Miriam Naor (now Israel's chief justice) on a nearly daily basis over three years. It ended in 1994 with a judgment of more than 600 pages. Most of the accountants entered into a plea bargain, in the framework of which they resigned from their profession. One of them, Dan Bavli, refused to accept the bargain and was convicted along with the bankers.

The defendants appealed their convictions to the Supreme Court, where the case was heard by a panel of five judges headed by Justice Dov Levin. (Shamgar, Barak, and Shlomo Levin, who had ordered Harish to indict the bankers, could not sit on this bench.) In its decision, 240 pages long, the court allowed substantial parts of the appeals. Bavli, represented by Hanan Melcer (now a Supreme Court justice) and Dan Sheinman, was acquitted on all counts. The bankers were acquitted, in a majority decision, of one of the central counts against them, intentional action by a director or manager that harms the bank's ability to meet its obligations.

On the whole, the Supreme Court displayed considerable sympathy for many of the bankers' claims, the very ones that had prompted the attorney general not to bring them to trial. In particular, the court noted the involvement of the authorities in fashioning the policy of supporting bank stock prices, and in granting "an irresponsible seal of approval to this negative phenomenon." The court also took cognizance of the administrative sanctions already imposed on the appellants, which banned them "from activity in their realm—the realm of banking," and the long time that had elapsed. The court thus canceled all the active prison sentences that the District Court had imposed, but left in place the fines and suspended sentences.[181]

In light of this notably unimpressive result, it is doubtful whether the Supreme Court's intervention in the attorney general's discretionary powers served any useful purpose, and whether the discretion of the justices was any more reasonable than that of Harish.

In fact, the Supreme Court's second-guessing of the attorney general's decision so as to compel him to bring people to trial against his better judgment runs counter to established past practice and does serious harm to the criminal process. It places the Supreme Court, which must preserve its neutrality, in a manifestly prosecutorial role. It is quite natural for persons indicted on the court's orders to feel that they are unlikely to get a fair trial.

True, the court took care to make it clear that it was not involving itself in the attorney general's position on whether the evidence was sufficient for an indictment. It was only reviewing the question of whether the public had an interest in a criminal prosecution. Nevertheless, it is difficult for a lower court to acquit (or even impose a light sentence) after the highest court has ordered an indictment. Furthermore, the decision advanced the court's sweeping activist approach another step forward. Soon the court would not hesitate to review determinations of sufficient evidence and plea bargains, as happened in the case of Israel's former president, Moshe Katsav, which I will examine shortly.

The prosecutorial cast that the Supreme Court took on is underlined by the fact that, so far, its review of the attorney general's decisions has all gone in one direction. In the cases in which it has chosen to intervene, it has always done so to order him to prosecute.

True, there have been a small number of attempts to petition the court against a decision by the attorney general to launch an investigation or bring a person to trial. But, to the best of my knowledge, none of them succeeded. The court has never instructed the attorney general to refrain from submitting an indictment. The most notable of these cases was a petition by Ehud Olmert, who would later become prime minister, against his arraignment on charges relating to violations of the campaign finance law in the 1988 elections. The attorney general decided to indict several people involved, but announced that he did not have sufficient evidence to justify an indictment against Olmert. His statement said, however, that a final decision on this matter would be rendered following the trial of the other suspects. In that trial, some of the defendants were convicted. Olmert's case was re-examined. This time the decision was to indict.

Olmert's attorneys made a simple claim in their petition against that decision to the Supreme Court. Prior to the trials of the other defendants, the prosecutors had claimed that there was insufficient evidence to charge him. Now the attorney general sought to base a case against Olmert on evidence garnered from the testimony of the defendants in the earlier trial—except that, at that trial, the prosecutors had claimed that the testimony given by these defendants was unreliable. If that were the case, how could the prosecutors now be basing an indictment on that same testimony? The Supreme Court recognized in principle that the court could order the attorney general to refrain from prosecuting a person. Yet the petition was denied on the ground that it was not clear that the prosecution had meant to claim that the whole testimony given by the defendants, rather than just part of it, was untrustworthy.[182] In the trial itself, Olmert was acquitted.[183]

An explanation for the Supreme Court's one-way intervention in prosecution decisions is that

[o]n the practical level, one must distinguish between a "mistaken" decision by the attorney general to press charges and a "mistaken" decision to refrain from pressing charges . . . we are here interested only in decisions of the second type. True, a decision of the first type is not immune from direct judicial review by the Supreme Court . . . but that rule applies to rare and exceptional cases, whereas the normal remedy for a defendant who argues that he was brought to trial as the result of an unreasonable decision by the attorney general is to plead an equitable defense,* the appropriate framework for the pursuit of which is the criminal process itself.[184]

Such one-way intervention, only to ensure that someone is brought to trial, places the Supreme Court at the head of the criminal prosecution and thus, at the very least, deprives the court of the objective appearance that it is required to preserve. It turns the entire justice system toward a prosecutorial stance, exacerbating Israel's already marked prosecutorial tendencies.

The case of Moshe Katsav, the Israeli president charged with a list of sex offenses, was a particularly striking one. A critical stage in the affair took place when the attorney general at the time, Menachem (Menny) Mazuz, sent, on January 2007, a letter to Katsav's attorneys, notifying them that he was considering, subject to a preliminary hearing, indicting the president for rape, several counts of sexual harassment, and other serious charges. That same day, Mazuz issued a press release detailing these charges. Katsav's lawyers immediately called a press conference in which they countered some of the accusations made by the women who had filed complaints about their client. Two days later, the Knesset's House Committee confirmed the president's official notice to them that he was temporarily unable to fulfill his duties.

The first charge in the draft indictment was based on accusations made by a woman, whose name was kept confidential, who had worked under Katsav when he served as minister of tourism. The charges involved a web of sexual harassment and two acts of rape. The second charge was based on the testimony of another woman,

* The so-called "equitable defense" is embodied in Section 149 (10) of the Israeli Criminal Procedure Law, providing that "[a]fter the commencement of the trial the defendant is entitled to make preliminary pleadings including . . . (10) The filing of the indictment or the conduct of the criminal proceedings is in material contradiction to the principles of justice and fair trial."

this one an employee at the President's Residence, who claimed that Katsav had harassed her sexually and committed three acts of forbidden consensual intercourse, accomplished by abusing his position of power over the woman. Two additional charges of sexual harassment involved two additional complainants.

Following the preliminary hearing Mazuz's position took a dramatic turn. He decided not to indict Katsav on the charges deriving from the testimony of the woman from the President's Residence, on the grounds of insufficient evidence. He also had doubts regarding the charges relating to the woman from the Tourism Ministry. Under the circumstances, Mazuz agreed to a plea bargain based on a list of charges that would not include rape but would include "indecent acts committed without consent under pressure," sexual harassment, and witness harassment. Katsav would be required to plead guilty to these charges and resign. He would receive a suspended jail sentence and would compensate his accusers, and also pay the state a sum of approximately $3,500 as compensation connected to a charge of using public money to give personal gifts.

The two sides signed the agreement and Katsav resigned, just a few weeks before his term was in any case set to end. Two days later the attorney general appeared on television and said that Katsav had behaved like a "serial sex offender." That same evening thousands demonstrated in Tel Aviv against the plea bargain. Given the legal culture that had developed in Israel by then, petitions to the Supreme Court were inevitable.

The court assigned a panel of five justices, headed by Chief Justice Dorit Beinisch, to hear the petitions. At that time I was serving as minister of justice, and in that capacity had no qualms about expressing my position that the Supreme Court had no business considering petitions of this sort. Since no one argued that the attorney general had acted in bad faith, it was my opinion that it would be a mistake for the Supreme Court to be drawn into ordering the state prosecutors to file charges, ratchet up the severity of the accusations, or block a plea bargain. Any such decision, I reasoned, would turn the court into chief prosecutor and thus encroach on its neutrality. At the same time, the rights of the accused would also be compromised when a lower court would hear his case after the highest court had already ruled that an indictment should be issued or the charges made more severe. Yes, the plea bargain with Katsav was problematic, with a huge disparity between the severity of the original charges and the relatively amenable resolution, but this did not justify the Supreme Court's intervention. (One reason such a disparity is problematic is that it can become routine practice. It creates an incentive for prosecutors to prepare extremely severe and not properly grounded lists of charges on the assumption that the defendant, fearing heavy punishment if convicted, will cave in and confess to less serious charges even if he believes himself innocent.)

The lawyers representing the attorney general had a difficult time defending the plea bargain. They had no alternative but to point out the weak chinks in the prosecution's case and the points that were liable to call into question the reliability of the women making the allegations against Katsav.

The justices issued a 200-page decision. The petition was dismissed by a majority composed of Eliezer Rivlin, Ayala Procaccia, and Asher Grunis. The two justices in the minority, Beinisch and Edmond Levy, maintained that the plea bargain should be revoked. The case should be returned to the attorney general, they said, who should consider charging Katsav with raping the woman from the Tourism Ministry and also charges relating to another woman. While this was a minority opinion, and only required that the attorney general "consider" or "reconsider," the intention was clearly that he charge the now-former president with rape. "The plea bargain with Katsav is characterized by gross incongruence between the actions ascribed to him in the plea bargain and the severity of the account of his actions that apparently emerges from the incriminating account of the woman from the Ministry of Tourism . . . which is still largely accepted by the attorney general even following the preliminary hearing," Beinisch wrote. "Under these circumstances, the attorney general's decision to reach the plea bargain under discussion here is glaringly inimical . . . to the public interest in conveying an effective and deterrent message against sex offenses, and for maintaining the principle of equality before the law."

But at this stage of the proceedings, Katsav had not yet been convicted. Given the presumption of innocence, was it not premature to speak of "an effective and deterrent message against sex offenses"? In my view, the most important passage in the judgment was written by Justice Grunis: "Interfering with the attorney general's decision in the case at hand would turn the court into a 'super-attorney general.' I cannot agree to that."[185]

Despite the fact that the petition was dismissed, the prosecutorial approach in the minority opinion should not be taken lightly. It came on top of the media coverage of the case, which was exceptional in its extent and in the damage it did to Katsav. Justices Levy and Rivlin addressed this latter issue, roundly criticizing Mazuz. According to Levy, a news item on the case "served as the first shot . . . in a media avalanche," following which "publication of privileged information did not cease throughout the investigation . . . In the reality of our times, even before a legal document leaves the attorney general's desk, it appears in large type in the daily papers . . . My criticism cannot pass over the attorney general and his subordinates . . . they must take account of their conduct with the media, not only in this case, but as an ongoing pattern. The evil consequences of this have been evident in the past, by which I mean other cases in which public figures were investigated or brought to trial, but it looks as if they have developed, in the current case, to the point of bursting. . . ."

Justice Rivlin also severely reproached Mazuz. Even prior to the plea bargain, he wrote, "the attorney general was interviewed on television and said that the investigation of President Katsav had turned up evidence that was 'extremely serious.' Two days after the plea bargain was reached, the attorney general was again interviewed on television and said that Katsav 'had for years conducted himself like a serial sex offender' . . . The conduct of a criminal proceeding . . . needs to be done cautiously, with kid gloves . . . Hanging in the balance are individual rights, the honor, on the one hand, of the victims, and on the other the suspects and defendants . . . All these require particular caution, both with decisions and with declarations. I fear that such caution did not typify the prosecution's conduct in this case. . . ."

The plea bargain remained in force, having barely survived the Supreme Court's review. But then came a new bombshell: Katsav decided to withdraw from the bargain, claiming his total innocence. He was indicted on serious charges, including rape, and a bench of the Tel Aviv District Court, composed of George Karra, Miriam Sokolov, and Judith Shevach, found the former president guilty on all counts.[186] By a vote of two to one, he was sentenced to seven years in prison (the judge in the minority thought that the sentence should be four years). Katsav's appeal of the conviction and the severity of the punishment was dismissed by a Supreme Court panel composed of Miriam Naor, Edna Arbel, and Salim Joubran,[187] and Katsav went to jail.

This affair came to its end leaving an uncomfortable feeling regarding the huge disparity between the plea bargain, which reflected the prosecution's lack of confidence in the evidence, and the outcome of the trial. This came on top of the media coverage, almost all of which condemned Katsav, and much of it based on material coming from the prosecution and the resulting hostile public atmosphere against him during the trial, as well as the problematic Supreme Court review of the plea bargain. As Dan Avi-Yitzhak, Deri's erstwhile defense attorney, put it, "There is almost no blunder that Mazuz did not make in this affair . . . Even a conviction on all counts . . . cannot overshadow the gravity of the damage this affair did to the prosecution system and public confidence in it."[188] None of this kept Mazuz from being appointed to the Supreme Court in November 2014.

II. SECOND-GUESSING APPOINTMENTS

The proceedings in the Bus 300 killings had long since been completed, but seven years after Shin Bet agents took into custody and killed two of the terrorists who had captured the bus, the affair reared its head once more. Yossi Ginossar, who had been forced out of the Shin Bet as a result, was appointed director general of the Israel Export Institute, and two and a half years later became chairman of the board of Amidar, a public housing company. Then Minister of Housing Binyamin Ben-Eliezer appointed him director general of his ministry. The Supreme Court was petitioned to disqualify Ginossar because of his actions in the Bus 300 affair.

The decision was rendered by Aharon Barak, who headed the bench that heard the case. He was joined by Justices Eliezer Goldberg and Eliahu Mazza. Ginossar had not been connected in any way to the murder of the terrorists, but Barak said in his opinion that "as a member of the Zorea Commission, he acted to conceal the role played by Shin Bet operatives in the affair. He was pardoned by the president for his part in the affair and was not brought to trial. Furthermore, Ginossar headed the team of interrogators in the Nafso affair . . . The interrogators used improper interrogation techniques and gave false testimony to the special military court that convicted Nafso. [Ginossar] was not brought to trial for this behavior."

The judgment contains one of Barak's favorite expressions, "imposing the rule of law on the rulers." A large part of the judgment was devoted to the question of whether transgressions committed by a candidate for a public position should be taken into account if he was not convicted of them (as Ginossar was not). Barak also addressed the nature of the pardon he had been given. Ginossar claimed that he had not wanted the pardon, as he maintained that he had acted within his authority and with the sanction of his superiors, and had agreed to request the pardon only after pressure was put on him to do so. He also argued that he had never been given the opportunity to prove his innocence. Barak rejected these claims and ruled that, under administrative law, a person may be held to have committed an offense even if he had not been convicted, and even if he had been pardoned. This ruling was inconsistent with a Supreme Court precedent made in *Reuven v. Legal Council*, which implied that a full pardon expunges a conviction and clears the defendant of any stain or defect.[189] The Crime Register and Rehabilitation of Offenders Law states: "A person whose conviction has been erased will be considered in all matters of law as if he had not been convicted, and every disqualification imposed as a result of conviction . . . is void from the day it was expunged." The law nevertheless permits various bodies, among them the government, to receive information about the expunged offenses for the purposes of appointments. Barak, recall, had maintained in his dissenting opinion that the president had exceeded his powers in pardoning the Shin Bet operatives, so it is hardly surprising that he gave the pardon no weight. The government's decision to appoint Ginossar director general of the Ministry of Housing was thus unreasonable in the extreme, and therefore illegal and void.[190]

Barak's ruling reflects the way in which the justices slowly turned their own values into obligatory rules, on the basis of the problematic equivalence he presumed between "unreasonable in the extreme" and illegality. Indeed, Barak quoted himself from a previous decision: "In an enlightened democratic country, a public figure . . . must maintain a proper moral level of behavior . . . for him to continue to serve in office." Ginossar's behavior in both cases was without a doubt shocking. Yet that is a separate issue from the question of whether the Supreme Court was correct to intervene in government appointments. The decision was handed down in March 1993, just a few months before the judgments were issued in the Deri and Pinchasi cases. In both those cases, it will be recalled, the Supreme Court also "legislated" a ruling that it was unreasonable (and therefore illegal) for the prime minister not to dismiss them.

The principal difficulty in the judgment in Ginossar's case was the huge uncertainty that it created and the complete dysfunction it generated in the process of making public appointments. The opinion in Ginossar's case offers a list of factors that should be taken into account, among them the severity of the offense, the amount of time that has passed since then (twelve years had gone by since the Nafso affair, eleven since the Bus 300 affair)—all this alongside the usual considerations regarding his qualifications.

When the court rejected Ginossar's appointment to director general of the Housing Ministry, the justices were aware of the fact that he had been appointed, not long before, to be chairman of the board of Amidar, a state enterprise of huge proportions. He continued to hold this position. Are we to conclude from this that he was not disqualified from holding this position, or that he was left there because no one bothered to petition the court to dismiss him from that post?

Barak stressed that the appointment "profoundly undermines public confidence in the public sector and public service." Since then, judicial decisions have reiterated innumerable times that the appointment of a person whom the court considers morally problematic "undermines public confidence" in government. But there is not a shred of evidence to back up this claim, just as there is no evidence that public confidence in government has risen since the Supreme Court began reviewing the moral aspects of public appointments. Further evidence of this disconnect comes from a debate some years later over the appointment of the mayor of Ramla, Brigadier General (ret.) Yoel Lavi, to head the Israel Lands Administration. There were clear indicators that showed that Lavi, whose case will be discussed in greater detail below, enjoyed public confidence, but that did not keep the court from asserting that his appointment would undermine public confidence. In other words, the court believes that such an appointment *ought* to impact public confidence, and on this basis over-rules it. The upshot is that the term "public confidence" has transformed from a consideration of fact into a legal fiction.

The role of the court is to guarantee that public administration operates according to the law. It seems doubtful whether its mandate includes fostering public confidence in state agencies. In fact, the court's intervention in such matters has produced a paradox—the more the court endeavors to ensure public confidence in government, the steeper the decline in public trust in the Supreme Court. In fact, under Barak's leadership, respect for the courts, including the Supreme Court, plummeted.

The court began to slide down a slippery slope. It did not limit itself to candidates with a record of criminal activity. A few years later it would turn out that any blemish on an appointee's record, alleged by any person at all, could justify Supreme Court review of the appointment. This could include improper behavior, or references to the appointee in the report of an investigative commission or court judgment. Even embarrassing, tasteless, or politically incorrect utterances made by an appointee at any time and in any context could be used against him.

Within a few years, the court had cast off all restraints in this regard, accepting no limitations regarding when the allegedly improper behavior or speech had occurred, its nature, or anything else. The absolute discretion claimed by the court led it to act in seemingly capricious ways. Often, it seemed to act with incomprehensible discrimination between candidates whose appointments reached the court.

Another appointment the Supreme Court sought to second-guess was that of Dan Halutz to the position of IDF deputy chief of staff. The issue involved the targeted killing, in July 2002, during the Second Intifada, of Salah Shehade, a senior Hamas commander in the Gaza Strip. Shehade was responsible for a large number of terrorist attacks in which many Israelis had died. An Israeli combat aircraft dropped a large bomb on a residential building in Gaza City, killing not only the targeted man but fourteen Palestinian civilians, among them several children. About 150 Palestinians were injured in the attack. Halutz had been commander of the Israeli Air Force at the time of the operation. In August 2003, while still serving in that capacity, Halutz responded to critics of the operation in an interview with Vered Levi-Barzilay in the newspaper *Ha'aretz*. He was upset—some protestors had gone so far as to spray-paint invective on the cars of pilots. The headline the newspaper gave to the interview was "Bleeding Hearts, Sick of You." Halutz told Levi-Barzilay: "If you still really want to know how I feel when I drop a bomb, I'll tell you—I feel a small tap on the aircraft, as a result of letting the bomb go. A second later it's gone, and that's it." Halutz's sentiments, and choice of words, are undoubtedly troubling, even taking into account his state of mind and his desire to stand behind the pilots who had been involved in the operation and who had not imagined that it would cause such carnage.

In 2004, Minister of Defense Binyamin Ben-Eliezer appointed Halutz to the post of the IDF's deputy chief of staff. It was clear that human rights activists would petition the Supreme Court to void the appointment, after no less than thirty citizens had, just a year before, filed suits asking the court to order the attorney general and chief military advocate general to open a criminal investigation of the operation against Shehade. Those earlier petitions were rejected by the court only five years later, in December 2008.[191] But in 2004, while those petitions were still pending, the same petitioners submitted another petition, demanding that Halutz be suspended until the court ruled on the earlier suits. They added an additional reason for doing so—Halutz's "moral stance," as reflected in the interview with *Ha'aretz*.

The claim apparently impressed the court, which wrote in its opinion: "We queried the counsel for the respondents if it would not be proper, before the court reached a decision on the petition, for the deputy chief of staff's response to be brought before the court . . . regarding the words attributed to him in the press and quoted in the petition . . . We expect to read in this response . . . also the respondent's position regarding the values reflected in those utterances."

It is hardly new for a governmental body to take an interest in the values of civilians and inhabitants, believers and heretics. Communist regimes, for example, were well aware of the danger presented by those who denied its doctrines, a danger that would be all the greater if such people were to find their way into key public positions.

The Israeli Supreme Court shares nothing with Communist regimes. On the contrary, its banner is that of liberal democracy, freedom of speech, and freedom of thought. But history also shows us that there can be a process in which the positions taken by different political theories can meet at their extremes. Oppressive theocracy can adopt features typical of totalitarian regimes and extreme liberalism can also sometimes display frighteningly oppressive tendencies. Indeed, oppression under the guise of liberalism is not an unfamiliar phenomenon.*

In this case the court rejected the petition, after Halutz apologized and offered an explanation.[192] He was thus able to continue to serve as deputy chief of staff and then as chief of staff. But the problematic principle that a politically incorrect remark could prevent a person from being appointed to a public post was not abandoned.

A woman soldier who served in 1995 under the command of Brigadier General Nir Galili accused him of rape. Galili acknowledged physical contact of a sexual nature with the soldier, but claimed that it was consensual, as part of a romance between the two, and that they had not included full sexual relations. Following an investigation by the Military Police, the IDF's advocate general decided not to charge him with rape. The grounds were the difficulty of determining which of the versions of the events in question was correct and the fact that the woman refused to testify in a military court. Galili was brought before a disciplinary panel in 1996, and, after being found guilty of behavior unbecoming an officer, an official censure was entered in his record. The chief military advocate general also recommended delaying his promotion by two years, and the chief of staff accepted this suggestion. More than two years later the chief of staff and minister of defense decided to promote Galili to a higher position and to the rank of major general. The woman who had accused him of rape petitioned the Supreme Court to forbid the promotion.

The opinion in the case, written by Justice Tova Strasberg-Cohen, is heavily tinged with moralistic language, with phrases such as "The IDF's might and fortitude are drawn from two sources: first, its moral fortitude . . . a high moral level in the whole and, specifically, in the relations between commander and subordinate . . . second, its military might." The court recognized that time had passed, nearly three years since Galili's conviction in the disciplinary proceeding, but "the period of time that

---

* I published a critique of this unusual decision in *Yedioth Ahronoth* under the title "Moral Police."

has passed cannot heal the moral blemish that has adhered to the respondent as a result of his unbecoming behavior."

The bottom line was astounding—the Supreme Court ruled that Galili could not be promoted to a higher rank, but that he could assume the higher position that the chief of staff and defense minister wished to appoint him to.[193]

One issue remained open. The court recognized that time had not yet run its course and that, on the face of it, Galili would be eligible to be promoted to the rank of major general at some future point. But the court's decision gives no indication of when that would be—after the passage of two more years, or perhaps in five or ten more years. The question did not arise in practice because, not long after the court handed down its judgment, Galili retired from the army.

The clear impression is that the high court's decision was tantamount to an additional punishment imposed on Galili for immoral behavior. But the Supreme Court is not free to turn itself into a vice squad. And as it is not, in cases like these, a criminal court, it clearly is not empowered to impose sentences of the type it imposed here. The theoretical basis for the ruling was the court's power to judge the reasonableness of decisions made by the chief of staff and defense minister. This basis, questionable in its own right, here turned into an instrument for imposing a more severe punishment on Galili than he had been given in the original proceeding.

In short, the Supreme Court decided that, from a moral point of view, Galili could continue to serve in the position he already held at the rank of brigadier general and advance to a more senior position. But he could not, morally, be awarded a higher rank. This questionable distinction came along with a sense that there were no rules, that the court saw no limits to its discretion, and that it had asserted its authority, completely unnecessarily, over the army's appointments and promotions.

In short, the court appointed itself the nation's pedagogue, and in that capacity it busied itself with the improper language used by public figures. In 2010 it received a petition calling for it to block the appointment of Yair Naveh to the position of the IDF's deputy chief of staff. The claim, based on an investigation published by *Ha'aretz*, was that Naveh had violated the court's rulings regarding targeted killings. The article quoted Naveh as saying: "Don't bother me with the Supreme Court's instructions, I don't know when Supreme Court instructions are issued or when they aren't." Later in the piece he asserted that, in practice, he had worked according to the rules, and the result was that the petition was rejected.[194] But none of the justices was prepared to let his remarks pass. Elyakim Rubinstein wrote that they prompted him to quote from "the deathless words of Ecclesiastes (9:17): 'Words spoken softly by wise men are heeded.'" Salim Joubran took Naveh to task: "We regret that . . . [the] respondent takes the liberty of expressing himself in a way that indicates contempt for the legal system and for the principle of the rule of law."

Naveh's remarks simply did not justify such reactions. It sounds as if the justices view the standing of the court and the principle they term "rule of law" as almost religious values that must be attended to with sacred awe. Bandying them about is sacrilege. Beyond that, I have serious doubts about the force of the court's rules regarding targeted killings. They appeared as an obiter dictum rather than as an integral part of the ruling in question, and they are a manifest example of problematic judicial legislation. I will return to this issue below.

Another case of public appointments involved the choice of a new national police commissioner in February 2007, a short time after I joined Ehud Olmert's cabinet. The minister of internal security's candidate was Inspector (ret.) Yaakov Ganot, who had served in a series of posts in the police and prison service. A few years earlier, Ganot had been commander of a force that tried to rescue two soldiers on the Lebanese border, an operation in which he lost one of his eyes and received a medal. In another case he entered alone a minefield to rescue a Druze citizen of Israel whose legs had been blown off by a mine, for which he was again decorated. He had been an exceptionally successful prison commissioner. As such, he looked like an excellent candidate, both to me and to Minister of Internal Security Avi Dichter.

But then a scandal broke out, regarding a court case in which Ganot had been accused of several offenses, among them bribery and breach of trust. They related to events that took place in 1992–1993, some fifteen years previously. The claim was, in brief, that while serving as deputy commander of the northern district, and later as commander, he had received a number of questionable benefits—among them, renovations to his home for which he either did not pay or paid a bargain price, and a party held in his honor.

Ganot had been acquitted of all these charges in the District Court. The state appealed to the Supreme Court, but the appeal was dismissed by a majority, leaving his acquittal standing.[195] Yet the majority opinion, written by Justice Eliezer Goldberg, had nevertheless criticized Ganot's behavior. It stated that in some cases doubt remained "as to whether they went beyond the bounds of a disciplinary infraction into the area of a criminal offense." Justice Itzhak Zamir concurred. When Ganot was presented as a candidate for police commissioner, Zamir, who had in the meantime retired from the court, launched a campaign against the appointment. He told Israel's national radio station, Kol Yisra'el, that Ganot was a "dishonest man." Immediately thereafter he was quoted on the website Walla under the headline: "Itzhak Zamir: Ganot Is Not Fit to Lead the Police." On another website, attorney Yossi Dar responded with the question: "Are we to accept a situation in which a judge who has completed his work on a specific case later becomes an 'expert witness' regarding the specific defendant who appeared before him, and publicly ascribe character traits to him?"

Ometz, a nonprofit organization, petitioned the Supreme Court to halt the appointment. The chairman of the Commission on Senior Appointments to the Public Service, Jacob Turkel, quickly declared that his commission would not take up the appointment until the Supreme Court rendered its decision. To his credit, Attorney General Mazuz maintained that there were no legal grounds for blocking the appointment and that he was prepared to defend the appointment before the court. But former Justice Zamir continued to speak out against it, now in an interview with Ha'aretz reporter Gidi Weitz. The headline was "Listen, We're Sick," and the bulk of the interview was a fierce attack on Ganot's appointment, which, Zamir claimed, was "an expression of the political leadership's contempt for society's moral standards, integrity, and values of equality and solidarity . . . this is how we encourage corruption."

Beyond the extreme sanctimoniousness and purism exuded by Zamir's declaration, it is hard to understand. Fifteen years had passed since the events for which Ganot was tried—and acquitted—took place. During that time he served in a number of senior and sensitive positions that required honesty and integrity. Not a single claim was made throughout that period that he was not qualified to serve in any of these positions. How long can a man be pursued because of an off-the-cuff remark by a judge?

If the issue is ethical standards, would it not be more correct to look at the broad picture and evaluate in that context the qualities of the candidate—a man who had demonstrated that he was willing to put his life at risk in order to save others, on the battlefield and in a minefield? Zamir likes to use the expression "it is not done" in reference to actions that are not prohibited by law but are nevertheless improper. I never before encountered a case in which a judge who had acquitted a defendant considered it proper to excoriate him in public. Indeed, "it is not done."

But Zamir won. Ganot withdrew his candidacy for police commissioner. He continued to serve in other public capacities, as director general of the Ministry of Transport and of the Ministry of Internal Security (in which capacity he oversaw the police force). In none of these cases did anyone seek to stymie his appointment or to allege that he did not fill these positions well. The state of Israel lost out and paid a heavy price for the fact that Ganot did not serve as police commissioner. Israeli citizens to this day suffer from a high crime rate, and the Israel Police Force is riven by rivalry and scandal. While there is no guarantee that Ganot's appointment would have remedied this, there are reasonable chances that it would have led to some improvements. Moreover, in principle, the government is responsible for the proper functioning of the police force. But how can it be held responsible when it becomes practically impossible to appoint the candidate it considers most qualified to head the police?

The Ganot case demonstrates how the Supreme Court has insinuated itself into public appointments and what damage that has caused. The civil service has a committee, chaired by a retired judge, that is charged with vetting and approving candidates for senior public positions. Presumably the committee thoroughly examines the record of all nominees and considers their successes and failures. I am pretty sure that the committee, on its own, would have approved Ganot's appointment as police commissioner. It was only fitting that they do so, just as they had approved him for other positions. But in fact it no longer operates alone but rather in the shadow of the morals squad that the Supreme Court has become. It is certainly possible that, despite the media attacks against him, the court would not have disqualified Ganot. But the very fact that the court took up the case, one that was likely to last for months and bring with it ever more strident attacks on Ganot in the press, was enough to bring him to withdraw his candidacy. Other qualified candidates, seeing how people like them are raked over the coals when appointed to a public position, must certainly have second and third thoughts about whether they really want to expose themselves and their families to such an experience.

One of the central factors that stripped the government of its ability to govern is that cabinet ministers, individually and collectively, are no longer able to exercise the authority, granted to them by law, to make appointments to positions key to the pursuit of their agendas and policies. That power has in practice been transferred to others, largely to the civil service and the legal system. The cause of this has been the concept of unreasonableness as defined by the Supreme Court. Arguably, it was "unreasonable" to appoint Ganot against the views of former Justice Zamir. It may be "unreasonable" to make an appointment to which the attorney general objects.

It may also be "unreasonable" to appoint a person to a position if a search committee has recommended someone else, as happened in the case of the head of the Tax Authority, discussed below.

True, a small number of top positions in each ministry are classified as "positions of trust" that may be filled by each cabinet minister as he sees fit. The most important of these is director general. But even here the prerogative has been whittled away. A good example is the case of Yossi Beilin, whom Prime Minister Ehud Barak appointed to head the justice portfolio in 1999. Upon entering the ministry, Beilin sought to replace its director general, Nili Arad, and appoint Shlomo Gur. This should have been a routine matter. But the Supreme Court intervened. Arad, who had long served as a senior attorney in the ministry, did not have to lift a finger. The Movement for Quality Government in Israel petitioned the high court to forbid Beilin to dismiss Arad. By the book, the court should not have dismissed the petition in limine—that is, outright—on the grounds that the movement had no standing. True, the revolutionary Supreme Court had established a rule that any person can file a petition in matters of public interest. But even according to the court this rule did not apply to cases in which the person who suffers direct injury is able to petition on her own—which Arad did not do. But that little hurdle did not stop the Supreme Court from issuing a temporary order preventing her removal from office pending a final decision on the case. "The matter now goes to the Supreme Court, where there is not a single justice who is not closely acquainted with the petition's heroine," Nahum Barnea and Shimon Shiffer wrote in *Yedioth Ahronoth*. But the matter was resolved elegantly. Arad was granted a nice promotion, to a judgeship on the National Labor Court,[*] excusing the Supreme Court from having to render a decision and leaving Beilin free to appoint his candidate to the position of director general.

Another justice minister, Yosef Lapid, sought to fill the post of attorney general with an appointment of his choice, but without success. Another illustration is provided by the case of the director of the Tax Authority. The government decided to form a search committee to recommend a candidate to this post. The committee recommended Moshe Asher. However, Minister of Finance Yuval Steinitz, who had a candidate of his own in mind, rejected the recommendation and sought to appoint a new search committee. Asher petitioned the Supreme Court. Steinitz clearly acted in good faith and genuinely believed that his candidate was the best man for the job. Nevertheless, the Supreme Court held that the recommendation of the search committee was "almost decisive" and ordered Steinitz to place Asher's name before the cabinet for approval.[196] At this stage, namely between the court's decision and before that matter was sent to a vote in the cabinet, Steinitz reached a compromise with Asher. Under it, Steinitz's man would serve in the position for a single year, after which Asher would be appointed.

The Supreme Court's ruling, which for all practical purposes forced an appointment against the responsible minister's better judgment, was part of a pattern—the government appoints a committee to examine a particular issue, the cabinet or responsible minister rejects the committee's findings, and then the Supreme Court

---

[*] The appointment was made by the Judicial Selection Committee, headed by the Minister of Justice Beilin.

rules that it is unreasonable not to accept the recommendations. In other words, a recommendation turns into a command, and an opinion into an order. The upshot is that the power of government is taken out of the hands of the ministers and vested in committees. Elected officials are thus stripped of their powers and left unable to implement the policies they were elected to pursue.

Another result is a split between authority and accountability. The cabinet minister remains responsible for the actions of his subordinates in his ministry, but divested of his power to take action. His powers have been transferred to a body accountable neither to the parliament nor the public, and which can seldom be held responsible for its errors.

The ideological basis for removing the power of appointment from the government and its ministers is the assumption, now axiomatic, that corruption has pervaded the political echelon of the executive and legislature to an extent that requires that they be placed under outside oversight and that governing powers be denied them. This piece of conventional wisdom is supported by brazen propaganda that paints Israel as a country in which corruption, notably at the political level, has spread to the point that it endangers the country's future. Anticorruption organizations and figures are seen as public crusaders fighting a holy war to save Israel from destruction. They—the police, the media, the state prosecutor's office, and the judges—are white knights battling the forces of darkness.[197] The fact that public servants and police officers are involved in numerous corruption cases in which no politician is implicated, does not seem to reduce the pressure to transfer power from democratically elected personalities to appointed officials.

III. INTERVENING IN POLICY

The legislative and executive branches of government have always, by common consent, had the power to make policy. The judiciary is not to intervene, for it lacks the means to evaluate the effects and implications of specific foreign, economic, and social policies. Yet in the era of the legal revolution, following Aharon Barak's appointment as chief justice, Israel's Supreme Court has steadily worn down this principle.

The Barak court had no compunctions about addressing economic policy. This was evident in its response to the program put forth by Benjamin Netanyahu in 2003, when he was serving as minister of finance, involving cuts in allowances and payments to the poor. The claim made by the petition filed against Netanyahu was simple: The legislation proposed by Netanyahu would cause harm to the weakest Israelis, whose difficulties were described most touchingly in the petition. Furthermore, the petitioners argued, the cuts constituted a violation of human dignity. The court first issued an order nisi, requiring the government to explain "why standards should not be established for dignified subsistence, as required by Basic Law: Human Dignity and Liberty." The case was then heard by a bench of seven justices, who rejected it by a vote of six to one (the lone justice in the minority being Edmond Levy).[198] In his majority opinion, the head of the bench, Chief Justice Barak, wrote at length about "the state's duty ... not to violate human dignity. . . ." He also ruled that the state was required "to maintain a system that ensures a safety net for those of few resources, so that their material situation not bring them to a position of lacking basic needs." The court rejected the petition on the grounds that "we have not been persuaded that the amendment to the Income Support Law in and of itself . . . violates human dignity." But it also stated that "we know that the economic situation of many families in Israel is very difficult, and that the poor stratum is very wide . . . We do not know whether the situation of any specific person has reached the state of harm to dignity in the legal-constitutional sense of that term. To arrive at such a judicial finding . . . we need a proper factual foundation."

The ruling seems incoherent. The court knows that "the economic situation of many families in Israel is very difficult." Evidence relating to specific cases was presented to it. And yet it refrained from providing a remedy on the problematic grounds of lacking a "proper factual foundation." Once again the court arrogated practically unlimited powers for itself and inserted itself into all issues, including income assurance, but then got cold feet when it came to actually exercising the powers it had assumed. Is the enlargement of income-support payments a constitutional right derived from the interpretation of the concept of human dignity? If so, by how much? Where will the money come from, and what will be the economic consequences? Instead of declaring that the matter is not justiciable in the absence of specific legislation empowering the court to deal with such a subject, the justices preferred to assert that it was, but that they nevertheless could not provide a remedy. It is hardly surprising, then, that their decision was vociferously attacked by the advocates of social equality.

On the other hand, the court has demonstrated its willingness to intervene in questions of resource allocation when it believes that this will not have macroeconomic consequences that will disrupt the national economy. Such was the case, decided in 2014, involving the construction of a *mikveh*, a Jewish ritual bath, in the town of Kfar Vradim, where about 6,000 primarily nonreligious Israelis live. Observant Jewish couples refrain from sexual relations during the woman's period and for a period thereafter, and the woman must purify herself ritually in a *mikveh* before relations can resume. There had never been a *mikveh* in Kfar Vradim, but several religious residents demanded that the local government build one—even though no few ritual bath facilities were available in nearby communities, just a short drive away. The religious families argued that those were not an option for women who need to immerse themselves on the Sabbath or holidays, when the rules of Sabbath observance prevent them from traveling outside the town. The local government established a committee to draft criteria for the construction of public facilities. The committee settled on a list of seemingly reasonable guidelines, among them the number of people expected to use the facility in question and the cost of maintaining it versus the number of users. In accordance with these standards, the committee ranked seventeen different public construction projects the town needed; the *mikveh* came in last. The local government thus decided not to build it for the time being.

The religious families went to court. Haifa District Court Ron Sokol wrote in his decision that no one denied that the petitioners were entitled to freedom of religion and worship. But the question at hand was the allocation of public resources, and on that basis there was no defect in the town council's decision. The petitioners appealed to the Supreme Court, which found it difficult to endorse such a logical decision, consistent as it was with the principle that it was not the courts' job to run the country or local authorities. The Supreme Court decision, written by Justice Uzi

Vogelman, stressed the importance of ritual immersion in Jewish religious practice and ordered Kfar Vradim to make the construction of a *mikveh* its first priority and to build one without delay. The justification for its intervention was that the town council's decision had been unreasonable.[199] But if anything is unreasonable here, it is the Supreme Court's decision, which by using the category of reasonableness reached an entirely unreasonable decision.

The ruling says nothing about the number of religious women who would use the ritual bath. But apparently that was not relevant to the court, whether their number was three, five, or thirty, or perhaps even just a single woman. Another figure notable for its absence is the question of other public construction projects that were likely to be postponed now that the *mikveh* was priority number one. That lacuna is, of course, characteristic of what happens when the Supreme Court takes upon itself to rule on an issue that is none of its business—that is, the allocation of resources to a given need that is brought before the court, without the court bothering to take an interest in where the resources will come from and at the expense of what other uses of those resources. A possible explanation of this pro-religious decision is that the religious and Hasidi parties are often highly critical of the court. The case provided the court with an opportunity to prove its nobility by defending the minority that criticizes it. The decision may also be politically expedient since it indicates to the religious parties that it is in their interest to support the court.

The decision raises a whole list of questions. First, what if, given the topography of Kfar Vradim and its harsh winter weather, it turns out that the proposed *mikveh* will not be accessible to families living in certain parts of the town. Does that mean that the local council must build a second and even third *mikveh* so that every religious woman in town will be supplied with an accessible way of immersing herself?

Second, what about the case in which a religious family moves into a town that has no *mikveh*? Is the local government then, at that very moment, required to make the construction of a *mikveh* its top priority? Finally, what if two or three Muslim or Christian families move into a Jewish town? Do they have the right to demand that the town build them a mosque or a church? Perhaps a church for each denomination? Has the court now created a right to demand that local governments build synagogues, churches, mosques, and ritual baths without any reference to the number of residents who need them? Must these be made top priorities?

IV. INTERVENTION IN DIPLOMACY

In the era of Chief Justice Barak diplomacy came also within the court's reach. One notable example is the court's consideration of arguments regarding the negotiations that Ehud Barak's government conducted with the Palestinians at Taba in January 2001. The talks took place after the fall of the government and Barak's announcement that he would resign and call a special election for prime minister. The conduct of negotiations on such a central issue after the government had lost the confidence of the Knesset was a public scandal of major proportions, and of course had no chance of success. Nevertheless, it was not a legal issue, and a court cognizant of its limitations would have declined to deal with this matter. But in the age of "all is justiciable" that is not the case, especially when the matter at hand is in the headlines.

A number of private individuals filed petitions against the prime minister. The central claim was that "the outgoing government is not empowered to conduct diplomatic negotiations" following its resignation, when it serves in a caretaker capacity.[200] This is a manifestly nonjusticiable claim that should have been dismissed by the court outright, stating succinctly that the matter lay outside its purview. But that is not how things were done in the era of Aharon Barak. The case was heard by an expanded panel of seven justices. In his decision, Chief Justice Barak held forth at length about the principle of the continuity of government and how a resigning prime minister continues to fulfill his duties until the establishment of a new government. He ruled, in the final analysis, that the conduct of negotiations in these exceptional circumstances did not exceed the bounds of the reasonable. In a minority opinion, Justice Turkel asserted that the conduct of such negotiations by a prime minister who had submitted his resignation was not reasonable, and as such the court should order him not to reach agreements with the Palestinian Authority nor any understandings that would tie the hands of the next government.

Aharon Barak preached that "all is justiciable" and that the Supreme Court was empowered to ensure that the government act within the bounds of reason. On these grounds, Turkel was clearly in the right—the conduct of negotiations at this time was entirely unreasonable. But if the subject is not justiciable, then it is not the court's business to take an interest in whether the government was acting reasonably. In other words, Chief Justice Barak ended up with the right decision, but for the wrong reasons. It was Justice Zamir who displayed the most acumen. He wrote in a concurring opinion that he knew of no case in which such a petition had been filed in any other country, because "it is accepted by all that oversight of diplomatic negotiations conducted by an outgoing government, even when there is a claim that the negotiations are unjustified or even unreasonable, lies in the hands of the legislature, or directly with the public, and not with the court." In other words, the issue is not justiciable. Zamir did not say that explicitly, perhaps because the idea that some issues are not justiciable had been rejected by the chief justice and the associate justices were not bold enough to use those words.

In January 2003, at the end of the term of Prime Minister Ariel Sharon's first government, Israel again held elections. This time the country reverted to its traditional system of a single vote for the Knesset, according to a proportional system. At Sharon's initiative, the separate poll for prime minister had been repealed. Likud won the election, and Sharon formed his second government.

Sharon's second term was a dramatic one on the economic front. Benjamin Netanyahu, who had retired from politics following his loss of the 1999 elections, now returned and assumed the position of finance minister. He carried out extensive reforms designed to free up Israel's economy. Among other things, he significantly reduced welfare and transfer payments to citizens, cut taxes, and privatized government companies. As a consequence of these policies the economy grew stronger, but Israel was transformed into a capitalist society in which the gap in income and wages between rich and poor approached that of the United States. Some of the issues the reforms raised reached the Supreme Court (how could they not?) and have already been discussed above.

The most important event on the Israel-Arab front during Sharon's second government was the withdrawal from the Gaza Strip in 2005, called the disengagement plan. This involved the evacuation of all the Israeli settlements in that territory, as well as some others in the northern West Bank. The plan was sharply opposed by many members of Sharon's Likud Party and led to a break between the two. Sharon bolted the party and established a new one, Kadima, which ran in the elections of 2006. Netanyahu returned to the leadership of Likud.

The evacuation of the Gaza Strip was instituted through legislation, which came before the Supreme Court. The issue was, on the face of it, a purely political one entirely vested in the government and the Knesset. Had such a case come before the classic Supreme Court, it would have been dismissed on the grounds that the issue was not justiciable. But now, instead of a brief decision stating that the issue was not in the purview of the court, the case was heard by a bench of eleven justices, who issued a decision of more than 300 pages.[201]

The decision opens dramatically and with no small measure of pathos: "These are difficult times. The nation is divided. The threat of violence hangs over us. The difficult and painful separation of Israeli settlers from regions in which they have lived for many years is about to take place." If one were to read this without knowing where it came from, the assumption would be that it must be a speech on the floor of the Knesset or at a public assembly. Then, hundreds of pages later, the court affirms, by a vote of ten to one, the disengagement law, but ordered higher compensation to be paid to some of the evacuees. Furthermore, the court claimed that this manifestly political decision was not political at all, but rather a "legal dispute." The minority opinion, written by Edmond Levy, states that "the settlement enterprise in Gush Katif [in the Gaza Strip] began more than thirty years ago, when visionaries and pioneers took up the challenge placed before them by the country's leaders and set out to settle tracts of land that were, for the most part, desolate at the time. They built houses, worked the land and turned it into a blooming garden, established enterprises that provided livelihoods not only to themselves but also employment to many of their Arab neighbors."

This and many other passages in Levy's dissent, including those that speak of the state of Israel's right "to demand sovereignty over the territories of the Land of Israel to the west of the Jordan River, including those areas slated for evacuation," sound just like the speeches made at conventions of those political parties that support this position. But Levy, like the justices of the majority, claims that he is writing a purely legal document. "Yes, we are judges and not politicians," he writes, "and our role is not to replace the legislative nor the executive branch." Like the opinions written by the majority, his dissent is full of references to precedents and laws, but they are nothing but veils meant to cover up the true face of his opinion—it is a political document, and the issue it addresses is none of the Supreme Court's business.

The ruling on the Gaza Strip evacuation demonstrates, first, how the concept that "all is justiciable" has blurred the lines between the judiciary and its fellow branches of government, and how the court has intruded itself into the territories of the other estates. It also demonstrates that, when this happens, judges largely tend to rule in accordance with the ideology of the political camp to which they belong. When the classic Supreme Court decided that it was not its job to rule on the question of establishing diplomatic relations with Germany, there was no way of knowing from the ruling whether Justice Yoel Sussman favored or opposed that policy, nor was his political ideology a factor in the ruling. The situation is entirely different when the court takes upon itself to rule on political issues over which the public is divided, even when it does its best to put these in legal guise.

In the end the court dismissed the petition against the disengagement plan. Perhaps some of the justices thought that by mandating higher compensation to some of the evacuees they could prove to the settlers that the court was "balanced" or "objective." Quite naturally, that did not work. Most right-wing Israelis are convinced that the Supreme Court tilts to the left, and that if that were not the case more of its justices would have joined the dissent of Justice Edmond Levy, himself a former member of a right-wing political party.

18

Political Agreements and Prizes

Political compacts, such as coalition agreements, are not justiciable. At least, that's what the classic Supreme Court thought. According to this quite reasonable rule, if, for example, two candidates on a Knesset list made an agreement that one would resign after a certain period so as to allow the second to take his Knesset seat, that pact was not subject to judicial review and would not be enforced by the courts. In other words, if the first Knesset member (MK) subsequently refused to vacate his seat for his colleague, the latter could not seek a judicial remedy.[202] Similarly, if one political party promised to another that it would vote in the Knesset or in the government a certain way and then did not, the other party, which did not receive the support it expected, would not be able to go to court to compel the wayward party to observe the agreement. Nevertheless, the classic Supreme Court also made it clear that a political agreement cannot sanction an illicit act. For example, if a coalition agreement required a cabinet minister to appoint to a public position a person who was disqualified by law from serving in that position, the court would declare the appointment null and void.[203]

Aharon Barak, who systematically did away with all the rules restricting the areas in which the court could intervene, also fought to overturn this tenet. One instance was a case in which Ya'akov Rubin, a candidate for president of the Israel Bar Association in 1985, brought suit against Menachem Berger, who had been elected to that post. Rubin demanded that the Supreme Court void pre-election agreements that Berger and his supporters had made with other persons and slates involved in the campaign.[204] Under the terms of these agreements, the signatories promised to support specific candidates for elective posts in the association. Among these positions were that of president and of the Bar Association's representatives on the Judicial Selection Committee, the statutory body that chooses Israel's judges.

In keeping with the old rules, the Supreme Court dismissed the suit. In its judgment, it pointed out that the compacts reached by the different parties did not apply to the attorneys who were the voting public in the Bar Association elections. Each voter could choose to support whatever candidate she wished. Justice Eliezer Goldberg also noted, briefly, that the agreements did not bind the representatives of the various slates serving in the association's governing bodies. But Barak, who agreed with the ruling, remarked in a concurring opinion that he had doubts about the rule that the two parties to such a pact could not sue each other over it. Deals of this sort were, he argued, gentlemen's agreements. Nevertheless, he asserted, "'a public gentleman' has a duty to honor public law." This obiter was more than a hint that, under certain undefined circumstances, politicians could go to court over a political compact—despite the established rule. Barak, it should be noted, saw nothing wrong with a pact that specified whom the Bar Association would appoint to the Judicial Selection Committee. But he disallowed in theory an agreement under which members of the committee would conclude deals in which members of the committee would agree to support each other's candidates for judgeships. Such a pact, he thought, would be detrimental to the public interest, and on those grounds the court would be duty-bound to invalidate it.

Again, this was an obiter, an aside in an opinion in which Barak accepted the classic court's rule about political agreements. But it served as an indication of where Barak intended to go. Another good question is whether Barak's assertion that deals to secure judicial appointments are invalid is in line with what really happens in the Judicial Selection Committee.

In the Dirty Trick of 1990, Israel's two major parties locked horns in a battle in which each sought to buy supporters in the Knesset who would tip the balance in their favor. To tempt legislators to support them, both large parties promised perquisites and benefits to small parties, wavering MKs, and splinter factions. Unsurprisingly, the matter came before the Supreme Court. The court first heard arguments regarding the financial guarantees that a splinter faction led by Yitzhak Moda'i had demanded from Likud. They were part of an agreement that included provisions aimed at ensuring that the latter would abide by the promises it gave the faction in exchange for its support. This matter ended when the attorney general notified the court that it was his position that the agreement to provide these guarantees was illegal and prohibited. This seems to have accorded with the court's view. In the face of the public uproar that the agreement set off, the two parties to the agreement set it aside.[205]

But the agreement, without the financial guarantees, came before the court anyway. The case gave Justices Menachem Elon and Aaron Barak an extensive platform for debate.[206] Elon opened his opinion by addressing the general issue of justiciability, fiercely attacking Barak's expansive view of this issue. The specific agreement at hand, he said, was not a matter for litigation and was not subject to judicial review. Agreements of this sort were, in the main, subject to the judgment of the public—that is, to public debate and to the decisions made by democratic procedures. In exceptional cases in which the court might be prepared to address such an agreement, the court should not order that the agreement be observed, or issue a restraining order or impose damages for violating it. At most, the court might issue a declaratory judgment. However, if the agreement included an illegal provision, the court could void that provision. In the case at hand, Elon ruled, the provision that required Likud to forgive a monetary debt that the Moda'i faction owed it was illegal. Granting a financial reward as part of a political agreement was unacceptable and thus null and void.

Barak took the opposite position. He ruled, as one might expect, that political agreements were subject to judicial review. He and Elon debated each other over many long pages, most of them filled with statements that were marginal to the issue at hand. But all the justices on the bench agreed about one thing in the ruling they handed down in 1990: Political agreements must be public.[207]

A political deal again came before the court in the form of an agreement between Yitzhak Rabin's Labor Party and Aryeh Deri's Shas. When Rabin won the 1992 election, Shas agreed to support him. Shas's participation in his government was vital for Rabin. Without Shas in the coalition, he would have led a minority government, dependent for its parliamentary majority on the outside support of two Arab parties. Shas's support became even more vital when Rabin signed the Oslo agreements with the PLO, agreements that set off a heated debate in the Israeli public and the Knesset. But in 1993, in the wake of the Supreme Court ruling that required Rabin to dismiss Deri and his Shas colleague Rafael Pinchasi from the cabinet, the party bolted the coalition. A month later, the Supreme Court handed down an opinion, based in part on Basic Law: Freedom of Occupation, permitting the importation of nonkosher meat, which of course angered the religious parties.[208]

In 1994 Rabin tried to tempt Shas back into the government. Shas sensed an opportunity to overturn the nonkosher meat ruling. A coalition agreement was drafted, stating in part that the signatory parties committed themselves to "repairing the violation [of the status quo in religious matters] by means of appropriate legislation." Specifically, the parties agreed to amend the Basic Law: Freedom of Occupation so as to enable the prevention of importation of nonkosher meat.

The Supreme Court was petitioned to invalidate the agreement. The case, *Velner v. Chairman of the Israel Labor Party*, came before a bench of five justices, which rendered its decision in February 1995, at the very end of Meir Shamgar's term as chief justice.[209] Barak, Shamgar's deputy, was slated to replace him half a year later. The majority, composed of Shamgar, Goldberg, and Mishael Cheshin, ruled against the petitioners, with Barak and Theodor Or in the minority.

The minority position is difficult to understand. Why should two political parties not be permitted to agree that a law should be changed, as the majority ruled that they could? Barak wrote in his dissent that he did not "at all question the Knesset's power to pass laws intended to change court rulings," but stated that the agreement "injures that standing of the judicial authority . . . [and] creates a possibility of infringing on the independence of the judicial process and the public's confidence in it." Such prejudice to "fundamental principles," Barak maintained, rendered the Labor-Shas compact invalid.

The dissent can only be understood against the background of the legal revolution that Barak dreamed of, advocated, and preached. That revolution was based on the Basic Law: Human Dignity and Liberty and Basic Law: Freedom of Occupation, both of which had been legislated about three years earlier. The proposed coalition agreement faced Barak with a practical problem that had until then been only theoretical and thus had not demanded his attention. He based his legal revolution on these basic laws, but the laws were subject to revision by the Knesset, which could thus change the constitutional structure that Barak sought to erect. Moreover, the most important law, the one on Human Dignity and Liberty, could be amended by a simple majority. Barak suddenly realized that the foundation of his constitutional theory was built on sand. The apparatus that had granted the Supreme Court huge powers, which allowed it to annul laws, could be snatched away from it by a show of hands in parliament.

In the end, the agreement never became operative (although the Labor government nevertheless amended the basic law so as to make it possible to prevent the import of nonkosher meat). Shas decided in the end not to give Rabin its support and eventually joined Benjamin Netanyahu's first government. In the meantime, the losing parties in the *Velner* case sought to overturn it by petitioning the court to bring the case before a larger panel of justices. But the court dismissed this petition in light of the fact that Shas had in the meantime decided not to join the coalition, thus rendering the issue moot.[210]

Another issue that came before the court was the awarding of prizes by public bodies. Section 33 of the Contracts Law (General Part) states that, in the case of a contract to award a degree or prize according to the decision of one of the sides or a third party, "the decision ... according to the contract is not a subject for litigation in court." But this provision did nothing to cool the Supreme Court's fervor for delving into this issue.

In 1977, Adiso Masala, a member of the Knesset, petitioned the Supreme Court, seeking to void the decision to award the Israel Prize, one of the country's top public honors, to Shmuel Schnitzer, an editor and columnist for *Ma'ariv*. The court ruled in favor of the petitioner and ordered the prize committee to reconsider its decision on the grounds that the committee had not been aware that Schnitzer had been convicted, in a disciplinary proceeding before the Ethics Appeals Board of the Israeli Press Council, for an article of his that had insulted the Ethiopian-Jewish community.[211] When Masala filed his suit, the matter became public and roused the media into a frenzy. The prize committee reconsidered his award but was unable to reach agreement. As a result, Schnitzer did not get the prize.

The incident set a precedent. Ever since, nearly every year when the Israel Prize recipients are announced, someone applies to the Supreme Court to cancel at least one of the awards. This is understandable in view of the fact that, in the course of the legal revolution, the requirement of standing was abolished, so that this kind of petition could be brought by any member of the public against any recipient of the prize. In 2008, when the court had begun to adopt a more moderate approach to the use of its powers, it heard a petition against the award of the Israel Prize to Zeev Sternhell, a senior Hebrew University political scientist. In dismissing the petition, Justice Hanan Melcer declared that the Israel Prizes "are not meant to be the subjects of litigation before this court."[212] Three years later the court was petitioned to deny the Israel Prize to Shimon Mizrahi, an attorney and chairman of the Maccabi Tel Aviv Basketball Club, for his contribution to sports in Israel. Justice Asher Grunis wrote in his opinion that "one could say that, just as Independence Day arrives each year on the fifth of [the Hebrew month of] Iyyar, so a petition will be submitted to this court each year after the Ministry of Education announces the winners of the [Israel] Prize." In this case, the petitioners made a number of charges against the award, among them that a member of the committee that chose the sports prize, Tal Brody, had a conflict of interest because he had played for Maccabi Tel Aviv. The petition was denied. Grunis noted that in a country of Israel's size it is almost inevitable that there would be some connection or other between the members of the prize committees in various fields and the candidates for the prize in those fields. The principal importance of this ruling was that in this case, for the first time, the petitioners were ordered to pay the legal costs incurred by the state and by Mizrahi himself, a sum of NIS 40,000 (about $11,000).[213] This seems to have had an effect. Since then, to the best of my knowledge, there has not been any petition to the Supreme Court seeking to challenge an Israel Prize award. But petitions on other matters by persons and entities without standing continue to flood the court.

19

Interference in Knesset Procedures

The principle of the separation of powers requires the different branches of government to respect each other. It also requires the courts to refrain from overinvolving themselves in the internal procedures of the democratically elected Knesset. But judges who believe they have a monopoly on determining what is just, reasonable, and legal will quite naturally place their own principles above the separation of powers.

The Supreme Court began to interject itself into the Knesset's proceedings at the end of the classic Supreme Court period. In 1981 the court overruled a decision by the Knesset's House Committee, which oversees and sets the parliament's rules and procedures, to suspend Knesset member (MK) Shmuel Flatto-Sharon from parliamentary activity.[214] The reason was that Flatto-Sharon had been convicted in Magistrates Court of conspiring to commit a felony and election bribery and was sentenced to nine months in prison and twenty-seven months' probation. The Supreme Court voided the decision on the grounds that the judgment against Flatto-Sharon was not yet final, as an appeal was pending, and that under the relevant provision of the Basic Law: The Knesset, as it then stood, the House Committee had no power to suspend an MK who was sentenced to less than one year in prison.* It was a rare ruling intervening in a decision of a Knesset committee. But it related to the suspension of an MK and was based on a specific provision in a basic law which, according to the court's interpretation, did not grant the Knesset's committee the power that it purported to exercise. As has happened in other areas, however, when the court addresses extreme instances, its intervention tends to push it down a slippery slope. It begins to take up less critical issues, and the litigation over them disrupts the process of government and blurs the separation of powers. The trend is clear—the court encounters a difficult and exceptional case and seeks justification for intervening. Once the justification is found, the court finds itself receiving petitions regarding much more routine and simpler issues that the court has no business taking up. But, having already crafted a justification for intervening in the work of the Knesset, the court finds itself unable to resist the temptation. Pretty soon "all is justiciable."

---

* The criminal proceedings in Flatto-Sharon's case ended only in 1984, when the Supreme Court affirmed his conviction. Flatto-Sharon was sentenced to three months in prison and fifteen months' probation: CrimA 71/83 Flatto-Sharon v. The State of Israel 38(2) PD 757 [1984] (Isr.).

I have already discussed the Supreme Court's groundbreaking ruling, which pried open the gates of the Knesset to Meir Kahane, the leader of the racist Kach movement, by refusing to disqualify his slate from running in elections. Kahane immediately began making a place for himself in the annals of Israeli jurisprudence. After taking his seat, he filed a petition against Knesset Speaker Shlomo Hillel. Hillel, Kahane charged, had refused to table two private-member bills Kahane had submitted. One of the bills stipulated that only Jews could hold Israeli citizenship, while non-Jews could only have the status of "sojourner," which would grant them only partial rights, conditioned on special duties and restrictions. Kahane's second bill was aimed at preventing assimilation. It mandated the establishment of separate beaches for Jews and Arabs and a prohibition against Jews marrying or having sexual relations with non-Jews. This was the democratic harvest of the Supreme Court's liberal decision to allow Kahane to run for the Knesset.

According to the Knesset bylaws, the speaker had to approve bills before placing them before the plenum. Hillel refused to sign off on Kahane's proposals. A Supreme Court panel headed by Aharon Barak rejected the claim that the subject was not justiciable and that the principle of the separation of powers required the court to refrain from intervening. Barak ruled that Kahane's bills "strike a blow at the fundamental principles of our constitutional regime, bring up horrifying memories, and are liable to do harm to the democratic character of the state of Israel." Despite this, Barak overruled the speaker's decision and asserted that Hillel had to place the two bills before the Knesset.[215]

Hillel did not move quickly to act on the ruling, so Kahane petitioned the court again, asking that the speaker be charged with contempt of court. This time the court dismissed his suit on the grounds that the previous ruling had been declaratory, rather than an order to act. A person could not be held in contempt of court for not carrying out a declaration.[216] The Knesset, for its part, responded by amending the Knesset bylaws to state explicitly that a bill deemed by the speaker to be racist or to deny the existence of Israel as a Jewish state would not be brought to the floor. Following that revision, Hillel refused to approve another bill submitted by Kahane. Kahane again sought remedy from the Supreme Court. He argued that the bylaws could not deny him the right to submit a bill, and that such a change would have to be made through legislation rather than in the bylaws.

This time, Meir Shamgar took the case himself rather than leaving it to Barak. He composed a bench of five justices that also included Deputy Chief Justice Miriam Ben-Porat and Justices Menachem Elon, Dov Levin, and Aharon Barak. Kahane's new petition was dismissed unanimously, halting (for the time being) the radicalization of human rights in Israel. Two of the justices, Elon and Levin, also indicated that they did not accept Barak's previous ruling and declared that, even prior to the amendment of the bylaws, the court should not have intervened in the speaker's decision.[217]

But Kahane did not give up. A year later he petitioned the court again, this time after a long dispute over his swearing-in to the Knesset. In that ceremony he had pledged allegiance to the state of Israel and promised to faithfully carry out his duties to the Knesset. However, at the ceremony he had added to the standard wording of the pledge a verse from the book of Psalms, "I will always obey your Torah, forever and ever." His declaration was accepted at this stage despite some hesitations, but in August 1984, in an interview published in the *New York Times*, Kahane referred to the additional verse in his pledge and stated: "I obey the laws of the Knesset as long as they don't disobey a higher law." Hillel consulted with the attorney general to see whether in making this explicit statement of his intent, Kahane had voided his pledge. At the attorney general's advice, Hillel demanded that Kahane take the pledge again. Kahane repeated the pledge and added the same verse as he did before. Hillel informed him that the addition of these words constituted a qualification of his pledge and were thus unacceptable. If he were unwilling to make the pledge verbatim, without any additions, he could not be seated in the Knesset. Kahane petitioned the Supreme Court, and the case was dismissed by Justices Ben-Porat, Elon, and Eliyahu Winograd (who was serving temporarily on the Supreme Court prior to his appointment as president of the Tel Aviv District Court).[218]

The Kach leader then opened up a new front in his legal war, assailing the Israel Broadcasting Authority (IBA) for refusing to air news reports about him and to quote anything he said that contained incitement or that was opposed to Israel's Declaration of Independence. A panel led by Barak accepted Kahane's suit and, in a judgment of more than fifty pages, ruled that Kahane's views should also be broadcast except in cases in which a pronouncement of his "constitutes a near certainty of disturbing the public order." This directive is far from being clear, as Barak and Justice Gabriel Bach disagreed about whether the IBA was required to broadcast statements of Kahane's that constituted a criminal offense. Bach thought not, whereas Barak maintained that the broadcaster should not necessarily refuse to air such a statement if, in doing so, he did not himself commit a criminal violation. Justice Shoshana Netanyahu concurred in issuing a rule absolute—that is, a ruling that must be carried out—against the IBA, but stated that it was not her intention "to require the respondents to carry out a criminal act."[219]

Following the 1985 amendment to the Basic Law: The Knesset banning parties that incite to racism from participating in the elections, Kahane was not allowed to run again in 1988. This helped dampen voices that supported the doctrines Kahane advocated. But the pace of Supreme Court petitions regarding Knesset proceedings only grew. MK Mohammed Miari, for example, asked the court to reverse a decision by the House Committee and the Knesset plenum to strip him of his parliamentary immunity from search and arrest and to revoke his freedom of movement throughout the country. The Knesset decided to do so after Miari spoke at a memorial rally for the former mayor of Hebron, Fahd Qawasmeh. The Knesset determined that participation in the event was an act of identification with Qawasmeh, as well as the PLO and its chairman, Yasser Arafat. The court ruled in Miari's favor in an opinion supported by three justices—Shamgar, Barak, and Shlomo Levin—against dissents by Ben-Porat and Elon. The justices in the majority held that the Knesset was authorized to strip one of its members of his parliamentary privileges only to prevent or reduce the chance of a future danger, not to discipline a legislator for something he had already done. Ben-Porat, in contrast, maintained that "behavior that expresses support for and bolsters the leadership of a hostile organization that aspires to destroy the state of Israel is not consistent with the fealty that a member of the Knesset owes to the state." She asserted that the House Committee and plenum, concerned about the possibility of Miari's future abuse of his privileges, were within their powers to strip him of them.[220]

The court continued to intervene in Knesset decisions regarding the privileges and immunities of its members. The question arose again in the case of Raphael Pinchasi, a Shas MK and deputy cabinet minister. The result was a saga that shows how a reasonable decision made by the Knesset was overruled by an unreasonable decision of the Supreme Court.

It began when the attorney general submitted a list of charges against Pinchasi, whom he accused of several offences, including fraud and conspiracy to commit a crime. The House Committee held six meetings, each one hours long, and recommended to the plenum that Pinchasi be stripped of his parliamentary immunity. The speaker presented the recommendation to the plenum, Pinchasi spoke for an hour in his defense, and in the end the Knesset voted to remove his immunity. Pinchasi challenged the decision in a petition to the Supreme Court, arguing that he was entitled in any case to substantive immunity—that is, irrevocable immunity against criminal prosecution for acts carried out in the Knesset and pursuant of his duties as an elected official. Beyond this, he argued, the Knesset debate over his case had been flawed. Barak, Shomo Levin, and Dov Levin accepted Pinchasi's claim, with Shamgar and Goldberg dissenting. Barak and the majority reiterated that they exercised "great restraint" in overseeing the Knesset's decisions, but also had the authority "to ensure the rule of law in the legislature."[221]

In the battle between "great restraint" (that is, not intervening) and "to ensure the rule of law in the legislature" (that is, intervene), the second won out. The court ruled that, since the indictment was not brought before the members of the Knesset and as they had not had a chance to study the minutes of the House Committee meetings, their decision was invalid.

The majority opinion in this case brings home the confusion caused when jurists critique the decisions of bodies to which juridical criteria do not apply. When an income tax official makes a determination of what the tax rate that a taxpayer should pay, it makes sense that a judge could examine whether the official had before him all the relevant information he needed to make his decision. When the Knesset decides on an issue within its purview, it is not the Supreme Court's job to ascertain whether all the legislators were proficient in the material relevant to the decision. To take this to an extreme, is it the court's job to determine whether the Knesset members who voted the Basic Law: Human Dignity and Liberty into law were briefed in all the law's details and implications?

Dan Avi-Yitzhak, the attorney who represented Pinchasi in the proceedings, maintained that the court's decision in Pinchasi's favor grew out of the fact that the petition was submitted by a leader of Shas, a party sharply critical of the court. The petition gave the court an opportunity, according to Avi-Yitzhak, to prove that it was a defender of the minorities who constantly vilify it. The court presumably operated on the assumption that the removal of Pinchasi's immunity would simply be reaffirmed in a repeat vote in the Knesset; it did not take into account that Shas had reached agreements with other parties that could change the result. In fact, Avi-Yitznak thought that it was these agreements that prompted Shas to submit the petition in the first place.

It was not long before the absurdity of the decision became apparent. Pinchasi's case returned to a Knesset now angry at the court's unjustified interference in its work. It decided not to withdraw Pinchasi's immunity, a decision that was the product both of the agreements Shas had reached and of the interest of many leg-islators in proving that the Knesset was sovereign to make whatever decisions it chose to. No one petitioned the court against this decision, although it would have been interesting to see how the justices would have addressed such a case. Would they have ruled that it was unreasonable *not* to strip Pinchasi of his immunity, meaning that the decision that the court had previously annulled was really the reasonable one?

However, the affair was not over. The court saw to it that Pinchasi would not have an easy time. Less than two months later it ordered the prime minister to dismiss Pinchasi from his deputy minister's post, as I have recounted above.

Pinchasi continued to serve in the Knesset, as he had been re-elected in 1996, but the new Knesset stripped him of his immunity. He went to the Supreme Court, arguing that once the previous Knesset had refused to do so, the new Knesset had no power to reconsider. The court dismissed this petition in a decision written by Chief Justice Barak.[222] Was this decision consistent with the majority opinion in the previous case, which termed the procedure for removing an MK's immunity "quasi-judicial"? Is a quasi-judicial body that rendered a decision in favor of a person free to reverse its decision? Especially given that there had been no real change in the cir-cumstances but only in the composition of the Knesset and the attitude of a majority of its members toward Shas? In the end, Pinchasi, stripped of his immunity, was tried in Magistrates Court on charges relating to campaign finance, not on charges of having received personal benefit. Following his conviction, he was sentenced to a suspended twelve-month term in prison and fined an amount equivalent to about $5,500.[223]

It is worth noting the timing of the Supreme Court's overruling of the Knesset's initial decision to strip Pinchasi of his immunity. It was the end of 1993, a time when judicial activism was setting one record after another. That was the year in which the Supreme Court began intervening in public appointments (Yossi Ginossar), in the composition of the government (Aryeh Deri and Pinchasi), and now it was interfer-ing in Knesset decisions. Chief Justice Shamgar was party to most of these decisions, even though in the Pinchasi case he tried to halt the court—but found himself in a minority. He was close to the end of his tenure, and it was clear that Barak would become chief justice in less than two years.

The Supreme Court's deep involvement in political issues and in petitions against the Knesset brought in its wake another exceptional development. Members of the Knesset increasingly petitioned the court on manifestly political matters, sometimes against the Knesset itself or against its speaker.

Menachem Mautner, of the Tel Aviv University Law School, examined this phe-nomenon. He found that since the end of the 1970s MKs have petitioned the court against the Knesset hundreds of times. Most of the petitioners belonged to parties of the left or center. His explanation was that, when the left was defeated in the polls and the right came to power, the secular-liberal culture that the left-wing parties championed lost its hegemony, to be replaced by a multicultural Israeli society with a strong religious component. The Supreme Court remained the stronghold of the liberal values that the center and left-wing parties represented. By petitioning the activist court with its secular-liberal leanings, the "former liberal hegemony" sought to preserve some of its power and set the country's agenda.[224]

Such wholesale appeal to the court by legislators is a phenomenon unique to Israel. After all, members of parliament have access to the media and can act in the framework of the legislature itself to pursue their goals. This practice of MKs seeking to impose their political agenda on the body in which they sit via the Supreme Court shows that the court has turned itself into a central arena of political battle, where it most likely has no place.

Another case of removing an MK's immunity arose in May 2003, when the Knesset voted on an economic reform bill submitted by Benjamin Netanyahu, then finance minister in Ariel Sharon's government. The floor debate was long and grueling, with votes being held late into the night. Some of the legislators stepped off the floor for a bit. After one of the votes, one MK claimed that someone had voted in place of an absent member of the coalition. Attorney General Elyakim Rubinstein ordered a police investigation.

One of the Knesset members suspected of voting in place of an absent colleague, Yehiel Hazan, asked his colleagues to remove his immunity. They complied, and Hazan was brought to trial on a charge of forgery with intention of obtaining a thing by deceit under aggravating circumstances, as well as of fraud and breach of trust.[225] He was convicted and sentenced to four months of community service and a two-month suspended prison sentence. Another MK suspected of being involved, Michael Gorlovsky, confessed of his own volition of voting in place of a colleague, Gilad Erdan. The Knesset Ethics Committee suspended him from the plenum and committees for four and a half months. But the attorney general found this insufficient and charged Gorlovsky with offenses similar to those he had filed against Hazan. Gorlovsky, unlike Hazan, did not agree to the removal of his immunity. The House Committee accepted his position and refused to recommend that it be removed.

A petition to the Supreme Court was not long in coming. The case was heard before a panel of seven justices headed by Chief Justice Barak. The question involved the considerations the House Committee was permitted to take into account in deciding whether to recommend the removal of an MK's immunity. One possibility was that the committee's discretion was limited to the question of whether the attorney general had, in drawing up charges against the legislator, acted on the basis of improper motives. Another possibility was that the committee had much broader discretion and could take into account, for example, the severity of the offense and the fact that the MK had already been punished by the Ethics Committee. In other words, in this latter view, the House Committee had the prerogative of considering the reasonableness of the attorney general's discretion. The law laying out the terms of the immunity enjoyed by members of the legislature places no limits on the House Committee. During the classic Supreme Court era, there were, by the way, differing opinions on this matter. The revolutionary court had no doubts. It reached a unanimous decision. Barak wrote the principle opinion, which stated that the House Committee's discretion is limited to examining the propriety of the attorney general's decision and whether it was based, unacceptably, on political considerations. Since no one had argued that that was the case, the court overruled the decision on Gorlovsky and instructed the committee to reconsider the matter.[226]

The justices seem to have assumed that the committee would understand that it was incumbent on it to remove Gorlovsky's immunity. But when the committee took up the matter, its members reacted sharply to the court's interference. One of them, Michael Eitan, like Gorlvosky a member of Likud, declared:

> Today I have come . . . not to defend Gorlovsky but rather the rule of law . . . when the law grants the committee powers, it also grants it discretion. It is not in any way possible for the court to make a decision that turns us into a rubber stamp, that gives us no discretion . . . That is an act of war against the Knesset by the court . . . the court has decided to restrict the House Committee's degrees of freedom . . . by what right? Are we the only ones subject to the law? . . . The court can interpret the law as it wishes . . . without owing any account to anyone, without explanation, and we are expected to be sycophants?

The committee certainly had good reason to believe that its decision had been reasonable and that the attorney general had taken too hard a line. He had not, the members believed, taken into account the circumstances surrounding the incident— the late hour, the marathon of votes, and the cumulative exhaustion these caused. The committee thus rejected the court's position and reaffirmed its position. By a vote of ten against six, it refused to strip Gorlovsky of his immunity. According to his biographer, "Barak was in shock."[227] The court's ruling, which for all intents and purposes stripped a member of the Knesset of his procedural immunity*—that is, his immunity, during his service as an MK, from prosecution for offences which he committed—demonstrated the Supreme Court's arrogance toward the Knesset. The House Committee's decision had been reasonable, certainly no less so than that of the attorney general. The fact that the committee refused to abide by the Supreme Court's decision, and by a decisive majority, is a manifestation of the hostility toward the court that I felt in the Knesset when I was appointed minister of justice. A full-scale clash was avoided this time because the Knesset immediately amended the immunity law, reversing the onus so that the attorney general did not have to ask the Knesset to remove a member's procedural immunity. Instead, an MK who wished to invoke his immunity was now required to take the initiative and ask the Knesset to grant it. The new law also laid out the grounds under which a legislator could ask for immunity. Among these are that the Knesset itself is pursuing proceedings against the MK, and that the nonpursuance of criminal charges "will not seriously impact the public interest." Under the new rules, the attorney general would not have to take the initiative. Instead, Gorlovsky could have asked the Knesset to grant him immunity. But he chose not to avail himself of this option. He was sentenced to two months of community service and a two-month probation.

---

* Procedural immunity is to be distinguished from substantive or material immunity, according to which certain acts committed by an MK in the pursuit of his parliamentary duties, are not considered an offense at all and do not entail civil or criminal liability. This immunity, unlike procedural immunity, is inalienable.

20

The Supreme Court and the Fight against Terror

Israel's battle against terror has compelled its government to take severe measures against its perpetrators. One of the measures used against terrorists is the demolition or sealing of their homes, carried out under the powers granted to the military commanders in the West Bank and Gaza Strip by the Defense (Emergency) Regulations. These were promulgated by the British Mandate in response to the wave of Arab terror of 1936–1939, and were later used by the British in their struggle against the Jewish underground. They remained in force after Israel was established, and Israel used many of them, although not those that allowed the demolition of terrorists' homes. These were now taken out of the drawer to battle terror.

The victims of home demolitions and sealings have petitioned the Supreme Court, most commonly on the grounds that the action punishes not only the terrorist himself but his entire family. The court has often allowed the action to proceed nevertheless. The precedent was set by the Meir Shamgar court,[228] and was applied under Aharon Barak as well. In general, however, the army has restricted itself to destroying only that part of the house in which the terrorist lives, in cases in which he shares a home with close family members. Such was the case, for example, with Musa Abd el-Kader Janimat, a suicide bomber who detonated himself in the Apropo Café in Tel Aviv in March 1997, killing three people and injuring dozens. Janimat lived in the village of Surif, in a building containing several units. He shared his own apartment with his wife and four children. The military commander of the area decided to demolish the terrorist's unit without damaging the adjoining one, where the terrorist's brothers and the rest of his family lived. The decision was affirmed by the Supreme Court over the dissent of Justice Mishael Cheshin, who maintained that the terrorist's widow and children should not be punished for an act committed by their husband and father.[229]

But in other kinds of cases relating to security, the Barak court made drastic changes. In the past the court had refrained from intervening in such cases; it now took a radically different approach. The self-confidence Barak displayed in expanding the court's powers in all areas did not overlook this one. His working assumption was that security was no different from any other subject. The court had the power to exercise its discretion in every field, to examine whether decisions and actions made by the government and military were reasonable, and ostensibly to "balance" security needs with other interests, just as it did in every other area. A notable example of this was the court's decision in the "bargaining chips" case.

In October 1986, during an attack on terrorist targets in Lebanon, an Israel Defense Forces (IDF) combat aircraft suffered a malfunction. Its two crewmembers had no choice but to eject and parachute into Lebanese territory. The pilot, Yishai Aviram, was recovered in a daring rescue operation, but the weapon systems officer, Ron Arad, was captured by members of the Shiite Amal militia, from which Hezbollah had split off following the First Lebanon War. Arad was held by an Amal commander, Mustafa Dirani, who handed him over to a senior Hezbollah commander, Abd al-Karim Obeid, who in turn apparently handed him over to Iranian forces, after which all trace of him was lost. Israel made huge efforts to free him or find out more about his fate, but his disappearance remains an open wound.

As part of the efforts to save Arad, or at least to gain information about him, an elite IDF unit kidnapped a number of Lebanese militants, among them Dirani and Obeid. They were tried, convicted, and sent to prison on charges of belonging to hostile organizations and for their involvement in actions against the IDF and against Israel's ally in southern Lebanon, the South Lebanon Army. After these two men and several others had served out their sentences, Israel continued to hold them under administrative detention, under orders signed by the minister of defense. These orders were extended from time to time with the sanction of the District Court, until an appeal was made to the Supreme Court.

A three-judge panel of the Supreme Court heard the case, under Barak's gavel. The two-to-one decision rejected the appeal and ruled that Israel could continue to keep the abducted men in prison.[230] The justice in the minority was Dalia Dorner. That did not end the matter, however. In her book on the Supreme Court, Nomi Levitsky relates that the international legal community was shocked by the decision when it was issued, and that, according to Dorner, who was in the United States at the time, the case "became the story most talked about in the legal community." Barak, Levitsky said, "was anxious about the magnitude of the criticism" outside Israel.[231] Deputy Chief Justice Shlomo Levin acceded to a request for a further hearing of the case, this time before nine justices. Barak switched sides and wrote an opinion overruling his previous opinion. He rejected the use of prisoners as bargaining chips and ruled that the minister of defense had no authority to order the administrative detention of a person who presented no danger.[232]

The end result was that the court ruled that the IDF had to release prisoners it had captured in its battle against terror. This despite the fact that terror organizations held Israeli prisoners indefinitely, without even providing any information about them. Three justices—Mishael Cheshin, Jacob Kedmi, and Jacob Turkel—remained in the minority. Cheshin noted: "The question that has thus come before us . . . and which will not let us go: is a country required to free the petitioners from prison, can we fight our enemies this way? Are they to hold our people while we will not be permitted to hold theirs?" Turkel wrote: "In my view, on the scales, one on one side and the other on the second, are the dignity and liberty of the detained people, enemy warriors, against the dignity and liberty of our prisoners and missing soldiers. Those who are currently imprisoned and those who will, God forbid, be prisoners in the future."

Cheshin rejected the claim that Israel was using these Hezbollah militants as bargaining chips or hostages, which would have been a violation of international law.

"The petitioners have in practice enlisted in the ranks of the enemy and their depiction [of the prisoners] . . . as hostages and bargaining chips . . . has the effect of coercing language and the truth. I am outraged by this description . . . The petitioners . . . have numbered themselves among the enemy's warriors, and as such they are not 'hostages' and not 'bargaining chips.'" It should be added that, even when a war ends, if one side refuses to engage in a prisoner exchange, the other side will also continue to hold its enemy prisoners until an agreement is reached. It would hardly be conceivable in such a case that these prisoners would be termed hostages. All the more so in the case of Hezbollah terrorists, who do not even have the right to be recognized as prisoners of war.

During a war, each side holds as prisoners the enemy soldiers it has captured and is not required to release them for the duration of the war. Given that the war with the Lebanese terror groups had not come to an end, there was no reason to release the prisoners. But Israel never made the claim that it was holding Hezbollah operatives because they were enemy fighters. The reason—an unjustified one—that Israel did not make this argument seems to have been a fear that if Israel were to claim that the Hezbollah operatives were prisoners of war, it would be necessary to grant them all the rights accorded to prisoners of war under international agreements.

International law has still not come to grips with the war against terror. The law of war as we have it evolved for the most part with regular armies in mind. It needs to be revised and adjusted when applied to groups that do not respect international law and that use civilian populations as human shields. The Supreme Court, having decided to address the subject, could have taken the opportunity to craft the rules in a way that would enable the conduct of this new sort of war in a reasonable way, rather than placing a burden on the fight against terror.

For example, the court could have recognized the concept of illegal fighters—terrorists—who should expect imprisonment as punishment for their offences. The court could also have ruled that there was no obligation to return them, even after they had served out their prison terms, on the grounds that they could be expected again to fight against Israel.

Following this court ruling, that required Israel to release Hezbollah terrorists that presented no danger, the Knesset passed a law on the incarceration of illegal fighters. The law authorized the IDF chief of staff to order the detention of anyone he deems would harm state security upon his release. This comes on top of a presumption that anyone belonging to a force that carries out hostile acts against Israel, or who has taken part in such an activity, is considered to be a person whose release would harm state security, so long as the opposite has not been proved. The law, nicknamed the Dirani and Obeid Law, was passed with difficulty, after jurists warned that it was "illegal" and "unconstitutional." This culture, which flowed from the Supreme Court to the legal community and the media, leads people to make unfounded declarations and raises needless concerns. It prompts lawmakers to add reservations and restrictions to the wording of laws so as to protect them from being nullified by the court. In many cases these qualifications go far beyond what is necessary and make the law unnecessarily complex and unwieldy. In the current case the law passed, and the arguments against it were shown to be baseless. A petition to the Supreme Court asking the law to be voided was dismissed.[233]

This "bargaining chip" decision did not do much for the two central plaintiffs. Following the ruling, Israel freed a group of Lebanese prisoners, but refused to release Dirani and Obeid. The government reiterated its position that letting them go would be detrimental to Israel's security. The two prisoners petitioned the Supreme Court again, but the court denied their suit.[234] However, the two Lebanese men continued to contribute to Israeli law. In 1998 they went to court to demand that they be allowed to meet with representatives of the International Red Cross. A panel of justices headed by Barak ruled in their favor.[235]

Dirani and Obeid were held by Israel until 2004, when Prime Minister Ariel Sharon concluded a controversial prisoner exchange agreement with Hezbollah. Under the agreement, an Israeli citizen held by Hezbollah was freed—Elhanan Tannenbaum, who was lured into a trap set by the terror organization following his involvement in a drug deal. Israel also received the remains of three of its soldiers. In exchange, Israel released 400 Palestinian prisoners and more than 30 other prisoners it held, mostly Lebanese, including Dirani and Obeid.

But the legal saga continued until recently. Mustafa Dirani, who resumed his terror activity, filed a damages claim in Israel from Lebanon regarding the torture he claimed to have been subject to in Israeli prison. According to the reasonable rule in such cases, adopted from English law and observed up until this point, enemy subjects are not permitted to file suit in an Israeli court. But radical liberalism had now flowed from the Supreme to the District Court, where Judge Amiram Binyamini decided to hear the suit. His decision to do so was appealed. Astonishingly, the Supreme Court, by a vote of two (Ayala Procaccia and Salim Jubran) to one (Hanan Melcer), endorsed the District Court's decision.[236] Toward the end of Asher Grunis's tenure as chief justice, after some balance had been restored to the Supreme Court, it held a further hearing and by a slim majority of four justices against three reversed this decision and ruled that the courts should not hear the suit of a terrorist living in a foreign country, so long as his organization was involved in hostilities against Israel.[237]

Another security issue that came before the Supreme Court was the "neighbor procedure" (sometimes called the "advance warning procedure"). This was a practice used by the IDF in operations aimed at capturing terror suspects, and according to the IDF was aimed at preventing the death or injury of innocent civilians. The commander of the force would get a local Palestinian civilian, often a neighbor or relative, to convey a warning to the residents of the house in which the terrorist was suspected of hiding out. The neighbor would inform them that the IDF was about to act and that it was possible that the suspect and people around him would be hurt. The civilian would seek to obtain the suspect's surrender, and if the suspect refused, the other residents of the house would be advised to vacate it prior to the IDF raid. The rules that the IDF drew up for the procedure had been approved by the attorney general, who maintained that they did not violate international law and noted that, during the year and a half that the procedure had been in use, not a single Palestinian had been hurt in the course of or as a result of its use. Nevertheless, the Supreme Court vetoed the procedure.[238]

In short, this was a protocol that saved human life and limb. Yet the court saw fit to outlaw it on the basis of abstract principles, with the help of a radical human rights interpretation of international law.

Another practice that the Supreme Court inserted itself into was that of targeted killings—that is, an attack, generally from the air, meant to kill a dangerous terrorist who could not be apprehended. Such attacks are daily occurrences in the war against terror waged by the United States and its allies in Afghanistan, Pakistan, and Iraq, and no other court in any other country has seen fit to intervene. But, unsurprisingly, the Israeli Supreme Court decided that the issue required its review. In doing so, it also blithely disregarded the fundamental principle that courts do not address abstract policy but rather concrete instances. In this case, the court did not order the practice to be stopped, but Barak saw fit to promulgate rules regarding the circumstances under which it could be used.[239] When the court issues rules about how to act against terrorists, setting a general policy rather than addressing a concrete example, it is quite blatantly legislating. It is yet another example of how the court has assumed legislative powers, making "judicial legislation" no less and perhaps more central than legislation passed by the Knesset.

Following Operation Defensive Shield of 2002, in which Israel responded to the bloody terrorism unleashed by the Second Intifada with a major military incursion into the West Bank, Ariel Sharon's government commenced the construction of a security fence in the West Bank that would protect Israeli citizens. The question of what route the fence would follow was a difficult and complex one. It had to serve its primary security purpose while also separating areas of Israeli habitation, including most of the Israeli settlements in the West Bank, from those where Palestinians lived. It also had to take into account Palestinian interests. The Palestinians fiercely opposed the fence, and said that if it were built it should be built along the Green Line, the boundary separating the state of Israel from the West Bank. The path planned for the fence in the end was long and convoluted. It cut across the terrain, separating Palestinian farmers from their orchards and fields. As a result, many Palestinians filed petitions against it. The Supreme Court, as usual, took upon itself to hear the cases and examine the security aspect of the fence as well. The result was endless delays in the construction of the fence, which has not yet been completed.

Another complication happened on the international level when, in December 2003, the Palestinians succeeded in getting the U.N. General Assembly to ask the International Court of Justice in The Hague to consider the legality of the separation fence. The International Court produced a majority opinion stating that the fence as it stood was inconsistent with international law and thus illegal.

Following the hearing in The Hague, the issue reached the Israeli Supreme Court once again and was this time brought before a panel of nine justices.[240] The court did not dispute the legal analysis offered by the International Court of Justice, but sharply criticized it on the grounds that it had not taken into account all the facts of the case and the security dangers involved. "I read the majority opinion of the International Court of Justice at the Hague," Justice Cheshin wrote, "and, unfortunately, I could not discover those distinguishing marks which turn a document into a legal opinion or a judgment of a court."[241] Barak, for his part, quoted himself from an earlier opinion to the effect that "the military commander is not authorized to order the construction of the separation fence if his reasons are political. The separation fence cannot be motivated by a desire to 'annex' territories in the area to the state of Israel." But, Barak ruled, "if it is necessary for military needs, the military commander is authorized to do so."[242] In a rule absolute, the court required the government to reconsider the path of the barrier around the Israeli settlement of Alfei Menashe, taking into account the needs of the affected Palestinians. True, in this case the court largely accepted the position of the Israeli government, but it nevertheless ruled on the assumption that it and not the elected government was the ultimate authority on security policy.

Even more astonishing has been the court's intervention in military operations while they were still in progress, a phenomenon that has no parallel anywhere else in the world.[243] One instance of this happened in May 2004, during an operation aimed at striking at the terrorist infrastructure and capturing suspected terrorists in Rafah, in the southern Gaza Strip. As part of the operation, the IDF set up a humanitarian center to address problems faced by the civilian population. That did not prevent a humanitarian organization, Physicians for Human Rights, from petitioning to the Supreme Court with an entire range of demands, among them that ambulances be allowed to pass through the combat zone without coordinating with the center, and the restoration of the electricity and water supply to the area. The petition was submitted to the court while the fighting was still underway. The court heard the case the next morning. In his ruling, Chief Justice Barak related that "Colonel Mordechai informed us orally about various matters that arose before us. Sometimes he asked for a little time to find out what was happening in the area of Rafah, while he contacted his men in the area who gave him details, and he passed them on to us."

The army asked that the petition be dismissed on the grounds that "extensive military operations are continuing in the area." But to no avail. During the hearing the army agreed (perhaps because it felt it had no choice) to most of the demands, and it was only on this basis that the petition was dismissed.[244] The Supreme Court was in essence functioning more as an overseer of the fighting forces than as a court.

Another wave of petitions reached the court immediately after Operation Defensive Shield was launched. The only reasonable ruling was given a year before, in January 2002, at the height of the Second Intifada but before this major operation. The most important thing about it is that it is only five lines long. It states: "The weaponry being used by the respondents with the goal of frustrating deadly terrorist attacks is not among the subjects that this court sees cause to intervene in."[245] But the same booklet in which this decision was printed includes no less than ten other decisions, all of them resulting from petitions submitted in the context of Defensive Shield. In each of these cases the IDF was required to explain, justify, and litigate with everyone who wanted to petition against it. It had to bargain and reach compromises with an entire range of petitioners, under the threat of a Supreme Court order. While a court order against the IDF was not issued in any of these cases, it is clear how they were handled. It can be summed up in a sentence from one of the rulings: "It would be best if the parties to the case before us reached an understanding."

Of special interest is the court's involvement in the IDF's actions in Bethlehem during Protective Shield. Israeli forces entered the city, which had been under sole Palestinian governance since the Oslo accords, on April 14, 2002. At that same time, thirty to forty Palestinian militants shot their way into the Church of the Nativity. Dozens of members of the Palestinian Authority security forces joined them, as did civilians unconnected to the militants. A total of some 200 people were thus sheltering in the church, cynically exploiting the sacredness of this site. Because of the sensitivity of the location, the IDF refrained from breaking into the building. But it imposed a siege.

It was just the moment to head for the Supreme Court. As the operation was underway, the office that oversees the compound for the Roman Catholic church, the Custody of the Holy Land, applied to the Supreme Court. The court dismissed the petition, noting that "at this moment the matter is the subject of contacts aimed at reaching an arrangement," and that it was sufficient "for the court not to intervene in a process underway at the height of a [military] operation."[246] But that was not the end of it. The next morning another petition was filed, this time by the Palestinian Authority's governor of Bethlehem, together with Knesset members Ahmad Tibi and Mohammad Barakeh. They demanded that Israel comply with "international law regarding the supply of food to the besieged fugitives." This petition, heard before a new panel of justices, was also dismissed, with Barak declaring: "Clearly, just as 'this Court will take no position regarding the manner in which combat is being conducted,' . . . we will not conduct the negotiations, and will not guide them. Responsibility for this issue rests on the shoulders of the executive branch and those acting on its behalf." Such a statement would be quite reasonable if it were the sum total of the judgment. But a closer reading shows that the IDF was required to explain its actions, and that the court deliberated at length on this subject. The central claim of the petitioners was that civilians and not just fugitives had taken refuge in the church compound and that "the armed Palestinians are preventing these civilians from exiting the compound, and the only way to ensure the provision of food to the civilians is by providing enough food for all who are in the compound." It was obvious that at least some of this food would be appropriated by the militants. According to the ruling the court issued, "[t]his situation troubled us. On April 30, 2002, we held a special session in order to be updated on this issue. We asked how it can be ensured that extra food—beyond the essentials—be provided to the civilians who remain in the compound. We asked whether respondents would be willing to allow civilians to leave the compound, receive extra food, and return to the compound. We received a positive answer." Only after this was the petition denied.[247]

The court thus intervened in a military process, offered operative proposals of its own, and all parties involved understood that if these proposals were not accepted the court would intervene more vigorously. True, in the Rafah case Barak asserted that "clearly this court will not take any position with regard to the conduct of the fighting so long as the lives of soldiers are at risk,"[248] but it seems unlikely that the litigation before the Supreme Court and the negotiations over the measures that need to be taken did not tie the hands of military commanders and did not affect the operation.

In an interview he gave after leaving the court,[249] Justice Turkel responded to the Hebrew version of this book and its claims regarding litigation before the Supreme Court during military operations. Turkel said that such hearings often discomfited him. "I sat in a hearing of precisely that sort," he related:

The claim was that IDF soldiers were blowing up water and electric lines and that some of the population in the region was cut off [from these utilities]. Chief Justice Barak presided over the bench and asked the representative of the State Attorney's Office to find out what was really happening there . . . They said, instead of us conducting a telephone conversation with the commanders in the field, we'll bring in an officer of the IDF's Humanitarian Staff. . . .

The officer in question stood before us and recounted how this business works, and what was being done in the specific case under discussion to solve the problem. He gave instructions from within the courtroom itself . . . I have to say that, deep inside me, I had a very uncomfortable feeling. There we were, sitting in court, and not as one of the military bodies charged with intervening in military operations. I did not say anything, but my feeling of discomfort leads me to agree with Daniel Friedmann's comments, and not only on this subject . . .

In this area, too, the Supreme Court continued its practice of not requiring public petitioners to pay court costs, even when their claims are baseless. In one case, Adalah, the Legal Center for Arab Minority Rights in Israel, asked the court to annul a decision of the military prosecution not to open a criminal investigation of injuries inflicted on civilians and damage to property in the Gaza Strip during military operations in 2004. Chief Justice Dorit Beinisch ruled that "the opening of a criminal investigation is not an automatic process. It must arise from a real suspicion that criminal violations were, indeed, committed."[250] The fact that civilians suffered injury or that their property was damaged during a conflict with a murderous terror organization whose members found shelter among the civilian population "does not constitute, per se, cause for an investigation of a criminal nature."[251] Even though the petition was entirely without foundation, was phrased in the most general terms, and was filed only after a long delay, the court decided not to impose costs on Adalah, "due to the importance of the material with which the petition deals."[252]

The struggle against the Hamas regime in the Gaza Strip in the years 2007–2008 also served as an excuse for the Supreme Court to supervise the supply of electricity and fuel to an area under hostile rule. That is the subject of chapter 29.

21

The Court as Legislator and the Wonders of Interpretation

In a democracy, the task of legislating is assigned to an assembly of representatives. The judge's job is to apply the law to the specific case that is brought before him. If the law is unclear, the judge must interpret it. When the law can be interpreted in several possible ways, the judge must choose one of them. That choice is a quasi-legislative act, in particular if the choice will obligate judges in the future, or if they choose to rule likewise. In Anglo-American jurisprudence, judges have historically had a broad area in which to make rules, in other words to legislate. This has caused some uneasiness and has prompted the crafting of a theory according to which the judge does not legislate but rather only "discovers" and declares the law.

This approach can be found in Israeli jurisprudence of the period prior to the legal revolution. Justice Moshe Etzioni wrote that "[t]he authority to make laws lies solely with the Knesset and not with the court. For my part, I see the role of the judge to be not a law maker but a law declarer."[253] But in those cases in which the judge establishes a new rule, one not observed in the past, he in fact crafts a law and does not only "discover" or "declare" it. The theory of discovery or declaration is, as is well known, a total fiction.

A legal fiction is a lie accepted by common consent. That is, it is an untrue statement that everyone treats as true even though they know it is not. Such fictions have played an important role in legal history. With regard to the legal fiction that the law is "discovered," François de La Rochefoucauld's aphorism that "[h]ypocrisy is a homage that vice pays to virtue" is apt. Judicial virtue consists of applying, not creating, the law. The discovery doctrine is simply an attempt to paper over the fact that this virtue vanishes when a judge exceeds his authority by assuming the power to legislate.

There are rules of judicial restraint that are meant to ensure that the judge will not encroach on the legislature's preserve more than is absolutely necessary. The first of these is that the judge must defer to the legislature and view himself as carrying out its instructions. As Justice Yoel Sussman wrote in the pre-revolutionary era, "In interpreting the word of the legislature, the judge should not give the legislature's pronouncement the meaning he, the judge, wishes, and must not aspire to achieve the purpose he thinks fit. Such interpretation is tantamount to sabotage of the legislative endeavor." Instead, he said, the judge must seek to understand the legislature's purpose and to interpret the law accordingly.[254]

The second rule is that "judicial legislation is always a byproduct of the judicial act. It does not stand on its own." Furthermore, "the judge legislates incidental to his ruling, and only for its purposes."[255] In other words, a judge cannot declare a legal rule simply because she wishes to do so. She can only do so in the context of a dispute that is being heard before her. The legislature, in contrast, is free to take up any subject it sees fit.

The corollary of this rule is that obiter dicta—tangential remarks that a judge includes in a ruling but which are not essential to the decision—do not obligate in future cases and are not taken as legitimate elements of judicial legislation. Justice Sussman went so far as to say that a court has no authority to even voice such subsidiary remarks. "It is neither our job nor our prerogative to make incidental remarks, and the more we refrain from doing so the better."[256] This restraint was cast to the winds by Israel's legal revolution. One of its salient characteristics is long legal rulings that go off on multiple tangents. A prominent example is the famous *Mizrahi Bank* ruling,[257] in which the Supreme Court, basing itself on the Basic Law: Human Dignity and Liberty, declared its power to void laws. The ruling, 340 pages long, is constructed entirely out of obiter dicta that together constitute a tactic in the court's campaign to usurp power and trespass on the legislative realm.

This ruling is just one of many issued by the revolutionary court that cast aside all judicial restraint and invaded legislative territory. Supreme Court rulings of the Aharon Barak era are full of long and detailed incidental remarks that were then taken by other judges to be binding rules. An example I have already addressed in chapter 20, is a ruling on a petition that sought to forbid the Israel Defense Forces (IDF) to carry out targeted killings. Clearly a general suit of this sort, one that did not focus on any specific act, ought not be heard by the court and should have been dismissed out of hand (in limine). Legal scholars and philosophers can debate hypothetical scenarios in articles and books, but the court should not seize the seat of the legislature and declare general rules that it promulgates without reference to a specific case brought before it.

Barak nevertheless wrote a long decision in the case.[258] His final conclusion: "Thus it is decided that it cannot be determined in advance that every targeted killing is prohibited according to customary international law, just as it cannot be determined in advance that every targeted killing is permissible according to customary international law." Each individual action must be examined on its own. The conclusion is correct and should have been obvious according to the rules of judicial restraint, but Barak arrived at it only after pages and pages of discussion, full of legal references on issues that might arise in a host of contexts, none of which were in fact before the court.

This document is formally a court ruling but is in fact a scholarly theoretical legal essay. Barak may well have intended to write a work that could serve not only as guidance for the IDF but also as a beacon to the world beyond Israel in its war against terror. There is certainly a place for such a work, but not in the framework of a court ruling. In contrast, consider a ruling handed down a few years later by Deputy Chief Justice Eliezer Rivlin in *Capital Markets Trustees Association v. State of Israel*.[259] Basing himself on American law, Rivlin ruled that the court should not hear a dispute that at this stage was only hypothetical. He called it the "ripeness rule," stipulating that a court should not consider a case that had not yet reached maturity. Neither should the court address a theoretical issue. In other words, he ruled that such situations are not justiciable. It may be that this ruling, from 2012, indicates that the Supreme Court is now acting more judiciously. Perhaps it is stepping back from the judicial activism of the revolutionary era and its transformation of the Supreme Court into a super-legislature that promulgates rules that it considers desirable, even when such judicial legislation has no basis in the context of the question before the court.

The revolutionary court also deviated from the rule of judicial deference to the legislature. This fundamental rule demands that the judge interpret the text in a way that accords with the intent of the legislators, as it is reflected by the text itself and taking into account what was deliberately not included in the letter of the law. In other words, the judge has little discretion when the text is clear and leaves no room for judicial activism. A characteristic example is the rule that prevailed in the past stating that the courts have no discretion in interpreting a contract whose "language is clear ... and leaves no room for doubt or interpretation," as Justice Haim Cohn wrote.[260]

Barak took the exact opposite approach, arguing that there is no such thing as clear and unambiguous text. Every text contains ambiguities and needs to be construed, although "not all contracts are equally unclear."[261] Barak has crafted an entire theory of interpretation, publishing no less than six books on the subject. Obviously, if all laws and all contracts are unclear, the judge has discretion in each case to choose the interpretation he thinks appropriate. This grants the judge extensive legislative power where he should not properly have it. Barak's doctrine is a notable departure from Cohn's claim that there are clear texts about which the judge has no room for maneuver and which he must apply as written.

The legal revolution, from the time of the Shamgar court, was characterized by "anti-legislature" rulings in which various heuristic techniques enabled the court to achieve the results it wanted without having to grapple seriously with the text of the law as passed by the legislature. A good illustration is the way the process for a further Supreme Court hearing has developed. In Israel, unlike in the United States, the justices of the Supreme Court do not sit as a single bench and hear all cases together. Instead, cases are assigned to panels of justices, most often three in number. This practice opens up the possibility that, following a ruling by such a tribunal, a petitioner may seek to have the issue re-examined by a larger panel of justices. Section 30 of the Courts Law authorizes the Supreme Court to hold a further hearing on "a matter which the Supreme Court has ruled by a panel of three." For decades this very clear rule was understood according to its simple meaning. Justice Sussman put it clearly in his book *Civil Procedure*, which was the bible of Israeli jurisprudence in this field: "If the number of judges was greater than three, there is no further hearing. The same is true when a single Supreme Court justice rules, as in the case of a request of leave to appeal."

This sentence still appears in the most recent edition of the book, edited by Justice Shlomo Levin, published in 1995. The rule was followed for decades, until *Nachmani v. Nachmani* reached the Supreme Court.[262]

The Nachmanis were a childless couple. Ruth Nachmani lost her ability to become pregnant by natural means. She and her husband, Daniel, thus sought to have children by having her egg cells fertilized outside her body and then implanted in the womb of a surrogate. After fertilized eggs were prepared, the couple separated.

Daniel moved in with another woman, who bore him a daughter. Ruth asked the hospital where her fertilized eggs were stored to release them so that she could have them implanted in the womb of a surrogate in the United States. Daniel refused to give his consent.

The case went through the lower courts and eventually came before the Supreme Court, where a panel of five justices was assigned to hear it. A majority of the justices ruled in Daniel's favor, stating that parenthood could not be forced on him against his will. Since the legal issues in play were complex ones, it was heard from the start not by the usual tribunal of three, but by five justices. That was in keeping with long practice—when a case presents difficult questions, it is assigned to a large bench so that the issue can be decided authoritatively without need for a further hearing. That was, in fact, the clear intent of the legislature, in specifying that a further hearing could take place only when the case was heard originally by three justices.

But Ruth Nachmani sought to revise the decision and asked for further hearing before a larger panel. Chief Justice Meir Shamgar agreed. Daniel challenged this decision, and this matter of procedure was itself heard by a panel of eleven justices, headed by the new chief justice, Barak. By a majority of eight to three, the panel endorsed Shamgar's decision to bring the case before a larger panel, even though it had been heard by five justices.[263] What happened here is simply that the court did not like the law that limited its discretion and thus decided to "amend" it so as to allow a further hearing in instances in which the legislator provided that it ought not to be available.

The Nachmani case itself then came before a bench of eleven justices. A majority, in a decision of more than one hundred pages, overruled the determination of the five-judge panel and ruled in Ruth Nachmani's favor.[264]

In the end, Ruth did not have a baby. Her right to use the egg cells was affirmed, but the surrogacy did not succeed. The huge amount of legal energy expended on the case was for naught. But the rule that revoked the legislator's limitation on further hearing remained as a precedent (although to the best of my knowledge it has not been invoked since).

A similar phenomenon was evident in *Apropim Housing and Promotions*,[265] a controversial case which involved the interpretation of contracts. The origin of the case was the efforts of the ministry of housing, then headed by Ariel Sharon, to encourage the construction of apartments for the masses of immigrants who were arriving in Israel from the Soviet Union. Sharon crafted a program under which the government would commit itself to buying apartments from builders who contracted with the ministry. The ministry drafted a uniform framework contract that served as the basis for its agreements with builders.

Apropim was one of the construction companies that contracted with the government to build residential buildings. A dispute arose with regard to the interpretation of one of the sections of the contract. It stated that the price at which the government would buy the apartments in development areas—areas on the Israel's periphery—would be reduced by 5 percent for each month of the contractor's delay in meeting certain obligations under the contract. Apropim completed the construction of its project after a five-week delay. The government informed Apropim that it was deducting 6 percent from the purchase price. The question was whether the government could do so—that is, whether the section in question that imposed a sanction (in fact, a fine) on the contractor for delays in fulfilling his obligations applied to the completion of construction, or only to other delays.

The District Court ruled that the language of the relevant section of the contract was clear and that it obviously did not apply to a delay in the completion of construction, only to other delays. The Supreme Court agreed that this indeed was the meaning of the words of the contract, yet it reached a different result. Justice Barak, writing for the majority, ruled that the purpose of the contract, along with the principle of good faith, required the court to interpret the relevant section "by changing its language so as to achieve its purpose" and thus apply it to a delay in the completion of construction as well. The result ran counter to fundamental rules of contract law, among them the rule that, when there is doubt, a contract should be interpreted against its drafter (in this case, the government), and the rule that a contract should be interpreted wherever possible so as to not impose a penalty on one of the parties.

Another difficulty lay in the rhetoric of the ruling, which gave a feeling that no contract is clear, everything is open, and that any result can be reached through interpretation. The ruling itself contains statements like "no words are 'clear' in and of themselves" and "what seems to be clear may turn out to be unclear in light of circumstances."

The ruling set off a storm in the legal community. It seemed to completely upend all legal certainty. Barak seemed to have turned interpretation into a tool by which he could control everything. It seemed as if there were no way for two parties to draft a contract that would say what they wanted it to say, since in the end the courts could interpret it as they saw fit, even if that interpretation did not accord with the contract's language. The problem with Knesset legislation is similar. If a judge can interpret Knesset language in a way that will grant the law the content he sees fitting, logical, right, or moral, even if it is not consistent with the language of the law, the judge can become a super-legislator.

There are undoubtedly instances in which deviation from literal interpretation is justified, in particular when a literal reading leads to absurd or completely unreasonable result. But the Apropim case created the impression that the wordings of the contract (and by implication also the wordings of a statute) are secondary to what the judge considered just and reasonable.

When the question of contract interpretation arose once more in the Supreme Court, a majority of a panel led by Chief Justice Barak reaffirmed the Apropim rule.[266]

During my tenure as justice minister I pursued a policy of putting more lawyers from the private sector in the courts. After Barak retired in 2006, such a candidate, Yoram Danziger, was chosen by the Judicial Selection Committee. Danziger, who had worked as a private attorney and was highly experienced in contract and commercial law, rejected the Apropim rule in several rulings. "I believe," he wrote, "that despite the rules of interpretation laid down in the Apropim rule . . . it is proper that in a place where the language of an agreement is clear and unambiguous . . . decisive weight should be given to it in construing the agreement.[267]

This time the Knesset decided to intervene. In January 2011 it amended Section 25 of the Contracts Law to say that if the intention of the parties (in the words of the law "an assessment of the thinking of the parties") is evinced "explicitly in the language of the contract, the contract will be interpreted in keeping with its language." Clearly, this amendment was meant to void the Apropim rule and to order the courts to attribute proper and, in many cases, decisive weight to the language the parties had used in their agreement. The amended section is not, however, worded well, and in any event did not prevent two Supreme Court justices, Eliezer Rivlin and Salim Joubran, from declaring that the amendment "is nothing but an adoption of the exegetical method brought into use in the Apropim case, while stressing the significant place of the language of the contract in the interpretive process—a place that . . . in practice it never lost."[268] Such a statement brings home the huge difficulty that Israeli legal culture, as molded by Barak, had with accepting the preeminence of the legislative branch and its authority to change rules established by the courts.

The Knesset certainly did not accept the relegation of the language of contracts to a dark corner. Justice Neal Hendel had no trouble making a clear statement that the legislature's presumption is that words can be clear and that it is the judge's job to implement their clear intent.[269] This approach is based on the fundamental principle that a judge's duty is first of all to read every law in accordance with the legislature's intent, and not to privilege judicial rulings over legislation. But during the legal revolution the Supreme Court used value-based or results-based interpretive methods to turn itself into a central player in the legislative field, thus fundamentally undermining the separation of powers.

22

The Supreme Court Writes a Constitution

The Supreme Court's use of legal interpretation as a source of power has been most forcefully evident in its arrogation of the authority to write a constitution for Israel.

Constitutions derive their unique status from the fact that they are promulgated by bodies specifically authorized to do so, usually as the result of a formal process. The constitution has special authority because it stands superior to regular legislation, and because it is more difficult to amend or repeal a constitution than it is to change or undo regular legislation.*

Israel has no official document enacted by the Knesset or any other authorized body that is labeled "constitution." But after the Knesset passed, in 1992, the Basic Law: Human Dignity and Liberty, Aharon Barak declared a constitutional revolution. An official seal was placed on this three years later in the *Bank Mizrahi* ruling upon Barak's accession to the post of chief justice. In deciding that case, the court included an obiter dictum—that is, a tangential remark not germane to the case before it—asserting that the Basic Law: Human Dignity and Liberty authorized it to declare acts of the Knesset as unconstitutional. That assertion set off a controversy that continues to this day, with Barak's opponents arguing that the court's assertion of this prerogative was fundamentally illegitimate.

"The day a constitution is given is a festive holiday. All know that a figure of authority is promulgating a constitution, here the constitution is to be given, here it is given," Justice Mishael Cheshin wrote in his opinion in the *Mizrahi* case. Former Chief Justice Moshe Landau later said, in reaction to the ruling, that the Israeli constitution is "the only one in the world to be created by judicial fiat."[270] Barak

---

* This refers, of course, to a formal constitution. The term "constitution" or "constitutional law" is sometimes used in a substantive or material sense, referring to the body of laws and traditions that represent the main features of the legal system. Thus, for example, the Law of Return can be regarded as part of Israel's material constitution even though it does not formally enjoy a superior status with regard to other laws and can be changed by ordinary legislation. England has no formal constitution, but it is of course possible to speak of the English constitution in the material sense. By the same token, Israel does not have a formal constitution, but has always had legislation that can be regarded as part of its material constitution. But such legislation does not enjoy a status higher than that of other legislation and cannot provide grounds for invalidating subsequent conflicting legislation.

himself acknowledged that his "constitutional revolution" took place "almost surreptitiously."[271] As Landau argued, "who has ever heard of a country's constitution
being approved 'almost surreptitiously'? A constitutional revolution must take place
openly and consciously. A constitution . . . cannot be passed by means of legislative
grab."[272]

So does Israel really have a constitution? When was it approved, and was there a
formal ceremony that marked its approval or ratification?

Most members of the Twelfth Knesset apparently had no idea that they were carrying out a constitutional revolution when they passed the Basic Law: Human Dignity
and Liberty in 1992. It would be interesting to know how many of them were aware
at the time that the law would grant the Supreme Court the authority to overturn
laws passed by the Knesset. In fact, few of them were present at the time. The Knesset
passed the law by a vote of thirty-two against twenty-one, with one abstention. In
other words, a majority of the members did not even show up to vote. Apparently,
they did not conceive that it was a vote for a sea change in Israeli jurisprudence. As
one of them, Michael Eitan of Likud, declared on the floor of the Knesset, "No one
spoke of it being a revolution, and no one told us that we were carrying out a constitutional change of any sort. There was a vote. A few months later the Israeli public is
notified that a revolution took place . . . the first revolution ever carried out without
public knowledge."

Years later Eitan recounted the Knesset debate that preceded the passage of the
law. He claimed that the word "constitution" was not mentioned at any point. Most
members of the Knesset did not believe that they had the authority to promulgate a
constitution. Only years later did they learn from Barak that that was precisely what
they had done. "It is the first time I hear that a country can get a constitution retroac-
tively," Eitan said while serving as a member of the cabinet in Benjamin Netanyahu's
second government.[273] Aryeh Deri called it a deception.[274]

On the other hand, a number of Knesset members, among them Amnon
Rubinstein, maintain that it was clearly understood that the purpose of the two new
Basic Laws—Human Dignity and Liberty, and Freedom of Occupation—was to
enable judicial review of Knesset legislation. Yet Rubinstein himself points out that
the attempt to "entrench" Basic Law: Human Dignity and Liberty failed in a Knesset
vote. He also recognizes the difficulty inherent in the concept that the Knesset can
bind itself.[275] These points are further discussed below.

In response to the charge of illegitimacy, an argument emerged that the Knesset
actually wears "two hats," being both the legislative branch of the Israeli government
and a constituent assembly as well. In the latter capacity it is authorized to write and
amend a constitution, even if the Knesset had never in its history presumed to craft
a document called a constitution.

This takes us back to 1949, when Israel, a newborn country, held its first elections.
The elections chose a Constituent Assembly that was meant to write a constitution.
But instead of doing so, it decided to change its name to "Knesset" and serve as a legislature. A year later the Knesset resolved, in what was called the *Harari* Resolution,
that Israel's constitution would be constructed not as a single document but stage by
stage, via the passage of a series of basic laws.

The "two hat" theory claims that the Knesset is a legislature, as it has always been,
but one that can turn itself into a constituent assembly. This magical act is a role

reversal that requires no special ceremony or procedure. It does not have to happen on a certain date or at a certain juncture, but can happen any day of the year and any hour of the day. It can also take place several times a day. All that is needed is to attach the magic word "basic" to the name of a law.

Under this theory the Knesset as a constituent assembly can bind the Knesset as a legislature. That leads to another question. Does the Knesset have the power, in its capacity as a constituent assembly, to "entrench" a law by resolving that it can only be amended by a special majority of the Knesset? Suppose the Knesset passes a law providing that this law or basic law cannot be revised or modified except by an act passed by an absolute majority of all members of the Knesset—that is, it requires sixty-one aye votes? I agree with what Justice Cheshin wrote in the *Bank Mizrahi* case, that such an act poses no difficulty. It creates a technical rule, which serves a procedural role. It has the same status as when the Knesset determines for itself what quorum is required for the passage of a law. A legislature can determine, by law or even as part of its bylaws, that no law can be passed unless, say, at least a third of its members participate in the vote. Such a rule does not subvert the fundamental principle that laws must be passed by majority vote. It simply establishes what conditions the majority must meet in order to wield its power.

The problem arises acutely, however, when a present majority seeks to restrict a future majority and to deny it the right to wield its power. Such a move runs counter to the fundamental rule that each Knesset is sovereign. It also violates the fundamental assumption that a constituent assembly is the highest organ and thus operates without restriction. If it is unrestricted, its only restriction is that it cannot restrict itself, and certainly not a constituent assembly that might be elected in the future. If it did so, it would create a restriction that violates the presumption that there is no restriction upon it. Such a restriction can be instituted, in principle, only by a body or institution that stands above the Constituent Assembly. But no body stands above the Knesset in its capacity as Israel's Constituent Assembly. The "two hat" theory, which is today the only extant constitutional theory in Israel, maintains that the Knesset, acting as Constituent Assembly, stands above the Knesset in its capacity as a legislature. But the Knesset as Constituent Assembly does not stand above itself when it resolves to resume its role as a Constituent Assembly.

Can the Knesset, for example, decide that, in the future, it may enact a basic law only by a majority of sixty-five or seventy votes? Such a rule would be of profound significance. Can the Constituent Assembly bind not only itself but also the majority of every future Knesset, no matter what the circumstances? And what majority is needed to institute such a restriction? Can the Constituent Assembly decide by any majority, even a two to one vote, that a given law can only be amended in the future by a majority of seventy or eighty members of the Knesset or perhaps only if all 120 members of the Knesset agree? Even the supporters of the theory that the Knesset can turn itself into a Constituent Assembly concede that there is no satisfactory answer to these difficulties.[276]

The Basic Law: Jerusalem, the Capital of Israel was passed in 1980 while Menachem Begin was prime minister. It included no entrenching provision and could be revised or repealed by a simple majority vote. In 2000 a provision was added forbidding any change in the city's boundaries and the transfer to any foreign political or governmental power any authority with regard to the territory of Jerusalem. These provisions, and only they, are entrenched—they can be changed only by the vote of sixty-one members of the Knesset. Now presume that a regular majority of the Knesset believes that this safeguard is insufficient and needs to be made stronger. According to the flawed theory that the Knesset, in its capacity as a Constituent Assembly, can restrict itself in the future, a chance majority can resolve that Israel cannot give up any territory at all except by a vote of 70 or 100 or even all 120 members of the Knesset. Such a result is clearly unacceptable.

I see no problem with determining that certain laws are called basic laws. Nor do I see a difficulty deciding on a restriction that requires a majority of sixty-one to amend or repeal them. But requiring a majority of greater than sixty-one raises a problem of principle. The "two hats" theory offers no solution. This subject has not been addressed in a systematic way, and the opening it leaves raises doubts about the nature of the constitution that Israel may or may not have.

Amazingly, Basic Law: Human Dignity and Liberty is not entrenched at all. That is, it does not state that it can be changed only by a vote of sixty-one of the Knesset. As a matter of fact, such a provision was proposed but failed to win a majority. It is thus uncontroversial that it can be revoked or amended by a simple majority, even of two against one. In the pre-revolutionary era, the Supreme Court ruled that subsequent laws take precedence over earlier laws, including non-entrenched basic laws.[277] In contrast, the activist Supreme Court treated the new basic laws that the Knesset passed in 1992, even though they are not entrenched, as standing above regular laws. In other words, the *Bank Mizrahi* decision negated the previous rule by which subsequent ordinary laws take precedence over previous basic laws, at least when these basic laws are not entrenched. This reversal of an important rule was not unique. The revolutionary court struck down, one after another, rules established in the previous era and which had been regarded as fundamental principles of the Israeli legal system.

The Israeli Supreme Court's invention of a constitution for the state of Israel was without precedent. Barak compared it to the famous U.S. Supreme Court decision *Marbury v. Madison*.[278] But this comparison is inapt. In the *Marbury* decision, Chief Justice John Marshall ruled that the U.S. Constitution grants the courts the power to review legislation and to annul laws that are inconsistent with it. But the Basic Law: Human Dignity and Liberty is entirely unlike the U.S. Constitution. Chief Justice Landau noted correctly that the *Marbury* rule was established "on the basis of a rigid constitution serving as the country's supreme law . . . whereas in Israel no such law exists. Rather, it is all a legal construction of the court itself, including the idea of judicial superiority."[279]

Judge Richard Posner also rejected any similarity between *Marbury* and what happened in Israel. The U.S. Constitution states clearly that it is a constitution, and it clearly serves as the supreme law of the United States of America.[280] In contrast, Basic Law: Human Dignity and Liberty can be revoked or modified by a simple majority— it requires nothing more than that. All that is required is that the revoking law itself be termed a basic law. If so, what sort of constitution is it? The question why this has not been done to date will be addressed in chapter 36.

Yet, despite this, the court was able to persuade itself that Israel has a constitution. As a result, even though the word "constitution" does not appear in any legislation passed by the Knesset, the expressions "constitutional" and "unconstitutional" appear countless times in Supreme Court decisions, as if it were clear to all that Israel in fact has promulgated a formal constitution. This assumption has made its way into the parlance of the legal community. Attorneys, jurists, law students, and even the public at large speak of the "constitutionality" of legislation and jurists frequently advise Knesset members to refrain from introducing one piece of legislation or another on the grounds that it is "unconstitutional."

Another question is what human rights are in fact protected by Basic Law: Human Dignity and Liberty. The law lists a number of protected values—life, body, and the personal freedom and dignity of all persons, as well as a person's right to his or her property, privacy, and intimacy. Further rights, relating to work, are protected by Basic Law: Freedom of Occupation. However, a long list of rights which are generally considered fundamental, and which in other countries are constitutional rights, are not mentioned in these two laws. Among these are the right to equality, freedom of speech, marriage, fair trial, and the right to be safe from retroactive punishment, from vaguely worded criminal charges, and self-incrimination. At least with regard to some of these rights, such as equality and freedom of marriage, it is clear that the omission was deliberate, so as to obtain the consent of the religious parties. Had they been included, the law would almost certainly not have passed. Judges must interpret the law consistently with the intent of the legislature, not according to what they think the legislature should have done. As Chief Justice Landau so colorfully put it, one cannot push rights "through the window" that "the basic law itself sent out through the door."[281]

The Supreme Court simply disregarded this fundamental principle. Convinced that it had managed to legislate a constitution, it also decided to determine its contents. The technique was a simple one—the two words "human dignity" can contain pretty much everything the court wants. They can be read to include freedom of speech and the right to equality.

One can certainly imagine situations in which discrimination infringes on a person's dignity. One example is when an applicant for a job or membership in an organization is rejected because of the color of his skin. But the Supreme Court's notion that the right to equality as contained within the term "human dignity" has gone way beyond what the members of the Knesset who passed the law ever imagined. For example, it is very difficult to find in the law any basis for the court's decision to invalidate the Tal law, discussed in chapter 9, which in practice enabled many *yeshiva* students to avoid mandatory military service. (To be precise, the court did not explicitly invalidate the law but forbade its extension.[282]) The inequality of Israel's military induction system is outrageous, but it is difficult to see how the Tal law, even though it enshrined inequality, infringed on the dignity of Israel Defense Forces soldiers. By the same token, it is hard to see any harm to human dignity in the fact that men serve a longer term of mandatory service than women do, or in the fact that religious women may choose not to serve in the army whereas nonreligious women have no such option. On the contrary, it is clear that the legislators intended to preserve such distinctions and inequalities when they refrained—not by chance or oversight—from including the right to equality in the basic law.

By the same method we learned that human dignity forbids the establishment of privately run prisons.[283] Prisons in Israel are overcrowded, and living conditions inside them are deplorable. There is thus a prospect that privately run prisons could improve prisoners' quality of life (would prisoners themselves refuse to serve their terms in a private prison if they were given the choice?). The issue of privately run prisons is a broad one and has many aspects which cannot be discussed here. Some argue that maintaining prisons is a uniquely state function that should not be delegated. This reasoning may well have laid behind the majority decision in the private prisons case. Yet it is doubtful whether such a position can be packed into the words "human dignity." In contrast, the Supreme Court recognized the power of the attorney general to authorize private attorneys who are not public employees to serve as prosecutors in criminal cases.[284] The appointment of such a "private" prosecutor in a criminal trial is a much more momentous innovation than a private prison. Prosecutors decide who to indict and when to seek an indictment, whether to take a case to trial or drop it, and what sentence, including a prison sentence, to ask for. In contrast, a private prison is simply a means of implementation of a prison sentence handed down by a court outside its own walls. Can a person, jurist or not, conclude from the words "human dignity" that they forbid private prisons but allow private prosecutors? The words of the poet T. S. Eliot in his poem *Burnt Norton* are apt: "Words strain/Crack and sometimes break, under the burden."

The only possible conclusion is that the Supreme Court has been writing a constitution. The words "human dignity" have served as the platform from which it has launched that effort. The connection between these words and what the court calls a constitution is an invention of the Supreme Court itself.

Another example is the court's decision regarding the compensation awarded the Israeli settlers who were evacuated from the Gaza Strip. The Disengagement Plan Implementation Law, passed by the Knesset in 2005, provided for an "individual grant" as compensation for the suffering and agony caused by the evacuation. The sum was determined in accordance with the number of years each person twenty-one years of age or more had lived there. This minimum age came before the Supreme Court, and the court invalidated the condition. A reading of the judgment shows that the court maintained that the provision was unreasonable. "It is difficult to understand why the legislature chose the age of twenty-one," the opinion states. Awarding compensation in this way is unfair, the court found, and, without actually making a ruling, the court opined that this condition violated the principle of equality.[285] The fact that equality is not mentioned—deliberately so—in Basic Law: Human Dignity and Liberty was no obstacle to the court's determination that it fell under the rubric of human dignity.

Another decision relating to the ambit of "human dignity" was handed down at the very end of Chief Justice Barak's tenure. This time the issue was one of survival. The Citizenship and Entry into Israel Law (Temporary Order) denied the right of residence and citizenship in Israel to Palestinians from the West Bank and Gaza Strip who married Israeli citizens. Such cases generally involved a Palestinian from the territories marrying an Arab citizen of Israel. The law allowed certain exceptions— for example, the interior minister was empowered to grant permits to reside in Israel to Palestinian men from the territories over the age of thirty-five and Palestinian women over the age of twenty-five. The law was classified as a temporary order, which could be extended periodically. It was enacted in the wake of the Second Intifada, during which it transpired that a number of Palestinians from the territories who were residing in Israel had abetted terrorist attacks in which fifty Israelis had been killed and more than a hundred wounded. The law was challenged before the Supreme Court, which rendered its decision in May 2006. The court split six to five, with Barak in the minority.[286] The court grappled first with the question of whether the rights in question were in fact "constitutional" rights. The petitioners argued that they had a right to family life and that they were being denied equality. If an Israeli citizen married a person from, say, Europe or the United States, the couple could live in Israel freely, whereas if the spouse was from the West Bank or Gaza Strip the couple was treated differently. But neither the right to family life nor the right to equality are mentioned in Basic Law: Human Dignity and Liberty, and their omission is not coincidental. They were deliberately left out because otherwise the law could not have been passed. The large parties, aware that they depended on the support of the religious parties to form governments, were unwilling to pass the law without the consent and cooperation of the religious factions, while the religious parties refused to agree to any provision that might breach the rabbinic courts' monopoly over marriage and divorce. The rabbinic courts operated according to Jewish religious law, which does not recognize a right to equality.

However, that did not stop Barak from declaring that the concept of "human dignity" guaranteed by the basic law includes the rights to equality and family life. He acknowledged the security risk involved when Palestinians from the territories settled in Israel through marriage to Israelis, but declared that this did not justify a blanket ban against all such spouses. Rather, each case should be examined on an individual basis, to evaluate the level of risk, and that should be the basis for a decision to allow or prohibit the spouse from joining his or her Israeli partner. Mishael Cheshin, for his part, maintained that the right to family life is not a constitutional right. He related what had happened in the Intifada, when

> [t]ens of thousands of terror attacks originating in the territories have struck children, the elderly, women and men indiscriminately and mercilessly . . . The economy of the State of Israel has been seriously undermined. . . . Many citizens have become fearful of everyday occurrences, such as travelling on buses, visiting shopping malls and eating out in restaurants.[287]

According to Cheshin, the law was thus justified for security reasons.

Barak did all he could to enlist a majority behind him, but without success. Cheshin's majority opinion was issued after he had already retired from the bench, and by the end of that year Barak had already retired as well.* Both justices were clearly involved in the case emotionally and not just intellectually. On May 16, 2006, a few days following the decision, Yuval Yoaz, a journalist at Ha'aretz, reported that Barak had written to a colleague at Yale that he had lost on a technicality, but that fundamentally a majority of the justices endorsed his position. According to Yoaz, "Justice Barak's estimation is that if the Knesset votes to extend the amendment to the Citizenship Law in its current form, the Supreme Court will invalidate it." Barak believed this to be the case because Justice Edmond Levy, who had voted against Barak's position, had stated in his opinion that in the end the legislature would have

---

* Cheshin's opinion was rendered in accordance with an Israeli law that authorizes a judge who has retired to issue judgments during the three months following his retirement, in cases in which the hearing was completed during his tenure.

to replace the blanket prohibition with a case-by-case procedure. Otherwise, Levy wrote, it was doubtful "whether the law will continue to be able to pass judicial review in the future as well."

Yoaz explained to his readers that "Barak and jurists at Yale . . . have a longstanding professional connection. Each year Barak spends his annual vacation at the Yale campus, during which time he teaches legal seminars." This raises a question regarding the reference group to which Israel's chief justice was looking—is it the Israeli public, which was facing a wave of bloody terror and a danger to its very existence, or the liberal professors living securely in Connecticut? Cheshin spoke about the decision in an interview with *Ha'aretz*. "Justice Barak," he asserted, "is ready for thirty to fifty people to be blown up as long as there are human rights. I do not agree. He think one way, I think another. I'm happy that I was in the majority." A few days later Cheshin apologized to Barak in the same newspaper.

The background to this litigation was a threat to Israel's security, but it is also important to consider the demographic issue. The fact that Israel is a Jewish state and the national home of the Jewish people is not a reason to deny citizenship or residency to the non-Jewish spouse of an Israeli. The problem arises when the spouse in question belongs to a society hostile to Israel. When an Israeli, whether Jewish or Arab, marries a Norwegian, Briton, or German, that spouse clearly has the right to live in Israel. None of those countries of origin seeks to destroy Israel or overrun it. The situation is different when the spouse is a Palestinian noncitizen. Many Palestinians believe that Israel is an illegal country, born in injustice and devoid of any right to exist. Notably, in the elections held in the West Bank and Gaza Strip in 2006, Hamas, a party that denies Israel's right to exist, won a majority. Since then, Hamas has only grown stronger. No country is bound to allow the massive entry into its borders of a hostile population, not even by way of marriage. On top of that, when such marriages take place, the couple nearly always, almost without exception, chooses to live in Israel. The Palestinian demand for a right of return to the places their families once lived in what is now Israel presents an existential danger to Israel, and the fact that the Supreme Court might facilitate the realization of this right via marriage does not make the danger less grave. True, in his opinion Barak noted that "human rights are not a recipe for national annihilation," but the practical consequence of his position, had it been accepted, would have been just that.

Notably, however, the attorney general did not make this demographic argument before the Supreme Court. We can't know what his reasons were for this omission, but it is important to note, here as well, how Supreme Court judgments have changed the nature of the position of attorney general. Recall that the Supreme Court also ruled that the attorney general actually controls the government from the legal point of view. He can refuse to defend the government's position before the court if he believes it unconstitutional, and he may decline to raise a particular argument in court even if there are reasonable prospects that it would be accepted, in particular if he identifies with the approach of the radical faction of the Supreme Court's justices.

The issue of marriages with residents of the territories arose again toward the end of the tenure of Chief Justice Dorit Beinisch, but Barak's prediction proved wrong. The court once again decided, by a six-to-five vote, not to invalidate the law.[288] It has been extended a number of times since then and remains in force to date. Beinisch, too, found herself in the minority.

23

Appointments to the Supreme Court

Aharon Barak was appointed chief justice three months after the assassination of Prime Minister Yitzhak Rabin. His term came to an end a few months after Ehud Olmert formed his government. Upon his retirement, Barak, who had been appointed to the Supreme Court at the age of forty-two, had served on the court for twenty-eight years, the longest term served by any justice in the Supreme Court's second era (in the previous era, Moshe Landau served for a bit longer, nearly thirty years).

Another fact that stands out regarding the young age at which Barak joined the court is that when, by virtue of seniority, he acceded to the chief justice's chair, he was still—after serving on the court for seventeen years—the youngest justice on the bench. This enabled him not only to wield decisive influence over the choice of a large number of Supreme Court justices but also to determine, in accordance with the tradition of seniority by which chief justices are chosen, who would succeed him.

The classic Supreme Court was notably stable in its composition. Many justices, among them Shimon Agranat, Yoel Sussman, Moshe Landau, Zvi Berinson, Alfred Witkon, and Haim Cohn, served for twenty years or more. The court during the Barak area saw rapid changes in the composition of the bench, while only a relatively small number of judges served on the court for a considerable period. Just one justice, Shlomo Levin, served for more than twenty years, from 1980 to 2003. A few others—Dov Levin, Gabriel Bach, Eliezer Goldberg, and Theodor Or—served for about fifteen years. All of them retired during Barak's tenure as chief justice.

When Barak was appointed chief justice there were thirteen judges on the bench. Less than a decade later only two of these remained, Eliahu Mazza and Mishael Cheshin. All others who served from 2004 onward were appointed largely at Barak's urging.

The post of deputy chief justice, to which Supreme Court justices are also appointed by seniority, is also worth noting. When Barak rose to be chief justice, Shlomo Levin took the deputy post. Levin was succeeded by Or, who was followed by Mazza and then Cheshin. In other words, four justices held this post under a single chief justice. All of them retired before Barak did.

Length of service on the Supreme Court is of great significance, as a judge acquires influence not only by virtue of his talents and ability but also because of his experience. Barak's period is notable not only for the relatively small number of senior justices but also for the fact that most of the justices who opposed his far-reaching activist approach and his doctrine that "all is justiciable" had retired before Barak became chief justice. Among these were Meir Shamgar, Miriam Ben-Porat, and Menachem Elon.

Barak became something of a super–chief justice, with power far greater than that wielded by any of his predecessors. This was due not only to his seniority, his personal abilities, and his control of the appointment process but also from the lack of any significant force that opposed him. He was thus able to impose his ideology on the court and to dictate his positions almost without opposition. True, a small number of justices took stances different from his on security and other issues, among them Shlomo Levin, Mishael Cheshin, and Jacob Turkel. But when they disagreed with Barak, they almost always found themselves in the minority.

Paradoxically, the only justice who was able to convince Barak to change his position was Dalia Dorner, the court's most radical member on human rights issues. Like other extremists on human rights, she almost completely disregarded the injury done to one group by the grant of disproportionate rights to another group. Barak seems to have been unable to accept a situation in which another justice emerged as more of a champion of human rights than he was. A good example is the way Barak was swept up in Dorner's wake on the issue of the Hezbollah prisoners in Lebanon.

The two first appointments of the Barak era were Jacob Turkel and Dorit Beinisch, which came just three months after his accession to the post of chief justice. The appointments were approved by the Judicial Selection Committee on November 13, 1995, immediately following the week of mourning for Prime Minister Yitzhak Rabin. Rabin's assassination left a caretaker government (a term that does not appear in Israeli law but which is nevertheless used to describe this situation). Barak seems to have been able to exercise his prestige to persuade Justice Minister David Libai to call a meeting of the Judicial Selection Committee despite the exceptional circumstances. Perhaps he stressed to Libai the importance of the continuity of government, or perhaps he made other arguments. Whatever the case, it leaves open the question of what the rush was.

Beinisch won many supporters in the State Attorney's Office during her tenure there, but she had opponents as well. As she made her way up the ladder to the top of the office, there she often found such an opponent seeking to block her promotion, but, luckily for her, the obstacles never ended up stopping her advancement. She served as deputy state attorney, under Yona Blatman, during the tenure of the national unity government in the 1980s. Blatman was slated to retire in 1988, at a time when the minister of justice was Avraham Sharir, an advocate of a tough approach to terrorists. Sharir's candidate to replace Blatman was Plia Albeck. But elections were held that November, after which Yitzhak Shamir formed a new government in which Sharir did not serve. The new justice minister was Dan Meridor, who was one of Beinisch's most enthusiastic admirers.[289] Beinisch got the job in early 1989.

By 1994, Beinisch's name was submitted to the Judicial Selection Committee as a candidate for appointment to the Supreme Court. Chief Justice Shamgar, who was then approaching retirement, decided at the last moment to oppose her nomination when the committee voted. He never explained why. The committee voted instead to seat Tova Strasberg-Cohen. Itzhak Zamir, a close friend of Barak's, was also appointed in that year.

Shamgar continued to oppose Beinisch's appointment as long as he served as chief justice. But once he reached the mandatory retirement age of seventy, Shamgar could not prevent Barak from nominating her. What Shamgar could have done while still in office, however, was to ensure that Beinisch would not be Barak's successor as chief justice when Barak himself had to retire. When Beinisch took her seat on the bench, she became the youngest justice then serving and thus the one who would accrue the most seniority by the time Barak's tenure came to an end. Under the traditional seniority system, this meant that she would become chief justice. In securing her appointment, Barak was thus naming his heir apparent. Shamgar could have prevented this eventuality by ensuring the appointment of a younger justice before he left the court. He failed to do so.

In the period following Rabin's assassination, the country's political leadership was in no less a state of shock than the public at large, and this at a time when the country faced difficult challenges. This atmosphere no doubt made it easier for Barak to push through such a controversial appointment. True, Beinisch's candidacy won considerable support, but she was hardly a consensus candidate. Rabin, notably, had not been a fan of hers. Some of her opponents may well have recalled her opposition to the deportation of the Hamas activists to Lebanon and to the pardon granted to the Shin Bet operatives involved in the Bus 300 incident. In both those cases she had stood against the united position of the political leadership, including that of Shimon Peres, who served after the assassination as acting prime minister and was the obvious candidate to form a new government. But in the upheaval of that time her appointment sailed through with relative ease. Later Beinisch would become the chief advocate of prohibiting the appointment of judges in such transitional periods, despite the fact that she herself had benefited from just such an appointment. Here is an example of how the law is manipulated, in the name of the rule of law, by those who decide what the law means.

In 1996, a year after Barak became chief justice, it looked as if he would face a difficult time appointing justices to his liking. Benjamin Netanyahu was elected prime minister, and his choice for minister of justice was Yaakov Neeman, a fierce opponent of judicial activism and a man with firm ideas about what direction the justice system needed to go and what kind of judges it needed. One member of the Judicial Appointments Committee was Dror Hoter-Yishai, president of the Israel Bar Association and another ardent opponent of Barak's approach. But everything soon worked out in Barak's favor, thanks to the criminal code. Both these members of the committee were forced out of their posts when trumped-up criminal charges were filed against them—a story I will tell below. Barak regained control of the committee.

The next appointment, in 1997, was Izhak Englard, a law professor at the Hebrew University, another close friend of Barak's. My colleague at the Tel Aviv University law school, Menachem Mautner, has pointed out that there was no better indication of the Barak court's monolithic nature than the fact that both the chief justice's co-authors of a seminal work on torts, Cheshin and Englard, served with him.[290] In fact, on numerous issues Cheshin adopted a position opposite to that of Barak, but he nevertheless came from the same cultural and intellectual environment. Englard was sixty-four years old when he was appointed, and retired while the younger Barak was still in office.

Three years after England's appointment, Eliezer Rivlin gained a seat on the Supreme Court. Two more appointments, made in 2001, attracted special attention because the two new justices were quite different. Ayala Procaccia graduated at the top of her class both as an undergraduate and graduate law student at the Hebrew University of Jerusalem, clerked for Justice Shimon Agranat, and earned a PhD from the University of Pennsylvania. As a judge on the Magistrates Court she attracted notice when she voided a Jerusalem municipal ordinance forbidding businesses to operate on the Sabbath, thus allowing cinemas to open and public recreational activities to be held on Friday nights.[291] Despite Barak's prestige, her appointment did not go through easily. He knew that the religious members of the appointments committee were likely to oppose her. Suddenly a new candidate was brought up by the minister of justice, Meir Sheetrit—Edmond Levy. Levy was quite a different candidate, one unlike all the others on the bench. He was religiously observant, Mizrahi by ethnicity, and from an entirely different sociocultural milieu than the rest of the justices. True, no few Sephardi and religious justices had served on the court—indeed, by tradition, there was a "Sephardi seat" and a "religious seat," but these men always hailed from the country's social and economic elite. None of them came from what is often called the "Second Israel," the Mizrahim who immigrated to Israel from Islamic countries after the establishment of the state of Israel. Many of them remain in a socially disadvantaged group.

Levy was a different case entirely. His family immigrated from Iraq to Israel in 1951, when he was ten years old. They first lived in one of the poverty-stricken immigrant tent and shanty camps established in Israel during the mass wave of immigration of the state's early years, and then moved to Ramla, in those days a no less poverty-stricken city in the country's geographic center but distant from its centers of power. He later became active in Herut, the party led by Menachem Begin, which eventually merged with other parties to form Likud. He served as Ramla's deputy mayor and crossed swords with the mayor, Aharon Abuhatssira, of the National Religious Party. As part of coalition negotiations, the two men had agreed—at least so it has been maintained—to rotate the post of mayor between them, but following disagreements between the parties, the rotation agreement was not implemented. In the end Levy decided to leave politics. He was appointed a judge on the Israel Defense Forces military court, then moving on to the Magistrates Court, from which he was promoted to the District Court. He specialized in criminal law, and he presided over the panel that tried Rabin's assassin, Yigal Amir.

Sheetrit was certainly well within his authority to propose Levy on the basis of his background and his personal experience of an immigrant camp, but the media and the public immediately latched onto the candidate's erstwhile affiliation with Herut. No mention of that can, however, be found in the biography he supplied for the Supreme Court's website, in what would seem to be a deliberate attempt on his part to consign that chapter of his life to oblivion. Another sign that politics seems to have left him with a bad taste in his mouth is that his judicial opinions take politicians to task with unusual ferocity, sometimes even when such vituperation is not called for.

Barak and Sheetrit, by virtue of their positions as the two most influential members of the selection committee, reached an accommodation that led to the appointment of two justices of diametrically opposed backgrounds, judicial philosophies, and political persuasions. This soon became apparent, for example in 2003, when the court sanctioned the candidacies of both Azmi Bishara and Baruch Marzel for the Knesset.[292]

Bishara, leader of the Balad Party, took part in Hezbollah rallies, spoke in favor of "resistance" to the state of Israel, and would later flee the country after coming under investigation suspected of severe security violations. Marzel had been active in Kach, the racist movement founded by Meir Kahane, but later joined Herut–The National Movement (not the same Herut Party that had been led by Menachem Begin). The candidacies of both men were challenged on the basis of a law forbidding the candidacy of any person whose actions explicitly or implicitly involve racial incitement (Marzel) or support of the armed struggle of an enemy state or terrorist organization against the state of Israel (Bishara). Their case was heard before a bench of eleven justices, who could be divided into four groups. The majority ruled that both should be allowed to run. The second group thought that both should be disqualified. A third group, made up of Edmond Levy and Jacob Turkel, maintained that Bishara should be disqualified and Marzel allowed to run, perhaps indicating that these two justices held right-wing political views. A fourth group, made up of Beinisch and Procaccia, took the opposite position. They sought to allow Bishara to run and to disqualify Marzel, a position in keeping with left-wing political views.[293] The two newest members of the court thus found themselves on opposite poles. One common view is that these two extremes have much in common and that the extremes on both sides of the political spectrum resemble each other in many ways. Both Levy and Procaccia were willing to overrule nonjusticiable decisions made by the Knesset and the government. Levy went astoundingly far in another of his minority opinion, cited above, in which he advocated that the court void the government's plan to disengage from the Gaza Strip. Procaccia, for her part, wrote a minority opinion at the end of 2006 in which she favored voiding a government decision to appoint a government committee to examine the prosecution of the Second Lebanon War,[294] a decision I will discuss in chapter 27.

It was now 2002, and Barak had to consider the composition of the court he would leave behind him. He had been chief justice for seven years, and he had four years more to serve in the post. The picture at this point did not look all that wonderful from his point of view. No few justices had retired, and others were about to. Barak decided to seek an amenable younger candidate from the academic world. (England, appointed under Barak's court, was older than the chief justice and was due to retire shortly.)

Academic appointments ought to be exceptional; jurists lacking in practical experience ought to be appointed only under special circumstances, or when the candidate is an exceptional one. This was the rule regarding Supreme Court appointments from Israel's earliest years. In fact, up until this point only three justices with solely academic qualifications had ever been appointed to the court—Rabbi Simha Assaf, immediately after Israel was founded; Menahem Elon, who held the "religious" seat; and Izhak England. (In 2012 another such appointment was made—Daphne Barak-Erez, no relation to the former chief justice.)

In 2002 there were two obvious qualified academic candidates for the open seat. One was Nili Cohen, former rector of Tel Aviv University. The other was Ruth Gavison, a professor at the Hebrew University law school and a notable figure in the field of human rights (she was a founding member of the Association for Civil Rights in Israel and served as its president from 1996 to 1999) and the question of religion-state relations. But Barak had no intention of allowing Gavison, a vocal advocate of limiting judicial activism and critic of many of Barak's rulings, to sit on the bench. A few years later Gavison won the Israel Prize and was elected to the Israel Academy of Sciences and Humanities.

Barak thus turned to Cohen, who had a shining academic career.* Mautner termed her "an outstanding jurist and a beloved teacher."[295] In 1994 Cohen was elected the university's deputy rector, and three years later she was chosen, by an overwhelming majority of the university Senate, for the post of rector, a post she filled with great success until 2001. But when it became public knowledge that Cohen was Barak's choice for the upcoming opening, an uproar ensued, one with a level of vitriol seldom seen in judicial appointments. In her book on the court, Nomi Levitsky related that Dorit Beinisch "made every effort to torpedo the appointment ... from morning to night she engaged in preventative actions, devoted days on end to the effort, tirelessly going from room to room, visiting judges in their chambers, closing the door behind her, and sitting down to tell them about Cohen and lay out her drawbacks and inadequacies."[296]

This was not the end of the matter. Cohen was informed, obliquely, that a certain Supreme Court justice had told one of her acquaintances that there was a problem of "financial irregularities." No one had ever made such an allegation against her, but soon thereafter the university comptroller told Cohen that he had received a complaint regarding a pay supplement she had granted to adjunct instructors. The payment in question had been made four or five years previously and had been approved by the Planning and Budgeting Committee, the body that oversees Israel's higher education budget. The complaint made it sound as if someone were trying to dig up dirt about Cohen, even though her integrity had never before been questioned.

In principle, the university's financial affairs were overseen by its president. The president at the time the payment had been made was Yoram Dinstein, who had since left that post. Dinstein declared, in fairness, that he had approved the payment. The matter thus came to an end and was not even mentioned in the comptroller's annual report.

But apparently that was not enough. Supreme Court justices received a letter of complaint from a former faculty member in the university's life sciences faculty. The faculty member's contract had ended and she had not received tenure. The faculty had recommended her dismissal and was unambiguously opposed continuing her employment, a position endorsed by the dean, Eliora Ron, and her two predecessors, Joseph Loya and Isaac Barash. What, then, did this biologist want from Cohen? Who had urged her to write the letter, and how did it reach the Supreme Court justices? It was all a big secret. But when the three deans learned of the letter, they together authored a letter expressing their consternation about it and asserting that Cohen had no role in the affair. They further added that "Professor Nili Cohen excelled at her position as rector, a post she filled with great aptitude and fairness. She proved herself to be an exceptional academic leader, furthered research and teaching, and

---

* Nili Cohen wrote her doctoral dissertation under my guidance, and we have been frequent co-authors, among them of a four-volume treatise on contracts.

her human relations were exemplary." (The letter was written after Cohen was no longer rector, so the authors were not beholden to her in any way.)

Cohen demanded to see the complaint letter but was turned down. When she continued to insist, Bark told her that the letter had been lost. Why was the letter kept from her, in violation of all the most basic rules of fairness that the court preaches? Presumably, it contained something that would have been discomfiting for someone, and perhaps it would have testified to the circumstances under which it was written and whether it was prompted by a conversation between the complainant and some other person.

When the picture clarified, Barak told Cohen that he still wanted to propose her as a candidate. Cohen refused to allow her name to be placed before the Judicial Selection Committee. It was clear that her appointment would not go through and that she would have been nominated only in order to wash the Supreme Court's hands of the affair and to make a show of considering her appointment on its merits. In 2015, she was elected president of the Israel Academy of Sciences and Humanities.

This technique of quashing appointments was developed in the State Prosecution. Yaakov Neeman was compelled in August 1996 to resign as justice minister after a baseless charge of false testimony was filed against him. Reuven (Ruvi) Rivlin's appointment to the same post was thwarted in 2001 when a baseless investigation was carried out against him (Rivlin is now the president of the state of Israel). It did not remain there but was rather, so it seems, taken up by the Supreme Court.

The foiling of Nili Cohen's appointment was depicted in the media as a victory by future Chief Justice Beinisch over Barak. But Barak in fact handed her this victory, one for which the court paid a heavy price. Given his status as a super–chief justice, Barak could have pushed through any appointment he truly wanted. He did so in the case of Elyakim Rubinstein in the face of opposition by many of his colleagues. He also placed his stamp of approval on the problematic appointment of Edna Arbel, despite the huge opposition that her appointment aroused, in particular outside the court. At that time Yosef (Tommy) Lapid was minister of justice, and in that capacity he did as Barak wished. Barak could thus easily have pushed through Cohen's appointment, which was supported by Justices Theodor Or and Ayala Procaccia, given that she was much admired outside Beinisch's small circle.

Barak complained at the time of the level of criticism levied at him, in comparison with the way Shamgar had been treated. "When I jump into an empty pool, I come out wet," he remarked. "When Shamgar jumps into a full pool, he comes out dry."* But such an incident could not have occurred on Shamgar's watch. First, Shamgar had refused to appoint Beinisch. Second, it is inconceivable that he would have allowed such meddling among justices serving under him.

The entire affair was covered extensively by the media and caused the court much damage. It showed that the battles over appointments to the court were political at base and were no less vicious than political fights. It also showed the public that when judges got involved in such fights, they displayed no moral superiority to anyone else. They behaved just like politicians. It led to some tough questions.

---

* To this statement Shamgar remarked briefly: "[W]ho jumps into an empty pool?", MEIR SHAMGAR, AN AUTOBIOGRAPHY 214 (2015) (Isr.).

Supreme Court justices are chosen by a committee whose composition is provided for by law. But it transpired that, at least with regard to appointments to the Supreme Court, the Judicial Selection Committee was not much more than a rubber stamp. The real decisions were made by the sitting justices.[297]

It turned out that the Supreme Court justices sitting on the Judicial Selection Committee did not act independently, in accordance with their own judgment, but rather as delegates representing their colleagues (although there were some exceptions to this). This is problematic given that the law governing such committees clearly requires their members to exercise independent discretion. Press reports about the committee's operations, based on sources within the Supreme Court, painted an even sorrier picture. According to these reports, the justices viewed themselves as a "family," and no one was allowed to join the family if any one of its members was opposed, for any reason whatsoever. This picture, of a court operating as a family business with a veto granted to each of its members, is outrageous, to say the least.[298]

A few months following the tempest over Nili Cohen's appointment, in June 2003, Asher Grunis was appointed to the court with the support of Deputy Chief Justice Shlomo Levin. At the same time Miriam Naor was also appointed. Both of them were District Court judges, and their candidacies sailed through the committee. (In 2012, Grunis, in accordance with the seniority system, ascended to the post of chief justice, and when he retired in 2015 he was succeeded by Naor.)

But the calm was short-lived. A huge storm broke about a year later, when the last round of appointments of the Barak era came before the committee. There were four seats to fill. Two of the new justices were District Court judges Esther Hayut and Salim Joubran, the latter becoming the first Christian Arab to serve on the Supreme Court.* The other two were Attorney General Elyakim Rubinstein and State Attorney Edna Arbel. In accordance with an established practice that had evolved in the court, all four had been vetted and approved at a gathering of the sitting justices prior to the meeting of the Judicial Selection Committee. The first two appointments were approved without incident. But Rubinstein and Arbel received the justices' stamp of approval only after a long battle.

Barak seems to have intended for Rubinstein to fill the "religious seat" on the court, but some of the other justices were solidly opposed, among them Dalia Dorner. Since she was one of the court's three representatives on the Judicial Selection Committee, Barak was concerned that she would act independently and vote against Rubinstein's appointment. Rubinstein seemed to be a worthy candidate in many respects—he had been an outstanding law student, and as attorney general he had been less prosecutorial than some. But he was religious and as such did not come from the same sociocultural environment to which the justices who had served in the State Attorney's Office, such as Beinisch and Arbel, belonged.

Arbel's appointment seemed much more problematic. She had displayed a notable prosecutorial approach as state attorney. I, at least, have a hard time understanding the logic behind her appointment. But the justices evinced little opposition, perhaps

---

* He was preceded by Abdel Rahman Zuabi, a Muslim justice who served on the Supreme Court in 1999. But Zuabi's appointment was a temporary one, and after it expired he resumed his District Court judgeship.

because they were aware of her close ties to Beinisch, who, it was increasingly clear, would be the next chief justice. In the end, as Levitsky relates, an understanding was reached, and both Rubinstein and Arbel were approved by the justices. Their names were brought before the Judicial Selection Committee in May 2004, two months after Dorner's retirement, thus averting any possibility that she might spoil the arrangement.

Outside the court, attitudes to these two appointments were the exact opposite. There was little opposition to Rubinstein, but much to Arbel. The committee received letters opposing her appointment on a number of grounds. One allegation was that, while serving as state attorney, Arbel had asked a cabinet minister, Limor Livnat, to further her husband's appointment to the board of a government corporation. (Arbel denied the charge and said that the request to Livnat had been made by someone else.) Another issue was her decision to indict Yaakov Neeman. Amnon Dankner of *Ma'ariv* wrote an article declaring that, given her role in the investigation, indictment, and prosecution of Neeman, "putting Arbel in Israel's top judicial institution would be like placing an idol in the Temple—a scandal and a disgrace."[299] Arbel claimed that she had not been responsible for the case, as she stated in a letter she wrote to the committee. Against her, Attorney General Michael Ben-Yair claimed that he disqualified himself from involvement in the *Neeman* case because he had doubts about the indictment that Arbel had decided to make. Justice Minister Lapid claimed that Ben-Yair had been party to the decision, as the documents submitted to him show.

The case was discussed in a series of newspaper articles. One, headlined "Edna Arbel Did Not Report Truthfully," reported Ben-Yair's position.[300] Another article bore the headline "Lapid Revealed Documents Contradicting Ben-Yair's Claim about Arbel."[301] A further article in *Ma'ariv* was headlined "The Former Attorney General Versus Lapid," with a subhead stating that "Michael Ben-Yair today sent a letter to the minister of justice in which he accused him of attacking him in order to defend Arbel."[302] Ya'akov Ahimeir, another prominent journalist, wrote that only a national commission of inquiry into the operation of the State Attorney's Office could restore public confidence in that body and in the Supreme Court.[303]

Whatever the case was, Neeman's trial was one of the most notable judicial scandals ever to occur in Israel and required investigation. But, as in many other cases of prosecutorial malfunction, that never happened.

Another journalist, Yoav Yitzhak, submitted an objection to Arbel's appointment. He offered several reasons, among them her alleged request from Livnat and her alleged involvement in the wiretapping conducted by the head of the Police Investigations Unit, Moshe Mizrahi. Yitzhak also petitioned the Supreme Court, asking it to issue an interlocutory order enjoining the Judicial Section Committee from approving Arbel's appointment as long as his objection had not been investigated. The court denied his petition on the grounds that the selection committee would look into it. But the question of whether that was actually done remains open.

Minister of Tourism Benyamin (Benny) Elon, the other member of the cabinet serving on the Judicial Selection Committee, proposed that the consideration of Arbel's nomination be postponed until the complaints against her had been probed, but Lapid refused. According to press reports, Barak claimed that even if some of the charges were true, they would not disqualify her from membership on the court. Note the glaring contradiction between the position on the claims raised against Arbel and the completely unfounded ones raised against Nili Cohen.

In the end, all four nominations went through. Three were approved unanimously. Elon voted against Arbel, and one of the Knesset's representatives on the committee, Shaul Yahalom of the National Religious Party, related that he voted in her favor only because his vote would not have made a difference and because he had been promised that Tel Aviv District Judge Devorah Berliner, who was religious, would be given at least a temporary appointment to the high court. Barak, for his part, denied that there had been any such deal.

Soon afterward Arbel found herself in the midst of another potential affair. It turned out that her resume, posted on her page on the Supreme Court's website, indicated that she had a master's degree from Bar-Ilan University. The truth was, however, that while she had indeed pursued graduate studies at that institution, she had never completed the requirements for a degree. Nana10, an Israeli news and entertainment website, published an item headlined "The Court Presents: 'Refurbishing' Edna Arbel's Resume." It related that a day after the error was exposed, the resume on the website was corrected to say that she had pursued studies for a graduate degree. According to the reporter, the Ministry of Justice's press secretary told him that the mistake had been made by the staff of the Judicial Selection Committee.[304] In "The Rule of the Dark Apparatus," an article that appeared in Ma'ariv's weekend magazine in March 2007, Ben-Dror Yemini compared the fix to Arbel's resume to the case of Knesset member Esterina Tartman of Yisrael Beitenu, whose political career came to an abrupt end when it turned out that she had misreported her academic credentials.

The post of justice minister, like many other political positions in recent years, has changed hands frequently. During Barak's tenure as chief justice he had worked with no fewer than eight justice ministers—and that does not include Netanyahu, who held the portfolio for a time while serving as prime minister.

Court appointments have clearly reflected the sitting minister's political inclinations. Under Libai, who worked in close cooperation with the legal establishment, Turkel and Beinisch were appointed during turmoil that followed Rabin's assassination, which created conditions that suited Barak. True, Neeman, the first justice minister in Netanyahu's first government, had his own ideas about the judicial system, ones that did not always sit well with Barak's. But Neeman was forced out after just a couple of months in office and the danger passed. Tzachi Hanegbi, who gained the portfolio soon after Neeman's resignation, served until the 1999 elections. Hanegbi's record was clearly not in line with that of previous ministers of justice.*

---

* In 1982, while Hanegbi was a university student, he was involved in a brawl at the Hebrew University campus in Jerusalem. The Magistrates Court convicted him of brawling in a public place and imposed a fine and probation. In another incident, Hanegbi, along with several others, submitted a complaint to the police alleging that employees of the student travel association (ISSTA) had committed "the biggest fraud in Israeli aviation history." The complaint led to the indictment of several ISSTA employees and associates, among them Pinchas Maoz, an external legal adviser for the association. Maoz was exonerated by the Magistrates Court. In its verdict, the court referred to Hanegbi's testimony as "having not always had truth as its guiding light." Following the trial, Maoz demanded that Hanegbi be charged with perjury or false testimony. The attorney general decided against an indictment on the grounds that a conviction was unlikely. A petition against the decision was filed with the Supreme Court, which in turn decided,

While serving in this post he was involved in the Bar-On–Hebron affair, but a petition to the Supreme Court calling for his dismissal from his post was denied.[305] Hanegbi largely deferred to the judicial branch and did his best to do its bidding, winning him many kudos from Barak. This approach may well have redounded to his personal benefit—the fact that he continued to serve as minister of justice, rather than being compelled by the system or the Supreme Court to resign, was not to be taken for granted. Had a minister of justice not so beloved of the legal establishment found himself in Hanegbi's situation, it is doubtful if he would have been allowed to retain his post. On Hanegbi's watch, Izhak Englard, an old friend of Barak's, was appointed to the court.

The 1999 elections for prime minister were won by Ehud Barak. Yossi Beilin received the justice portfolio. The judicial system was astonished to discover that Beilin had independent ideas and had a hard time accepting this. The result was a head-on collision between Beilin and the top echelon of the ministry. At one point the Supreme Court even tried to teach him a lesson and gave him a hard time when he sought to appoint the man he had chosen to be director general of his ministry.[306]

Beilin's top candidate for the Supreme Court was Mordechai Kremnitzer, a member of the Hebrew University law faculty, human rights activist, and advocate of radical judicial activism, more radical even than Barak's. Kremnitzer's political opinions can be learned from the fact that in 2008 he was active in the New Movement, a group that a year later ran for the Knesset together with Meretz, the Jewish party furthest to the left on the Israeli political spectrum. Kremnitzer's foray into politics did not lead to impressive results, as the combined slate won only three seats. Beilin's attempt to get Kremnitzer onto the court failed because Barak would not hear of it. Beilin himself later left Labor for Meretz.

After Prime Minister Ehud Barak's resignation in December 2000, Ariel Sharon was elected. Like the two prime ministers who had preceded him, who also won direct elections for the prime minister's post, Sharon found himself under criminal investigation, which proceeded while he was in office. One investigation, involving an allegation of bribery, was closed in 2004. Another, regarding donations he had received for his campaign in Likud's internal elections, was still in progress when Sharon suffered a stroke in January 2006 and went into a coma.

Sharon's first justice minister was Meir Sheetrit, who also displayed a large measure of independence. In the area of appointments, this was displayed in his nomination of Edmond Levy for a seat on the court.

"after much hesitation—by a hairsbreadth" not to intervene: HCJ 3846/91 Pinchas Maoz v. The Attorney General 46(5) PD 423 [1992] (Isr.). These affairs were also discussed in another petition filed against Hanegbi: HCJ 1993/03 The Movement for Quality Government v. Ariel Sharon 57(6) PD 817 [2003] (Isr.). Hanegbi, who was appointed justice minister in 1996, left office in 1999 along with the Netanyahu government in which he served. He later found himself under investigation for acting in conflict of interest in connection with a nonprofit organization with which he had been associated. The police file against him was closed by Attorney General Rubinstein, but the Knesset Ethics Committee reprimanded him and decided to deprive him of two months' salary. In 2010 he was acquitted of a number of charges brought against him but was found guilty of perjury in the Jerusalem Magistrates Court.

Sharon, leading Likud, formed a second government after the elections of 2003. Likud's largest coalition partner was Shinui, a liberal secularist party led by Yosef (Tommy) Lapid. Shinui was the dark horse of those elections, winning a surprising fifteen seats. Lapid received the justice portfolio. From Barak's point of view, it was an ideal appointment.

Lapid was a lawyer by training and a journalist by profession. Prior to his cabinet appointment he had been one of the fiercest public critics of Barak and the activist Supreme Court.[307] But, once minister of justice, it was as if Barak had waved a magic wand and transformed Lapid entirely. Lapid declared unqualified fealty to the court and became the chief justice's trusty servant. His tenure proved to be a relatively short one, only a year and nine months, but it was a busy one in terms of appointments to the court. No less than six new justices were added to the bench, and all of them were names proposed by the court itself. The first of these were Grunis and Naor, followed by Hayut, Joubran, Rubinstein, and Arbel—the last four at the meeting of the Judicial Appointments Committee that set off a media storm.

For Barak, this final round of nominations marked the end of an era in which he had an almost free hand in nominations to the bench. A year later Sharon brought Labor and Shas, the Mizrahi-Haredi Party that was Lapid's nemesis, into his coalition. Shinui walked out. The new justice minister was Tzipi Livni, then a member of Likud. She served for about a year and a half and proved to be much less congenial for the chief justice than Lapid had been. Livni had her own ideas about appointments to the high court. Her top candidate was Ruth Gavison. Gavison, as I have noted, is a jurist of the first order, with a fine international reputation. Politically and in her advocacy of human and minority rights, she is a woman of the center-left, but she is also an unashamed supporter of Israel's right to ensure that it remains a Jewish state. In this context, she has displayed a willingness to work with people and groups on the right to reach broad agreements on issues such as the role of Jewish culture in Israeli society and religion-state relations. Gavison is also a vocal opponent of Barak's philosophy and practice of judicial activism.

Barak adamantly opposed her appointment. Gavison, he maintained, "has an agenda," a rather problematic way of putting it given that he himself had a very clear agenda of granting the court power over all other branches of government. His problem with Gavison was clearly not that she had an agenda but rather that her agenda and his were opposed. This time their disagreements did not remain within the ivory tower and reached the media, as each side sought to gain a majority on the Judicial Selection Committee. It was not clear at all who would win, and a single vote on the committee could have been decisive. In the meantime, Livni, who was the statutory chair of the committee, delayed convening it. As it happened, the two members representing the Israel Bar Association were slated to be replaced. In the meantime, the public was witness to retired members of the court itself acting as Barak's choir as they campaigned uncompromisingly in support of his position.

On November 16, 2005, retired justice Itzhak Zamir wrote an article for *Yedioth Ahronoth* with the headline "Unfit and Illegal." He censured Livni for not convening the committee. "The workload is intolerable. The price is being paid not only by the justices but also by the public," he declared, warning that "it would be a disgrace" if Livni's behavior "were to come before the court." The timing of the article was inauspicious, as just as it was published Livni announced that the committee would meet in January.

But the wind in the Supreme Court suddenly changed direction. Tova Tzimuki, a journalist at *Yedioth Ahronoth*, reported that "sources close to the Supreme Court claim that it would be illegal to convene the committee on the eve of elections."[308] Former justice Dalia Dorner attacked the decision to hold the committee meeting just prior to national elections. "The decision is illegal," she insisted, "and exceeds the bounds of the reasonable." What about the shortage of justices on the bench? Dorner said that there was nothing terrible about it. "We have waited for ten months," she said. "The Supreme Court can hold out for a few more." In other words, while Zamir claimed that it was illegal not to convene the committee, Dorner maintained the opposite. Both suggested that a petition to the Supreme Court was called for, in the one case to order the justice minister to call a committee meeting and in the other to forbid her to do so. And all this in order to defend the justices' control of appointments to the high court.

During the uproar over Gavison's appointment, the chief justice switched roles. Instead of playing a member of the Judicial Selection Committee leading a crusade against the minister of justice, he took the part of a justice of a court handing down rulings. A few days before the committee's meeting in January 2006, the court ruled on a petition regarding the new composition of the Kiryat Ono Religious Council.[309] The case revolved around the fact that Prime Minister Sharon, who at the time held the authority to approve the memberships of religious councils, had not done so in the case of the city of Kiryat Ono. Following the resignation of his government and when the date for national elections was set, the question came before the court. Barak headed the bench that heard the case. He did not write the judgment, which was assigned to Justice Procaccia. She focused on the issue of appointments during an election campaign. Section 30 of Basic Law: The Government, which addresses the issue of the continuity of government, states explicitly: "When a new Knesset has been elected or the government has resigned ... , the outgoing government shall continue to carry out its functions until the new government is constituted." But that very clear statement was no obstacle to the Barak court, which authorized itself to legislate as it saw fit even if in doing so it contradicted the laws passed by the Knesset. Procaccia thus ruled that a caretaker government needed to maintain a balance "between restraint and action." In instances in which it was not clear whether those involved in the appointments would remain in office following the election, "the view has been accepted that it is proper that appointments to positions in the public service not be carried out by the agents of the administration ... except in instances in which filling a particular position is a really vital need." She affirmed the prime minister's decision to put off the appointment of a new religious council for Kiryat Ono.

It is hard to see how this ruling squares with a previous one, handed down on a petition by Hillel Weiss, a professor at Bar-Ilan University and outspoken right-wing political activist.[310] In that case, the court authorized Ehud Barak, then prime minister of a caretaker government, to engage in critical negotiations with the Palestinians—a matter of importance and implications far beyond those of the appointment of a religious council, and which ought to be pursued only by a government that enjoys the confidence of the Knesset and electorate.

There is no need to expand on the problematic nature of a court decision that establishes a rule touching on an issue that at that very moment stands before the Supreme Court and the minister of justice. Furthermore, anyone familiar with the theory of precedent should have known that the "rule" established in the *Kiryat Ono* case had no bearing on the Judicial Selection Committee. Not every notion raised by a judge in an opinion is a binding rule. There is a name for such marginal speculations—they are obiter dicta and are not binding. The rule established by a judgment is limited to what is called the *ratio decidendi*, the rationale used by the court in reaching its decision. In the case in point the prime minister refused to address the composition of a religious council, and all that was ruled in the case was that his decision to refuse to do so was legitimate. That is not the same thing as saying that he was forbidden to appoint a religious council under the circumstances. It goes without saying that nothing about the prime minister's decision in this case is anything like the decision of the Judicial Selection Committee. Notably, the glaring fact that Dorit Beinisch had been appointed to the Supreme Court under a caretaker government is not mentioned in the ruling.

Livni seems to have understood that the committee should not be convened at that time and in any case that her chances of securing Gavison's appointment were not very bright. Attorney General Menachem (Menny) Mazuz agreed that the meeting should be postponed. The upshot was that no Supreme Court seats were filled during Livni's term as justice minister. As a number of justices had retired by this time, Barak was left with a court of only ten justices, far below its statutory membership of fifteen.

To complete the picture, it should be noted that the court had a candidate of its own. Dan Meridor had long been active in politics, largely in Likud, and as justice minister had appointed Beinisch to the post of state attorney. At this particular juncture, however, he was not serving in any political post. It is hard to see him as a serious candidate for the court. His standing as a jurist certainly did not qualify him, but as I have already noted, he was one of Beinisch's greatest admirers. The idea of putting him on the court says much about the priorities of the justices themselves in choosing their colleagues. Livni, however, would not hear of it. The justices realized that, in the wake of the Rubinstein-Arbel affair, they had no chance of securing Meridor's appointment without the support of the justice minister. It fell by the wayside.[311]

To sum up, a total of twelve justices were appointed during Aharon Barak's eleven-year tenure as chief justice. Eleven of these were candidates proposed by the court itself. No figure or body outside the court really had any say in these nominations, even though only three out of the nine members of the Judicial Selection Committee were Supreme Court justices. Only one appointment during this period, Edmond Levy, was proposed by the minister of justice. In other words, even though the law stipulated that sitting Supreme Court justices were a minority on the committee, in practice the court's sitting justices—all of them, not just the three who were officially members of the committee—served as a de facto nominating board that for all practical purposes usurped the power of the statutory committee. As ministers of justice came and went at a rapid pace, and since most of them deferred to the court, the justices were able to maneuver the nominating process in a way that allowed them to determine, in almost every case, who their colleagues would be. When Dorner said,

"We have waited for ten months. The Supreme Court can hold out for a few more," it was clear that she meant that the court should simply wait until it could arrange the appointments it wanted.

But this time the justices were disappointed. The post of justice minister continued to operate like a revolving door, but the nominating process did not revert to being controlled by the Supreme Court. Livni was succeeded by Haim Ramon; Barak did not succeed in reaching an accord with him.

Another aspect of Barak's nominating tactics is that they did not ensure that the Supreme Court's members were as varied or as qualified in their backgrounds and legal philosophies as they should have been. The court that Barak left upon his retirement in 2006 was the least impressive court in Israel's history. Of course, worthy men and women were appointed to the bench under his leadership, but so were a number of people of less impressive standing, while highly qualified candidates were quashed. On top of this, the court was morally bruised. The acrimonious nominating process showed the public that Supreme Court justices were no different from politicians. When their interests were at stake, they behaved no better than the public figures that they claimed the power to criticize and overrule.

Another jarring fact about the revolutionary court was the large number of justices who had come to it from the public prosecution. Many of them had never had a client they had to defend nor a commercial enterprise that they represented. This was one of the most salient differences between the revolutionary and classic courts. The Supreme Court established when Israel was founded had been composed almost entirely of figures with experience as private attorneys.

This shift had already begun when Attorney General Meir Shamgar was appointed to the court, and became more pronounced three years later when Shamgar's successor as attorney general, Barak himself, joined the court. Neither man had ever worked in the private sector. The result was a court that became much more heavy-handed in criminal cases, both in its interpretation of the law and in its extensive use of the very vague charge of breach of trust, which the court can basically fill with whatever content it wishes and thus, for all intents and purposes, to impose retroactive punishments for deeds committed far in a public figure's past.[312]

Not even four years had gone by following Barak's move to the court when State Attorney Gabriel Bach joined him. In his footsteps came another former attorney general, Itzhak Zamir. The phenomenon took off after Barak became chief justice, with the appointment of State Attorneys Beinisch and Arbel and yet another former attorney general, Elyakim Rubinstein. Beyond the number of justices of this background, it is also telling that three successive chief justices—Shamgar, Barak, and Beinisch, who together led the court for about three decades, from 1983–2012—all stood at the helm of the state prosecution authority. The sense was that the prosecution and the court lived in symbiosis.

The blunt belligerence of the court's involvement in the appointments process under Barak, and the sense that it had gone too far, prompted the Knesset to action. The change was rather modest, but given the menace of criminal law that cast a shadow over the political system, this was a significant achievement. Two provisions were added to the Courts Law in 2004, immediately following the controversy over the appointments of Arbel and Rubinstein. One provision requires an eighteen-month cooling-off period before an attorney general or state attorney can be appointed to the Supreme Court. The other stipulates that the members of the Judicial Selection Committee must vote in accordance with their own individual judgment, unbound by the decisions of the bodies they represent on the committee. This provision may look strange to anyone unfamiliar with the way the process has worked. Indeed, this has always been the rule—the Knesset has never instructed its two representatives on the committee how to vote. But the Supreme Court did not honor this rule, rather expecting that its three members vote as a block in accordance with decisions made in advance by the justices on the court. In other words, the new provision was intended to tell the court that it had to obey the law.

24

The Role of Criminal Law

A short time after Aharon Barak was appointed chief justice and Benjamin Netanyahu elected prime minister, a wave of criminal investigations and trials of central political figures swept the country. Unprecedented in Israel and most likely without parallel in any other democracy, it was the second such period in Israeli history. The first occurred during Yitzhak Rabin's initial term as prime minister in the mid-1970s. In fact, every prime minister who has served from 1996 to the present—Benjamin Netanyahu, Ehud Barak, Ariel Sharon, and Ehud Olmert—has come under criminal investigation, in some cases multiple times. On top of that, there has been a long list of criminal investigations of cabinet ministers and other public officials. It is as if a cloud of suspicion hangs over everyone in public service.

At times there was justifiable cause for an investigation, but in no few cases the impression has been that the suspicions are baseless or trivial, involving the kinds of deeds that hardly called for a criminal investigation and certainly not for criminal punishment. These latter sorts of investigations and trials have utterly undermined the central government, which often operated in an atmosphere of anxiety and fear. Expansive use was made of the vague offense of breach of trust, which has become a catch-all accusation wielded by a prosecution unable to make a case for any concrete offense. Consequently, cabinet ministers have found themselves suspected of criminal activities in connection with events that took place long in the past, at a time when no one thought that the actions under investigation were problematic in any way.

This phenomenon has placed huge power in the hands of the courts, the Supreme Court in particular, as well as in the attorney general and State Attorney's Office. What Amnon Dankner called "symbiosis" between these authorities has also emerged.[313] A great number of public prosecutors have been appointed to the courts. The personal connections between the people occupying these positions have become augmented by ideological agreement. In the meantime, the state bureaucracy has grown much more powerful. A minister who listens to the advice he receives from his ministry's staff can cite that in his defense, while those who have rejected such advice have found that, by rejecting "the recommendations of the professional cadre," they have brought suspicion upon themselves.

Two other changes that brought on more criminal investigations were the primary system by which many parties now choose their Knesset slates and the two direct elections for prime minister held in the 1990s. These two innovations created a situation in which candidates required large amounts of money, opening up opportunities for the rich and well-placed to leverage political contributions into political clout. With that danger in mind, the Knesset aimed to ensure that election campaigns did not spur corruption and that every candidate would have an equal opportunity no matter what his financial resources and connections. It enacted campaign finance laws that provided for state funding of political campaigns and fundraising rules for candidates. Among these were limits on private contributions. Violations of some of these rules were classified as criminal acts. Of course, candidates and their advisers immediately began searching for loopholes in the law that would enable them to benefit from private contributions that were not explicitly forbidden by the new laws. Campaign finance laws were also circumvented, for example, by setting up organizations without any direct ties to candidates but which campaigned on their behalf. The system created an entire legal industry devoted to parsing what kinds of donations were legal and which ones criminal.

Taken as a whole, the cases brought against political figures over the last thirty years should worry every Israeli citizen. While a few of the investigations were indeed called for, and produced solid evidence that led to convictions, most demonstrate prosecutorial overreach and raise the question of why and how could this have happened.

I. MINISTER OF JUSTICE NEEMAN IS FORCED OUT OF OFFICE AND PUT ON TRIAL

When he took his post, Netanyahu's minister of justice, Yaakov Neeman, immediately embarked on replacing Attorney General Michael Ben-Yair, who had been appointed by the government of Yitzhak Rabin. Neeman most probably made this move in consultation with Netanyahu. But it turned out that Neeman was himself replaced before he managed to put someone else in the attorney general's chair. He resigned when he was indicted on baseless charges.

Neeman later related that he had met with Ben-Yair a few days before he entered the government. According to Neeman, he told Ben-Yair that, since he had been appointed attorney general by Rabin's government, Netanyahu did not want him to continue to serve in the post. However, Neeman told Ben-Yair, he did not have to leave immediately. In the past, a minister of justice would have had no problem replacing the attorney general. But times had changed. The minister found himself ejected from office in a gambit that served the interests of the judicial system.

Neeman had been a professor of law and then became a leading partner in one of Israel's largest law offices, Herzog Fox & Neeman. He is religiously observant. His views on the law and the legal system differ utterly from those that the radical Supreme Court instilled in the system. As such, his rapid dismissal served the cause of advancing the legal revolution and helped bolster the justices' control over appointments to the court on which they sat.

The affair began when a journalist, Yoav Yitzhak, filed a petition with the Supreme Court demanding that it declare Neeman unfit to serve on the grounds that he had persuaded a witness in Aryeh Deri's trial, Martin Brown, to perjure himself. The basis for this charge was a memorandum written by a police officer. The officer wrote that Brown had told him about a conversation in which Neeman had asked Brown, "How is it that you are helping the police?" The memorandum had for years been part of the material collected in the Aryeh Deri investigation, and no one up to this point had thought there was any reason to investigate Neeman or to suspect that he had done anything wrong. But at this particular point in time it was suddenly leaked to the press. The document seemed to be a rather tenuous foundation for an investigation of any type, but the Supreme Court required Neeman to respond, which he did in an affidavit.

Before going on to Neeman's response itself, it is worth considering the question of why he had to submit a statement to the court in the first place. Why was the petition not dismissed out of hand as soon as it was filed? The answer is that the Supreme Court had turned its process into a lash to be used against public figures. Anyone could go to the Supreme Court and seek to stymie any government appointment on the basis of any shred of evidence, whether it came from the media or was simply a rumor. Instead of refusing to hear such questionable petitions, the court instituted a practice, which became almost automatic, of requiring the target of the petition to respond to the charges. As a consequence, public figures felt obligated to provide detailed statements about their past actions.

In his affidavit, Neeman addressed the fact that "the Israeli Supreme Court is being asked to rule on a constitutional question of the appointment of a minister of justice, on the basis of reports lacking all substance that have been deliberately planted in the media." Further on in the document Neeman wrote, "I never said these things, or anything like them, to Mr. Brown. The opposite is true." (Even if Neeman had said them, it is hard to see how they could serve as the basis for a claim that Neeman had engaged in witness tampering.) But Attorney General Ben-Yair informed the court that he would order a police investigation.

Not long thereafter, Neeman himself was indicted, on a charge of perjury. The basis for the charge was a section of the affidavit he had submitted to the Supreme Court supplying information about his meetings with Brown and his connection to Deri. The affidavit had been prepared by an attorney in Neeman's firm, Ehud Sol, and it turned out that Sol had made a mistake regarding an important date. Sol later explained the source of the error and insisted that he and not Neeman was responsible, but in its judgment the Magistrates Court stressed a fact that showed something about how the indictment had been made: "This is the place to note the fact that Attorney Sol, writer of the affidavit, was not interrogated at any point by police investigators. His version of events was heard first when he took the stand as a witness for the defense. The prosecution has no explanation of why Sol was not interrogated. After all, no one disputes the importance of interrogating the author of the affidavit."

The fact that a central witness had not been investigated by the police and that his testimony had not been considered before the indictment was issued raised difficult questions about the dubious and problematic conduct of the prosecution in this case. But, as in many other cases, no one bothered to look into it. The court acquitted Neeman.[314] Yet he would not return to the justice ministry for another thirteen years, until he received the post again in 2009.

Neeman's replacement as justice minister was Tzachi Hanegbi, a man whose background did not accord with what had previously been expected of the person given this portfolio (see Chapter 23). His policy was to capitulate to the justice system. As such, from Aharon Barak's perspective, Hanegbi was an ideal minister. He supported everything Barak wanted to do, and in turn Barak praised him to the skies.

II. THE TRIALS OF RAFAEL EITAN AND AVIGDOR KAHALANI

Rafael (Raful) Eitan was another right-wing cabinet minister to find himself indicted in 1996. He entered politics after serving as the chief of staff of the Israel Defense Forces (IDF). During his long military career he had displayed exceptional determination and bravery. He received a Medal of Courage and twice returned to active duty after being badly wounded. His chosen vehicle for politics was a new party he founded, Tzomet, which won much support thanks to the public's admiration of him as a soldier, farmer, and representative of classic Israeli values. In 1996 he led his party into a coalition with Netanyahu. According to the coalition agreement he was to be appointed minister of internal security (the portfolio responsible for the police force). But after he was indicted, the attorney general ruled that Eitan could not serve in this post and he took the agriculture portfolio instead. The indictment involved a matter that can only be called less than nothing, and is one of the great legal scandals ever to have occurred in Israel. No one would believe that such things could happen if it were not written in the judgment itself.[315]

The affair began in the wake of an internal struggle in Tzomet over the choice of a director general for the movement. The complainant was one of the candidates for the post. Defendant number four, as cited in the indictment, was an army reservist who used his position to print out personal details about the complainant from an army computer. This defendant was brought up before an IDF disciplinary panel and given an official reprimand, but this did not prevent him from being cited as a defendant in the criminal case that resulted from the incident. The print-out in question reached the hands of two other defendants, one of whom, according to the indictment, showed it to Eitan, who copied from it information regarding the complainant's education and the fact that he had been sentenced to a term in military prison for absenteeism. After doing so, Eitan met with the defendant.

The judgment in the case carries on the story from there. "During this meeting," it relates, Raful

> presented the complainant with the information he had received from the army data base and asked him if it was in fact true that he lacked a college education, in contradiction to his presentation of himself, and if he had indeed been a "deserter" from the IDF. The complainant, who hesitated in replying, was asked by . . . [Eitan] to answer "yes or no" and not to "beat around the bush." When the complainant acknowledged that he had been a "deserter," [Eitan] told him . . . that, as a former chief of staff, he would not consent to having a deserter in his movement, and that he could be neither director-general or a member of the movement, [and] also added . . . that he would not publicize the information if the complainant left the movement.

The court offered an extensive analysis of the triviality defense, that is, the claim that the matter is so trifling that it does not justify a criminal proceeding. The judges quoted at length from my article "Judicial Discretion in Criminal Trials" with regard to what was later termed "equitable defense."* They ruled that Eitan could claim in his defense Section 18 of the Protection of Privacy Law, inasmuch as he had acted in keeping with a legal, moral, or professional obligation. The court stated: "We are speaking of the head of a movement . . . He has a social, professional, and moral duty to ensure that those standing at the head of the movement, filling its posts, and representing it act in accordance with criteria that reflect the character of the movement and the values it holds."

In short, Eitan was acquitted on the spot. Witnesses were not even called, as the court ruled that the facts as presented in the indictment, to which Eitan admitted, did not constitute an offense. To put it simply, the prosecution submitted an indictment on an act that was not culpable, and the indictment was thrown out of court unceremoniously. The indictment against the two other defendants, those who had received the print-out from the computer, was also struck down. The attorney general then decided to suspend proceedings in the case of defendant number four, who had printed out the information from the army computer.

As usual, no one went back to check why a ridiculous indictment had been filed against a cabinet minister, and who was responsible for doing so. Michael Ben-Yair, attorney general at the time, left that position before the acquittals of Neeman and Eitan.

Netanyahu, Neeman, and Eitan were not the only members of the Netanyahu government to catch the eye of the legal system. I have already recounted the investigation of Hanegbi in the Bar-On—Hebron case. Another instance was that of Avigdor Kahalani, who was given the internal security portfolio after Eitan was disqualified. Kahalani also entered politics following an impressive military career. He was badly wounded in the Six Day War but returned to active duty. In the Yom Kippur War he commanded an armored battalion on the Golan Heights, fought valiantly, and played an important role in halting the Syrian advance and saving the Golan. He was awarded the medal of valor, Israel's highest military decoration. Elected to the Knesset in 1992 on the Labor Party slate, Kahalani left that party after the Oslo agreements and helped found and lead a new party, the Third Way, which won four Knesset seats in the elections of 1996. He served as a member of Netanyahu's cabinet throughout his first government, until July 1999. The investigation against him, and the resulting trial, happened thereafter.

Toward the end of Kahalani's service in the government, the police launched a secret investigation of Ofer Nimrodi, editor of the daily newspaper *Ma'ariv*. Kahalani, it was alleged, had, at Nimrodi's request, provided him with information about the investigation. He was indicted in the Tel Aviv Magistrates Court in 2000. After two years of proceedings, the court decided that there was no basis to the charges, and he was acquitted.[316]

---

* When I published the article in 1983, it constituted the first step in the recognition of the so-called "equitable defense" in criminal law in Israel. Under this principle, a defendant can plead that "the filing of an indictment or the conduct of criminal proceedings is in material contradiction to the principles of justice and fair trial (sec. 149(10) enacted in 2007 and embodied in the Criminal procedure Law [Consolidated Version] 1982."

III. NEW INVESTIGATIONS AGAINST NETANYAHU

In September 1999, a few months after leaving the post of prime minister, the media began reporting suspicions against Netanyahu and his wife Sara regarding their relations with a moving contractor, Avner Amadi, who had performed a variety of jobs for the couple during Netanyahu's term in office. A series of charges built up, some of which the couple was supposed to pay out of their personal funds, and the rest of which was to be paid by the government. The State Attorney's Office could hardly be expected to pass over the opportunity to investigate a senior political figure yet one more time. This time the suspicions involved bribery, breach of trust, attempted fraud, and obstruction of justice. Another suspicion was that the Netanyahu family had illegally taken for itself gifts given to the prime minister that were, by law, public property. When the investigation was completed, the police recommended bringing Netanyahu, his wife, and two members of their staff to trial.

After long discussions in the State Attorney's Office, Attorney General Elyakim Rubinstein decided to close the cases against the former prime minister and his wife on the grounds of "evidence insufficient to the demands of a criminal trial." Instead, he published a "public report" in which he explained that his decision had been a hard one. "There was a consensus among those involved," he wrote, "that this is not the proper way to behave in the governing system—not to allow a large debt to build up towards a private person ... The Netanyahus did not see to it that the debt was paid, neither out of their own pocket to the extent it was a private debt, and not, with regard to the extent to which it touched on the period of his service as prime minister, in an orderly and proper way from the public purse." After the prime minister and his wife had undergone a nightmarish year, the case against them ended with a scolding. The cases against the other defendants were closed as well.

The attorney general's opinion made it clear not only that there had been disagreement among the government's lawyers but also that State Attorney Edna Arbel had been given an adequate opportunity to present her prosecutorial position. Her position had been that the prime minister and his wife should have been brought to trial on some of the charges. Once the dispute was made public, *Haaretz*, under the terms of Israel's Freedom of Information Law, asked the District Court to order that Arbel's opinion be made public. The court denied the petition, and *Haaretz* appealed to the Supreme Court. There a panel allowed the petition by a vote of six to one, Justice Edmond Levy remaining in the minority. It instructed the attorney general to publish "briefly but comprehensively" Arbel's reasons for maintaining that the Netanyahus should be indicted.[317]

In the final analysis, the Amadi affair looks like one of the most absurd proceedings ever pursued against a public official. Amnon Rubinstein, author of one of the seminal texts on Israeli constitutional law and a former cabinet minister for Meretz, pulled no punches:

> The State Attorney's Office has ordered the criminal investigation of every prime minister in the last twenty years ... and the police have seen to it that every such investigation receives local and international media coverage, and yet no one has been brought to trial. The record was set in the criminal investigation of former Prime Minister Benjamin Netanyahu in the Amadi affair ... It was a civil

matter . . . what does it have to do with a criminal investigation? . . . Netanyahu and his wife were interrogated for many long hours, each session lasting seven or eight hours! In the end the state attorney recommended indicting them for an offense that was a product of its own ingenious imagination. The attorney general, Elyakim Rubinstein, justifiably rejected the state attorney's recommendation, but in the meantime the news that a former prime minister of Israel had been interrogated for fraud had been reported all over the world.[318]

IV. THE INVESTIGATIONS OF EHUD BARAK AND ARIEL SHARON

Ehud Barak, the prime minister elected to replace Netanyahu, entered office in May 1999 and left it in January 2001. His was the shortest term of any Israeli prime minister, but that did not save him the ordeal of criminal investigation. Following his election, the police began looking into charges that political action organizations had collected illegal donations in support of Barak's election bid. The police inquiry ended several years later with a whimper, without producing any indictments. The question is why the case had to remain open for so long, hanging like Damocles' sword over Barak's head.

The next prime minister to be investigated was the next one to be elected, of course. Ariel Sharon defeated Barak in 2001. Eighteen years earlier, the Kahan Commission, in its report on the massacres at the Sabra and Shatila refugee camps in Beirut during the First Lebanon War of 1982, had recommended that he be dismissed from the post of minister of defense. Now elected prime minister, he suffered an even worse collision with the justice system.

One subject that came under investigation was the purchase of farmland in the area of Lod by an Israeli businessman, David Appel, and Dror Hoter-Yishai, an attorney. Appel wanted to change the zoning of the land so that he could build on it. Sharon, who had served as housing minister, was alleged to have helped further this change in illegal ways. The investigation was closed when it became clear that nothing Sharon had done had involved any favoritism or intervention specifically on Appel's behalf.

But that was not all. Sharon and his younger son, Gilad, were also investigated in what was called the Greek Island affair. This, too, involved Appel and a grandiose plan of his to build several vacation resorts, to the tune of $16 billion. One of the resorts was to be built on the Greek island of Patroklus, not far from Athens; part of the property involved had been declared a protected archaeological site. As a result, Appel's plan ran into difficulties with the Greek authorities. To overcome them, Appel sought to establish contacts with figures in the Greek government and, in early 1999, arranged for Greece's deputy foreign minister, who was visiting Israel, to meet Ariel Sharon, then Netanyahu's foreign minister. A few months later, the mayor of Athens visited Israel as the guest of Jerusalem's Mayor Ehud Olmert. Appel invited the Greek mayor and his entourage, along with Ariel Sharon (now an opposition member of the Knesset) and his son Gilad to a dinner. It is hard to see what the problem with such an event might be.

The really problematic part of the Greek Island affair was that Appel had hired Gilad Sharon as a consultant on the project. Gilad worked for some time on the project, but following disagreement between the parties a new contract was signed, under which Appel and his corporation paid Gilad $400,000 for past services and promised him a substantial salary of $20,000 a month for future work. In addition, the younger Sharon was to receive a bonus of $1.5 million when Appel obtained permits to build on the island, and a further bonus when the resort opened its doors. Gilad continued to work for another year, receiving in total $640,000 from Appel. Despite these huge sums, and the fact that Gilad Sharon had no special expertise in Greek islands, the tourism industry, or archaeology, the recently appointed attorney general, Menachem (Menny) Mazuz, concluded that Gilad's job was not a fictitious one, and that there was no proof that Appel had hired him in order to be able to gain the older Sharon's assistance. While Sharon, of course, knew that his son was working for Appel, there was no evidence that he had specific information about what his son was being paid.

On top of this, a dispute broke out between State Attorney Arbel and her staff on the one hand, and on the other, the attorney general and the team he had appointed to consider the issue. The senior prosecutors handling the Greek Island affair concluded in December 2003 that Appel should be charged with bribing Sharon—but that there was not sufficient evidence to indict Prime Minister Sharon. A month later, in January 2004, when Mazuz took up his position, the case was reopened, and in March Arbel submitted a new opinion to Mazuz recommending the indictment of Ariel and Gilad Sharon. Three months later Mazuz issued his decision not to indict them, on the grounds of insufficient evidence. Mazuz also spoke of "marking targets," a remark that could be interpreted not only as a rejection of the prosecutorial stance of the State Attorney's Office but also as skepticism about the prosecutors' motives. Mazuz was referring, of course, to things that had happened under his predecessors. But what can politicians and the public think when they read a headline that says "Mazuz: Edna Arbel Made It a Goal to Indict Sharon"? Mazuz's remarks were sharply criticized by other justice ministry lawyers. Later it was reported that he sat down with the staff of the State Attorney's Office to assure them that they enjoyed his confidence.

The decision to close the case was roundly criticized by the public, following the lead of Sharon's political opponents and those who disagreed with his policies. A petition to the Supreme Court was the inevitable next step, the petitioners including Knesset member (MK) Yossi Sarid of Meretz and Eitan Cabel of Labor. The case was heard by a panel of seven justices presided over by Aharon Barak. The majority opinion, signed by six of the seven, was written by Eliahu Mazza, who denied the petition on the grounds that the court had no cause to intervene in the attorney general's decision. Mishael Cheshin, in the minority, maintained that the court should issue an order nisi regarding the payments to Gilad Sharon.[319] This brought an end to the affair and ensured some quiet so that Sharon could run the country. But there were other complications waiting in line.

One of them was the Cyril Kern affair. Kern was a South African friend of Sharon who gave him a loan to pay for his election campaign. The suspicion was that the money had actually been given as a gift, and that its real source was not Kern but Martin Schlaff, an Austrian-Jewish billionaire. Another case had to do with Sharon's financing of his primary campaign within Likud for the internal elections of September 1999, when he beat out Ehud Olmert and Meir Sheetrit for party leader. Omri Sharon, Sharon's older son, served as his right-hand man in this campaign and helped him win his victory. He himself was chosen for the Likud slate to the Knesset and became a central figure in the party. But the state comptroller found irregularities in the funding of Ariel Sharon's campaign, and this led to a police investigation. Omri took responsibility for violating campaign finance laws and, in 2005, six years after the elections in question, he was brought to trial. He confessed to receiving a donation that was above the legal maximum and of spending on the campaign sums above those allowed by law. He also pled guilty to falsifying corporate documents and perjury. In February 2006, about a month after his father suffered a stroke and lost consciousness, Omri was sentenced to a nine-month prison term and a fine of NIS 300,000 (about $65,000).[320] On appeal to the District Court, the sentence was reduced to seven months.[321] A further appeal to the Supreme Court was dismissed.[322]

The investigation of Ariel Sharon continued throughout his term as prime minister. To sum up: In the primary campaign finance case, his son Omri was convicted. The Greek Island and Lod zoning cases were closed, and in January 2013 the State Attorney's Office announced that the Cyril Kern case against Ariel and Gilad Sharon would also be closed—more than ten years after it began.

V. THE INVESTIGATION OF RUVI RIVLIN

One of the most serious cases of a problematic investigation of a public figure, one that, once again, ended with no charges being filed, involves Reuven (Ruvi) Rivlin, a senior Likud figure and today president of Israel. Rivlin was slated to receive the justice portfolio in the first Sharon government. Just as the cabinet was being put together, in March 2001, the State Attorney's Office suddenly announced that he was under investigation. It declared that that he could not be appointed justice minister, but that he could receive the communications portfolio. Meir Sheetrit became minister of justice instead. This was the second time, after the Neeman affair, in which the legal system frustrated the appointment of a justice minister who was not to its liking. This time, too, it was a scandal, as the accusations against Rivlin were baseless.

The basis, such as it was, had to do—once again—with David Appel. Appel, as we have seen, figured in a number of corruption investigations. As a result of these suspicions the police tapped his phone—but, as Appel was well connected with many senior Likud figures, the tap on his phone gave the police an opportunity to listen to them as well. The police lifted a few sentences from the transcripts of Appel's conversations with Rivlin that, with the help of a vivid imagination, they were able to concoct into a full seven ridiculous and vacuous charges. Rivlin was summoned for a day-long interrogation, but even though nothing emerged from it, it led to his disqualification for the justice portfolio. Another serious aspect of the affair was that this extremely dubious investigation remained open for years—it ended only in 2004, under Mazuz's orders.

Mazuz's decision on the case reveals much about how absurd the allegations were. One of them was that Rivlin had helped Appel's children obtain visas to the United States. Rivlin, it was said, had spoken to the director general of Israel's foreign ministry (who, of course, was also interrogated), who told him that he had sent Appel's children to the U.S. embassy, where they had received pretty much the same service received by all Israelis who apply for visas. No one involved received anything in exchange for what they had done. The case was closed. Another accusation was that

Rivlin, then a member of the Judicial Selection Committee, had passed on information about that body's proceedings. While the committee's meetings are formally
secret, news of its deliberations appears regularly in the press, and no investigations
of these leaks had ever been pursued. This case was closed as well.

The whole affair says much about what concerns the legal system and what it is
willing to do to bring down a public figure who is not to its liking, or at least to prevent him from gaining a position that would give him the authority to make changes
in the legal system. The most important part of the Rivlin case, like so many others,
is that no one afterward investigated or looked into the question of what led to such a
problematic investigation being opened in the first place, why it began precisely as he
was about to be appointed justice minister, and why the investigation remained open
for so many years. Rivlin himself has spoken out more than once and coined the now
popular expression "the rule of law gang" to refer to his accusers.

VI. AVIGDOR LIBERMAN

Another Israeli leader to be investigated was Avigdor Liberman. It began while he
held the post of director general of the Prime Minister's Office in Netanyahu's first
government and lasted for ten years. Any number of allegations were looked into.
Liberman resigned that post at the end of 1997 and went into business, returning to
politics in 1999 when he founded Yisrael Beitenu, a secular right-wing party supported largely by Israelis who had immigrated, as Liberman himself had, from the
former Soviet Union. The situation in which a public figure—any person, in fact—
finds himself under continuous investigation for more than a decade, with new allegations regularly popping up, is intolerable. It happens because there is no oversight
over the work of the attorney general and the public prosecution. It was only in
December 2012 that Attorney General Yehuda Weinstein decided to close the principal case, involving allegations that Liberman had received large sums from overseas,
some of them after he returned to politics, because of insufficient evidence. But he
was indicted on a problematic count of breach of trust, involving the appointment
of an ambassador, Ze'ev Ben Aryeh, who had, according to the charges, formerly illegally provided Liberman with information about a criminal investigation against
him. Following the indictment, Liberman resigned his post as foreign minister in
Netanyahu's second government. He was acquitted in 2013.

VII. DROR HOTER-YISHAI ON TRIAL

Dror Hoter-Yishai was elected president of the Israel Bar Association in 1991, during
the second half of the Meir Shamgar era. He became a strident opponent of Aharon
Barak and his judicial policy and became a critic of the judicial selection process as
well. In 1995, the year of Barak's accession to the post of chief justice, Hoter-Yishai
was re-elected, beating out four other candidates. It was more than a hint that many
lawyers supported his position on these issues and that they were dissatisfied with
the state of the legal system.

The situation came to a head in November 1996, when the Haredi daily *Yated
Ne'eman* published an interview with the Bar Association chief. His impression was
that the secular press supported Barak without reservation, and that his own views

could appear in the large dailies only in the form of paid advertisements. He thus decided to speak out in a Haredi publication, where he could offer a stringent critique of the current state of the legal system in a sympathetic environment. He argued that when the Supreme Court exceeded its proper authority, it had more difficulty addressing those matters that were properly under its purview. "The legal system has collapsed," he declared.

> The situation requires intensive care. We have for years repeatedly warned that the court system does not do its job properly, that the courts, instead of judging . . . preoccupy themselves with all sorts of high matters . . . The Supreme Court must not become a super-legislator or a super director-general [of a ministry] . . . It is not true that all is justiciable . . . I think that anyone who tries to drag the court into areas that do not belong to it damages the legal system, and the Supreme Court . . . should not be dragged into those areas.

By overstepping its bounds, Hoter-Yishai argued, the court system had slowed down to a snail's pace, "to the point that people have even killed themselves as a result of not receiving a judgment in [reasonable] time."

He also criticized the use of the concept of "reasonableness" as a foundation or judicial review.

> If you begin to check reasonableness and proportionality, you are actually saying "I am the manager," because you privilege your judgment over his. I don't only check to see if he is acting in accordance with the law . . . but actually examine to see if I would decide that way or in some other way.

He also criticized judges who spent their time writing books and teaching college for high fees. "Judges should do us the honor of not taking on any work other than that of adjudicating, instead of writing learned books that lawyers buy for good money . . . It always comes at the expense of something . . . a judge, who today earns one of the highest salaries in government service . . . can supplement his salary generously at the colleges or by writing books." He also disparaged Attorney General Ben-Yair and the way in which Neeman was ousted from the justice ministry.

Immediately following the publication of the interview in *Yated Ne'eman*, Hoter-Yishai was attacked on all sides with unheard of virulence. Critics even called for a criminal investigation on charges of contempt of court. A few days later the press revealed that the State Attorney's Office had drafted charges against Hoter-Yishai of tax violations and deliberately not reporting income. There was nothing to back up such accusations, but an indictment was filed a short time later.

Three weeks after the interview appeared, the chairmen of the Bar Association's district offices had an emotional discussion with Aharon Barak and four other Supreme Court justices. The justices felt injured. They seem to have expected the Bar's district committees to denounce Hoter-Yishai's statements. Barak stressed, however, that if Hoter-Yishai had been speaking as an individual and not in the name of the organization he headed, "there is no argument, and it is his right to express his opinion." In the air was a threat that the justices would boycott Bar Association events. What was said in fact was that there would be no such boycott, "but each justice will act as he sees fit."

That same day, on December 17, 1996, the Bar Association's Central Committee discussed the issue. Hoter-Yishai received considerable support. In the end the committee passed a proposal by Yosef Shapira, chairman of the Jerusalem district (who was later a judge and has since July 2012 served as state comptroller), stating that it made note of Hoter-Yishai's avowal that his statements to *Yated Ne'eman* were intended as constructive criticism. They reflected his personal opinion and had not been said at the behest of the Central Committee, and "had not been meant to be disrespectful to any justice." Furthermore, the Central Committee declared that it viewed cooperation with the courts as important, but "without diminishing its duty and right to voice criticism." The proposal passed by fourteen votes against one. Another proposal, condemning Hoter-Yishai's statements and calling on him to resign, was voted down. A day later, Hoter-Yishai was indicted.

The indictment was problematic in the extreme. It involved the Bar Association president's father, Aharon, a well-known public figure who had founded the IDF's legal branch and served as the first chief military advocate general. Hoter-Yishai senior had bought, together with a partner, a tract of farmland, on which they planted an almond orchard. The land was purchased in 1959, when Dror was thirteen years old.

In 1989, a company trespassed on the land, dumping thousands of tons of junk metal on the property. The younger Hoter-Yishai represented his father and his father's partner in suing the company. Following a lengthy legal battle, the company removed the refuse and paid compensation to the owners. The tax authorities did not assess the owners for this sum, nor did it claim that Dror had received any of this compensation. The two owners of the property argued that the money they received was not income but rather reimbursement for damages they had suffered as a result of the trespass and the company's refusal to clear the property. The State Attorney's Office argued, however, that the payment, at least in part, was in fact a rent paid by the company for use of the property, and as such subject to taxation.

The dispute was a civil one, and as such, criminal proceedings are difficult to justify. It is even harder to explain why they were directed against Dror Hoter-Yishai, who was not an owner of the property, especially given that no criminal charges were filed against his father and the partner. Also dubious is the surfeit of charges brought against the Bar Association president, among them nonreporting of income and tax evasion, given the fact that the income under dispute had not been his. Other charges included abetting the concealment of income, fraudulent misrepresentation, and even abetting or causing his father's partner to declare that the payment he had received was tax-exempt. The fact that the partner was himself a tax adviser and well informed about tax matters did not prevent the prosecution from involving the younger Hoter-Yishai in his affairs.

The trial was heard by Judge Ziva Herman-Hadasi of the Magistrates Court. In the end, Hoter-Yishai was acquitted of most of the charges, but convicted on two counts involving his father's tax returns.[323] Hoter-Yishai, in addition to claiming that the indictment had been groundless, charged that the trial had been conducted improperly and that the proceedings had gone on for too long. He had a clear interest in a rapid process, given that the trial interfered with his ability to fulfill his duties as Bar Association president and even led him to resign from his seat on the Judicial Selection Committee. He claimed that he had made every effort to expedite the proceedings, and had even agreed that the court should receive all the statements that witnesses had made to the police, forfeiting his right to cross-examine them in court. None of this helped. The prosecution's conduct caused the trial to drag on, and the court spread the sessions over a long period, holding only two per month.

What happened after the verdict tends to support Hoter-Yishai's claim. He announced that he had no intention of making arguments regarding his sentence and asked that it be given immediately, so that he could appeal right away. The judge did not agree, instead deferring to the prosecution's demand. She scheduled arguments in the sentencing to three weeks later. It is hard to see what possible justification there could have been for this. Such a delay is generally granted at the request of the defendant. Here the defendant asked for an immediate sentence, so that he could appeal. Yet the judge preferred the prosecution's position. Three weeks later, she imposed a six-month suspended prison sentence and a fine of NIS 50,000.

A side story to Hoter-Yishai's saga is a note that was discovered in the courtroom on the day Judge Herman-Hadasi convicted him. Written in the hand of Judge Edna Bekenstein, later president of the Tel Aviv Magistrates Court, it read: "Ziva, I came to congratulate you! Edna." Aside from the note's gossip value, it says no little about the atmosphere in which the trial was conducted and the desire to get rid of Hoter-Yishai.

Hoter-Yishai indeed appealed. To the system's credit, the appeal process was rapid, and three months later he was acquitted on all counts (although in one case it was a majority ruling).[324]

Beyond the specific aspects of the case, it needs to be seen in context. Hoter-Yishai's indictment followed Ya'akov Neeman's appointment as justice minister in Netanyahu's government and a year after Hoter-Yishai had been elected president of the Bar Association and a member of the Judicial Selection Committee. For the Supreme Court, and for Aharon Barak, who had just recently ascended to the chief justice post, this created a new and discomfiting situation on that key committee. Neeman had his own ideas about the judicial system as a whole and about judicial appointments in particular, while Hoter-Yishai was an outspoken and bitter opponent of Barak and judicial activism.

But it did not take long for these problematic members of the committee to be removed. Not two months had gone by and Neeman was indicted. He resigned and was replaced by a minister much more amenable to the system, Tzachi Hanegbi. Soon thereafter, Hoter-Yishai was indicted. He resigned from the committee and was replaced by Haim Klugman, the Bar Association's director general and a former director general of the justice ministry. In other words, two indictments changed the balance of power on the Judicial Selection Committee. Note that both Neeman and Hoter-Yishai were acquitted in the end, but Neeman did not return to the justice ministry and the chairmanship of the Judicial Selection Committee for another thirteen years, while Hoter-Yishai had to run several more gauntlets.

In March 1997, the Movement for Quality Government in Israel petitioned the Supreme Court to demand Hoter-Yishai's ouster from the top post at the Bar Association, arguing that the indictment filed against him and his public pronouncements disqualified him.[325] The petition remained in abeyance for several long months as Hoter-Yishai's trial proceeded. After his conviction in the lower court, in

February 1998, the petitioner asked for an urgent hearing and for the court to order the attorney general to open an investigation of further statements Hoter-Yishai had made following his conviction. The request was rejected by Justice Dorner on the grounds that it raised questions that had not been raised in the original petition. With regard to ordering the attorney general to start an investigation, Dorner remarked that "the petitioner applied to the attorney general only on February 18, 1998, such that his application to this court is premature, not to mention hasty. Furthermore, it turns out that in the meantime the attorney general has ordered an investigation opened."

In May the Movement for Quality Government submitted a revised version of its petition, but more than a year later, in September 1999, the movement asked to cancel its suit. The apparent reason was that Hoter-Yishai's term as Bar Association president had come to an end and he was not re-elected. The bottom line was that from March 1997 to the end of his term, Hoter-Yishai headed the Bar Association under the shadow of a Supreme Court petition seeking his ouster from a post to which he had been democratically elected. For most of the time he was unable to serve on the Judicial Selection Committee.

Of Hoter-Yishai's indictment and the demand that he leave his position, whatever was the cause of these proceedings, a journalist, Evelyn Gordon, wrote that the message was conveyed very clearly—anyone who raises his voice against the Supreme Court needs to be prepared for more than a merely ideological war.[326]

The scandal of the baseless criminal proceedings against Neeman and Hoter-Yishai did not shake the unchallenged standing of the legal system, which continued to act as if nothing whatever had happened that might require repair or reflection.

Some voices were raised, however. One was that of another journalist, Amnon Dankner, who wrote an article in *Ma'ariv* under the headline "Hoter-Yishai is right: The acquittal of the Bar Association president uncovers serious flaws in the work of the state prosecution." He connected the dots between this affair and that of Ya'akov Neeman, who upon taking over the justice ministry "sharply and publicly criticized the State Attorney's Office. He also indicated that he would ask the then attorney general, Michael Ben-Yair, to resign. And look, before long the prosecution filed a severe indictment against him that . . . it turned out, had nothing serious to it." In short, Dankner wrote, "Justice, as they say, must also be seen, and on the face of it what emerges from these two affairs is not justice, but an itching suspicion that critics of the system are being targeted. . . ."

Hoter-Yishai's saga continued even after his acquittal on the tax charges. Klugman, who took his place on the Judicial Selection Committee, resigned from that post, and a meeting of the Bar Association's National Council was scheduled to choose another person for the post. The leading candidate was Hoter-Yishai. Then, on July 15, 1998, precisely the day the council was slated to meet, Hoter-Yishai was indicted once again, this time for contempt of court. The basis for the indictment were blunt remarks he made against Judge Herman-Hadasi and against her verdict, at the stage when the prosecution asked for a postponement of the hearing on his sentence. Hadas Magen, in the financial daily *Globes*, quoted Hoter-Yishai saying: "If the court intends to postpone the hearing on this subject, it would be just one more proof of the illicit symbiosis in this case between court and the prosecution." The headline was "Hoter-Yishai: The court's subterfuges stink."

Hoter-Yishai informed the Bar's National Council of the new indictment, but the Council nevertheless chose him to rejoin the Judicial Selection Committee. A few days later, however, the Movement for Quality Government petitioned the Supreme Court yet again, and on July 22 the court ordered Hoter-Yishai to give cause why he should not recuse himself from the Judicial Selection Committee. This time he decided not to resign, on the grounds that the indictment had been known to the body that chose him for the post (beyond this, the charge was so baseless that he would have been justified in disregarding it).

This time, even the media, largely hostile to Hoter-Yishai, protested that the prosecution had gone too far. For example, *Haaretz* economic columnist Nehemia Shtrasler wrote: "Is only the blood of judges red? . . . Do all other human beings not have dignity? . . . Is an attack on the prime minister on his family not more critical? . . . Is an attack . . . on members of the Knesset not a serious blow against democracy?" American law professor Alan Dershowitz wrote a letter to the *Jerusalem Post* protesting the charge against Hoter-Yishai. Appearing under the headline "The right to criticize," Dershowitz also explained why judges should not judge those who critique them.

In November 1998, some four months after the new indictment, in a hearing before Judge Ehud Rakam of the Magistrates Court, the prosecution was persuaded to reach a compromise that was in effect the withdrawal of an indictment that should never have been made in the first place. As part of the agreement, Hoter-Yishai declared that he "had not said the things included in the indictment with the intention of harming the legal system or disrespecting the judge." In the wake of this declaration, the indictment was expunged and he was acquitted. The agreement also stipulated that the withdrawal of the indictment would not be followed by a "chain reaction" in the media, which presumably meant that Hoter-Yishai would not take advantage of the withdrawal of the indictment to criticize the prosecution in the media. The Supreme Court petition calling for Hoter-Yishai's dismissal from the Judicial Selection Committee was denied, since it no longer had any rationale.[327]

But Hoter-Yishai's tribulations were not yet over. In December the Central Committee of the Israel Bar Association met. On its agenda was a request by Judge Ziva Herman-Hadasi that two law school graduates be assigned to perform their apprenticeships as her clerks. Hoter-Yishai recused himself from voting on the matter, but he did not refrain from making a comment on Herman-Hadasi's fitness to train young lawyers. The prosecution jumped at the opportunity and declared his comment an "ostensible violation" of the apology he had made in the compromise arrangement. (Hoter-Yishai denied that his statement in court constituted an apology.) Uzi Vogelman of the State Attorney's Office (today a Supreme Court justice) maintained that "contempt of her honor the judge continues . . . Under these circumstances, we will consider a resumption of criminal proceedings against Hoter-Yishai for contempt of court."[328] The idea that an indictment that had ended in an acquittal could be resumed on the grounds that the agreement that had ended it had been breached hardly lends respect to the prosecution. It is a judicial invention. In fact, Hoter-Yishai had not breached any compact, since his declaration regarding Herman-Hadasi had not related to the previous proceeding.

About two months later a new indictment was filed against him, no less baseless than the others. The case was heard in Haifa by Judge Amirav Rand, who accepted

Hoter-Yishai's claim that there was no reason for him to even respond to such an unfounded accusation. The prosecution was ignominiously sent home.

About a month after Hoter-Yishai's first indictment, the Bar-On–Hebron scandal exploded. Hoter-Yishai found himself embroiled in that as well. In a brief, State Attorney Edna Arbel maintained that "[f]rom the material, it appears that MK Deri, Attorney Hoter-Yishai, and businessman David Appel, who have social and business ties, sought Ronnie Bar-On's appointment to the post of attorney general. The three worked assiduously to achieve their goal." Hoter-Yishai's interest in the improper appointment, she said, was that "at the time . . . the State Attorney's Office was about to decide on the question of indicting Hoter-Yishai."

It is not clear what Arbel's basis for this statement was. Hoter-Yishai denied any connection to the Bar-On affair, other than his stated opinion that it would be best if the next attorney general was chosen from the ranks of the country's private attorneys. He was called in for questioning by the police several times. At one point, one of the police interrogators told him that, even though it was obvious to them that he had not been involved in the Bar-On appointment, his name would appear in the final report "in a way that would tarnish his good name and taint his image."

Hoter-Yishai wrote to Arbel to alert her to the baseless insertion of his name into the affair, but it was to no avail. One might expect the state attorney at least to have noted the fact that Hoter-Yishai denied any involvement in the matter and to have laid out the evidence supporting her claim that he was. But none of that appears in her opinion, which was released while he was on trial for alleged tax violations. Naming him in a controversial political-legal scandal was liable to further poison the atmosphere against him. Arbel's brief contrasts with that of Attorney General Rubinstein, who omitted Hoter-Yishai's name from the opinion he issued just a few days later.

Just a year later, Hoter-Yishai filed a libel suit against Arbel. It recounted the unfounded criminal indictment that had been filed against him, as well as his interrogation in the Bar-On–Hebron affair even though "it was clear from the outset that he had nothing to contribute to the investigation." He charged that Arbel had "inserted unfounded statements" about him in the report she issued, without giving him any practical opportunity to tell his side of the story. She had deliberately slandered him, he maintained. Yet his suit was soon dismissed, and the dismissal was confirmed by Justice Dalia Dorner of the Supreme Court, on the grounds that the state attorney issues her opinions in her official capacity and that as such she enjoys immunity from civil suits, even if "libel is committed carelessly or maliciously."[329] The question is whether there was any justification for this expansion of immunity and its application to opinions of the state attorney even when the people named there have had no real chance to defend themselves from serious accusations made against them in such opinions. At the very minimum, Arbel should have been told to re-examine Hoter-Yishai's claim that his name was mixed unnecessarily into an affair to which he was unconnected. If it turned out that he was correct, she should have been instructed to issue an appropriate correction. But that is not what happened.

In addition to all this, it turned out that Hoter-Yishai had been called in for questioning dozens of times, in a wide variety of police investigations. Nothing emerged against him in any of these cases. In one such instance, for example, Hoter-Yishai was ordered to report to the police on November 24, 1999. He did not appear, and asked to be questioned in his office. That same day police interrogators appeared in his office and demanded that he come with them. He refused. The interrogators told him he was under arrest, but Hoter-Yishai still refused to go with them. The police went to the Tel Aviv Magistrates Court to request an arrest warrant, while Hoter-Yishai asked the court to free him from arrest. Judge Eliyahu Becher decided that the case should be heard the next day before the court's deputy president, Zecharia Caspi, and that in the meantime Hoter-Yishai would be set free under certain conditions. The police were not satisfied with that. That same afternoon they went to the District Court. The court clerk consulted with the justice on duty that day, Edmond Levy (later appointed to the Supreme Court), who ruled that there was no urgency and that the police could submit an appeal the next morning.

At this point the State Attorney's Office stepped in. Nava Ben-Or (now a District Court judge) went to the Supreme Court. To his astonishment, Hoter-Yishai was called in to a night session before Justice Zamir in an appeal of a District Court decision that has not yet been rendered (its only decision was that the issue would be heard the next day; a decision of the Magistrates Court cannot be appealed directly to the Supreme Court). The hearing went on, midnight passed, and in the early hours of the next morning Justice Zamir composed a learned opinion.[330] The case, he said, presented

> difficult legal questions … In fact, no appeal was submitted to the District Court and no decision was rendered by the District Court … is it possible and proper under the law for the Supreme Court, under these circumstances, to hear an appeal of a Magistrates Court ruling? And if we maintain that the District Court rendered an opinion, although an unwritten one, it is a decision not to hear the appeal of the Magistrates Court ruling that same day, only the next day. Is it proper for the Supreme Court to discuss the appeal of such a decision?

Zamir had another question as well. "Can an arrest order legitimately be issued by me in the middle of the night, when the Magistrates Court has decided that the arrest warrant request will be heard by it early the next morning?"

It is unfortunate that Zamir did not pose this question, the answer to which is obvious, before he convened his midnight session. In fact, he decided in the end that the lower court should address the matter, as would have happened had he left the case alone. But he ruled that the appeal would remain in abeyance, so that he could render a decision in light of developments. Zamir made no secret of his sympathy for the prosecution. "The clear principle," he ruled, "is that the police must act equally toward all people … a person may not demand that he be treated as more privileged than a common person … every person asked by the police to report to the police to provide testimony or be interrogated should do so."

Zamir had nothing to say about the prosecution's behavior, about its exaggerated prosecutorial fervor, about its loss of all sense of proportion, or about the nighttime race to the Supreme Court following reasonable decisions by two lower courts. He offered no explanation of what was so urgent, and why he consented to preside over a nighttime session as if it were a matter of a criminal who was about to escape or who presented a clear and present danger to the public, when everyone knew that just a few hours later the Magistrates Court would convene to consider the matter.

Zamir noted that the police "believed that the respondent's detention was highly important." Is that sufficient? Can a court accept such claims uncritically?

Zamir wrote about equality, but Hoter-Yishai argued that "the police are hounding [me], and not treating [me] like every other suspect." Was this claim, based on the principle of equality, not worthy of inquiry? Zamir makes no reference to it. At the same time, he gives serious consideration to every one of the prosecution's claims. But is it not the court's responsibility to exercise oversight of the police and prosecution? The impression, on the contrary, is that the state's attorneys feel—especially when standing before Zamir, who, as a former attorney general, had stood on the prosecution side—quite at home there. The Supreme Court likes to hold forth about human rights. Zamir's decision shows a reality that is quite different.

The story of the night session has a short epilogue. Hoter-Yishai was interrogated by the police in connection with a real estate transaction, but nothing came of it. More than ten years have gone by since then, and in that time there have been no developments in this urgent police inquiry, which apparently has been closed.

In sum, during his second term as president of the Bar Association, Dror Hoter-Yishai was indicted no less than three times, each indictment raising serious questions. In each case he was acquitted or the prosecution was compelled to withdraw the indictment or agree to have it expunged. On top of this, he was repeatedly and incessantly summoned for police interrogation, with the Supreme Court's night session testifying to the obsessive prosecutorial nature of all these proceedings. It is hard to escape the impression that the criminal code was misused here, way beyond what is proper in a democracy that respects human rights.

It did have results. In the Bar Association elections of 1999, Hoter-Yishai was defeated by his rival, Shlomo Cohen. The improper criminal proceedings against him almost certainly contributed much to his loss. Hoter-Yishai made mistakes. He spoke out too bluntly and made uncalled for ad hominem attacks when he spoke about the salaries and other income earned by judges. It was nothing new for judges to have teaching positions or to write books, and no one had ever suggested there was anything improper about it. But the years have shown that his fundamental claims about the legal system are solid ones, many of them accepted today by the public at large.

25

Guilty until Proven Innocent

I. THE DIMINISHING CHANCES OF ACQUITTAL

The growing number of judicial appointments coming from the state prosecution was not confined to the Supreme Court. The Supreme Court justices, recall, wield considerable influence over appointments to the lower courts as well. Supreme Court justices hailing from the prosecution have displayed a notable tendency to look there to fill District and Magistrates Court vacancies. Most of the judges thus appointed specialize in criminal law, and as such the criminal cases that reach the District and Magistrates Courts are largely assigned to them. Thus, the chances that an accused person will find himself facing a judge (or panel) with roots in the prosecution are very high. When the financial newspaper *The Marker* checked in 2007, it found that 30 percent of the 611 sitting judges on all levels had reach their posts from the prosecution, and that an additional 14 percent had served in other government positions. Hence, although public lawyers constitute a mere 10 percent of the total number of practicing attorneys, they form 44 percent of the bench.[331]

The prosecutorial proclivity that developed in the Supreme Court spread to the lower courts. The result could be seen not only in the rules of criminal law but also in practice, in the percentage of convictions. Judges began to broaden the scope of vague offenses, such as breach of trust, and made it easier to obtain a conviction on the basis of dubious evidence. Furthermore, they discarded the traditional rule that, in case of doubt, the law should be interpreted in favor of the defendant.

Aharon Barak devoted an entire book to this issue, laying out his philosophy of interpretation—*Purposive Interpretation in Law*. The central idea expounded by the book is that a legal text should be interpreted in light of its purpose, that is, "the values, goals, interests, policies, and aims that the text is designed to actualize."[332] He also distinguishes between the subjective aspect of the purpose, meaning the intention of the legislator or party to a contract, and the objective aspect. The latter does not necessarily have anything to do with the author of the language, but may rather reflect societal values, among them justice and morals. Clearly, this grants great power to the judge, who is at liberty to determine, in light of his view of society's values, what the law's objective purpose is.

The concept of purposive interpretation was applied to criminal law as well. It was adopted by the Knesset, presumably under the influence of the jurists who drafted an amendment to the Penal Code in 1994. The amendment sought to integrate Barak's principle of purposive interpretation with the principle of interpreting in the defendant's favor. However, it is clear that the purposive interpretation takes precedence. The new section (34U) provides that in cases in which several possible purposive interpretations of a law are reasonable, the one that is most lenient to the defendant should be applied. In other words the lenient interpretation will not be applied if it is inconsistent with the purposive interpretation of the penal provision.

The ruling in *Yissascharov v. Chief Military Prosecutor* is an exception in this move toward stringent application of criminal law.[333] The case was heard by a panel of nine justices, and the majority opinion was rendered (seven years after the case was heard!) by Dorit Beinisch. She declared that the court could, at its discretion, exclude evidence that had been obtained illegally. In the case at hand, it was a confession by the accused, but in principle the rule applied to other instances as well, such as evidence obtained via illegal search and seizure. The approach is liberal, but its result was not liberal at all. In fact, the rule has hardly ever been used so as to acquit a defendant of any significant charge against him.[334]

Under the revolutionary court, the percentage of convictions reached illogical proportions. In 1990, 95.4 percent of indictments ended in conviction, but that was apparently not enough. In 2005 the figure reached an astonishing 99.9 percent.[335] In other words, only one, or perhaps two out of every 1,000 defendants in criminal trials was acquitted. In 2007 the figure declined somewhat—only 98.6 percent of defendants were convicted, but it remains utterly unacceptable.*

True, these figures do not present the entire picture. In some cases the prosecution drops charges, and this is not included in the statistics. There are also cases in which a single indictment is issued against several defendants, some of whom are acquitted and others are convicted. Such a case is counted by the figures as a conviction. Similarly, in many cases a single person is accused of several offenses. It is sufficient for him to be convicted of a single count for the case to be counted as a conviction, even if he was acquitted on most counts. Furthermore, sometimes a person is cleared of a serious charge but the court convicts him of a lighter charge. In addition, a large number of convictions take the form of plea bargains in which a person is convicted of lesser or fewer charges that carry a lighter sentence than those included in the original indictment.

In fact, a study conducted by the Supreme Court's Department of Information and Research shows lower conviction rates.[336] The study examined a random sample of criminal cases heard by the Magistrates and District Courts between May 2010 and May 2011. It found that the prosecution dropped charges in 15 percent of the cases that came before the Magistrates Courts, and that in more than 5 percent of the cases in which a defendant had confessed to the crime the courts nevertheless refrained from convicting him. Frequently, defendants were convicted on only some counts or of less serious crimes than they were originally charged with. According to the authors of the study, the 99 percent conviction rate is misleading. They recognize, however, that when a case is litigated to the end, "the percentages of full acquittals are indeed very low (less than one percent)."

---

* I do not know if there is a connection between this modest decline in the conviction rate and my repeated declarations, while I was justice minister, that this level was unreasonable.

Not all these qualifications bear equal weight. The fact that a defendant accused of a serious crime is in the end convicted of a lesser one may be a relief of a sort to him, but he has nevertheless been convicted of a crime, and the pall of that conviction will hang over him for many years thereafter, affecting his reputation, his ability to find work and to obtain visas to enter other countries. The same is true of a person acquitted on all counts but one. The impression is that the courts are reluctant to embarrass the prosecution by issuing blanket acquittals—the approach seems to be that the prosecution ought to "get something." That should not be encouraged. It gives the prosecution an incentive to heap up charges and issue lengthy indictments, in the hope that at least one accusation will stick. The bottom line is that, however you qualify it, the level of convictions is unreasonable.

Furthermore, these same qualifications were true in earlier years and thus do not explain the steady rise in the conviction rate, as reflected in government statistics: 77.8 percent in 1961, 92.3 percent in 1981, 95.4 percent in 1990, and 99.9 percent in 2005. It seems likely that the declining number of acquittals reinforces itself. The clearer it becomes to a defendant and his counsel that the chances of acquittal are close to nil, the greater his incentive to plead guilty or seek a plea bargain. Each such pleading or bargain in turn pushes the percentage of convictions up further.

A similar picture emerges in criminal appeals to the Supreme Court. A study of the allowance or denial of appeals from 1948 to 1994 shows that the state's chances of winning an appeal on a criminal case were 70.1 percent, while a defendant's chances were only half that, 34.9 percent. Neither is that the complete picture, as another study shows that the state's advantage, that is, its chances of winning an appeal as opposed to those of the defendant, were lower until 1981, after which they rose considerably, during the period of the judicial revolution.[337]

A later study, looking at the years 2006–2007, shows that when the state appealed judgments in criminal cases it won no less than 81.1 percent of the time, while defendants won only 15.1 percent of the time.[338] This may be explained, perhaps, by the fact that the prosecution tends to appeal only when it estimates that it has a reasonable chance of winning, whereas a defendant may well seek an appeal even if his chances of success are low, as he has nothing to lose. But that can only be a partial explanation. It cannot account for the drastic differential these figures show.

The implications of these figures are immense. First, they show that the prosecution has gained huge powers. The fate of a defendant is for all intents and purposes sealed when the state or police prosecutors decide to indict him. If he goes to trial, he can try to bargain over the punishment and the counts on which he will be convicted, but his conviction on some offense is nearly guaranteed.

The second implication is political. A public figure knows that the critical point comes when a complaint is made against him. From that point onward his fate lies in the hands of the State Attorney's Office, but not only his fate. The doom of the government he sits in or the party he belongs to is also determined.

II. BREACH OF TRUST, FRONT AND CENTER

The trial of Shimon Sheves, director general of the Prime Minister's Office during Yitzhak Rabin's second government, took place after Rabin's Labor Party had lost power and Ariel Sharon was prime minister. Sheves no longer held a public post, such that his trial did not have the same implications as one of proceedings against a figure at the center of the political stage. Yet, in the end, his conviction on the hazy charge of breach of trust boosted the prosecutorial inclinations of the judicial system and further empowered the prosecution. It demonstrated that the State Attorney's Office and the police could conduct investigations and achieve convictions in circumstances that no one had ever thought previously could be a basis for a criminal inquiry or trial.

The facts of the case are fairly complicated. The main issue is that Sheves, as a public office-holder, took action in matters affecting two businessmen personally close to him. One case involved upgrading a businessman's connections with a foreign country, the anticipated result being closing profitable defense contracts with the country in question. In the end, no such contracts were signed. In the second case, he helped a building project move forward. In the first case, the businessman deposited money in Sheves's private bank account, while in the second Sheves received payments from two other businessmen, not directly involved in the building project, after he left office.

The case was tried in the Tel Aviv District Court before judge Edmond Levy, who acquitted Sheves on a count of bribery in the first case, but convicted him of an attempt to receive a bribe and of breach of trust. In the second case, Levy acquitted him of bribery and breach of trust. The sentence was three years in prison, one of which was on probation, and a fine of NIS 50,000 (about $12,200 at the time).[339] Sheves appealed both the conviction and the sentence to the Supreme Court, while the state appealed his acquittal on the charge of breach of trust in the second case (but not his acquittal on the bribery charge). Justices Dalia Dorner and Eliahu Mazza, in the majority, acquitted Sheves on the first count, on the grounds that it had not been proven beyond reasonable doubt. In the second case, Mazza criticized Sheves on the grounds of conflict of interest, but ruled that his involvement in his friend's building project had been inconsequential and that "it could certainly be that his actions constituted a disciplinary violation involving an ethical and public fault." But not every ethical fault needs to have a criminal label attached to it. Mazza found that, in this case, Sheves's behavior had not reached the level required for a criminal conviction. The bottom line was that, in the appeal, Sheves was acquitted on all counts.[340]

The reader may well feel uncomfortable about Sheves's acquittal when he clearly acted, to say the least, in a manner unbefitting a public official. But, once the bribery charge failed, the judges in the majority based their ruling on the imperative to exercise caution and to seek to avoid convicting a government official on the vague charge of breach of trust. Miriam Naor, in her minority opinion, agreed with the justices in the majority in voting to acquit Sheves of the charges in the first case, but maintained that he should be convicted of breach of trust in the second case.

The state did not accept this result and petitioned for a further hearing by a larger panel. Justice Mishael Cheshin granted this request, after the prosecutors declared that if they won the case, the state would forego their demand for a prison term. Presumably the state's attorneys made this commitment because they understood that without it their request would be denied. Indeed, further hearing in this case was hardly appropriate on two counts. First, the state should generally refrain from asking for a further hearing of a case in order to seek the conviction of a defendant who has already been acquitted by the Supreme Court. Second, by law, a further hearing is to be allowed only if the legal issue at stake is of an "importance, difficulty, or novelty" that justifies it. But Mazza's decision acquitting Sheves established no new rule. He simply applied the law to the facts. Other judges may have disagreed with the way he did so, but that in and of itself does not justify a further hearing. It seems, rather, that an exceptional hearing was allowed in order to give the court a chance to expand the boundaries of the problematic category of breach of trust and to signal to the legal system that the court was adopting a tougher prosecutorial approach to this offense than it had previously taken.

That is indeed what happened. Eight justices voted to convict Sheves of breach of trust in both cases, with only Mazza remaining in the minority.[341] The court recognized that "the boundaries of breach of trust are hazy," but ruled that its validity should be recognized. One of the salient instances of the violation was when a public official took action in a matter in which he had a conflict of interest, the court declared. Yet the court also sought not to broaden the category too much. "Conflict of interest in and of itself is not sufficient," the court declared; "another 'aggravating aspect' is also required." This could, for example, be material damage to the public's confidence in government officials, their integrity, or the standards of public administration.

I need hardly say more about the imprecision of all these tests, given that even the definition of "conflict of interest" is unclear. For example, is it a conflict of interest for a public official to promote a project that an activist in his political party has a vested interest in? Is it a conflict of interest if he seeks to promote a subordinate with whom he has a history of cooperation stretching over many years?

In one of his articles, Aharon Barak notes that a "vague criminal law" would not meet the standards set by Basic Law: Human Liberty and Dignity.[342] He refers specifically to Section 198 of the Penal Code, which imposed criminal sanctions on "[a]ny person who does any act which may cause or tend to a public mischief." If so, why does this not apply to breach of trust? Moreover, some fifty years earlier, the classical Supreme Court strongly denounced the section relating to public mischief, on the grounds that such an offense, lacking clear boundaries, in practice authorizes the courts to create new offences about which the public has not been warned and enables retroactive punishment for acts that were not regarded as a crime when committed.[343] As a result, this problematic section was seldom invoked.* But the revolutionary Supreme Court, despite its human rights rhetoric, was completely undeterred by the prospect of retroactive punishment. In his ruling in the Sheves case, Justice Cheshin sought to make a distinction between causing public mischief and breach of trust. But given the fuzziness of these terms, it is difficult, if not impossible, to distinguish between the difficulties raised by the two. He also pointed out that the public mischief offence was applied generally, while breach of trust applies only to public officials. But it is difficult to see why this is relevant and why it is permissible to deprive public officials (a term which, in any case, the Penal Code defines very broadly) of basic human rights.

The Sheves verdict, in which Basic Law: Human Dignity and Liberty is not even mentioned, deserves to be compared to the ruling in an American case, *Skilling v. U.S.*, handed down in 2010.[344] Jeffrey Skilling was the chief executive officer of the

---

* During my tenure as justice minister, Knesset member Yoel Hasson introduced a private member's bill to revoke this section. I supported it, and the bill passed in 2008.

Enron Corporation, which crashed into bankruptcy. Several of the company's officers, Skilling among them, were indicted on several counts, among them honest services fraud, that is, "to deprive another of the intangible right of honest services." This provision was enacted by the U.S. Congress with the intent of including under the category of fraud deceptions and ruses that prevent a person from receiving the honest service to which he is entitled. In the past, it had been invoked to hold workers responsible for furthering their individual interests in violation of their obligation to act in good faith toward their employer. Among other things, it had been used to charge workers who had not revealed to their employees a conflict of interest that might influence their actions on their jobs. Despite the different wordings, there is considerable similarity between the broad American definition of the honest services fraud provision and the Israeli section on fraud and breach of trust (although the American provision is not confined, as the Israeli one, to public servants but rather also imposes an obligation on the employees of private businesses). Skilling's attorneys argued that this type of offence was unconstitutional, on the grounds that a criminal law had to be worded in a manner such that a normal person could understand what he is forbidden to do. Otherwise the law could be applied arbitrarily and with prejudice.

The U.S. Supreme Court accepted this argument in the main. Justice Ruth Bader Ginsburg, who wrote the leading opinion, maintained that the offense should not be struck down entirely, because the court took care not to invalidate laws passed by Congress if it could resolve the issue by means of interpretation. As such, the offence should be confined to situations lying at the heart of the issue, that is, bribery and kickbacks. In this, the justices rejected the possibility of convicting a defendant on this count simply because he had acted in a situation of conflict of interest. Unlike Ginsburg, some of the judges considered that the provision should be struck down in its entirety. Skilling's conviction of depriving another of the "intangible right of honest services" was thus quashed. The U.S. Supreme Court added that if Congress wished to expand the bounds of criminal responsibility, it would have to do so using clear language, laying out well-defined rules that would remove any concern that due process might be violated. The case was remanded to the Court of Appeals to deal with questions that remained open regarding Skilling's convictions on other counts. In 2013 in the course of the proceedings, his lawyers reached an agreement with the prosecution under which his term in prison was reduced from twenty-four years to fourteen.

The U.S. Supreme Court was careful to preserve the fundamental principles of criminal law and the human rights they protect. The same cannot be said of its Israeli counterpart. The Israeli court's ruling on the issue of fraud and breach of trust empowers the prosecution to hound suspects in a broad range of cases and creates exactly the sort of situation that the American ruling seeks to prevent, one in which the law can be applied selectively, arbitrarily, and prejudicially. It also raises the question of how such a ruling can be consistent with Basic Law: Human Dignity and Liberty and with the fundamental principles of human rights.

The *Sheves* ruling of 2004 granted the prosecution and the criminal investigation apparatus huge powers. It did not take long for those powers to be exercised. The hazy and unbounded charge of breach of trust became the flagship of the prosecution and the courts in their battle against public figures.

26

The Attorney General Reigns Supreme

I. COUNSEL AS COMMAND

When Aharon Barak was appointed to the Supreme Court in 1978, Itzhak Zamir replaced him as attorney general, serving in that post until 1986. In 1985, when the Shin Bet affair had yet to explode in full force, Zamir issued a puzzling guideline according to which the president was not empowered to pardon criminals prior to their conviction. Zamir's intention was to establish a rule that would bind the government and the president. When the subject reached the Supreme Court, Barak sought to give Zamir's rule the force of a Supreme Court ruling. He failed. Barak remained in the minority, with Meir Shamgar and Miriam Ben-Porat ruling, in keeping with precedent, that Zamir's opinion was wrong.

This failure was not the end of the matter. Eventually, Zamir and Barak successfully put into place a number of subversive tenets that have virtually no parallel anywhere else in the world. They turned the rule of law into the rule of lawyers, and for all intents and purposes turned the attorney general into the Israeli government's commander in chief. Zamir and Barak pushed through this transformation in Israeli jurisprudence by taking an uncompromising and extreme position on two issues. The first was the force of opinions issued by the attorney general and the extent to which the government was obligated to act in accordance with them. The second was how the state and its governing bodies would be represented in court, and who could determine when and why the state, government, or any officer or institution of the state body was entitled to such representation.

Recall that the debate over the powers of the attorney general broke out during the tenure of the first person to hold that post, Yaakov-Shimshon Shapira. It intensified considerably when Minister of Justice Dov Yosef clashed with Attorney General Gideon Hausner. A committee headed by Justice Shimon Agranat was appointed in 1962 to examine the issue. It concluded that the attorney general had independent decision-making powers with regard to criminal proceedings. In this area, the committee asserted, he is not required to obey orders from the justice minister, even though he is required to take into consideration the government's policy (for example, to fight a certain category of offenses) and to consult with the minister about cases with security or public implications. The committee's ruling was seen as a victory for the attorney general, but he was less successful in other areas. Hausner maintained that, when he issued an opinion, it was to guide the government "as long as the court has not ruled otherwise." The justice minister thought, for his part, that "the government would do best generally to accept the attorney general's advice," but that it had no obligation to do so. In this regard, the Agranat Committee adopted Yosef's opinion, to the effect that proper administration requires "that the government generally relate to the legal opinions [of the attorney general] as reflecting existing law. However, the government is permitted to decide that, in a particular case, it should act in accordance with its own discretion."

The attorney general's Hebrew title is an important piece of evidence in this regard. A literal translation would be "legal adviser to the government." As that job description clearly states, his job is to advise. If his recommendations become binding, he ceases to be an adviser and becomes a judge, and the opinions he renders have the status of judicial rulings. All the government can do if it does not like his ruling or considers it to be erroneous is to petition the Supreme Court to overrule him. The absurdity of a government petitioning against its own legal counsel hardly requires amplification. Beyond that, it raises the question of who is to represent the government in such a proceeding. Is the attorney general, who is the government's lawyer, meant to represent the government and argue against his own legal opinion? It seems unlikely that he would do so, and if he did, that he would do it well. Hence the Agranat Committee's ruling that the attorney general's opinion does not bind the government is logical and reasonable.

Zamir was not persuaded. In 1986, just before he left the post under conditions that were for him problematic, he gave a lecture on the attorney general's role. One can sympathize with how he felt at the time, but his feelings hardly justify the way he presented the Agranat Committee's position. "The committee ruled unambiguously in favor of the attorney general," he wrote. That is, "Where there are differences between [the attorney general and the government], the final decision lies in the hands of the attorney general."* This is, to say the least, far from representing what the committee's report actually says. It is true with regard to the attorney general's authority in specific criminal cases, but the opposite is true with regard to opinions the attorney general authors on legal matters.

Zamir laid out the rules that made the attorney general powerful. "Rule one, which also finds expression in the Agranat committee report . . . says that the attorney general's opinion reflects the law, as far as the government is concerned . . . The consequence is that the government must act . . . in accordance with the attorney general's opinion." But the committee said the exact opposite, and said so quite explicitly—the government is free to act in any given matter "in accordance with its own discretion."

Some years later, when Zamir again wrote about the Agranat Committee report, he was more cautious. He termed the committee's report "lukewarm," and maintained

---

* During my tenure as minister of justice, Dan Avi-Yitzhak produced, at my request, a comprehensive comparative study on the position of attorney general in different countries. The study was used to draft legislation laying out and setting limits on the attorney general's duties and obligations. The study showed that the Agranat Committee's determination, that an opinion rendered by the attorney general does not bind the government, is consistent with practice and law in the other countries examined.

that "the meaning . . . is not entirely clear." In fact, the meaning is crystal clear, but it conflicts with Zamir's theory.

Zamir bolstered his rule that the government must act in accordance with the attorney general's opinion with a second rule. "The state's representation in court is invested entirely and exclusively in the attorney general. This means that if a government authority refuses to act in accordance with the attorney general's opinion, it will have no one to defend it in court."

Where does this second rule come from? What is its source in law? Zamir does not say. But Ruth Gavison has noted that not only did the Agranat Committee not advocate Zamir's rules, but in fact rejected them explicitly.[345] Gavison's co-author of an article on the subject, Eitan Levontin, notes that "the unavoidable conclusion is that [Zamir's rules] . . . present an inaccurate portrayal of the Agranat committee report."[346] In short, the rules have no basis in law or in logic. Their origin lies in the attorney general's desire to take control of the government, a desire that no doubt grew stronger because of what happened to Zamir in the Shin Bet affair. The law states: "In every proceeding to which the state is party, the state will be represented by the attorney general or his agent."[347] But this clearly refers to civil proceedings and not to representation before the Supreme Court in cases regarding administrative and constitutional matters. Its purpose is to save the government the trouble of issuing the attorney general a power of attorney each time he has to appear in court to represent the state in a civil suit. Furthermore, it is clear that any legal counsel must act in accordance with his client's instructions. If he cannot or is not interested in doing so, he must resign and enable his client to choose a different lawyer.

Zamir's rules not only have no basis in law, but lack any grounding in the legal tradition. Attorney General Haim Cohn never dreamed that he could refrain from representing the government when he did not agree with it. It is said that Attorney General Meir Shamgar told the government that he would not defend its position in the Helen Seidman conversion case,[348] but the matter never came to a head, and nowhere was it implied that the government could not, in such a case, hire another lawyer to represent it. According to one version of the controversy surrounding Yitzhak Rabin's illegal American bank account, Attorney General Aharon Barak informed Minister of Finance Yehoshua Rabinowitz that if he decided to allow Rabin to pay a penalty in lieu of facing criminal charges, he, Barak, would himself petition the Supreme Court to order Rabin's indictment. In such a case, Barak said, Rabinowitz would have to hire a private attorney to defend him, as no one in the State Attorney's Office would agree to do so. Rabinowitz would also have to pay this attorney's fees out of his own pocket, as Barak would not allow the government to fund it. But all this shows that even Barak did not think he could forbid the finance minister from hiring a private attorney to represent him. In fact, it is not clear at all on what authority Barak declared that he would prevent the state from paying the fee of a private attorney representing the finance ministry. Could he, for instance, prevent such payment even if the Supreme Court demonstrated that Rabinowitz had been correct by ruling in his favor?

Zamir maintained that his rules reflected the law. The rules were put to the test in the 1980s in the case of the banning of Yitzhak Laor's play *Efrayim Goes Back to the Army*. The Film and Play Review Board, a former state body that then had to approve every film screened and play staged in Israel, refused to sanction its performance on the grounds that "it presents the military government in a false, distorted, malevolent, and malicious way, even comparing it to the Nazi regime." The board was asked to reconsider its decision. A state attorney, Renato Yarak, represented the attorney general at the board's session. Yarak informed the commission that it would be difficult to defend a ban on the play before the Supreme Court. The board nevertheless affirmed its previous decision. As expected, Laor petitioned the Supreme Court to overturn the proscription. Zamir refused to defend the board's decision before the court. The case was heard by a panel chaired by Barak.

In his decision, Barak briefly surveyed the matter of the board's representation. He noted that Zamir had refused to defend the board on the grounds that it had made its decision in contravention of the instructions he had given it. Zamir did not, however, prevent the board from hiring a private attorney. Zamir explained his willingness to allow this on the grounds that the board was not a "regular government body" and thus "it would not be proper to prevent the board from presenting its reasoning and explaining its decision to the Supreme Court." (And had it been a "regular government body," would Zamir have had the authority to prevent the board from having its day in court?)

In his opinion, Barak related these events without comment, presumably because he agreed with the assumptions on which Zamir based his actions. On the issue at hand, the court voided the board's ban and allowed the play to be staged.[349]

Zamir also refused to represent Shin Bet chief Avraham Shalom in one of the Bus 300 cases. Zamir and State Attorney Dorit Beinisch had instructed the police to investigate the claim that Shin Bet agents had killed the two terrorists apprehended when the hijacked bus was intercepted. It is not surprising that Zamir would not represent Shalom in such a case, but in this case Zamir also refused to allow the Shin Bet chief to hire a private attorney to defend him. What can justify such a decision?

Prime Minister Shimon Peres maintained that, given that Zamir had a conflict of interest in the case, Shalom deserved to receive legal counsel from a nongovernment lawyer. Peres thus decided that Shalom would be represented by Ram Caspi, a prominent private attorney. The justice ministry's staff was furious. Zamir claimed a monopoly on representing government officials even when this meant that an official would be denied legal representation. Yechiel Gutman, a lawyer who wrote a book about the Shin Bet affair, quotes Zamir as saying, "Caspi came in as an adviser, a helper, whatever. I came out publicly against it ... I spoke about this phenomenon of court counselors and the rule of law ... Their positions do not empower them to go and ask opinions from a private attorney."[350]

It is easy enough to understand the feelings of a person who thinks he has a monopoly and then suddenly discovers that he has competitors whom the customers prefer. But Zamir's chagrin doesn't make his position any more acceptable. It's obviously easier on the attorney general when public officials are required to accept his rulings submissively without even considering whether his opinion is correct or not. But such legal clout does not sit well with the fundamental demands of fairness or with human rights. Zamir claimed an exclusive privilege to sanction the retention of private legal services by government officials, but the idea that he can deprive them of any representation and deny them their day in court is unacceptable.

The issue of the Shin Bet chief's representation before the Supreme Court resolved itself when Zamir was replaced by Yosef Harish. Harish took a more reasonable stance. As Gutman quotes him:

> I decided that I would defend the state in all Supreme Court suits against it because I think that neither the attorney general, the state attorney, nor any other lawyer [in government service] can claim the luxury of not appearing [in court] in any matter about which he feels uncomfortable appearing. When is he permitted not to appear? Only when the government's position is indefensible . . . [when] it stands contrary to the great principles of law, morality, the rule of law—only then.

Tellingly, just a few years later, toward the end of his term, Harish adopted a position not fundamentally different from that taken by Zamir. The cases in point were those of Aryeh Deri and Raphael Pinchasi. In his ruling in the Pinchasi case, Aharon Barak wrote:

> The attorney general is the authorized interpreter of the law for the executive branch . . . and his interpretation obligates it internally . . .
> . . . This view derives its vitality from our constitutional tradition. The tradition was consolidated by the report of the committee of jurists on the powers of the attorney general (1962). Since then it has become part of Israel's common law.

Barak baffles with this claim. Where did this "constitutional tradition" come from? Why is it constitutional? Does he mean that it cannot be changed except by means of a constitution or basic law? Moreover, his statement is simply incorrect. As I have already shown, the Agranat Committee's report says something else entirely—that the government may choose to reject the attorney general's position. The committee's position was accepted by Chief Justice Yitzhak Olshan, who wrote that "with regard the first type of his powers [to render a legal opinion for the government], the attorney general's views, advice, and decisions do not obligate the government or its members when they have requested his guidance or opinion."[351]

What happens when the attorney general errs in interpreting the law, as Zamir did in his account of the president's power of pardon? For Barak and Zamir, the answer is clear—the executive branch must act in accordance with the mistaken opinion, in the name of the rule of law.[352] In one of his rulings, Justice Yoel Sussman adduced the term "doublethink," a word from newspeak, the language imposed by the regime in George Orwell's novel *1984*. Doublethink is, Sussman noted, "the ability to hold two contradictory beliefs simultaneously and to believe in both of them."[353] According to the new approach, the rule of law is to be preserved by means of requiring the government to act in accordance with the opinions of the attorney general, even if, in doing so, the government violates the law.

Yet the Supreme Court nevertheless promoted the attorney general to the position of the government's chief commanding officer. His opinion constitutes an order. But what is the scope of such an order? The answer seems simple—the attorney general's opinion is binding only on legal issues. But the tangle that the Supreme Court produced undermined even the simple and understood. If everything is justiciable, including the question of whether the government acts reasonably, the inescapable conclusion is that every government act or decision falls under the purview of the attorney general.

The best illustration of this is the way in which the attorney general gained control over government appointments. As I related in Chapter 17, the Supreme Court has assumed the power to declare the appointment of a person to a public position "unreasonable" and thus illegal. It can do so, for example, if the candidate is on record as having said, at some point in his life, something improper. This attitude was taken up by the attorney general, who acted accordingly in 2008 when a new director of the Israel Lands Administration was appointed. A search committee examined all the candidates and found three of them right for the job. Housing Minister Ze'ev Boim, under whose ministry the authority fell, wanted to appoint Yoel Lavi, the mayor of Ramla and an army reserve colonel. The saga began.

More than a year earlier, in a newspaper interview, Lavi was asked about the demand made by one of his city's Arab inhabitants regarding the change of a street name. The street had been given a "Zionist" name, and the Arab asked that the street be given an Arab name. Lavi's reaction was, "Why should I change the name? Because some Jamal wants to change the name, or because some Mohammad wants to change the name? Let him go change his God, what's the big deal? They can all fuck themselves." To this he added a tirade against a journalist who had written about Arab street names. Lavi published an apology in *Ha'aretz* a short time later.

This was not his only outburst. He told a *Ma'ariv* correspondent about an exchange he had with one of the city's Arab inhabitants during an election rally. The Arab complained that Lavi had erected a sign reading, "The people with the Golan," opposing Israeli withdrawal from the Golan Heights in the framework of an agreement with Syria. Lavi told the journalist that his response was: "I didn't come here to talk with you about national issues. I came to take care of the fact that you don't have water mains, sewage systems, roads, and sidewalks. If the Arab community wants to tangle with me on national issues, I'll be the first to shoot you. I have good life experience. Each time I've shot at an Arab I survived and he didn't. Go to hell." The newspaper article raised a public outcry and a demand for a police investigation. But none was forthcoming.

Attorney General Menachem Mazuz adopted the style of the Supreme Court. He spoke of the need to shore up "public trust" in government. He ruled that Lavi's racist remarks made him unfit to serve as director of the Israel Lands Administration. To this Mazuz added two other reasons for disqualifying Lavi. First, Lavi was under criminal investigation on suspicion of prejudicing good governance and integrity. Second, Lavi was affiliated with Boim's political party, Kadima, and when such a political connection existed between the minister making an appointment and the candidate, there had to be an explicit reason why the political candidate should be preferred to a candidate without political affiliation.

Neither of these reasons is persuasive. The police investigation had to do with a vague suspicion that should not have been taken seriously. Such investigations take years to complete, and it is unreasonable for them to paralyze public officials indefinitely. The fact is that, to this day, years after the offenses were supposedly committed, no indictment has been made. When the police take years to investigate the fuzziest of charges, the fact that a person is under investigation cannot in and of itself disqualify a person for public office indefinitely.

Neither should political party affiliation disqualify a candidate. The search committee ruled that Lavi was qualified for the job. It is no crime to belong to a political party—without parties, there can be no democracy. The idea that party members should be discriminated against is unreasonable and undemocratic. It is part of the super-piety and mistrust of public figures that has spread through Israel's law enforcement agencies. (Unfortunately, it has even made inroads into the law. In the same spirit, Section 18c of the Government Corporation Law forbids the appointment to the post of director or director general of a government corporation any person "who has a personal, business, or political link to any government ministers," unless the candidate possesses "special qualifications in the corporation's field of activities" or "other special qualifications.")

In addition to voiding Lavi's candidacy, Mazuz made another demand—that his name not even be brought before the cabinet, the body with the final power to make the appointment. The demand was baseless, but Boim gave in—further evidence of the attorney general's overweening power and the extent to which cabinet ministers fear crossing him.

A different candidate was chosen for the job. But Yoel Lavi filed suit against the prime minister and attorney general. The decision, rendered by Chief Justice Beinisch, affirmed Lavi's disqualification on the grounds of his racist outbursts. His apology was to no avail. The claim that his appointment would undermine public confidence in government was reiterated. Lavi had answered that charge with a counterargument that might seem unassailable to anyone not acquainted with legal complexities. He pointed out that he had won the recent mayoral elections in Ramla with the support of a large portion of the city's Arab inhabitants. In other words, despite whatever insulting remarks he might have made, he enjoyed the support of the public, the Arab public included. Beinisch's response to this was that "public confidence" is a "normative concept that is not measured in general elections, but rather measured by legal criteria in keeping with the fundamental values of Israeli society." You have to read it to believe it—what this means is that "public confidence" is a fictional concept, with no grounding in reality. It is rather a creation of the court. A person can enjoy public confidence in the real world, successfully pass the test of the polls, and still be considered, in the fictional-legal world, to be undermining public confidence in government. That happens in the fictional world crafted by the Supreme Court in its role as the nation's moral compass.

The Supreme Court affirmed the attorney general's substantive position while criticizing him for preventing the issue from coming before the cabinet. "The duty and responsibility to decide lies with the body to which the law grants the power of decision ... and the attorney general may not himself enforce the opinion that he rendered in his advising-interpretive capacity ... The determination made by the attorney general ... created an undesirable situation in which the authorized authority did not have the opportunity to exercise the power of decision placed in its hands." Yet the court did not void Mazuz's ruling and ordered the government to desist from appointing Lavi.[354]

This reasoning highlights the absurdity of the rules the Supreme Court established regarding the attorney general. It ruled that the government must accept the attorney general's rulings even if they are mistaken and even if the government does not agree with them. Yet the same court criticized the attorney general for not giving

the cabinet the opportunity to do its job "and take upon itself the public responsibility accompanying the decision." But why should the government have "public
responsibility" for an action it did not want to take? The cabinet, after all, did not
seek to disqualify Lavi. It wanted to appoint him. Here is another instance of flawed
jurisprudence—a court ruling that takes powers away from the government and
hands them over to the attorney general or to the Supreme Court, while at the same
time maintaining that the government remains responsible for the exercise of that
very same power of which it was deprived. This absurd situation was demonstrated
by Mazuz, who for all intents and purposes maintained that if he was authorized to
decide that Lavi was disqualified, why should the cabinet waste its time discussing
and voting on his appointment? Why should he not decide for them?[355]

When that is said and done, the force of a decision by the attorney general is
dwarfed by the matter of representation. As I have already noted, Prime Minister
Rabin resolutely opposed the dismissals of Deri and Pinchasi. Yet he was represented
before the Supreme Court by State Attorney Beinisch, acting on behalf of Attorney
General Harish—who argued the opposite of her "client's" position. When Pinchasi's
counsel asked how the state attorney could represent two opposite positions, that of
the attorney general and that of the prime minister, Barak replied that there was no
contradiction. The real "prime minister's position" is that which the attorney general
decides is the legally correct one. The fact that the prime minister himself maintains
otherwise is not relevant. As Barak put it, "It should not be said that the state attorney
pleaded before us in the name of two clients whose interests are contradictory. She
pled before us in the name of the single authorized authority—the prime minister.
True, the position of Mr. Yitzhak Rabin, the prime minister, differs. The attorney
general agreed to bring that to our attention. That is his privilege. But that is not the
position that was represented to us."[356]

It's unbelievable. Barak reasons here that the prime minister is not a person
elected by the public who composed a government that received the confidence of
the Knesset. Rather, the prime minister is a legal fiction, a phantom created by the
court and the attorney general who is, in their view, the "reasonable prime minister."
This phantom prime minister, usurping the real one, is the one who is represented
by the attorney general, and only the phantom's claims are brought before the court.

One of the questions that Barak's assertion prompts is why he bothered writing an
opinion of nearly thirty pages in the Pinchasi case. According to the theory of the
phantom prime minister, all he needed were a few lines. He could have stated that the
petitioners demanded Pinchasi's removal from the government. Since State Attorney
Beinisch argued, in the name of the fictional prime minister, that the petitioners
were correct, there was in fact no dispute between the parties to the suit. Both sides
agreed that Pinchasi should be fired, so the court needed merely to confirm that this
is what was to be done.

Two rules were thus established that raised the attorney general to the position of
Israel's utmost authority, with only the Supreme Court above him. In other words,
judicial activism expanded into the actual administration of government. No longer
is the attorney general bound by the plain meaning of his Hebrew title—rather than
the government's adviser, he is its commander in chief. This has nothing to do with
human rights or any concrete dispute. It has to do with the way the state is run and
who runs it. One could, of course, argue that a country ruled by officers who were

not democratically elected will be a better guarantor of human rights. But history pretty convincingly shows the opposite.

Furthermore, these rules lack any shred of legitimacy and betray the fundamental principles of natural justice. The ruling is not an error but rather a very real deviation from the bounds of legitimacy.

Less than two months after the Supreme Court ruled that Deri and Pinchasi could no longer serve in the cabinet, on November 1, 1993, Harish resigned his post. As he wrote to Rabin following his refusal to represent him before the Supreme Court, "It is clear to me that the position I have taken requires me to accept personal accountability. I am prepared for that, immediately." In other words, he consented to leave.

It is ironic that Harish ended his tenure following a dispute quite similar to that which brought an end to the term of his predecessor, Itzhak Zamir. The two cases nevertheless display some notable differences. By replacing Zamir, the national unity government of the time achieved its goal of ending the Shin Bet episode without a police inquiry, indictments, and a coalition crisis. In contrast, Harish's replacement by Michael Ben-Yair changed nothing for Deri and Pinchasi. They still had to resign.

The Shamgar commission, appointed in the wake of the Bar-On–Hebron affair, was composed of some of the country's leading legal figures. In addition to former Chief Justice Shamgar, its members were Ruth Gavison, one of the country's preeminent legal scholars and human rights activists, as well as three former justice ministers: Haim Zadok, Moshe Nissim, and David Libai. It heard testimony from a number of witnesses and produced a report written in light not only of the Bar-On–Hebron affair but also of Barak's ruling in the Pinchasi case, handed down five years earlier. As one might expect, the government accepted its report and recommendations. In practice, however, only some of those recommendations—those relating to the manner of appointing the attorney general and the length of his term—were implemented.

The Shamgar Commission accepted the Agranat Committee's position that opinions rendered by the attorney general obligated the entire executive branch, but also that "the government may act otherwise than the attorney general advises." In other words, it rejected the baseless rule established by Barak in his Pinchasi ruling. Shamgar had concurred in that ruling, yet the commission he chaired reverted to the correct position taken by the Agranat panel. But this made no difference. The Supreme Court continued to adhere to its erroneous position and to insist that the government was bound to submit to and obey the attorney general's rulings—as we saw in the Lavi case.

With regard to the government's representation in court, the Shamgar Commission tried to have it both ways. It did its best to resolve the uncomfortable situation that the Pinchasi case produced, that is, the prospect of the attorney general appearing before the Supreme Court as the representative of the prime minister and his cabinet while arguing before the court a view opposed to that of the government. The commission was aware of the harsh critique leveled at that ruling by former Justice Haim Cohn. "The attorney general," Cohn maintained, "cannot gag [the government or any one cabinet minister] and impose his opinion on them, nor is it fitting that he do so."[357]

The commission's language was equivocal: "In cases not involving clear and present illegality, it is appropriate for the attorney general to permit the representation [by a private attorney] of a state agency that disputes his opinion . . . There are circumstances . . . in which a governing authority should not be denied its day in court."[358]

In other words, on the one hand the Shamgar Commission recognized the government's right to representation, but on the other hand it reiterated that the government, or any of its agencies or officers, could receive external representation only with the consent of the attorney general, permission that he is expected to give. However, the commission did not say why such permission is necessary or what the government was to do if the attorney general nevertheless refused to grant it. Should the government then petition the Supreme Court against its own legal counsel? Who would represent the government in such a case? Would the attorney general have to allow the government to be represented by a private attorney in this case?

One might think that this minimalist position taken by a commission headed by a former chief justice would be adopted, but that, it turned out, was not the case. The State Attorney's Office's Department of Constitutional and Administrative Law continued to act in the spirit of Barak and Zamir.[359] In other words, it continued to assert that, in the name of the rule of the law, it could gag the government and its ministers, forbid them to differ with the attorney general, and deny them their day in court.

The commission also recommended ending a practice that had commenced with the Menachem Begin government, when the attorney general began to attend every cabinet meeting. His participation should be limited, Shamgar and his colleagues suggested, to meetings addressing legal issues on which his opinion is needed. In practice, however, governments, apprehensive of the consequences of excluding him from their deliberations, have deferred to the attorney general in this regard. He is invited to all meetings and decides for himself which to attend and which to skip.

The commission considered the conflict of interest that is built into the post—the attorney general is, on the one hand, the government's lawyer, and on the other heads the state prosecution, which conducts investigations against members of the cabinet and other government officials and decides whether to bring them to trial. Nevertheless, the commission decided in the end, despite the burgeoning number of such criminal investigations of public figures, not to split the post in two.

The real innovation in the commission's recommendations had to do with the process of appointing and dismissing the attorney general. Shamgar and his colleagues proposed the establishment of a professional public committee chaired by a former Supreme Court justice, named by the sitting chief justice. Its other members would be a former justice minister or attorney general chosen by the cabinet, a member of the Knesset elected by the Knesset's Constitution, Law, and Justice Committee, an attorney named by the Israel Bar Association's National Council, and an academic legal expert selected by the deans of the country's law faculties. The government would not be obligated to accept the commission's recommendation, but could not name a person to fill the post itself. It could only ask the commission to recommend a different candidate. The cabinet accepted this recommendation.

At first glance, this appointments committee seems well balanced in its constitution. In practice, however, it is another symptom of one of the notable ills of Israeli governance—government by committee. Theoretically the committee is professional and objective. But the fact is that the worldview of a jurist, be he a judge or an attorney general, cannot but affect his professional judgment. When the post to be filled is one of such great power, ideological considerations can be decisive. The very idea that the law can be objective or neutral is a fantasy. That is certainly the case in Israel, where all is justiciable and where public jurists have an enormous range of discretion over questions of morality and reasonableness. In practice, this supposedly objective committee to recommend candidates for attorney general has represented opposing interests. According to Barak's agenda, the attorney general ought to support the expansion of the Supreme Court's powers and block legislation or other measures aimed at constraining that power. To some extent, in this view, the attorney general serves as a representative of the court sitting in and pulling the strings of the executive branch. The cabinet's interests are different. It seeks an attorney general who will help it promote its policies and is not ardent about investigating its members. The representatives from the Bar and the law faculties have ideologists as well, which may lead them to support or oppose the Supreme Court.

Unsurprisingly, then, the committee has been a total failure. When Elyakim Rubinstein reached the end of his term, it was constituted under the chairmanship of former Supreme Court Justice Gabriel Bach. Minister of Justice Yosef Lapid wanted to appoint a private attorney rather than someone from within the government legal system. He proposed two such candidates to the committee, Eli Zohar and Yoram Turbowitz. Zohar bowed out because it transpired that he was a close friend of Lapid's, a fact that sufficed to raise unjustified objections to his appointment. The committee refused to recommend Turbowitz on the grounds that he was insufficiently experienced. The government thus lost the ability of appointing an attorney general to its own liking. Lapid's son Yair (who later served as finance minister in 2013–2014), maintained in a book published after his father's death, that his father had wanted to appoint Zohar, a close friend of his, because he believed that "the State Attorney's Office has become a closed junta, in which everyone . . . thinks the same way." The younger Lapid wrote in reaction to the opposition to Zohar: "It's ridiculous. According to the ethical rules that the purists are trying to impose, you can appoint someone you hate . . . but if you like someone you have to rule him out from the start." He added that "the [legal] system's working assumption is that everyone is corrupt . . . the system believes only those who grew up within it." An outside candidate for a public position will find himself the target of "slanders and intrigues, malicious reports and ugly leaks from behind the scenes."[360]

After deliberating, the committee proposed three candidates, presumably because its members were unable to agree on a single one. They were Menachem Mazuz, the deputy attorney general, and two District Court judges, Uzi Vogelman and David Cheshin. Vogelman was supported by the Supreme Court and by Dorit Beinisch in particular (Vogelman would receive a Supreme Court appointment while Beinisch was chief justice). From the cabinet's point of view, Mazuz was preferable because he was not close to the sitting Supreme Court justices, nor did he belong to the Beinisch-Arbel circle in the State Attorney's Office. He was chosen, only to clash with Arbel soon thereafter. But the most important outcome was that the cabinet lost its ability to choose the person it regarded as right for the job. It was permitted only to choose among the candidates proposed by the appointments committee, even though none of them was the justice minister's first choice. Lapid's plan to appoint an attorney from the private sector was thwarted.

The committee convened again when Mazuz came to the end of his term. This time its chairman was former justice Theodor Or. In the meantime the government had amended its previous decision about the committee to require it to propose at least three candidates.*

The process ended in a fiasco, with the politicization of the committee evident for all to see. Two of the committee's members, former Justice Minister Moshe Nissim and Knesset member Yariv Levin of Likud, proposed a private attorney, Yehuda Weinstein, as well as District Court Judge Noam Sohlberg, a religious jurist who lives in an Israeli settlement in the West Bank (in 2012 Sohlberg was appointed justice of the Supreme Court). Both candidates were highly qualified and amenable choices for the Netanyahu government. But that is not how Or and the academic member of the committee, Eyal Benvenisti (himself a candidate for a Supreme Court seat), saw it. They proposed Daphne Barak-Erez, a law professor whose views on judicial activism were close to those of Barak. (Barak-Erez was later appointed to the Supreme Court while Beinisch was chief justice.) They also proposed a private attorney, Zvi Agmon, a former law partner of Justice Mishael Cheshin.

Clearly the disagreement was of a political nature—relating to the candidates' ideologies and their relations with figures and factions in government and the judiciary. The fact that committee members Nissim and Levin were members of Likud did not make their position more political than that of Justice Or and Professor Benvenisti. This time the committee found itself unable to achieve a compromise—none of the candidates received, as the rules required, the support of at least four of the five members. The committee thus ended its deliberations without forwarding any candidates to the cabinet. The cabinet, left to its own devices, chose Yehuda Weinstein. Of course, the appointment was challenged before the Supreme Court (how could it not be?), but the suit was denied.[361]

The committee's total failure to agree on any candidate, much less offer the government a choice of three, resulted, of course, from the fact that its members represented different interests and philosophies of law and government. It also proves the naivety, and perhaps the blindness, at the foundation of the Shamgar Commission's recommendations. They were based on the faith that key government posts could and should be filled impartially and virtuously according to supposedly objective and professional criteria, when the fact is that ideological and personal considerations are inevitable and decisive. There was no reason to strip the cabinet of its prerogative of appointing the attorney general. The problematic choice of Ronnie Bar-On did not justify shifting the responsibility to a committee, just as a military or economic failure does not mandate handing over the power to make policy in these fields to the courts. It would be no less absurd to argue that if a court makes a mistaken ruling (say, by convicting an innocent man), the consequence should be the transfer of the judicial power to the executive branch. But during his first term, Netanyahu's government was weak and frightened. Both the prime minister and his justice minister were under criminal investigation, so they saw no choice but to accept the Shamgar Commission's recommendations.

---

* The amendment was my initiative, proposed while I was justice minister.

The Shamgar Commission did get one thing right, however. It proposed that the attorney general be limited to a single six-year term. It is certainly unacceptable for the person holding such a powerful post to serve indefinitely. Furthermore, legal and political realities are likely to make it difficult for the government to dismiss an attorney general, especially if he is overseeing criminal investigations of cabinet ministers. In keeping with this recommendation, Mazuz's tenure came to an end in January 2010, and Weinstein was appointed.

The march of fiascos continued with the appointment of a new committee to replace Weinstein, whose term expires in February 2016. The committee headed by former Chief Justice Asher Grunis was unable to agree on three candidates as required by the government and by its terms of appointment. Only one candidate, Avichai Mandelblit former military advocate general and cabinet secretary, got four votes. All the members of the committee supported him except Grunis. The former chief justice considered him qualified for the job but sought to invent a new rule that has no legal basis, that the cabinet secretary needs a cooling period before being appointed attorney general. The end result was that the committee's failure to agree on three candidates left the government free to appoint any qualified person regardless of the committee's recommendation. Mandelblit was however amenable to the government, which decided on January 3, 2016, to appoint him. As expected, a petition against it was submitted to the High Court of Justice immediately after the government approved the appointment. A panel of five justices dismissed the petition.[362]

The debacle of the search committees led the Minister of Justice, Ayelet Shaked, to propose that the government decides to do away with this method of appointing the attorney general so that from now on the power to do so would revert to minister of justice and the government, unfettered by external interests and elements. If this happens, an important element of the legal revolution would be removed.

II. THE ATTORNEY GENERAL AS PROSECUTOR AND LEGISLATOR

The attorney general's power to issue orders to the elected government was augmented by another aspect of his power—his position at the head of the state prosecution. He can order the indictment of any person, including members of the Knesset, cabinet ministers, and even the prime minister. No less significant is the authority to order the opening of a criminal investigation. The damage done to a public figure in either case is enormous. His reputation is undermined and his ability to fulfill his duties is compromised. He is often forced to leave his post, and he may find himself disqualified to hold public posts in the future—even if the investigation ends without an indictment or his trial ends in an acquittal.

The attorney general's prosecutorial powers have been augmented by court rulings that have dramatically expanded the boundaries of criminal liability, in particular that of public officials, through the massive invocation of vague charges such as breach of trust and obstruction of justice. The potential for criminal investigations has thus expanded astonishingly and has invested huge discretionary powers in the attorney general. He can launch an investigation of a cabinet minister and bring him to trial for making political appointments, while not investigating or indicting another minister for the same actions. Political life and death lie in his hands.

The combination of his powers as counsel and adviser along with his indictment powers reinforce each other. Even when he offers advice on a question that is not a legal one (assuming that there remains any issue in Israel that no longer has a legal aspect), the cabinet or the public official who received the advice will necessarily be wary of rejecting it. For example, what if a cabinet minister wants to form a committee to examine an issue in the purview of his portfolio but the attorney general opposes it. The attorney general would obviously not threaten the minister with the opening of a criminal investigation. He hardly needs to. The simple fact that the minister fears that he might find himself under investigation if he crosses the attorney general is enough. That is, in fact, the way many cabinet ministers feel when they find themselves in such a situation.

One of the few areas in which the attorney general was not granted formal powers by law is in the area of legislation. If the cabinet or one of its ministers wishes to submit a bill to the Knesset, the attorney general has no authority to stop it. But his prosecutorial powers create a de facto situation in which it is very difficult to enact a law that he strongly disagrees with. Such is the case with, for example, bills seeking to divide the attorney general's powers between two separate posts, or to create a mechanism for overseeing his actions. Initiatives to rein in the Supreme Court's power may also run into the attorney general's opposition if he supports the court's activist ideology.

Another phenomenon that has enlarged the attorney general's influence is his practice of issuing directives. The practice began with Meir Shamgar in 1968. To Shamgar's credit it should be noted that he stressed that these were not tantamount to legislation. He thus avoided making them public at first and considerably restricted their application. They were meant for the most part to provide guidance in concrete cases by quoting from the relevant laws and summarizing court rulings touching on the subject. These directives gradually, however, began to take on larger dimensions and to spill over into other areas. Now, thanks to the Supreme Court, they have full legal force and government agencies and authorities are required to abide by them. In other words, they are tantamount to law.

The phenomenon of internal directives is familiar in administrative law. They may address internal working procedures in an administrative unit, and they serve largely to guide government bodies in the exercise of their discretion in areas under their purview.[363] For example, the office responsible for issuing gun licenses may establish criteria for receiving such a permit. Conditions may include, among others, having reached a minimum age, working at an occupation that makes carrying a gun necessary, and the lack of a criminal record.

But the directives issued by the attorney general are on an entirely different plane. Itzhak Zamir included them under the category of internal directives, but noted that "the attorney general's directives have a special status. For government authorities, these directives reflect established law, or interpret it authoritatively, and thus are obligatory on government authorities."[364]

Directives from the attorney general may include instructions of an internal nature. For example, the attorney general may offer the prosecution instructions regarding plea bargain agreements, such as when they can be reached, with whom, and with what conditions. The attorney general may also instruct the prosecution about the time frame for reaching a decision in criminal investigations. But once the concept was brought into the world, these directives began to expand gradually into areas that cannot be considered internal matters. Furthermore, the number of such directives is enormous. Shelves of thick binders contain the attorney general's instructions regarding all areas of administration and government. They have become quasi-legislation. No longer are they addressed only to the staff reporting directly or indirectly to the attorney general but rather to the entire executive branch, including the cabinet.

One example is Directive 1.1708, issued by Attorney General Menachem Mazuz in October 2004. It forbids cabinet ministers and deputy ministers to handle requests from members of the political body that chooses them (for example, a party central committee that elects the party's candidates for its slate in elections to the Knesset). The intent is to prevent "conflicts of interest, ulterior motives, favoritism, and discrimination." Presumably Mazuz meant well. But it is one thing to say (even if it is mistaken) that an opinion issued by the attorney general addressing a concrete legal issue obligates the government. It is another thing entirely for the attorney general to lay down rules for future behavior, in a range of situations, when the specific circumstances are not yet known. Any such generalization inevitably takes on the nature of legislation. That is, the attorney general becomes a lawgiver as well as a judge. His rulings obligate the government and all its institutions. At the same time, the attorney general is the government's only lawyer. He holds a monopoly on representing the government and its agencies. On top of that, he is the chief prosecutor for the public as a whole and for the public agencies that must act in accordance with his instructions. A fundamental principle of administrative law is the principle of legality, according to which no administrative authority may exercise any powers other than those granted to it by law. This tenet long ago fell by the wayside with regard to Israel's attorney general. As I have shown, supported by the Supreme Court he has radically arrogated powers in the absence of any legislative basis for doing so.

What, then, happens to a cabinet minister who disobeys a directive from the attorney general? The question arose when the attorney general decided not to order a criminal investigation against Binyamin Ben-Eliezer, minister of national infrastructure, for his alleged involvement in political appointments. The Supreme Court was petitioned to reverse the decision. The court sharply criticized Ben-Eliezer and went so far as to say that he had acted "in contravention of the attorney general's directives." The court apparently was completely unaware of the problematic nature of these directives and automatically assumed that they were binding and that their breach by the minister was wrong. Yet, the attorney general was never granted the power to legislate, and certainly not to create new criminal offenses. His directives certainly do not profess to establish criminal offenses directly, but the question is whether they can do so indirectly. Does disobeying a "legislative" directive by the attorney general constitute an offence of breach of trust? The question remains open. In Ben-Eliezer's case, the court chose, despite its censure of Ben-Eliezer, not to intervene in the attorney general's decision not to open a criminal investigation against him.[365]

PART THREE

Partial Restraint

27

The Olmert Government and the Second Lebanon War

The elections for the Seventeenth Knesset, held in the shadow of the disengagement from the Gaza Strip, were set for March 2006. Prime Minister Ariel Sharon reached dizzying heights of popularity, but his Likud Party was riven from within. Many of the party's Knesset members had opposed the evacuation of the Israeli settlements in the Gaza Strip (as well as three in the northern West Bank). Sharon reached the conclusion that he would not be able to accomplish his goals as the leader of a party in conflict with itself. He decided to bolt Likud and found a new party, Kadima.

Several Likud Knesset members left the party with him. Some figures in the opposition Labor Party also switched their allegiance to the new faction, among them Shimon Peres and Haim Ramon. The result was a center party that, its leaders and supporters hoped, would end the long-standing virtual tie between Israel's right and left. Opinion polls showed the new party winning 40 seats in the 120-member Knesset.

But then fate stepped in, as it often does in private lives and history. In mid-December 2005, as he and his supporters labored to found Kadima, Sharon suffered a minor stroke. He carried on as if nothing had happened, but on January 4, 2006, he suffered a massive stroke that sent him into a coma from which he never awoke. The government and Kadima were left rudderless, with elections only three months away. Vice Prime Minister Ehud Olmert became acting prime minister and the man who would lead the new party into the elections. In the meantime, the region did not remain static. That same January, the Palestinian Authority (PA) held elections to its legislative council. The two major political forces in the Palestinian territories were Fatah, led by the incumbent head of the PA, Mahmoud Abbas, and Hamas, the radical Islamist movement. Israel's position was that Hamas was a terrorist organization and, as such, should not be allowed to participate in the elections. But the United States, which sought to promote unrestricted democracy among the Palestinians, did not agree. Sharon's government had no choice but to accept the Palestinian Authority's demand that Palestinians living in East Jerusalem also be allowed to participate in the vote. East Jerusalem, it should be recalled, had been annexed by Israel following the Six Day War of 1967. While that annexation had not been recognized by any other country, under Israeli law the city's Arab inhabitants were residents of

Israel, not the Palestinian Authority. In the end, Hamas won a stunning victory in the Palestinian elections, which were held after Olmert became acting prime minister.

Olmert made a key decision prior to the Israeli elections. He ordered the evacuation of Amona, an unauthorized Israeli settlement in the West Bank, and the demolition of the homes that had been built there. The demolition was carried out in the face of violent clashes between the police and the settlers and their hundreds of supporters, among them members of the Knesset. For the settlers it was a test case following the evacuation of the Gaza Strip. Fearing that the next step would be a similar Israeli withdrawal from the West Bank, they sought to draw a red line and ensure that no other settlement suffer the same fate. Dozens of civilians and police personnel were injured. While the evacuation and demolition were carried out, the opponents were successful in creating a deterrent against any further move of the same sort. Olmert nevertheless issued his Realignment Plan, meant to be the second act following the withdrawal from the Gaza Strip. Israel, he proposed, should withdraw unilaterally from a large part of the West Bank. Then the elections arrived.

Kadima won twenty-nine seats, emerging as the largest party in the Knesset. Compared with its standing in the polls before Sharon's incapacitation, the results were a disappointment. On the other hand, for the first time in Israeli history a brand-new party had won an election. Likud, headed by Benjamin Netanyahu, for its part, suffered a stunning setback—it won only twelve seats. Labor won nineteen, and its leader, Amir Peretz, agreed to join Olmert's coalition. Peretz received the post of defense minister. Shas would have preferred a right-wing government, but with the right defeated, it joined Olmert's coalition as well. But Olmert found that his far-reaching plans to reach an accommodation with the Palestinians were overtaken by other events. The fizzling out of the Second Intifada and the disengagement from Gaza had led to a period of calm—but it was short-lived. Palestinian militants ratcheted up their rocket attacks on southern Israel. At the same time, Hezbollah, the de facto ruler of southern Lebanon, presented an ever-growing threat as it gained sophisticated arms and improved its training. Less than two months after the elections, the Olmert government found itself facing an axis of evil on its southern and northern frontiers.

On June 25, 2006, Hamas terrorists penetrated Israel through an underground tunnel, emerging near the Israeli farming village of Kerem Shalom. They attacked an Israel Defense Forces (IDF) outpost and a tank stationed there. An officer and a noncommissioned officer were killed, while a third soldier, Gilad Shalit, was captured and taken into the Gaza Strip. A few days later the IDF apprehended dozens of Hamas personnel in the West Bank, among them members of the Palestinian Authority cabinet and Legislative Assembly. The IDF carried out a series of operations in the Gaza Strip under the collective rubric of Operation Summer Rains. Fighting continued for five months before a ceasefire was achieved. Three Israeli soldiers and two civilians had been killed. The Palestinians suffered hundreds of losses, most of them terrorists. Hamas undertook to stop rocket fire from the Gaza Strip, but one of the major goals of the operation, gaining the release of Shalit, was not achieved.

While the conflict in the south was at its height, a new front opened in the north. On July 12, just two and a half weeks after Shalit's capture, Hezbollah launched a rocket and mortar attack against Israel's north. A contingent of its fighters attacked an IDF patrol along the border fence. Three soldiers were killed and two others,

Ehud Goldwasser and Elhanan Regev, were captured (it later transpired that they had been killed in the attack, but the presumption at the time was that they had been taken alive). Five more soldiers were killed when IDF forces entered Lebanon in an attempt to rescue Goldwasser and Regev. Clearly, Israel could not let this Hezbollah attack pass without a response. The policy of containment, or restraint, instituted by Prime Minister Ehud Barak after he withdrew Israeli forces from southern Lebanon in 2000, came to an end. That very day Israel launched a major operation, which came to be called the Second Lebanon War.

In presenting the military operation to the Knesset, Olmert offered a broad range of goals. He sought, he said, "to change the equation," that is the tit-for-tat ritual in which Hezbollah would attack, Israel offer a moderate response, after which Hezbollah would attack again, and so on. Instead Israel would seek to force Hezbollah out of southern Lebanon and achieve long-term calm on Israel's northern border. Another goal was the release of the captured soldiers. The security cabinet decided on an aerial bombardment of Dahiya, the Beirut neighborhood where the Hezbollah command's headquarters was ensconced, deep underground.

Hezbollah's leader, Hassan Nasrallah, responded, as expected, with a rocket barrage against Israel. The government faced a dilemma. The First Lebanon War of 1982, in which Israel suffered heavy losses and ended up strengthening Hezbollah, remained fresh in Israeli memory. Israel's leaders thus preferred to avoid a large-scale ground invasion. But the Hezbollah bombardments left them with no choice. Hezbollah waited in ambush in tunnels, much as Viet Cong guerillas had done in their battle against U.S. forces in Vietnam. They forayed out of their lairs to attack Israeli forces, disappearing back into the tunnels when they were done. At the beginning of August the ground invasion was extended deeper into Lebanon, until a ceasefire was declared on August 14. The fighting grew especially fierce just prior to the ceasefire. In the two days before it took force, twenty-four Israeli soldiers were killed.

The IDF's losses totaled 111, with more than 600 soldiers wounded. A full 44 Israeli civilians were killed and many injured. Between 500 and 700 Hezbollah militants died in the war. Hundreds of thousands of Lebanese civilians fled the war zone, and the damage to property and infrastructure was huge. That did not keep Hezbollah from declaring victory. But Nasrallah acknowledged that, had he known that Israel would respond so forcefully, he would not have ordered the attack that set off the war.

The Israeli public felt battered and let down. For the first time since Israel's establishment, a war was fought not only on the front but also in the rear. Israeli civilians found themselves facing daily rocket attacks that continued despite Israel's air strikes in Lebanon. While the war achieved some important aims—it re-established Israeli deterrence, and peace returned to the Galilee as soon as the fighting ended—the ground invasion, so costly in lives, looked like a failure. The furious public blamed the government, especially Prime Minister Olmert, Minister of Defense Amir Peretz, and IDF Chief of Staff Dan Halutz. Olmert's government faced a further difficulty, an outgrowth of Israel's system of government. His foreign minister and the number two leader in Kadima, Tzipi Livni, set her eyes on the party leadership and the prime minister's chair, while Ehud Barak, who had retired from politics following his crushing defeat in 2001, returned to challenge Peretz for the leadership of Labor.

Immediately after the ceasefire, Peretz appointed a committee to examine the conduct of the war. Its members were former IDF Chief of Staff Amnon Lipkin-Shahak, former air force chief Herzl Bodinger, General (ret.) Ilan Biran, and Eli Horowitz, an industrialist. But Halutz opposed the committee. It did not start its work and was soon dissolved. Paradoxically, the abortive committee actually furthered the investigation of the war. The fact that Peretz had insisted on an investigation, compelled Olmert to appoint a government commission of inquiry under the chairmanship of retired Judge Eliyahu Winograd. It was fairly clear that the odds were that its findings would not be amenable to the government and prime minister. The Agranat Commission, established after the Yom Kippur War, was led by a respected chief justice, but was attacked from all quarters when it placed blame for the mismanagement of that war solely on the commanders of the Israeli army while absolving Israel's political leadership. The Kahan Commission, which investigated the Sabra and Shatila massacre during the First Lebanon War, charged Prime Minister Menachem Begin and Minister of Defense Ariel Sharon with responsibility, and the public largely accepted its conclusions. Given the public outrage at the outcome of the Second Lebanon War, the members of the Winograd Commission must have realized that the public would turn against them if they did not lay responsibility for the war's failures at the feet of the top civilian leadership.

That should have been clear to Olmert was well, yet he felt he had no choice. All he could do—barely—was to ensure that the Winograd Commission had the status of a government commission of inquiry, rather than a national commission of inquiry. The main difference between the two is that members of the government commission are appointed by the cabinet while those of the national commission are appointed by the chief justice. However, as far as their powers and operations are concerned there is little difference between the two. Its appointment gave the government some breathing space, but not very much. Halutz, facing public fury, did not wait for the commission's report and resigned. Gabi Ashkenazi, the director general of the defense ministry and a reserve general, was appointed in his place.

It was the third commission of inquiry into a military debacle. The Agranat and Kahan commissions, formed under the terms of the Commission of Inquiry Act, were appointed by the chief justice of the Supreme Court. The Winograd Commission was, in contrast, appointed by the cabinet. The government's insistence on controlling the appointments grew out of the politicians' loss of confidence in that kernel of the legal system that under the banner of "the rule of law" placed the judiciary over all other branches of government. It was not that the cabinet ministers no longer trusted all judges, but they were suspicious of that faction of judges and lawyers who had become dominant under the leadership of Aharon Barak. The politicians' mistrust of the justices of the Supreme Court, with just a few exceptions, manifested itself in other ways as well. In the past, for example, Justices Miriam Ben-Porat and Eliezer Goldberg, after their retirement from the Supreme Court, had been appointed state comptroller. But in 2005 the Knesset preferred a judge from the district court, Micha Lindenstrauss, and in 2012, when the two leading candidates were Deputy Chief Justice Eliezer Rivlin and District Court Judge Yosef Shapira, the latter was elected. That does not mean (as Lindenstrauss proved quite well) that a district court judge would seek the good graces of politicians, but it was clear that the members of the

Knesset had concerns about appointing a member of the Supreme Court who belonged to the group supporting the legal revolution.

Winograd, the cabinet's choice to head the government commission of inquiry into the conduct of the Second Lebanon War, was also a retired district court judge. The other members were two scholars, Ruth Gavison and Yehezkel Dror, and Reserve Generals Menachem Einan and Haim Nadal.

Unsurprisingly, the decision to establish the Winograd Commission, like many other nonjusticiable decisions that resulted in large headlines in the press, came before the Supreme Court, with petitioners asking the court to order the government to appoint a national commission of inquiry. In any other country such a suit would have been tossed out of court, but not in Israel. The sense after the war was that the government had lost all support from the public. A Supreme Court ruling requiring the government to appoint a national commission of inquiry would have been absurd, but it would most likely have been popular. However, this time logic prevailed, if only by a one-vote margin. A four-justice majority consisting of Eliezer Rivlin, Asher Grunis, Salim Joubran, and Esther Hayut voided the order nisi and permitted the Winograd panel to begin its work. Three justices—Ayala Procaccia, Miriam Naor, and Elyakim Rubinstein—maintained that the government's decision should be voided. They considered that the legal provisions regarding a government commission of inquiry did not apply to the type of issues that the Winograd panel was charged with investigating. Procaccia went so far as to maintain that the government's decision was unreasonable and that the cabinet had a conflict of interest in the matter. The justices in the minority nevertheless did not accept the petitioners' demand that the court order the government to establish a national commission. They proposed voiding the decision and sending the matter back to the government. Most likely, however, had their position prevailed, the government would have had no option, from a public point of view, other than to decide on a national commission appointed by the chief justice.[366]

The Knesset confirmed my appointment as minister of justice in the Olmert government on February 7, 2007. I had not been a member of the cabinet when it decided on the Winograd Commission. The commission submitted an interim report on April 30, 2007, a little over two months after my appointment. The report addressed the initial days of combat, prior to the ground invasion. Ostensibly, there had been no special problems in this stage, which was generally viewed, at least by the public, as militarily successful. In the days prior to the release of the interim report I heard some ministers estimating that it would be relatively benign. Olmert had formed his government just a few months before the war, and developments in the years prior to the war, in particular the strengthening of Hezbollah and the failure to stop its recurring attacks, had not been the responsibility of the Olmert cabinet.

But these expectations were disappointed. The partial report turned out to be extremely critical of three men: Olmert, Peretz, and Halutz. While on the first page of its introduction the members of the commission cited a number of the war's achievements, the tone changed immediately thereafter.

> Nevertheless, for the first time . . . a war in which Israel was involved ended without Israel achieving a clear military victory . . . The rocket fire on the rear continued throughout the war, until the very last minute, and ended only due to the

cease fire . . . A paramilitary organization of several thousand fighters was able to withstand the strongest army in the Middle East for many long weeks. It would be difficult to overstate the far-reaching implications of this result.[367]

The claim that this was the first time Israel had fought a war that "ended without Israel achieving a clear military victory" is hardly incontestable. The same could and has been said, for example, of the War of Attrition of 1967–1970, the Yom Kippur War of 1973, and the First Lebanon War of 1982. But, with this as its starting point, the commission proceeded to present the Second Lebanon War as having ended in the worst military outcome in Israeli history. The War of Attrition wore out both sides, and Egypt immediately violated the agreement that ended it by deploying surface-to-air missiles along the west bank of the Suez Canal. An exhausted Israel made no response. At the end of the Yom Kippur War, Israel declared victory but found itself in a precarious military situation. And while Israel seized control of a sizable territory in the First Lebanon War, it was forced, after suffering losses far greater than those of the Second Lebanon War, to withdraw from a large part of it (and later from the rest).

The commission offered a lengthy analysis of Israel's policy of containment and restraint, in which it responded to Hezbollah attacks with only moderate force. The policy originated under Ehud Barak's government, following Israel's final and full withdrawal from Lebanon. On October 7, 2000, Hezbollah attacked an IDF patrol on Mount Dov (the lower western spur of the part of Mount Hermon controlled by Israel) and captured three soldiers. It later turned out that the three had been killed during the attack, but that was not known at the time. Israel hardly responded. Israeli governments from that time onward pursued the same policy, which led ultimately to the attack and abduction of July 12, 2006, the trigger that set off the Second Lebanon War. Obviously, the three men the commission charged with responsibility for the conduct of the war—Olmert, Peretz, and Halutz—were not the authors of the policy that led to it. Halutz, in fact, had vocally opposed that approach.

The Winograd Commission noted that this policy of restraint stood in contradiction to public statements by Ehud Barak following the withdrawal from Lebanon. Barak declared then that Israel would respond with force to any violation of its sovereignty. The withdrawal, Barak argued, would make it easier for Israel to respond militarily to Hezbollah attacks. In fact, however, Israel did not launch military responses but rather pursued a policy of restraint. As the commission pointed out, this

in fact enabled Hezbollah to gain military strength . . . and to act provocatively against Israel in southern Lebanon and along the [border] fence. The combination of these capabilities . . . granted the organization an advantage and a real ability to act against Israel. This permitted Hezbollah . . . [to carry out] an ongoing initiative in which it acted at times and in ways appropriate for its interests, without any military response from Israel . . . It created a balance that was very problematic for Israel for a long period.

Despite the criticism of the containment and restraint strategy, it had offered some clear benefits, the commission noted, and as such the commission preferred not to take a firm position on whether it was correct or incorrect. Having resolved not to hold anyone responsible for the policy that led to the war, it put the full weight of its authority behind the one issue that remained: the decision to launch "a broad and deliberate military action." The commission charged that "it was not based on a plan prepared in advance . . . The decision was made without a serious examination of the army's readiness and . . . without a cautious consideration of the possible scenarios of how the campaign would progress." The commission sharply criticized the decision-making procedure, in particular the fact that "there were no . . . in-depth and comprehensive discussions of the operation's contours, goals, and the ways to achieve them."

The assignment of personal responsibility to the three leaders was worded sharply. The commission held the prime minister "responsible, ministerially and personally, for the defects in the decisions that were made, and the defects in the process of making them." The minister of defense "did not demand and did not examine the army's plans, did not ascertain its readiness and its deployment." The chief of staff "failed in not being organized and prepared for an event that could have been anticipated, and in not informing the political leadership about the complexity of the arena."

In his defense of the appointment of the Winograd Commission, the state representative declared to the Supreme Court that the commission was bound by the rules of natural justice.[368] Yet it failed to give the persons that it criticized so harshly an opportunity to defend themselves. This failure can hardly be justified by the fact that the commission refrained from recommending that the three men take any specific action, such as resignation.

In a book he wrote following the war, Halutz criticized the Winograd Commission for its failure to abide by the rules of natural justice.[369] Yet, neither he nor the others criticized by the commission petitioned the Supreme Court to quash its findings. But the way the commission acted raised concern regarding the next stage of its investigations and its final report. The IDF Military Defense Counsel submitted a petition to the Supreme Court regarding the way the commission was required to enable persons who are likely to be harmed by its final report to defend themselves. In reply, the commission's counsel declared that "the commission pledges to notify anyone who is liable to be harmed by the report and to inform him what harm can be expected; to grant him the right to examine the evidence relevant to the expected harm; and to grant him the right to make arguments before the commission. . . ."[370] In its interim report, the Winograd Commission certainly did not act in line with this declaration.

The commitment made by the commission's counsel satisfied the IDF Military Defense Counsel, and the petition was withdrawn. Some two months later, the Winograd Commission announced that in its final report it would not include any personal conclusions or recommendations. A new petition was submitted to the Supreme Court to instruct the commission to cancel this decision, so that it would remain open to it to make personal findings and recommendations. The petition was dismissed.[371]

The public responded harshly to the interim report. A few days after it was released, an estimated 100,000 Israelis protested in Rabin Square in Tel Aviv, calling on Olmert and Peretz to resign. Referring to a speech Olmert had made in which he claimed to be working for the public, one of the speakers at the rally, the novelist Meir Shalev, declared: "Mr. Prime Minister, you work for us . . . you're fired." The crowd cheered.

A day after the commission submitted its interim report, Eitan Cabel, who served in the Olmert government as a minister without portfolio representing the Labor Party, submitted his resignation. He called on the prime minister to follow his example. A day later, at her request, Foreign Minister Livni met with Olmert and told him that, in light of the report, he would do best to resign. Had Olmert done so, it should be noted, Livni, who also held the post of vice prime minister, would have become acting prime minister. Olmert was not persuaded. Livni then declared that she had no intention of resigning herself. She would, she said, push for the implementation of the Winograd Commission's recommendations from within the government.

The phenomenon of a cabinet minister calling on the prime minister to resign while at the same time continuing to serve in his government is one of the wonders of the Israeli system. Olmert could, of course, have dismissed her. The standards of good government required him to do so, but he did not. The report left him politically weak. While he enjoyed the support of most of Kadima's cabinet ministers and Knesset members, he preferred not to make a move that would have split his party. Like other prime ministers before him, he found himself having to lead a government that included a person who was trying to replace him.

The internal strife within the Labor Party had already reached a high level even before the interim report came out. Internal elections for the party leadership were scheduled for a month hence. The leading candidates were Ehud Barak, Amir Peretz, and Ami Ayalon, a former Shin Bet chief. Peretz, the current party leader, was knocked out in the first round, and Barak defeated Ayalon in the runoff. He wasted no time. On June 17, 2007, Olmert and Peretz were conferring at the prime minister's residence in Jerusalem. There was a knock on the door, and the superintendent of the residence brought in two urgent faxes. Both were from Ehud Barak. One was addressed to the prime minister, notifying him that, in furtherance of the party's decision to make him leader, he, Barak, would henceforth serve as defense minister. Barak asked Olmert to take the necessary steps to put that into effect. The second fax, a copy of the first, was addressed to Peretz. Olmert later related that he was left speechless, while Peretz walked out of the meeting. Olmert suggested to Barak that Peretz be given the immigrant absorption portfolio, and even offered to give him this post at the expense of Kadima's quota of cabinet members, but Barak refused. He was prepared at most for Peretz to serve as a minister without portfolio, but Peretz demurred.

Olmert had no choice. Without the Labor Party his government would lose its majority. The cabinet ministers approved Barak's appointment in a telephone poll, and the next day the appointment was brought before the Knesset. Three days later Barak was minister of defense and Peretz outside the government. A month after the foreign minister called on the prime minister to resign so that she could fill his shoes, the cabinet found itself with a new senior minister who also aspired to take Olmert's place.

The Winograd Commission submitted its final report in January 2008, some nine months after the release of the interim report. The final report exhibited none of the harsh language of the interim version. The commission refrained entirely from making recommendations regarding specific figures in the government or the army. While it pointed at defects in a number of areas, it did not hold any particular persons responsible. "We held the three leaders personally responsible [in our interim report]," the final report stated,

> even though we found considerable flaws in the actions and in the failures of many others in the political and military system, and despite the fact that a large part of the background conditions to their decisions were dictated to these three by facts and processes for which they were not responsible ... We do not wish to create a situation in which political or military leaders will prefer to refrain from a necessary military response out of fear of failure or of a commission of inquiry. Too much hesitation and apprehension can be very dangerous for the state of Israel under the circumstances in which it exists and acts.

The report identified failures and malfunctions, but on a number of central issues it in fact cleared the prime minister of blame. Nevertheless, the final report did not mitigate the effect of the interim report, which was to convey the message that a leader who decides on a vital military operation endangers his political future. Every military operation, after all, involves risks and may lead to unexpected outcomes. In contrast, a decision to avoid a military engagement will never lead to the appointment of a commission of inquiry and seldom involves any political risk. Thus, from a political leader's point of view he is best off not acting at all. This way the risk is not to him but to the country.

The severest public outcry focused on the large-scale ground operation that began on August 11, 2006, just before the ceasefire. This phase of the war was costly—many soldiers lost their lives. In his testimony before the Winograd Commission, Olmert explained his reasons for approving the action, and his chief of staff, Yoram Turbowicz, told of his contacts with Stephen Hadley, national security adviser to President George W. Bush, regarding the decision of the Security Council that was being prepared in response to the war. The commission accepted Olmert's explanations and concluded that the security cabinet's decision to approve Olmert's recommendation to launch the final ground maneuver "was reasonable in the framework of the political and professional judgment of the decision makers." In the big picture, the Winograd Commission report underlines the difficulty of predicting the results of a legal proceeding. In its interim report, the commission addressed the opening of the military operation, which was generally considered successful, at least by the public, yet it worded its findings in a devastating way. Its final report addressed the rest of the operation. The public and press had vociferously condemned the government's and army's handling of the war, in particular during its final stages, but the report turned out to be a measured one. In short, in both instances the decision makers found that the results were the opposite of what they had expected.

The interim report had another long-range effect. After its publications, cabinet discussions of military affairs became longer, with the same points often being made over and over again as the ministers repeatedly went over the same ground so that no one could argue that they made decisions without careful consideration. But just as it is a mistake to prepare for the next war on the basis of the previous one, neither is it wise to prepare for the next commission of inquiry on the basis of the conclusions reached by the previous one. After all, a new commission will almost certainly find other subjects to focus on.

The storm over the Winograd Commission's interim report had barely subsided when, in June 2007, Hamas staged a military coup in the Gaza Strip. It was a dramatic stage in the internal Palestinian strife between Hamas, which had won the Palestinian elections the previous year, and the Fatah faction headed by Mahmoud Abbas, the president of the Palestinian Authority. The Hamas takeover was bloody and exceptionally brutal. Fatah members were cast out of windows on the upper floors of buildings, while others were kneecapped. Some Fatah partisans fled through Israel to the West Bank. It was clear that Hamas would exploit its control of the Gaza Strip, with its population of more than a million, to ratchet up its terror war against Israel and make common cause with radical forces in the Muslim world.

In reaction, the Israeli government decided to forbid Gaza Strip residents from entering Israel, even to visit family members held in Israeli prisoners. The Supreme Court dismissed suits against this policy.[372]

Olmert had labored to reach an accommodation with the Palestinians. Negotiations were pursued in part at direct meetings between Olmert and Abbas in Jerusalem and at the Annapolis summit of November 2007. The summit produced a declaration of the intention to reach a peace agreement before the end of 2008. Those hopes were not realized, but the declaration of intentions strengthened Israel internationally by making it clear that it sincerely sought peace. Olmert offered a plan based on the borders of June 4, 1967, just before the Six Day War. These borders would be modified to incorporate large blocks of Israeli settlements in the West Bank into Israel proper; the Palestinians would receive territory from Israel in exchange. He also offered an accommodation in Jerusalem, and said he was willing to take a small number of Palestinian refugees into Israel over the space of several years. It was the best offer Israel had ever made to the Palestinians, one that, just a few years before, they could barely have dreamed of. But they failed to accept it.

Another challenge faced by the Olmert government was an impending nuclear threat. Iran has been active in the nuclear field for many years, but it transpired that there was an additional danger much closer to Israel. Syria was developing a nuclear installation at a secret site. Israel's response to this challenge is recounted in the memoir written by President George W. Bush, *Decision Points*. The Syrian reactor was located in Deir az-Zor and was built according to the North Korean model. Bush relates that Olmert asked him to order an American attack on the site. But, as American intelligence services were unable to demonstrate clearly that a nuclear weapons program was being pursued at the site, Bush told Olmert that the United States would not destroy the reactor. A disappointed Olmert told him that a nuclear-armed Syria would constitute a threat to Israel's very survival.

On September 6, 2007, the Deir az-Zor facility was bombed and destroyed. Foreign media attributed the attack to Israel. According to Bush, "Prime Minister Olmert's execution of the strike made up for the confidence I lost in the Israelis during the Lebanon war." Further material published outside Israel helps paint a picture of the complicated situation that followed Ehud Barak's assumption of the defense portfolio in June 2007, just three months before the attack on the Syrian reactor. According to this information, Barak opposed an attack and demanded that it be postponed for several months—despite the fact that there was good reason to believe that during this time the reactor would become "hot." Bombing it at this stage would be dangerous and could even contaminate the Euphrates River, which flowed not distant from the site. Barak argued that a delay was necessary to prevent a repeat of the Second Lebanon War, for which preparations had been inadequate. Olmert, for his part, suspected that Barak's calculations were political.

According to these reports, Olmert insisted on going forward with the attack. The question was brought before the security cabinet, where Barak switched sides and voted in favor of an attack. The Israeli media, basing themselves on foreign media reports, kept the Israeli public informed about these events. One Israeli reporter wrote:

> Olmert and others reached the conclusion that Barak was motivated by personal political rather than professional considerations, growing out of the fact that they were waiting for the report of the . . . Winograd Commission on the Second Lebanon War. Ashkenazi, [Mossad chief Meir] Dagan, and especially Olmert concluded that the defense minister was hoping that Olmert would be forced out of office and that he, Barak, would replace him or serve as defense minister in an alternative government . . . and that in such a government . . . a successful attack in Syria would be credited to him.[373]

Barak, of course, rejects these claims, claiming that he feared that Olmert was acting overhastily.

In his book, Bush also relates that he urged Olmert to state publicly that the attack had been an Israeli one, so as to isolate the Syrian regime. But Olmert told Bush that "he wanted total secrecy. He wanted to avoid anything that might back Syria into a corner and force Assad to retaliate."[374] It certainly would have been in Olmert's personal political interest to comply with Bush's request, as it would have painted him as a hero. But he insisted on setting his personal political benefit aside in favor of the national interest. It is all the more to Olmert's credit that he did this at a time when, following the Winograd Commission's interim report, his political fortunes could have used a boost. Olmert's public-mindedness stood in notable contrast to that of Menachem Begin, who rushed to take credit for the bombing of Iraq's nuclear reactor in 1981.

On Bush's account, the issue at the time was whether to pursue diplomatic or military means in the face of Syria's nuclear program. The Syrians hoped that the project's secrecy would protect it. Had they surrounded the reactor with major defenses, it would have indicated that the site contained a valuable military asset. But when, without their knowledge, their secret was discovered, it remained defenseless for all intents and purposes. A diplomatic initiative would have told the Syrians that their secret had been uncovered. That would have led them to deploy massive defenses and given them an opportunity to prepare a response to any attack on it, making an attack much more difficult and risky. If the diplomatic initiative were to fail—and there was every reason to believe that it would—and an attack inevitable, it might then have ignited the entire region.

28

The Olmert Investigations

Ehud Olmert has been the subject of multiple criminal investigations, on numerous occasions, most of them unconnected to each other and some of them picayune. Most of the investigations were closed, sometimes years after they were opened, without charges being filed. But, hydra-like, each time one investigation ended, others appeared. In 1996, Olmert was brought to trial on charges that he had violated campaign finance laws. It is doubtful whether the charges had any substance, and indeed Olmert was acquitted.

In 2001, while Olmert was mayor of Jerusalem, his name came up as part of the investigation of David Appel and his involvement in several dealings. One of these was the Greek Island affair, in which, as already noted in chapter 24, Prime Minister Ariel Sharon and his son Gilad also came under investigation. The inquiry ended without indictments. Olmert's involvement was connected to his hosting of a visit by the mayor of Athens, apparently at Appel's request. In 2002 the police recommended charging Olmert with bribery and breach of trust. But Attorney General Menachem Mazuz decided in 2004 to close the case without filing charges.

It is hard to see what is nefarious about elected officials promoting business and helping businessmen in their contacts with foreign officials. Is it a crime when the president of the United States invites American businessmen to accompany him on state visits to China or Russia, so as to encourage commerce between the countries? In Israel, however, any such initiative immediately raises eyebrows and leads to ominous references to the capital-government complex—a term that has become a synonym for corruption. The legalization of every aspect of life in Israel undermined politicians and created a situation in which every elected official is automatically suspect, if not of actual corruption, then of suspicious or unreasonable motives.

Olmert was a vigorous public official who sought to promote projects in the areas that came under his purview. His view of how to do this did not always match the position taken by the bureaucracy and its professional advisers, and he was often criticized for acting against expert advice.

One example comes from Olmert's tenure as industry minister. While he served in that post, the ministry's Investment Center dealt with an application by Dimona Silicate Industries Corporation, which planned to build a factory that would produce raw materials for the rubber and plastic sectors, to receive the status of an approved enterprise. Such status brought with it government assistance and tax breaks. In 1992 the corporation was granted the status, but due to a number of difficulties the factory was not built, and the approved enterprise status was revoked in 1997. In 2001 the corporation reapplied, but its application was not taken up for some time. The entrepreneur, Ephraim Feinblum, hired a lawyer, Uri Messer, who had once been Olmert's law partner, to represent him. In December 2003 the approved enterprise status was reinstated, and in 2004 the cornerstone for the factory was laid. A comptroller's report on the affair, published in April 2007, came down hard on Olmert. It faulted the involvement of the industry minister and his staff "in specific activities that fall under the roles and authorities of the professionals in the Investment Center." Olmert, the comptroller wrote, also had a conflict of interest in the matter in that the negotiations were with his former partner. "And when the conflict of interest includes within it a financial aspect, the public servant involved demonstrates the connection between capital and government." (It should be noted that in this case Olmert's connection was not with the investor but with his attorney.) The comptroller referred to the case of Shimon Sheves, who was convicted of breach of trust. Such a reference was more than a hint that the comptroller believed that Olmert had committed a criminal offense. As such, the attorney general had to decide whether to open a criminal investigation.

There was certainly a valid question in this case, one that has come up many times in Israel. Which connections are legitimate and which are out of bounds between government decision makers and lawyers representing those affected by their decisions? For example, what about a judge who decides a case in which one of the parties is represented by an attorney who is a close friend of the judge, or a lawyer formerly in the public service who represents private clients before the same government authority that previously employed him? Rules can be made, but the claim that the judge or the government official in such a situation is automatically committing a crime is unreasonable. Olmert was acting as any good government minister should, seeking to further projects he considered important through exercise of his own judgment rather than acting as a simple yes-man to the bureaucrats working under him. That getting a factory built in Dimona was in the public interest hardly needs defending—it would have provided jobs in an Israeli city suffering from high unemployment and furthered the development of the Negev region, a goal of all Israeli governments throughout the country's history.

The state comptroller's report about the deal was one more in a series focusing on Olmert's actions that began a year earlier, in 2006. That was the year Olmert was elected prime minister and thus automatically became a target of investigation. He was investigated for anything and everything. The poor performance of the Israel Defense Forces' ground forces in the Second Lebanon War, which caused his popularity to plummet, made him an easy target. Every criticism and investigation against him, justified or not, was supported and cheered by the media.

In fact, the police had already launched a bribery investigation against Olmert three months before his election victory. He had supposedly received valuable gifts—expensive pens for a collection Olmert was proud of. Half a year later the attorney general decided that there was no cause to file charges. The attorney general's decision to close the case was challenged before the Supreme Court, but the court did not intervene.[375] In March 2006 State Comptroller Micha Lindenstrauss released a report on Olmert's sale of his apartment in Jerusalem to a billionaire businessman, Daniel Abrams, for a sum that was allegedly above the market value. The Olmert family continued to live in the apartment as paying tenants for a time following the sale, again for rent that was alleged to be lower than the going rate for such a residence. The inquiry found that the price Olmert received had been reasonable, and while the rent he paid had been somewhat low, it had not been proved that it lay "outside the bounds of the reasonable."

That same month, Attorney General Mazuz looked into another complaint, this one regarding a home Olmert had purchased on Cremieux Street in Jerusalem. The suspicion was that he had paid considerably less for his new home than it was actually worth. Mazuz found no cause for a criminal investigation, but nevertheless referred the case to the state comptroller, who handed it over to his adviser on corruption affairs, Yaakov Borovsky, to decide whether there was cause for a more comprehensive investigation. In September 2006, after the fiasco of the war, such an investigation got underway. Staff members from the comptroller's office met with the prime minister and interrogated him on the purchase of the apartment, on the suspicion that in exchange for a bargain price, Olmert had helped push a building project through the bureaucracy. The comptroller sent the case back to Mazuz, who now ordered an investigation. All this was, of course, reported by the media.[376] Even before this, in August, a *Ha'aretz* columnist predicted that a police investigation of the Cremieux Street affair would soon begin. "All the odds are that two months from now . . . [Olmert] will no longer be prime minister," Ari Shavit wrote.[377]

The comptroller's investigation raised the question of whether he was, in fact, not exceeding the bounds of his authority in investigating a claim of this sort. In principle, the state comptroller's job is to investigate government activities. If, in the course of doing so, he suspects that a criminal offense has occurred, he should hand the matter over to the attorney general. The Cremieux Street affair did not involve a government agency, but rather an alleged benefit received by a public official. That falls under the purview of the police or the attorney general, and the latter, as noted, initially saw no cause for a criminal investigation. Once that determination had been made, it was hardly reasonable for the comptroller to launch a separate investigation to see whether Olmert had nonetheless committed a criminal offense.

As if that were not enough, at about the same time as the Borovsky investigation, the press reported that that comptroller was about to recommend that the attorney general commence a criminal investigation against Olmert and others on suspicion of bribery in connection with the government tender offering for the sale of the controlling interest in Bank Leumi (the Israeli government had taken over ownership of the country's large banks during the bank stock crisis of 1983 and was seeking to privatize them). In addition, in August 2006 the comptroller issued and submitted to the attorney general a report implicating Olmert in making political appointments in the Small Business Authority.

The profusion of press reports on suspicions against and investigations of Olmert redounded on Lindenstrauss. In early November, five respected figures published an open letter in *Ha'aretz* claiming that the state comptroller was causing damage to the Israeli government. The signatories were Amnon Rubinstein, a former cabinet minister and legal scholar; Shlomo Avineri, a respected political scientist and former director general of the Ministry of Foreign Affairs; Yoav Dotan, the dean of the Hebrew University law school; Yaffa Zilbershats, a legal scholar at Bar-Ilan University; and Arye Carmon, director of the Israel Democracy Institute. They charged that the comptroller's office was leaking information about the investigations to the press. Dotan told the news website Ynet that "the impression is that the attorney general's office has been bombarded by the state comptroller with all kinds of requests for investigations, and that everything that reaches the attorney general . . . also reaches the media in parallel. This undermines the executive branch."[378]

Following the war, the media and public turned increasingly against Olmert. That same month the Knesset's State Control Committee lent Lindenstrauss its full backing and denounced the signers of the open letter. It had nothing to say in favor of Olmert, whose private matters had come, one after the other, under Lindenstrauss's magnifying glass.

Mazuz had his own problems at the time. He had already indicted a member of Olmert's cabinet, Haim Ramon, on a charge of indecent conduct. The case, discussed in detail in Chapter 30, was being heard in the Tel Aviv Magistrates Court. Suddenly, the question arose: How had such a problematic indictment been made? A large swathe of the public and the media felt that criminal law was being improperly invoked. This time the advocates of the "rule of law" did not stand behind Mazuz. Many of them felt uncomfortable with the fact that Ramon had been charged with such an offense, especially as the trial proceeded and it turned out that the case was a weak one. On top of that, it transpired that wiretap transcripts of relevance to Ramon and his defense had not been provided to his lawyers, despite their repeated requests for them. The wiretaps demonstrated that the woman had been scandalously cajoled into submitting a complaint against Ramon. Mazuz feared, rightly so, that Ramon would be acquitted. The Bank Leumi affair came as a blessing from heaven.

In fact, the Bank Leumi case was totally without foundation. The tender had been a public one, and the conditions for all bidders were the same. The bidder whom Olmert supposedly sought to boost dropped out and never submitted a bid. Ram Caspi, attorney for another bidder, Nochi Dankner (who did not win in the end), maintained that the tender had been conducted in a model way. According to Dankner, "It is nothing but a despicable and contemptible slander."[379] But State Attorney Eran Shandar decided on a criminal investigation of Olmert. (Mazuz recused himself from the case because his sister was legal counsel to the Finance Ministry, which had put out the tender.)

In fact, the investigation served Mazuz very well. In January 2007, prior to my appointment as justice minister, Olmert notified Mazuz that he intended to ask the cabinet to appoint a governmental committee of inquiry to look into the handling of the Ramon case. Mazuz forbade him to do so, largely on the grounds that the prime minister himself was under investigation at the time. The Bank Leumi case would later benefit Mazuz in another way. When it came time to replace Shandar, Mazuz categorically opposed my demand that the search committee for a new state attorney propose three candidates. He argued that giving the government the discretion to choose one of three candidates might, at a time that the prime minister was under investigation, grant the government undue influence over the new state attorney, who would be responsible for pursuing the case. The result was that the search committee, which Mazuz chaired, offered the cabinet a single candidate, Moshe Lador.

When the investigation in the Bank Leumi case was completed, the police announced that there was insufficient evidence to prove a criminal violation. Yet the unsubstantiated case was kept open. Only more than a year later, after the government's fall, did Lador announce that he would close it. The investigation had been justified, he insisted. But he never explained why the case against the prime minister had been kept open for so long. What was clear was that the attorney general and the State Attorney's Office found it convenient to have the case hanging over Olmert's head.

The investigation of Olmert's Cremieux Street house also ended with a whimper, but, of course, only after the government had already fallen. In March 2009 the police submitted the material to the state attorney, noting that no evidence of any crime had been discovered. The case was closed that July.

The State Comptroller issued his trenchant report about Dimona Silicate Industries in April 2007. The prime minister was highly critical. He charged that Lindenstrauss was persecuting him and declared that he had no confidence in the state comptroller. One can certainly understand how Olmert felt in the face of this wave of investigations against him by the comptroller and the public atmosphere it created. But his behavior turned out to be a tactical error. He declared his lack of confidence in Lindenstrauss at almost the same time that the Winograd Commission issued its interim report, with its sharp criticism of the prime minister. While most of the investigations produced no indictments, the sheer quantity of investigations and the consequent media furor—prior to, during, and following the investigations—created a public atmosphere hugely hostile to Olmert. On top of this came the Winograd report, the internal infighting within Kadima, and pressure from the Labor Party. Given these conditions, Olmert's blunt condemnation of the comptroller was inept, and may well have spurred Lindenstrauss to make the tone and content of his reports more severe. Other politicians did not act as Olmert did, and came out of the investigations better.

In retrospect, it is clear that the government did not fall because of anything produced by these investigations, but they made Olmert highly unpopular and vulnerable. And, given all the material that accumulated in investigations of him and published in the media, it was clear that he would not go scot-free. Accusations were fired in all directions, and investigators labored to find something, anything, that would incriminate him. In November 2007 the police seized the computers in the Ministry of Industry, Trade, and Labor, a portfolio Olmert had previously held. That led to the Investment Center inquiry. In July 2008 the State Attorney's Office and the police issued a joint statement on the Rishontours case. Rishontours was the travel agency that had handled Olmert's overseas travel; and he was suspected of arranging double compensation for his travel expenses and pocketing the difference. The suspicion related to the time before he became prime minister. Investigators examined all the documents stored in his office manager's computers. The prime minister himself was interrogated no less than fourteen times. No stone was left unturned.

Does such a hunt, investigation after investigation in every possible direction, respect human dignity? How does the Israeli legal system permit such a thing to happen, without restraint and without oversight? And all the more so against a sitting prime minister? The questions remain unanswered. All these investigations were in full swing as Hamas's bombardment of southern Israel intensified, reaching a point where the terrorist faction was firing hundreds of missiles each month and the country was on the verge of war.

In May 2008, on the eve of Holocaust Memorial Day, just a week before Independence Day, the police conducted a search of the prime minister's office.

Like all the other investigations and searches performed by the police in relation to Olmert, it was carried out with full media coverage, as senior figures in the police force dropped broad hints that a new investigation of Olmert was underway, something far more serious than any of the others. The day before the police had interrogated Morris (Moshe) Talansky, an American businessman and old friend and associate of Olmert's, and his office manager, Shula Zaken. Zaken's interrogation was reported on television that same night. On the day after Holocaust Day, May 2, the front page of *Yedioth Ahronoth* bore the headline: "Dramatic development. Olmert to be interrogated this morning under warning. The suspicion: a cash bribe from an American businessman." A court order was issued forbidding the press to report on the matter.

The gag order created a paradoxical situation. The press circumvented the court order, publishing bits of information leaked to it about the case, apparently by people within the law enforcement system. But the prime minister, whose name was dragged through the mud, was helpless to defend himself because of the ban.

The drama reached its climax the night following Independence Day. The gag order was lifted, and the public learned that Talansky was lynchpin in the new scandal. He had told the police that he had conveyed envelopes containing cash gifts to Olmert. Olmert denied that he had received any money illegally, but that did nothing to appease the public. Immediately thereafter the state attorney demanded that Talansky be deposed in court, to that his testimony could later be admitted in Olmert's trial. Such early testimony, prior to indictment and trial, was necessary, the state attorneys claimed, because Talansky was scheduled to return to the United States and there was reason to believe that he would not return to testify at the trial. The request further amplified the furor. It meant that Talansky would give public testimony against Olmert before the prime minister had even been charged with a crime, when it was still unclear whether an indictment would be forthcoming and, if so, what the charge would be. Despite the fact that the testimony—the reliability and significance of which could not be determined at the time—was liable to topple the government in the midst of a missile attack from the Gaza Strip, Attorney General Mazuz and State Attorney Lador were not deterred.

An attorney general should take such considerations into account and weigh them against the speculative value of such early testimony. Indeed, it subsequently transpired that the early testimony had been unjustified. "There was no real professional justification for hearing early testimony from Talansky, as was not only proved afterward but also could have been understood from the start,"[380] Dan Avi-Yitzhak wrote. Yehuda Weinstein, who would later serve as attorney general, said that "this decision was legally wrong."[381]

The District Court nevertheless approved the request for early testimony. An appeal of that decision was dismissed by the Supreme Court.[382] Once again, the courts trusted the prosecutors and refrained from exercising any real oversight.

Talansky began testifying at the end of May. Olmert was vilified in banner headlines. The day after Talansky finished testifying, Ehud Barak called a press conference and demanded that the prime minister step aside. If Olmert did not resign, Barak announced, the Labor Party would seek early elections. A day later Foreign Minister Tzipi Livni seconded Barak's call for Olmert's resignation at a press conference of her own. Kadima, she said, should prepare for every possible eventuality, including elections. Olmert's close associates viewed these statements as tantamount to a putsch.[383] While Barak and Livni may not have coordinated their actions, the effect was of a united front against the prime minister. But both these politicians, while hoping to replace Olmert as prime minister, soon found themselves going in different directions.

The government was in a precarious position. The opposition Likud Party submitted an early elections bill. Labor threatened to support it, unless Kadima called an internal election for a new leader. Olmert had no choice—he announced that Kadima would hold a leadership election no later than the end of September. At first he declared that he would be a candidate, but then the Rishontours investigation hit the headlines. Olmert decided not to run and announced that he would resign as party leader as soon as a replacement was elected. The two candidates were Tzipi Livni and Shaul Mofaz. Livni won by a small margin.

A few days after the election, on September 21, 2008, Olmert submitted his resignation as prime minister. Under Israeli law, the resignation of a prime minister turns the government into a caretaker government pending the formation of a new government or new elections. Livni tried to form a government herself. On paper, she should have had no problem doing so. Everyone expected her to form a government reassembling the existing coalition, with the same program and the same parties. After all, Kadima had done what Labor demanded. It had a new leader. But Barak's appetite was not assuaged. He made more demands.

The fact is that Labor's bargaining position was weak. The polls showed that it would do badly in a new election (as indeed happened). Livni agreed to name Barak "deputy prime minister and the most senior government minister," but refused to give him the post of vice prime minister. I was told that Livni also consented to give Labor a veto over all legislation touching on the legal system. That demand was not a difficult concession for her to make, or at least so it seemed at the time, but having given in on this point she soon found herself facing further demands.

Shas presented an even more difficult problem. The party had moved to the right, and Likud was pressing it not to support Livni. The party demanded more financial support for large families and a written commitment from Livni that she would conduct no negotiations with the Palestinians over the status of Jerusalem. Livni in the end failed to form a government, and new elections had to be called.

Two months following Olmert's resignation, Attorney General Mazuz announced that he had decided to indict him in the Rishontours case, pending a hearing at which Olmert would be able to present his side of the story. Olmert had his hearing, and Mazuz issued the indictment. It was the first of a series of charges and indictments of Olmert following his exit from public office. At the time, however, Olmert was still in office, since under Israeli law the sitting prime minister continues to serve until a new government is established. The next day Livni, speaking before a gathering of Kadima leaders, called on Olmert to resign. But Olmert could not, by law, leave his post until a new government was formed. What Livni actually wanted was for Olmert to declare himself incapable of carrying out his duties, so that Livni, his vice prime minister, could become the acting prime minister. But Olmert refused. He had no reason to cooperate in his own ouster. Furthermore, Operation Cast Lead in the Gaza Strip was already on the horizon, and it was better for Israel that Olmert remain at the helm.

Subsequent to his resignation, Olmert was indicted on a number of charges, all of them relating to the period prior to his term as prime minister. The first indictment included the Talansky, Rishontours, and Investment Center affairs. The bribery count, which had been the basis for the hue and cry about the Talansky affair, was dropped. Instead, Olmert was accused of breach of trust. In July 2012, he was acquitted in the Talansky case, the one which had toppled his government. He was also acquitted in the Rishontours case. In the Investment Center case he was convicted of breach of trust. The state attorney appealed.

Prior to the end of that trial, Olmert was indicted yet again, along with several others, among them his longtime secretary and office manager Shula Zaken, on charges of bribery, most of which in connection with building permits issued for the Holyland construction project in Jerusalem. In 2014, Olmert was convicted on two charges of bribery, the main one related to a payment of NIS 500,000 (about $130,000) made to his brother, in connection with the Holyland building project. The other charge related to another project and was concerned with a payment of NIS 60,000 (about $16,000) made to his secretary and allegedly transferred to him. He was sentenced to six years in prison. Olmert appealed. Shula Zaken was also convicted in the Holyland case, but before being sentenced, and facing the likelihood of a very long term in prison, she had changed her tune. After a long period in which she had refused to testify against her former boss, she reached a plea bargain with the prosecution under which she agreed to testify against her former boss. In accordance with the plea bargain she received a relatively mild sentence of eleven months in prison. I am on record as saying that Olmert's conviction in the main charge, namely the one relating to the payment of NIS 500,000 to his brother, was unwarranted.[384] On December 29, 2015, the Supreme Court acquitted Olmert of this charge but confirmed his conviction of bribery in connection with the payment of NIS 60,000 and reduced his sentenced from six years in prison to one and a half years.

Throughout this two-year period, between 2012 and 2014, the state attorney's appeal of Olmert's acquittal in the Talansky and Rishontours affairs was still pending in the Supreme Court. At this very late stage the Supreme Court decided, in a highly unusual step, to accept the prosecution's application and remit the Talansky case back to the District Court so that it could hear Zaken's testimony. In the wake of her new testimony, Olmert was convicted of breach of trust and fraud, and was sentenced to eight months in prison. Olmert appealed this verdict as well.

This is not the place to enter into a detailed analysis of the merits of these verdicts. Suffice it to say that because of the harsh and hostile atmosphere created by the media and his opponents, Olmert did not get fair trials.

Zaken's testimony also led to additional charges of obstruction of justice against Olmert, regarding which he reached a plea bargain. According to the plea bargain, Olmert would plead guilty to two of these charges and be sentenced to six months in prison, overlapping the prison sentence that was already imposed on him and pay a fine of NIS 50,000. On February 10, 2016 the Jerusalem Magistrates Court confirmed the plea bargain but modified it so that one month of the prison sentence will be in addition to the other sentences imposed on him. Such modification of a plea bargain is highly exceptional.

29

War in the Shadow of Criminal Investigations

The bombardment of Israel's south by Hamas rockets and mortars intensified as the government was rocked by internal strife and the prime minister was under constant investigation. Something had to be done to stop it. The bombardments had grown worse after Hamas staged its coup in Gaza in June 2007, wreaking fear and destruction in the Israeli towns and farms on the strip's perimeter. Furthermore, captured Israeli soldier Gilad Shalit remained a prisoner, and Hamas made huge demands for his release.

Some cabinet ministers, myself included, thought that Israel had to topple Hamas. The Jewish state, we argued, could not tolerate an illegal and hostile regime, supported by Iran, on its southern border. The Second Lebanon War and the Winograd Commission's interim report were still fresh, but in my view the current crisis was of an entirely different sort. Hezbollah in Lebanon enjoyed strategic depth; its fighters had places to retreat to. Even if the Israel Defense Forces (IDF) were to once again seize control of southern Lebanon, Hezbollah's leader, Hassan Nasrallah, could regroup his forces north of the Litani River to harass Israel's forces and then reoccupy the south once the IDF pulled out. Hezbollah also enjoyed an open border with Syria, through which it could receive a steady supply of weapons, equipment, and troop reinforcements as the fighting proceeded.

Hamas had none of these strategic advantages. For all intents and purposes, the Gaza Strip was under siege. Egypt, the only other country with which it had a border, was then ruled by Hosni Mubarak, who loathed Hamas and was unlikely to offer it any assistance. Hamas had no chance of winning a fight against Israel. Furthermore, Israel's reasons for ending Hamas rule were clearly justified and enjoyed international support. Israel's allies understood and accepted that Israel could not sit by idly while its civilians were being targeted by a terror organization.

Defense Minister Ehud Barak held to the policy Israel had pursued before the coup, when the Palestinian Authority had controlled Gaza. Rockets had been fired on Israel then, though on a much more modest scale, but Israel had sought to avoid a crisis with the Palestinian Authority's leaders, with whom Israel sought to reach a peace agreement. It thus kept its responses moderate, in the form of occasional air strikes or limited ground actions. Israel also targeted militants involved in firing rockets and terror activities. This ritualistic response did nothing to mitigate the rocket fire—on the contrary, it intensified. Hamas steadily extended the range of its homemade Qassam rockets, which eventually began falling on Ashkelon, an

Israeli city not far north of the Gaza Strip. In September 2007 rockets hit an IDF basic training camp and injured several soldiers. At the end of February 2008 the IDF embarked on Operation Hot Winter, in which air and ground forces attacked terror infrastructure in the Hamas-controlled territory. The IDF killed more than one hundred militants, but rather than deterring rocket fire on Israel, it caused the Palestinians to escalate their attacks to a rate of hundreds of launches each month. Israel declared the Gaza Strip a "hostile entity." The Ariel Sharon government had promoted disengagement from Gaza with the claim that, once Israel had withdrawn its civilian settlements and its troops from the Strip, it would no longer bear responsibility for the humanitarian needs of its inhabitants. In principle, that was correct, but became subject of controversy. International humanitarian organizations and a number of legal experts argued that Israel continued to be responsible at least for certain aspects of the humanitarian situation in Gaza. Israel's leaders had also assumed that once they had declared the Gaza Strip regime a "hostile entity," Israel would be within its rights to enforce a siege of Gaza and reduce its supply of electricity and fuel. The issue reached the attorney general, and shortly afterward came before the Supreme Court. How could it not?

The court, led by Chief Justice Dorit Beinisch, closely scrutinized all aspects of the question. In November, in an interim procedure, an officer who gave evidence on behalf of the state informed the court that Egypt would supply a transformer that would improve the operation of the Gaza electrical power station. "In connection with this datum we wish to receive all the relevant information on the way the additional transformer will affect the supply and regulation of electricity to Gaza," Beinisch declared. The court also required the state to provide affidavits containing "details about the destinations of the electric lines whose supply will be restricted, noting the different places, including vital facilities, if any, which receive their electric supply through these lines."[385]

It took the court two months to deny the petition. But this is hardly an example of the court's nonintervention in security matters. In fact, simply by consenting to hear such a suit the court exerts pressure on the government and puts it in an impossible position. IDF officers are required to appear in court and to submit affidavits explaining every detail in the military operations under their command to the satisfaction of the judges. Indeed, the court said as much:

> Col. Nir Press, the commander of the Coordination and Liaison Authority, appeared before us during the final hearing and supplied details of the relevant data and information upon which the respondents rely . . . and insisted that the amount of fuel and electricity entering the Gaza Strip is sufficient for the proper functioning of all the humanitarian services in the territory; Col. Press further told us of contact that he made with Palestinian representatives for the routine monitoring of the functioning of the humanitarian services in the Gaza Strip . . . [W]e were convinced by the respondents' declarations that they intend to continue to allow the supply of industrial diesel fuel at the same level as prior to the implementation of the reductions, namely 2.2 million litres per week.[386]

It is hard to believe that any other court in the world would have taken up the implications of sanctions imposed by its country against an area under enemy control, much less make a determination of exactly what quantity of fuel the enemy should receive.

But it happened when the Israeli government sought a way to stop Hamas's bombardments of Israeli towns and villages. The court also took up the issue despite Israel's explicit commitment to avert a humanitarian crisis in the Gaza Strip, despite Hamas's terror campaign, and specifically to ensure that the electricity supply to the region's hospitals not be cut off. That did not mean, however, that Israel had to make sure that electricity also reached the workshops that were manufacturing Qassam rockets.

While Israel was fighting under the watchful gaze of its Supreme Court, Hamas brazenly attacked the border crossings where Israel delivered supplies to the besieged population. It also fired rockets at the electric power station in Ashkelon, which supplied electricity to the Gaza Strip. At the time, Israeli jurists feared that if a rocket damaged the power station and thus interrupted the supply of electricity to the Palestinians, Israel would be held responsible by the international community. From January through June 2008 the blitz reached a level of 200 projectiles per month; in April alone 500 rockets and mortar shells were fired at Israel. Hamas had no problem with the fact that the Gaza Strip's population was suffering dozens of casualties each month. Yet the Israeli government could not tolerate the terror, death, and destruction that were paralyzing the inhabitants and economy of a large circle of territory around the Gaza Strip.

On top of all this, Gilad Shalit remained a prisoner. Hamas refused even to allow representatives of the International Red Cross to visit him. Overthrowing the Hamas regime was also vital to any future Israeli-Palestinian peace accord, under which Gaza would become a port city serving the economies of both Palestinians and Israelis rather than a depot for terror materiel. It looked as if the international community would support such an action. After all, Hamas was officially classified as a terror organization that had seized control of the Gaza Strip illegally, and this while President George W. Bush was pursuing an aggressive antiterrorism policy.

It was clear that reoccupation of the Gaza Strip, or at least a large part of it, would be problematic for Israel in a number of ways. It would cost the lives of soldiers, and, once captured, the territory would have to be administered. Israel had no interest in ruling it. Who could do so once Hamas was out of the picture? On top of all this, such a military operation would be expensive, as would the cost of administering the territory until some resolution of its status could be achieved. Yet, despite all these problems, it seemed that the benefit of overthrowing the murderous Hamas terror regime outweighed the cost of doing so.

It was precisely during March, April, and early May 2008, with Qassams and mortars falling on Israel daily, that the Talansky affair hit the headlines. The prosecution's handling of the affair demonstrated that all it was concerned with was gaining an advantage in its attempt to convict Ehud Olmert. The fact that Israel was locked in battle with Hamas made no difference.

In the meantime, Amos Gilad, director of the Defense Ministry's Political-Military Affairs Bureau, was involved in talks, mediated by Egypt, to achieve a ceasefire with Hamas. It was a sharp departure from Israel's policy up until that time of not negotiating with terror organizations (except on the release of Israeli prisoners). Clearly, Ehud Barak was behind these talks, and it is hard to believe that Prime Minister Olmert had not approved, or that he was at least aware of them. But Olmert was then in the midst of the Talansky scandal, and even members of his own party were trying to oust him. Barak himself had declared that if Kadima did not replace Olmert, he and his Labor Party would demand new elections.

In June, Barak placed a ceasefire agreement before the government. Barak was eager to see it approved. Olmert supported it but, in my estimation, only reluctantly. I was one of the opponents in the cabinet. The Defense Ministry's position was that the agreement would promote Shalit's release. I didn't believe it. It was obvious to me that the opposite would be the case, as events soon proved. After the ceasefire was approved, Hamas denied that it had made any promises regarding Shalit.

The agreement provided for a six-month armistice. Israel would allow more provisions and supplies into Gaza. It did not apply to the West Bank, where Israel was pursuing Hamas terrorists, even though Hamas had wanted it to. In my view the agreement was the most serious mistake the government in which I served made.

The fact was that Hamas saw Israel's consent to a ceasefire as a sign of weakness. As Hamas saw it, Israel had concluded that it could not stop the rocket attacks by military means. With Hamas seeing the armistice as a victory, I and many others estimated that armed conflict would inevitably break out again. George W. Bush was still president, but would not be for much longer. The United States would hold elections that November, just as the six-month term of the ceasefire was coming to an end. No one knew at the time what the outcome of the elections would be and what the new president's position on the conflict would be. Clearly, putting off an offensive against Hamas would mean, for Israel, conducting it under less optimal conditions, in which more Israeli lives would be lost.

Elections were approaching in Israel as well. While more than two years remained in the Knesset's and the government's statutory term, the Talansky scandal made it likely that the poll would be moved up to early 2009. Was the decision to reach the ceasefire agreement affected by electoral considerations? Were there those who thought that it would be better to fight Hamas just before the elections, in the hopes of gaining votes in the wake of a successful operation? Or were there politicians who thought it might be possible to extend the ceasefire until the elections and thus claim credit for bringing peace to the south?

For the first and only time I spoke out against a decision made by the government in which I sat. I told Olmert in advance that I intended to do so; being of two minds himself about the decision, he consented to my doing so. I informed the public of my reservations about the ceasefire, which was dangerous and would not help release Shalit. He would not even get the right to visits by the Red Cross.[387]

In the meantime, Shalit's parents petitioned the Supreme Court to forbid the opening of the border crossings with the Gaza Strip. Astoundingly, the court issued a temporary order to keep the crossings closed, inserting itself into a manifestly nonjusticiable matter. While the court in fact revoked this order the next day and dismissed the suit,[388] the court had nevertheless encroached on the executive.[389] Amos Gilad and the Shalit family met in the court room, where Gilad tried to persuade the family that "the cessation of hostilities is the only hope for bringing Gilad's release." Other Defense Ministry officials added that "we have no doubt that the cease fire in fact increases the chances of bringing Gilad Shalit home via a deal with Hamas, rather than the opposite."[390] It is not clear what the source of this optimism was; in any case, it was soon proved wrong.

The negotiations over Shalit's release continued, intermittently and with periodic crises, for a long time thereafter. Hamas made insolent demands, among them the release of hundreds of Palestinian terrorists held by Israel. I was certain that no Israeli government would agree to them, but I was wrong.

Hamas continued to attack Israel even as the ceasefire was in force, but there was nevertheless a drastic reduction in the number of rockets and mortar shells fired at Israel. At the same time, more and more weapons were smuggled into the Gaza Strip. The Qassam rocket was improved and was capable of reaching a longer range. Hamas erected ever more defenses and dug myriad tunnels through which its operatives could enter Israeli territory. It also improved the training of its combat units. The calm period ended at the beginning of November 2008, when Israeli forces uncovered a tunnel that Hamas had intended to use to penetrate and attack Israeli territory. The IDF demolished the house that stood over the entrance to the tunnel within the Gaza Strip, killing seven Hamas operatives. The terror organization responded by barraging Israel and staging attacks along the border. The shelling of Israel continued all through November and December.

In the meantime both the United States and Israel underwent political changes. Israel was heading toward new elections. In the United States, Barack Obama was elected president and would enter the White House in January 2009. A month before that, Olmert's caretaker government had to decide how to respond to the collapse of the ceasefire and the new torrent of rockets falling on Israeli cities and villages.

It was not a good time for Israel's government to be making such a weighty decision. Olmert was certainly not affected by electoral considerations. But that was not the case with two figures in his government who sought to replace him. Both of them—Minister of Defense Ehud Barak and Foreign Minister Tzipi Livni—headed parties that would soon be facing the voters. They must have been aware of the possible effect of a military operation and its outcome on the forthcoming elections.

President Bush, sympathetic to Israel, was about to reach the end of his second term, and Obama's position was not yet clear. On top of these political problems, Israel found itself facing what looked to be an unusually severe winter. Rain and mud would make it much more difficult for its army and air force to fight and easier for Hamas to defend itself.

One possibility was an extension of the ceasefire. But Hamas's impudence was unbounded. Encouraged by the fact that Israel had given in to many of its terms in the previous ceasefire, Hamas leaders assumed that Israel had lost its self-confidence and said that they would agree only if Israel would also agree to cease military operations in the West Bank and to remove the siege on Gaza, making it easier for Palestinians to enter and leave the territory. But it was clear to the government that a new ceasefire agreement, even one in which Israeli did not give in to Hamas's new demands, was unacceptable.

On December 27, 2008, half a year after the ceasefire was reached; three months after Olmert's resignation, putting him and his government into caretaker status; and just a month and a half before the elections, Israel launched Operation Cast Lead.

The question was what the nature of the operation should be, and what goals it would seek to achieve. The government set the goals at the minimum that Israeli interests required—the cessation of the bombardment of Israeli territory. Ehud Barak opposed any broader goals, even though Israel's strategic interests required the end of the Hamas regime and the return of Gilad Shalit. The operation began with an aerial attack against military targets in the Gaza Strip. Hundreds of terrorists were killed, along with some civilians. Hamas, like all terrorist organizations, refused to say how many of its guerrillas had been killed and inflated the number of civilian deaths by counting terrorists as civilians. But bombing from the air had major limitations. Terrorists melted into the civilian population. Homes, mosques, and schools served as arms depots and terrorist hideouts, taking advantage of the fact that Israel wished to avoid harming innocent bystanders. Hamas even located its command headquarters in Gaza's Shifa hospital, disguising its commanders as medical personnel. It also transpired that Hamas had taken advantage of the armistice reached in June to improve the technology and capabilities of its homemade rockets and to arm itself with long-range missiles smuggled in from the outside. Thanks to the ceasefire, the cities of Ashdod and Beersheva were now in range and suffered casualties during the operation.

A week later Israel launched a ground operation. IDF forces cut the Gaza Strip in two, but its forces advanced slowly because of the difficulties presented by combat in densely populated built-up areas. Houses were booby-trapped, and these had to be located and demolished. Barak, for his part, wished to keep the ground operation from becoming too broad and going too deep into enemy territory. He thus sought to end it at an early stage.

Hamas had suffered much heavier casualties than the IDF. Israeli forces did not penetrate Gaza City itself, but it was clear that the toppling of the Hamas regime was within reach. Its leadership had hunkered down below ground in fear. It was the right moment to reach a deal for Shalit's release, even if that meant extending the operation. But Ehud Barak was eager to bring it to an end, and the IDF withdrew without Shalit. The government settled for a period of calm in the south.

On January 17, 2009, Israel declared a unilateral ceasefire, and a few days later IDF ground forces had withdrawn from the Gaza Strip. The defense minister had succeeded in imposing his will on the cabinet. Hamas remained in control, and Gilad Shalit remained a prisoner.

Nine Israeli soldiers were killed in Operation Cast Lead, and four Israeli civilians were killed in Hamas's barrages. Palestinian losses were estimated by Israel at 1,166 dead, between a quarter and a third of them civilians.

Of course, no account of the operation is complete without addressing the role of the Supreme Court. Once again, during Operation Cast Lead, human rights organizations petitioned the Supreme Court and demanded that it intervene while the bullets and rockets were still flying. IDF officers had to appear in court while combat was in progress to explain their actions and tell the court what they were doing to protect the civilians among whom the terrorists were fighting. Among the charges leveled by the petitioners was that the Gaza Strip was short of electricity and there was a need to ensure the operation of hospitals, clinics, and the region's water and sewage systems. The IDF informed the court that it had established a "humanitarian command center" meant "to solve the difficulties of coordinating the evacuation of the wounded" and that "actions were being taken to repair the electrical infrastructure." But that did not satisfy Beinisch. She noted in her ruling that the officers responsible for the humanitarian situation in the Gaza Strip had not appeared before the court. (Why the astonishment? They were busy addressing the problem in the field.) The court therefore ordered "the state's representatives to submit an up-to-date and detailed response, accompanied by an affidavit from the senior echelon responsible for humanitarian arrangements in the Gaza Strip." The justices did not accept the claim that the suit should be dismissed on the grounds that it was not justiciable. It was denied in the end, but only after the IDF testified regarding the repair of Gaza's electric lines and the supply of fuel for the Palestinian power station, and after the army assured the court that "200,000 liters of diesel oil for transport, 234 tons of cooking gas, water hygiene and purification kits, and bottled water were also brought into the Gaza Strip in the course of the fighting."[391]

What took place in the Supreme Court was not adjudication. The justices did not rule in a justiciable dispute. They functioned as an oversight body, exerting incessant pressure on the IDF to act in a way consistent with so-called liberal values. The court also placed the onus of proof on the IDF, requiring it to show that it was acting in accordance with the strictest possible standards, in a way that may well have put its own soldiers and Israeli civilians at risk. All that is required to impose a heavy burden of proof on the state is a suit that may well be based on nothing more than media reports, rumor, or hearsay regarding a specific incident. It should be obvious that the court itself cannot offer solutions to concrete problems the army encounters, such as Hamas's use of ambulances to transport combatants and war materiel. It should also be obvious that the justices lack the capacity to evaluate pitched battles in the alleyways of refugee camps from their chambers in Jerusalem. But none of that kept the Supreme Court from making itself into a central player in events lying outside its realm of knowledge and capabilities. In this it carried on with what it had done in 2004, under Aharon Barak's leadership, with regard to the IDF's operation in Rafah. The only indication in the court's ruling that its oversight of Operation Cast Lead might be problematic was a comment by Justice Asher Grunis to the effect that "I see no need to address the question of justiciability."[392] If the justices supposed that their close oversight of the military in wartime to ensure its adherence to international law and humanitarian values would ensure that Israel would be lauded worldwide for its moral conduct of the war, they were quickly proven wrong. The U.N. Human Rights Council appointed an international commission to report on allegations that Israel had committed humanitarian violations during the conflict. Chaired by a South African judge, Richard Goldstone, the commission issued a tendentious report execrating Israel for war crimes and crimes against humanity.

After a ceasefire was declared, Egyptian President Hosni Mubarak hosted a summit at Sharm el-Sheikh to seek arrangements for a long-term truce between Israel and Hamas. Following the summit, Prime Minister Olmert hosted the leaders of the five leading European countries at his official residence in Jerusalem. Chancellor Angela Merkel of Germany, President Nicolas Sarkozy of France, Prime Minister Gordon Brown of the United Kingdom, Prime Minister José Luis Rodríguez Zapatero of Spain, and Prime Minister Silvio Berlusconi of Italy, along with Prime Minister Mirek Topolánek of the Czech Republic provided an impressive display of international support both for Israel and for Olmert personally. They explicitly endorsed Israel's right to defend itself as it had done in the recent conflict. Astoundingly, Israel's international standing plummeted soon thereafter, when Benjamin Netanyahu returned to power. When the reprehensible Goldstone Report was issued soon thereafter,* Israel found itself helplessly trying to defend itself against slanders and condemnations from all directions.

---

* I criticized the report in an article in the *Jerusalem Post* entitled "Goldstone Report: The Terrorists' Magna Carta," Oct. 30, 2009.

Israel held its elections a short time after Operation Cast Lead. Several parties invited me to run on their lists, but I declined. When the votes were counted, the block of right-wing and religious parties had a clear majority. The center-left had been defeated.

Nevertheless, Kadima won more seats in the Knesset than any other party—twenty-eight, only one less than in the previous election. While many of its former voters moved to the right, it picked up votes from the left and center. It was the second time the legal system had toppled a government, first Yitzhak Rabin's first government in 1977, and now Olmert's government. In the aftermath, both times, the center-left was defeated by the right-wing Likud.

Netanyahu presented his government on March 31. Kadima was left leading the opposition. Labor suffered an embarrassing decline to only thirteen seats in the Knesset. That did not, however, prevent Ehud Barak from dragging his party into a coalition with Likud, even though the positions of the two parties were diametrically opposed. It did not take long for Labor to split. The party left the government, but Barak remained and formed a five-member splinter faction called Haatzma'ut (Independence), four of whose members were given cabinet posts.

Tzipi Livni, who had sought to replace Olmert, in March 2012 suffered a stinging defeat in an internal Kadima leadership contest. Unwilling to serve under her victorious rival, she resigned from the Knesset. In January 2013 she fielded a slate of her own in the elections to the Nineteenth Knesset, Hatenua, which won only six seats. She joined Netanyahu's third government as justice minister. Barak's Haatzma'ut did not run, and he retired from politics. In December 2014, Netanyahu dismissed Livni and his main coalition partner, Finance Minister Yair Lapid, leader of the centrist Yesh Atid (There Is a Future) Party that had, in the previous elections, surged to garner nineteen seats. Netanyahu called new elections. Livni and her faction went into partnership with Labor in a block called the Zionist Camp, with her receiving second place after Labor's new leader, Yitzhak Herzog. Netanyahu won the elections and formed his fourth government. Livni remained in opposition.

Shalit would remain captive for two more years after Operation Cast Lead. Public calls for the government to give in to Hamas's demands increased. In the end Netanyahu caved in. In October 2011 the Netanyahu government reached an agreement with Hamas for the return of the abducted soldier. In exchange, Israel released more than a thousand Palestinian prisoners, including many who had been sentenced to life in prison for carrying out horrifying terror attacks. The government also gave in to a demand that no previous government had agreed to—to include Arabs of Israeli citizenship among those released. Israel's only condition was that some of the prisoners released would be sent into exile overseas.

Prime Minister Netanyahu violated all the principles he had advocated in the past. The agreement was a disgraceful defeat for Israel and a great victory for Hamas. But, paradoxically, Netanyahu's popularity and prestige zoomed to new heights. Israel had undergone a cultural transformation—surrender was now seen as triumph and capitulation as leadership. But skepticism about the agreement has increased ever since.

30

The Ramon Trial

The evening following Hezbollah's deadly attack in the north on July 12, 2006, in which eight soldiers were killed and two abducted, the cabinet was summoned for an emergency meeting. The ministers decided on a military response which soon turned into the Second Lebanon War. Just before the cabinet met, a smaller forum convened in Prime Minister Ehud Olmert's office to be briefed and to discuss the security situation. One of the participants was the minister of justice, Haim Ramon. After the smaller meeting ended and while waiting for the cabinet to convene, Ramon bantered with an army officer who worked in the prime minister's office. The officer, who was just about to complete her term of service, told Ramon that she would be taking an overseas trip with a friend. She invited Ramon to join them. She then asked him to pose for a photograph with her. The photograph was taken in an adjoining room. It shows her with both her arms around Ramon's body. She reported that, after the picture was taken, Ramon suddenly kissed her and inserted his tongue into her mouth. Ramon's version is different—he maintains that the officer initiated the kiss. The two of them emerged from the room, were photographed again, and the officer gave Ramon her telephone number.

When the officer told her commander and a few friends her version of the events, she did not tell her friends that she gave Ramon her phone number. Neither did she mention that she had suggested to him—jokingly, she would later claim—to accompany her on her travels. Her commander told the head of the Police Investigations Unit, Yohanan Danino, about the kiss, and Danino decided that an investigation was in order. Precisely a week later the officer left a farewell letter for her commander in which she wrote: "I'm flying out two days from now ... I will take that story to the grave with me. Shula [Zaken, Olmert's secretary] and we'll bury it here between four walls." The next day a police officer and the Israel Defense Forces chief of staff's adviser on women's affairs tried to persuade her to file a complaint with the police, but she refused.

That wasn't enough. That Saturday the officer was summoned to a meeting with the prime minister's military secretary, Major General Gadi Shamni, at a café. Shamni did all he could to convince her to file a complaint. They were later joined by Police Brigadier General Miri Golan, who managed to get the officer to change her mind. But it would take some time before these means of persuasion came into light. That same night the complainant flew to Central America. Police officers were later flown there to take her testimony.

A day before the meeting at the café, State Attorney Eran Shandar had met in his office with several senior police officers. With the knowledge of Attorney General Menachem Mazuz, Shandar endorsed the officers' request to go to court to request permission to perform wiretaps. The justification was a suspicion of obstruction of justice, presumably that the officer was being pressured not to complain or to change her story. A later investigation by the state comptroller found nothing wrong with this decision, but I find it difficult to understand why a wiretap was justified. Nothing at all in her farewell letter, in which she said she would take the story to the grave, offers the faintest hint that someone was trying to pressure or influence her.

The main charge against Ramon was committing an indecent act, a count that offers no ground for wiretapping. The addition of the charge of obstruction of justice provided the necessary justification for a tap that, along the way, was likely to bring in evidence relating to the original charge, which on its own could not justify such an action. In fact, the police asked Judge Uri Goren for permission for wiretaps as part of its investigation of both charges, even though the state attorney had refused to countenance it for the indecent act charge. The police did not inform Judge Goren that the request for the wiretap to investigate that charge had not been approved by Shandar. Goren authorized both parts of the request. The officer's phones were tapped, as were those of her commander and Zaken, the prime minister's secretary.

It soon became clear that the wiretaps had boomeranged. If the police investigators had hoped that Ramon would incriminate himself by trying to influence witnesses, they were disappointed. The taps turned up not a scrap of evidence for that and, worse, produced material that was very inconvenient for the prosecution. They showed that the officer had no interest at all in complaining. In fact, she opposed doing so with all her might. But she was no match for the pressure applied to her, pressure that went far beyond anything that could be considered legitimate. She was recorded saying that Golan told her: "If you fly out without submitting a complaint, he [Ramon] will be able to sue you for libel." In fact, there was no such risk, but the officer did not know that. In another conversation, Shamni told the officer's commander that Golan had told the officer: "This man [Ramon] will appoint the next chief justice." The commander responded: "Do you get what job he chose, what chutzpah." In a different conversation, the officer said: "Everyone told me that that shit should sit in jail." The impression is that the investigation was also motivated by the belief that Ramon was not fit to be justice minister and could not be allowed to appoint the next chief justice. The country therefore had to be saved from him.

Judge Goren had authorized the wiretaps for forty-eight hours, but they were stopped just a day after they began. No transcripts or summaries were prepared. Someone seems to have realized that they had not produced the material that the investigators were looking for.

The next stage was to bifurcate the two charges against Ramon. Two different investigation files were opened, one for committing an indecent act and the second for obstruction of justice. The documentation of the wiretaps was put in the second file, which was closed. No mention of the wiretaps appeared in the indecent act file, even though the wiretaps had produced information relevant to the charge—information that could be of use to Ramon in his defense. Ramon and his counsel received only the material in the first file.

Ramon resigned, and his trial began in September 2006 in the Tel Aviv Magistrates Court, before three judges: Hayuta Kochan, Daniela Shirazi, and Daniel Be'eri. During the trial, Ramon learned of the secret wiretaps from an inside source in the police force. On October 22 his lawyer, Dan Sheinman, wrote to the prosecutor in the trial, Ariela Segal-Antler, asking to receive the material. "In the framework of the investigation against your client in this matter no wiretaps were made," the prosecutor replied the next day. Sheinman again asked if there had been wiretaps. Segal-Antler repeatedly denied that there had been any. At this point the Tel Aviv district attorney, Ruth David, asked for the documentation relating to the wiretap and the recordings themselves. After David perused the material, Sheinman was summoned to the State Attorney's Office and it was conveyed to him. The trial, keep in mind, was in progress at the time, and the officer who had filed the complaint against Ramon had already testified.

The investigation and trial aroused much criticism, even from dyed-in-the-wool feminists. The well-known novelist Yochi Brandes penned an article that appeared in *Ha'aretz* under the title "Girls, We've Gone Too Far. "In a society that has healthy checks and balances, this story would have been shunted to the margins of the media and the cabinet minister would have starred, to his detriment, in the gossip columns," she wrote. "The justice system would not have dreamed of wasting its resources on such trifles . . . Such a kiss is at most a matter of bad taste. Is that a reason to destroy a person's personal and professional life? Have we lost our senses? If we don't distinguish between the important and the trivial, it will harm not just men but us as well."

Mazuz and Shandar went to battle. *Ha'aretz* interviewed Shandar and the newspaper offered a teaser under the headline "Shandar on Ramon: He wasn't flirting, she didn't consent." The newspaper's readers were informed that the full interview would be published in the issue that would appear on Yom Kippur eve. Mazuz appeared on Channel Ten and asked a rhetorical question: Would you want what happened to the officer to happen to your daughter? The question he didn't ask was whether a parent would want any of his children to undergo the nightmare of a criminal trial, one that put their futures at risk, because of a single isolated stupid action.

Shulamit Aloni, a lawyer by training, a former cabinet minister, and one of the country's leading advocates of women's rights, responded to Shandar and Mazuz in an article for the news website Ynet. The headline was "The state attorney has already passed judgment on Ramon." She asked: "Why have Mazuz and Shandar passed judgment on their superior, and why have they done all they could to arouse hostile public opinion?" Ramon should not even have been charged, she wrote. "There is no criminal violation here . . . it is contempt for the law" and would ultimately hurt women.

The sense that something was wrong with the process spread. Former Tel Aviv District Attorney Miriam Rosenthal voiced her unease at a gathering of criminal lawyers held in Eilat close to the end of the trial. She spoke out against the Prevention of Sexual Harassment Law. Women, she said, are strong and know how to say "no." Chief Justice Dorit Beinisch, who rose to head the Supreme Court three months earlier, was present. She took the podium to speak about weak woman who were dependent on male employers for their livelihood. "We certainly need to be cautious, but the prosecution did not abuse the law." According to a journalist who was present, Beinisch added, regarding the possibility that her words would be understood in the context of Ramon's trial, "don't mix current events with things that are not connected to them."[393]

Section 39(a) of the Code of Ethics for Judges states: "A judge speaks through judgments and decisions. A judge usually is not interviewed, nor does he relay information to the media."[394] While these rules were issued several months after the convention in Eilat, the rule that a judge speaks through his judgments and decisions is an old and recognized one. Beinisch's statement at the gathering was made at a particularly bad time, just when Ramon faced the court's decision. She may well have believed that, in speaking of the Prevention of Sexual Harassment Law, she was addressing a purely theoretical issue. Or perhaps she did not have Ramon's trial in mind. But the question is how her remark was understood, and whether she should have been aware of how it was likely to be construed even though she said that it should not be connected to any case underway. It can safely be assumed that some believed it to be a veiled hint to Ramon's judges about how to act in the case.

Ramon's verdict was handed down on January 31, 2007. It was entirely baseless, and the way the judges reached their decision to convict a man who should have been acquitted is worrisome. It was a case in which the testimony of one party stood against the testimony of the other. Conviction under such circumstances is obviously problematic. While judges are supposed to be able to distinguish between truth and falsehood, in Israel confidence in their ability to do so has been shaken again and again. In Israel there is a very high risk of innocent people being found guilty, and I have already noted in chapter 25, the high rate of convictions in criminal cases. Experience shows that when a case involves the word of one side against the word of the other, without any objective data to back up either, there is a high probability that the judge will prefer the testimony of the prosecution witness, especially if the judge himself reached the bench from the prosecution.

In fact, in Ramon's case there were no few objective facts, and they supported his claims. Characteristically in sexual harassment cases, one person files a complaint and then several other putative victims follow with their own accusations against the suspect. In the Ramon case, the wiretaps showed Miri Golan of the police telling the officer that as soon as she made an official complaint "ten more will complain after you." Yet, conspicuously, no other women came forward to claim that they had been victims of Ramon's advances.

Furthermore, the photograph of the complainant with Ramon, showing her embracing him with both arms, does not seem to be an ordinary souvenir photo that a woman working in a cabinet minister's office would have taken with a superior. The standard would be something more reserved and respectful. In this case, the picture speaks volumes. Moreover, the officer and Ramon were photographed again, after the kiss, and in that picture the officer does not seem to be at all upset, as she later claimed to be. On top of all that, there is the officer's invitation to Ramon that he join her on her coming trip, followed by her supplying him with her telephone number.

Despite all this, the verdict was notably one-sided. The court explained away each of these facts. The complainant's invitation to join the trip was made facetiously, the judges maintained. But even if it was, wasn't it the kind of humor that Ramon might well have interpreted as intimating an interest in him? The judges explained the fact that she did not tell her friends that she gave Ramon her phone number by asserting that "she understood that she had made a mistake, [and] felt ashamed and bad about herself." The fact that she gave Ramon her number is explained away with the claim that the victim of a sex crime often acts in seemingly inexplicable ways. The officer, the judges maintained, "acted like a robot, without thinking, and under pressure." But the robot image is inconsistent with the explanation the officer offered her commander, according to which she seemed to be acting rationally and out of utilitarian motives—given that, she said, she might want in the future to work in Ramon's office.

The judges also methodically dismantled the testimony of the defense witnesses. Cabinet Secretary Israel Maimon, a man whose integrity and truthfulness have never been doubted, told the court that the officer had also invited him to go to Costa Rica with her, saying that they could have a good time together. He described the conversation as "a flirt with a sexual insinuation." The officer did not deny having such a conversation with Maimon, but the court had trouble understanding how the cabinet secretary could interpret it as sexual allusion. It seems difficult, however, to understand such an offer in any other way, and it is quite likely that many Israelis would have taken it exactly as Maimon did.

The court's bias was also evident in a number of remarks hostile to the defendant. Ramon seems to have said at some point that he was being framed. The court ruled that Danino, head of the Police Investigations Unit, ordered the case looked into before he even knew which of the cabinet ministers was involved. That, the court maintained unpersuasively, "pulled the rug out from under the baseless claim that someone sought to frame the defendant." Ramon certainly had cause to believe that, had the same weak evidence been adduced against someone else, no indictment would have been forthcoming. The court did not suffice with rejecting the claim. It added: "Statements like 'they falsely accused me' [and] 'they framed me' are generally the refuges of criminals, including elected officials, who hide behind baseless claims in order to save themselves from the noose of investigation and trial that tightens around their necks." It would be interesting to know what the judges think a person who sincerely believes he is falsely accused or being framed is supposed to say. What words is he permitted to use so that the judges would not think that he is a criminal seeking refuge?

According to Ramon, the officer was not telling the truth about certain aspects of the incident. The court reacted sharply to this claim. "It is clear to us," the judges said, "that these are not lies or fabrications made by the complainant, and for that reason portraying her as a liar indicates the defendant's clear interest in sullying her name and defaming her, while at the same time washing his hands of any personal guilt. It is precisely this interest that points to a clear sense of guilt on the part of the defendant." The logic of the court was then that the defendant's attempts to defend himself and to deny the version of events presented by the main prosecution witness prove that he felt guilty. If that is the case, what is a defendant supposed to do when he is convinced that the prosecution witness is not telling the truth? The material shows that Ramon believed that the officer consented to his kiss. In fact, the court did not find that he knew that she did not consent. Nevertheless, the judges ruled, he acted recklessly. Such a finding had nothing to support it, and the judges were certainly wrong in convicting a man simply because he acted imprudently. From a broader perspective, the court's bias in its treatment of the evidence and testimony gives the impression that the judges were seeking to cover up a weak case with strong language. The fundamental requirement that a defendant should only be convicted if proven guilty beyond reasonable doubt evaporated.

Two days following the judgment I published a furious critique of it. Five days later the Knesset approved my appointment to the post of minister of justice. I was reminded of the butterfly effect—how a remote and irrelevant incident can have unpredictable consequences. A cabinet minister kissed an army officer, and I became justice minister.

A ceremony was held at the Ministry of Justice to mark the change in ministers. Tzipi Livni welcomed me, happy to be relieved of her extra portfolio. She expressed full confidence in the law enforcement system. "There are no frame-ups here," she declared, standing behind Mazuz and against Ramon. It was clear to me that Kadima's intraparty conflicts would make my job difficult.

My appraisal of the Ramon trial was hardly unique. In fact, hardly anyone had anything good to say about the court's decision. The following morning, *Ha'aretz* ran an editorial declaring that "criminal justice should have kept itself away from this case, and bringing it to court is an indication of the overly-energetic and pressured activity of the investigative and prosecutorial authorities ... It is another aspect of how Israeli society has become adversarial to a sickening point and of the deferment of decisions on matters of morals and behavior to judges, as if their opinions on such questions regarding what elicits disgust and revulsion carries more weight than that of any other person."

The next day an article appeared in *Ma'ariv* under the headline "A Judgment with a Black Flag." The term "black flag" is a significant one in Israeli jurisprudence, taken from a seminal case in which soldiers were convicted of the murder of Arab civilians even though they claimed to have acted in accordance with their superior officers' orders. In that case, the court ruled that an order that, as the court put it, has a black flag flying over it cannot be cited as a defense against a criminal charge. Ben-Dror Yemini, a senior commentator for the newspaper, wrote: "The moment our courts are transformed into tribunals serving moral vigilantes, we are taking giant steps toward [becoming] Saudi Arabia and Iran. Not Denmark or Sweden."

George Fletcher, a noted American jurist with expertise in criminal law, also roundly criticized Ramon's indictment and trial. He highlighted the errors in the judgment and said that Israel made excessive use of criminal proceedings. "The impression, in Ramon's case is that criminal procedure was used to achieve a political outcome," he claimed. "If judges here really understood criminal law, they would expunge the conviction in its entirety."[395]

Former cabinet minister Amnon Rubinstein, a well-known legal scholar, seconded Fletcher's critique. "The wholesale use of criminal law cheapens it," he argued, "and the appointment of police prosecutors to judicial seats, without any cooling-off period, diminishes the status of the courts."[396]

Another criminal law expert, Mordechai Kremnitzer, was no less categorical. "The Haim Ramon case was problematic in terms of how it was handled by the prosecution and the court," he wrote. "I assumed that they had something in their files to prove criminal intent. I did not see that something in the trial, and yet that was enough for a conviction. I don't really understand how. I therefore think that both systems, the judges and the general prosecution, suffer from a problem of professionalism."[397]

In fact, there was hardly a serious jurist willing to defend the indictment and judgment. One notable exception was Itzhak Zamir, who came to the defense of Attorney General Mazuz.[398] Zamir told *Ha'aretz* correspondent Gidi Weitz: "I definitely don't think [Mazuz] made a mistake . . . He had no choice but to file charges against Haim Ramon . . . Haim Ramon made lots of mistakes. He did not take a lot of opportunities to bring the affair to an end. Had he said 'Forgive me, I made a mistake, I thought you wanted, it turns out you didn't, I hurt you, I'm sorry,' he would have put an end to the matter."[399]

This extraordinary claim that Mazuz really had no choice but to indict, displays an unimpressive use of a technique of shoring up a weak claim by wording it in an extreme form. Mazuz also adopted the unconvincing claim that the whole matter could have been resolved with an apology and that this would have cleared the affair of any criminal aspect.[400] Apparently he had no better justification for filing charges. But since when does an apology by a criminal make an indictment superfluous? In any case, Mazuz's weak argument is inconsistent with the facts. In his police testimony, Ramon said that "if I had had even the shadow of a thought that I did something improper, I would ask her apology, I would tell her I'm sorry." He said much the same thing in court. Furthermore, if an apology saves a person from indictment, wasn't it Mazuz's job to explain that to Ramon and suggest that he offer one?

The defense of Mazuz by Zamir, a former attorney general and a retired Supreme Court justice, demonstrates the exaggerated prosecutorial inclination that had developed in the Attorney General's Office and which also infected the Supreme Court. Zamir's defense of the mistaken indictment was part of a campaign that accompanied the legal revolution, one that offered unreserved support for the Supreme Court, judicial activism, and criminal proceedings against public figures, all while criticizing anyone who disagreed.

The court sentenced Ramon two months after convicting him and after I had replaced him as minister of justice. In many respects, the judges' decision on his sentence was the polar opposite of their earlier decision. In convicting Ramon they used blunt, harsh, and hostile language. But in sentencing him they not only displayed empathy but actually minimized the nature and seriousness of the "crime." It was, they wrote, "on the lowest level of violations of this type." The kiss, they noted, had been a single, isolated, and unpremeditated act that followed an inane conversation. It lasted for no more than two or three seconds and ended right there. Yet the judges did not revoke his conviction (which courts are authorized to do—they may impose community service without a conviction). "The defendant's punishment must be tiny," they wrote, and imposed on him 120 hours of service and a compensation payment of NIS 15,000 (about $3,750) to the officer. They rejected the prosecution demand to define Ramon's act as one involving moral turpitude, citing Section 42a(a) of Basic Law: The Knesset, according to which a member of the Knesset convicted in a final ruling of an offense that the court determines to be one of moral turpitude automatically loses his membership in parliament. In other words, Ramon would continue to serve in the Knesset and the door was also open to his return to the cabinet.

I can only speculate on what happened between conviction and sentencing. It may well be that, following the public uproar over its decision and my appointment to the portfolio Ramon previously held, the court sought to moderate the result. Also, it may have sufficed that Ramon, who was regarded as a figure inimical to the legal revolution, was ousted from the influential post of justice minister. There was thus no need to go further. Whatever the case, the judges had already done grave damage to public confidence in the courts. Ramon's trial had dramatic results. His was hardly the first case in which cabinet ministers had been indicted under questionable circumstances, but in those past cases the courts had done their work properly. Yaakov Neeman was acquitted, and in Rafael Eitan's case the prosecution had been thrown out of court red-faced. What was different this time was that the court failed to do its job and showed itself to be no less prosecutorial than the prosecution. For other public figures it was a sign that no one would defend them against predatory prosecutors. There is something symbolic, perhaps not just symbolic, in the fact that the system's fervor to convict Ramon was manifested a few months after the accession of Dorit Beinisch to the post of chief justice, and just a short time after her problematic statement at the convention of attorneys in Eilat.

The decision in the Ramon case put huge power in the hands of the attorney general. The prosecution had always been enormously powerful, but it now transpired that every indictment, no matter how unsubstantiated, was almost tantamount to conviction. In the past there had been a chance of acquittal. Now that approached zero. Fear of the attorney general reached a level that is difficult to describe. I could see the surrealistic effect of this during my service in a cabinet in which many of my colleagues were terrified of voicing any disagreement with him.

Ramon did not appeal his conviction. He would have seemed to have excellent chances of getting it overturned by a higher court, but it is impossible to know in advance what the outcome of any court proceeding will be. Furthermore, there was no way of estimating what effect Beinisch's statement would have on the appeals bench. His conviction did Ramon considerable damage, but that damage was mitigated by the determination that his act did not involve moral turpitude. Had he appealed, the prosecution would certainly have done the same, demanding a determination of turpitude. While the chances that the prosecution request would be accepted were probably small, Ramon had already seen just how mistaken a court ruling could be. Even the small chance that the appeal would leave him worse off than he already was turned out to be enough to deter him.

But the prosecution could have appealed anyway. Why did the attorney general not decide to appeal Ramon's light sentence and the determination that his offense did not involve moral turpitude? Clearly, Mazuz had no motivation to assume any risk. From his point of view, Ramon's conviction, as doubtful and problematic as it might have been, was enough to lend credence to the indictment he had insisted on—for a one-time act of two or three seconds, the lowest level of violation that bore no moral turpitude.

After completing his 120 hours of community service, Ramon was eligible to return to the government. I publicly supported his doing so. His conduct in the kissing affair was improper and was certainly nothing to be proud of, but his unjustified conviction was, in my opinion, a much more severe punishment than he deserved and one that more than atoned for his indiscretion. It was also an opportunity to counter the self-righteousness and purism that had spread through the Israeli public, encouraged by the Supreme Court's rhetoric. The prime minister agreed. Olmert appointed him to the post of vice prime minister for special assignments, especially in the diplomatic arena.

The inevitable Supreme Court petition was heard by Justices Ayala Procaccia, Asher Grunis, and Edna Arbel. The case should have been summed up in a few sentences stating that the Knesset had ratified the appointment, and, in the absence of any legal grounds for disqualifying it, the petition should be dismissed. Instead, the panel produced a lengthy document of more than sixty pages, and decided the case by majority vote.[401] The most reasonable of the opinions—and the briefest— was produced by Justice Grunis. He opened by declaring that "in a case like this, in which the Knesset confirms the addition of a minister to the cabinet, on the basis of a proposal by the prime minister and a cabinet decision, it is doubtful whether there are any grounds for the Supreme Court's intervention." With regard to the claim that Ramon's appointment was unreasonable, he wrote: "[T]he court is no better placed than any citizen of the state to determine whether the decision is unreasonable."[402] Grunis's opinion stands out in that it does not address moral issues of the type that his two colleagues' opinions are replete with. Justice Procaccia's decision, some thirty pages long, relentlessly repeats overused phrases regarding appointments, includ- ing the need to ensure the public's confidence and to weigh the "ethical quality and moral virtues of the candidate."[403] The court, she argues, may apply the test of rea- sonableness to a cabinet minister. However, the final conclusion she reached was the correct one: "There is no basis for exercising judicial review of the Knesset's decision to approve the Government's notice concerning the appointment of MK Ramon as a cabinet minister."[404]

Most astonishing is Edna Arbel's minority opinion. Unsurprisingly, it is replete with statements like: "The government's ability to rule also depends ultimately on public confidence in it." In her view, "The decision to appoint MK Ramon at this time gives rise to a difficulty in the ethical sphere because it inherently undermines the values of the rule of law."[405] As such, she determines, Ramon's appointment should be invalidated. The fact that the government decided on and the Knesset ratified his appointment by a large majority was no obstacle. She had no sense of the arrogance she displayed in arguing that the court should nullify a decision made by the execu- tive and the legislature.

If the issue is public confidence, in my estimation public confidence in the Supreme Court was diminished far more by the notorious session of the Judicial Selection Committee that appointed Arbel than whatever level of damage, if any, was done by Haim Ramon's return to the cabinet.

There is also a moral issue at stake here. Ramon was convicted. In the legal world, a conviction is final and binding, and under Israeli law, if the conviction is explicitly labeled as not bearing turpitude, then there is no obstacle to the convicted person's service as a government minister. Of course, morality is not bound to or limited by the court's findings. People, including the prime minister, his cabinet, and the mem- bers of the Knesset, may disagree with the conclusion reached by the judges and are permitted to think that Ramon's conviction was baseless. If that is what they thought in this case, and as long as the judges who ruled in Ramon's case deliberately left the door to future government service open, the government and Knesset were fully within their rights and prerogatives in rehabilitating Ramon politically by bringing him back into the cabinet.

But instead of respecting the independence and judgment of the country's elected officials, the Supreme Court majority evinced gross contempt for the Knesset and its legislation. Both Arbel and Procaccia declared, in keeping with previous rulings, that the Supreme Court has the power, in principle, to overrule a cabinet appointment on the grounds of unreasonableness. This runs directly counter to the basic laws stating that a Knesset member or cabinet minister's tenure ends automatically when they are convicted by a court of a crime of moral turpitude. The only reasonable interpretation of the basic law is that if the offense of which the politician was convicted was not one of moral turpitude, then he may be appointed to the cabinet. It is unreasonable to claim that a decision to do so can be subverted by the court's determination that the appointment is unreasonable.

There is an epilogue to the story, involving the presiding judge in the panel that convicted Ramon, Hayuta Kochan. Kochan's name was included in the list of candidates for promotion to the District Court, a list prepared before I was appointed minister of justice. I assume that her name was put forward by the former chief justice, who by the law governing the Judicial Selection Committee is empowered, as is the justice minister or any three members of the committee acting together, to nominate candidates. But after my appointment, Chief Justice Beinisch took her off the list. According to a news report, Beinisch telephoned Kochan to inform her of her removal. The reason she allegedly gave was that I, the minister of justice, was seeking to get back at her for her conviction of Ramon.[406] Another news outlet offered a more tempered version of what Beinisch allegedly told Kochan—that, given my criticism of the Ramon ruling, she thought that I would not want to see her on the list of candidates.

My office issued a clarification stating that I had not been involved in any way in Kochan's removal from the list. Following that, the Supreme Court's press secretary, speaking for Beinisch, issued a statement asserting that Kochan had been struck from the list "because of the needs of the Magistrates Court." That statement infuriated the president of the Tel Aviv Magistrates Court, Edna Bekenstein, who wrote Beinisch a sharply worded letter saying that no one had consulted with her and that using the needs of her court as a reason for removing Kochan from the list was an attempt to throw dust in the eyes of the public.

Beinish came in for harsh criticism over the entire affair, some of it in unprintable language. Some of her detractors were certainly not biased against the chief justice. Ze'ev Segal, a law professor and columnist on legal affairs for *Ha'aretz*, wrote that "Beinisch owes us an explanation . . . The current state of affairs, in which the president [of the Tel Aviv Magistrates Court] claims that the chief justice is not telling the truth, cannot be passed over in silence. The chief justice must offer the public an explanation of a statement that ostensibly deals a heavy blow to her credibility." In 2009, Minister of Justice Neeman appointed Kochan to a temporary position on the District Court. A year later she retired.

The Ramon affair demonstrated a threefold failure in the justice system—the indictment, the verdict, and the wiretap and its consequences. In its ruling, the court addressed the issue of the wiretaps that were not handed over to Ramon's lawyers in a timely fashion, and Major General Yohanan Danino, head of the Police Investigations Unit, testified at the trial that the "mishap" would be looked into. The court noted that "given Major General Danino's promise that the matter would be examined in-depth, we refrain from making a determination that the products of the wiretaps were not conveyed to the defense maliciously . . . We determine that, at the least, this is a matter of real negligence on the part of the prosecution."

While awaiting the court's judgment, the prime minister and attorney general had a harsh exchange. Olmert wanted to appoint a government commission to study the scandal. But Mazuz forbade him to do so, telling Olmert that he would see to it that the affair was looked into. The prime minister, he claimed, was not permitted to address the subject because of conflict of interest—he was himself under investigation, in the Cremieux Street house and Bank Leumi affairs, which later ended without indictments.

But one could just as persuasively have argued that the person who had a conflict of interest was the one who had decided to launch those investigations—that is, Mazuz himself (and State Attorney Shandar). Recall that prior to the elections, in March 2006, Mazuz had concluded that there was no cause for a criminal investigation of Olmert in the Cremieux Street case. Nevertheless, the state comptroller assigned a member of his staff, retired senior police officer Yaakov Borovsky, to look into the affair, and the results of that inquiry were submitted to Mazuz. On September 24 the media reported that the attorney general had decided to order a police investigation. This was just a few days following the beginning of Haim Ramon's trial. The wiretap issue had not yet blown up, but it was already clear that Mazuz had gotten himself into a hard place in the Ramon affair. The case against Ramon was extremely weak, and Mazuz must have realized that there was a very real chance of acquittal. If Ramon were found not guilty, Mazuz, who was already the subject of withering public and press criticism for having indicted Ramon, would find himself in a precarious position. He said as much in an interview with Ari Shavit:

> This case produced the harshest attack on the system level of the police, the prosecution, and the court. It was frightening . . . The most frightening moment came on the eve of the trial. I remember that we were sitting in this room and we tried to think of what would happen if Ramon were acquitted . . . It was clear to us that if he was acquitted, the consequence was liable to be devastating for the [legal] system. It would be a tsunami.

Seeing the tsunami on the horizon, Mazuz decided that the police should investigate Olmert's purchase of a house on Cremieux Street. Clearly, turning the prime minister into a crime suspect would severely weaken his position. Furthermore, any power he had to act against the attorney general would entirely evaporate. Did Mazuz have a conflict of interest in ordering the investigation?

The Bank Leumi case reached Mazuz's desk at about the same time. Here Mazuz recused himself and handed the case over to State Attorney Eran Shandar. In the meantime, the secret wiretapping in the Ramon case had come to light, and both Mazuz and Shandar found themselves in even more difficult straits. At the end of October 2006 Shandar ordered a preliminary examination of the Bank Leumi case, and on January 16, 2007, some two weeks prior to the verdict in Ramon's trial, he decided on a full-scale investigation of Olmert's role in the Bank Leumi affair. The issue of conflict of interest arose also with regard to Shandar. He had handled the Ramon case and had signed off on the wiretaps (which Mazuz also approved). It may well be that neither of them was involved in the decision to split the Ramon case into two. They presumably also played no role in the prosecution's initial denials that there had been wiretaps. Nevertheless, in my estimation it was clear that both of them had a clear interest in assuring that neither the government nor the prime minister seek to examine what was going on in the Ramon case or to take any measures with regard to it. Shandar's decision to investigate the Bank Leumi affair, coming on top of Mazuz's decision to investigate the Cremieux Street affair, crippled the prime minister. It rendered him powerless to remedy the failures in the legal and justice system that the Ramon case had brought to light. It kept the government from exercising oversight of the attorney general, the state attorney, and the prosecution. Mazuz's vociferous objections also prevented the government from appointing an investigative commission to look into the system and recommend changes. I do not mean to say that the decisions to investigate the prime minister were made in order to prevent any inquiry into what happened in the Ramon case. But that is the nature of conflicts of interest. It is not necessary to show that the conflict actually affected the actions of the people involved. The very fact that the conflict of interest exists requires them to excuse themselves from handling the matter.

At the end of November 2007 the police recommended closing the Bank Leumi case. But this did not prevent the new state attorney, Moshe Lador, from keeping it open for another year. He ended it only in December 2008, after Olmert announced his resignation. In March 2009, the police recommended closing the Cremieux Street investigation as well, but the prosecution actually did so only four months later, following the fall of Olmert's government and the establishment of Netanyahu's second administration.

In practice, then, Mazuz remained in control of the Ramon investigation. In consultation with the police chief, he appointed a retired judge, Shalom Brenner, to examine the wiretap issue and the reason why "some of the material was not conveyed in a timely fashion" to Ramon's lawyers. In other words, the attorney general appointed a one-man investigative commission of his own, an act without any legal basis. The legal imagination can always find some way to justify actions of this sort, such that this is an inherent power of the attorney general, and that any officeholder can establish an apparatus for looking into failures that took place in his area of responsibility. But if that is the case, the authority of the examiner will be limited in scope. He will have no statutory authority, be unable to subpoena witnesses, and will not be able to take testimony under oath.

In this specific case there was something discordant about an investigation devoid of legal authority set in motion by the people in whose offices the failure occurred, a failure that had repercussions much beyond their own bailiwicks, impeding the work of the justice minister and the operation of the government. The proper way to address the situation was for the attorney general to ask for the establishment of a government commission of inquiry, but that is exactly what Mazuz did not want. He preferred an inquiry confined in boundaries he set himself, conducted by a person of his choosing. In short, he wanted to use the so-called principle of "rule of law" to circumvent the law governing the establishment of official inquiries of the type that were appropriate for this situation.

After my appointment as justice minister, Ramon's lawyer, Navot Tel-Zur, asked me to appoint a government commission of inquiry to look into the affair. I wrote to Judge Brenner, who was already deep into his investigation, to ask whether he would be willing to take upon himself the powers of a government commission. I sent Mazuz a copy of the letter. Turning the investigation into one conducted by a government commission would have required appointing additional members to a commission that Brenner would head. Brenner notified me that he was already close to completing his inquiry, and thus had no interest in being involved in a government commission.

In his report, Judge Brenner made several important points. State Attorney Shandar had, he found, sanctioned the police's application to receive court approval for wiretaps on the grounds of suspicions of obstruction of justice. The charge of committing an indecent act, Brenner affirmed, could not serve as a justification for wiretaps. Nevertheless, the head of the police investigation, Chief Superintendant Eran Kamin, had also asked court sanction for a wiretap with regard to the indecent assault charge. "I found no explanation, not any acceptable one or any at all, as to why Kamin . . . made up rules for himself and added . . . the indecent act charge [to the request]," Brenner wrote.

With regard to the police, Brenner found that "beyond any doubt, both Chief Superintendant Golan and Chief Superintendant Kamin knew and/or should have known that once wiretap orders were given with regard to indecent act as well, all the products of these wiretaps became . . . investigation material . . . in Ramon's case as well, and that . . . this material had to be made available to the defense attorneys immediately upon his indictment." Furthermore, "neither Golan nor Kamin gave any satisfactory explanation as to the failure to transcribe the passages by the complainant that clearly indicated that she did not wish to submit a complaint."

Regarding the two prosecutors who handled the wiretap issue—District Attorney Ruth David and her associate Ariela Segal-Antler—Brenner stated that they were "presumed to have known" that in this case wiretaps were also carried out *on the complainant*, and yet neither of them asked herself what had been recorded in these conversations . . . The presumption is that both of them knew and, at the very least should have assumed that . . . something spoken by the complainant must certainly have been recorded. I would have expected them to display more interest in the possibility that the material recorded was relevant to the investigation."

His final conclusion: "*Nevertheless . . . I was persuaded that malicious intent, as Ramon claims, on the part of those who handled his case, did not exist here. Major negligence there certainly was*" (emphasis in the original). The word "nevertheless" is indeed apt. The sum total of circumstances cast a pall over the entire affair. These began with the failure to transcribe the complainant's conversations, which were extremely detrimental to the police and the prosecution's case, continued with the bifurcation of the case, and reached its climax with the denial that any wiretaps had been performed. Still, despite his censure of the way the case was handled, Judge Brenner limited himself to systemic recommendations. Among these was that "in no instance should any police investigation be bifurcated." He did not say whether any measures should be taken against the prosecutors and others responsible for the case.

Brenner submitted his report to Mazuz. It then transpired that lengthy discussions had already been held in Mazuz's office about the lessons to be drawn from the Ramon case. In the end, the participants reached a consensus that all that was needed were some systemic fixes, such as revising working procedures. No one should be held personally responsible. I was astonished at the time by the lenience displayed toward the officials involved in the case. I later learned that this was the way things were done in the prosecution. The prosecutors controlled the system, and like all rulers, they believed that those who ran the control apparatus deserved immunity. It seems unlikely that a similar failure in some other government office would have been given such a pass, but prosecutors and police investigators get special treatment—even when the defects that came to light in the Ramon case were much more serious transgressions than those with which Ramon himself was charged.

I was not willing to accept this approach, but I had no interest in getting bogged down in the issue and wanted to bring it to an end. I suggested to Shandar that a letter be inserted into the personal files of the responsible prosecutors noting that they had not done their job properly. In retrospect, I think that this compromise went too easy on the prosecutors and the police given the serious nature of their conduct. I was wrong to propose it. But to my astonishment, even this indulgent offer was rejected. Perhaps I should not have been surprised, given the sense of superiority and dominion that prevailed in the prosecution. (After I left office, I was told that Mazuz had wanted to accept my proposal, but that when the prosecution refused he had not tried to impose his opinion on them.)

I thus had no choice but to address the outrage. Here, however, I ran into a problem. Theoretically, a member of the cabinet bears responsibility for any errors perpetrated by his ministry's staff. Yet ministers in fact lack the requisite power to address such failings. This is particularly true of the justice minister, whose authority to intervene in the operations of his ministry's staff is extremely limited. The opening of police investigations and the filing of indictments lies under the discretion of the ministry's chief officers, the attorney general and state attorney. But these two figures are not answerable to anyone. As such, there is a separation of responsibility and authority. The minister of justice may not order the investigation of a particular individual. Even the initiation of disciplinary proceedings requires the cooperation of the chief officers. This barrier between the justice minister and the legal system was established, of course, out of concern that the minister would take advantage of his office to incriminate political rivals. But no one seems to have considered the fact that the law-enforcement system is not necessarily objective and that it may have interests of its own.

In the Ramon case it was clear to me that any procedure that depended on the law-enforcement apparatus would not go anywhere. The central problem was how to enforce the law on the law-enforcement system. I thus decided to request an outside opinion from a retired judge, Vardi Zeiler. Since police officials were also involved in the Ramon affair, I needed the consent of Minister of Internal Security Avi Dichter. He agreed that we would together ask Zeiler to take on the task. We asked him to recommend what measures ought to be taken in the wake of Judge Brenner's report and the other questions that the affair had raised. Mazuz was angry. He thought that the Brenner report and the procedural changes it proposed should be the end of it. I, of course, was not willing to accept that.

Zeiler produced a thorough and comprehensive report. He laid out the many issues that the Ramon affair had raised and pointed out the limitations that Judge Brenner had faced, lacking as he did statutory authority and the power to call witnesses and to take testimony under oath. The matter required an inquiry by a body with appropriate powers. He recommended the establishment of a government commission of inquiry.

It goes without saying that Zeiler's report made no impact on Mazuz, who had approved of the tapping of Ramon's phones (he was involved in the affair at least on this count, not to mention his overarching responsibility for the conduct of a case against a cabinet minister). He did all he could to prevent an investigation. Dichter also inalterably opposed a commission of inquiry. When I asked him whether any disciplinary action had been taken against the police officials involved in the Ramon case, I was told that such action had been considered and rejected.

The next stage took place in the Knesset. In December 2006, just after the wire-taps had been exposed and before my appointment as justice minister, that body's House Committee had decided, over Mazuz's objections, that the Constitution, Law, and Justice Committee would serve as a parliamentary commission of inquiry into the affair. That committee held an important session on March 31, 2008, slightly less than two months after Zeiler submitted his report. The session was chaired by Michael Eitan of Likud because the committee's chairman, Menachem Ben-Sasson, was a member of Kadima and it seemed best that a member of the opposition preside. The verdict in the Ramon case had noted Major General Danino's promise that the wiretaps would be "probed deeply." The members of the committee debated whether Judge Brenner's inquiry constituted the in-depth examination that Danino had promised. Judge Zeiler appeared before the commission and told it that the Brenner report was insufficient and that a government commission of inquiry was needed. The meeting then adjourned until June 3.

In the interim, Morris Talansky arrived in Israel for the Pesach holiday and the scandal of the payments he had been making to Olmert hit the headlines. He first testified to the police on April 29. His interrogation had not ended, but the State Attorney's Office rushed to court on the eve of Israel Independence Day (less than a week following Talansky's first session with the police) with an urgent request that Talansky be deposed early, prior to Olmert's indictment. The request was highly un-reasonable. It must have been clear to Mazuz and Lador that if Talansky were to testify in court, it would cause severe damage to the prime minister and might well topple the government. The court nevertheless approved the request, and Talansky began to testify on May 27, 2008, in a case in which no charges had been filed and might never be. Political developments, hardly unexpected, made it clear that the government's days were numbered.

About a week following Talansky's pre-trial testimony, the parliamentary com-mission of inquiry held its second session. I was present. So was Lador, who spoke at length against a further inquiry. He did not persuade the committee. It passed the following decision: "The Zeiler report raises the question of whether the com-mitment made to the Magistrates Court, regarding an in-depth probe by the law-enforcement authorities, was in fact honored. We request of the minister of justice, given that there is a report that he ordered, that he respect it and act in accordance with its recommendations." All the committee members, of all parties, coalition and opposition, who took part in the vote supported this resolution. None abstained, and none voted against.

Clearly, it was incumbent on me to ask the cabinet to appoint a government com-mission of inquiry in accordance with Section 8a of the Government Law. But it was not that simple. One difficulty is that the law refers to the case of a minister appoint-ing a panel to examine an issue that falls under his responsibility. The minister in question can, with the approval of the minister of justice, ask the cabinet to grant the panel the powers of a commission of inquiry. What had occurred in the prosecution fell under my portfolio, but the police were Dichter's territory. I thus had no choice but to restrict my request to the prosecution. (Of course, the cabinet had the power to expand the commission's mandate to include the police, even over the objections of the internal security minister.)

Even so, it was difficult to get the matter onto the cabinet's agenda. Mazuz was opposed and fought tooth and nail to keep the issue off the government's table. I was astonished. His attitude showed just how low things had sunk. It seems rather obvious that a cabinet minister ought to be able to raise any issue he thinks important before the cabinet. And, unless the prime minister sees some reason to prevent it, a discussion should be held. If the attorney general opposes the minister's proposal, he can voice his objection during the cabinet debate. I find it totally illogical to permit the attorney general to forbid any issue to come before the government, and in this case I was certainly not going to accept it. (When Mazuz forbade the cabinet to discuss the appointment of Yoel Lavi to head the Israel Lands Administration, the Supreme Court put him in his place.) But it was no simple matter. The technical task of drawing up the agenda for cabinet meetings is performed by the cabinet secretary. Ovad Yehezkel, who held that post at the time, was himself under investigation on suspicion of engineering political appointments (the investigation ended without indictment some time later). And the prime minister himself was under investigation. Yehezkel was clearly in an uncomfortable situation. On the one hand, the justice minister was demanding that he put a subject on the agenda, while his fate lay in the hands of the attorney general, who opposed any discussion of the matter. It was only after weeks of argument that I was able to get my proposal for a government commission of inquiry on the cabinet's agenda.

On July 3, 2008, just three days before the discussion was to take place, Mazuz sent the ministers a letter laying out his objections to my proposal. He used the most extreme language. "I categorically oppose this proposal," he wrote,

> which in my view constitutes an abuse of power and controverts proper government procedures, subverts the separation of powers, and constitutes a shattering of all norms by the minister of justice (and those who support his initiative), in the framework of what seems to be a vendetta against the law-enforcement system . . . [It is concerned with an investigation conducted] against a senior minister, a close friend and political associate and partner of the prime minister.

Mazuz also stated in his letter that "in an exceptional decision, a parliamentary commission of inquiry into the subject of wiretaps was established, and which has been considering the matter for a year and a half." He neglected however to mention that the parliamentary commission had unanimously called for the adoption of Judge Zeiler's recommendation for a government commission of inquiry. The attorney general's concern about the separation of powers is also surprising—after all, the law-enforcement apparatus is part of the executive branch, meaning that the cabinet bears both public and parliamentary responsibility for its proper functioning. As such, the cabinet is certainly within its powers to appoint a commission of inquiry in the matter. As for the vendetta charge, I can only note that I was prepared to put the whole subject to rest with a letter placed in the personal files of those involved. The prosecution prevented that.

It was not an easy meeting. Talansky's early testimony had shaken the government. Tzipi Livni and Ehud Barak were demanding Olmert's resignation. Four days previously Dichter had called a press conference and demanded that Kadima hold a primary to choose a new party leader to replace Olmert.

Mazuz and Lador participated in the cabinet meeting, as did Police Commissioner Dudi Cohen. They roundly opposed a commission of inquiry. To this day I am mystified as to what their reasons were, except that they were seeking to protect their subordinates. It seems that people who perform investigations do not themselves like to be investigated. The meeting dragged on, and there was no clear majority in support of my proposal. The Labor ministers were largely opposed. Kadima was split—Livni and Dichter were against. Ramon had recused himself from the vote, but took part in the debate, for which he was criticized. In my view, the fact that he had been the victim of an unjustified indictment and mistaken verdict was no reason to gag him. Furthermore, the attorney general was present and could respond to any charges that Ramon made. Prime Minister Olmert, under investigation and in difficult circumstances following Talansky's early testimony, did not participate in the debate and announced that he, too, would not take part in the vote. This was just one more demonstration of how the investigations of the prime minister magnified the power of the attorney general and the law-enforcement system while weakening the executive branch.

As it was not clear how the votes would fall, I decided to accept a compromise proposed by Labor, one that fell between appointing a government commission and silencing the whole matter without any further inquiry. The compromise, which received an overwhelming majority in the cabinet, was to hand the issue over to the state comptroller. Only Dichter voted no.

I can state with near certainty that, had the prime minister not been disqualified by Mazuz from dealing with the investigation of the wiretaps, a government commission of inquiry would have been appointed. But the preliminary testimony by Talansky, which knocked the government off balance, put an end to any real possibility that that would happen.

Why was Olmert said to have a conflict of interest when he sought an investigation of what was going on on Mazuz's turf, while Mazuz was held not to have any conflict of interest as he directed the investigation of Olmert? Wasn't it clear that there needed to be an investigation of him and his subordinates in the matter of the wiretaps in the Ramon case? Were Mazuz's interests not conflicted when he chose to have the investigation conducted by Judge Brenner instead of allowing the appointment of a government commission of inquiry? Were they not similarly conflicted when he disqualified Olmert from involvement in the matter of an inquiry? The decision to rush to depose Talansky prior to the trial itself was also made in a state of conflict of interest. As I see it, Mazuz had a clear interest in preventing the appointment of a commission of inquiry (just how emotional an issue it was for him is evident in his letter to the members of the cabinet). It should have been clear to him that Talansky's early testimony was likely to destabilize and perhaps even topple the government, and thus prevent the establishment of a government inquiry.

In its letter to the comptroller, the cabinet requested the comptroller's opinion "on the matter of wiretaps in criminal investigations . . . and complaints of recent years on this matter." This was much less than Judge Zeiler and the Constitution, Law, and Justice Committee had recommended and than I had thought proper. Nevertheless, it was the first time that an Israeli government had discussed a serious case of failure involving the investigation and trial of a cabinet minister. A series of early scandals of this sort that I have mentioned in chapter 24, which had seriously impeded governance, had not been addressed by the cabinet. The law-enforcement system had stayed on course without being forced to take stock and without any measures being taken against those responsible. This time, at least, something had been done.

The police and prosecution, which were accustomed to having politicians capitulate to them without question, spoke up against what had happened. A bit more than two months following that cabinet meeting, *Haaretz* published an interview with Police Commissioner Cohen, conducted by Ari Shavit. Cohen lashed out at the government: "On a matter of this sort you propose a commission like the Winograd commission? On a matter of this sort the cabinet holds a four-hour discussion? It's hallucinatory. It's simply hallucinatory." This phenomenon, of public officials attacking the government they serve, was as good an example as any of the weakness of the central government. Cohen also targeted me, and I thought he had gone too far. I demanded that Olmert bring the issue up at a cabinet meeting. In a properly run country, a police commissioner who spoke so harshly against the government would have been dismissed. That can't be expected in Israel. But the cabinet did discuss it, and sharply criticized Cohen, making it clear to him that he had crossed a red line and did not enjoy absolute immunity. The police commissioner wrote the government a letter of apology, in which he explained that "he had not meant to criticize the government or any of its ministers."[407] From that point onward, to the best of my knowledge, no police official has publicly criticized the government, or me.

In the interview he gave Ari Shavit at the end of his tenure, Mazuz spoke of the Ramon case as one which "in the legal balance seems like the tiniest and simplest case of all the public ones I dealt with." He had a hard time understanding what seemed to him as a contradiction. "It was precisely this case that led to the harshest systematic offensive against the police, the prosecution, and the courts," he said. In his view, the attack was so fierce that it put the rule of law in jeopardy. Mazuz did not understand why such a storm broke out. He called it a "delegitimization campaign." He did not comprehend that what seemed to him to be a contradiction explained the events very well. The public-at-large suddenly realized that this tiniest of his cases—and to my mind, the most problematic—was enough to oust a cabinet minister. The intolerable ease with which it was possible to get rid of Ramon revealed just how powerless democratically elected officials were in the face of an aggressive bureaucratic apparatus.

The investigation conducted by State Comptroller Micha Lindenstrauss covered the general issue of wiretaps and several specific complaints about them. The larger part of his report addressed the Ramon case. The comptroller found that the state attorney's decision to request a wiretap permit on suspicion of witness tampering was reasonable. The failure to convey the wiretap material in a timely fashion to Ramon's defense attorney, Lindenstrauss determined, was not done "maliciously, but it clearly involves real negligence on the part of those who did the work: Police Brigadier General Miri Golan . . . , Chief Superintendant Eran Kamin, District Attorney Ruth David, and Prosecutor Segal-Antler." In his conclusion, Lindenstrauss reiterated that the flaws "point to personal failures by the four involved in the matter, which are tantamount to real negligence even though they were done without malice, and it should be considered whether to take personal measures against them. The attorney general should consider his position on the matter with attention to all the relevant factors." The comptroller also stated that the limitations period on disciplinary measures was not an obstacle to administrative measures, for example, delaying promotion.

I was not convinced that the case had been investigated fully. An investigation of a different sort was required on numerous counts: the failure to transcribe the wiretaps that were discomfiting for the police and prosecution; the bifurcation of the case, with the material relating to the wiretap placed under the obstruction of justice case that was then closed; the fact that there were people in the police force who knew that the wiretap material was relevant to Ramon's defense, as is evidenced by the fact that word of the wiretaps was leaked to Ramon.

The comptroller's report was issued a year and a half after Olmert's government came to an end. The justice minister at the time was Yaakov Neeman. Mazuz had also retired from his post, and the new attorney general, Yehuda Weinstein, recused himself from every matter having to do with Haim Ramon, because at a certain point he had offered Ramon advice relating to his trial. Lindenstrauss's report thus came before State Attorney Lador. Lador rejected the comptroller's recommendations and took no measures at all against the prosecutors and police officers involved in the affair. Not only that, but he supported the appointment of Ariela Segal-Antler to the post of Tel Aviv district attorney. She received the promotion, while the criticism of her negligence in the Ramon case remained stuck in the comptroller's report.

But that was not the end of the affair. It lacked one vital element—a petition to the Supreme Court, without which no affair is complete. The two prosecutors, David and Segal-Antler, asked the court to intervene in the comptroller's determination that their handling of the wiretap material was negligent. In the normal course of events, the state attorney should have defended the comptroller. Lador decided not to. But the State Attorney's Office is not a private business. The fact that two senior government prosecutors seek vindication from the Supreme Court does not excuse it from doing its job. True, the state attorney is free to announce that he will not defend a state body when there is no basis for such a defense and no chance it would succeed, but in this case there was a very good chance that the suit would be rejected. The comptroller obtained the services of a private attorney, the prosecutors' suit was denied, yet the court refrained from imposing court costs on the petitioners.[408] The state, for its part, had to pay a large sum to cover the fees of the private lawyers hired by Lindenstrauss, money that could have been saved if the State Attorney's Office had taken on the case.

There is an epilogue to the story of the two prosecutors. Ruth David left her post as Tel Aviv district attorney in 2010 and joined the firm of a well-known lawyer, Ronel Fisher. In the meantime, Lador managed to have Segal-Antler appointed district attorney for Tel Aviv despite the sharp condemnation of her handling of the Ramon affair by everyone who had examined the case.

Fisher was later arrested on suspicion of offering suspects secret information from their police files, which was then used to obstruct their investigations. He was also suspected of managing to close cases in exchange for bribes which he conveyed from his clients to a police officer. In May 2015 he, the police officer, and several other people were indicted. One of the others was Ruth David. She stands charged of obstruction of justice and receiving property obtained by felony. In the wake of the indictment, the question arose of whether to re-examine the cases she handled as a district attorney in which the defendants were represented by Fisher.

31

The Decline in the Supreme Court's Standing

The classic Supreme Court enjoyed enormous prestige, the product of years of carefully considered and balanced rulings. It served as a civil rights watchdog, respected the government and the Knesset, acted with restraint, and recognized the limits of its powers.

This began to change in significant ways under Chief Justice Meir Shamgar's leadership. The Shamgar court claimed much greater powers and inserted itself into issues that were outside its purview. Even so, the court retained its standing as the highest and unquestioned arbiter of the law of the land. Shamgar himself scrupulously nurtured his esteem and nonpartisanship. The politicians admired him and helped him with legislation that broadened the authority of the chief justice.

While the Supreme Court under Aharon Barak retained its cachet at first, respect for it gradually began to crack, and the almost complete immunity from criticism that the court enjoyed began to evaporate. One fault line became apparent when, in 1995, Dror Hoter-Yishai was elected to a second term as president of the Israel Bar Association. Hoter-Yishai was a fierce critic of the Barak court's judicial activism. His re-election, at a time when his views on the court had received considerable publicity, was a sign that the court was no longer immune to criticism nor above public controversy.

One early and acerbic critic was Amnon Dankner, a prominent journalist, who wrote a scathing article for *Ha'aretz* at the beginning of January 1996 entitled "The Law Church." The legal system, he wrote, was "taking on a religious character in the sense that it claims to be a sole and final arbiter of the truth, which it hands down in its rulings." He also critiqued Barak's method of legal heuristics, arguing that his interpretations were tantamount to legislation, often in clear contravention of the intention of the Knesset.

More fierce criticism of the Barak court appeared in an exceptional interview that former Chief Justice Moshe Landau granted, eighteen years after his retirement, to *Ha'aretz* correspondent Ari Shavit.[409] Landau's basic position was that "even after retirement, judges should refrain from speaking publicly about matters of public controversy. So I have done and so I have advised my fellow-judges to do." But at this point, after a long silence (except for articles in legal publications), he decided to set aside this rule because "things have gone too far." On the personal level, Landau liked and admired Barak ("he is a prodigy . . . a man who can digest huge quantities of academic and legal material . . . Barak has wonderful personal qualities. He . . . is a most likeable man who is prepared to help others"). Landau also praised Barak's political acumen. Barak, he said, had "a keen aptitude for navigating the Israeli governmental system. He makes a personal imprint on the entire legal community."

Despite all this, Landau maintained that the judicial policy Barak pursued was a great danger to the country. Landau also spoke of Barak imposing his own preferred moral values on society, "and that is tantamount to judicial dictatorship." When asked whether Barak had a tendency to amass too much power, Landau replied: "Yes. Governing power. And, as I see it, that is not right. It leads to a dead end. Because the court is getting into water that is too deep for it. Into a morass of political opinions and beliefs. It is dangerous both for the country and for the court."

The Supreme Court, Landau maintained, had lost its sense of humility. "It displays arrogance and hubris. Plato, in his *Republic*, suggested entrusting the government of the republic to a class of sages who were specially trained and educated for this purpose. Sometimes it seems to me that most of the justices on the Supreme Court see themselves more or less as governing sages." Landau also spoke of the consequences of this policy for the work of the courts and service to Israel's citizens. "Another problem of the activist approach," he said, "is that many lawyers and citizens have been getting the feeling that the court is preoccupied with high matters and is not available for day-to-day ones, the interests of the common citizen. The sense is that the justices prefer to write dissertations and establish values and deal with general philosophy, and that they are less interested in the drab work of regular judging and conflict resolution."

Landau's warning did not resonate as one might have expected. Yet the barriers that had protected the court began to break down, and the immunity from criticism it had hitherto enjoyed was shaken. This was evident in particular in the problematic process of appointing new justices. The Knesset also turned critical, often fiercely so. "Neither the Mizrahi community nor the Arab community has access to the court," claimed Knesset member David Azoulay of Shas. He demanded a change in the way justices were appointed, in which sitting justices "brought their friends onto the court." He wanted "appropriate representativeness . . . until then, I will continue to ask where justice is?" In June 2000, four members of the Knesset from Yisrael Beitenu introduced a draft of a Basic Law: Constitutional Court, which proposed to strip the Supreme Court of powers and dramatically weaken it. The bill went nowhere, but it was a sign of the public mood.

Public opinion polls also showed the decline in the court's prestige. In 1996, at the beginning of the Barak era, a survey showed that 85 percent of the public had confidence in the Supreme Court.[410] That level of trust seems to have continued for several years more. Another survey, in 2000, at the midpoint of Barak's tenure as chief justice, showed that 80 percent of the Jewish public said they had great confidence in the Supreme Court. But trust in the court eroded over time. In 2002, it was 70 percent, and in 2003, it was 65 percent. In February 2007, half a year following Barak's retirement, only 56 percent declared the same level of confidence. There have since been only small fluctuations. In 2011, just before Dorit Beinisch's retirement, it sank to 54 percent, while in 2012 and 2013, after Grunis became chief justice, the level of confidence rose a bit, to 57 and 56, respectively (the level of confidence of the Israeli Arab population in the Supreme Court in 2012 and 2013 was 49 percent).[411]

The irony is that the court's overbearing intervention in government activity and public administration, including in the matter of public appointments, was almost always justified by the court by the need to preserve "public confidence" in government. This buzz phrase became a mantra in Supreme Court decisions. But while it seems doubtful that the court's aggressive and invasive activity has increased public confidence in the other branches of government, it certainly badly eroded public trust in the court itself. Tellingly, public confidence in the lower courts also declined drastically. In 2000, a full 61 percent of the Jewish public said they had great confidence in the court system, but this dropped by 2007 to only 36 percent. The entire legal system was in crisis.[412]

The decline was caused by a number of factors. The first was the court's arrogance, as summed up in the "all is justiciable" principle that Barak imposed on the legal system. This idea is rejected by most Israeli jurists and was not accepted by any of the chief justices who preceded Barak—even Shamgar.

A second factor is the court's intervention in public appointments and the gap between its actions and its rhetoric in this regard. Its rulings exude sanctimoniousness and purism. But when the court itself is involved in appointments to the judiciary, its conduct is no better than that of the politicians, sometimes even worse.

Menachem Mautner of the Tel Aviv University law school has noted that

> for many years . . . the justices of the Supreme Court have claimed that Israel's appointment procedure [to the judiciary], being "professional" rather than "political," is "the best in the world." But looking at the record of the court's involvement in the appointment process in the past three decades, particularly when it has had to do with appointments to the ranks of court itself, one cannot but arrive at the sad conclusion that it has been this involvement, more than anything else, that has contributed to the exposure of the political normative system underlying the court's conduct and to the deterioration in the court's status and legitimacy.[413]

The press has often raised questions about nepotism in the courts. The children of Supreme Court justices were represented disproportionately among clerks for members of the high court and lower courts, as well as elsewhere in the public law system.[414] In her book on the Supreme Court,[415] Nomi Levitsky offers a detailed account of the process by which new Supreme Court justices were appointed during the time of the legal revolution, and the picture is not pretty. I have already related how the Judicial Selection Committee chose Attorney General Elyakim Rubinstein and State Attorney Edna Arbel for slots on the court, arousing furious criticism from observers of the court such as Amnon Dankner. Another journalist, Hadas Magen of *Globes*,[416] reported the reaction of Michael Eitan, then chairman of the Knesset's Constitution, Law, and Justice Committee. The judicial branch, Eitan claimed, had become so powerful that it did not realize that it was sailing on the *Titanic*, "dancing on the deck, while public trust in the integrity and level of judges cracks [below]." These appointments led the Knesset to legislate a cooling-off period to prevent sitting attorneys general and state attorneys from being appointed to the high court.

Along the same lines, the kid-glove treatment that a judge accused of fabricating trial records received from her judicial colleagues opened the court up to harsh criticism. Justices Mishael Cheshin and Eliezer Rivlin, forming the majority in a disciplinary panel that heard her case, sentenced her to a reprimand and transfer to a different circuit. District Court Judge Musia Arad, in the minority, held that the judge should be removed from the bench. Meirav Arlosoroff, a correspondent for *The Marker*,[417] wrote that "the mishap of the disciplinary ruling ... represents the normative dullness into which the Israeli legal system has sunk in recent years, and along with that the system has lost its standing as the country's conscience." In the end, the Judicial Selection Committee decided to overrule the panel and dismiss the judge.

The third cause of decline in the Supreme Court's standing during the Barak era is related to its overinvolvement in security issues, often even while military operations are in progress. Here the difference between the approaches of Shamgar and Barak really stands out. Shamgar displayed the necessary deference on security matters, according great respect to the judgment of the security forces. Barak maintained that security issues needed to be closely supervised by the court. The difference was evident as early as the pardons granted to Shin Bet officials in the Bus 300 affair, discussed in Chapter 10. Behind the legal question lay the concern that the scandal would destroy an organization vital to Israel's security. The Israeli government and the president believed that a pardon was a clear and present need. For Barak, the damage to the Shin Bet was not a consideration. As far as he was concerned, the court had to pursue the goal of justice without regard to the consequences, even if it meant ruling against precedent.

Other prominent examples were the temporary injunction against the deportation of Hamas terrorists to Lebanon[418] and the order to free a group of Hezbollah terrorists and allow them to return to Lebanon after they completed their prison terms.[419]

The fourth factor is the feeling that the legal system has taken control of all other branches of government. In doing so, it has caused paralysis and red tape that weighs heavily on the administration of the country. Judicial activism is often justified on the grounds that the courts must protect human rights from being trampled by the government. But the radical court's activist rulings have often addressed matters of administration that have nothing to do with either human rights or violation of the law. The question of whether a national commission of inquiry should be appointed to study the Second Lebanon War is not a human rights issue, but rather a matter of proper administration, and so is the ruling that the attorney general's opinion is binding on the government. The wide-ranging rulings touching on public service appointments fall into the same category. The question of whether a person who has some blemish on his record or who has made an insulting or controversial public statement is fit for a public position is a matter of administration, not of rights.

The fifth factor that has brought the Supreme Court low is its inability to fulfill the promise inherent in the doctrine that "all is justiciable," which creates the illusion that the law is a panacea to every ailment. The court's insinuation of itself into nearly every public issue has created a demand for judicial review of matters that the court had never before dreamed of taking up and is unable to resolve. Thus, the court has refrained from intervening when the government has cut welfare payments to the poor.[420] This led to criticism by advocates of social justice. As they see it, if the court has ruled that Basic Law: Human Dignity and Liberty protects a host of rights that are not explicitly mentioned in the text of the law—such as freedom of expression and equality—why does it not recognize the right to a minimum income or to proper housing?

The decline in the court's standing can also be attributed to the feeling that the courts are no longer functioning as they are supposed to. During the legal revolution, there has been a noted decline in the Supreme Court's performance of its major function, which is to hear and decide everyday disputes. The court prefers to address high principle, philosophy, and general issues of public administration, at the expense of the quotidian needs of Israel's citizens and commercial bodies. Former Chief Justice Landau said exactly this in the interview in which he spoke out against the Barak court.

32

Changes and Reform Proposals

Many members of the Knesset truly believed that, when that body passed Basic Law: Human Dignity and Liberty and Basic Law: Freedom of Occupation, it had no intention of granting the Supreme Court the power to declare laws unconstitutional. When the court did so, they termed it a power-grab by the court. In this view, if there is indeed a place for judicial review of legislation in the Israeli system of government, it would best be accomplished by a special constitutional court, distinct from the Supreme Court.

Chief Justice Aharon Barak's reaction to the idea was curt: "That cockroach should be killed while it is still a small one." But the "cockroach" is very much alive and still under discussion. So is the feeling that the Supreme Court has been acting illegitimately, both in its manner of interpreting Knesset legislation, which it views as merely a "first draft";[421] in its rulings that have expanded its own powers; and its brute intervention in decisions made by the cabinet and Knesset, on the grounds of "unreasonableness."

I believe that the system needs to be put back in balance. This is not only a pressing interest of the Knesset and of the government but also imperative for the Supreme Court itself. The court has a vital interest in dissipating the feeling that it has been acting illegitimately, and that it has committed, as U.S. Judge Richard Posner put it, legal piracy. In 2002 the government appointed a commission headed by Yaakov Neeman to consider the issue. The commission for all intents and purposes adopted Barak's approach and recommended legislation that would explicitly grant the Supreme Court (but not lower courts) the authority to annul laws. The only ostensible concession to the Knesset was a suggestion, inspired by Canadian practice, that the Knesset have the power to override the voiding of a law by passing it again by a special majority. According to the proposal, this would require a special majority of 70 in the 120-member Knesset, and the new law would remain in force for only five years. It is not easy to understand how the commission reached such far-reaching conclusions, which endorsed the Supreme Court's position as supreme over the other branches of government. Under Israel's fractured and divided political system, it is nearly impossible to get seventy members of the Knesset to agree on anything, such that the override provision was largely meaningless. Neither did the commission take under advisement that officially ratifying the Supreme Court's role as a Constitutional Court would require a change in the way justices are selected. A Constitutional Court's judges require a selection system in which sitting judges have less power over court appointments than they do today. It is hardly surprising, then, that the commission's proposal never went anywhere.

As I saw it, the most important task was to put the constitutional issue in order. The court's powers, I maintained, had to be explicitly laid out in legislation. Under no circumstances should the government permit the continuation of the uniquely Israeli innovation of a Supreme Court that for all intents and purposes writes the country's constitution and decides what the relationship between the different branches of government should be. Legislation is needed to clearly and explicitly address three central issues: if, how, and under what circumstances the Supreme Court has the power to void legislation passed by the Knesset; the crafting of a method of selecting justices for the high bench that is appropriate to the powers granted to the court by law; and clear rules regarding the court's intervention in matters that are not justiciable.

The first of these was the most urgent. At the time, the court had before it a petition demanding that it void a law that restricted the possibility that Palestinians living in the West Bank and Gaza Strip or in Arab countries could gain the right to reside in Israel by marrying an Israeli citizen. The court had rejected such petition by a one-vote margin at the end of Barak's tenure, and in 2007, a similar petition had once again come before the court. The forecast was that this time there would be a court majority for voiding the law. (In the end it did not do so, but at the time the danger that it would looked very real.) I saw this as an existential issue for the state of Israel, and a solution had to be proposed.

One possibility was the establishment of a separate Constitutional Court. My predecessor as justice minister, Haim Ramon, told me that he had considered this option. Another possibility was the Neeman Commission's proposal. It was unacceptable, and there was no chance that the Knesset would pass it in its original form. However, I thought the Knesset might accept the Neeman proposal if the number of votes needed to override a Supreme Court annulment of a law was set at sixty-five or sixty-one rather than seventy. Even this raised the theoretical issue of whether the Knesset could restrain itself and future Knessets by requiring a special majority, whether sixty-five or seventy, for any particular purpose.

I consulted with the leader of the Labor Party at the time, Defense Minister Amir Peretz. He opposed any legislation regarding the Supreme Court that the court itself opposed. I believed that a majority of the Knesset's members supported my view, but it was not politically possible to pass a basic law if a party central to the ruling coalition opposed it.

Peretz's spirited defense of the Supreme Court did him little good. A few months later he was defeated in Labor's internal leadership elections. In June 2007 Ehud Barak replaced him as defense minister.

I met with Ehud Barak at his home after he won the post of Labor's leader and of minister of defense, accompanied by Dov Weissglas, Prime Minister Ariel Sharon's chief of staff. We discussed issues relating to the legal system. Barak minced no words in speaking out against the way the legal system was working, with his ire directed in particular at a long-running investigation of a number of nonprofit organizations suspected of having been used to funnel illegal money into his campaign for prime minister in 1999. The investigation had begun during his term as prime minister and had dragged on for years. He thought the investigation to be totally unjustified on the grounds that he had acted on the basis of an opinion rendered by the attorney general. Ehud Barak expressed no opposition to reforming the legal system in principle, although he wanted to know the details before declaring his support of any particular proposal.

But Barak was not on the same wavelength on this issue with most of Labor's Knesset members, who strongly supported the Supreme Court's position and were opposed to any override provision that required less than seventy votes. Barak made no attempt to convince Labor's nineteen Knesset members (MKs) to change their position.

Since any change required the amendment of Basic Law: The Judiciary, it was necessary to obtain the agreement of all the coalition parties. Coalition agreements usually grant every party a veto on any change in the basic laws. But even in the absence of such an agreement it is seldom possible to pass legislation that one of the coalition parties strongly opposes. Such a move may cause that party to leave the coalition, toppling the government. With Labor opposed, there was no way to pass a reform at this point. I nevertheless carried on with the process of drafting a bill so that it would be ready if a solution presented itself later on. My goal was to gain the support of Shas, Ehud Olmert's second major coalition partner. Ostensibly, that should not have been a problem, given that this party, like the other religious parties, preferred to see controversial issues decided by the Knesset and not the Supreme Court. On the other hand, Shas was extremely wary of passing any basic laws at all because of its lack of confidence in the way the Supreme Court would interpret the new legislation. Following extensive discussions, I obtained Shas's agreement to a provision that would enable sixty-one Knesset members to override a Supreme Court nullification of a law passed by the Knesset.

On the face of it, any governing coalition should be able to muster sixty-one votes for such a purpose. But, in fact, it made overriding a Supreme Court decision fairly difficult. Most laws are passed by much smaller majorities. Party discipline is not all that strong, and just a few wayward MKs could prevent such an action.

A bill in this spirit was prepared by the justice ministry, with my involvement. It granted the Supreme Court the right to void laws inconsistent with Basic Law: Human Dignity and Liberty and Basic Law: Freedom of Occupation, as well as other basic law provisions that were "entrenched," that is, which required a majority of Knesset members (at least sixty-one) for their amendment. The bill required that a ruling to void a law had to be issued by a bench of at least nine justices, of which at least two thirds voted to void the law. The Knesset would be able to override such a ruling by passing legislation with the votes of sixty-one of its members, and that only if no more than fifty-five MKs opposed the bill.

As I saw it, this arrangement would rehabilitate the Supreme Court's standing, avert the establishment of a separate Constitutional Court, and legitimize the court's powers to declare laws unconstitutional. True, it opened up a possibility that court rulings might be overturned, but the legislature's power to supersede court rulings with subsequent legislation has always been recognized as its prerogative. Yet, there was every reason to believe that the override provision would also be invoked only seldom. But the Supreme Court saw it differently. Aharon Barak wanted much greater power for the court—he wanted it to be supreme over the Knesset. So he opposed the amendment.

I was able to bring the proposed amendment to Basic Law: The Judiciary before the cabinet only when the Olmert government's end was clearly in sight. As I expected, the Labor ministers opposed the proposal. Kadima split along the usual lines. Tzipi Livni, preparing to contend for the post of Kadima's leader, opposed the amendment. I had trouble understanding her reasons. She argued that, since a public commission had recommended an override provision of seventy votes, she could not support my proposal. That being her position, some of the other candidates for the Kadima leadership lined up behind her on the issue.

In the end the proposal was passed by the cabinet with a one-vote margin and was placed before the Knesset. It was now the summer of 2008. The first reading was set for the Knesset's winter session, which was scheduled to begin in October. I was certain that it would pass overwhelmingly, since the right-wing party, Likud, would support it. But Olmert resigned in September, the Knesset was paralyzed, and only consensual issues were brought before it. Subsequently, Benjamin Netanyahu's new government made no attempt to further the amendment.

The major victim was the Supreme Court itself. During my term as justice minister the court did not void a single law, but after I left that position, it ruled on a case that had been pending for several years, declaring unconstitutional a law that permitted the establishment of private prisons on the grounds that it contradicted Basic Law: Human Dignity and Liberty.[422] Minister of Finance Yuval Steinitz fiercely criticized the court for "intervening in the economic realm callously, irresponsibility, and almost negligently." Knesset Speaker Reuven Rivlin (now president of Israel) also spoke out stridently, questioning the legitimacy of the court's action. An interview he granted to the news website Ynet was headlined "The rotten fruit of the legal revolution." Rivlin declared that "a restrained and gradual process has been abandoned in favor of creativeness and revolution. Instead of choosing the path of dialogue and a profound internal process, it was decided to break the conventions that were intertwined."

There were other reforms that I furthered while I was justice minister. My first initiative in this direction was the Term Law, in fact an amendment to the Courts Law. It aroused the ire of the Supreme Court, principally because it limited the term of the chief justice to seven years (both Meir Shamgar and Aharon Barak served in the post for more than a decade, and there was no legal limit to how long a chief justice could serve). The justices seem to have been no less upset that the bill restricted the presidents of the lower courts in the same way. The practice at the time was that the presidents of the lower courts served a term of four years, which could be renewed by the minister of justice with the consent of the chief justice. The consequence was that the presidents of the lower courts were beholden to the chief justice and the justice minister. I thought that this dependence was unhealthy, but the Supreme Court apparently liked it. The Labor Party did not oppose the change, however, and my bill was approved by the Ministerial Committee for Legislation without any problem. The Knesset's vote on the bill was astounding. Despite the fact that the legislators knew of the Supreme Court's opposition, forty-nine voted in favor and only five against, with one abstention. The opponents came from the far left of the political spectrum—Meretz and the Arab parties.

I know of no other instance in which the Knesset lent the Supreme Court such a stinging rebuke. One would have thought that the vote would have lit all the court's red lights. Each time the Knesset rejected unreasonable positions taken by the high court, I had the impression that a sense of liberation pervaded the Knesset. The MKs felt as if they had been set free after a long series of humiliations and sermonizing by a haughty court certain that it represented the absolute truth. The arguments against the Term Law were weak and unconvincing. The Knesset had been given a chance to make its voice heard, and it had done so clearly and distinctly.

The significance of the Term Law was summed up by Ya'akov Ahimeir in *Ma'ariv*:

One may well ask if the Supreme Court justices have come to terms with the astounding margin by which the law was passed by the Knesset . . . The five opponents were MKs from Meretz and Hadash, while those voting in favor were legislators belonging to the center-right-religious factions, including the Labor faction. In other words, the Supreme Court's base of support has become very small. Chief Justice Beinisch sent the [Knesset's Constitution,] Law [and Justice] Committee a memorandum in which she laid out her reasons for opposing the law; retired justices appeared before the committee personally . . . but it is worth noting that sitting judges personally called and urged the members of the committee to pass the law over the objections of Chief Justice Beinisch . . . Credit for the achievement goes to [Justice] Minister Friedmann. The law ends the growing dependence between the Supreme Court and the lower courts. The previous situation was fundamentally military, the relationship between commander and subordinate.

At the time, I recalled what former Chief Justice Moshe Landau had said in the interview he granted *Ha'aretz* in 2000:

I warned Aharon Barak against this eventuality . . . I told him that he was living inside this beautiful court building as if it were an aquarium. But neither he nor the justices who are with him are sensitive to what is going on outside the aquarium . . . They are not sufficiently attentive to what the public feels and to things that even many lawyers feel. And those are very harsh things.

A few months later the Labor Party began to take a different position regarding the reforms I had proposed, including measures that were not connected to the basic laws. I don't know what caused this change of heart, and why Ehud Barak, the party leader, now took a public position not in line with the views he had expressed to me privately at his home. Neither do I know if there was any connection to positions I took on security issues that Barak did not like. Perhaps it had to do with the very strong instinct in the political system that "nice" behavior toward the legal system is a good way of protecting oneself against criminal investigations and other unpleasant things. Or perhaps Barak had other reasons. Whatever the case, from that point onward I had to fight within the coalition on every issue that the Supreme Court opposed. I sometimes succeeded nevertheless.

I also prepared a proposal for an amendment of Basic Law: The Judiciary on the constitution of the Judicial Selection Committee. My proposal made a distinction between the process of choosing Supreme Court justices and that of judges to lower courts. In the former case, I proposed, only two sitting Supreme Court justices (as opposed to three) would serve on the committee—the chief justice and one other. For this purpose the committee would also be supplemented with two other members, to be chosen by the cabinet—a former judge and a person, not a member of the cabinet, from the field of science, economics, education, or the social sciences. The committee would also include a scholar chosen by the presidents of the country's research universities. This would increase the membership of the Judicial Selection Committee to eleven members, and make its membership more heterogeneous.

With regard to choosing judges for the lower courts, I thought that the committee's composition should be changed in one central way. Instead of three members of the Supreme Court, the committee should include the chief justice and two retired District Court judges, selected by the presidents of the District Courts. I had two reasons. First, District Court judges are better acquainted with candidates for the Magistrates and District Courts. Second, it was not healthy for the Supreme Court to control the professional futures of members of the state prosecution who seek judgeships, and of Magistrates Court judges who wish to move up to the District Courts. But this proposal did not make any progress during my service as justice minister.

The issue of justiciability was the third issue in my memorandum. I promised Aharon Barak that I would not move forward with this issue before discussing it with him. Indeed, before making my proposal public, I sent it to him and to Meir Shamgar as well. I found their positions to be notably divergent. Shamgar pointed out that their opposing views on this issue found expression in the *Ressler* decision,[423] in which the Supreme Court denied a petition on the issue of the government's noninduction of *yeshiva* students into the army. Barak, Shamgar said, had distinguished between normative justiciability (according to which any issue can be considered on the basis of legal criteria) and institutional justiciability (according to which certain legal issues may remain under the purview of another branch of government). Nevertheless, Shamgar maintained, in Barak's approach normative justiciability undermines institutional justiciability, with the result that "the court does not forgo taking up almost any issue." Barak, for example, opposed the *Reiner* decision,[424] in which the court had ruled that the credentialing of the German ambassador to Israel was not justiciable. Shamgar stressed that Barak's position had been a lone one in the *Ressler* case, and that the two other justices who had shared the bench with him (Shamgar himself and Miriam Ben-Porat) opposed his position. In Shamgar's view, when the political nature of an issue dominates, it is not justiciable and the court should not take it up.

I based the explanatory text that I attached to my legislative proposal on this subject largely on Shamgar's position. Yet Shamgar opposed legislation on the subject "given the special sensitivity necessarily aroused by all legislation touching on the powers of the court, which is without question a vital institution for liberal democracy." As such, he maintained, it was better to leave the matter to the court itself.

Aharon Barak reiterated that he did not maintain that everything is indeed justiciable. He noted once again his view that there is "institutional non-justiciability." Yet it was evident that he felt uncomfortable with such an eventuality, as "what it means is giving a state authority a free hand to act in contradiction of the law and even arbitrarily. It creates a black hole of a lack of judicial review. This black hole permits harsh violations of the law in the area in which there is no judge and no law. That is the heavy cost of non-justiciability." (With regard to Barak's black hole theory, it should be noted that such a black hole can be found, first and foremost, in the Supreme Court's rulings, which are not subject to any oversight.)

Once again, during my tenure as justice minister the court did not void any law passed by the Knesset, even though it heard petitions asking it to do so. Many cases of this sort drag on for many long years before a decision is rendered, a delay that is hard to justify. It could be that the discussions among the justices take a long time, but it is also possible that the court is awaiting a convenient time to issue its rulings. It may, for example, be taking account of public reaction or the Knesset's reaction. For example, it may well be that the court refrained from voiding any laws during my tenure because it feared that it would spur the passing of the override provision.

33

Changes in Appointments to the Supreme Court

In the three years prior to my appointment as justice minister in 2007, no less than six justices retired from the Supreme Court after reaching the mandatory retirement age of seventy: Theodor Or, Dalia Dorner, Eliahu Mazza, Jacob Turkel, Mishael Cheshin, and Aharon Barak. All these were central figures, and, without them, the court looked somewhat anemic.

No new justices had been appointed since May 2004 when, during Yosef (Tommy) Lapid's term as justice minister, Esther Hayut, Salim Joubran, Elyakim Rubinstein, and Edna Arbel were added to the court. Justice Minister Tzipi Livni's term had been marked by fierce contention between her and Chief Justice Aharon Barak over the candidacy of Ruth Gavison, which had stymied the entire appointments process. Since justice ministers seldom serve for long in today's Israel, the sitting justices no doubt expected that they could get the appointments they wanted if they just waited out Livni. New elections were on the horizon and that meant a new justice minister would soon take over. The same thing has happened at other junctures when the high bench found itself facing an independent-minded justice minister. All they needed was a bit of patience. But this time it didn't work.

Barak and his colleagues had not noticed that times had changed. The unreserved confidence and respect that the Supreme Court had previously enjoyed among the public and politicians had evaporated. Under the Barak court, the appointments procedure became controversial. During the latter half of his term as chief justice, public approval of the court system in general and of the Supreme Court in particular plummeted. The chances grew that the court would face a justice minister who would not content himself with being a rubber stamp for the court. That happened when Haim Ramon took on the justice portfolio. And, indeed, under his stewardship not a single judge was appointed to any court.

On top of the vacancies that needed to be filled, there was the issue of naming a chief justice and deputy chief justice for the Supreme Court. Deputy Chief Justice Cheshin had retired in February 2006. Under the customary seniority rule, Dorit Beinisch was in line to replace him, but she did not get the appointment because the Judicial Selection Committee needed to affirm it and the committee was not convened. With Barak slated to retire the following September, it looked as if the court would be left leaderless. It very nearly happened. But, in the end, the court was saved from chaos at the last minute. Meir Sheetrit, who held the justice portfolio temporarily following Ramon's indictment and resignation, convened the committee a week before Barak's retirement. It confirmed Beinisch as chief justice and Eliezer Rivlin as her deputy.

The court and Ramon, prior to his resignation, did manage to reach a consensus on some temporary appointments to the Supreme Court. By law, the justice minister has the power to make temporary appointments to the court with the consent of the chief justice, without requiring the approval of the Judicial Selection Committee. Ramon deferred to Barak in this regard, approving two of the chief justice's candidates, Jerusalem District Court Judge David Cheshin and Tel Aviv District Court Judge Devora Berliner. Ramon, like other justice ministers, apparently did not appreciate the full significance of such appointments, and neither did the Knesset or the public. Since temporary appointments, which must be of sitting District Court judges, can last for no more than a year, they would seem to be of little impact. In fact, however, they were the central tool by which the Supreme Court exerted control over both the District Courts and appointments to the high bench.

The system worked as follows: When a vacancy opened up on the Supreme Court, three or four District Court judges could be appointed to the available seat for short periods, one after another. Each temporary justice was cut off during that period from her work on the District Court, to which she returned when her interim appointment ended. Each time a District Court judge left and then returned to her benches, the work of those courts was disrupted. Furthermore, the temporary judges were often insulted if they did not receive permanent appointments to the high court. Top judges have sometimes resigned following what they felt was a rejection. Furthermore, brief revolving-door temporary appointments caused many District Court judges to defer unduly to the justices of the Supreme Court, since their chances for promotion to the high court depended on the whims of its sitting members. Furthermore, it created a class distinction on the high court itself. The temporary justices had an inferior standing, and given their hopes for a permanent appointment, their independence of judgment was open to question. In addition, temporary appointments had to be District Court judges, and District Court judges were generally required to serve as temporary justices before being elevated to the high court permanently. The practice created a baffling distinction between justices who had ascended to the court from the position of attorney general, state attorney, the academy, or private practice and those who had ascended from the lower courts. Perversely, judges with years of experience on the bench needed to undergo an "apprenticeship" when men and women who had never served as judges took up their gavels directly. Finally, to the best of my knowledge, temporary appointments were not practiced by any other court of last resort in the world.

Temporary appointments served the Supreme Court in two ways. First, during periods of adversarial relations between the court and a justice minister, the court was generally able to persuade the minister to allow temporary appointments. It solved the problem of case overload and enabled the justices to wait for a more auspicious time to promote their candidates for permanent appointments. The other thing that temporary appointments did was help the justices wield nearly exclusive power over appointments. From time to time the justices invented rules that, while they had no basis in law, granted them a huge advantage in the appointments process. One of these so-called rules was that no District Court judge should be appointed to the high bench without first having served in a temporary position. Since a temporary appointment required the consent of the chief justice, this in practice gave the head of the court a veto over the appointment of judges from the lower courts to the Supreme Court. This prerogative came on top of the huge power that the sitting justices already exercised over the appointment of their colleagues, given that they held three of the nine seats on the Judicial Selection Committee.

As I saw it, such a veto was unlawful. It circumvented the Judicial Selection Committee and prevented it from exercising its discretion to appoint an appropriate District Court judge to the Supreme Court. I was thus determined to eliminate temporary appointments. At the time, only ten permanent justices were serving on the court. Cheshin's and Berliner's temporary appointments were about to expire. It was very clear that permanent appointments to the court would not happen any time soon, and the Supreme Court was in a state of open crisis. Exceptionally, I consented to Chief Justice Beinisch's request to allow the appointment of two temporary justices to replace those whose terms were ending. It was the beginning of a messy situation.

I had my own candidates for the temporary positions. One was Judge Isaac Amit of the Haifa District Court. Since I needed Beinisch's consent, I thought it only proper that I consult with her before sounding out Amit himself. It seemed the fair thing to do. If I were to speak to Amit first and he were to consent to the appointment, only to encounter Beinisch's opposition, I would create an embarrassing situation for both of them. I did not know Amit personally, but he was a first-class candidate (and was later appointed to a permanent seat under Justice Minister Yaakov Neeman). I assumed that, if appointments were made on the basis of merit, there was every chance that the chief justice would agree. To my surprise, when I raised his name with Beinisch, she said that she would convey me her answer a few days hence. I waited but received no communication from her. Only two days after the promised date did Beinisch inform me that Amit could not join the Supreme Court because of the caseload he had on the District Court. I decided to look into that myself. I spoke with Amit, who confirmed that he was indeed overloaded and could not take on a temporary appointment to the high court. (Some months later, he tried again to persuade me that this was the case, and added that it had not been easy for him to persuade his colleagues that this was the real reason for turning down my offer.) In any event, Beinisch's conduct, which saved her from having to express her opinion as to whether Amit was a worthy appointment, hardly seemed commendable. I decided that in the future I would speak directly to the candidate, and only afterward inform the chief justice and let her make whatever inquiries she wished.

My next candidate was Judge Neal Hendel of the Beersheva District Court. I spoke with him, received his consent, and told him that his appointment was contingent on Beinisch's agreement. But when I gave his name to the chief justice, she replied that she did not agree. She noted that he was religiously observant, but did not offer any reason for her opposition. I had to tell Hendel that Beinisch was opposed. Hendel later received, under Justice Minister Neeman, a permanent appointment to the high court. Beinisch consented then, because it was clear that the round of appointments at that time could not be completed if she did not agree to Hendel.

From Hendel I proceeded to Judge Yosef (Sefi) Elon, also of the Beersheva District Court. (Elon was the son of former Deputy Chief Justice Menachem Elon, and a fine judge on his own merits.) He agreed. I told Beinisch that my choices for the two temporary appointments were Uzi Vogelman, a candidate I knew she wanted, and Elon, her interest in whom I doubted. For me it was the last stand. If Beinisch agreed, fine. If not, I would make no temporary appointments. After all, I thought the system was flawed from the start. Beinisch, however, agreed.

I consulted with Beinisch several times on permanent appointments. She insisted that a District Court judge could be a candidate for the high court only if he had served as a temporary justice first. This was a long-standing rule, she maintained, arguing that it was important that candidates prove themselves in a trial run. I took the other position. Among other things, I pointed out that she was not a personal example of the rule she was so assiduously defending. How could she make a temporary appointment a precondition when she herself had not had one, nor had the two chief justices who preceded her?

I reached the conclusion that the appointment procedure needed to be put into law. I had a proposal prepared that did away with temporary appointments. The draft came before the Ministerial Committee on Legislation on May 14, 2008, the day President George W. Bush arrived for his second visit to Israel. A welcoming ceremony was held at Ben-Gurion Airport.

Ehud Barak asked Olmert to make me withdraw the bill. The prime minister refused. On my way to the ministerial committee meeting that followed the ceremony, Barak called me and insisted that I take the proposed legislation off the agenda. If not, he said, it would be the end of cooperation between us. Having no idea what cooperation he was speaking of, I refused. The committee overwhelmingly favored the proposal. The only opponents were the two Labor representatives, Shalom Simhon and Ami Ayalon. Simhon offered a compromise proposal, according to which the committee would issue a unanimous call to appoint to the high court judges who had not had temporary appointments. I decided to accept the compromise, even though it angered some of my colleagues. The problem with it was that there was good reason to fear that the sitting justices would disregard the committee's position, no matter that it was unanimous. In retrospect, I may well have erred. It was time to put an end to temporary appointments. On the other hand, it is not clear that the compromise did any real damage. The Talansky scandal was already in the air, and the government's days were clearly numbered. While I might have managed to get my bill through the parliamentary process to a final vote before the Seventeenth Knesset came to an end, there is no way to be certain.

I nevertheless persisted, to the end of my tenure, in my policy of not making temporary appointments to the Supreme Court. My successor, Yaakov Neeman, understood the importance of the issue and accepted my recommendation that he continue it. In practice, that put an end to the baseless rule that the Supreme Court had invented. Under the circumstances, Beinisch had no choice but to make do. During Neeman's term she agreed to the appointments of five District Court judges who had not held temporary appointments—Neal Hendel, Isaac Amit, Zvi Zylbertal, Noam Sohlberg and Uri Shoham.

Another critical issue for me was the appointment of private-sector attorneys to courts on all levels. In the twenty-five previous years, attorneys general and state attorneys had increasingly been placed directly on the Supreme Court bench. State and police prosecutors were also appointed to other judgeships. The great majority of criminal cases were by that point being heard by judges whose experience lay mostly in the prosecution. The consequence was astronomical conviction levels. On top of this, there was a notable shortage of judges with experience in civil and commercial law.

I wanted to change that by appointing to the bench lawyers who had represented defendants and who had heard their stories about police interrogations and the pressure put on them. I also thought it vital that Israel have judges who had put together large business deals and who had grappled with government bureaucracy and regulation. The first appointment to the Supreme Court under my watch was Hanan Melcer. He was acceptable to the sitting justices, but they resisted the appointment of another private-sector attorney to their club. For my part, I felt that a single justice who hailed from the private sector would not be able to make a sufficient impact. I believed that at least two were needed to bring about some sort of change in the court's approach.

I had a prospect of putting together a majority on the Judicial Selection Committee because the two Bar Association representatives were likely to support appointments from the private sector. I usually had the support of one of them, Pinhas Marinsky, in any case. The chairman of the Bar, Yuri Guy-Ron, leaned more toward Beinisch's side, but clearly had an interest in private-sector appointments. But this presented another problem. I found that no few senior private attorneys refused to have their names put forward.

Despite this, I was able to propose two first-class candidates: Yoram Danziger and Dalia Tal. The committee approved Danziger, but I was not able to obtain a majority for Tal. In fact, I found that under Beinisch it was not easy to get women appointed to the Supreme Court. The only one approved during her tenure was Daphne Barak-Erez, and that at the very end of Beinisch's term.

It was the first time since Israel's Supreme Court was first constituted that two private attorneys were appointed consecutively. The bench now had twelve permanent justices, leaving three seats still vacant. Beinisch wanted these spots filled by District Court judges. That was acceptable to me, especially given that there was no shortage of qualified candidates. But Beinisch's insistence that such candidates serve first in a temporary position complicated the situation.

I supported the candidacy of Yehudit Tzur on the basis of her rulings in the field of human rights, and because I wanted to see more women on the Supreme Court. I therefore thought her appointment was especially important. Rumor had it that she was close to Beinisch, but it turned out that Beinisch was not at all pleased that she had consented to have her name put forward. From Beinisch's point of view, Tzur was abetting my effort to put an end to the temporary justice rule.

As a matter of fact, the temporary appointment regime was highly unpopular among District Court judges, who felt it discriminated against them. Tzur's willingness to be a candidate demonstrated her courage and independence, which only strengthened my conviction that she ought to be on the Supreme Court. But Beinisch held the opposite view and the disagreement between us continued. As determined as I was about Tzur's appointment, Beinisch was no less determined to stymie it. One possible compromise was that Tzur agree to a temporary appointment prior to a permanent one. The problem was that I was firmly opposed to the rule and wanted to put an end to it. But the suggestion became moot when Tzur announced that, given that she was a well-known and senior judge, she saw no reason to acquiesce to the trial period that the sitting justices insisted on.

At the time, the Knesset's Constitution, Law, and Justice Committee was considering a bill submitted by Knesset member Gideon Sa'ar of Likud to require Supreme Court appointments to receive seven votes out of the nine members of the Judicial Selection Committee. Such a bill could not in practice be approved by the Knesset committee without the consent of the justice minister. After long hesitation, I decided to support it. I presumed that the Supreme Court would not object—after all, the existing situation made it theoretically possible for a minister of justice to push through an appointment to the court over the opposition of the three Supreme Court justices who were members of the committee. In practice, this rarely happened, as the three justices were usually able to get at least two other member of the committee to support them on appointments to the Supreme Court. The law was enacted. The upshot was that neither the chief justice nor the minister of justice would be able to push through an appointment to the high court without the consent of the other. Each of them could be almost certain of the support of two other members of the committee, enabling each to veto any candidate not to their liking. The new provision should also be of interest to game theorists—since any three members of the committee could band together to block a candidate, it granted considerable bargaining power to each individual member of the committee.

I continued my negotiations with Beinisch after the law passed, but we did not reach an agreement. While I cannot be certain, it was my distinct impression that the chief justice was prepared to accept a single appointment of a District Court judge without requiring a temporary appointment first, so long as it was not Yehudit Tzur, who had agreed to have her candidacy put forward by me without clearing it with Beinisch first. In the meantime, something changed among District Courts judges. They now saw that there was a real possibility that the temporary appointment system would come to an end, and as such they were no longer as hesitant to become candidates for the Supreme Court without having previously served on a temporary appointment. I spoke again with Isaac Amit, and he agreed to be a candidate.

I decided to convene the Judicial Selection Committee even though I had not reached an agreement with the chief justice. I hoped that we might be able to overcome our differences during a meeting of the committee and fill the vacant seats on the Supreme Court. Kadima held its leadership election five days prior to the date set for the committee meeting, and Tzipi Livni was elected party leader. Olmert announced his resignation the day before the meeting. Under Israeli law, a prime minister's resignation brings about the resignation of the entire government, turning it into an interim ("caretaker") cabinet that serves until a new government obtains the confidence of the Knesset. That did not mean that I had to cancel the Judicial Selection Committee meeting. I realized, however, that the chief justice might use that as an excuse to prevent it. I consulted with Attorney General Menachem Mazuz, who agreed that there was no reason why the committee could not appoint judges at this time.

Nevertheless, when the members of the committee gathered the next day in my office, Beinisch announced that, given the government's resignation and previous rulings by the Supreme Court, the committee could not do business. Her two colleagues, Justices Ayala Procaccia and Edmond Levy, backed her on this. I took the opposite position, and called in Mazuz to present his opinion about why the committee could indeed meet. All the other members accepted Mazuz's ruling. I pointed out to the three justices that they did not, as members of the committee, have judicial powers, nor did they have the status of a Supreme Court bench. After all, the entire Judicial Selection Committee is subject to judicial review. The Supreme Court had in any case ruled that the attorney general's opinion is binding on all administrative bodies, including the Judicial Selection Committee. It thus also bound them in their capacity as members of this committee.

However, the three justices, led by the chief justice, ignored Mazuz's ruling. This meant also disregarding their own court's ruling concerning the binding power of the attorney general's opinions. They refused to take part in the meeting. This is what they call "rule of law." While I believed that the justices' action was unlawful, I decided to cancel the meeting.

That same evening, the Israel Bar Association held a gathering in Jerusalem. Beinisch and I both spoke there. I reminded the audience that Beinisch, who opposed appointments to the high court under an interim government, had been herself appointed in precisely such circumstances, after the week of mourning that followed Yitzhak Rabin's assassination. I said that I did not think this cast any doubts on the legality of her appointment. The assembled lawyers broke out in laughter.

But that was not the end of it. Another meeting of the Judicial Selection Committee was scheduled for six weeks hence, this time for the purpose of making appointments to the lower courts. It was not clear if the justices would boycott this meeting as well on the same faulty grounds. After all, these were appointments almost entirely devoid of political significance. Furthermore, it was vital to make such appointments as the lower courts were seriously overburdened. I nevertheless thought it best to notify Beinisch that if the justices intended to refuse to participate, I would not hold the meeting. About two weeks before the scheduled session she notified me that "according to court rulings and in accordance with prevailing legal and public policy," judicial appointments could not be made, not even to the lower courts. In this she stood against the wishes of members of the Knesset from both sides of the aisle.

Beinisch's refusal was roundly criticized in the public and press. Legal journalists were unanimous in declaring her move a serious mistake. The absurdity of the position taken by the three justices on the committee was all the more obvious given the fact that the Olmert government decided, during this pre-election period, to carry out Operation Cast Lead in the Gaza Strip, just as the Benjamin Netanyahu government would decide in November 2012, in similar circumstances, on another Gaza operation, Operation Pillar of Defense. In other words, a "caretaker" government (recall that under Knesset legislation, such a government has exactly the same powers as it did before it resigned) can go to war, but the Judicial Selection Committee is supposedly barred from appointing judges, even to the Magistrates Court. Another paradox is that the prohibition that the justices invented against judicial appointments after a government's resignation or during an election period was ostensibly meant to strengthen public confidence in government. Clearly, the justices' behavior in this case did the precise opposite, increasing public reservations about the high court.

Unfortunately, there was no choice but to wait until after the elections. After the accession of the new Netanyahu government, it became clear just how costly the justices' refusal to allow judicial appointments had been for the public, the courts, and no less so for the Supreme Court itself. Beinisch's appointments policy lay in ruins. A newly constituted Judicial Selection Committee convened only in August 2009, nearly a year after the one Beinisch had sabotaged. The courts, including the high court, had to wait many long months for their vacancies to be filled. The meeting, chaired by the new justice minister, Yaakov Neeman, appointed three justices to the Supreme Court according to the new rule requiring the approval of at least seven of the committee's nine members: Isaac Amit, Neal Hendel, and Uzi Vogelman. Beinisch explicitly supported Vogelman, who formerly worked with her in the state attorney's office. She had previously opposed Hendel categorically, denying him even a temporary appointment. It was apparently the first time in the history of the Supreme Court that a chief justice was compelled to accept the appointment of a candidate she emphatically opposed. The reason presumably lies in the fact that Neeman continued my policy of declining to make temporary appointments. In this situation, when it became crucial for the depleted Supreme Court to fill its ranks, Beinisch had no choice but to resign herself to this result. It was also solid proof of the flaw in the so-called rule regarding temporary appointments. Amit and Hendel, who had never been granted a temporary appointment, now won permanent seats on the court, breaking that prejudicial and unacceptable rule invented by the Supreme Court. The rule lost out once again in January 2012, at the very end of Beinisch's term, when three District Court judges were appointed to the court. Uri Shoham, Zvi Zylbertal, and Noam Sohlberg had not held temporary appointments first.

Beinisch's only achievement was preventing the appointment of her erstwhile friend Yehudit Tzur. Tzur ended up resigning, depriving the bench of a first-class judge.

Finally, the "rule" about not making appointments during election periods fell by the wayside after Asher Grunis ascended to the chief justice's chair in 2012. The Judicial Selection Committee met in December of that year and made several appointments to the lower courts. It was one of the signs that judicial activism had been curbed and that the justices are limited in their ability to invent baseless rules that damaged the court system.

District Court appointments were largely made from among Magistrates Court judges, a high proportion of whom are graduates of the prosecution. I wanted to change this as well by appointing private attorneys directly to District Court seats. Once again, it was difficult to get high-quality lawyers to agree to be candidates. Most such figures have well-established practices that bring them high incomes and are thus not enthusiastic about leaving their firms. I was nevertheless able to persuade more such men and women to accept appointments than had been possible previously. Another District Court appointment made during my tenure was that of Moshe Yoad-Cohen of the Public Defender's Office, an appointment that I considered of importance in countering the tendency to fill judicial vacancies with judges of prosecutorial background.

34

Snail-Paced Justice

The courts were in crisis when I became justice minister. The Judicial Selection Committee had not met for several years, rendered dysfunctional by the dispute between Tzipi Livni and Aharon Barak over the appointment of Ruth Gavison. When Meir Sheetrit held the justice portfolio for an interim period in 2006, he convened the committee to choose a new chief justice and deputy chief justice from among the sitting members of the Supreme Court, but no new justices were settled on. As I have already recounted, when Barak retired, the court was left with only ten justices; five seats were vacant. No few seats were vacant on lower courts as well, and these courts in fact desperately needed even more judges. At my first meeting with Prime Minister Ehud Olmert, when he offered me the justice ministry, we agreed to the creation of eighty-five new positions, augmenting the benches by 15 percent. It was the largest ever expansion of Israel's court system.

On top of the shortage of judges, the system suffered from procedural and administrative problems. I instituted a number of reforms. One of these was the previously mentioned Term Law, which mandated fixed terms for the presidents of the various courts. But there were many other serious problems as well.

The Supreme Court was an especially serious issue. It had adopted the position that "all is justiciable" and was increasingly producing decisions of huge length going off on innumerable tangents on which justices engaged in arcane disputes over social and moral theory.

When this practice of unnecessarily long decisions made its way down to the lower courts, it contributed no little to further braking the already slow wheels of justice. On top of this, as the Supreme Court expanded its authority, it created more work for itself and for the lower courts as well. Each decision that a given issue was subject to judicial review (for example, whether the award of an Israel Prize could be revoked) brought a trail of petitions in its wake. The Supreme Court's declaration that it had power to annul laws passed by the Knesset led to a long series of petitions demanding that the court declare a huge variety of laws unconstitutional.

The severity of the problem can be illustrated by reference to a decision handed down by Justice Ayala Proccacia on her final day on the court. The case had to do with an Interior Ministry regulation regarding foreign nationals who resided and worked lawfully in the country—specifically women workers who had given birth to children in Israel. The regulation required such women to leave Israel with their babies. If they wished to return to Israel to complete the legal period under which licensed foreign nationals may work in the country, they could do so only if they left their children behind. The regulation was an outrageous one; one can only wonder how government officials committed to the values of a Jewish and democratic state concocted such a rule. The Supreme Court quite properly struck it down. But no less perturbing than the regulation itself was how long it took the Supreme Court to issue its decision—six years after the petition was filed, and this in a case (one of many) in which the Supreme Court was the court of both first and last resort.[425] The delay had only partially to do with the vacant seats on the court, as it postdated the round of appointments that restored the court to its full complement of fifteen justices. It also came after the court's caseload was reduced by the transfer of many categories of cases that had once come directly under the purview of the Supreme Court to administrative benches in the District Courts. The delay was colorfully described by one of Israel's best-known defense attorneys, Avigdor Feldman, in a blog post on his website, headlined "Justice Proccacia's Peacock Feather."

Civil suits were in even worse shape. It had become routine for rulings in civil cases appealed to the Supreme Court to be rendered only three years later. Sometimes it took much longer, this after years of previous litigation in the District Courts. It was not uncommon for such cases to languish in the courts for a decade before a final decision was issued.

Other courts suffered from similar problems, first and foremost the Tel Aviv District Court. This largest of Israel's District Courts serves the country's commercial capital. At that time it had fifty judges, who were responsible not just for cases originating in the Tel Aviv metropolitan area but also for those coming from the nearby Central District.

At first I wanted to add judges to the court, but it turned out that the courthouse did not have enough courtrooms and chambers to accommodate them. Another concern was that a larger court would be difficult to manage properly. It seemed preferable to create a new District Court for the country's central region that would relieve the Tel Aviv court of close to half of its caseload. It was a good idea, but it soon became clear that it would not be easy to implement.

I saw no reason to consult with Chief Justice Dorit Beinisch, since the establishment of new courts falls under the purview of the justice minister, and the chief justice has no standing in such decisions. Former Chief Justice Barak later criticized me for creating, "without any real discussion with the chief justice of the Supreme Court, a new District Court in Petah Tikva." Clearly, Israel's chief justices were demanding to be the head of the court system, authority that no law granted them. I had no objection to granting them that title and the honor that goes with it, but I maintained that it did not grant the chief justice any additional powers and certainly none of the powers vested by the Knesset in the justice minister.

For the new court to succeed, it needed a president with good administrative abilities. After lengthy consultation, I determined that the best person for the job was Judge Hila Gerstel, vice president of the Tel Aviv District Court. I had no previous acquaintance with her. But a new obstacle presented itself. The law gives the minister of justice the power to appoint presidents of the lower courts, but during the term of Chief Justice Meir Shamgar the law had been amended to require the chief justice's consent for such appointments. It was part of the revolutionary court's project of expanding the chief justice's powers. What was the legal nature of this provision? In my view, the power of appointment clearly remained with the justice minister. The chief justice's role was not that of a partner in the decision, but merely a check on the minister's choice. For example, the chief justice could refuse to sign off on the appointment based on an improper motive, or one of an unqualified person. But it is not a discretionary power that enables her to veto the appointment of a highly qualified individual simply because she prefers that someone else be given the post. I was certain that Beinisch could have no justifiable reason to oppose Gerstel's appointment.

Beyond the technical legal issue, my impression was that the consent provision, which also applied to temporary appointments to the Supreme Court, was transforming the chief justice into the decisive force in the system, one to whom the justice minister had to defer. The legal question of whether the chief justice's role was solely a check on the minister was shunted off to the sidelines. In the end, Beinisch gave her consent—but only after lengthy arguments and after making me wait for quite some time.

The new Central District Court was inaugurated eight months into my term as justice minister. All the problems it presented, including the issue of a building for it to occupy, were quickly resolved. The new court was housed temporarily in an appropriate building in Petah Tikva, a Tel Aviv suburb. The question was where its permanent seat would be. Several cities in the region were interested. Such a court is an economic asset to any municipality, bringing with it direct employment and associated economic activity. I consulted with Gerstel and Finance Minister Ronnie Bar-On, and we chose the city of Lod. The judges may well have preferred Petah Tikva, more prosperous and with easy access to Tel Aviv and to the areas north of it, but Bar-On and I thought that Lod should get the nod. That city, plagued by poverty and inhabited by both Jews and Arabs, needed an economic boost. It is to the credit of Gerstel, the other judges, and the employees of the new court that they recognized the importance of the decision and accepted it without objection. Unfortunately, the planning process for the new courthouse was a lengthy one; the cornerstone of a new and impressive structure was laid only after I left the ministry and was replaced by Yaakov Neeman. Construction was completed in August 2012.

The new court has proved itself to be one of the country's most efficient ones. But one can't escape the incessant refrain. The decision to found the new court in Lod could not pass without a petition to the Supreme Court. The Petah Tikva municipality demanded that the Supreme Court decree that the court had to remain there. The petition had no chance, and, in the end, the municipality withdrew it. Then Ramla, Lod's neighboring city, also petitioned the high court, only to withdraw its suit as well.

35

The Media Battle

My appointment as justice minister was greeted enthusiastically in the government and Knesset, but not by the Supreme Court. At noon on the day the Knesset was slated to approve my appointment, former Deputy Chief Justice Mishael Cheshin declared in a radio interview: "My father was a justice on the first Supreme Court. I was one afterward . . . it is my home. If anyone raises his hand against the Supreme Court, I will cut it off." What emerges from this statement is that this retired justice felt a sense of ownership over the court. That is typical of people who hold on to unchecked power for a long time. They gradually forget that it is not a private enterprise of their own and that the body they serve on belongs to the public as a whole.

Cheshin's statement set off a vociferous media campaign against me. It enjoyed the support of Chief Justice Dorit Beinisch and her associates, with the backing of a choir of retired judges.[426] There had never been anything like it in Israel in connection with the relations between the justice minister and chief justice. While I am hardly objective, it seems to me that the campaign, and the attempt to delegitimize me, failed. That seems clear from the huge support I garnered in the Knesset during my period of service. Polls of the public and of the legal profession also confirmed the support I enjoyed. From my point of view, the aggressive media crusade against me boomeranged and ended up damaging the Supreme Court. The group of judges who orchestrated the struggle were no doubt encouraged and cheered by their close associates in what former Chief Justice Moshe Landau termed the "aquarium," meaning the Supreme Court building, but they were blind to what was happening outside and had no sense of how the public and the legal profession felt. At an earlier time such campaign might have knocked a justice minister off balance—but those times were gone. The standing of the Supreme Court had been shaken, and criticism of its actions had increased prior to my appointment. The pronouncements issuing from the court and its acolytes had lost much of their potency.

The campaign succeeded only on one count. The uproar lasted for months, and over time the public found it difficult to remember who had started it and who was lashing out without restraint. Little by little, both sides—one of which was me—came to be seen as equally responsible for the escalation. But I spoke much more moderately than did those attacking me, and I was not the one to drag the media into the struggle. It all began with Cheshin's declaration, just a few hours before the Knesset approved my appointment. Less than a month later Dorit Beinisch sent me a fierce letter. She assailed the agenda for a meeting of the Judicial Selection Committee set for two days later. The letter made its way to the press. *Yedioth Ahronoth* reported it on March 6, 2007, under the headline "Frontal confrontation between the justice minister and the chief justice." I had chaired a meeting of the committee a week before at which new judges had been approved. Following that meeting questions were raised about the procedure, regarding, for example, the recording and publication of its minutes. I thought it only proper not to rush to make further appointments without addressing those issues. Also, I wanted the members of the committee to receive more information about the candidates. I thus decided to devote the next meeting largely to procedural matters. Beinisch charged that "for a long period no judges have been appointed to the District and Magistrates Courts," but her letter followed the previous meeting in which new judges had in fact been designated. It was true that prior to my entry into the Justice Ministry no new judges had been appointed for a long time, but clearly I was not to blame, just as I was not responsible for the dispute between my predecessor, Tzipi Livni, and the Supreme Court that had created that situation. Since I had just taken office, I deserved to be given some slack to make inquiries and preparations.

The Terms Law which had been my initiative and which had garnered wide support was passed by the Knesset in July 2007. Beinisch strongly and publicly opposed it, even after its passage. Apparently, she regarded a graduation ceremony at the University of Haifa law school, held in the same month the law passed, as an appropriate occasion to make her views known. But the media was not convinced. I have already mentioned, in chapter 32, Ya'akov Ahimeir's response in *Ma'ariv* to Beinisch. Tova Tzimuki, legal affairs correspondent for *Yedioth Ahronoth*, wrote that "Chief Justice Beinisch, who holds to conservative positions and refuses to allow any breath of change, tried to thwart the law passed yesterday by issuing an opinion opposing it, which she sent to the Constitution [Law and Justice] Committee. She also sent two personal representatives to the committee, retired Justices Itzhak Zamir and Theodor Or. For naught. Beinisch can paint [Justice] Minister Friedmann any color she likes. It is hard to argue with the practical and rational logic of his reform. She has no monopoly on the truth."

Another stage in the media storm swirled around the addition of the eighty-five new judgeships that the prime minister approved at our first meeting. Following negotiations with the director of the Finance Ministry's Budget Department, Kobi Haber, we agreed that the new positions would be added gradually over the course of a few years. However, the need to staff the new District Court, that I established,[427] required some changes in that schedule. I sent Haber a letter at the beginning of July thanking him for his agreement to allow six judges from the 2008 quota to be appointed already in 2007. Copies of that letter were sent to several other people, among them Courts Administration Director Judge Moshe Gal. A few days later I received another letter from Beinisch. She asserted that she, the chief justice, was in charge of the court system. She complained that I had not sent her a copy of my letter to Haber and that, in general, I was not including her and consulting with her on court issues. She also noted that my letter did not say that the cost of the additional judgeships should not be cut from other parts of the court system's budget. She concluded by writing: "Unfortunately, it is difficult to avoid the impression that the announcement of the additional [positions] does not provide a real response to the system's needs, and that it seems to be intended for publicity."

I was not expecting a letter of appreciation for achieving a significant number of new judgeships, but I felt that the chief justice's last sentence went beyond the acceptable. I responded briefly the next day, observing that the Courts Administration was well informed about the budgetary issues and adding that her letter "speaks of a chief justice who is 'in charge of the system.' I know of no provision of law that states that, but if I have perhaps missed it, I would be grateful if you would bring to my attention the legal provision to that effect." A month later, this exchange of letters was the subject of a discussion I had with former Chief Justices Meir Shamgar and Aharon Barak.

Media uproars of the kind created by Beinisch's letter do no good to the Supreme Court and certainly do not strengthen its standing. That seems to have been understood. I received an invitation to discuss the matter with Shamgar and Barak. We agreed to meet at my home, in part to avoid the media spotlight, but reports and film crews nevertheless staked out the entrance to my building. As always, the conversation with the two former chief justices was amiable. They told me that they had understood in their time that, as chief justices, they headed the judicial system, even though the law does not state that explicitly. I told them that my letter regarding the status of Chief Justice Beinisch was a response to her discourteous letter. I asked them whether either of them would have written such a letter to a justice minister. It was a rhetorical question, as the answer was quite clear.

We summed up the discussion in writing. The main point was recognizing the chief justice's position as head of the judicial system and of the justice minister's standing as responsible for the administration of the courts—all in keeping with the powers granted to them by law and in the spirit of a long tradition of mutual respect. Quite naturally, each of us preferred to stress the points he thought most important. For my part, I attributed little importance to matters of honor and had no difficulty with calling the chief justice the head of the judicial system. On the other hand, I was not prepared for that honorary title to grant the chief justice any powers that lawmakers had not granted her. That was the reason for the phrase "all in keeping with the powers granted to them by law." The decision to establish a new District Court, for example, comes under the sole authority of the minister of justice. That is what the law says. Likewise, the decision to locate the new court in Lod or any other city lies within the power of the justice minister, in consultation with other relevant government authorities.

To complete the picture, Aharon Barak approached Prime Minister Ehud Olmert soon after I entered office, proposing that he lead a commission to draft a proposal for the establishment of an independent Judicial Authority. I assume that this proposal was supported by other justices. Clearly, my opinion was required. I suspect that they believed that I would oppose the initiative and that this would provide grounds for attacking me. As such, they were no doubt astonished when I offered my full support. I was prepared to give up my own powers over the court system and hand them over to an appropriate body that would guarantee the independence of the courts, without subordinating them to the power of any single figure. I was not prepared, however, to refrain from using the authority granted the justice minister by law, or to use those powers only as directed by the chief justice. But after I had agreed to establish a commission chaired by Barak, it turned out that he was not interested, and the commission never came into being. I can only suppose that, in the end, Barak and Beinisch decided against such an independent authority, realizing that it would not provide the chief justice with all the powers they wished that post to have, and would mandate the establishment of oversight procedures and means of accepting responsibility for the system's slowness and dysfunction.

Less than two weeks after my meeting with Shamgar and Barak, interviews with me and Beinisch appeared in the press. I was interviewed by Orit Shohat and Ze'ev Segal of *Ha'aretz*. The headline was "Saving the Court from itself." The subhead read, in part, "Not a word about Dorit Beinisch." I presented my view that constraining the authority of the Supreme Court would actually strengthen it, and that the over-expansion of its judicial purview had actually hurt the court and shaken its standing. And, indeed, I said nothing at all critical of the chief justice. The previous evening, on August 16, 2007, *Globes* published an interview that Beinisch gave to Noam Sharvit in which she was quoted as saying that "the confrontations with the [justice] minister have distracted me ... not only from my work as a judge but also from plans I had ... he simply doesn't allow things to move." This despite the fact that she acknowledged, in the interview, that I established a new District Court and that I had obtained dozens of new judicial positions. In the first six months of my service, new judges had been appointed to all courts, including the Supreme Court. What was it that I was not allowing to move? The only specific item cited by Beinisch was the establishment of a Court of Appeals, a proposal that had been rejected by the Or Committee and which was unacceptable.* She also mentioned the need to transfer administrative cases from the Supreme Court to lower courts, but did not bother to mention that I had accepted this request and acted to remove a range of subjects from the Supreme Court's purview and transfer them to administrative courts. Her interview clearly did not accord with the understanding I had reached with Shamgar and Barak.

The next day Tzimuki reported in *Yedioth Ahronoth* that the truce that Barak and Shamgar had brokered between the chief justice and the justice minister seemed to have collapsed. "Unprecedentedly, Beinisch gave an interview and attacked the minister of justice," she wrote. The interview had shocked the entire legal system, "as chief justices have never granted interviews to the press while in office, with the exception of legal journals." Tzimuki suggested that Beinisch had decided to give the interview because she wanted to preempt my interview in *Ha'aretz*. But, the veteran legal correspondent noted, "Beinisch did not know that Friedmann had been careful to respect her."

The denouement of that month's saga was presented in two comprehensive articles that appeared in *Yedioth Ahronoth*'s weekend magazine. One was authored by a former president of the Jerusalem District Court, Vardi Zeiler. The headline was "Don't be fools—there is no defect in any of the proposals suggested by Daniel Friedmann that makes the discussion illegitimate." The article listed no less than

---

* The Supreme Court has long looked for ways to reduce its load, and a number of committees have been appointed to study the issue. One idea was to establish a Court of Appeals to hear appeals from the District Courts, with appeals allowed from that court to the Supreme Court only with special leave. The judges of the District and the Magistrates Courts strongly opposed this idea, which was not endorsed by any committee that dealt with the matter.

fifteen shortcomings in the legal system, among them protracted procedures, the courts' intervention in matters outside their purview while neglecting cases that do not grab headlines, the unhealthy concentration of power in the hands of a small group, and conditioning the promotion of a District Court judge to the Supreme Court on holding a temporary appointment to the high court first. He then presented my proposals, noting that none of them was unacceptable.

An opposing article was written by retired Justice Itzhak Zamir. It criticized each and every one of my proposals. I found no acknowledgment of the serious problems faced by the court system, with the exception of the vague "there is room for criticism of the legal system."

The media offensive against me also included a rash of articles and pronouncements by Aharon Barak, many of them in April 2008. They were notable for their extremism and use of apocalyptic language. An item in *Ha'aretz* on April 4, promoting an interview that would appear in the weekend edition, was headlined "Friedmann's initiatives are the beginning of the end of the legal system" (according to Barak). *Ma'ariv* told its readers that a "first-ever interview" with the former chief justice" would appear the following Friday. The headline was "Friedmann is turning us into a third-world country." The next day an article by Barak himself appeared in *Yedioth Ahronoth*, under the headline "The court is being destroyed before our eyes."

Simultaneous appearances in three newspapers may seem like overkill. Responses to the attack were not long in coming. Radio correspondent Eitam Lahover spoke on the air with newscaster Ya'akov Ahimeir: "The minister of justice hasn't had such a gratifying moment since entering office. He has won the sweeping support of dozens of members of the Bar Association's Tel Aviv and Central District Committees, as well as from former justice minister Yaakov Neeman, who has stood by him in the well-publicized debate between him and the justices of the Supreme Court." Commentator Ben-Dror Yemini was even more acerbic in an article that appeared in *Ma'ariv's* weekend magazine a few days later:

It is doubtful whether anyone is more guilty of the decline in the Supreme Court's position than Chief Justice Barak . . . According to all the polls, there is no other man who has caused such an ongoing, dramatic decline in public confidence [in the court] . . . Anyone looking for examples can find them in his megalomaniac declarations that "all is justiciable," in the legal revolution . . . But the ruins he left behind him are not enough. He continues his destructive campaign. "An attempt to put a pistol to the court's head," he said this week regarding Professor Daniel Friedmann's attempts to save the legal system. There is, of course, no connection, not even a weak one, between Friedmann's reform proposals and Barak's hysterical reactions.

I also responded, in an article entitled "Castle in the air" in *Yedioth Ahronoth*. I wrote that Barak had constructed a constitution for Israel out of nothing, endowing the Supreme Court with powers it had never before had, and had abolished accepted rules that had been in force for many long years. I cited the concerns voiced by former Chief Justice Moshe Landau about the court and Barak.

At about the time I became justice minister, the American jurist Richard Posner wrote a scathing review of Barak's book *The Judge in a Democracy*.[428] Posner, formerly a law professor and at the time a judge on the U.S. Federal Appeals Court, slammed Barak much more acerbically than anyone in Israel had done. He cited a character-ization of Barak by another prominent American jurist, Robert Bork, to the effect that the Israeli chief justice "establishes a world record for judicial hubris." In this he agreed with Chief Justice Landau, who claimed that the Supreme Court had lost its humility. Posner referred to Barak as an "enlightened despot," listing the powers that the Israeli Supreme Court had assumed for itself at Barak's inspiration. Posner wrote that while a state could grant such powers to its judges, "only in Israel . . . do judges confer the power of abstract review on themselves, without benefit of a con-stitutional or legislative provision . . . Such an approach can accurately be described as usurpative." Posner also called Barak a "legal buccaneer," saying that Barak took as a given that judges have vested authority to overrule laws. Barak's method of inter-preting legislation amounted to "using the statues themselves as first drafts that the court is free to rewrite." Posner's article was translated into Hebrew and published in *Yedioth Ahronoth.*

Barak Medina, a Hebrew University law professor, came to Barak's defense. In articles published in both Hebrew and English,[429] he charged that Posner did not understand the Israeli legal system. Posner himself had admitted that, but noted that, in his book, Barak was proposing a general theory of the judge in a democracy, one that Posner could not agree with.[430]

Posner's article had a huge impact. His carefully argued critique empowered Israeli critics of the expansion of the Supreme Court's power. Previously, any at-tempt to appraise Barak's innovations critically had been utterly delegitimized. In some cases, such as those of Neeman and Dror Hoter-Yishai, unjustified crimi-nal charges had even been filed against persons considered inimical to the legal revolution. As political scientist Shlomo Avineri put it when Barak repudiated the candidacy of Ruth Gavison, a potent critic of the law-enforcement system, for the Supreme Court: "Anyone who tries to raise doubts about the Supreme Court's powers may find that he is required to sacrifice, if not his life, then his future in the legal profession."[431]

Criticism of Barak and his legal doctrine had constantly been delegitimized by charging that it involved ulterior motives. At a swearing-in ceremony for new judges held just a few weeks after Posner's article was published, Chief Justice Beinisch de-clared: "Judges have become in large measure the targets of improper criticism . . . In recent years we have seen a deliberate tendency [to achieve] improper goals, aimed at placing the legal system in negative light. Those involved are seeking power and influence in the political arena, are suspect of having encounters with legal and court institutions and are thus seeking to weaken them, and are or were accused of crimes."

Up until this point, such delegitimization could place the critic out of bounds, or at least deter him from repeating his critique. Following Posner, that was no longer possible, and criticism was loudly voiced. Among the critics were leading intellectu-als and scholars such as Amnon Rubinstein, Shlomo Avineri, Shimon Shetreet, Ruth Gavison, and Yoav Dotan. They were joined by prominent figures in the media, arts, and legal profession, such as Boaz Okon, Gadi Taub, Amnon Dankner, Ben Caspit, Ben-Dror Yemini, and Moshe Gorali. To these should be added former Justice Minister Yaakov Neeman and attorneys such as Yiron Festinger and Haim Misgav, who had no hesitations about speaking to the media.

I enjoyed impressive public support, as could be seen in public opinion polls. Immediately following my appointment, when my opinions were well known, Arutz Sheva published a poll showing that 40 percent of the public supported my appointment, as against only 15 percent who were opposed. Two months later, *Globes* published a survey showing that 67 percent of Israel's lawyers supported me and only 17 percent were opposed. In September 2007, *Ma'ariv* published a public opinion survey including approval ratings for different government ministers. I came in second place, after Tzipi Livni, or third place if the occupants of other offices were included (Dalia Itzik, speaker of the Knesset, had a higher rating than I did). Ben Caspit explained that the figures showed that my campaign "did not lack public backing."

In January 2008, the readers of *Praklitim*, a magazine published by the Israel Bar Association, chose me as man of the year. Of the 2,790 lawyers who voted, 45 percent supported me. Beinisch received 29 percent. Half a year later, following Barak's volley of attacks on me, the Voice of Israel published a survey of its own. The question was who people preferred as justice minister—me, Gideon Sa'ar of Likud, or Ophir Pines-Paz of Labor. I received 31.1 percent, Sa'ar 19.9 percent, and Pines-Paz 16.8 percent.

The Court Today

Moderate Rulings, Radical Principles

The Olmert government came to an end at the beginning of 2009. Ehud Olmert left politics as a result of the legal proceedings against him. In the elections held later that year, his party, now led by Tzipi Livni, won twenty-eight seats in the Knesset, as compared to twenty-seven for Likud under Benjamin Netanyahu. The election results reflected Israel's political instability and the weakness of its largest parties, neither of which won even a quarter of the seats in parliament. Despite Kadima's one-seat advantage, it was Netanyahu who formed a government, with the support of the Haredi and right-wing parties. It was the second time that the legal system had, by forcing the resignation of a sitting prime minister, caused government to pass from the center to the right (the first time was when Yitzhak Rabin resigned in 1977 in the wake of the revelation of his foreign bank account). Netanyahu appointed Yaakov Neeman as his justice minister, reinstating him in the post he had been forced out of thirteen years previously by means of a trumped-up indictment. Neeman tried but failed, just as I had, to divide the attorney general's job into two, with the responsibility for prosecutions invested in a separate office. Because of the strong opposition of the legal system, neither was he able to institute an oversight mechanism for the state prosecution. The legal system again showed that it could block measures and legislation that it did not like, even when those proposals enjoyed public support and majorities in the cabinet and Knesset.

Prime Minister Netanyahu proved himself unwilling to endorse any such initiative if the attorney general opposed it. In fact, since returning to the prime minister's office in 2009, he has consistently avoided any steps that could be considered an attempt to restrain the powers of the legal system. It is unclear why. It may well be that he has not forgotten the criminal investigations he was subject to during his first term—the Bar-On–Hebron and Amadi affairs—when his political future lay in the hands of the legal system and hung by a hair. On top of that, Israel's political leaders have a deep and abiding faith that anyone who tries to act against the will of those dominating the legal system incurs serious personal risk. They are very much aware of the fate of those politicians who opposed legal activism. But there may be other considerations as well.

Nevertheless, Neeman did succeed in appointing an attorney general from the private sector, Yehuda Weinstein, following the utter failure of the search committee established for this purpose to carry out its mission. Weinstein was the first attorney general in thirty-five years who did not come to the job from public service or the academic world. Perhaps along with the fact that the political system did not attempt to curtail the powers the legal system had claimed for itself, after Weinstein's appointment, criminal procedures against public figures subsided. That did not affect Ehud Olmert, however. The investigations and trials against him did not abate, and the prosecution even appealed his acquittals.

Temporary appointments to the Supreme Court ceased, although the law allowing them remained in force. Neeman refused to serve as a rubber stamp for appointments that members of the Supreme Court sought. The result was a more balanced choice of new justices for the high court. One example was the appointment of Judge Neal Hendel. Chief Justice Dorit Beinisch, who had at first refused to give him even a temporary slot, now had no choice but to accept him on the court.

In 2013 Netanyahu won another election and formed his short-lived third government. Tzipi Livni, whose new Hatenua Party won only six seats in the Knesset, joined his coalition and returned to the justice ministry for two years. Under her watch, the attorney general agreed to the establishment of an internal oversight mechanism for the prosecution, a measure that did not require new legislation. Weinstein, however, complied only after he was assured that the oversight system would be established by means of administrative decisions instead of via legislation, that it would be put under his purview, and that the attorney general himself would be exempted from its supervision. Hila Gerstel, whom I had appointed president of the Central District Court, became the head of the overseeing office and has since issued reports highly critical of the state attorney's office. However, the watered-down mechanism, which she heads, faces great difficulties in doing its job, notably as the state attorneys virulently oppose it. They even imposed work sanctions to gain a change that would ensure that the oversight would not address the personal failures of any specific attorney. There is no doubt that legislation is needed, and the matter is still pending.

Plagued by dissention in his coalition, Netanyahu called elections again, for March 2015, and won them handily. His new coalition was based on his own Likud Party; the Haredi parties; Habayit Hayehudi (The Jewish Home), a right-wing religious party; and a single centrist faction. But all these parties together have only sixty-one Knesset seats, a razor-thin Knesset majority that makes it difficult for the government to function. The justice portfolio is now in the hands of Ayelet Shaked of Habayit Hayehudi, who is attempting to carry out significant reforms in the legal system. But given Netanyahu's reluctance, it is not clear what she will be able to accomplish.

Dorit Beinisch retired in early 2012, replaced by Asher Grunis. Chief Justice Grunis advocated a much more modest approach to judicial review in contrast to the judicial activism of his predecessor. The appointment of new justices with a broader range of views on the court's proper powers and role, along with the fact that it has now become legitimate to criticize the court, and even to do so sharply, has considerably curbed the court's activism.

I have already cited some decisions typical of this new approach, among them the judgment that imposed costs on petitioners who wanted the court to disqualify a candidate for the Israel Prize. The court's firm stand on the suit will no doubt limit, or even bring to an end, suits of this sort.[432] A suit that asked the court to void a law governing admissions committees in community settlements, which was passed in order to constrain the scope of the *Ka'adan* decision,[433] was also denied.[434] The Supreme Court also upheld the Boycott Law, which stipulates that anyone who knowingly issues a public call to boycott Israel, or a person or body because of their association with Israel, may be liable to civil suit. It did, however, void a section of the law under which courts could award damages even if the plaintiff had not proven that he suffered actual loss, while leaving the law as a whole with all its other provisions standing. In other words, the court recognized the state's right to defend itself. As Justice Hanan Melcer wrote in the majority opinion, "The law is included in the framework of the state self-defense doctrine."[435]

On the other side is the Supreme Court's ruling on amendments to the Prevention of Infiltration Act of 1954. The most significant and comprehensive of the amendments was passed in 2012, in response to a wave of Africans who were crossing Israel's border with Egypt's Sinai Peninsula. Their numbers soared, with more than 60,000 citizens of different African countries making their way illegally into Israel in the years 2006–2013. Many of them came from Sudan and Eritrea. The infiltrators themselves claimed that they were refugees, while the Israeli government claimed that most of them were entering Israel in search for work and improvement of their quality of life. Some of them were deported, while others left Israel under pressure to do so or in response to economic incentives offered them. An estimated 50,000 remained. They have concentrated in several places, among them southern Tel Aviv. The Israeli residents of the neighborhoods where large numbers of refugees live have suffered greatly. The flow of infiltrators was reduced to a trickle following the construction of a border fence, completed in 2012 at the cost of more than $270 million. The fence is hardly impenetrable, however, and, as such, it seems likely that the possibility of reaching Europe also contributed to the reduction of the number of infiltrators entering Israel. There is thus a risk that, as resistance to their entry into Europe grows, the number entering Israel will pick up.

Whatever the case, Israel's government has taken steps to reduce the motivation for entering Israel, embodied in amendments to the law. As might be expected, these amendments were challenged before the Supreme Court. The first ruling in this matter was handed down in September 2013 by a panel of nine justices. They voided most of the amendments, most importantly the one that empowered the state to hold infiltrators in custody (which the petitioners argued was tantamount to imprisonment) for up to three years without trial, so long as their cases were still under inquiry.[436] Following the ruling, the Knesset passed the amendment again after softening some of its provisions. The custody period was limited to one year and opened up the possibility that they could be held at an open facility, the Holot camp in the Negev desert, which they could enter and leave as they please so long as they reported back in at noon and in the evening. The law again reached the Supreme Court, which issued a new ruling in September 2014, a year after its first one. A majority of a panel of nine justices again voided the provision, over the dissensions of Chief Justice Grunis and Justice Hendel. The dissenting justices maintained, however, that the infiltrators should be required to report only once a day, in the evening, and should not be required to do so at noon as well. The court's ruling was widely criticized by political leaders, especially from the right.

Minister of the Interior Gideon Sa'ar, one of the architects of the new provisions and generally a supporter of the Supreme Court, was highly critical of the ruling. He demanded that Basic Law: Human Dignity and Liberty be amended, just as Basic Law: Freedom of Occupation had been amended to block the importation of nonkosher meat, when Rabin was prime minister. Such a move had the support of a majority in the Knesset, but Netanyahu, in keeping with his established policy, firmly opposed doing so. Instead, the Knesset yet again passed a revised version of the amendment to the Prevention of Infiltration Act. The amendment was challenged a third time before the Supreme Court, where the case was again heard by a panel of nine justices, this time headed by the new chief justice, Miriam Naor. The law, now much attenuated, permitted holding an infiltrator for a period of up to three months in custody and for twenty months in an open facility (meaning the Holot camp), where he would have to report in once a day. The ruling was handed down a year later, in August 2015. The court approved the three-month custody provision, a period that would be used to identify the infiltrator or to carry out procedures to remove him from Israel. But the open facility provision still seemed excessive to most of the justices. They voided it, but the majority opinion indicates that they would acquiesce in a term of one year rather than twenty months.[437]

However, the most important indication of the court's retreat from the extreme activism of the Aharon Barak and Dorit Beinisch eras came during Operation Protective Edge, Israel's operation in the Gaza Strip in the summer of 2014. While the operation lasted for forty-nine days, not a single petition regarding the conduct of the operation, nor any demand that Israel provide humanitarian aid to the residents of Gaza, was brought before the Supreme Court. This was an extremely positive development in comparison with the military operations conducted during the Barak and Beinisch periods. Apparently the citizens, human rights organizations, and Knesset members who had filed such petitions in the past, realized that they had no chance in the Grunis court. The only petitions were indirectly related to the military action. One demanded that the court instruct the Israel Broadcasting Authority to broadcast a commercial in which the names of the Palestinian children killed in the Gaza Strip were recited. The second demanded that the court order the government to fortify Bedouin settlements in the Negev against rocket attacks from the Gaza Strip. The court dismissed both suits.[438]

Another case had to do with terrorists who had been sentenced to prison in Israel. In the past, the Supreme Court had mandated that they receive a set of privileges, in keeping with the radical approach to human rights that the court had applied to them as well. During my term as justice minister, Israeli soldier Gilad Shalit was still languishing in Hamas captivity, where he received not a shred of the rights and dispensations enjoyed by Hamas prisoners in Israel. A ministerial committee I chaired formed a professional team to examine the conditions under which Hamas operatives were confined. The intention was to restrict the rights of members of terror organizations to the minimum required by international law. In the wake of our decision and the team's work, the Israel Prison Service stopped allowing security prisoners to take distance-learning courses with the Open University of Israel. A group of prisoners challenged the decision but lost their case in the District Court, after which they appealed to the Supreme Court. A panel composed of Chief Justice Asher Grunis and

Justices Hanan Melcer and Uri Shoham affirmed the District Court ruling, declaring: "We have found no rule, including in constitutional law, establishing the right of a prisoner to pursue higher education during his stay in prison." The justices also affirmed that treating security prisoners differently from criminals was legitimate and that it did not constitute invalid discrimination. The ruling was then confirmed by further hearing before a larger panel.[439]

Yet, while the court grew less radical in its rulings, it did not change any of the rules established by the revolutionary court that augmented the power of the legal system and expanded its authority. As a result, one still encounters, from time to time, rulings like that which required a local authority to give priority to the construction of a ritual bath (*mikveh*) over other public institutions.[440]

Another example of the far-reaching powers claimed by the Supreme Court relates to Knesset legislation that amended the Knesset Elections Law by raising the threshold for seats in the Knesset to 3.25 percent. Under Israel's proportional electoral system, a party must receive a certain minimum percentage of votes to gain seats in the Knesset. The threshold had originally been 1 percent, but it had been raised a number of times, and this was not the first time that such legislation had been challenged in court. It had happened when the Knesset raised the threshold from 1 to 1.5 percent, before the enactment of Basic Law: Human Dignity and Liberty. At that time, a panel of three justices denied the suit in a one-page ruling and imposed costs on the petitioner.[441] This time, prior to the 2015 elections, the suit was heard before a panel of nine justices who produced a judgment of no less than eighty pages. It was another example of how the court imposes on itself an unnecessary burden by agreeing to hear an issue that ought not be within its purview. Once a majority of the Knesset's members—meaning at least sixty-one*—had decided to raise the threshold, the court had no business meddling in it. In the event, a majority of the justices denied the suit, with Justice Salim Joubran remaining in the minority.[442] Nevertheless, all the justices insisted that the court had the authority to intervene in such a decision, on the basis of Basic Law: Human Dignity and Liberty—which itself had been voted into law, as described in chapter 22, by only thirty-two members of the Knesset.

To boil down this lengthy and gratuitous ruling, the justices were most concerned by the possibility that raising the threshold would result in denying Knesset representation to minorities, in particular the Arab minority. In fact, the election results showed that Arab representation was not hurt at all—actually, it increased. The three Arab parties, facing the prospect that alone each one would fail to reach 3.25 percent of the vote, united and ran as a single list. The case demonstrates that the court has become more modest about second-guessing laws passed by the Knesset, while nevertheless maintaining and even expanding its claim that, in principle, it may intervene in anything it wants to.

---

* The reason that the threshold legislation passed by a majority of more than sixty stems from the requirement of Section 4 of Basic Law: The Knesset, under which elections to the Knesset must be based on equality. This section, which is entrenched, provides that it can only be modified by a majority of Knesset members. The threshold provision is considered to be in conflict with the requirement of equality and hence the requirement that it be passed by a majority of over sixty.

The bottom line is that the Supreme Court remains, at least in theory, as powerful as it was in its most radical phase, and this despite the fact that the Knesset could easily strip it of its power to void laws and limit its jurisdiction on nonjusticiable issues. After all, the court bases its power on legislation, notably on Basic Law: Human Dignity and Liberty, and that law can be amended by a simple plurality vote in the Knesset.

The obvious question, then, is why the Knesset has not done so, despite the widespread dissatisfaction with the court's overweening power. There are a number of reasons. One is that Israeli governments are coalitions. The opposition of a single party in the governing coalition to a change in a constitutional matter can prevent it from happening. In Israel, even when the ruling party is a right-wing one that advocates reining in the Supreme Court, it generally brings a center or left-wing party into the coalition, and these parties generally advocate allowing the Supreme Court to retain the powers it has acquired for itself. Furthermore, despite the fact that many legislators oppose the Supreme Court's aggressive position, most Knesset members accept that it is right and proper for legislation to be subject to judicial review, within bounds. Some maintain that such review ought to be performed by a special constitutional court made up of judges chosen in a different way than other judges are. Another approach is that the Knesset ought to be allowed to override a Supreme Court decision to void a law, although there is disagreement about exactly how many votes should be required to do so.

Another factor that makes legal reform difficult is the fear of criminal proceedings. Politicians in Israel firmly believe that anyone who tries to restrain the prosecutors and courts may well find himself under criminal investigation. The fear is not paranoid—it is based on experience, which shows just how easy it is for some vague suspicion of breach of trust or financial irregularity to be dredged up from a politician's past. A criminal investigation, even if it does not go to trial, and a trial, even if it ends in acquittal, can drag on for so long and be so expensive for a public figure to defend himself from, and so damaging to his career, that most are deterred from proposing or supporting any reform that the system opposes. Furthermore, and ironically, the Supreme Court's move toward a more moderate use of the power it has taken itself has somewhat lowered the political motivation to repair the system.

One important change that has occurred is the judicial selection process. The only official modification that has been made is to raise the number of votes needed in the Judicial Selection Committee to name a judge to the Supreme Court. The composition of the committee has not changed. But the politicians involved in the process have become much more assertive. Justice ministers who have held the post since my own tenure no longer agree to make temporary appointments to the high court. This has, for all intents and purposes, ended a situation in which the sitting justices wielded almost exclusive power to fill the bench, although they still retain considerable influence.

From the Supreme Court's point of view, the situation is a sensitive one. It stands firm on retaining the dominance it has assumed for itself but is very much aware of how easy it would be for the Knesset to strip it of that power. It has to walk a fine line between the principles it proclaims and the fear that rulings that elected officials and the public fiercely oppose may impel the Knesset to pull the rug out from under the Supreme Court's excessive power. This may explain why the court refrained from striking down legislation that allows the government to deny Palestinians from the territories who have married Israeli citizens from receiving the rights of citizenship or residency in the country. Recall that Chief Justice Aharon Barak insisted that such marriages should automatically qualify Palestinians for such rights.[443] In addition, voices on the court itself are now expressing doubts about excessive activism, a sentiment unheard of on the Barak court, although they remain in minority. One such voice was that of Chief Justice Grunis, who retired in January 2015, to be replaced, in accordance with the seniority system, by Miriam Naor. At a ceremony held in his honor in June of that year, retired Justice Eliezer Rivlin, who had served as deputy chief justice under Beinisch, addressed the issue. He praised the prudential rules developed by American courts that keep them from overstepping their bounds. One of these is the rule regarding standing to petition the courts (the revolutionary court in Israel eliminated this requirement and allowed anyone to petition the courts about anything). Another such rule prevents the courts from judging matters of policy. Rivlin also praised Grunis's opposition to unrestrained use of the concept of reasonableness as grounds for intervening in the decisions of other branches of government. "It is worth reconsidering," he said,

> the mistaken assumption that establishing more elastic threshold conditions and expanding the scope of justiciability empowers the court. The contrary is true— threshold mechanisms, filtering mechanisms, are tools that have been provided to the courts in order to protect them from intervening in highly controversial matters, from intervention in matters assigned to the other branches of government.

This is the current, uncomfortable, status quo. The legal rules restricting the Supreme Court's ability to second-guess the other branches of government have been eliminated, but the court exercises care in wielding the excess power that it retains. That is hardly ideal, but it is better than the situation under the revolutionary court, which daily brandished powers that the court should never have been allowed to acquire in the first place.

Notes

1. The English text of the law can be found at: http://www.israellawresourcecenter. org/israellaws/fulltext/lawandadministrationord.htm.
2. DANIEL FRIEDMANN, THE EFFECT OF FOREIGN LAW ON THE LAW OF ISRAEL 19, 46–47 (1975).
3. THEODOR HERZL, HERZL'S WRITINGS: THE JEWISH STATE Vol. A 68 (S. Perlman trans.,) (Isr.) (1953). An English translation is available at: http://www.zionism-israel.com/js/Jewish_State_29.html.
4. *Id.* at 229–38. An English translation is available at: http://tinyurl.com/pxzackk.
5. Daniel Friedmann, *The "Unmarried Wife" in Israeli Law*, 2 ISRAEL YEARBOOK ON HUMAN RIGHTS 287 (1972).
6. CA 135/68 Bareli v. Director of Estate Duty 23(1) PD 393 [1969] (Isr.).
7. Mil. Court MR 3/57 The Military Prosecution v. Major Malinsky 17 PSM 90 [1958] (Isr.).
8. For more information about the massacre and trial, *see* DANIEL FRIEDMANN, BEFORE THE REVOLUTION—LAW & POLITICS IN THE AGE OF INNOCENCE 243–53 (2015) (Isr.).
9. YITZHAK RABIN & DOV GOLDSTEIN, PINKAS SHERUT [SERVICE NOTEBOOK] 549–51 (1979) (Isr.); MICHAEL BAR-ZOHAR, AS THE PHOENIX: SHIMON PERES—THE BIOGRAPHY 428–33 (2006) (Isr.).
10. *See* Yair Sagy, *Supreme Authority: On the Establishment of the Supreme Court of Israel*, 44 MISHPATIM 7 (2013) (Isr.) (for further discussion of the matter, including the minutes of the justices' meeting where the issue was discussed).
11. CrimA 118/53 Manderlbrot v. The Attorney General 10 PD 281 [1956] (Isr.); CrimA 186/55 Mizan v. The Attorney General 11 OD 769 [1957] (Isr.); MIRIAM BEN-PORAT, THROUGH THE ROBE 63 (Shachar Alterman ed.) (2010) (Isr.).
12. Nir Keidar, *Ben-Gurion and the Battle to Appoint a Sephardi Justice to the Supreme Court*, 19 MECHKAREY MISHPAT [LEGAL RES.] 515 (2002) (Isr.).
13. HCJ 64/51 Daud v. The Defense Minister 5 PD 1117 [1951] (Isr.).
14. HCJ 329/51 Daud v. The Security Areas Appeal Committee 6 PD 229 [1952] (Isr.); HCJ 840/97 Sabit v. The Israeli Government 57(4) PD 803 [2003] (Isr.); HCJ (further hearing) 6354/03 Sabit v. The Israeli Government (June 18, 2004), Nevo Legal Database (by subscription) (Isr.).
15. HCJ 10/48 Ziv v. Gubernick 1 PD 85 [1948] (Isr.).
16. HCJ 7/48 Karbutali v. The Defense Minister 2 PD 5 [1949] (Isr.).

17. HCJ 98/69 Bergman v. The Finance Minister 23(1) PD 693 [1969] (Isr.). An English
    • translation is available at: http://elyon1.court.gov.il/files_eng/69/980/000/Z01/
    69000980.z01.pdf.
18. Ibid., p. 4.
19. Ibid., p. 10.
20. HCJ 186/65 Reiner v. The Prime Minister 19(2) PD 485 [1965] (Isr.).
21. HCJ 73/53 Kol Ha'am v. The Minister of Interior 7 PD 871 [1953] (Isr.).
22. HCJ 144/50 Scheib v. The Defense Minister 5 PD 399, 407 [1951] (Isr.).
    An English translation is available at: http://elyon1.court.gov.il/files_eng/50/
    440/001/Z01/50001440.z01.pdf, p. 10.
    The decision reiterated a ruling rendered shortly after the establishment of the
    State which held that in the absence of legislative authorization the executive is not
    entitled to prevent a person from working in the profession of his choice: HCJ 1/49
    Bejerano v. Minister of Police 1 PE 121 [1949] (Isr.). These decisions were precur-
    sors of the Basic Law: Freedom of Occupation enacted in 1992 (replaced in 1994).
23. HCJ 262/62 Peretz v. The Chairman of the Local Council & Population of Kfar
    Shamnryahu 16 PD 2101 [1962] (Isr.).
24. HCJ 143/62 Funk-Schlesinger v. The Minister of Interior 17 PD 225 [1963] (Isr.).
25. However, when both partners are Jewish Israel citizens who were married abroad
    in civil marriage, the Rabbinical Court has the authority to dismantle the mar-
    riage: HCJ 2232/03 Ploni v. The Tel-Aviv-Yaffo Regional Rabbinical Court 61(3)
    PD 496 [2006] (Isr.).
26. CrimA 217/68 Isramax v. The State of Israel 22(2) PD 343 [1968] (Isr.).
27. HCJ 72/62 Rufeisen v. The Minister of Interior 16 PD 2428 [1962] (Isr.).
28. HCJ 58/68 Shalit v. The Minister of Interior 23(2) PD 477 [1970] (Isr.).
29. An English translation is available at: http://www.mfa.gov.il/mfa/mfa-archive/
    1950-1959/pages/law%20of%20return%205710-1950.aspx.
30. HCJ 18/72 Shalit v. The Minister of Interior 26(1) PD 334 [1972] (Isr.). For further
    discussion, see below.
31. An English translation is available at: http://www.mfa.gov.il/mfa/mfa-archive/
    1950-1959/pages/law%20of%20return%205710-1950.aspx.
32. ElecA 1/65 Yeredor v. The Chairman of the Central 16th Knesset Elections
    Committee 19(3) PD 365 [1965] (Isr.).
33. HCJ 253/64 Jiryis v. The Haifa District Commissioner 18(4) PD 673 [1964] (Isr.).
34. HCJ 5666/03 Kav Laoved v. The National Labor Court in Jerusalem (Oct. 10, 2007),
    Nevo Legal Database (by subscription) (Isr.).
35. HCJ 390/79 Duikat v. The State of Israel 34(1) PD 1 [1979] (Isr.).
36. HCJ 285/81 Al Nazar v. Commander of Judas and Samaria 36(1) PD 701 [1982]
    (Isr.).
37. HCJ 4481/91 Bargil v. The State of Israel 47(4) PD 210 [1993] (Isr.).
38. Moshe Sharett, Personal Journal Vol. 2 510, 518 (1978) (Isr.).
39. CrimA 2321/55 The Attorney General v. Gruenwald 12 PD 2017 [1958] (Isr.).
40. CrimA 232/55 The Attorney General v. Gruenwald 13 PD 2189 [1958] (Isr.).
41. Amir Oren, *Investigations on Top—From the Dayan Precedent to the Katsav Affair*,
    Ha'aretz, May 13, 2011 (Isr.).
42. Details about the affair can also be found in Yechiel Gutman, A Storm in the GSS—
    The Attorney General versus the Government from the Tubiansky Affair

TO THE BUS 300 AFFAIR 393–406 (1995) (Isr.); NOMI LEVITSKY, YOUR HONOR—
AHARON BARAK, BIOGRAPHY 141–46 (2001) (Isr.); YOSSI DAR, AHARON BARAK & THE
PLEASURES OF THE RULE OF LAW 33–113 (2002) (Isr.); BARUCH LESHEM, ZIGEL—THE
FULL STORY OF THE CORRUPTION INVESTIGATIONS 78–101 (1988) (Isr.).

43. ASHER YADLIN, TESTIMONY 21 (1980) (Isr.).

44. OR 290/76 Yadlin v. The State of Israel 31(1) PD 671, 672 [1976] (Isr.).

45. ASHER YADLIN, TESTIMONY 54 (1980) (Isr.) (where Yadlin refers to the foundation available to Sharett); *see also* MOSHE SHARETT, PERSONAL JOURNAL Vol. 3 843
(1978) (Isr.).

46. YITZHAK RABIN & DOV GOLDSTEIN, PINKAS SHERUT [SERVICE NOTEBOOK] 556
(1979) (Isr.).

47. *Id.*

48. YECHIEL GUTMAN, A STORM IN THE GSS—THE ATTORNEY GENERAL VERSUS THE
GOVERNMENT FROM THE TUBIANSKY AFFAIR TO THE BUS 300 AFFAIR 413–14
(1995) (Isr.); NOMI LEVITSKY, YOUR HONOR—AHARON BARAK, BIOGRAPHY 148
(2001) (Isr.).

49. YITZHAK RABIN & DOV GOLDSTEIN, PINKAS SHERUT [SERVICE NOTEBOOK] 556
(1979) (Isr.).

50. CrimA 234/77 Yadlin v. The State of Israel 32(1) PD 31 [1977] (Isr.).

51. YITZHAK RABIN & DOV GOLDSTEIN, PINKAS SHERUT [SERVICE NOTEBOOK] 560
(1979) (Isr.). A detailed description of the meeting with Rabin can also be found
in NOMI LEVITSKY, YOUR HONOR—AHARON BARAK, BIOGRAPHY 157 (2001) (Isr.)
(according to which Barak also directly spoke with Leah Rabin).

52. CrimA 767/76 The State of Israel v. Maman 31(2) PD 673 [1977] (Isr.).

53. YITZHAK RABIN & DOV GOLDSTEIN, PINKAS SHERUT [SERVICE NOTEBOOK] 561
(1979) (Isr.).

54. YOSSI DAR, AHARON BARAK & THE PLEASURES OF THE RULE OF LAW 127 & n. 137
in p. 411 (2002) (Isr.).

55. NOMI LEVITSKY, YOUR HONOR—AHARON BARAK, BIOGRAPHY 161–62 (2001)
(Isr.).

56. ARIEL BENDOR & ZE'EV SEGAL, THE HAT MAKER—DISCUSSIONS WITH JUSTICE
AHARON BARAK 219–20 (2009) (Isr.).

57. LEAH RABIN, STEPPING IN HIS PATH 181–82 (Amos Carmel ed.) (1997) (Isr.).

58. OrderA 6/77 Mizrahi v. The State of Israel 31(3) PD 265, 269 [1977] (Isr.).

59. LEAH RABIN, HIS WIFE ALL THE TIME 214 (1988) (Isr.). Leah Rabin repeated the
argument that the case against Abba Even was closed because "no one politically
targeted him" in her book STEPPING IN HIS PATH 182 (1997) (Isr.).

60. NOMI LEVITSKY, YOUR HONOR—AHARON BARAK, BIOGRAPHY 241 (2001) (Isr.).

61. HCJ 194/93 Segev v. The Foreign Minister 49(5) PD 57 (1995) (Isr.).

62. CrimA 308/75 Pesachowitz v. The State of Israel 31(2) PD 449 [1977] (Isr.).

63. HCJ 852/86 Aloni v. The Justice Minister 41(2) PD 3 [1987] (Isr.).

64. HCJ 448/87 Nakash v. The Justice Minister 41(2) PD 813 [1987] (Isr.).

65. CrimA 6182/98 Sheinbein v. The Attorney General 53(1) PD 625 [1999] (Isr.).

66. David Weiner, *All Israel Is Responsible for Each Other—Between Extradition and
Jewish Commitment, in* DAVID WEINER BOOK 219, 220 (Dror Arad-Ayalon, Yoram
Rabin, Yaniv Vaki, Maya Rapaport eds.) (2009) (Isr.).

67. CrimA 173/75 The State of Israel v. Ben-Zion 30(1) PD 119 [1975] (Isr.).

68. HCJ 387/76 Ben-Zion v. The Police Minister 31(1) PD 484 [1976] (Isr.).

69. Nomi Levitsky, Your Honor—Aharon Barak, Biography 201 (2001) (Isr.).

70. An English translation of the Kahan Commission Report is available at: http:// www.mfa.gov.il/mfa/foreignpolicy/mfadocuments/yearbook6/pages/104%20 report%20of%20the%20commission%20of%20inquiry%20into%20the%20e.aspx.

71. Dov Weissglas, Arik Sharon, Prime Minister—A Personal Outlook 38–51 (Rami Tal ed.) (2012) (Isr.).

72. Nomi Levitsky, Your Honor—Aharon Barak, Biography 220 (2001) (Isr.).

73. HCJ 389/80 Dapey Zahav Ltd. v. The Israel Broadcasting Association 35(1) PD 421 [1981] (Isr.).

74. Nomi Levitsky, The Supremes—Inside the Supreme Court 78–79 (2006) (Isr.).

75. This is what happened with the justiciability issue discussed in HCJ 910/86 Ressler v. Minister of Defense 42(2) PD 441, 446 [1988] (Isr.) regarding the army draft of *yeshiva* students, an issue that will be discussed in chapter 9. Barak was also left in minority in HCJ 428/86 Barzilay v. The Government of Israel 40(3) PD 505 [1986] (Isr.) regarding the president's authority to pardon, another issue that will be discussed in chapter 10.

76. Nat'l Labor Court 53/3-160 El Al Israeli Airlines Ltd. v. Danilowitz PDA 26:339 [1993] (Isr.).

77. HCJ 721/94 El Al Israeli Airlines Ltd. v. Danilowitz 48(5) PD 749 [1994] (Isr.).

78. Aharon Barak, *The Constitutional Revolution: Protected Basic Rights*, 1 Law & Governance 9 (1992) (Isr.).

79. CA 6821/93 Mizrahi Bank v. Migdal Kfar Shitufi 49(4) PD 221 [1995] (Isr.).

80. DK [*Divrey Knesset*—Knesset Proceedings] 144a (1995) 5246 (Isr.).

81. DK 125 (1992) 3783 (Isr.).

82. Amnon Rubinstein, *The Tales of the Basic Laws*, 14 L. & Bus. J. 79 (2012) (Isr.).

83. DK 154 (1996) 4478 (Isr.); Gideon Sapir, The Constitutional Revolution, Past, Present, Future 70–80 (2010).

84. Elections Appeal 2/84 Neiman v. Chairman of the Central Elections Committee for the 11th Knesset 39(2) PD 225 [Decision from 28.6.84, written verdict was given on May 2005] (Isr.).

85. HCJ 253/64 Jiryis v. The Haifa District Commissioner 18(4) PD 673 [1964] (Isr.).

86. Elections Appeal 1/88 Neiman v. Chairman of the Central Elections Committee for the 12th Knesset 42(4) PD 177 [1988] (Isr.); Elections Appeal 2858/92 Movshowitz v. Chairman of the Central Elections Committee for the 13th Knesset 46(3) PD 541 [1992] (Isr.).

87. Elections Appeal 2/88 Ben Shalom v. The Central Elections Committee 43(4) PD 221 [1989] (Isr.).

88. Elections Approval 11280/02 The Central Elections Committee v. Tibi 57(4) PD 1 [2003] (Isr.).

89. Barak Medina, *40 Years to the Yeredor Case: The Rule of Law, The Law of Nature and the Limits to the Legitimate Discourse in a Jewish and Democratic State*, 22 Law Studies 327, 370 (2006) (Isr.).

90. HCJ 11225/03 Bishara v. The Attorney General 60(4) PD 287 [2006] (Isr.).

91. The decision is from February 18, 2015. The detailed decision was rendered some 10 months later: Elections Approval 1095/15 The Central Elections Committee for the 20th Knesset v. Zoabi (Dec. 10, 2015), Nevo Legal Database (by subscription) (Isr.).

92. HCJ 40/70 Becker v. The Minister of Defense 24(1) PD 238, 246 [1970] (Isr.). An English translation is available at: http://elyon1.court.gov.il/files_eng/86/100/009/Z01/86009100.z01.pdf.

93. HCJ 910/86 Ressler v. The Minister of Defense 42(2) PD 441, 464 [1988] (Isr.).

94. HCJ 1635/90 Zharzhevsky v. The Prime Minister 45(1) PD 749, 766 [1991] (Isr.).

95. HCJ 2148/94 Gelbart v. The Chairman of the Hebron Massacre Investigation Committee 48(3) PD 573, 600 [1994] (Isr.).

96. HCJ 3267/97 Rubinstein v. The Minister of Defense 52(5) PD 481 [1998] (Isr.).

97. HCJ 6427/02 The Movement for Quality Government in Israel v. The Knesset 61(1) PD 619 [2006] (Isr.).

98. HCJ 6298/07 Ressler v. The Knesset (Feb. 21, 2012), Nevo Legal Database (by subscription) (Isr.).

99. A detailed description of the affair can be found in Yechiel Gutman's book, *A Storm in the GSS*, and in Ilan Rachum's book, *Parashat Ha-Shabak* [The Shin bet affair]. The affair is also portrayed in Gidi Weitz and Nadav Asael's film, *A, Take Them Down*.

100. Joel Markus, *It Need to Be Seen Alright*, HA'ARETZ, June 24, 1986 (Isr.); ILAN RACHUM, PARASHAT HA-SHABAK [THE SHIN BET AFFAIR] 76–78 (Carmel 1990) (Isr.).

101. HCJ 4723/96 Avivit Atiyah v. The Attorney General 51(3) PD 714, 732 [1997] (Isr.).

102. YECHIEL GUTMAN, A STORM IN THE GSS 77–78 (Yedioth Ahronoth 1995) (Isr.).

103. HCJ 177/50 Reuben v. The Chairman and the Members of the Legal Counsel 5 PD 737, 751 [1951] (Isr.).

104. HCJ (further hearing) 13/60 The Attorney General v. Matana 16 PD 430, 469 [1962] (Isr.).

105. HCJ 428/86 Barzilay v. The Government of Israel 40(3) PD 505 [1986] (Isr.).

106. *See also* NOMI LEVITSKY, YOUR HONOR—AHARON BARAK, BIOGRAPHY 195 (2001) (Isr.).

107. The two affairs are linked in both the Landau Report and in Ilan Rachum's book, *Parashat Ha-Shabak* [THE SHIN BET AFFAIR], which discusses both.

108. CrimA 124/87 Nafso v. The Military Advocate General 41(2) PD 631 [1987] (Isr.).

109. Igal Sarna & Anat Tal-Shir, *Nafso Speaks Out*, YEDIOTH AHRONOTH, May 29, 1987 & June 2, 1987.

110. COMMISSION OF INQUIRY INTO THE METHODS OF INVESTIGATION OF THE GENERAL SECURITY SERVICE REGARDING HOSTILE TERRORIST ACTIVITY (1987) (Isr.). An English translation available at: http://www.hamoked.org/TimelineFramesPage.aspx?returnID=timelinetorture&pageurl=http://www.hamoked.org/Document.aspx?dID=Documents1643%22, p. 1.

111. Ibid., pp. 10–11.

112. Ibid., p. 33.

113. Ibid., p. 34.

114. HCJ 88/88 Nafso v. The Attorney General 42(3) PD 425 [1988] (Isr.).

115. The Landau Commission Report, above note 110, at 71-72.

116. Mordechai Kremnitzer & Re'em Segev, *The Use of Force in Shin Bet Interrogations—The Lesser Evil?*, 4 MISHPAT VE-MIMSHAL [L. & GOV'T] 667 [1998] (Isr.); Daniel Statman, *The Question of Absolute Morality Regarding the Prohibition of Torture*, 4 MISHPAT VE-MIMSHAL [L. & GOV'T] 161 [1998] (Isr.).

117. HCJ 5100/94 The Public Committee Against Torture v. The State of Israel 53(4) PD 817 [1999] (Isr.). An English translation is available at: http://elyon1.court. gov.il/files_eng/94/000/051/a09/94051000.a09.pdf, p. 23.

118. *Cf.* Meir Dan Cohen, *Decision Rules and Conduct Rules: On Acoustic Separation in Criminal Law*, (1984) 97 HARV. L. REV. 625 (1984).

119. MICHAL SHAKED, MOSHE LANDAU – JUDGE 532 (2012) (ISR.).

120. HCJ 320/80 Kawasama v. Minister of Defense 35(3) PD 113 [1980] (Isr.).

121. *Id.*

122. NOMI LEVITSKY, YOUR HONOR—AHARON BARAK, BIOGRAPHY 183–188 (2001) (Isr.).

123. HCJ 5973/92 The Association of Civil Rights in Israel v. The Minister of Defense 47(1) PD 268, 289 [1993] (Isr.).

124. CrimA 281/82 Abuhatssira v. The State of Israel 37(3) PD 673 [1983] (Isr.).

125. HCJ 3094/93 The Movement for Quality Government in Israel v. The Government of Israel 47(5) PD 404 [1993] (Isr.).

126. HCJ 4267/93 AMITI—Citizens for a Proper Governance and Integrity v. The Prime Minister of Israel 47(5) PD 441 [1993] (Isr.).

127. My correspondance with Dan Avi-Yitzhak, May, 20, 2012 (Isr.).

128. CrimC (Jer) 305/93 The State of Israel v. Deri 1999(1) PM 10 [1993] (Isr.).

129. CrimA 3575/99 Deri v. The State of Israel 54(2) PD 721 [2000] (Isr.).

130. CrimA (Further Hearing) 5576/00 Deri v. The State of Israel 54(3) PD 601 [2000] (Isr.).

131. HCJ 6302/01 Deri v. The Attorney General 56(6) PD 725 [2002] (Isr.).

132. Re-Trial 8483/00 Deri v. The State of Israel 57(4) PD 253 [2003] (Isr.).

133. Noam Sharvit, *Adv. Yigal Arnon to "Globes": Aryeh Deri Was Marked. They Decided to Convict Him at Any Price*, GLOBES, Feb. 5, 2007.

134. CrimC (Jer) 1872/99 The State of Israel v. Deri 25 Dinim Shalom 227 [2003] (Isr.).

135. AdminA (Jer) 8774/08 Deri v. The Jerusalem Municipal Election Administration (unpublished Oct. 2, 2008) (Isr.).

136. The facts of the affair are summarized in a brief submitted on April 18, 1997, by State Attorney Edna Arbel to Attorney General Elyakim Rubinstein.

137. HCJ 237/97 Pines v. The Israeli Prime Minister (unpublished Mar. 3, 1997) (Isr.). The chain of events is described in Ze'ev Segal's article, *Hovering Shadows over the Rule of Law*, 4 MISHPAT VE-MIMSHAL [L. & GOV'T] 587, 593 (1998) (Isr.).

138. The full text of the report is quoted in Ze'ev Segal's article, *Hovering Shadows over the Rule of Law*, 4 MISHPAT VE-MIMSHAL [L. & GOV'T] 587, 597-598 (1998) (Isr.).

139. HCJ 2534/97 Yona Yahav v. The State Attorney 51(3) PD 1 [1997] (Isr.).

140. Labor ran a joint slate with some smaller factions under the name of One Israel (Yisra'el Ahat).

141. A number of private individuals filed petitions against the prime minister conducting these negotiations. The petitions were denied: HCJ 5167/00 Weiss v. The Prime Minister 55(2) PD 455 [2001] (Isr.). The case is discussed in Chapter 17.

142. An English translation of the Or Report is available at: http://www.jewishvirtual-library.org/jsource/Society_&_Culture/OrCommissionReport.html.

143. For example: HCJ 721/94 El Al Israeli Airlines Ltd. v. Danilowitz 48(5) PD 749 [1994] (Isr.).

144. HCJ 153/87 Shakdiel v. The Minister of Religious Affairs 42(2) PD 221 [1988] (Isr.).

145. HCJ 58/68 Shalit v. The Minister of Interior 23(2) PS 477 [1970] (Isr.).

146. HCJ 72/62 Rufeisen v. The Minister of Interior 16(4) PD 2428 [1962] (Isr.).

147. HCJ 2859/99 Makarina v. The Minister of Interior 59(6) PD 721 [2005] (Isr.).

148. CA 448/72 Shik v. The Attorney General 27(2) PD 3, 6 [1973] (Isr.).

149. CA 653/75 Shelach v. The State of Israel 31(2) PD 421 [1977] (Isr.).

150. CC (TA) 25477-05-11 Yoram Kaniuk v. The Minister of Interior (Sept. 27, 2011), Nevo Legal Database (by subscription) (Isr.); HCJ 7489/11 Yoram Kaniuk v. The Minister of Interior (Dec. 25, 2011), Nevo Legal Database (by subscription) (Isr.).

151. HCJ 147/70 Staderman v. The Minister of Interior 24(1) PD 766 [1970] (Isr.).

152. Translation: The New JPS Translation according to the Traditional Hebrew Text, p. 598. The different names for the Jewish people are at the center of the book, MEIR STERNBERG, HEBREWS BETWEEN CULTURES: GROUP PORTRAITS AND NATIONAL LITERATURE (1998).

153. *See* URI AVNERY, OPTIMISTIC 152–81 (2014) (Isr.), for a detailed discussion regarding Canaanites and the attempt to distinct between "Jewish" and "Hebrew."

154. CA 630/70 Temerin v. The State of Israel 26(1) PD 197 [1972] (Isr.).

155. CA 8537/08 Ornan v. The Ministry of Interior (Oct. 2, 2013), Nevo Legal Database (by subscription) (Isr.).

156. *See* Chapters 1 & 2.

157. CAP 8256/99 Plonit v. Ploni 58(2) PD 213 [2003] (Isr.).

158. HCJ 3045/05 Ben Ari v. The Director of the Population Administration in the Ministry of Interior 61(3) PD 537 [2006] (Isr.).

159. HCJ 807/78 Ein Gal v. The Film and Play Review Board 33(1) PD 274 [1979] (Isr.).

160. HCJ 4804/94 Station Film Co. Inc. v. The Film Review Board 50(5) PD 661 [1996] (Isr.).

161. HCJ 4804/94 Station Film Co. Inc. v. The Film Review Board 50(5) PD 661 [1996] (Isr.). For an English translation, *see* http://elyon1.court.gov.il/files_eng/94/040/048/Z01/94048040.z01.pdf, p. 18.

162. HCJ 243/62 Israel Filming Studios Inc. v. Gary & The Film and Play Review Board 16 PD 2407 [1962] (Isr.).

163. HCJ 316/03 Bakri v. The Film Review Board 58(1) PD 249 [2003] (Isr.).

164. An English translation is available at: http://elyon1.court.gov.il/files_eng/03/160/003/L15/03003160.l15.pdf, p. 13.

165. An English translation is available at: http://elyon1.court.gov.il/files_eng/03/160/003/L15/03003160.l15.pdf, p. 22.

166. Ibid., p. 25.

167. HADASSA BEN-ITTO, THE LIE WOULDN'T DIE: THE PROTOCOLS OF THE ELDERS OF ZION (2005).

168. CA 8345/08 Ben Natan v. Bakri (July 27, 2011), Nevo Legal Database (by subscription) (Isr.).

169. *See* CA 8954/11 Ploni v. Plonit (Apr. 24, 2014), Nevo Legal Database (by subscription) (Isr.), in which the court enjoined the publication of a book that infringed the plaintiff's privacy.

170. HCJ 4541/94 Miller v. The Defense Minister 49(4) PD 94 [1995] (Isr.).

171. HCJ 6698/05 Ka'adan v. Israel Lands Administration 54(1) PD 258 [2000] (Isr.).

172. Brown v. Board of Education of Topeka, 347 U.S. 483 (1954).

173. HCJ 528/88 Avitan v. Israel Lands Administration 43(4) PD 297 [1989] (Isr.).

174. HCJ 114/78 Burkan v. The Treasury Minister 32(2) PD 800 [1978] (Isr.); Shimon Shitrit, *The Ruling in the Ka'adan Case Wasn't Necessary*, NEWS 1, http://www.news1.co.il/Archive/003-D-2714-00.html.

175. HCJ 2311/11 Sabach v. The Knesset (Sept. 17, 2014), Nevo Legal Database (by subscription) (Isr.).

176. HCJ 156/56 Shor v. The Attorney General 11 PD 285 [1957] (Isr.); Justice Shamgar was willing to expand the judicial review to cases in which there was a substantial distortion on justice: HCJ 665/79 Vinograd v. The Attorney General 34(2) PD 634, 641 [1980] (Isr.).

177. HCJ 329/81 Nof v. The Attorney General 37(4) PD 326, 334 [1983] (Isr.).

178. Preceding this case was another case which, by majority opinion, compelled the attorney general to order the police to investigate claims about a *sub-judice* offense concerning newspaper reports describing John Demianiuk's ongoing trial. The reporter was subsequently indicted and convicted in court, but won on appeal: HCJ 223/88 Sheftel v. The Attorney General 43(4) PD 356 [1989] (Isr.).

179. HCJ 425/89 Tzufan v. The Chief Military Advocate General 43(4) PD 718 [1989] (Isr.).

180. HCJ 935/89 Ganor v. The Attorney General 44(2) PD 485 [1990] (Isr.).

181. CrimA 2910/94 Yeffet v. The State of Israel 50(2) PD 221 [1996] (Isr.).

182. HCJ 6781/96 Olmert v. The Attorney General 50(4) PD 793 [1996] (Isr.). *See also* HCJ 1563/96 Katz v. The Attorney General 55(1) PD 529 [2001] (Isr.).

183. CrimC (TA) 329/96 The State of Israel v. Olmert, PM 1997(3) 46 [1997] (Isr.).

184. HCJ 5675/04 The Movement for Quality Government in Israel v. The Attorney General 59(1) PD 199, 209 [2004] (Isr.) (Justice Eliyahu Matza).

185. HCJ 5699/07 Ploni (A) v. The Attorney General 62(3) PD 550 [2008] (Isr.).

186. CrimC (TA) 1015/09 The State of Israel v. Katsav, PM 2010(4) 282 [2011] (Isr.).

187. CrimA 3372/11 Katsav v. The State of Israel (Nov. 10, 2011), Nevo Legal Database (by subscription) (Isr.).

188. Dan Avi-Yitzhak, *Beginning with Sharon and Ended with Olmert*, 6 THE LAWYER [ORECH HADIN] 16, 20 (2010) (Isr.).

189. *See also* HCJ 957/89 Tzadik v. The Israel Bar Association 44(2) PD 431 [1990] (Isr.); CrimFH 9384/01 Al Nisasra v. The Israel Bar Association 59(4) PD 637 [2004] (Isr.).

190. HCJ 6163/92 Eizenberg v. The Minister of Construction 47(2) PD 229 [1993] (Isr.).

191. HCJ 8794/03 Hess v. The Chief Military Advocate General (Dec. 23, 2008), Nevo Legal Database (by subscription) (Isr.).

192. HCJ 5757/04 Hess v. The Deputy Chief of Staff 59(6) PD 97 [2005] (Isr.).

193. HCJ 1284/99 Ploni v. The Chief of Staff 53(2) PD 62 [1999] (Isr.).

194. HCJ 8707/10 Hess v. The Defense Minister (Feb. 3, 2011), Nevo Legal Database (by subscription) (Isr.).

195. CrimA 4148/98 The State of Israel v. Ganot 50(5) PD 367 [1996] (Isr.).

196. HCJ 8134/11 Asher v. The Minister of Finance (Jan. 29, 2012), Nevo Legal Database (by subscription) (Isr.).

197. *See* YOSSI SHAIN, THE LANGUAGE OF CORRUPTION AND ISRAEL'S MORAL CULTURE 15 (2010) (Isr.) (criticizing this phenomenon).

198. HCJ 366/03 Commitment for Peace and Social Justice Society v. The Minister of Finance 60(3) PD 464 [2005] (Isr.). The Supreme Court had already rejected a petition against the cutting of pensions for the elderly as part of Netanyahu's economic plan of 2002 and 2003: HCJ 5578/02 Manor v. The Minister of Finance 59(1) PD 729 [2004] (Isr.).

199. AdminA 662/11 Sela v. The Head of the Kfar Vradim Local Council (Sept. 9, 2014), Nevo Legal Database (by subscription) (Isr.). I published an article criticizing this case in *Yedioth Ahronoth* on November 12, 2014.

200. HCJ 5167/00 Weiss v. The Prime Minister 55(2) PD 455 [2001] (Isr.).

201. HCJ 1661/05 The Hof Aza [Gaza Coast] Local Council v. The Israel Knesset 59(2) PD 481 [2005] (Isr.).

202. HCJ 501/80 Zoabi v. Abu Rabia 35(2) PD 262 [1980] (Isr.); Nili Cohen, *The Political Agreement*, 1 HAMISHPAT [THE LAW] 59 (1993) (Isr.).

203. HCJ 313/67 Axelrod v. The Minister of Religions 22(1) PD 80 [1968] (Isr.).

204. HCJ 669/86 Rubin v. Berger 41(1) PD 73 [1987] (Isr.).

205. HCJ 1523/90 Levy v. The Prime Minister of Israel 44(2) PD 213 [1990] (Isr.).

206. HCJ 1635/90 Zharzhevsky v. The Prime Minister 45(1) PD 749, 766 [1991] (Isr.).

207. HCJ 1601/90 Shalit v. Peres 44(3) PD 353 [1990] (Isr.).

208. HCJ 3872/93 Meatrael Inc. v. The Prime Minister 47(5) 485 [1985] (Isr.).

209. HCJ 5364/94 Velner v. Chairman of the Israel Labor Party 49(1) PD 758 [1995] (Isr.).

210. HCJ(FH) 808/95 Amiti, People for Good Governance & Integrity v. The Attorney General 49(1) PD 837 [1995] (Isr.). Another question was whether or not a further hearing was an option after a verdict rendered by a panel of five justices. This issue will be discussed in chapter 21.

211. HCJ 2205/97 Masala v. The Education & Culture Minister 51(1) PD 233 [1997] (Isr.).

212. HCJ 2454/08 The Legal Forum for the Land of Israel v. The Minister of Education (Apr. 17, 2008), Nevo Legal Database (by subscription) (Isr.).

213. HCJ 2324/11 Gil v. The Minister of Education (Apr. 26, 2011), Nevo Legal Database (by subscription) (Isr.).

214. HCJ 301/81 Sharon v. The Knesset Committee 35(4) PD 118 [1981] (Isr.). An English translation is available at: http://versa.cardozo.yu.edu/sites/default/files/upload/opinions/Flatto-Sharon%20v.%20State%20of%20Israel.pdf.

215. HCJ 742/84 Kahane v. The Speaker of the Knesset 39(4) PD 85, 96 [1985] (Isr.).

216. HCJ 306/85 Kahane v. The Speaker of the Knesset 39(4) PD 485 [1985] (Isr.).

217. HCJ 669/85 Kahane v. The Speaker of the Knesset 40(4) PD 393 [1986] (Isr.).

218. HCJ 400/87 Kahane v. The Speaker of the Knesset 41(2) PD 729 [1987] (Isr.).

219. HCJ 388/85 Kahane v. The Managing Board of the Israel Broadcasting Authority 41(3) PD 255 [1987] (Isr.).

220. HCJ 620/85 Miari v. The Speaker of the Knesset 41(4) PS 169 [1987] (Isr.).

221. HCJ 1843/93 Pinchasi v. The Knesset 48(4) PD 492 [1993] (Isr.).

222. HCJ 5368/96 Pinchasi v. The Attorney General 50(4) PD 364 [1996] (Isr.).

223. CrimC (TA) 8074/96 The State of Israel v. Raphael Pinchasi, PM 1997(4) 15 [1997] (Isr.).

224. MENACHEM MAUTNER, LAW AND CULTURE IN ISRAEL AT THE THRESHOLD OF THE TWENTY FIRST CENTURY 138–39 (2008) (Isr.); MENACHEM MAUTNER, LAW & THE CULTURE OF ISRAEL 102–03, 115–27, 144 (2011).

225. CrimAR 1915/07 Hazan v. The State of Israel (June 18, 2007), Nevo Legal Database (by subscription) (Isr.).

226. HCJ 11298/03 The Movement for Quality Government v. The Knesset Committee 59(5) PD 865 [2005] (Isr.).

227. NOMI LEVITSKY, THE SUPREMES—INSIDE THE SUPREME COURT 357–58 (2006) (Isr.).

228. HCJ 6026/94 Nazal v. IDF Commander in Judea and Samaria 48(5) PD 338 [1994] (Isr.).

229. HCJ 2006/97 Janimat v. OC Central Command 51(2) PD 651 [1997] (Isr.).

230. AdminA 10/94 Plonim v. The Defense Minister 53(1) PD 97 [1997] (Isr.).

231. NOMI LEVITSKY, THE SUPREMES—INSIDE THE SUPREME COURT 242 (2006) (Isr.).

232. CrimA (further hearing) 7048/97 Plonim v. The Defense Minister 54(1) PD 721 [2000] (Isr.).

233. CrimA 6659/06 Ploni v. The State of Israel (June 11, 2008), Nevo Legal Database (by subscription) (Isr.).

234. AdminA 5652/00 Obeid v. The Defense Minister 55(4) PD 913 [2000] (Isr.).

235. HCJ 794/98 Obeid v. The Defense Minister 55(5) PD 769 [2001] (Isr.).

236. CA 993/06 The State of Israel v. Dirani (July 18, 2011), Nevo Legal Database (by subscription) (Isr.).

237. CA (further hearing) 5698/11 The State of Israel v. Dirani (Jan. 29, 2013), Nevo Legal Database (by subscription) (Isr.).

238. HCJ 3799/02 Adalah v. OC Central Command 60(3) PD 67 [2005] (Isr.).

239. HCJ 769/02 The Public Committee Against Torture in Israel v. The State of Israel 62(1) PD 507 [2006] (Isr.).

240. HCJ 7954/04 Maraaba v. The State of Israel 60(2) PD 477 [2005] (Isr.). Official English translation is available at: http://elyon1.court.gov.il/files_eng/04/570/079/A14/04079570.a14.pdf.

241. Ibid., p. 65 (of the English translation).

242. Ibid. p. 10.

243. For a critique, see Prof. Shlono Slonim in Malvina Halberstam, Judicial Review, A Comparative Perspective: Israel, Canada, and the United States, 31 CARDOZO L. REV. 2393, 2433–36 (2010).

244. HCJ 4764/04 Doctors for Human Rights v. The IDF Commander in Gaza 58(5) PD 385 [2004] (Isr.).

245. HCJ 5872/01 Barakeh v. The Prime Minister 56(3) PD 1 [2002] (Isr.).

246. HCJ 3436/02 The Castodia Internazionale della Terra Santa v. The State of Israel 56(3) PD 22, 24 [2002] (Isr.).

247. HCJ 3451/02 Almadani v. The Defense Minister 56(3) PD 30 [2002] (Isr.).

248.   HCJ 4764/04 Doctors for Human Rights v. The IDF Commander in Gaza 58(5) PD 385, 392 [2004] (Isr.).

249.   Interviewed by Liat Natovich-Kushinsky, published online on July 27, 2014 (Isr.).

250.   HCJ 3292/07 Adalah—The Legal Center for the Arab Minority Rights in Israel v. The Attorney General (Dec. 18, 2011), Nevo Legal Database (by subscription) (Isr.). An official English translation is available at: http://elyon1.court.gov.il/ files_eng/07/920/032/n06/07032920.n06.pdf, p. 15.

251.   Ibid.

252.   Ibid., p. 26.

253.   CA 373/72 Tepper v. The State of Israel 28(2) PD 7, 15 [1974] (Isr.).

254.   Yoel Sussman, Miktzat Matamei Parshanut [A Little Taste of Interpretation], Jubilee Book to Pinchas Rosen (Haim Cohn ed. 1962) (Isr.).

255.   Aharon Barak, Judicial Discretion 149, 162 (1987) (Isr.).

256.   CrimA 424/63 The Attorney General v. Shalbi 18(2) PD 478, 481 [1964] (Isr.).

257.   CA 6281/93 Mizrahi Bank v. Migdal Kfar Shitufi 49(4) PD 221 [1995] (Isr.).

258.   HCJ 769/02 The Public Committee against Torture in Israel v. The State of Israel 62(1) PD 507 [2006] (Isr.). An English translation is available at: http://elyon1. court.gov.il/files_eng/02/690/007/A34/02007690.a34.pdf, p. 50.

259.   HCJ 3803/11 The Capital Market Trustees Association v. The State of Israel (Feb. 5, 2012), Nevo Legal Database (by subscription) (Isr.).

260.   CA 383/77 Asphalt and Negev Stone Products Ltd. v. The State of Israel 33(1) PD 641, 642 [1979] (Isr.).

261.   Aharon Barak, Interpretation in Law—Contract Interpretation 60 (2001) (Isr.). Elsewhere, however, Barak acknowledges the possibility of a clear text: Aharon Barak, Purposive Interpretation in Law 51 (2003) (Isr.); on the role of interpretation and the development of purposive interpretation in the Supreme Court's judicial legislation, see also Menachem Mautner, Law & The Culture of Israel 90–95 (2011).

262.   CA 5587/93 Nachmani v. Nachmani 49(1) PD 485 [1995] (Isr.).

263.   CMR 1481/96 Nachmani v. Nachmani 49(5) PD 598 [1996] (Isr.).

264.   CA (further hearing) 2401/95 Nachmani v. Nachmani 50(4) PD 661 [1996] (Isr.).

265.   CA 4628/93 The State of Israel v. Apropim Housing and Promotions (1991) Ltd. 49(2) PD 265 [1995] (Isr.).

266.   CA (further hearing) 2045/05 Vegetable Growers Association v. The State of Israel 61(2) PD 1 [2006] (Isr.).

267.   CA 5856/06 Levy v. Norkeit Ltd. PM 2008(1) 840 [2008] (Isr.); CA 3676/07 National Insurance Institute of Israel v. The Israeli Phoenix Insurance Company Ltd. (June 20, 2010), Nevo Legal Database (by subscription) (Isr.).

268.   CAR 3961/10 National Insurance Institute of Israel v. Sahar Suits Company Ltd. Migdal Insurance Company Ltd. (Feb. 26, 2012), Nevo Legal Database (by subscription) (Isr.).

269.   FamAR 8300/11 Ploni v. Ploni (Aug. 2, 2012), Nevo Legal Database (by subscription) (Isr.).

270.   In a symposium published in Hamishpat in 2000 (Isr.).

271. Aharon Barak, *The Risks and Chances*, HALISHKA—THE JERUSALEM DISTRICT BAR ASSOCIATION MAGAZINE 14 (1995) (Isr.).

272. Moshe Landau, *Giving Israel a Constitution Using Judicial Ruling*, 3 MISHPAT VE-MIMSHAL [L. & GOV'T] 697, 702 (1996) (Isr.).

273. Malvina Halberstam, *Judicial Review, A Comparative Perspective: Israel, Canada, and the United States*, 31 Cardozo L. Rev. 2393, 2422 (2010).

274. GIDEON SAPIR, THE CONSTITUTIONAL REVOLUTION, PAST PRESENT AND FUTURE 80 (2010) (Isr.).

275. Amnon Rubinstein, *The Story of the Basic Laws*, 14 L. & BUS. 79 (2012) (Isr.).

276. *Id.*

277. CrimA 107/74 Negev Automobile Service Station Ltd. v. The State of Israel 28(1) PD 640 [1974] (Isr.).

278. Marbury v. Madison, 5 U.S. 137 (1803).

279. Moshe Landau, *Giving Israel a Constitution Using Judicial Ruling*, 3 MISHPAT VE-MIMSHAL [L. & GOV'T] 697, 706 (1996) (Isr.).

280. Malvina Halberstam, *Judicial Review, A Comparative Perspective: Israel, Canada, and the United States*, 31 CARDOZO L. REV. 2393, 2418 (2010).

281. Moshe Landau, *Giving Israel a Constitution Using Judicial Ruling*, 3 MISHPAT VE- MIMSHAL [L. & GOV'T] 697, 701 (1996) (Isr.).

282. HCJ 6298/07 Ressler v. The Israeli Knesset (Feb. 21, 20112), Nevo Legal Services (by subscription) (Isr.); for further discussion on the matter, *see* Chapter 9.

283. HCJ 2605/05 The Academic Center for Law and Business, Human Rights Department v. The Finance Minister (Nov. 19, 2009), Nevo Legal Services (by subscription) (Isr.).

284. HCJ 8340/99 Gorali, Cochan and Associates v. The Attorney General 45(3) PD 79 [2001] (Isr.); HCJ 1783/00 Haifa Chemicals v. The Attorney General 47(3) PD 652, 656 [2003] (Isr.).

285. HCJ 1661/51 The Hof Aza [Gaza Coast] Local Council v. The Knesset 49(2) PD 481, 642–46 [2005] (Isr.).

286. HCJ 7052/03 Adalah—The Legal Center for Arab Minority Rights in Israel v. The Interior Minister 61(2) PD 202 [2006] (Isr.).

287. An English Translation is available at: http://elyon1.court.gov.il/files_eng/03/520/070/a47/03070520.a47.pdf, p. 131.

288. HCJ 466/07 Galon v. The Attorney General (Jan. 11, 2012), Nevo Legal Services (by subscription) (Isr.).

289. NOMI LEVITSKY, THE SUPREMES—INSIDE THE SUPREME COURT 73 (2006) (Isr.).

290. Menachem Mautner, *Appointing Justices to the Supreme Court in a Multi-Cultural Society*, 19 MECHKAREY MISHPAT [LEGAL RES.] 423, 459 (2003) (Isr.).

291. CrimC (Jer.) 3471/87 The State of Israel v. Kaplan PM 5748(2) 26 (1987) (Isr.).

292. Elections Approval 11280/02 The 16th Knesset Central Elections Committee v. Tibi 57(4) PD 1 [2003] (Isr.).

293. Elections Approval 11280/02 The 16th Knesset Central Elections Committee v. Tibi 57(4) PD 1 [2003] (Isr.). Other aspects of this case are discussed in Chapter 8.

294. HCJ 6728/06 Ometz NGO v. The Prime Minister of Israel (Nov. 30, 2006), Nevo Legal Services (by subscription) (Isr.).

295. MENACHEM MAUTNER, LAW & THE CULTURE OF ISRAEL 167 (2011).

296. NOMI LEVITSKY, THE SUPREMES—INSIDE THE SUPREME COURT 21 (2006) (Isr.).

297. An accrue of critique articles regarding the Supreme Court appointments is included in Yiron Festinger's book, WHOSE HOUSE IS THIS? Part III—Friend Brings Friend—The Private Mansion 73–96 (2006) (Isr.).

298. I criticized the appointments process, including the "family" phenomenon, in an article I published in *Yedioth Ahronoth* on November 4, 2003. The familial argument, as raised by Barak was also described in Anat Berckowitz's article "Towards the Round of Supreme Court Appointments: Internal Differences Regarding the Question of Staffing the Future Justice Positions" published in *Globes* in December 2002.

299. Amnon Dankner, MA'ARIV May 4, 2004.

300. Yoav Yitzhak, MA'ARIV, June 16, 2010.

301. Yuval Yoaz, HA'ARETZ, June 22, 2004.

302. Yinon Kadri, MA'ARIV, June 22, 2004.

303. MA'ARIV, June 27, 2004.

304. An article by Yossi Gurevich, June 28, 2004.

305. HCJ 2533/97 The Movement for Quality Government v. The Israeli Government 51(3) PD 47 [1997] (Isr.).

306. *See* Chapter 17.

307. In an article published in 1993, Lapid spoke of the fact that "in Israel there are two governments," one chosen by the Knesset and another "called High Court of Justice": YOSSI DAR, AHARON BARAK AND THE PLEASURES OF THE RULE OF THE LAW 149 (2002).

308. Tova Tzimuki, *Because of Gavison: The Supreme Court Demands to Postpone the Appointment of Judges until after the Elections*, YEDIOTH AHRONOTH Nov. 27, 2005 (Isr.).

309. HCJ 8815/05 Landstein v. Spiegler (Dec. 26, 2005), Nevo Legal Database (by subscription) (Isr.).

310. HCJ 5167/00 Weiss v. The Prime Minister 55(2) PD 455 [2001] (Isr.).

311. Yuval Yoaz recounted the affair in an article entitled *From the Knesset to the Supreme Court?*, HA'ARETZ, May 2, 2005 (Isr.).

312. An early example can be seen in CrimA 884/80 The State of Israel v. Grossman 36(1) PD 405 [1981] (Isr.), which was decided by majority just a few years after Barak's appointment to the Supreme Court.

313. Amnon Dankner, *Weakening the Link*, MA'ARIV, June 11, 2006 (Isr.).

314. CrimC (Mag-TA) 7771/96 The State of Israel v. Neeman (Sept. 15, 1997), Nevo Legal Database (by subscription) (Isr.).

315. CrimC (Mag-Hi) 5040/96 The State of Israel v. Eitan (Feb. 19, 1997), Nevo Legal Database (by subscription) (Isr.).

316. CrimC (Mag-TA) 12121/00 The State of Israel v. Kahalani (July 31, 2002), Nevo Legal Database (by subscription) (Isr.).

317. CA 7759/01 Ha'aretz Newspaper Publisher Ltd. v. The Justice Ministry 58(5) PD 150 [2004] (Isr.).

318. Amnon Rubinstein, *Tzehok miShilton haHok* [Mockery of the Rule of Law], MA'ARIV, Feb. 16, 2007.

319. HCJ 5675/04 The Movement for Quality Government in Israel v. The Attorney General 59(1) PD 199 [2004] (Isr.).

320. CrimC (Mag-TA) 4837/05 The State of Israel v. Sharon (Feb. 14, 2006), Nevo Legal Database (by subscription) (Isr.).

321. CrimA (TA) 70569/06 Sharon v. The State of Israel PM 2007(2) 11030 (2007) (Isr.).

322. CrimA 6152/07 Sharon v. The State of Israel (Jan. 28, 2008), Nevo Legal Database (by subscription) (Isr.).

323. CrimC (Mag-TA) 7848/96 The State of Israel v. Hoter Yishai 12(2) Misim 493 (1998) (Isr.).

324. CrimA (TA) 523/98 Hoter Yishai v. The State of Israel (June 15, 1998), Nevo Legal Database (by subscription) (Isr.).

325. HCJ 1668/97 The Movement for Quality Government v. The National Council of the Israel Bar Association (Feb. 24, 1998), Nevo Legal Database (by subscription) (Isr.).

326. Evelin Gordon, *Judicial Activism and the Non-Existing Discussion*, 3 Tchelet 44, 56 (1998) (Isr.). The article was written while Hoter-Yishai's trial was still pending.

327. HCJ 4568/98 The Movement for Quality Government v. The National Council for the Israel Bas Association (Nov. 18, 1998), Nevo Legal Database (by subscription) (Isr.).

328. Uzi Vogelman's letter from Dec. 20, 1998.

329. CA 6356/99 Hoter Yishai v. Arbel 56(5) PD 254, 265 [2002] (Isr.).

330. CrimC 8362/99 The State of Israel v. Hoter Yishai (Nov. 25. 1999), Nevo Legal Database (by subscription) (Isr.).

331. Arnon Ben-Yair, "When 10% of the Sector Provides 50% of Judges it Lowers the Level of the Judiciary" The Marker, Feb. 25, 2007 (Isr.).

332. Aharon Barak, Purposive Interpretation in Law 89 (2005) (referring to Fuller).

333. CrimA 5121/98 Yissascharov v. The Military Advocate General 61(1) PD 461 [2006] (Isr.). An English translation is available at: http://elyon1.court.gov.il/files_eng/98/210/051/n21/98051210.n21.htm.

334. Boaz Sangero, *The Exclusionary Rule Set in the Yisascharov Case Regarding Illegally Obtained Evidence—Gospel or Disappointment? Opinion and Invitation for a Further Hearing*, 19 Mishpat ve-Tzava [L. & Mil.] 67 (2007) (Isr.).

335. Central Bureau of Statistics, 16 The Statistical Abstract of Israel 621 (1965) (Isr.); Central Bureau of Statistics, 2006 The Statistical Abstract of Israel 11.4 (2007) (Isr.).

336. Oren Gazal-Eyal, Inbal Galon, & Keren Wishchel-Margal, Department of Information and Research, Supreme Court of Israel, May 2012.

337. Yoram Shahar & Meron Gross, *Accepting and Rejecting Supreme Court Applications*, 13 Mechkarey Mishpat [Legal Res.] 329 (1996) (Isr.).

338. Theodore Eisenberg, Talia Fisher, & Issi Rosen-Zvi, *Israel's Supreme Court Appellate Jurisdiction: An Empirical Study*, 96 Cornell L. Rev. 693, 718 (2011).

339. CrimC (TA) 40387/99 The State of Israel v. Sheves (Dec. 1, 2000), Nevo Legal Database (by subscription) (Isr.).

340. CrimA 332/01 The State of Israel v. Sheves 57(2) PD 496 [2003] (Isr.).

341. CrimA (further hearing) 1397/03 The State of Israel v. Sheves 59(4) PD 385 [2004] (Isr.).

342. Aharon Barak, *The Constitutionalization of the Legal System Following the Basic Laws and Its Implication on Criminal Law (Substantial and Procedural)* 13 Mechkarey Mishpat [Legal Res.] 5, 18 (1996) (Isr.).

343.   CrimA 53/54 Eshad Temporary Center for Transportation v. The Attorney
       General 8 PD 785 [1954] (Isr.).

344.   561 U.S. 358 (2010).

345.   Ruth Gavison, *The Attorney General: A Critical Review of New Trends*, 5 Plilim
       [Crim. L.] 27, 95–96 (1996) (Isr.).

346.   Eitan Levontin, Representing the State in Court 83 (2009) (Isr.) (PhD
       diss., The Hebrew University in Jerusalem).

347.   The Law to Amend Civil Procedure (The State as a Party), 5718-1958, SH No.
       251 p. 118 (Isr.).

348.   Yechiel Gutman, A Storm in the GSS—The Attorney General versus the
       Government from the Tubiansky Affair to the Bus 300 Affair 312 (1995)
       (Isr.); Evelyn Gordon, *How the Government Lost Its Right to Legal Representation*,
       4 Tchelet 57 (1998) (Isr.).

349.   HCJ 14/86 Laor v. Council for the Critique of Films and Plays 41(1) PD 421 [1987]
       (Isr.). A request for a further hearing was denied in HCJ (further hearing) 3/87
       Council for the Critique of Films and Plays v. Laor 41(2) PD 162 [1987] (Isr.).

350.   Yechiel Gutman, A Storm in the GSS—The Attorney General versus the
       Government from the Tubiansky Affair to the Bus 300 Affair 84 (1995)
       (Isr.).

351.   Yitzhak Olshan, Din Ve-Dvarim—Zichronot [Debate—Memoirs] 365
       (1978) (Isr.).

352.   HCJ 4267/93 AMITAI—Citizens for Right Administration and Integrity v. The
       Prime Minister of Israel 47(5) PD 441, 473 [1993] (Isr.).

353.   HCJ 121/68 Electra (Israel) Ltd. v. The Minister of Commerce and Industry 22(2)
       PD 551, 560 [1968] (Isr.).

354.   HCJ 4646/08 Lavi v. The Prime Minister (Oct. 10, 2008), Nevo Legal Database (by
       subscription) (Isr.).

355.   For a devastating critique of the court's decision, *see* Eitan Levontin, *Supposed
       Truth and Truth as It Is: 50 Years to the Agranat Committee Report*, *in* Levontin
       Book—Legal Articles in Honor of Avigdor Levontin 131, 173–75 (2013)
       (Isr.).

356.   HCJ 4267/93 AMITAI—Citizens for Right Administration and Integrity v. The
       Prime Minister of Israel 47(5) PD 441, 473 [1993] (Isr.).

357.   Haim Cohn, *The Qualifications of Public Servants*, 2 Mishpat ve-Mimshal [L. &
       Gov't] 265, 285 (1994) (Isr.).

358.   The Public Committee for Examining Ways to Appoint the Attorney
       General and Other Issues Regarding His Tenure Report 76 (1998) (Isr.).

359.   Uzi Vogelman, *The State Attorney's Department of Constitutional and
       Administrative Law*, 6 Mishpat ve-Mimshal [L. & Gov't] 173, 174 (2001) (Isr.);
       Eitan Levontin, Representing the State in Court 83 (2009) (Isr.) (PhD
       diss., The Hebrew University in Jerusalem).

360.   Yair Lapid, Memoirs After My Death—The Story of Yoseph (Tommy)
       Lapid 375, 377 (2010) (Isr.).

361.   HCJ 29/10 The Headquarters for The Country of Israel v. The Attorney General
       (Jan. 25, 2010), Nevo Legal Database (by subscription) (Isr.).

362.   HCJ 43/16 Ometz NGO v. The Israeli Government (Jan. 17, 2016), Nevo Legal
       Services (by subscription) (Isr.).

363. HCJ 80/54 Nochimovsky v. The Minister of Interior 8 PD 1491 [1954] (Isr.); Itzhak Zamir, The Administrative Authority (1996) (Isr.); Daphne Barak-Erez, Administrative Law 227–58 (2010) (Isr.).

364. Itzhak Zamir, Administrative Power 776 (1996) (Isr.).

365. HCJ 5305/08 The Foundation for Promoting Good Governance v. The Attorney General (Nov. 24, 2009), Nevo Legal Database (by subscription) (Isr.).

366. HCJ 6728/06 Ometz NGO v. The Prime Minister of Israel (Nov. 30, 2006), Nevo Legal Database (by subscription) (Isr.).

367. Page 18 of the partial report.

368. HCJ 6728/06 Ometz NGO v. The Prime Minister of Israel (Nov. 30, 2006), Nevo Legal Database (by subscription) (Isr.).

369. Dan Halutz, Begova Ha-Eiynaim [Eye to Eye] 495 (2010) (Isr.) (see the chapter titled "Natural Justice? Not in the Vinograd Committee").

370. This statement appeared in HCJ 6666/07 The Military Legal Defense v. The Examination Committee of the 2006 Lebanon war (Sept. 30, 2007), Nevo Legal Database (by subscription) (Isr.). This petition was filed after the interim report, which as it turned out, showed that the committee did not give the persons whom it criticized an apt opportunity to defend themselves. However, even before, in HCJ 6728/06 Ometz NGO v. The Prime Minister of Israel (Nov. 30, 2006) (Isr.), as part of the petition demanding to establish a national committee of inquiry (instead of the Winograd Committee), the state representative declared that the committee must enable any person who may be hurt by it to exercise his or her right to be heard.

371. HCJ 8723/07, 8923/07 The Movement for Quality Government in Israel and The Military Legal Defense v. The Examination Committee of the Northern War chaired by Judge Vinograd (Nov. 27, 2007), Nevo Legal Database (by subscription) (Isr.).

372. HCJ 5268/08 Inbar v. OC Southern Command (Dec. 9, 2009), Nevo Legal Database (by subscription) (Isr.).

373. Itamar Eichner, Doctor Ehud and Mister Barak, Yedioth Ahronoth, Aug. 18, 2012. His article relies on the book of Yossi Malman & Dan Raviv, The Shadow War—The Mossad and the Intelligence Community 464 (2012) (Isr.). A detailed description can also be found in David Makovsky, The Silent Strike, New Yorker, Sept. 17, 2012.

374. George W. Bush, Decision Points 421 (2010).

375. HCJ 8749/06 Ometz NGO v. The Attorney General (Dec. 27, 2006), Nevo Legal Database (by subscription) (Isr.).

376. Shani Mizrahi, An Investigation Against the Prime Minister Will Commence in the Cremieux Affair, Ma'ariv, Sept. 25, 2006 (Isr.).

377. Ari Shavit, The House in 8 Cremieux Street, Ha'aretz, Aug. 17, 2006 (Isr.).

378. Article by Meital Zoor and Miri Hasson, The Comptroller: I Will Continue Fearlessly With the Battle For Integrity, Ynet (Nov. 2, 2006), www.ynet.co.il/articles/0,7340,L-3322708,00.html (Isr.).

379. Nochi Dankner on the Olmert affair and the Bank Leumi Tender, Globes, Oct. 26, 2006 (Isr.).

380. Dan Avi-Yitzhak, Opened with Sharon, Finished with Olmert, 6 Orech Hadin [The Attorney] 16, 21 (2010) (Isr.).

381. Ella Levy-Weinrib, *The Talansky Testimony Brought to Olmert's Expulsion and It Had No Room Legally*, GLOBES, Aug. 7, 2008 (Isr.).

382. CrimA 4345/08 Olmert v. The State of Israel (May 20, 2008), Nevo Legal Database (by subscription) (Isr.).

383. TZVI AVISAR, SHARON—FIVE YEARS LATER 179–82 (2011) (Isr.).

384. *With No Evidence*, YEDIOTH AHRONOTH, May 16, 2014 (in this article I did not deal with the other conviction relating to the payment of IS 60,000).

385. HCJ 9132/07 Albasioni v. The Prime Minister (Jan. 30, 2008), Nevo Legal Database (by subscription) (Isr.).

386. This English translation is available at: http://elyon1.court.gov.il/files_eng/07/320/091/n25/07091320.n25.pdf, pp. 11–12.

387. Shlomo Tzezana, ISRAEL HAYOM, June 23, 2008; Dorit Gabay, MA'ARIV, June 23, 2008.

388. HCJ 5551/08 Shalit v. The Israeli Government (June 23, 2008), Nevo Legal Database (by subscription) (Isr.).

389. Ben-Dror Yemini, *Activism with No Boundaries*, MA'ARIV, June 23, 2008.

390. Shmuel Mitelan, Mia Bengal, Amir Rapaport, & Dudu Bezeq, MA'ARIV, June 23, 2008.

391. HCJ 201/09 Doctors for Human Rights v. The Prime Minister, 63(1) PD 521 (2009) (Isr.). An English translation is available at: http://elyon1.court.gov.il/files_eng/09/010/002/n07/09002010.n07.pdf, p. 21.

392. Ibid., p. 25.

393. Noam Sharvit, GLOBES, Dec. 3, 2006 (Isr.).

394. An official English translation is available at: http://elyon1.court.gov.il/eng/ethic.doc, p. 18.

395. Amnon Rubinstein, *Flaws Revealer*, MA'ARIV, Mar. 12, 2007 (Isr.).

396. *Id.*

397. Quoted by Ella Levy-Weinreb, *LeHarbeh Anashim Yesh Heshbon Patua'h Ito* [Many People Have an Open Account with Me], GLOBES, Mar. 7, 2008 (Isr.).

398. One legal scholar who spoke out in defense of the verdict was Orit Kamir, *Yesh Parshanut Aheret, Harbeh Yoter Peshutah* [There is Another Interpretation, Much More Simple], HA'ARETZ, Mar. 12, 2007.

399. Gidi Weitz, *Listen, We're Sick*, HA'ARETZ, Feb. 27, 2007 (Isr.).

400. In an interview with Ari Shavit, HA'ARETZ, Feb. 3, 2010 (Isr.).

401. HCJ 5853/07 Emuna—The National-Religious Woman Movement v. The Prime Minister (Dec. 6, 2007), Nevo Legal Database (by subscription) (Isr.).

402. An English translation is available at: http://elyon1.court.gov.il/files_eng/07/530/058/r07/07058530.r07.pdf, p. 2.

403. Ibid., p. 15.

404. Ibid., p. 13.

405. Ibid., p. 58.

406. Tova Tzimuki, *The Price of Conviction?*, YEDIOTH AHRONOTH (Isr.).

407. Yonatan Lis & Barak Ravid, *The Inspector General Following the Interview in Ha'aretz: I Did Not Mean to Criticize the Government*, HA'ARETZ, Sept. 28, 2008 (Isr.). The article also provides details from the government meeting, including the statement of Minister Ami Ayalon: "*In an orderly country, the Inspector General should have been fired.*"

408. HCJ 4870/10 Blum-David v. The State Comptroller (June 23, 2011), Nevo Legal Database (by subscription) (Isr.).

409. Ari Shavit, *Interview with Moshe Landau*, HA'ARETZ, Oct. 6, 2000 (Isr.).

410. According to a poll conducted by Ephraim Yaar, Tamar Harman, and Arye Nadler, The Peace Index Project (Tel-Aviv University, 1996); Issachar Rozen-Zvi, *Haim Hashoftim Kibnai Adam*? [Are Judges Human?] 8 MISHPAT VE-MIMSHAL [L. & GOV'T] 49, 96 [2005] (Isr.).

411. ARYE RETNER, THE LEGAL CULTURE IN ISRAEL—EMPIRICAL STUDIES (2013) (Isr.); Revital Hovel, HA'ARETZ, Aug. 4, 2013 (Isr.).

412. On the declining trust in the court, *see* MENACHEM MAUTNER, LAW & THE CULTURE OF ISRAEL 162–69 (2011).

413. *Id.*, 165.

414. An example can be seen in Shabtai Azriel, *The Petition Is Denied and Send Warm Regards to Mom*, HA'ARETZ, Oct. 14, 2005 (Isr.). Another example is Einat Berkowitz, *Justice Barak as a Fable*, HA'IR, Nov. 25, 1994 (Isr.). *See also* MENACHEM MAUTNER, LAW & THE CULTURE OF ISRAEL 165–66 (2011).

415. NOMI LEVITSKY, THE SUPREMES—INSIDE THE SUPREME COURT 12-44 (2006) (Isr.)

416. Hadas Magen, *A member of the Judicial Selection Committee: Most Objections in The Committee Were Not Related to Arbel But to Rubinstein*, GLOBES May 11, 2004 (Isr.).

417. Meirav Arlosoroff, *Hila Cohen Is Right*, THE MARKER Sep. 12, 2005 (Isr.).

418. *See* Chapter 12.

419. *See* Chapter 20.

420. HCJ 366/03 Commitment to Peace and Social Justice Foundation v. The Minister of Finance 60(3) PD 464 (2005) (Isr.).

421. Richard A. Posner, *Enlightened Despot*, NEW REPUBLIC, Apr. 23, 2007.

422. HCJ 2605/05 The Academic Center for Law and Business, Human Rights Department v. The Finance Minister (Nov. 19, 2009), Nevo Legal Database (by subscription) (Isr.).

423. HCJ 910/86 Ressler v. The Defense Minister 42(2) PD 441 [1988] (Isr.).

424. HCJ 186/65 Reiner v. The Prime Minister 19(2) PD 485 [1965] (Isr.).

425. HCJ 11437/05 Kav Laoved v. The Ministry of Interior (Apr. 13, 2011), Nevo Legal Database (by subscription) (Isr.).

426. One can learn a great deal about Beinisch's media activity from senior legal correspondent Anat Peleg's: ANAT PELEG, OPEN DOORS 65, 70, 151, 152, 162 (Aliza Wolach ed.) (2012) (Isr.).

427. Chapter 34 above.

428. Richard A. Posner, *Enlightened Despot*, NEW REPUBLIC, Apr. 23, 2007, at 53 (reviewing AHARON BARAK, THE JUDGE IN A DEMOCRACY (2006)), *available at* http://www.newrepublic.com/article/enlightened-despot.

429. Barak Medina, *Four Myths of Judicial Review: A Response to Richard Posner's Critique of Aharon Barak's Judicial Activism*, 49 HARV. INT'L L.J. ONLINE 1 (2007).

430. Malvina Halberstam, *Judicial Review, A Comparative Perspective: Israel, Canada, and the United States*, 31 CARDOZO L. REV. 2393, 2426 (2010).

431. Hillel Sommer, *Richard Posner on Aharon Barak: Things You See from There, Are Not Seen from Here*, 49 HAPRAKLIT [THE ATTORNEY] 523, 533, n. 82 (2000) (Isr.).

432. HCJ 2324/11 Gil v. The Minister of Education (Apr. 26, 2011), Nevo Legal Database (by subscription) (Isr.), discussed in Chapter 18.

433. HCJ 6698/05 Ka'adan v. Israel Lands Administration 54(1) PD 258 [2000] (Isr.), discussed in Chapter 16.

434. HCJ 2311/11 Ori Sabach v. The Knesset (Sept. 17, 2014), Nevo Legal Database (by subscription) (Isr.).

435. HCJ 5239/11 Uri Avnery v. The Knesset (Apr. 15, 2015), Nevo Legal Database (by subscription) (Isr.).

436. HCJ 7146/12 Naget Serg Adam v. The Knesset (Sept. 16, 2013), Nevo Legal Database (by subscription) (Isr.).

437. HCJ 8665/14 Desta v. The Knesset (Aug. 11, 2015), Nevo Legal Database (by subscription) (Isr.).

438. HCJ 5228/14 BEZELEM—Israeli Information Center for Human Right in the Territories v. Israel Broadcasting Authority (Aug. 13, 2014), Nevo Legal Database (by subscription) (Isr.).

439. HCJ (further hearing) 204/13 Salah v. Israel Prison Service (Apr. 14, 2015), Nevo Legal Database (by subscription) (Isr.). The court held, however, that prisoners who were close to completing their studies should be allowed to do so.

440. AdminA 662/11 Sela v. The Head of the Kfar Vradim Local Council (Sept. 9, 2014), Nevo Legal Database (by subscription) (Isr.), discussed in Chapter 17.

441. HCJ 4329/91 Saar v. Constitution Law and Justice Committee (Nov. 4, 1991), Nevo Legal Database (by subscription) (Isr.).

442. HCJ 3166/14 Gutman v. The Attorney General (Mar. 12, 2015), Nevo Legal Database (by subscription) (Isr.).

443. *See* Chapter 22.

INDEX

Surnames starting with "al-" are alphabetized by the subsequent part of the name.

Caspi, Ram, 86, 240, 270
Caspi, Zecharia, 229
Caspit, Ben, 334
Central Elections Committee, 24,
  65–68, 71
Cheshin, David, 247, 318–319
Cheshin, Mishael
  appointment to Supreme Court, 54, 54*
  background of, 53–54
  on Barak's "all is justiciable"
    policy, 75–76
  Bar-On appointment, 122
  on Basic Law: Human Dignity and
    Liberty, 62
  on constitutional promulgation, 189
  on demolition of terrorist homes, 175
  disagreeing with Barak, 198
  on discipline for judicial
    misconduct, 306
  on family life as right, 195–196
  on protecting Supreme Court from
    critics, 329
  on religion and the state, 165
  retirement, opinion issued in, 195*
  retirement from Supreme Court, 317
  on security fence, 179
  on Sharon alleged improprieties, 220
  on Sheves verdict and breach of
    trust, 235
  term on Supreme Court, 197
  on terrorist prisoners as bargaining
    chips, 176–177
Cheshin, Shneur Zalman, 16, 21, 29, 53
Christian Phalange forces. See Sabra and
    Shatila massacre
Church of the Nativity, 180–181
Citizenship. See Nationality and citizenship
Citizenship and Entry into Israel Law
    (Temporary Order), 194–195
Citizenship Law cases, 194–196,
    356nn286–288
Civilians in war on terrorism. See
    Terrorism/War against terrorism
Classical era, 1–47. See also Agranat,
    Shimon; Barak, Aharon; Olshan,
    Yitzhak; Smoira, Moshe
  compared to revolutionary court, 211
  legislator immunity in, 172

political agreements in, 163–164
prestige of, 303
stability of court in, 197
Clinton, Bill, 107, 125, 127
Coalition governments
  amendment of Basic Law: The
    Government and, 311
  amendment of Basic Laws, effect
    on, 342
  Begin, 57
  Ben-Gurion, 7
  Jewish-Arab cooperation in, 71–72
  Levy and, 200
  Netanyahu, 119, 122, 282
  Rabin, 99, 165–166
  Sharon, 208
Code of Ethics for Judges, 286
Cohabitation
  cases involving, 135
  Disabled Persons Law (Provident
    Payments and Rehabilitation,
    1949), 8
  recognition in law, 8–9, 9*
Cohen, Dudi, 299, 300
Cohen, Nili, 201–203
Cohen, Shlomo, 230
Cohn, Haim
  as attorney general, 29, 30, 239
  on contract interpretation, 185
  on democracy's need for protection, 24
  on deportations of Palestinians, 101
  on indictment use, 29, 30
  on presidential pardon, 87
  on religious courts, 8
  on role of attorney general apropos
    executive branch, 245
  on standing, 38
  term on Supreme Court, 197
  in Yeredor case, 66
Commission of Inquiry Act, 258
Commissions of inquiry
  Agranat Commission (1974), 11,
    16, 258
  Bejski Commission (1985), 142–143
  Constitution, Law, and Justice Committee
    to act as (Ramon case), 297
  Kahan Commission (1983), 47, 128,
    219, 258

375